D0517366

THE CHRONOLOGY OF BRITISH HISTORY

THE CHRONOLOGY OF BRITISH HISTORY

ALAN AND VERONICA PALMER

CENTURY
London Sydney Auckland Johannesburg

First published in Great Britain in 1992 by
Century Ltd
20 Vauxhall Bridge Road
London SW1V 2SA

Copyright © Alan and Veronica Palmer 1992

All rights reserved. No part of this publication may be
reproduced, stored in a retrieval system, or
transmitted in any form or by any means, electronic,
mechanical, photocopying, recording or otherwise,
without prior permission in writing from the publisher.

A catalogue entry for this book is available from the British Library.

ISBN 0 7126 2173 3 (hardback)

ISBN 0 7126 5616 2 (paperback)

Designed by Humphrey Stone
Maps by First Edition
Diagrams by Neil Hyslop

Typesetting by SX Composing Ltd, Rayleigh, Essex

Printed and bound in Great Britain by
Butler and Tanner Ltd, Frome and London

CONTENTS

INTRODUCTION

For generations of schoolchildren the learning of historical dates has been an educational blight, deadening their imagination to the exciting mystery of times past. The rote recital of the accession years of England's kings and queens became an exercise of questionable value, soon forgotten. There were, of course, gifted teachers who devised ways to jog the memory: for example, a fictitious telephone number (BROM 4689) put in the right order Marlborough's battles: Blenheim 1704; Ramillies 1706; Oudenarde 1708; Malplaquet 1709. In those days, before coded exchanges were introduced, BROM 4689 was easy enough to remember. Yet was the mnemonic worth inventing? Four letters and four digits may brand four battles on the mind, but why? The trick teaches no history; it says nothing of Marlborough's campaign, the wearying march from Meuse to Danube or that sickening final slaughter in the wooded slopes above Malplaquet. Dates remembered in this fashion are mere milestones, notched numbers beside a featureless track.

In this chronology, however, dates are not so much milestones as signposts, pointing the way laterally across a period in time. By this means it is possible to relate the general events of the past to what was happening in the arts and sciences, in scholarship, literature, music and popular entertainment. At the same time, by providing a long and continuous reel of history from earliest times until the present day, we hope to counter that weakness of all examination syllabuses, the limiting of historical understanding to a narrow period of years or to a specialised topic, studied in isolation. Not that we intend this chronology to serve solely as a companion guide for students of history. All who read widely must gain in understanding from relating their particular interests to past society as a whole. History is not, in fact, disappearing beyond our range of vision. It is a moving staircase, which a chronology gives the reader an opportunity to observe. A sense of continuity enriches our experience of both past and present by illuminating, however briefly, all that stands on each step along the escalator of time.

The pattern upon which this book has been contructed needs some explanation:
Units of time The reader will find our entries made, not regularly under each year, but under varying units of time, listed at the top of the page. In pre-history these units cover several thousands of years. In the middle ages and for the early modern period each unit is for five years, although the units are shorter during such eventful periods as the 1580s and 1640s and at the start of the eighteenth century. From 1791 until 1854 the units cover two years; they then revert to a year at a time.
Mythical events and doubtful dates Some 'historical' characters (King Arthur, Hengist, Horsa, St Ninian among them) and some alleged events, such as the

battle of Aylesford or the tussle of St Columba with a monster in the River Ness) are most probably mythical; and asterisks have therefore been used to mark characters or events that seem little more than fables. Dates printed in italics are doubtful, although there is no question that the events they record took place.

Classifation Events are classified under eight headings: general and political; fine arts and architecture; literature and scholarship; music and drama; re-creation and fashion; religion and education; science and invention; voyages of exploration. The book is concerned solely with what happened in the United Kingdom or in Britain's overseas possessions. But in order to help readers fit what was happening in Britain into a world picture, we have added a ninth heading 'events elsewhere'.

Abbreviations These are explained on page 10.

Calendars Dates before September 1752 follow the Julian Calendar; thereafter the jump of eleven days is made and the Gregorian ('New Style') Calendar duly followed. Dates marked in brackets (N.S.) in the early eighteenth century show continental usage, much of western Europe having adopted the Gregorian Calendar on its inception in 1582.

Lists and Diagrams The prime purpose of these lists is to enable the reader to trace the succession of important office-holders and to gain some impression of events difficult to include in any narrowly chronological chart, such as changes in population and the gradual coming of speedier communication across the country as a whole. Since the early eighteenth century the effective head of government has, of course, been the Prime Minister. In medieval England the principal statesman was occasionally the Justiciar but often the Chancellor and sometimes the Chamberlain; we have therefore merely picked out the years in which there was an outstanding political figure, rather than attempt to list all the Justiciars and medieval Chancellors. The longest (almost) unbroken chain of succession is provided by the greater church dignitaries: the Archbishops of Canterbury and York, and three senior bishoprics (London, Winchester, Durham); and we have therefore given separate lists to these. Explanatory notes are given at the start of the lists, or beside the diagrams, where these are felt to be useful. No attempt has been made to give a comparative table of the value of the pound sterling or the cost of living, as (at least outside the present century) there can be no uniform system for deciding on what to base any estimate. The diagram of the cost of bread in London shows the considerable fluctuations in all such assessments.

Maps The nineteen maps were chosen to help understand particularly involved periods of British history. As well as showing parts of the United Kingdom, they illustrate three important wars in which English/British troops fought in Europe, and the spread of empire into North America, India, Australasia and Africa.

Indexes There are two indexes, neither of which include entries relating to the 'events elsewhere' heading or to material in the lists and diagrams. Both indexes refer to years rather than to pages. The longer index – People and Places – gives births and death dates of people mentioned in the chronology, where such information is known. The shorter index lists topics.

Readers using the more recent years included in the chronology may wish to complement the material by referring to back-numbers of newspapers, many of which are on microfilm in the larger reference libraries. It is partly for this reason that we have tried, where possible, to give the dates and places of the first performance of plays, etc., in case readers should want to see for themselves what contemporary critics thought of these occasions.

Our debt to the established histories and works of reference in incalculable. We have found the volumes of the *Oxford History of England* particularly helpful, but we also wish to acknowledge the value and total reliability of the Royal Historical Society's *Handbook of British Chronology* (third edition, London 1986).

In the early stages of work on this book we were greatly helped and encouraged by the enthusiasm of our commissioning editor, Linden Lawson. And we appreciate, too, the wise counsel and good sense of Julian Shuckburgh, at whose suggestion the lists and diagrams were added to the original core of the chronology.

ALAN PALMER
VERONICA PALMER
Woodstock, Oxfordshire
April 1992

LIST OF ABBREVIATIONS

Ψ	Battle	FM	Field Marshal
AD	Anno Domini	Gen.	General
Archbp	Archbishop	HRE	Holy Roman Emperor
Adm.	Admiral	I.	Island, Isle
Bp, Bpp	Bishop, Bishops	Is	Islands
c.	circa	K.	King
Cap.	Captain	Maj.	Major
C.-in-C.	Commander-in-Chief	Mqs	Marquis
Col.	Colonel	NY	New York
Comm.	Committee	P.	Prince, Princess
Commn	Commission	Q.	Queen
d.	died	R.	River
D.	Duke, Duchess	Rom.	Roman
DD	Dukes	St	Saint
E.	Earl	Ty	Treaty
EE	Earls	Vct	Viscount
Emp.	Emperor	W. Emp	Western Emperor

THE CHRONOLOGY

250,000—3,000 BC

250,000 BC	First human skull from Swanscombe, Kent.
200,000 BC	Neanderthal remains in Pontnewydd cave, Clwyd.
26,000—10,000 BC	Late Ice Age cave-dwellers, stone and bone tools used (Creswellian culture). Engraved bone tools found. Sites: Creswell Crags, Derbyshire; Kent's Cavern, Devon; Mendip caves; ceremonial burial in Paviland cave, Gower peninsula, Wales.
18,000—14,000 BC	Height of last glaciation, with ice south to York, on higher ground in Wales.
by 8,300 BC	Mesolithic period begins. Ice melts, forests form, but Britain still connected to Europe by land. Hunting, fishing, herding of deer or reindeer general in N. Europe and Britain. Settlements made by lakes and sea. Sites: Thatcham, Berks; Star Carr, Yorks; Isle of Oronsay, Scotland.
by 6,500 BC	English Channel formed.
4,000—3,000 BC	Neolithic period begins, farming introduced from NW Europe. Large hilltop enclosures (causewayed camps) built (Windmill Hill culture). Sites: Windmill Hill, Wilts; Hambledon Hill and Maiden Castle, Dorset. Long barrows, containing multiple burials as well as animal bones and domestic débris, grouped near enclosures. Flint mined: Findon and Worthing, Sussex; plain pottery made, wheat grown.

Events Elsewhere

3,500—3,000	First Sumerian city states at Uruk and Ur (Iraq). Cuneiform writing developed in Sumeria.
3,100	Egyptian kingdom established. Hieroglyphic writing in Egypt.

3,000—1,400 BC

3,000—2,400 BC	Circular henge monuments begin to replace enclosures as centres for local population or tribe. Wessex emerging as most important centre in England. Sites: Stonehenge and Woodhenge, Wilts. Large wooden buildings, palaces or assembly halls built inside henges. Sites: Woodhenge; Tara, Ireland. Small houses, round barrows built, long barrows continue. Sites: Silbury Hill, Wilts. In SE Britain earthen barrows with internal wooden chambers found. Sites: West Kennet, Wilts. In Scotland, NW Britain chambered cairns or barrows with stone interiors ('megaliths') made. Sites: Quanterness and Maes Howe, Orkney. Stone circles and houses built in Scotland. Sites: Stenness and

Skara Brae, Orkney. In Ireland stone passage tombs made. Sites: Tara and Bends of Boyne. Flint mining centred on E. Anglia. Sites: Grimes Graves.

from 2,440 BC   Stonehenge largely abandoned.

from 2,300 BC   Central European Beaker people, named from distinctive pottery artefacts, reach Britain. Possibly warriors, gradually evolving into ruling class. Barley grown, metal (copper) work begins, gold jewellery found. Individual tombs made, stone circles, henge monuments developed further. Sites: Avebury, Wilts; Rollright Stones, Oxon.

1,800–1,400 BC   Early Bronze Age marked by increased wealth, use of bronze tools and weapons, rule by wealthy class and domination of SE Britain (Wessex culture). Individual burials, later cremations, in round barrows found, sometimes with rich grave goods. Sites: Hove, Sussex; Rillaton, Cornwall; Mold, Clwyd; many in Wilts. Trade with Europe, especially Brittany, increased. New Stonehenge built, with sarsen stones brought 20 miles and blue stones from Prescelly mountains, Wales.

Events Elsewhere

2,000   First palaces of Minoan Crete. Greeks settle at Mycenae, Tiryns.
1,650–1,480s   Minoan power at height. Linear B (early Greek) script in Crete.

1,400–100 BC

---

from 1,400 BC   Wessex culture disappears, possibly as result of climatic change. New centres emerge in Thames valley, Fen country, and N. Wales. Pottery urns made, for domestic use and cremation burials in old barrows or new flat cemeteries. Farming increased, field systems developed, horses ridden and driven. Tools and weapons mass-produced by new bronze-casting technique. Stone hut circles and hillforts built for defence. Sites: Deverel and Rimbury, Dorset; Gwithian and Trevisker, Cornwall; Rams Hill, Berks; Ivinghoe Beacon, Bucks; Grimthorpe, Yorks; Dinorben, Clwyd.

800–450 BC   Celtic culture spreads through Britain. Iron working, adopted through contact with or immigration by Celtic peoples of Europe, starts with sword making (Hallstatt culture), later extends to other weapons and tools. Hillforts further developed, containing numerous small houses. Walled farmsteads found, especially in west and north. Wheat grown, 2-ox plough introduced, sheep and cattle farming common in north. Wool woven for clothing. Trade with Europe cross-channel, tin exported to Mediterranean by Atlantic route. Sites: Little Woodbury, Wilts; Bodrifty, Cornwall; Staple Howe, N. Yorks; new fortifications at older sites like Ivinghoe Beacon, Maiden Castle. First British port: Mount Batten, Plymouth, Devon.

from 450 BC	Hillforts surrounded by extra ramparts and ditches, entrances further fortified. Forts built on cliffs and promontories, often centres for sea-borne trade. Sites: Hengistbury Head, Dorset.
from 400 BC	Parisi from N. France move into Humberside area, chieftains are buried with chariots (Arras culture). Sites: Garton Slack and other Yorkshire sites. Small separate forts ('brochs') begin to be built in Scotland. Sites in Caithness-Orkney region.
330–320 BC	Pytheas of Massilia (Marseilles), Greek sailor, circumnavigates Britain, describes Cornish tin trade with Mediterranean at Land's End and St Michael's Mount or Plymouth.
from 300 BC	Increasing influence of European Celtic peoples, through trading contacts or invasion, shown by introduction of art forms common in La Tène culture from Brittany and Normandy. Sites: Brentford, Thames valley; St Mawgan and other sites in Cornwall.

Events Elsewhere

1,150	Trojan War.
753	Foundation of Rome.
587	Nebuchadnezzar, K. of Babylon, destroys Jerusalem.
530	Prince Gautama founds Buddhism in India, Nepal.
500	Confucianism developed in China.
490	Ψ Marathon. Greeks repel Persian invasion.
480–479	Greeks defeat second Persian invasion (Ψs Salamis, Plataea).
334	Alexander the Great begins conquest of East.
323 Jun. 10	Alexander dies lord of Egypt, Persian empire, part of India.
221	Great Wall of China begun.
by *146*	Rome supreme power in Mediterranean.

---

100 BC—AD 40

from 100 BC	Celtic culture throughout Britain. Belgic people arrive, Catuvellauni occupying territory north-east of R. Thames and west to Chiltern hills, Trinovantes settling in Essex. Mixed and arable farming increases in S. Britain, north stays mainly pastoral. Coinage introduced.
80–50 BC	Second wave of Belgic invasion (Atrebates, Regni) settles in Sussex, Berkshire, E. Hampshire. Settlements on low ground ('oppida') behind dykes. Sites: St. Albans, Herts; Colchester, Essex; Chichester, Sussex; Silchester, Hants; Bagendon, Gloucs. Lake villages built: Glastonbury and Meare, Somerset. Cremation burials, in urns or buckets, some with rich grave goods. Druids in charge of religion and education.

55 BC	Julius Caesar, Proconsul of Gaul, receives British envoys, sends Commius, Atrebates' chief, back to Britain with them. Commius seized by British. Tribune C. Volusenus reconnoitres coast.
Aug. 26–27	Caesar and 2 legions sail to Britain, probably from Boulogne, land between Deal and Walmer, defeat British in skirmishes. Commius freed.
30–31	Storm prevents arrival of cavalry transports, damages beached Roman ships. Romans defeated in skirmish by war chariots, but repel enemy from beaches. Britons promise hostages, Romans return to Gaul.
54 BC *Jul.*	Caesar invades Britain with 5 legions and 2,000 cavalry, lands in Kent, crosses R. Stour, defeats Britons. Ships damaged in storm and repaired. Caesar defeats British coalition under Cassivellaunus, K. of Catuvellauni, crosses R. Thames. Trinovantes appeal to Romans against Catuvellauni, assist Caesar. Caesar takes Cassivellaunus' oppidum (probably Wheathampstead, Herts). Kentish tribes attack Roman naval camp and are defeated.
Sep.	Hostages taken, tribute fixed. Catuvellauni agree not to molest Trinovantes. Romans return to Gaul.
50 BC	Commius joins Gallic revolt, flees to Britain. He becomes chief of British Atrebates, with capital at Silchester, Hants, and issues coinage. Trade with Europe centres on SE Britain.
34–27 BC	Octavian (Emperor Augustus) plans British expedition, but makes alliance with Trinovantes (capital Colchester) and Atrebates.
25–20 BC	Tincommius, chief of Atrebates, issues coins Roman in type with word 'rex' (king). Iceni (E. Anglia) become rich, warlike tribe, using gold for ornament, especially torcs (collars). Hoards found at: Snettisham, Bawsey and N. Creake, Norfolk; Ipswich, Suffolk.
AD 7	Catuvellauni under Cunobelin (Cymbeline) conquer Trinovantes, establish capital at Colchester, hold most of SE Britain, expanding into Sussex and Kent. Cunobelin issues coins with 'rex'. Catuvellauni monopolize increased trade with Roman empire.
AD 40	Emperor Gaius (Caligula) threatens to invade Britain from Boulogne.

Events Elsewhere

44 BC *Mar. 15*	Caesar assassinated.
31 BC *Sep. 2*	Ψ Actium: Octavian defeats Antony and Cleopatra, becomes supreme at Rome, takes name Augustus.
BC 30	Crucifixion of Jesus Christ. Beginning of Christianity.

AD 41–60

by AD 43	Cunobelin succeeded by sons Caratacus and Togodumnus, who expand into lands of Dobunni (Oxford to Somerset), take Atrebates' kingdom.
43	Aulus Plautius, commander, with legions II Augusta, IX, XIV, XX, and about 20,000 auxiliary troops, invades Britain from Boulogne.
by May	Roman army lands at Richborough, Kent, possibly with 2nd landing near Chichester. Britons defeated in skirmishes, Dobunni surrender to Rome, Romans under Vespasian force crossing of R. Medway and win decisive battle. Britons retreat across R. Thames, pursued by Romans. Togodumnus is killed, Caratacus flees to Wales.
Aug.–Sep.	Emperor Claudius arrives with reinforcements, including elephants, personally supervises capture of Colchester. Claudius accepts surrender of Catuvellauni and other tribes, appoints Aulus Plautius first Governor of Britain, returns to Rome.
43–47	Governorship of Aulus Plautius. Vespasian, commanding legion II from base at Fishbourne, Sussex, conquers SW Britain to Exeter, taking Isle of Wight, reducing 20 hillforts, including Maiden Castle, Dorset; he accepts surrender of Durotriges (Dorset), Dumnonii (Devon), bases legion II at Exeter.
	Legion IX advances north-east to eventual base at Lincoln, legion XIV through Midlands. Legion XX establishes base at Colchester. Military bases built also at Gloucester and St Albans, forts on both sides of Severn-Humber frontier line.
	Client kingdoms recognized outside Roman province: Iceni (E. Anglia); Regni Atrebates (Sussex); Brigantes (N. England).
	Foundation of London. Romans build first bridge across R. Thames, near London Bridge, and military base on north side at Cornhill. Commercial centre and port develop on site of City of London. Headquarters of Procurator (financial administrator) in London. Military roads built, many converging on London: Watling Street (Richborough-London-Towcester-later Wroxeter), Ermine Street (London-Lincoln-later York), Stane Street (London-Chichester) and London-Colchester road. Fosse Way (Exeter-Lincoln) marks frontier of Roman province.
47	Ostorius Scapula, Governor, defeats raiding Welsh tribes led by Caratacus.
48	Ostorius disarms tribes south of frontier, including allies. Iceni resist, but are defeated. Romans defeat Deceangli (NE Wales).
49	Colchester, now provincial capital, made 'colonia' (settlement of veteran soldiers) and centre of imperial cult, with temple of Claudius.
	Mendip lead-mines, Somerset, worked by Roman army but demilitarized by AD 60.
49–51	Silures (SE Wales) attack Romans. Ostorius, with legions XIV and XX,

pushes up R. Severn and builds forts to cut off S. Wales.

51   Caratacus leads Ordovices (N. Wales) into battle against Romans on upper
      R. Severn, flees to Brigantes (N. England) after defeat, is betrayed to
      Romans. He is exhibited at Rome in chains, but pardoned. Silures continue
      guerrilla warfare.
      Foundation of St Albans as 'municipium' (self-governing town). Silchester
      city centre developed: baths, amphitheatre, forum.

52   Ostorius dies. Didius Gallus, Governor, continues to contain Welsh tribes
      with forts, builds legion XIV base at Wroxeter.

58   Suetonius Paulinus, Governor, campaigns in Wales. Julius Agricola becomes
      military tribune (junior officer) under Paulinus.

Events Elsewhere

54   Emperor Claudius dies, succeeded by Nero.

AD 61–80

60–61   Paulinus takes Anglesey, last stronghold of Druid priesthood, destroys sacred
        groves and garrisons island.

61   Rebellion of Iceni (E. Anglia), caused by Roman attempt to seize kingdom
        after king's death. His widow, Boudicca (Boadicea), resisting officials of
        Procurator Decianus Catus, is flogged, her daughters raped. Boudicca rouses
        Iceni and Trinovantes (Essex) who resent foundation of Colchester. Britons
        destroy Colchester, massacre Roman settlers, defeat legion IX under Petilius
        Cerialis. Paulinus hurries south with legion XIV and part of XX, abandons
        London as indefensible, withdraws towards north. Britons sack London, St
        Albans, are defeated by Paulinus in pitched battle in Midlands. Boudicca kills
        herself. Paulinus punishes rebels and neutral tribes alike. New Procurator
        Julius Classicianus intervenes to prevent further uprising. Paulinus removed
        from office after imperial inquiry.

62–68   S. Britain calm. Cornwall occupied. Legion II Augusta moves to Gloucester;
        Exeter now civilian town. Legion XIV leaves Britain.

68   Vettius Bolanus, Governor, attacks anti-Roman faction now in power among
        Brigantes (N. England), without success.

71   Petilius Cerialis, Governor, conquers Parisi (Humberside) and Brigantes, with
        legion IX and legion XX under Agricola. Legion II Adiutrix sent to Britain,
        posted to Lincoln. Legion IX moved to new fortress at York.

74   Julius Frontinus, Governor, conquers Silures (S. Wales), builds fortress at

			Caerleon for legion II Augusta. He begins conquest of Ordovices (N. Wales) and fortress at Chester for legion II Adiutrix.
78			Agricola, now Governor, finally subdues N. Wales.
79			Agricola completes conquest of NW Britain and legionary fortress at Chester.
80			Agricola, with legions IX and XX, advances to R. Tay, fortifying Carlisle and Corbridge.
75–80			Agricola encourages Romanization in architecture, education and dress: town centres developed in Cirencester, Exeter, Lincoln, St Albans; Governor's palace and basilica built in London; main palace at Fishbourne built; villas appear in SE Britain.

Events Elsewhere

64	*Jul.*	*18*	Great fire of Rome.
68	*Jun.*	*9*	Death of Nero.
69			Year of Four Emperors: civil war in empire, Vespasian victorious.
70			Vespasian's son, Titus, sacks Jerusalem.
79			Vespasian succeeded by Titus.
	Aug.	*24*	Vesuvius erupts, destroying Pompeii and Herculaneum.

AD 81–120

81	Agricola establishes Forth-Clyde frontier with forts; large fort at Newstead on R. Tweed; Votadini (E. Lowlands) become unreliable allies.
82	Agricola subdues SW Scotland, by sea from Cumbria. Coast of Galloway occupied, with view to possible invasion of Ireland.
83	Campaigning by land and sea against 'Caledonii' north of Forth-Clyde line. Romans reach Aberdeenshire, begin fortress for legion XX at Inchtuthil on R. Tay, and build forts to close off glens.
84	Ψ Mons Graupius (?Mt Bennachie, Aberdeenshire): Caledonii under Calgacus defeated. Army advances to south coast of Moray Firth. Fleet sails round N. Scotland, visiting Orkneys.
85	Agricola recalled to Rome. New roads to north built by Agricola: Carlisle-Scotland; Dere Street (York-Corbridge-Scotland); Stanegate (Carlisle-Corbridge). Wales and N. Britain defended by system of forts and roads. Naval base at Dover for British fleet ('classis Britannica').
from 87	Fighting in N. Britain, and Scotland. Romans withdraw to Forth-Clyde frontier, abandon Inchtuthil.

90–98	Lincoln and Gloucester become coloniae.
by 100	Legion II Adiutrix withdrawn from Britain. 3 legionary fortresses are rebuilt in stone and occupied until end of Roman period: Chester (legion XX); Caerleon (legion II Augusta); York (legion IX). First public baths in London and Bath; temples and theatres built: Canterbury theatre, AD 90.
by 105	Romans leave Scotland, Tyne-Solway line made frontier. Scottish and northern forts abandoned and burnt, including Newstead and Corbridge.
118	Pompeius Falco, Governor, suppresses revolt of Brigantes (N. England) allied to Scottish tribes.

Events Elsewhere

97–98	Historian Tacitus writes *Agricola*, biography of his father-in-law and description of Roman Britain to AD 85.
by 100	Christian gospels written.
113–117	Trajan's Parthian war. Greatest extent of Roman empire.
117 *Aug.*	Trajan dies near Antioch, succeeded by Hadrian.
	Cult of Mithras, Persian god, spreads in Roman army.

AD 121–160

122	Emperor Hadrian visits Britain, decides to build wall from Tyne to Solway as frontier. Hadrian's friend, Platorius Nepos, is appointed Governor. Legion VI arrives in Britain, eventually replacing legion IX in York. Legions II, VI, XX begin building wall.
	Forum and fort in London completed.
120	Fenland in E. Anglia drained: Car Dyke (Cambridge-Lincoln) constructed, canal network and roads built.
122–139	Building of Hadrian's Wall: 75 miles long, from Wallsend on east coast to Barrow-on-Solness on west coast, 2–3m thick (originally wider); east section stone, rest turf to be replaced by stone later; 80 milecastles (small forts) built along wall, 1,500m apart; 160 turrets in pairs between milecastles, 500m apart; larger forts about 10km apart (Housesteads, Chesters). Ditches dug: north of wall, 8m wide, 3m deep; south of wall ('vallum'), 35m wide, 6.5m deep. Wall garrisoned by auxiliary troops. Bridges built across Tyne.
by 130	Town centres redeveloped: Wroxeter (AD 129–30), Leicester, Silchester, 2nd forum of London.
139	Emperor Antoninus decides to retake Scottish Lowlands.
	New Governor, Lollius Urbicus, begins advance to Clyde-Forth line.
	Corbridge reconstructed as base, forts in Lowlands rebuilt: Newstead largest.

	In Hadrian's Wall gates of milecastles removed, vallum filled to make causeways through to north. Pennine forts stripped of troops for northern advance.
142–144	Turf wall, 3m high, 4.3m wide, built from Bridgness on R. Forth to Old Kilpatrick on R. Clyde. Ditch to north 12.2m wide, 4m deep, forts at 2-mile intervals along wall, with small forts between, garrisoned by auxiliary troops. Military road built to south.
154–155	Serious revolt of Brigantes in Pennines, put down by Governor Julius Verus, forces Roman retreat from Scotland again. Forts in Lowlands and on Antonine Wall destroyed. Brigantes lose territory, probably to new 'civitates' (tribal units) based on Carlisle and Corbridge.
from 158	Hadrian's Wall refortified.
160	Antonine Wall reoccupied; Newstead and other lowland forts rebuilt.

Events Elsewhere

134	Rebellion of Jews, ends in dispersal from Palestine.
138 Jul. 10	Hadrian dies, succeeded by Antoninus.

AD 161–200

162–163	N. England restive. Calpurnius Agricola, Governor, reconstructs forts along Hadrian's Wall. Antonine Wall finally abandoned.
169–175	Forts built or rebuilt in Wales, possibly as result of revolt.
175	5,500 Sarmatian cavalry, conscripted from captives taken north of R. Danube, sent to N. Britain.
180	Scottish tribes cross Hadrian's Wall, ravage country, defeat Roman troops. Ulpius Marcellus, Governor, begins campaign against them.
185	Marcellus, after punitive campaigns beyond Antonine Wall, retreats to Hadrian's Wall. Troops withdrawn from Newstead and other lowland forts. Federation of tribes (Maeatae), living both sides of Antonine Wall, are in treaty relationship with Rome, tribes of far north (Caledonii) give guarantees not to attack.
	Mutiny in army in Britain, deputation of 1,500 sent to Rome to complain of the appointment of non-senatorial legionary commanders. Helvius Pertinax made Governor, puts down several mutinies.
187	Pertinax resigns through unpopularity with army.
192	Clodius Albinus, Governor, proclaimed Emperor, but bought off by chief

rival Septimius Severus with junior partnership and title 'Caesar'.

196	Albinus proclaims self 'Augustus', takes troops to Gaul to overthrow Severus, now supreme in Rome.
197	Ψ Lyons, Albinus defeated. Severus appoints Virius Lupus Governor, with own relative Varius Marcellus as Procurator. Lands of Albinus' supporters confiscated to Emperor. Pennine forts rebuilt. Maeatae (S. Scotland) raid south as far as Hadrian's Wall, Caledonii (N. Scotland) prepare to help them. Lupus bribes Maeatae to make peace.
by 200	Pottery industry established, especially in Oxfordshire: Oxford (Cowley, Headington) and Churchill. Earthwork defences built round towns, stone wall begun round London. Temples to Mithras built: 4 on Hadrian's Wall, 1 in London (London temple possibly not until AD 240).

Events Elsewhere

161	Emperor Antoninus dies, succeeded by Marcus Aurelius. Tribes from north of R. Danube begin to threaten Roman empire.
166	Roman soldiers bring plague from East back to Rome.
180	Marcus Aurelius succeeded by son Commodus.
192	Praetorian guard kill Commodus, try to auction empire.
197	Severus establishes self as sole Emperor, with title 'Augustus', using 'Caesar' as title for son and heir Caracalla.

AD 201–260

206	Alfenus Senecio, Governor, begins to repair Hadrian's Wall, appeals to Emperor for help against Scottish tribes.
208	Emperor Severus journeys to Britain with wife, sons Caracalla and Geta, and takes command. York, imperial headquarters, raised to status of colonia.
208–209	Severus and Caracalla march through Fife to Aberdeen against Caledonii, Geta administers province. Caledonii, though never brought to battle, agree terms, giving up some territory. Fort built at Cramond on Firth of Forth, legionary fortress at Carpow on Tay estuary. Christianity reaches Britain; possible date for martyrdom of St Alban (v. 250–259).
210	Maeatae (S. Scotland) revolt. Caracalla sent on punitive expedition against them.
211	Caledonii (N. Scotland) join Maeatae (S. Scotland) in revolt. Severus

	prepares new expedition against them.
Feb. 4	Severus dies at York.
	Caracalla, now joint Emperor with Geta, abandons Scotland, renewing treaties with Scottish tribes, and returns to Rome.
by 216	Britain divided into two provinces: Upper Britain (south and west) with 2 legions based at Caerleon and Chester; Lower Britain (north) with 1 legion at York, auxiliary troops in forts and on Hadrian's Wall. Peace in N. Britain until *c.* AD 300.
by 220	Saxon (N. German) pirates raid SE coast. Defensive coastal forts built: Reculver, Kent; Brancaster, N. Norfolk.
	Serving Roman soldiers allowed to marry; small Romano-British towns ('vici') develop round forts, along Hadrian's Wall (Corbridge, Old Carlisle). Large private town houses built: St Albans (AD 215–40). New stone theatres: Canterbury (AD 210–20).
250–259	Christians persecuted in Britain, possibly period of St Alban's martyrdom (*v.* 208–209).
259	Latinius Postumus, Roman commander on Rhine, rebels, proclaims Germany, Gaul, Spain and Britain as separate 'Empire of the Gauls'.

Events Elsewhere

212	Caracalla murders Geta. As sole Emperor, he grants citizenship to all subjects of Roman empire.
244	Murder of Emperor Gordian III begins 40 years of chaos in empire outside Britain: up to 55 emperors, many murdered; galloping inflation; population decreases; barbarian tribesmen serve in army.

AD 261–300

from 270	Saxon raids increase. Fortresses built at: Burgh Castle, Suffolk; Richborough, Kent; Portchester, Hants; coast defended by chain of forts from Brancaster to Portchester known later as 'Saxon Shore'.
270–290	Stone walls built round towns (St Albans, AD 273). Fishbourne palace burnt. Dover naval base run down, fleets use north-east ports on estuaries of Humber, Tees, Tyne.
277	Restrictions on British wine production lifted by imperial edict.
277–278	Unrest caused by Emperors' attempts to maintain unity, restore currency. Emperor Probus sends Moorish general Victorinus to put down British revolt, settles Burgundian and Vandal prisoners in Britain.

286–287	Belgian soldier, Mausaeus Carausius, given naval command at Boulogne to deal with raiding Franks (NW Germans) and Saxons in Channel. To avoid execution for embezzling captured pirate treasure, Carausius flees to Britain, proclaims self Emperor. He controls part of N. Gaul, issues coinage, including only Roman coin with Vergil quotation, 'expectate veni' (come, O long-awaited).
289	Carausius defeats Emperor Maximian in naval battle.
293	Julius Constantius appointed Caesar, takes Boulogne, defeats Franks allied to Carausius. Carausius murdered by finance minister Allectus, who seizes power in Britain, employs Frankish mercenaries.
296	Constantius commands recovery of Britain. 2 Roman fleets: 1st from Boulogne under Constantius driven back by weather; 2nd from Le Havre under prefect Asclepiodotus lands near Southampton, passing British fleet in fog. Roman army defeats Britons near Silchester, Allectus killed. Romans prevent retreating Franks from sacking London. Constantius hailed as saviour of London.
297	Start of rebuilding for forts on both sides of Hadrian's Wall, some possibly damaged by northern raiders. Caledonii now first called Picts ('picti' - painted people). Constantius returns to Gaul.
by 300	York fortress massively rebuilt as chief military headquarters.

Events Elsewhere

274	Emperor Aurelian reunites Roman empire.
284	Diocletian becomes Emperor, divides empire into east and west: Diocletian Eastern Emperor, Maximian Western; each has title 'Augustus'.
293	Tetrarchy established to rule Roman empire: each Augustus adopts 'Caesar' as heir: Constantius Western Caesar, Galerius Eastern Caesar. Diocletian begins administrative reforms of empire, separating civil from military administration, dividing provinces into large groups of smaller units.

AD 301–360

301	2 British products appear in Diocletian's edict fixing prices throughout Roman empire: woollen goods (hooded cloak, rug) and beer (at twice price of Egyptian beer).
306	Constantius, now Western Emperor, returns to Britain with son Constantine, campaigns in N. Scotland, defeats Picts.
Jul. 25	At York: Constantius dies; army proclaims Constantine Emperor.
by 314	Diocletian's reforms take effect, dividing Britain into 4 smaller provinces,

	civil government separated from military. Commander-in-Chief ('dux') based at York, commands permanent army of Britain. Count ('comes'), imperial nominee, sent in charge of task force in crisis.
314	Christian Church hierarchy appears. 3 British bishops (York, London, ?Lincoln), 1 priest, 1 deacon, attend Council of Arles.
to 340	Period of prosperity, much villa building with finest mosaic art.
343 *Jan./Feb.*	Constans, Western Emperor, unexpectedly visits Britain, deals with trouble on northern frontier and Saxon Shore, threat of internal revolt. Pevensey Fort built.
after 343	Count Gratian leads task force to Britain.
350	Pagan Magnentius seizes western empire, with British support.
353	Constantius II, Eastern Emperor, defeats Magnentius, rules alone. He sends imperial notary Paul to punish British supporters of Magnentius, put down paganism. Many arrests, confiscations.
355	Julian appointed Caesar in charge of Britain and Gaul.
359	Julian reopens lower Rhine for export of British corn, building fleet of 600 ships; Britain becomes granary of army in W. Europe. 3 of up to 25 British bishops attending Council of Rimini are poor enough for imperial subsidy.
360	Picts, aided by Scots from Ireland, attack northern frontier. Julian sends reinforcements to Britain.
by 360	Christianity spreads to countryside: private chapels built in villas at Lullingstone, Kent; Hinton St Mary, Dorset; church at Silchester, Hants. Treasures including vessels for use in Christian ceremonies buried: Mildenhall, Suffolk; Water Newton, Cambs.

Events Elsewhere

303	Diocletian decrees persecution of Christians.
305	Diocletian and Maximian abdicate.
312	Constantine wins Ψ Milvian Bridge, Rome, becomes senior Emperor.
313	Edict of Milan: Constantine legalizes Christianity.
324	Constantine, now sole Emperor, founds Constantinople (Istanbul).
360	Julian becomes sole Emperor, attempts to restore paganism.

AD 361–400

361–380	Pagan revival: new shrine of Celtic god Nodens at Lydney, Gloucs.
367	Concerted land and sea invasion of British province by Picts, Irish Scots,

Attacotti (cannibals, probably island tribe), some Saxons. Hadrian's Wall overrun, C.-in-C. Fullofaudes captured and Nectaridus, count of Saxon Shore, killed. Army deserters and runaway slaves roam country.

368   Count Theodosius sent with task force, sets up headquarters in London, announces amnesty for deserters, restores administration with new Governor Civilis and C.-in-C. Dulcitius.

369   Theodosius routs invaders, begins refortifying frontier; Roman troops no longer kept north of Hadrian's Wall. Watch towers built on north-east coast from Filey to Huntcliff; Welsh forts rebuilt; naval base at Holyhead. Bastions supporting catapults added to external town walls.

382   Magnus Maximus, Spanish general formerly serving under Theodosius, defeats Picts and Scots.

383   Maximus usurps western empire, taking troops from Britain. Forts abandoned: legionary fort at Chester; Welsh forts of Brecon, Cardiff, Forden Gaer; some Pennine forts.

388   Maximus defeated, killed in Italy. Last Roman coinage minted in Britain.

389–390   Task force sent by Emperor Theodosius (son of Count) against Picts.

396–398   Vandal Stilicho, chief minister of Western Emperor Honorius, sends (possibly leads) expedition to defeat Picts and Scots by sea.

397   *St Ninian, a British bishop trained in Rome, arrives in Galloway, founds monastery ('Casa Candida') at Whithorn, converts lowland kingdoms.

by 400   Irish Scots raid and settle in Wales (Lleyn and Gower peninsulas, Pembrokeshire), Devon and Cornwall. 3 British kingdoms established north of Hadrian's Wall: Strathclyde, Gododdin (Votadini), Galloway (possibly established by Maximus). Period of prosperity in SE Britain, but towns garrisoned, mainly by auxiliary troops. Christianity extends to kingdoms north of Hadrian's Wall and S. Ireland.

Events Elsewhere

391   Theodosius, advised by St Ambrose, Bp of Milan, bans paganism.
395   Roman empire permanently divided between East and West.
by 400   Huns appear in central Europe.

AD 401–450

401   Stilicho withdraws troops from Britain for defence against Goths. Caernarfon fort and Yorkshire coast forts abandoned.

402	Last issue of Roman coinage found in Britain.
405	Niall of Nine Hostages, High King of Ireland, leads raids on south coast of Britain.
406 *Dec. 31*	German tribes cross R. Rhine on ice, overrun Gaul, threaten Britain.
407	Constantine III, last of 3 successive usurping Emperors proclaimed by army in Britain, crosses Channel and drives Germans from Gaul.
408–409	Army rebels against Constantine III, Germans invade Gaul again, Saxons raid Britain. Britons expel Roman administration.
410	Emperor Honorius tells British towns to defend themselves, without help from Rome. Hadrian's Wall abandoned, or garrisoned by local troops.
420–430	*British bishop Fastidius writes *On the Christian Life*.
by 425	British kingdoms, with Christian Celtic culture, begin to emerge. 'Heresy' of British theologian Pelagius adopted by many wealthy Britons, including Vortigern ('high king'), ?Welsh ruler later described as ruling all Britain. Coel Hen ('Coel the Old' ? = 'Old King Cole') ruler in Wales or N. Britain in same era.
429	St Germanus, Bp of Auxerre, sent to Britain by Pope, defeats Pelagian 'heretics' in public debate, travels about preaching. After visiting St Alban's shrine, Germanus helps British troops rout Picts and Saxons, teaching them to shout 'Alleluia'.
430	Vortigern settles Saxons under *Hengist and *Horsa in Kent, round London and on coast near Wash and Humber estuary, to defend kingdom against Pictish raids, Roman intervention and rival 'king' Ambrosius. *Vortigern moves Cunedda, chief of Gododdin, Scotland, to N. Wales to resist Irish raids, founding the royal house of Gwynedd. Coinage no longer used.
431	Pope sends Bp Palladius to Ireland. Mission alleged to have failed. Palladius dies in Britain on way home.
432	St Patrick, a Briton captured by raiders and enslaved in Ireland as a youth, sent back as bishop and converts all Ireland.
446–447	Britons appeal unsuccessfully to Aetius, chief minister of Western empire, for help against Saxons, Picts and Scots. Return visit of St Germanus. Pelagian 'heretics' exiled.
447–450	Extensive settlement in Britain by Angles (from Schleswig-Holstein), Saxons and Jutes (from Jutland), collectively known as English. Vortigern's Saxon allies revolt, join invaders.
450	End of most Romano-British town and villa life. Some Britons migrate to Brittany, others to Cumbria, Wales and SW Britain. British kingdoms develop further outside area of English invasions.

Events Elsewhere

402		Western imperial court removed to Ravenna, Italy.
410		Goths under Alaric sack Rome.
418	*Apr. 30*	Emperor Honorius bans Pelagian 'heresy'.
434		Attila, K. of Huns, begins to move against Roman empire.

AD 451–500

455   *Ψ Aylesford: Horsa killed, Saxon victory. Alternative date for St Patrick's mission to Ireland.

470–500   Monasticism arrives in Britain: first foundations: Llanilltud (Llantwit Major), Wales, where St Illtud began famous school; Tintagel, Cornwall; *Glastonbury, Somerset. Later monasteries in Ireland.

477   *Aelle and 3 sons land at Selsey to found South Saxon kingdom (Sussex).

by 490   First phase of English settlement completed: Angles in E. Anglia, along east coast to Humber estuary, inland to York; Saxons in Sussex, Essex, Hertfordshire; Jutes in Kent, S. Hampshire, I. of Wight. British resistance centred on refortified Iron Age hillforts: Congresbury and South Cadbury, Somerset. Earthwork defence built from Bristol Channel to Marlborough Downs (Wansdyke).

491   *Aelle takes Pevensey fort.

495   *Cerdic and son land near Southampton, to found West Saxon kingdom (Wessex).

500   Ψ Mount Badon (?Liddington, Wilts): Britons, under *King Arthur or Ambrose Aurelianus, defeat English army, under *Aelle, K. of Sussex. English advance to west halted. Britain divided into British, mainly Christian, north and west and pagan English east.

Events Elsewhere

451	Attila invades Gaul, is defeated in battle by Romans.
453	Attila invades Italy.
486	End of Roman rule in Gaul, now divided into Frankish kingdoms.

AD 501–550

501	Irish Scots from Antrim settle in I. of Man, SW Scotland. *Fergus and 3 sons found kingdom of Dal Riada Scots in Argyllshire.
516	Alternative date for Ψ Mount Badon (*v. 500*).
by 523	St Brigid founds Kildare, first religious house for women in Ireland.
527	Further Saxon invaders found kingdom of Essex.
534–548	Theodoric, K. of Franks, employs English mercenaries in German wars, settles them in Germany, claims overlordship of Britain.
537	*Death of King Arthur in battle near Hadrian's Wall.
546–550	British priest Gildas writes *On the Destruction of Britain*, main written source for post-Roman British history, but without dates.
by 547	St David founds monastery at St David's, Wales.
547	Angles led by K. Ida land at Flamborough Head, Yorkshire, and establish kingdom of Bernicia, with capital Bamburgh, Northumbria.

Events Elsewhere

527–565	Reign of Justinian in eastern empire: he reconquers west, issues new code of Roman law and builds Santa Sophia Church in Constantinople.

AD 551–600

560	Aelle is first K. of Angles of Deira (Yorkshire). Ethelbert becomes K. of Kent, later marries Christian princess Bertha, daughter of Frankish K. of Paris.
563	St Columba, Irish bishop, descendant of K. Niall, arrives in Iona, Scotland, founds monastery which becomes chief centre of Celtic Church in Britain. Columba leads mission to Picts, converts or makes treaty with Brude, K. of Picts (d. 584), in his capital at Inverness, *overcomes monster in R. Ness.
563–583	*St Brendan, abbot of Clonfert, Ireland, explores N. Atlantic, founds monastery on Tiree, Hebrides.
571	E. Anglia becomes kingdom.
574	Columba ordains Aidan K. of Argyll Scots.
575	K. Aidan and Columba visit N. Ireland, make treaty with Irish Scots.

577	Ψ Dyrham, Somerset: K. Ceawlin of Wessex, 'Bretwalda' (overlord of S. English kingdoms), defeats 3 British kings, expands Wessex to Severn estuary.
585	Kingdom of Mercia established, in valley of R. Trent.
593	K. Ethelfrith joins Bernicia and Deira to unite Northumbria.
600	Ψ Catterick: Britons from Lothian, N. Wales and N. England assemble at Edinburgh, attack Northumbria and are defeated.

RELIGION AND EDUCATION

| 597 | Pope Gregory I sends mission to England under St Augustine. 40 priests land in Kent, are accepted by K. Ethelbert, now Bretwalda.
By Christmas Augustine is made bishop, over 10,000 English are baptised. |
| by 600 | St Kentigern (Mungo): mission to Strathclyde; founds first church and city of Glasgow. |

AD 601–620

603	K. Ethelfrith of Northumbria defeats Dal Riada (Argyll Scots) under K. Aidan, expands kingdom into central and E. Lowlands.
613/616	Ψ Chester: Ethelfrith defeats kingdom of Powys; Northumbrian power extends to Solway Firth, separates Britons of Wales from Scotland.
616	Ψ R. Idle (S. Yorks): K. Redwald of E. Anglia, now Bretwalda, defeats and kills Ethelfrith, and makes exiled Edwin K. of Northumbria. Edwin conquers British kingdom Elmet, centred on Leeds, Yorks.
by 616	K. Ethelbert of Kent issues first written English laws.

RELIGION AND EDUCATION

601/602	Augustine made Archbishop; Christ Church (later cathedral) at Canterbury founded.
601–604	Augustine fails to establish authority over Celtic bishops.
604	K. Ethelbert of Kent founds St Paul's Cathedral, London, and Rochester Cathedral.
610–615	St Columbanus, Irish monk, founds monasteries in France and Italy. Irish monasteries become centres of learning for Europe.
by 616	*K. of Essex founds monastery on Thorney Island, Middx, later site of Westminster Abbey.
616	After Ethelbert dies, Kent (temporarily) and Essex return to paganism. Bps of London and Rochester flee to France.

612   Mohammed begins preaching.

AD 621–640

621–630   Ship burial at Sutton Hoo, Suffolk. Tomb thought to be that of K. Redwald of E. Anglia.

628   Ψ Cirencester: Mercians under Penda against Wessex men. Wessex cedes lands along R. Severn and Cirencester to Mercia.

by 632   K. Edwin of Northumbria attacks N. Wales, takes I. of Man and Anglesey, and besieges Cadwallon, British K. of Gwynedd, on Anglesey.

632 *Oct.* 12   Ψ Hatfield Chase, Yorks: K. Cadwallon of Gwynedd and K. Penda of Mercia defeat and kill K. Edwin. Northumbria ravaged and divided.

633   Oswald, returned from exile on Iona, defeats and kills Cadwallon, restores united Northumbrian kingdom, becomes Bretwalda.

638   Northumbrians attack and possibly capture Edinburgh.

RELIGION AND EDUCATION

627   Bp Paulinus, brought to Northumbria by K. Edwin's Kentish consort, baptises Edwin at York, becomes Bp of York, and converts Northumbria and kingdom of Lindsey (centred on Lincoln).

631   Burgundian St Felix is first Bp of E. Anglia at Dunwich, Suffolk; he and Irish monk St Fursey convert E. Anglia.

632   Paulinus flees to Kent after Ψ Hatfield Chase and becomes Bp of Rochester. Northumbria mainly reverts to paganism.

634   K. Oswald of Northumbria brings St Aidan from Iona as bishop and founds monastery on Lindisfarne (Holy Island) for Aidan. Northumbria is reconverted to Celtic Christian tradition.

635   St Birinus from Italy begins to convert Wessex and becomes Bp of Dorchester-on-Thames, Oxon.

Events Elsewhere

622   Islam founded.

AD 641–660

by 641	Northumbrian power extends north to Forth or beyond.
642 *Aug. 5*	Ψ Maserfelth (?Oswestry, Shropshire): K. Penda of Mercia defeats and kills K. Oswald of Northumbria; Oswald is canonized saint. Northumbria is divided again: Bernicia under K. Oswy, Oswald's brother; Deira subject to Mercia.
654	Ψ Winwaed (near Leeds, Yorks): K. Oswy defeats Mercians and allies, including British kings, kills K. Penda. Oswy, now Bretwalda and K. of reunited Northumbria, rules most of Mercia.
657	Mercia regains independence and expands south to Thames valley.
from 658	Wessex expands to west, driving British from Dorset and Somerset.

FINE ARTS AND ARCHITECTURE

650–675	Book of Durrow, earliest surviving Irish illuminated manuscript, possibly originally from Northumbria (c.f. 698)
after 653	St Cedd builds chapel of St Peter, Bradwell-on-sea, Essex, re-using Roman foundations and bricks: oldest surviving brick church in England.

LITERATURE AND SCHOLARSHIP

643	*Widsith* is earliest surviving example of English heroic verse.

RELIGION AND EDUCATION

653	Cedd begins to convert Mercia and later as bishop converts Essex.
657	St Hilda founds Whitby Abbey, Yorks, for monks and nuns.
660	Wine appointed first Bp of Winchester by K. of Wessex.

AD 661–680

665–670	Mercia controls S. England.
672	K. Egfrith of Northumbria campaigns north of Forth and defeats Picts.
678	Ψ R. Trent: Mercians defeat K. Egfrith and prevent Northumbrian expansion south of Trent.
by 680	British kingdom of Rheged (Cumbria, W. Lowlands) is finally conquered by Northumbria.

FINE ARTS AND ARCHITECTURE

674   Ripon Minster begun in Italian style.
680   Basilica-style church at Brixworth, Northants, built by Italians.

LITERATURE AND SCHOLARSHIP

675   St Aldhelm, abbot of Malmesbury, writes Latin verse and letters.
678   First possible date for *Beowulf*, earliest surviving English epic poem (*v. 793*).
680   Caedmon, lay brother of Whitby Abbey, composes earliest surviving English religious poetry.

MUSIC AND DRAMA

after 669   English churches are first outside Rome to use Gregorian chant.

RELIGION AND EDUCATION

664   Synod of Whitby settles dispute over date of Easter between Celtic and Roman traditions: Colman, Bp of Lindisfarne, speaks for Celts; St Wilfrid, later Bp of York, for Rome. K. Oswy of Northumbria decides for Rome. Colman and Celtic monks go to Iona, then Ireland. St Cuthbert is made prior of Lindisfarne, combining Celtic tradition and obedience to Rome.

669   Theodore of Tarsus is appointed Archbp of Canterbury by Pope to reorganize English Church; he makes Canterbury centre of learning, teaching Latin, Greek, humanities, Roman law.

672 *Sep.* 26   Synod of Hertford gives see of Canterbury authority over all English Church, with power to divide dioceses and make new bishops.

674   Foundation of monastery at Monkwearmouth/Jarrow, Northumbria. Books brought from France and Rome begin great library there.

677   St Wilfrid, Bp of York, resists reorganization, is expelled from Northumbria and preaches to Frisians of Dutch coast.

680   Wilfrid is reinstated by Pope, imprisoned in Northumbria and expelled; in exile he converts Sussex, last pagan English kingdom. York diocese is divided: bishops at York, Ripon, Lincoln, Hexham, Lindisfarne, Abercorn.

Events Elsewhere

by 680   Muslim Arabs control Middle East and N. Africa.

AD 681–700

684   K. Egfrith of Northumbria campaigns in N. Ireland.

685 *May* 20   Ψ Dunnichen Moss, nr Forfar, Scotland: Picts defeat, kill K. Egfrith of Northumbria. End of English rule north of Forth.

685   K. Cadwalla of Wessex takes I. of Wight, Kent, Surrey, Sussex.

688	Cadwalla is baptised by Pope, dies in Rome. K. Ine succeeds him.
by 690	Wessex extended to E. Devon, including Exeter.
694	K. Ine writes code of laws for Wessex.
695	New laws codified in Kent.

FINE ARTS AND ARCHITECTURE

by 685	Abbey churches of Monkwearmouth/Jarrow built in stone by French masons in Roman style, with first English use of coloured glass.
bef. 698	Illuminated Gospel Book of Durrow (Ireland) completed.
698	Lindisfarne Gospels begun.
700	Carved stone crosses: Bewcastle, Cumbria; Ruthwell, Dumfriesshire.

LITERATURE AND SCHOLARSHIP

688	St Adomnan, abbot of Iona, begins *Life of St Columba*.
by 700	*Dream of the Rood*, poem attributed to Caedmon.

RELIGION AND EDUCATION

684	St Cuthbert made Bp of Hexham, later of Lindisfarne.
688	Glastonbury Abbey refounded by K. of Wessex.
691	Wilfrid, now Bp of Ripon, seeks reinstatement at York as Bp of all Northumbria but is exiled to Mercia, founding many monasteries there.
692	Synod of Tara, Ireland: all Irish Church accepts authority of Rome.
695	English mission under St Willibrord from Northumbria, later Archbp of Utrecht, begins to convert Frisians (Netherlands).

Events Elsewhere

687	Venice elects first Doge.

AD 701–720

710	K. Ine of Wessex, with K. of Sussex, attacks British K. Geraint of Dumnonia, adds all Devon to Wessex.
711	Picts attack Northumbria south of Forth, are heavily defeated.
716	Ethelbald becomes K. of Mercia; Mercian ascendancy begins.

FINE ARTS AND ARCHITECTURE

by 716	*Codex Amiatinus*, illuminated Bible, produced at Jarrow Monastery.

LITERATURE AND SCHOLARSHIP

703 Bede, monk at Jarrow, writes manual of chronology.
711 Writing of Latin riddles popular pastime for monks.

RELIGION AND EDUCATION

705 St Wilfrid reinstated as Bp of Ripon and Hexham, not York.
716 St Boniface, monk from Exeter, joins mission to Frisians.
717 Nechtan, K. of Picts, after taking advice from abbot of Jarrow, Northumbria, adopts Roman Easter, expels Celtic monks.
719 Boniface commissioned by Pope to evangelize Germany.

Events Elsewhere

711 Arabs invade Spain and S. France.

AD 721–740

722 K. Ine of Wessex unsuccessfully invades Cornwall.
736 K. Ethelbald of Mercia, now overlord of Kent, Wessex and Middlesex (including London), is described as 'King of Britain'.

LITERATURE AND SCHOLARSHIP

725 Bede's second chronological work introduces dating from Christ's birth (*Anno Domini*).
731 Bede completes *Ecclesiastical History of English*.

RELIGION AND EDUCATION

722 *Nov. 30* St Boniface, English missionary, made Bp to the Germans.
725 Monks from Ireland first visit Faroes.
732 Boniface made Archbp in Germany, organizes dioceses in Bavaria.
735 Egbert, pupil of Bede, becomes first Archbp of York, founds great cathedral school at York.

Events Elsewhere

732 Ψ Poitiers, France: Charles Martel, K. of Franks, defeats Arabs, halts Muslim advance in Europe.

AD 741–760

750	K. Edbert of Northumbria defeats Britons of Strathclyde, takes Kyle, Ayrshire.
752	Ψ Beorhford (unidentified): Wessex defeats Mercia, temporarily gains independence.
756	K. Edbert of Northumbria, allied to Picts, takes Dumbarton, capital of Strathclyde.
by 757	Wat's Dyke built from R. Severn to R. Dee, first attempt to define Mercian frontier with Wales.
757	K. Ethelbald of Mercia murdered, Mercian domination of S. Britain ended. After civil war Offa becomes King.
760	Mercians and Welsh fight at Hereford.

RELIGION AND EDUCATION

746/747	Council of Clofeshoh (?Brixworth, Northants), with K. Ethelbald of Mercia presiding, calls for more Church discipline, condemns monastic abuses and decrees liturgy to be sung to music sent from Rome.
747	St Boniface, now Archbp of Mainz, writes to K. Ethelbald of Mercia, condemning his treatment of monks and nuns.
749	K. Ethelbald of Mercia frees Church by edict ('privilege' of Gumley, Leics) from economic obligations to King.

AD 761–780

by 764	K. Offa of Mercia overlord of Kent.
771	Offa defeats men of Hastings, subdues all Sussex.
774	Offa described as 'King of the English'.
776	Ψ Otford: Kent regains independence from Mercia for 10 years.
778	Offa ravages Dyfedd.

RELIGION AND EDUCATION

by 761	Angus I, K. of Picts, founds abbey of St Andrews, Fife (v. 834, alternative date).
767	Alcuin becomes head of York Cathedral school.

784	K. Offa of Mercia campaigns in Wales, begins to build Offa's Dyke, 150 miles long with rampart and ditch, from Severn estuary to N. Wales, probably joining Wat's Dyke (*v.* 757). Dyke defines Welsh-Mercian frontier, abandoning some English territory to Wales.
after 786	First Viking raid on England, at Portland, Dorset.
787	K. Offa of Mercia has son anointed King: first consecration of King in England.
787	K. Offa of Mercia issues silver 'penny' coin bearing his name and portrait.
by 789	K. Offa of Mercia establishes diplomatic and trade relations with Charlemagne, K. of Franks.
789	K. Offa of Mercia proposes to marry his son to Charlemagne's daughter. Charlemagne breaks off relations, imposes trade embargo on English.
792	K. Offa of Mercia's daughter marries K. of Northumbria. Offa visits Rome.
793 *Jun.* 8	Vikings sack Lindisfarne, Northumbria.
794	Vikings raid Orkneys and Jarrow.
795	Vikings raid Iona and Skye.
796	Charlemagne makes trade agreement with K. Offa of Mercia, in earliest surviving letter from European to English ruler. Offa ravages Dyfed. Vikings raid Irish coast.
Jul. 26	K. Offa of Mercia dies. Wessex regains independence.
796–798	Kentish rebellion against Mercia, finally suppressed.

FINE ARTS AND ARCHITECTURE

780	Book of Kells, illuminated Gospels, begun on Iona.

LITERATURE AND SCHOLARSHIP

793	Last likely date for *Beowulf* (*v.* 678).
800	(?Mercian) poet Cynewulf writes English religious poems, including *Elene*, story of St Helena's journey to Palestine.

RELIGION AND EDUCATION

782	English scholar Alcuin becomes master of Charlemagne's palace school at Aachen.
786	Papal legates visit England, hold councils in Mercia and Northumbria.
788	K. Offa of Mercia induces Pope to divide see of Canterbury and make Lichfield, Staffs, an archbishopric.

795 *Feb.–Aug.*   Irish monks visit Iceland.

Events Elsewhere

800 *Dec. 25*   Charlemagne crowned Holy Roman Emperor in Rome.

AD 801–820

801   Unsuccessful Northumbrian invasion of Mercia.

802   Vikings raid Iona. Egbert becomes K. of Wessex.

806   Vikings burn Iona, kill 68 monks.

815   K. Egbert of Wessex conquers Cornwall.

817   K. Cenwulf of Mercia in dispute with Wulfred, Archbp of Canterbury, over Church lands.

FINE ARTS AND ARCHITECTURE

807   Books of Kells taken from Iona to be finished at Kells, N. Ireland.

LITERATURE AND SCHOLARSHIP

800   Earliest date for Welsh cleric Nennius to have begun *Historia Brittonum* (described by himself as 'heap of all I found'), first source of K. Arthur story.

RELIGION AND EDUCATION

803 *Oct. 12*   Council of Clofeshoh (?Brixworth, Northants): Archbishopric of Lichfield abolished.

807   Abbot Cellach of Iona founds new monastery at Kells, N. Ireland.

AD 821–840

821   Archbp of Canterbury submits to K. Cenwulf of Mercia and pays fine.

822   Mercians invade Wales, destroy Deganwy fortress and subdue Powys.

825   Ψ Ellendun (Wroughton, Wilts): K. Egbert of Wessex defeats Mercians, subdues Essex, Kent and Sussex. End of Mercian supremacy.

829   K. Egbert of Wessex temporarily conquers Mercia and is acknowledged as overlord by Northumbria.

835   Vikings raid Sheppey, Kent.

| 838 | Ψ Hingston Down, Cornwall: K. Egbert of Wessex defeats combined army of Cornish and Danes. |

| 839 | Vikings defeat Picts. |

LITERATURE AND SCHOLARSHIP

| 829/830 | Latest date for Nennius's *Historia Brittonum* (*v.* 809). |

RELIGION AND EDUCATION

| by 834 | Angus II, K. of Picts, founds abbey of St Andrews, Fife (*v.* 761, alternative date). |

AD 841–860

| 841 | Norwegians (Norsemen) build fortified harbours in Ireland, including Dublin. |

| 842 | Vikings raid: London; Rochester, Kent; Southampton. |

| 843 | Kenneth MacAlpin, K. of Dal Riada Scots since 840, becomes K. of Picts also; kingdom now centred on Forteviot, Perthshire. |

| 851 | First recorded naval battle in English history, off Sandwich, Kent. Kentish ships defeat Danish fleet.
Ψ 'Aclea' (Oakley, somewhere south of Thames): K. Ethelwulf of Wessex defeats Danish army.
Danes spend first winter in England, at Thanet, Kent.
Danes attack Norwegian colonists in Ireland and W. Scottish isles, and take Dublin. |

| 853 | Olaf *'the White' restores Norwegian power in Ireland. |

| by 860 | Norse colonies established in Orkneys, Shetlands and Hebrides. |

| 860 | Ethelbert becomes K. of Wessex. |

RELIGION AND EDUCATION

| 849/850 | Dunkeld Abbey, Perth, refounded; St Columba's relics brought there. |
| 852 | St Swithin made Bp of Winchester. |

VOYAGES AND EXPLORATION

| 853 | K. Ethelwulf of Wessex sends youngest son Alfred to Pope Leo IV's court in Rome: Pope robes Alfred as consul. |
| 855 | K. Ethelwulf and Alfred spend year in Rome and at court of Franks. |

865		Ethelred becomes K. of Wessex. 'Great Army' of Danes, led by K. Ivar 'the Boneless' and K. Halfdan, lands in E. Anglia.
866	*Nov. 1*	Danes take York.
867		Danes defend York, defeat Northumbrians, impose puppet king on Northumbria and winter in Nottingham; Northumbria and Mercia buy peace from Danes.
869	*Nov. 20*	Ψ Hoxne, Suffolk: Danes under Ivar defeat and kill St Edmund, K. of E. Anglia.
870		Danes invade Wessex, taking Reading, Berks. K. Olaf of Dublin attacks Strathclyde and sacks Dumbarton.
871	*Jan.*	Ψ Ashdown, Berks: Wessex army under K. Ethelred and brother Alfred defeats Danes; after losing later battles, Wessex buys peace from Danes. Ethelred dies, succeeded by Alfred. Danes winter in London.
874		Danes appoint puppet king of Mercia; Danish army splits into two.
875–876		Halfdan leads northern Danish army against Picts and Strathclyde; Danes divide Northumbria, taking southern part for Danish kingdom of York.
877		Southern Danish army under Guthrum attacks Wessex, takes Exeter and retreats to Gloucester. Part of army settles in E. Mercia, later known as 'Five Boroughs' (Derby, Leicester, Lincoln, Nottingham, Stamford). Danish K. Halfdan invades Ireland, is defeated and killed by Norsemen at Ψ Strangford Lough.
878	*Jan.*	Guthrum's southern Danish army takes Chippenham, Wilts, conquers most of Wessex.
	Easter	K. Alfred retreats to Athelney, Somerset, builds fort and begins guerrilla warfare. Ψ Countisbury Hill, Devon: new Danish army from Wales defeated.
	May 11/12	Men from Somerset, W. Hampshire, Wiltshire, join Alfred to defeat Danes under Guthrun at Ψ Edington, Wilts. Danes make peace; Guthrum is baptised with Alfred as godfather. Danish army settled in E. Anglia; Guthrun K. of E. Anglia. K. Rhodri the Great of Gwynedd dies; S. Welsh Kings submit to Alfred as overlord.

RELIGION AND EDUCATION

875	Monks leave Lindisfarne with St Cuthbert's body and, after wandering for 7 years, settle at Chester-le-Street, Durham.

862   Swedish Vikings found Novgorod; beginning of Russian state.
after 863   St Cyril, evangelist of S. Slavs, invents Cyrillic script.
867–870   Eastern Orthodox Church separates from Rome.
870   Norwegians begin to colonize Iceland.

AD 881–900

886   K. Alfred frees London from Danes, restores city to Mercia. Alfred and 'all
              English councillors' make treaty with K. Guthrum and E. Anglians: E.
              England between RR Thames and Tees declared Danish territory (later
              'Danelaw'), where English and Danes are equal in law.

after 887   K. Alfred begins to build fortresses ('burhs'): Cricklade, Wilts; Wallingford,
              Oxon; Wareham, Dorset. New law code issued, based on laws of KK
              Ethelbert, Ine and Offa.

892   New Danish army under Hastein invades from France; Danes of York and E.
              Anglia join Hastein.

893   Ψ Buttington Island in R. Severn: Welsh Kings join K. Alfred to defeat
              Danes, who retreat to Chester and Wales.

894   Danes march south-east to Thames estuary, finally towing ships up RR
              Thames and Lea, and camping at Ware, Herts.

895   K. Alfred blockades Danish fleet by obstructing R. Lea; Danes retreat to
              Bridgnorth, Shropshire, leaving ships. Alfred builds battle fleet.

896   Danish army disperses to Northumbria, E. Anglia and France.

899 *Oct. 26*   K. Alfred dies, succeeded by son Edward 'the Elder'.

900   Scots under K. Constantine II invade British kingdom of Strathclyde; British
              nobles migrate from Strathclyde to Wales.

FINE ARTS AND ARCHITECTURE
after 886   London rebuilt; streets between Cheapside and R. Thames laid out.
              Winchester replanned: Old Minster and palace with painted walls built.
              'Alfred Jewel', possibly jewelled bookmark (found 1693 at Athelney).

LITERATURE AND SCHOLARSHIP
887   K. Alfred begins translating Latin works of Pope Gregory I, Bede, Orosius,
              Boethius and St Augustine into English.
892   *Anglo-Saxon Chronicle* compiled in English; copies distributed to churches.

893	Asser, Bp of Sherborne, writes *Life of Alfred*.

RELIGION AND EDUCATION

by 887	K. Alfred assembles circle of scholars and learns to read Latin.
894	K. Alfred plans to have all free-born boys taught to read English.

Events Elsewhere

898	Magyars from S. Russia under leader Arpad found Hungary.

AD 901–920

902	K. Edward of Wessex puts down rebellion of cousin allied to Danes. Irish drive Norwegians from Dublin; Irish Norsemen begin to colonize NW England, especially the Wirral peninsula, Cheshire.
910	Danes from York invade W. Mercia. Ψ Tettenhall, Staffs: Wessex victorious, 3 Danish kings killed.
911–918	Ethelfleda, K. Alfred's daughter, 'Lady of the Mercians', rules Mercia after her husband's death, and builds 10 fortresses against Danes, including Tamworth.
911	K. Edward transfers London and Oxford from Mercia to Wessex.
914	Wessex repels new Danish army raiding in Wales. Irish Norsemen under Ragnald invade Northumbria, defeat Northumbrians and Scots at Corbridge, Northumbria.
by 914	Norwegian Sihtric retakes Dublin.
915	K. Edward of Wessex occupies Bedford, builds fortress.
916	K. Edward of Wessex advances into Essex, builds fortress at Maldon.
917	K. Edward of Wessex and Ethelfleda of Mercia campaign in Midlands and E. Anglia; Derby taken, Danish K. of E. Anglia killed. Apart from armies of Leicester, Lincoln, Nottingham, Stamford, all Danes south of Humber submit to Edward.
918	Ethelfleda of Mercia dies; K. Edward of Wessex rules Mercia after seizing Tamworth; Danes in remaining 4 of Five Boroughs submit to Edward. Princes of Gwynedd, Dyfed and W. Wales pay homage to Edward. Norwegian Ragnald leads new Viking fleet from Ireland against Northumbria, fights Scots and Northumbrians in indecisive battle.
919	Ragnald seizes York, makes self King. K. Edward builds fortresses on R. Mersey.

| 920 | Sihtric leads Norse attack on Cheshire. |
| | K. Edward advances to Bakewell, Derbyshire, builds fortress and is acknowledged overlord by Constantine II, K. of Scots, K. Ragnald of York, K. of Strathclyde and all Northumbria. |

FINE ARTS AND ARCHITECTURE

| 901–915 | Irish-Norse sculpture in NW England: Gosforth cross, Cumbria. |
| 910–915 | Embroidered vestments in St Cuthbert's tomb, early example of Winchester school of decoration (with acanthus leaves); part of K. Athelstan's gift to shrine (*v.* 934/935). |

RELIGION AND EDUCATION

| 906 | Agreement of Scone: Constantine II promises Bp of St Andrews to uphold laws of Scottish Church. |

Events Elsewhere

| 911 | Viking Rollo becomes first Duke of Normandy. |

AD 921–940

924 *Jul.* 17	K. Edward dies, succeeded in Mercia by son Athelstan.
925 *Sep.* 4	K. Athelstan crowned K. of Wessex at Kingston, Surrey.
926–930	K. Athelstan of Wessex issues law codes at Grately, Hants, and Exeter, Devon.
927	K. Sihtric of York dies; K. Athelstan of Wessex drives heirs out of England, occupies York, seizes treasures and destroys Danish fortifications.
Jul. 12	At Eamont Bridge, Cumbria, KK of Scots and Strathclyde, and English of N. Northumbria acknowledge K. Athelstan as overlord.
927–928	K. Athelstan defeats Welsh princes. At Hereford Welsh agree to pay tribute and to keep R. Wye as boundary between England and S. Wales.
	K. Athelstan subdues Cornwall, sets boundary of Cornwall at R. Tamar and expels all British from Exeter.
928	K. Athelstan's sister Edith marries German prince Otto, later Holy Roman Emperor.
931 *Mar.* 24	K. Athelstan holds first General Council of all England at Colchester.
934	K. Athelstan's army invades Scotland, fleet ravages east coast of Scotland up to Caithness.
935	K. Athelstan's coinage bears title 'King of all Britain'.

936	K. Athelstan sends escort to restore nephew Louis as K. of Franks; helps godson Alan of Brittany return home and defeat Viking invaders.
937	Ψ 'Brunanburh' (?): K. Athelstan defeats coalition of Scots, Strathclyde and Irish Norsemen under Olaf Guthfrithsson.
939	K. Athelstan sends English fleet to Europe, supporting K. Louis of Franks against Germans; expedition fails.
Oct. 27	K. Athelstan dies, succeeded by brother Edmund. Olaf Guthfrithsson invades again and takes York.
940	K. Olaf, supported by Archbp Wulfstan of York, invades Midlands; by Ty of Leicester K. Edmund grants Olaf Five Boroughs.

FINE ARTS AND ARCHITECTURE

| 934/935 | Bede's *Life of St Cuthbert*, illuminated and with frontispiece depicting K. Athelstan (earliest contemporary portrait of English king) given by Athelstan to Cuthbert's shrine (*v.* 910–915). |
| by 939 | Malmesbury Abbey rebuilt; Athelstan buried there. |

RELIGION AND EDUCATION

| 940 | St Dunstan becomes abbot of Glastonbury, begins reform and revival of English monasticism, following European Benedictines. |

Events Elsewhere

| 930 | 'Althing', world's oldest legislature, founded in Iceland. |

AD 941–960

941	K. Olaf of York dies, succeeded by Olaf Sihtricsson.
942	K. Edmund of Wessex recaptures Five Boroughs.
944	K. Edmund takes York.
945	K. Edmund invades Strathclyde, grants Cumbrian part of kingdom to Malcolm I, K. of Scots.
946	K. Edmund tries to restore nephew, K. Louis of Franks, to throne.
May 26	K. Edmund murdered, succeeded by brother Eadred.
947	Archbp Wulfstan of York and Northumbrian Council, after first accepting K. Eadred, invite Eric 'Bloodaxe', deposed K. of Norway, to be K. of York.
948	K. Eadred invades and ravages Northumbria, burns Ripon Minster and forces Northumbrians to exile Eric. Malcolm I ravages Northumbria to R. Tees.

949	Olaf Sihtricsson, now K. of Dublin, returns as K. of York.
949/950	Death of Hywel Dda (the Good), Anglophil P. of Gwynedd, reputed compiler of first written Welsh law code.
952	Archbishop Wulfstan imprisoned by K. Eadred. Eric 'Bloodaxe' restored as K. of York.
954	K. Eric of York killed on Stainmore, Yorks. Eadred now K. of all England. Scots under K. Indulf take Edinburgh and Lothian.
955 *Nov. 23*	K. Eadred dies, succeeded by nephew Eadwig.
956	K. Eadwig quarrels with St Dunstan. Dunstan exiled.
957	Mercia and Northumbria rebel, and choose Eadwig's brother Edgar as King. Edgar makes Dunstan Bp of Worcester and London.
959 *Oct. 1*	K. Eadwig dies; Edgar succeeds as K. of England, and makes Dunstan Archbp of Canterbury.

MUSIC AND DRAMA

from 957 — Archbp Dunstan, himself a musician, encourages use of organ in churches, installs organ in Malmesbury Abbey.

RELIGION AND EDUCATION

from 957 — Archbp Dunstan encourages K. Edgar to refound abbeys, including Bath, Exeter, Malmesbury and Westminster Abbey.

AD 961–980

962/963	K. Edgar issues law code, allowing legal autonomy to Danish territory in England.
967	Mathghamhain, K. of W. Munster, with brother Brian Boru, defeats Norsemen near Tipperary, and sacks Limerick.
971	Kenneth II, K. of Scots, plunders as far south as Stainmore, Yorks.
973	Coronation of K. Edgar at Bath by Archbps Dunstan and Oswald, with ritual used for later English monarchs. Edgar sails to Chester, receives homage from 6 kings (1 of Scots, 2 of Strathclyde, 2 from Wales, 1 Viking of the Isles) and is rowed by them on R. Dee. *Edgar grants Lothian to K. of Scots.
975	K. Edgar dies, succeeded by son Edward.
978 *Mar. 18*	K. Edward murdered at Corfe Castle, later canonized, succeeded by half-brother, Ethelred 'the Unready' (without counsel).

| 980 | Vikings raid again: Danes in south and west, Irish and Manx Norsemen in Wales. |
| | Maelsechnail (Malachy) II, High K. of Ireland, defeats Dublin Norsemen at Tara. K. Olaf Sihtricsson leaves Ireland for Iona. |

FINE ARTS AND ARCHITECTURE
| by 970 | Many churches have bell-towers: St Mary's Deerhurst, Gloucs. |
| after 971 | Winchester school of illumination flourishes: *Benedictional* of St Ethelwold; Foundation Charter of Winchester New Minster. |

MUSIC AND DRAMA
| 970 | Dramatization of Resurrection story in Easter Day liturgy ('Quem quaeritis?') introduced to English churches. |
| | Organ is installed in Winchester Cathedral. |

RELIGION AND EDUCATION
961	St Oswald made Bp of Worcester, founds and refounds abbeys: Ramsey, Cambs; Evesham and Pershore, Worcs; Winchcombe, Gloucs.
963	St Ethelwold made Bp of Winchester, restores severe monastic discipline and refounds abbeys: Ely and Peterborough, Cambs.
970	Council at Winchester regulating monastic revival approves *Regularis Concordia*, adaptation of European Benedictine ritual to include prayers for English king and royal family.
971 *Jul.* 15	During rebuilding of Winchester Cathedral, St Swithin's body is moved to new shrine.

AD 981–1000

981–988	Danes raid Dorset, Devon and Cornwall.
985–986	Irish, Norsemen and Danes raid Hebrides.
991 *Mar.* 1	Ty between K. Ethelred and D. Richard I of Normandy, arranged by Pope's envoy to end hostility caused by Normandy's protection of Viking raiders; each agrees not to assist the other's enemies.
Aug.	Danish fleet of 93 ships, probably led by Olaf Tryggvason, later K. of Norway, sacks Ipswich and occupies Northey Island in Blackwater, near Maldon, Essex.
10	Ψ Maldon: Danes victorious; English pay first Danegeld (£10,000). Ethelred makes treaty of peace and mutual assistance with Olaf; trade regulated and £22,000 Danegeld agreed.
993	Danes raid Northumbria.
994	Olaf of Norway and Swein 'Forkbeard' son of Danish King, lead Danish

invading army in unsuccessful siege of London and ravage south-east; Danegeld (£16,000 + provisions) paid. Swein pillages Wales and I. of Man on way home. Olaf, baptised and confirmed at Andover with K. Ethelred as sponsor, swears not to return to England.

997	K. Ethelred's law code, issued at Wantage, Berks, defines legal position in Danelaw; Scandinavian custom of trial by sworn jury of 12 introduced.
997–998	Danes raid south and west coasts, and S. Wales.
999	Danes raid Kent, sailing up R. Medway to Rochester. Maelsechnail and Brian Boru, joint High KK of Ireland, take Dublin; Norse kingdom, subjected to Irish, pays tribute.
1000	Danes spend year in Normandy. English naval expedition ravages I. of Man; combined land and sea attack on Cumbria fails.
1000	English navy attacks Cotentin peninsula, Normandy.

LITERATURE AND SCHOLARSHIP

990–995	Aelfric, monk of Cerne Abbey, Dorset, writes *Catholic Homilies*, 80 sermons for use throughout Church's year.
996/997	Aelfric writes English verse *Lives of the Saints* and begins to translate Old Testament.
1000	Heroic poem *The Battle of Maldon* composed.

Events Elsewhere

982	Norwegian Eric 'the Red' discovers Greenland.
987	Hugh Capet chosen as first King of France.
1000	Leif Ericsson, son of Eric 'the Red', lands on N. American coast and discovers 'Vinland' (Newfoundland).

AD 1001–1010

1002	Truce with Danes. Danegeld (£24,000) paid. K. Ethelred marries Emma, sister of D. of Normandy.
Nov. 13	Massacre of Danes in England ordered by K. Ethelred; dead include sister of K. Swein of Denmark.
1002–1005	Brian Boru makes self High K. of Ireland, described in *Book of Armagh* as 'Imperator Scotorum' (Emperor of Irish).
1003–1005	Danes raid Devon and E. Anglia.
1006–1007	Danes raid south-east coast, ravage from I. of Wight to Reading and

Wallingford in winter. Danegeld (£36,000) paid.

1008	K. Ethelred issues laws for protection of Christianity, drafted by Archbp Wulfstan II of York, at King's Enham, Hants.
1009	New English fleet built, but 100 ships lost through treachery.
Aug. 1	Danish fleet occupies Sandwich; army attacks London, burns Oxford.
1010	Danes under Thorkell 'the Tall' defeat E. Anglian army at Ψ Ringmere, Norfolk, ravage E. Anglia and Mercia.

AD 1011–1020

1011	Danes take Canterbury and capture Archbp, later St, Alphege.
1012 Apr.	Danes are paid Danegeld (£48,000), but kill Archbp Alphege before leaving England. Danish leader Thorkell, with 45 ships and crews, leaves Danes, joins English.
1013 Jul.	K. Swein of Denmark, with son Cnut, sails up RR Humber and Trent to Gainsborough, Lincs, and is accepted as King in Danelaw.
	Danes conquer Mercia and Wessex; by Christmas all England submits to Swein. K. Ethelred flees to Normandy, following Q. Emma and sons Edward and Alfred.
1014 Feb. 3	K. Swein dies; Danish army chooses Cnut leader. English invite K. Ethelred to return.
Apr.	Cnut withdraws to Denmark. Ethelred's son Edmund 'Ironside' seizes Five Boroughs as independent ruler. Thorkell joins Cnut.
23	Ψ Clontarf, Ireland: Irish defeat Norsemen. Brian Boru killed.
1015 Aug.	Cnut invades England, conquers Wessex, Mercia and Northumbria.
1016 Apr. 23	K. Ethelred dies, succeeded by son Edmund.
May	Edmund retakes Wessex; Cnut besieges London.
Oct. 18	Danes defeat English in Ψ Ashingdon, Essex; treaty between Cnut and Edmund leaves Edmund K. of Wessex only.
Nov. 30	Edmund dies, Cnut chosen K. of England.
1017	K. Cnut divides England into 4 districts: Wessex under self; earls rule E. Anglia (Thorkell), Mercia (Leofric), Northumbria (Eric the Norwegian).
Jul.	Cnut marries K. Ethelred's widow, Emma.
after 1018	K. Cnut issues 2-part law code (ecclesiastical and secular), probably drafted by Archbp Wulfstan II of York, based on laws of KK Edgar and Ethelred.
1019–1020	K. Cnut, now K. of Denmark, sends letter to England promising to protect English from Viking attacks if they remain loyal to him.

Ψ Carham on R. Tweed: Malcolm II, K. of Scots, defeats Northumbrians, takes permanent possession of Lothian.

1020 Godwin, rival of Leofric, becomes E. of Wessex.

FINE ARTS AND ARCHITECTURE

by 1013 Greensted, Essex: earliest surviving wooden church built.
1020 K. Cnut adds rotunda to Bury St Edmunds Abbey; dedication of Ashingdon Church to commemorate battle.

LITERATURE AND SCHOLARSHIP

1011 Monk Byrhtferth of Ramsey writes *Manual*, scientific work on time.
1014 Archbp Wulfstan's homily, *Sermo Lupi ad Anglos* (from the Wolf to the English), proclaiming Danes as God's judgement on England.

AD 1021–1030

from 1023 Danish Siward E. of Northumbria.

1025/1026 K. Cnut leads fleet in indecisive Ψ Holy River, S. Sweden, against KK of Norway and Sweden.

1027 K. Cnut, in Rome on pilgrimage and to attend coronation of Conrad II as Holy Roman Emperor, negotiates tax-free route for English travellers to Rome; he sends letter home proclaiming his diplomatic success.
Cnut invades Scotland, receives homage from K. Malcolm II.

1028 K. (later St) Olaf of Norway exiled; K. Cnut, proclaimed K. of Norway, sends first wife Aelfgifu and son Swein to rule there. Harthacnut, son by Emma, made K. of Denmark.

LITERATURE AND SCHOLARSHIP

1023 Archbp Wulfstan II of York writes *Homilies*.

Events Elsewhere

1030 Ψ Stiklestad; Swein defeats and kills Olaf of Norway.

AD 1031–1040

1035 *Nov. 12* K. Cnut dies. English crown disputed between: son by Emma, K. Harthacnut of Denmark, supported by E. Godwin of Wessex; son by Aelfgifu, Harold

	'Harefoot', supported by EE Siward of Northumbria and Leofric of Mercia.
1036	Council of Oxford proclaims Harold Regent. Harold seizes royal treasury at Winchester from Emma. Emma sends for sons by Ethelred, Alfred and Edward; Alfred lands at Dover and is murdered by Godwin, by order of Harold; *Edward returns to Normandy after raiding Southampton.
1037	Harold I proclaimed K. of England; Emma exiled to Bruges, later joined by Harthacnut.
1039	Gruffyd ap Llewelyn, P. of Gwynedd, defeats English invading force.
1040 *Mar. 17*	Harold I dies.
Jun.	Harthacnut lands at Sandwich, makes peace with Godwin and becomes K. of England.
Aug. 14	Macbeth kills Duncan, K. of Scots, and usurps throne.

Events Elsewhere

1035	William 'the Conqueror' succeeds as D. of Normandy.
	Norway accepts Magnus Olafsson as King.
1038/1039	Ty between Harthacnut of Denmark and Magnus of Norway.

AD 1041–1050

1041	K. Harthacnut invites P. Edward to England as his heir.
1042 *Jun. 8*	Harthacnut dies; Edward elected King.
1043 *Apr. 3*	Edward 'the Confessor' is crowned at Winchester on Easter Day; he makes Swein and Harold, sons of E. Godwin of Wessex, earls.
Nov. 16	Edward accuses Q. Emma of treason, dismisses her confidant Bp Stigand of E. Anglia.
	E. Leofric of Mercia founds Coventry Abbey: legend of wife Godiva's naked ride in protest against taxes may originate from her generosity to abbey, 'denuding self' of possessions. City grows later around abbey.
1044	K. Edward reinstates Q. Emma and Bp Stigand.
1045 *Jan. 23*	K. Edward marries Edith, Godwin's daughter.
1046	E. Swein Godwinsson invades S. Wales with P. Gruffyd of Gwynedd, kidnaps abbess of Leominster and is exiled (1047).
1048	Last Viking raid on SE England; raiders flee to Flanders.
	K. Edward joins Emperor in war against Flanders, closing Channel with great fleet at Sandwich, Kent.
1049	Swein Godwinsson returns, murders his cousin, is exiled again.

| 1050 | Council of London: Robert of Jumièges, a Norman, made Archbp of Canterbury, is hostile to Godwin. Swein Godwinsson pardoned. Macbeth, K. of Scots, makes pilgrimage to Rome. |

| 1041–1042 | *Encomium Emmae* (Praise of Emma), biography of and commissioned by Q. Emma of England, written by monk of St Omer. |
| 1046 | *Exeter Book* (7th-century poems) presented to Exeter cathedral. |

Events Elsewhere

| 1047 *Oct. 25* | K. Magnus of Norway dies, succeeded by Harold Hardrada. |

AD 1051–1060

1051 *Sep.*	E. Godwin raises rebellion against K. Edward. Godwin family exiled: Godwin and sons Swein, Tostig and Gyrth go to Flanders, sons Harold and Leofwine to Ireland. Q. Edith sent to nunnery.
1051/1052	*D. William of Normandy visits Edward and is made his heir.
1052 *Mar. 6*	Dowager Q. Emma dies. P. Gruffyd of Gwynedd invades Herefordshire.
Sep. 14/15	Godwin and sons sail up R. Thames to London with large fleet, force Edward to reinstate them. Archbp Robert of Canterbury flees to Normandy, other Normans to Scotland. Stigand is appointed Archbp.
1053 *Apr. 15*	Godwin dies, succeeded as E. of Wessex by son Harold.
1054 *Jul. 27*	E. Siward of Northumbria and Malcolm 'Canmore', son of K. Duncan, invade Scotland, defeat K. Macbeth at Ψ Dunsinane. Malcolm occupies Lothian.
1055	Siward dies. Tostig Godwinsson made E. of Northumbria.
Oct. 24	P. Gruffyd, now ruler of all Wales, and exiled Aelfgar, son of E. Leofric of Mercia, sack Hereford. E. Harold, commanding English army in Wales, makes peace with Aelfgar.
1056	Ψ Glasbury on Wye: Welsh defeat and kill Bp of Hereford.
1057	Edward 'the Exile', son of K. Edmund 'Ironside', returns to England from Hungary and dies, leaving heir P. Edgar. E. Leofric of Mercia dies, his son Aelfgar is exiled again for treason. E. Harold's brothers, Gyrth and Leofwine, are made earls.
Aug. 15	Ψ Lumphanan, Mar: Malcolm of Scots defeats and kills Macbeth.
1058 *Mar. 17*	Malcolm kills Macbeth's stepson, becomes K. Malcolm III of Scots.

Exiled Aelfgar, allied to P. Gruffyd of Wales and supported by Norwegian fleet, attacks English coast; attack fails, but Aelfgar reinstated as E. of Mercia.

1059   Malcolm III, K. of Scots, visits Edward's court and pays homage.

FINE ARTS AND ARCHITECTURE
1060 *May 3*   Dedication of Waltham Abbey, Essex, built by E. Harold.

by 1060   Rebuilding of Westminster Abbey begun by K. Edward.

AD 1061–1065

1061   Ealdred, Archbp of York, and E. Tostig of Northumbria go on embassy to Rome.
Malcolm III, K. of Scots, raids Northumbria.

1062   Edwin succeeds as E. of Mercia.
(St) Wulfstan made Bp of Worcester.
Christmas   E. Harold raids Rhuddlan, N. Wales, headquarters of P. Gruffyd.

1063 *May*   EE Harold and Tostig invade Wales, conquer Gwynedd.
Aug. 5   P. Gruffyd of Wales killed by own men. Wales divided: north under princes paying tribute to England, south under independent princes.

1064/5   E. Harold in Normandy, on embassy from K. Edward or as result of shipwreck, joins D. William in campaign against Brittany. *He does homage to William and takes oath to assist him to English Crown.

1065 *Oct. 3*   Northumbrian rebels attack York, outlaw E. Tostig and choose Morcar, brother of E. Edwin of Mercia, as earl. Mercian and Northumbrian armies invade Midlands. Tostig exiled.

FINE ARTS AND ARCHITECTURE
1065   Dedication of Wilton Abbey, built by Q. Edith.
Dec. 28   Dedication of Westminster Abbey.

Events Elsewhere
by 1064   William of Normandy conquers Maine.

1066	Jan.	4/5	K. Edward dies. E. Harold chosen King.
		6	Edward buried in Westminster Abbey. Harold II crowned.
	May		Exiled Tostig, Harold's brother, attempts invasion, fails and retreats to Scotland.
	Sep.		K. Harold of Norway and Tostig sail up R. Humber, attack Yorkshire.
		20	Ψ Gate Fulford, Yorks: Norwegians defeat EE Edwin and Morcar.
		25	Ψ Stamford Bridge: K. Harold defeats Norwegians. Harold of Norway and Tostig killed.
		28	William of Normandy lands at Pevensey, Sussex. K. Harold settles Yorkshire and marches south.
	Oct.	14	Ψ Hastings: William victorious; K. Harold and brothers, Gyrth and Leofwine, killed.
	Oct.-Dec.		After attempt to choose P. Edgar, great-nephew of K. Edward, as King, London and SE England submit to William.
	Dec.	25	William I crowned K. of England in Westminster Abbey by Archbp Ealdred of York.
1067	Dec.		William I puts down revolt of Exeter, builds Exeter Castle.
			P. Edgar flees to Scotland with mother and sisters.
1068			William I defeats rebel EE Edwin and Morcar in York; he builds castles at Warwick, Nottingham, York, Lincoln, Huntingdon, Cambridge.
1069	Jan.	28	Northumbrians kill new Norman earl, attack York, but are defeated.
	Sep.		Danish fleet reaches R. Humber. Danes and rebels take York, burn Minster. Mercians revolt, but are defeated by William I at Stafford.
1069–1070			William I defeats English rebels and harries North and Midlands, devastating land from Shropshire to Durham.
1070	Spring		K. Swein of Denmark joins fleet in Humber. Danes and English rebels, led by Hereward 'the Wake' from Lincolnshire, occupy I. of Ely.
	Jun.	1	Hereward plunders Peterborough Abbey.
			Ty between Swein and William I: Danes leave England.
	Aug.	15	Archbp Stigand dismissed; Lanfranc, abbot of Caen, Normandy, appointed Archbp of Canterbury.
			Malcolm III, K. of Scots, invades England; he marries Margaret, P. Edgar's sister (St Margaret).

FINE ARTS AND ARCHITECTURE

1067	William I founds Battle Abbey on site of Ψ Hastings, to design based on St Martin's, Tours, with altar on spot where K. Harold was killed: one of several new monastic foundations from 1066 to 1100.
after 1070	St Augustine's Abbey, Canterbury, and York Minster rebuilt.

after 1066   Norman style of short hair, with shaven face and neck, supplants English long hair, moustaches and beards among noblemen.

AD 1071–1075

1071   William I defeats English rebels on I. of Ely. Rebel leader Hereward escapes to live as outlaw in 'Bruneswald' (Bromswold) on Northants border.
E. Hugh of Chester, first of Norman 'Marcher' (border) lords, begins to subdue Gwynedd.

1072 *Aug.*   William I invades Scotland up to R. Tay, receives homage of Malcolm III, K. of Scots.

by 1074   William I's second son, Richard, killed while hunting.

1075   Roger de Montgomery, a Norman, made E. of Shrewsbury, pushes Anglo-Welsh frontier west into Powys.
Revolt of Roger, E. of Hereford, Ralph, E. of East Anglia and Waltheof, E. of Northumbria, soon suppressed. Danish fleet arrives too late to join rebels.

FINE ARTS AND ARCHITECTURE
1071–1077   Canterbury Cathedral rebuilt by Archbp Lanfranc to design of his abbey in Caen.
1072–1073   Lincoln Cathedral begun by Bp of Fécamp.
by 1075   Norwich Castle built.
1075–1078   Old Sarum Cathedral begun.

RELIGION AND EDUCATION
1072 *Apr.*   Archbp Lanfranc holds first Church Council at Winchester: primacy of Canterbury over York established; bishops to hold diocesan synods and appoint archdeacon and chapter.
1075   Council of London: abuses reformed; rural sees (Dorchester, Lichfield, Selsey, Sherborne) moved to towns (Lincoln, Chester, Chichester, Salisbury).

Events Elsewhere

from 1072   William I campaigns each year in France, against French King and Count of Anjou.

AD 1076–1080

1076 *May 31*	Waltheof, E. of Northumbria executed. Walcher, Bp of Durham, given power of earl.
1077/1078	Robert, William I's oldest son, rebels in Normandy, flees to Flanders and is supported by French King.
1079	William I completes afforestation of New Forest, Hampshire, one of several royal hunting preserves, with severe penalties for poachers. *22 villages destroyed to make New Forest.
1080	Northumbrians rebel and murder Bp of Durham. William I's brother, Odo, Bp of Bayeux and E. of Kent, crushes rebels and harries countryside.
Autumn	William's son Robert, now reconciled to his father, leads campaign into Scotland as far as Falkirk.

FINE ARTS AND ARCHITECTURE

1077	Rebuilding of St Albans and Rochester cathedrals begun.
1078	'White Tower', first part of Tower of London, and Colchester Castle begun, similarly designed by Bp Gundulf of Rochester.
1080	Castle built on R. Tyne (Newcastle).

RELIGION AND EDUCATION

1076 *Apr.*	Council of Winchester: confirms rights of parish priest against overlord and powers of ecclesiastical courts; attempts to establish: celibacy of clergy, marriage ceremony in church as norm for all couples.
1077	Lewes, Sussex: first Cluniac abbey in England founded.
1080	William I refuses to acknowledge Pope Gregory VII as overlord.

AD 1081–1085

1081	William I leads campaign in S. Wales, as far as St David's.
1082	Bp Odo arrested, forfeits earldom of Kent and is imprisoned.
1085	K. Cnut of Denmark, allied to KK of France and Norway, threatens to invade England, but is prevented by revolt at home.
	William I imports large force of French, Norman and Breton mercenaries.
Dec. 25	Christmas Council: William orders survey of land ownership throughout England (*Domesday Book*).

1081   Ely Cathedral begun.

1082   Completion of Bayeux Tapestry: panorama embroidered in wool on linen, 230ft. × 20in., depicting Norman conquest of England; English work, probably from Canterbury, commissioned by Bp Odo of Bayeux.

1084   Worcester Cathedral begun by Bp Wulfstan.

AD 1086–1090

1086 *Aug. 1*   Council at Salisbury. All landowners of importance do homage to William I. Domesday survey finished, incorporated in 2 vols. of *Domesday Book* by 1088.

1087 *Sep. 9*   William I killed campaigning in Maine against French King: succeeded as D. of Normandy by first son Robert; as K. of England by third son William 'Rufus'; fourth son Henry left money.

     26   William II crowned by Archbp Lanfranc of Canterbury.

  Christmas   Bp Odo, pardoned by William I on deathbed, returns as E. of Kent.

1088 *Apr.*   Odo, supported by many Norman barons, rebels in favour of D. Robert. Bishops, except Durham, sheriffs and English subjects are loyal to William II. Robert fails to send troops to support rebels.

     July   William crushes rebels; Odo and Bp of Durham exiled to Normandy.

1089 *May*   Lanfranc dies. See of Canterbury, with other sees and abbacies, left vacant while William II enjoys revenues.

1090   William II buys allegiance of barons in Normandy and controls most of duchy east of Seine.

FINE ARTS AND ARCHITECTURE

1087   Old St Paul's Cathedral burnt down; rebuilding begins.

1088   'White Tower' of Tower of London built.

1089   Gloucester Cathedral, Tewkesbury Abbey begun.

RECREATION AND FASHION

by 1090   Long and facial hair returns for men. Long gowns with very long sleeves, often tied in knots, worn by both sexes. Court fashion thought effeminate.

Events Elsewhere

1088   Papal schism between Popes Urban II and Clement III: Urban recognized in France and Italy, but not in England.

1091	*Feb.* 2	William II invades Normandy, makes Ty of Rouen with D. Robert: William to keep part of Normandy already held (*v.* 1090) and help Robert to restore order and recover Maine. P. Henry resists loss of lands he bought (Cherbourg and Mont St Michel), and is expelled from Normandy.
	May	Malcolm III, K. of Scots, invades Northumberland.
	Autumn	William II and D. Robert campaign in Scotland together: Malcolm submits to William as overlord on same terms as to William I.
1092	*May*	William II takes Cumbria from Scots, advancing frontier to Tweed-Cheviot line and refounding Carlisle.
1093	*Mar.* 6	William II, gravely ill, appoints Anselm, abbot of Caen, to vacant see of Canterbury.
	Nov. 13	Malcolm III, K. of Scots, and oldest son killed at Alnwick, invading Northumberland.
	16	Q. Margaret of Scots dies; Malcolm's brother Donalbain becomes K. of Scots.
		Death of P. Rhys ap Tudor opens S. Wales to Norman occupation; castles built include Cardiff and Pembroke.
1094	*Feb.*	While preparing to invade Normandy, William II quarrels with Anselm about royal overlordship of Church lands and right to make Church appointments ('investiture'), and recognition of Pope (*v.* 1088).
	Mar. 19	William II invades Normandy without success; during absence Welsh drive Marcher lords from N. Wales and destroy all castles except Pembroke in S. Wales.
1095	*Jan.*	William II returns to England.
		Revolt of Robert de Mowbray, Norman E. of Northumberland, with barons of previous revolt (*v.* 1088). William takes castles of Newcastle (or Tynemouth) and Bamburgh, crushes revolt.
	Feb. 25	Council of Rockingham meets to debate William II's quarrel with Archbp Anselm; no decision reached.
		William II asks Pope Urban to depose Anselm in return for English recognition of his papacy.
	May	Papal legate arrives in England, accepts recognition, but refuses to depose Anselm. Enforced reconciliation between Anselm and King.

FINE ARTS AND ARCHITECTURE

1093	Durham Cathedral begun: first building in W. Europe with ribbed vaulting in roof.

SCIENCE AND INVENTION

1092 *Oct. 18*	Walcher, prior of Malvern, one of first W. Europeans to use astrolabe,

by 1095	observes and calculates exact time of eclipse of moon. Abacus used in England for calculation.

AD 1096–1100

1096		William II lends Duke Robert money to go on 1st Crusade, in exchange for 3-year lease of Normandy, and grants younger brother, P. Henry, 2 Norman counties.
1097		After 2 campaigns William II fails to reconquer Wales, but sets Edgar, son of Malcolm III and Margaret, on Scottish throne.
	Oct.	William exiles Archbp Anselm for deciding to visit Pope without royal permission.
1098		Norman expedition into N. Wales takes Anglesey, but is halted by Norwegian fleet led by K. of Norway; E. of Shrewsbury killed.
1100	*Aug.* 2	William II is killed hunting in New Forest, succeeded by P. Henry.
	5	Henry I is crowned by Bp of London; in coronation charter promises reforms of all William's abuses.
	Sep. 23	Anselm returns, but refuses to recognize royal overlordship of Church lands.
	Nov. 11	Henry marries Matilda, daughter of Malcolm III of Scots.

FINE ARTS AND ARCHITECTURE

1096	Norwich Cathedral begun.
1097	Westminster Hall built.

RELIGION AND EDUCATION

1100	Monastic order of Augustinian canons reaches England.

Events Elsewhere

1096	1st Crusade begins.
1099	Crusaders take Jerusalem; Godfrey of Bouillon made K. of Jerusalem.

AD 1101–1105

1101	*Apr.* 2	Henry I appoints Roger, a Norman monk, Chancellor.
	Jul.	D. Robert of Normandy lands at Portsmouth with army. Ty of Alton: Robert gives up claim to English throne in return for annuity of 3,000 marks (£2,000).

1102	Robert de Bellême, E. of Shrewsbury, rebels, is defeated and banished to Normandy, where he reduces duchy to anarchy; Welsh of Powys assert independence from Norman rule during earl's absence.
	Roger made Bp of Salisbury (consecrated 1107) and resigns as Chancellor.
1103	Archbp Anselm of Canterbury goes to Rome in attempt to settle dispute between Henry I and Pope over royal investiture of clergy; he fails and remains abroad.
1104	Henry I leads expedition to restore order in Normandy.
1105	Henry I campaigns in Normandy, takes Bayeux and Caen.

RELIGION AND EDUCATION

| 1102 | Council of London forbids marriage of clergy; disobedience to be punished by heavy fines. |

AD 1106–1110

1106 *Sep. 28*	Ψ Tinchebrai, Normandy: Henry I defeats brother D. Robert, imprisons him for life and reunites duchy with England.
1107	Agreement on investiture between Henry and Archbp Anselm. Henry gives up right to invest with spiritual dignities, but retains power of appointment and overlordship of Church lands.
	Bp Roger of Salisbury made Justiciar.
by 1107	Merchant gilds are established in towns, regulating trade; first recorded at Burford, Oxon.
1108	Flemish farmers and traders settle in S. Pembrokeshire.
by 1110	Exchequer (named after 'scaccarium', table ruled in squares and used like abacus for accounts) organized by Bp Roger as separate department, under Barons of Exchequer.

FINE ARTS AND ARCHITECTURE

1107	Winchester Cathedral tower falls, is rebuilt with rib-vaulting.
1108	Southwell Minster, Notts, begun.
from 1110	Anglo-Norman churches decorated with carved chevron pattern.

RECREATION AND FASHION

| by 1110 | Henry I has royal park at Woodstock, Oxford, walled, for hunting and keeping exotic wild animals. |

1108–1112   Walcher of Malvern produces lunar tables for 1036–1112 (*v.* 1092).

AD 1111–1115

1111   Henry I campaigns in Normandy against rebels led by exiled E. Robert of Shrewsbury and supported by Counts of Flanders and Anjou and K. Louis VI of France.

1112   E. Robert captured and imprisoned; Count of Anjou agrees to do homage for Maine, and to marry daughter to Henry's only son William.

1113 *Mar.*   Ty of Gisors with France recognizes English overlordship of Maine and Brittany.

1114 *Jan.* 7   Henry's daughter Matilda marries Emperor Henry V.
Bp Roger of Salisbury introduces pipe roll (double sheet of parchment rolled and tied) as permanent record of Exchequer accounts.

AD 1116–1120

1116–1119   Henry I campaigns in France against K. Louis VI of France, Counts of Flanders and Anjou, and Norman rebels.

1118   Peace made with Flanders.
May 1   Henry I's wife, Q. Matilda, dies.

1119 *Jun.*   Peace with Anjou confirmed by marriage between Henry I's only son P. William and Count of Anjou's daughter.
Aug. 20   Ψ Brémule: French are defeated; peace between England and France.

1120 *Nov. 25*   P. William drowned in sinking of 'White Ship' off Barfleur.

FINE ARTS AND ARCHITECTURE
1117   Rebuilding of Peterborough Cathedral, burnt down in 1116, begun.

RELIGION AND EDUCATION
1119   Pope confirms constitution of Cistercian monastic order ('Carta Caritatis') written by English abbot, (St) Stephen Harding.

AD 1121–1125

1121	Henry I marries second wife, Adeliza of Louvain.
1123	Louis VI of France and Count of Anjou support revolt in Normandy.
1124	Norman rebels defeated. Henry I attempts joint attack on France with son-in-law, the German Emperor. David I, son of Malcolm III, becomes K. of Scots. Galloping inflation in England ('pound could not buy pennyworth'): moneyers punished by castration and loss of hand.

FINE ARTS AND ARCHITECTURE
1121	Henry I refounds Reading Abbey.
1123	St Bartholomew-the-Great, Smithfield, London, is begun as part of priory and first London hospital founded by Rahere, courtier or court jester of Henry I. Rahere becomes first prior.

LITERATURE AND SCHOLARSHIP
1125	William of Malmesbury finishes *Gesta Regum Anglorum* and *Gesta Pontificum Anglorum*, secular and ecclesiastical histories of England.

AD 1126–1130

1127 *Jan.* 1	David I, K. of Scots, and all clerical and lay magnates of England take oath to accept Henry I's daughter Empress Matilda, now widowed, as heir to England and Normandy.
1128 *Jun.* 17	Matilda marries Geoffrey Martel, heir to Count of Anjou.
1129–1130	Earliest surviving pipe roll (record of Exchequer account).
by 1130	Establishment of craft gilds begins with weavers and cordwainers.

FINE ARTS AND ARCHITECTURE
after 1129	Winchester Bible begun.
1130	New choir of Canterbury Cathedral finished.

RELIGION AND EDUCATION
1126	Sees of Canterbury and York declared equal, but Archbp of Canterbury usually to act as papal legate. Henry of Blois, Henry I's nephew, made abbot of Glastonbury. David I, K. of Scots, founds Kelso Abbey.

1128	David I, K. of Scots, founds Holyrood Abbey, Edinburgh; guest house used by Scottish kings is beginning of later palace.
1129	First Cistercian abbey in England founded at Waverley, Hants.
	Council of London: clergy marriages banned again, unsuccessfully.
	Henry of Blois made Bp of Winchester.

RECREATION AND FASHION

by 1130   Gowns, often of silk or muslin from the East, are shorter for both sexes, collars and girdles richly decorated in Byzantine style. Women wear hair uncovered, in long (sometimes false) plaits.

AD 1131–1135

1133	*Mar. 5*	Henry Plantagenet, son of Count Geoffrey of Anjou and Empress Matilda, Henry I's daughter, born.
	Aug.	Henry I goes to Normandy and remains there.
1135		Geoffrey of Anjou stirs up revolt in Normandy.
	Dec. 1	Henry I dies of gastric attack after eating lampreys. His nephew Stephen of Blois hurries to England and is elected King.
	22	Stephen crowned.
	26	David I, K. of Scots, invades Northumberland.

FINE ARTS AND ARCHITECTURE

1131	Cistercian abbey of Rievaulx, Yorks, founded.
1132	Benedictine (later Cistercian) abbey of Fountains, Yorks, founded.
1134	Romanesque church, 'Cormac's Chapel', built on Rock of Cashel, Tipperary, Ireland.

RECREATION AND FASHION

1133   Bartholomew Fair, Smithfield, London, established by royal charter granting tolls to St Bartholomew's Priory (*v.* 1123). Held for 3 days from 23 Aug., it always involved popular entertainment, but later became greatest cloth fair in England.

RELIGION AND EDUCATION

1132   Theobald of Étampes, describing himself as a master of Oxford, teaches theology to over 60 students at chapel of St George's-in-the-Castle, Oxford.

AD 1136–1140

1136		Ty between K. Stephen and David I, K. of Scots: David's son granted Carlisle and other lands in England.
	Jan. 1	Welsh defeat and kill Norman colonists near Swansea, and capture Cardigan; general revolt of Wales.
		Pope confirms Stephen's claim to English Crown.
1137	Mar.	K. Stephen crosses to Normandy, fails in attempt to win duchy from Empress Matilda and her husband Geoffrey, Count of Anjou, and makes truce with them.
1138		Empress Matilda's half-brother, E. Robert of Gloucester, rebels against K. Stephen in support of her claim to English throne.
		David I, K. of Scots, invades and ravages Northumberland, reaches Lancashire and Yorkshire.
	Aug. 22	Ψ of 'the Standard', Cowton Moor, Yorks: Archbp Thurstan of York leads army under banners of saints to defeat Scots.
1139	Apr. 9	Ty of Durham between K. Stephen and David I, K. of Scots: David's son to have Northumberland, except for castles of Bamburgh and Newcastle.
		K. Stephen dismisses and imprisons Bp Roger of Salisbury (Justiciar), and deprives his family of official positions, confiscating their castles, money and arms. Clergy, especially Bp Henry of Winchester, become hostile to Stephen.
	Sep.	Empress Matilda and E. of Gloucester land in England and make Bristol headquarters; civil war ('Anarchy') begins.
	Nov. 7	Men of Gloucester destroy and plunder Worcester.
1140	Dec.	E. Ranulf of Chester seizes Lincoln.

LITERATURE AND SCHOLARSHIP

1136	Geoffrey of Monmouth writes *Historia Regum Britanniae* history of English kings 'especially of K. Arthur', dedicated to his patron, E. Robert of Gloucester; includes story of 'Merlin building Stonehenge'.

MUSIC AND DRAMA

1140	*Adam*, Anglo-Norman religious play, written in England: Latin stage directions prescribe settings, costumes and gestures.

RELIGION AND EDUCATION

1136		David I, K. of Scots, refounds Melrose as Cistercian abbey, with monks from Rievaulx, Yorks.
1138		David I, K. of Scots, founds Jedburgh Priory (later Abbey).
1139	Mar. 1	Bp Henry of Winchester appointed papal legate.
1140		Dryburgh Abbey founded.

1141	*Feb.* 2	Ψ Lincoln: EE of Chester and Gloucester, with Welsh support, defeat and capture K. Stephen.
	Apr. 8	Empress Matilda, supported by Bp Henry of Winchester, is elected Q. of England at Winchester.
	Jun.	Matilda enters London with help of Geoffrey de Mandeville, E. of Essex and Constable of Tower of London.
	24	Londoners, provoked by Matilda's arrogance and tax demands, expel her from Westminster during banquet; she flees to Oxford.
		Q. Matilda, Stephen's consort, with army of Flemish mercenaries, occupies London and wins back loyalty of Bp of Winchester.
	Jul/Aug.	Empress Matilda besieges Bp's palace in Winchester, and is besieged in turn by Q. Matilda's army.
	Sep. 14	Defeated army of Empress retreats; E. of Gloucester is captured.
	Nov. 1	K. Stephen is released in exchange for E. of Gloucester.
1142		P. Henry, son of Empress Matilda, comes to England, stays in Bristol.
	Sep. 26	K. Stephen takes Oxford and besieges Empress in Oxford Castle.
	Dec.	Empress escapes in white clothing over ice and snow to Wallingford, Oxon.
1143		Empress Matilda and E. of Gloucester hold W. England. Geoffrey de Mandeville, joining Empress's party for second time, is arrested and deprived of Essex castles and constableship of Tower; he seizes Ely and starts reign of terror in Cambridgeshire.
1144		Geoffrey, Count of Anjou, completes conquest of Normandy, and is recognized as duke by K. Louis VII of France.
1145		K. Stephen's army takes Faringdon Castle, Oxon, and confines Empress Matilda's party to Gloucestershire and West.

LITERATURE AND SCHOLARSHIP

1140–1142	William of Malmesbury writes *Historia Novella*, history of England to 1142, unfinished at his death.
by 1141	Ordericus Vitalis, Anglo-Norman monk, completes *Ecclesiastical History of England and Normandy*, in Latin.

RELIGION AND EDUCATION

1142	First Cistercian abbey in Ireland founded at Mellifont, Louth.

SCIENCE AND INVENTION

1142–1144	Adelard of Bath, astronomer, mathematician, philosopher and Arabic scholar, dedicates treatise on astrolabe to P. Henry.
1143	Robert of Chester, mathematician and astronomer, is part-author of first translation of Koran into Latin.

| 1144 *Feb.* 11 | Robert of Chester completes translation from Arabic to Latin of Morienus's treatise on alchemy, one of first translated in Europe. |
| 1145 | Robert of Chester finishes translation of Arabian mathematician Al-Khorawizmi's work on algebra (*also on arithmetic, introducing Hindu-Arabic numerals to Europe). |

AD 1146–1150

1146	E. Ranulf of Chester is arrested, released on surrender of castles and begins campaign of terror in North. Many of most violent barons go on 2nd Crusade.
1147	P. Henry arrives in England and is defeated in skirmishes with K. Stephen's forces; Stephen pays for his return to Normandy. K. Stephen defends Coventry against attack by E. of Chester; surrounding country laid waste.
Oct. 24	English crusaders, fighting for K. of Portugal against Moors, help capture Lisbon; English Gilbert of Hastings made Bp of Lisbon.
31	Death of E. Robert of Gloucester weakens Empress's party.
1148 *Feb.*	Empress Matilda leaves England for last time.
1149 *May* 22	P. Henry knighted by great-uncle David I, K. of Scots, at Carlisle. David cedes Lancashire north of R. Ribble to E. Ranulf of Chester, who acknowledges David overlord of Carlisle. David, Henry and Ranulf plan to capture York, but K. Stephen prevents attack. Stephen buys off Ranulf by grant of Lincoln; Henry leaves England.
1150	P. Henry made D. of Normandy. Worcester sacked and burnt.

Events Elsewhere

| 1146 | 2nd Crusade begins. |

AD 1151–1155

1151	K. Louis VII of France, supported by K. Stephen's son Eustace, makes war on P. Henry in Normandy.
Aug.	Ty between Louis and Henry: Henry does homage to Louis for Normandy and cedes Norman Vexin to France.
Sep.	Count Geoffrey of Anjou dies, succeeded by son P. Henry.

1152	*May 18*	P. Henry marries Eleanor of Aquitaine, ex-wife (divorced 21 Mar.) of Louis VII of France, and so becomes D. of Aquitaine. Henry defeats coalition of Louis, K. Stephen's son Eustace and own brother Geoffrey.
		K. Stephen besieges Wallingford, Oxon., last opposition stronghold in Thames valley.
	Dec.	E. Ranulf of Chester dies.
1153	*Jan.*	P. Henry invades England and takes Malmesbury; E. Robert of Leicester joins Henry, giving him control of Midlands.
	May 24	David I, K. of Scots, dies, succeeded by grandson Malcolm IV.
	Aug. 17	K. Stephen's son Eustace dies; Archbp Theobald of Canterbury and Bp Henry of Winchester mediate between P. Henry and Stephen.
	Nov. 6	Agreement between K. Stephen and P. Henry at Winchester (*Ty of Wallingford*): Henry to be Stephen's heir; lands restored to those who owned them under Henry I; castles built since then to be destroyed.
1154	*Oct. 25*	K. Stephen dies.
	Dec.	Henry II and Q. Eleanor crowned together by Archbp Theobald.
1155		Henry II appoints Thomas Becket, Archbp Theobald's clerk and archdeacon of Canterbury, as Chancellor.
		Henry reclaims royal castles and lands, defeating barons who oppose him and abolishing earldoms of York and Hereford.
		Pope Adrian IV, in papal bull *Laudabiliter*, approves English plan to conquer Ireland.

LITERATURE AND SCHOLARSHIP

1154 Henry of Huntingdon finishes *Historia Anglorum*.

RECREATION AND FASHION

1154 Short hair and shaving return for men, with simpler clothing. Short cloaks popular: 'Curt-Manteau' is Henry II's nickname. Women's head-covering includes 'barbette' (linen strip under chin, pinned on top of head), worn by Q. Eleanor, and 'wimple' (veil over head and round neck).

RELIGION AND EDUCATION

1152 Synod of Kells, Ireland. Pope attempts to reorganize Irish Church and reduce influence of monasteries: Archbp of Armagh invested as primate, with 3 other archbps (Cashel, Dublin, Tuam).

1154 *Dec. 4* English cardinal Nicholas Breakspear chosen Pope Adrian IV.

AD 1156–1160

1156 *Feb. 5* Henry II secures title to Normandy, Anjou and Aquitaine, by homage to K.

Louis VII of France.

Henry II suppresses revolt of brother Geoffrey in Anjou, and gives Geoffrey control of Brittany as Count of Nantes.

1157 *May*	Malcolm IV, K. of Scots, cedes Cumberland, Westmorland and Northumberland to Henry II.
Jul.	Henry II campaigns in N. Wales; P. Owain of Gwynedd submits, pays homage to Henry and withdraws frontier to R. Clwyd.
	German merchants from Cologne settled in 'hansa' (house), later the Steelyard, near London Bridge are given royal protection.
1158	Chancellor Thomas Becket goes on splendidly equipped embassy to Paris.
Aug.	Ty between Henry II and Louis VII of France: Henry's son P. Henry to marry P. Margaret of France; Norman part of Vexin to be returned to Henry; Henry to remain overlord of Brittany.
Sep.	Duke Conan of Brittany does homage to Henry II for duchy.
1159	Henry II leads expedition to claim Toulouse as part of Aquitaine. Louis VII of France defends city and Henry abandons siege.
1160 *Nov. 2*	Henry II has marriage of P. Henry and P. Margaret of France celebrated, and regains Norman part of Vexin.
	Malcolm IV, K. of Scots, subdues Galloway.

LITERATURE AND SCHOLARSHIP

1159 John of Salisbury, scholar, writer, Archbp of Canterbury's secretary, completes *Metalogicon*, first mediaeval work based on whole of Aristotle's system of logic, and *Polycraticus*, account of ideal state; he dedicates both works to Chancellor Thomas Becket.

AD 1161–1165

1162 *Jun. 3*	Chancellor Thomas Becket consecrated Archbp of Canterbury, then resigns chancellorship.
	Last collection of Danegeld, now simply royal tax.
1163 *Jan.*	Henry II returns from France and suppresses revolt in S. Wales, imprisoning P. Rhys ap Gruffyd.
Jul. 1	Henry II calls Welsh leaders and K. of Scots to court at Woodstock, to do homage; Welsh rebel again; Archbp Becket quarrels with Henry.
Oct. 1	Council of Westminster: Henry II claims power to punish criminal clerics after their conviction by Church courts, but Becket leads bishops to oppose King's proposal.
1164 *Jan.*	Council of Clarendon: in Constitutions of Clarendon Henry II codifies legal rights of Church and State, based on ancestral custom, aiming to prevent

	appeals to Rome by English clergy. Archbp Becket agrees to constitutions, but later repents.
Oct. 8	Council of Northampton: Becket is accused of embezzlement and contempt of court; other bishops, led by Gilbert Foliot, Bp of London, support Henry II. Becket flees to Louis VII of France.
	Ψ Renfrew: Malcolm IV, K. of Scots, defeats men of Argyll and W. Isles, and their Irish allies.
1165 Jul.	Henry II invades Gwynedd against Welsh PP Owain and Rhys, but unusually wet weather forces him to abandon campaign.
Dec. 9	Malcolm IV, K. of Scots, dies, succeeded by brother William 'the Lion'.

FINE ARTS AND ARCHITECTURE

by 1163	Henry II converts hunting-lodge at Woodstock, Oxford, into palace.
1165	Henry II builds pavilion with water garden (Evenswell, later called Rosamund's Bower) to a Moorish design in Woodstock Park, for mistress Rosamund Clifford.

LITERATURE AND SCHOLARSHIP

1162/1163	John of Salisbury writes *Life of Anselm*.

RELIGION AND EDUCATION

1161	K. Edward 'the Confessor' canonized.
1162	Archbp Becket decrees that Trinity Sunday (Sunday after Pentecost), the day of his consecration to Canterbury, be celebrated in England; Trinity Sunday later becomes general in Europe.
1163 May	Archbp Becket attends Council of Tours, and presses unsuccessfully for canonization of Anselm, presenting biography of Anselm *by John of Salisbury.
Oct. 13	K. Edward 'the Confessor's' bones translated to new shrine in Westminster Abbey.

AD 1166–1170

1166	Assize of Clarendon instituted by Council at Clarendon: duty of local juries to report and sheriffs to investigate serious crimes made law; accused to be tried by ordeal by water.
Mar.	Henry II leaves for France until 1170.
Jul.	Henry II deposes D. Conan of Brittany, grants duchy to own son Geoffrey and betrothes him to Conan's daughter Constance.
Aug. 1	Exiled K. Dermot of Leinster, Ireland, arrives in England.
1167	K. Dermot of Leinster does homage to Henry II, is allowed to recruit allies in England.

		P. Owain of Gwynedd takes Rhuddlan Castle, recovers ancestral lands in north; P. Rhys recaptures S. Wales, destroys Cardigan Castle.
Sep.	10	Empress Matilda, Henry II's mother, dies.
1167–1169		Henry II campaigns in France against rebels and K. Louis VII.
1169 Jan.		Ty of Montmirail between Henry II and Louis VII of France: Henry divides lands between sons: England, Normandy, Anjou to P. Henry; Aquitaine to P. Richard; Brittany to P. Geoffrey.
		Louis agrees to marry daughter Alice to P. Richard and tries to reconcile Henry to rebels and Archbp Becket.
May		Norman-Welsh barons, mostly of same family ('Geraldines'), land at Wexford in Ireland to restore exiled K. Dermot of Leinster.
1170 Apr.		'Inquest of Sheriffs': Henry II orders commission to inquire into financial dealings of sheriffs and other officials since 1166.
Jun.	14	P. Henry crowned joint-king (Young King) at Westminster by Archbp of York, an act which infringes rights of Archbp of Canterbury.
Jul.	22	Henry II offers to allow Archbp Becket to return to England and recrown Young King. Becket accepts; Henry remains in France.
Aug.	23	Richard de Clare, E. of Pembroke ('Strongbow'), leads new expedition to Ireland, takes Waterford and marries daughter of K. Dermot of Leinster.
Sep.	21	E. of Pembroke takes Dublin.
Nov.	23	Death of P. Owain of Gwynedd followed by quarrels over succession.
Dec.	1	Archbp Becket lands at Sandwich, Kent, having excommunicated or suspended opposing bishops; Archbp of York, Bpp of London and Salisbury complain to Henry II in Normandy, provoking his anger against Becket.
	29	4 knights, thinking to please Henry II, kill Archbp Becket in Canterbury Cathedral.

LITERATURE AND SCHOLARSHIP

1166	Monk of Ely writes down *Song of Cnut*, popular ballad in Old English *composed and sung by K. Cnut as he rowed past Ely.
1170	Roger of Hovedon or Howden begins *Gesta Regis Henrici*, history of Henry II's reign.
by 1170	John of Salisbury writes *Historia Pontificalis*, history of papal court as he witnessed its activities from 1148 to 1152.

RELIGION AND EDUCATION

| 1167 | English students are barred from attending Paris University; Oxford University's growth accelerated as result. |

1171	*May*	Dermot of Leinster dies, succeeded as king by son-in-law, E. Richard of Pembroke.
	Oct. 16	Henry II sails from Milford Haven to Ireland, is acknowledged by E. of Pembroke as overlord of Leinster; Irish princes submit to Henry.
	Nov.	Henry II builds palace in Dublin and holds Christmas court there.
1172	*Feb.*	Synod of Cashel: Irish bishops support Henry II fully.
	Apr. 17	Henry II leaves Ireland.
	May 21	Compromise of Avranches: Henry II absolved of Becket's murder by papal legates in return for recognition of Pope's authority over English Church and freedom of clergy to appeal to Rome; question of clergy's legal position in courts temporarily ignored.
		P. Rhys ap Gruffyd made 'Justice of South Wales'.
1173	*Jan.*	Count of Toulouse acknowledges Henry II as overlord.
	Mar.	Young King Henry demands share of revenues and right to rule in own territory, rebels against father Henry II and flees to French court with brothers Richard and Geoffrey; Q. Eleanor tries to join them, disguised as man, but is arrested and imprisoned. Rebellion of Henry II's sons supported: in England by dissident barons and William, K. of Scots, who invades Northumberland; in Normandy by Louis VII of France. Loyal armies campaign successfully against rebels in both areas.
1174	*Jul. 12*	Henry II fasts and is scourged at Becket's tomb in Canterbury Cathedral as penance for Becket's murder.
	13	William, K. of Scots, is captured at Alnwick, Northumberland.
	Sep. 30	Ty of Montlouis between Henry II and his sons' party: rebels pardoned, financial provision made for sons from their own revenues, but without increase of power; Q. Eleanor kept in custody.
	Dec.	William, K. of Scots, released in return for homage to Henry II.
1175		P. Richard given task of subduing remaining rebels in Aquitaine.
	Oct.	Ty of Windsor: Rory O'Connor recognized as High K. of Ireland under Henry II, in return for payment of tribute.

FINE ARTS AND ARCHITECTURE

| 1175 | | Master mason William of Sens begins to redesign choir of Canterbury Cathedral, burnt down in 1174. |

LITERATURE AND SCHOLARSHIP

| 1172/1173 | | John of Salisbury writes *Life of Becket*, whose secretary he was. |

RELIGION AND EDUCATION

| 1173 | *Feb. 21* | Becket canonized (St Thomas of Canterbury); his tomb in Canterbury Cathedral becomes pilgrim shrine. |

AD 1176–1180

1176	Assize of Northampton confirms provisions of Assize of Clarendon (*v.* 1166), with severer penalties for convicted.
1177	Council of Oxford: Henry II, ignoring Ty of Windsor (*v.* 1175) as unworkable, grants kingdoms of Cork and Limerick, and newly conquered Ulster to English barons; makes son John Lord of Ireland.
	Welsh princes David of Gwynedd and Rhys of S. Wales swear allegiance to Henry II and are confirmed in their lands as 'kings'.
Sep. 21	Non-aggression pact agreed at Ivry between Henry II and Louis VII of France; they promise to go on Crusade together.
1179	P. Richard completes military subjection of Aquitaine.
	Henry II meets Louis VII of France, on pilgrimage to St Thomas's tomb, Canterbury, at Dover.
Apr.	Henry II institutes Grand Assize, royal court where disputed property claims may be decided by jury instead of by single combat.
1180 *Sep. 18*	Louis VII of France dies, succeeded by son Philip II 'Augustus', with whom Henry II renews Pact of Ivry (*v.* 1177).
	Henry II institutes major reform of coinage: new silver coins of standard pattern struck and old coins called in; exchange to be carried out at new royal exchanges only and profits to go to royal treasury.

FINE ARTS AND ARCHITECTURE

1179	William of Sens, having fallen from scaffolding, is succeeded as chief mason at Canterbury Cathedral by William the Englishman.
	Working to William of Sens's design, he builds choir and Trinity Chapel (of St Thomas) in Early English Gothic style.
1180	Wells Cathedral begun.

LITERATURE AND SCHOLARSHIP

1179	Richard fitzNigel, Treasurer, writes *Dialogus de Scaccario* (Dialogue of the Exchequer) to explain working of Exchequer.
1180	*Tractatus de Legibus et Consuetudinibus Regni Angliae* (Treatise on Laws and Customs of England), attributed to Ranulf de Glanvill, Justiciar: first account of English law.

MUSIC AND DRAMA

1176 *Dec.*	1st Eisteddfod held at Cardigan, in castle of P. Rhys of S. Wales.
1180	'Shrewsbury Fragments': parts of Christmas and Easter plays, in mixture of Latin and English, to be performed in church.

1178   Henry II founds first English Carthusian abbey at Witham, Somerset, with Hugh of Avalon, later St Hugh of Lincoln, as first prior.

AD 1181–1185

1181   Assize of Arms stipulates weapons and armour each freeman is expected to own and to deploy in King's service.
Geoffrey, D. of Brittany, marries Constance (*v.* 1166).

1182–1183   Young King Henry supports discontented barons in Aquitaine against brother P. Richard and father Henry II.

1183 *Feb.*   Young King Henry and D. Geoffrey of Brittany, with Philip II of France, make war on P. Richard and Henry II.

Jun. 11   Young King Henry dies; collapse of rebellion in Aquitaine.

1184   Assize of the Forest: first codification of laws protecting royal forests.
Aug.   Henry II tries to persuade P. Richard to give up Aquitaine to brother P. John. Duke Geoffrey of Brittany and John fight against Richard.

1185 *Jan. 29*   Henry II offered throne of kingdom of Jerusalem, but declines.
Q. Eleanor, released from custody, takes charge of Aquitaine; Henry II seems to recognize P. Richard as his heir and swears to expedite Richard's marriage to P. Alice of France (*v.* 1169).

Apr. 25   P. John sent to Ireland with army, eventually to be K. of Ireland; he insults English barons and Irish chiefs, giving away their lands to his young drinking companions.

Dec.   P. John recalled; Henry II entrusts Ireland to E. of Pembroke.

FINE ARTS AND ARCHITECTURE
1184   Glastonbury Abbey burnt; rebuilding begins (to 1303).
1185   Knights Templar build great hall and round church, the New Temple, on north bank of R. Thames in London.

LITERATURE AND SCHOLARSHIP
1184/1186   Gerald of Wales, 'Giraldus Cambrensis', priest who served in royal household and accompanied P. John to Ireland, writes *Topographia Hibernica* (Topography of Ireland); he takes 3 days to read it to masters and scholars of Oxford University and also lectures there.

AD 1186–1190

1186		Henry II restores Edinburgh to William, K. of Scots, and allows celebration of William's marriage in royal palace at Woodstock.
	Jul.	Duke Geoffrey of Brittany killed in tournament in Paris; Philip II of France claims duchy and wardship of Geoffrey's unborn son (Arthur).
1187	May	Philip II attacks borders of Aquitaine, but makes truce with Henry II and P. Richard; all 3 agree to go on Crusade; Philip still supports rebels in Aquitaine and sets Richard against Henry.
1188	Nov. 11	Philip II and P. Richard meet Henry II at Bonmoulins; Henry refuses to expedite Richard's marriage to P. Alice of France or name him heir; Richard pays homage to Philip for French lands.
1189	May	Philip II and P. Richard campaign against Henry II in France.
	Jul. 4	At Colombières Henry II yields; he agrees to make Richard heir, arrange his marriage and pay indemnity of 20,000 marks (£13,333 6s 8d).
	6	Henry II dies, succeeded by Richard; Richard proclaims amnesty in England for offenders against forest law.
	Sep. 3	Richard I is crowned.
	Dec. 5	Richard frees William, K. of Scots, from agreement made with Henry II and restores Berwick and Roxburgh castles; William pays 10,000 marks (£6,666 13s 4d) to finance Richard on Crusade.
	12	Richard goes on Crusade, leaving Hugh Puiset, Bp of Durham, and Chancellor William Longchamp, Bp of Ely, as Justiciars and Regents and nephew Arthur of Brittany as heir instead of P. John.
1190	Feb.-Mar.	Jews are robbed and murdered in E. Anglia.
	Mar. 15–17	Jews besieged in York Castle by mob; most kill themselves and survivors are murdered. York is punished by fine.
		Bp Longchamp arrests Bp of Durham and rules alone as Chancellor, Justiciar and papal legate.
		P. Rhys of S. Wales rebels.

LITERATURE AND SCHOLARSHIP

1188	Gerald of Wales begins *Itinerarium Cambriae* (Journey in Wales).
by 1189	Gerald writes *Expugnatio Hibernica* (Conquest of Ireland, from 1169).

RECREATION AND FASHION

by 1190s	Chess becomes popular game in England.

RELIGION AND EDUCATION

1186	Prior Hugh of Witham (later St Hugh) becomes Bp of Lincoln.

Events Elsewhere

1189   3rd Crusade begins, led by Emperor Frederick 'Barbarossa', Philip II of France and Richard I of England.

AD 1191–1195

1191   P. John, aiming at succession to throne, opposes Chancellor, Bp Longchamp.
    Oct.   John and supporters depose and exile Bp Longchamp; Archbp of Rouen, Walter of Coutances, sent by Richard I, becomes chief Justiciar.
Richard I marries Berengaria of Navarre in Cyprus.

1192   John recognized as heir to throne, but continues to intrigue with Philip II of France and acquires royal castles of Windsor and Wallingford.

1193 *Feb.* 14   Richard I is captured on journey home from East and handed over as prisoner to Emperor; Hubert Walter, Archbp of Canterbury, sent by Richard to England to raise ransom; John stirs up rebellion.

1194 *Mar.* 13   Richard I returns to England, finds rebellion almost suppressed by loyal subjects; Richard confiscates lands of rebels, including John.
    Apr. 17   Richard I crowned again at Winchester.
    May 12   Richard I goes to Normandy, spends rest of reign in France; Bp Longchamp, reinstated as Chancellor, remains with Richard.
Richard meets John in Normandy, where he is hiding, and forgives him.
Archbp Walter, now Justiciar, regularizes election of coroners in all counties and defines duties: to hold inquests and keep records of Crown pleas. He sets up 'Exchequer of Jews', separate department for financial and judicial affairs of Jews.
Llewelyn 'the Great' becomes P. of Gwynedd.

1195   John defends Normandy against Philip II of France and has lands restored to him.
Ty of Louviers between Richard I and Philip II: Philip retains Norman Vexin.

LITERATURE AND SCHOLARSHIP

1191   Monks digging in ruins of old Glastonbury Abbey find alleged bones of K. Arthur and Q. Guinevere.
by 1192   Walter Map, archdeacon of Oxford, writes *De Nugis Curialium* (Courtiers' Trifles).

RECREATION AND FASHION

1194   Richard I licenses tournaments in England.
after 1194   Richard I encourages horse-racing as sport.

AD 1196–1200

1196	Assize of Measures establishes standard measure (ell) throughout England and regulates production of woollen cloth at 2 ells width.
	Richard I builds Château Gaillard on R. Seine, Normandy.
1198 *Jun.*	Richard I resumes war against Philip II of France.
	Richard reoccupies most of Norman Vexin, and makes alliances with German princes and counts of Boulogne and Flanders against France.
Sep.	Ψ Gisors: Richard defeats Philip.
1199 *Jan.* 13	Truce between Richard I and Philip II: each to keep lands seized.
Apr. 6	Richard dies of wound received in siege of castle of Châlus.
	England, Normandy accept P. John as Richard's heir; Aquitaine pays homage to dowager Q. Eleanor; Anjou, Maine to Arthur of Brittany.
25	John invested as D. of Normandy at Rouen.
May 27	John crowned K. of England at Westminster.
	Philip II renews war in support of Arthur's claims in France.
1200 *May* 22	Ty of Le Goulet: John cedes Norman Vexin and Evreux to Philip II, but is recognized as overlord of all other English lands in France.
Aug.	John marries Isabel, daughter of Count of Angoulême.
Oct. 8	John and Isabel crowned together at Westminster.
Oct.–Nov.	John tours Midlands and receives homage of William I, K. of Scots, at Lincoln.
Nov. 24	John acts as pall-bearer at Bp Hugh of Lincoln's funeral in Lincoln Cathedral.
	P. Llewelyn of Gwynedd takes Anglesey.

LITERATURE AND SCHOLARSHIP

1196	William of Newburgh begins *Historia Rerum Anglicarum* (History of England, 1066–1198), left unfinished at death.
1200	Layamon, Worcestershire priest, writes *Brut*, verse history of England to AD 689, one of earliest works in Middle English, with first vernacular accounts of Arthur, Lear and Cymbeline.

AD 1201–1205

1201 *Jul.* 11	Llewelyn confirmed in conquest of N. Wales and pays homage to John.
1202 *Apr.* 30	Philip II of France confiscates John's French lands, granting all except Normandy to John's nephew Arthur of Brittany.
Aug. 1	Ψ Mirabeau, nr Poitiers: John raises siege, rescues mother Q. Eleanor, and

captures Arthur and other rebel barons.

1203	Apr. 3	*John murders Arthur. Brittany and Maine revolt against John.
1204	Mar. 8	Philip II of France captures Château Gaillard, Normandy.
	Apr. 1	Dowager Q. Eleanor dies.
	Jun. 24	Philip completes French conquest of Normandy by taking Rouen. John visits Devon.
1205	Jan.	R. Thames freezes and can be crossed on ice.
	Spring	Famine and inflation.
	Mar.	Council at Oxford: barons promise obedience only in return for King's promise to maintain rights of England.
	by Jun.	Army and fleet prepared for invasion of France, but barons reluctant to go; Archbp Walter and William Marshal persuade John to abandon expedition.
	Jul. 13	Archbp Walter dies; Canterbury monks elect their subprior as Archbp.
	Dec. 11	John forces election of Bp Gray of Norwich as Archbp.
from 1205		John begins building royal navy.

LITERATURE AND SCHOLARSHIP

1202	Jocelyn of Brakelond writes *Chronicle of Bury St Edmunds* (1173–1202).

AD 1206–1210

1206		Llewelyn of Wales marries John's illegitimate daughter Joan.
	Mar.	Pope Innocent III rejects Bp Gray as Archbp of Canterbury (v. 1205).
	Jun. 7	John invades France to defend Aquitaine and campaigns in Poitou.
	Oct. 26	John and Philip II of France make 2-year truce at Thouars.
	Dec.	Pope persuades Canterbury monks to elect Stephen Langton Archbp. Langton stays in France. Canterbury monks exiled to France.
1207		John exiles Archbp of York to France and retains revenues of Canterbury and York.
		First appearance of Irish coin depicting harp.
		William Marshal, now E. of Pembroke, inherits Leinster, Ireland.
1208	May 23	Pope places England under interdict (ban on church services). Bpp of London, Ely, Worcester and Hereford flee to Europe; other bishops, including Norwich and Winchester, support John, who confiscates all Church property, later allowing loyal clergy to buy it back.
		Llewelyn of Wales takes Powys.
1209	Aug.	John marches to Norham Castle, preparing to invade Scotland; William, K. of Scots, buys peace with England.
	Nov.	Excommunication of John published in France.

| 1210 | *Jun.* 20 | John lands at Waterford, Ireland, receives Irish princes, builds castles and replaces barons by clergy as Justiciars. Stone castle begun in Dublin. |

FINE ARTS AND ARCHITECTURE

| 1208 | | Choir of Lincoln Cathedral, designed by Geoffrey de Noyes, finished; first use of decorated rib-vaulting. |

RELIGION AND EDUCATION

| 1209 | | Cambridge University begun by *c.* 3,000 students leaving Oxford after some Oxford students are hanged for murder. |

AD 1211–1215

1211	*Jul.*	John invades N. Wales, builds forts, confines Llewelyn beyond R. Conway. English occupy N. Cardigan, build Aberystwyth Castle.
1212		John sends William, K. of Scots, mercenaries to fight rebellion.
	Jun.	Welsh burn Aberystwyth Castle and rebel, led by Llewelyn.
	Sep.	John's punitive expedition in Wales halted by baronial plot.
		William Marshal keeps Irish barons loyal, and advises peace with Pope.
	Nov.	John sends peace mission to Pope.
1213	*May* 13–15	John yields to papal legate, receives Archbp Langton and cedes kingdom to Pope. Excommunication and interdict are lifted.
	30	English fleet defeats French invasion fleet off Damme, Flanders.
	Jun. 3	John makes truce with Llewelyn of Wales.
	Aug.	Archbp Langton dissuades John from campaign against northern barons who refused to serve in France.
1213–1214		'Unknown Charter of Liberties' drafted: list of barons' demands to be negotiated with King, similar to later proposals (*v.* 1215).
1214	*Feb.* 15	John lands at La Rochelle and campaigns in W. France.
	Jul.	After initial successes, John is forced back to La Rochelle.
	27	Ψ Bouvines: Philip II of France defeats English forces and allies led by Emperor Otto (John's nephew).
	Sep. 18	John and Philip make truce at Chinon.
	Oct. 15	John returns to England; barons, led by northerners, begin to demand charter of liberties from King.
	Dec. 4	William, K. of Scots, dies, succeeded by Alexander II.
		Llewelyn of Wales takes Shrewsbury.
1215	*Mar.*	John postpones negotiations with barons; both sides appeal to Pope.
	May 3	Barons, led by Robert Fitzwalter, renounce allegiance and attack Northampton; John offers concessions and orders mercenaries into London.

	17	Barons take London before mercenaries arrive.
Jun.	*15*	After mediation by Archbp Langton, John meets barons at Runnymede on R. Thames and agrees first draft of charter.
	19	'Magna Carta' (Great Charter) sealed and copies distributed. It confirms: rights of Church and barons against King; existing legal procedures; privileges of towns and merchants. It also establishes national standard weights and measures. 25 barons appointed to oversee working of charter. John appoints Hubert de Burgh Justiciar.
Aug.	*24*	Pope declares Magna Carta null and void.
Sep.		Barons take Rochester Castle and ask for French support. Archbp Langton, suspended by papal commission, goes to Rome to plead with Pope.
Nov.	*30*	John takes Rochester Castle after long siege.
Dec.		Alexander II of Scots invades England as far as Newcastle; John harries Midlands and North. Llewelyn of Wales conquers all S. Wales except Pembroke.

RELIGION AND EDUCATION

1214   Ordinance of papal legate defines rights of Oxford scholars against citizens and places Oxford University under authority of Bp of Lincoln, as Chancellor of University.

AD 1216–1220

1216	*Jan.*	John sacks Berwick and drives out Scots, raiding lowlands.
	Feb.–Mar.	John suppresses revolt in E. Anglia, but barons, supported by French troops, hold London.
	May 21	P. Louis of France lands in Kent to claim English throne.
	Jun.–Oct.	John campaigns against rebels in E. England.
	Oct. 19	After losing baggage train in Wash estuary, John dies at Newark.
	28	John's son Henry III crowned at Gloucester by Peter des Roches, Bp of Winchester; William Marshal appointed Regent.
	Nov. 12	Revised Magna Carta reissued at new King's Council at Bristol. Llewelyn of Wales divides S. Wales among native princes.
1217	*May 20*	William Marshal and Bp of Winchester defeat rebels at Lincoln.
	Aug. 24	French fleet destroyed off Sandwich.
	Sep. 12	Ty of Kingston: P. Louis of France accepts 10,000 marks (£6,666 13s 4d) to leave England; amnesty for rebels; restoration of lands, including royal castles, to previous owners; Scots surrender conquests in England. Archbp Langton of Canterbury returns from exile.
	Nov. 6	Magna Carta reissued with forest clauses expanded as separate Charter of the Forests.

1218 *Mar.*	Ty of Worcester recognizes Llewelyn of Wales as regent of royal castles in S. Wales during minority of Henry III.
1219 *May 14*	William Marshal dies. Llewelyn of Wales ravages his earldom of Pembroke.
1220 *May 17*	Henry III crowned in Westminster Abbey.

FINE ARTS AND ARCHITECTURE

1220 *May*	Henry III lays foundation stone of new Lady Chapel in Westminster Abbey, to be built in English Gothic style.
	Rebuilding of Salisbury Cathedral in Early English Gothic style begins (*v.* 1258).
1220	Rebuilding of Beverley Minster, Yorks, in Gothic style begins.

MUSIC AND DRAMA

by 1220	Easter plays performed outside churches: first recorded instance at Beverley Minster.

RELIGION AND EDUCATION

1220 *May*	Bp Hugh of Lincoln canonized.
Jul. 7	Canterbury Cathedral: St Thomas Becket's body translated to new shrine in Trinity Chapel.

SCIENCE AND INVENTION

by 1220	Michael Scot, Scottish scholar, begins translating Aristotle from Arabic to Latin, and writes on astronomy and alchemy.

Events Elsewhere

1216	5th Crusade begins.

AD 1221–1225

1221	Alexander II, K. of Scots, marries Henry III's sister Joan.
	Justiciar de Burgh marries Alexander II's sister Margaret.
1223	Pope declares Henry III of age to rule with limited powers.
	E. of Pembroke (son of William Marshal), seizes Carmarthen and Cardigan castles from Llewelyn of Wales.
	De Burgh leads army against Welsh, occupies Montgomery and builds castle there; E. of Pembroke retains Cardigan and Carmarthen.
1224 *by Apr.*	Royal castles taken in revolt against John are returned to King.
May 5	Louis VIII of France declares war on Henry III.
	French invade Poitou and Gascony.

1225 *Feb. 11*   Magna Carta and Charter of Forests reissued in definitive form; in return every householder to pay tax of 1/15 of movable property.
Henry III's brother Richard made E. of Cornwall and sent to defend Gascony.

LITERATURE AND SCHOLARSHIP

1225   *The Owl and the Nightingale*, early Middle English poem, written. *King Horn*, earliest surviving English verse romance, written.

RECREATION AND FASHION

1222 *Jul. 15*   London defeats Westminster in annual wrestling match; supporters riot; ringleaders are hanged or lose hands and feet as punishment.

RELIGION AND EDUCATION

1221 *Aug.*   First Dominican friars arrive and found houses in London (Blackfriars, Chancery Lane), Oxford and later Canterbury (1240).

1224 *Sep.*   First Franciscan friars reach England and found houses at Canterbury, London (1225, Greyfriars, Newgate St) and Oxford.

AD 1226–1230

1226   Cardigan and Carmarthen made royal castles.

1227 *Jan.*   Henry III declares self of full age.
     Mar.   Henry makes truce with French.
     May   Richard of Cornwall returns to England, quarrels with Henry and de Burgh and flees to escape arrest. Barons, already complaining of Henry's government, support Richard. Henry promises reforms and is reconciled to Richard.

1228 *Apr.*   De Burgh campaigns in S. Wales without success.

1229 *Oct.*   Henry III postpones French campaign and blames de Burgh for delay.

1230 *May 3*   Henry III begins campaign in France, landing at St Malo and marching south to Bordeaux with little fighting.
     Oct.   Henry returns to England, leaving small force in France.
Exchequer pipe roll for year lists property of 'Robertus (Robin) Hood', an outlaw in Yorkshire.

LITERATURE AND SCHOLARSHIP

1230   *Ancrene Wisse*, devotional book for nuns written by their chaplain, important example of early Middle English prose.

by 1229 · Robert Grosseteste, lecturer and 'master of scholars' at Oxford, is first master of new Franciscan school of theology there.

Events Elsewhere

1228 · 6th Crusade begins.

AD 1231–1235

1231 *by May* · Hubert de Burgh is now chief Marcher lord on S. Wales borders, controlling Montgomery, royal castles of Cardigan and Carmarthen, the Gower peninsula and much of Glamorgan; he plans to attack central Wales.

Jun. · Llewelyn ravages de Burgh lands, takes Cardigan Castle and defends conquests against royal army, forcing truce.

Bp of Winchester, returning from Crusade, negotiates 3-year truce between England and France.

Simon de Montfort arrives in England to claim inheritance as E. of Leicester and becomes Henry III's friend.

1232 *Jun.* · Bp of Winchester, planning to oust de Burgh, appoints nominees to offices in royal household.

Nov. 10 · De Burgh is arrested, stripped of offices and Welsh possessions, and imprisoned for life.

1233 *Jan.* · Bp of Winchester's party control Exchequer and highest financial posts; Richard, E. of Pembroke, leads baronial opposition to them.

Aug. · Henry III, with army prepared for Irish expedition, attacks E. of Pembroke in his castle of Usk.

Sep. · E. of Pembroke and Llewelyn of Wales in alliance defeat Henry.

1234 *Apr. 16* · E. of Pembroke is murdered in Ireland, defending his Leinster estates against attacks of royalist party.

Bp of Winchester's supporters are removed from office.

Jul. · Llewelyn of Wales makes peace with Henry III and retains Cardigan.

1235 · English forces conquer Connaught, Ireland.

Aug. · Truce with France is renewed for 5 years.

RELIGION AND EDUCATION

1233 · (St) Edmund Rich consecrated Archbp of Canterbury.
1234 · Robert Grosseteste becomes Bp of Lincoln.

AD 1236–1240

1236 *Jan. 14*	Henry III marries Eleanor of Provence, sister of Q. of France.
	Statute of Merton, first English statute, issued by Council: clarifies property rights. Council empowers secular rather than ecclesiastical courts to decide legitimacy cases.
Dec.	First reference to 'parliament', summoned for 20 Jan. 1237.
1237 *Jan.*	Henry III confirms Charters and enlarges Council by 3 barons, in return for general tax to be approved by barons.
Sep.	Ty of York: Anglo-Scottish border settled on Tweed-Solway line, Alexander II, K. of Scots, ceding claims to N. England.
1238 *Jan. 7*	Simon de Montfort marries Henry III's sister Eleanor; barons, led by Richard of Cornwall, oppose match and foreign influence on King.
Feb. 22	Henry promises reforms demanded by barons.
1240 *Apr. 11*	Llewelyn of Wales dies, succeeded by son David.
May 15	Ty of Gloucester: David does homage to Henry III for N. Wales; rights in rest of Wales to be subject of arbitration.

LITERATURE AND SCHOLARSHIP

by 1236	Roger of Wendover, monk at St Albans, writes *Flores Historiarum*, history of world from creation to 1235.

RECREATION AND FASHION

1237	Henry III, beginning his collection of wild animals, has leopard house built in Tower of London.

RELIGION AND EDUCATION

1240 *Nov. 16*	Archbp Edmund Rich dies; Q. Eleanor's uncle, Boniface of Savoy, is appointed Archbp of Canterbury.

SCIENCE AND INVENTION

by 1236	Roger Bacon, Franciscan friar and scientist, is one of first lecturers on Aristotle's *Physics* and *Metaphysics* at Paris University.

AD 1241–1245

1241	Henry III leads expedition into N. Wales.
Oct.	New treaty with David of Wales; David makes Henry his heir.
1242 *Feb. 2*	Barons in Council refuse taxation.

	May	Henry III leads expedition to France to support revolt in Poitou against French rule.
	Jul. 21–22	Richard of Cornwall extricates Henry from confrontation with main French army at Taillebourg; defeated in skirmish, Henry retreats.
1243	*Sep.*	Henry III renews truce with (St) Louis IX and returns home.
	Nov. 23	Richard of Cornwall marries Sanchia of Provence, sister of QQ of England and France, and renounces rights to Gascony.
1244	*Aug.*	Scots threaten border and Irish Sea. Henry III blockades Scotland and musters army at Newcastle. Alexander II, K. of Scots, renews Ty of York (1237): Alexander's son to marry Henry's daughter.
	Nov.	Council refuses tax and proposes reforms: barons to elect judicial and financial officers of administration and 4 'conservators of liberties' to supervise King's activities and spending. Henry III rejects proposals, relying for income on feudal obligations, taxes paid by Jews, and loans from Richard of Cornwall.
1245		Henry III campaigns in N. Wales against David.

FINE ARTS AND ARCHITECTURE

1245		Henry III begins building of new Westminster Abbey, in Gothic style influenced by French cathedrals and Sainte Chapelle in Paris; Henry de Reyns, trained in France, is first architect to work on Abbey (1245–53).

Events Elsewhere

1242	Alexander Nevsky defeats Teutonic Knights near Pskov, Russia.
1244	Muslims retake Jerusalem.
1245	7th Crusade begins.

AD 1246–1250

1246	*Feb.* 25	David of Wales dies, succeeded by nephews Owen and Llewelyn.
1247	*Apr.*	Ty of Woodstock: Welsh princes recognize Henry III as overlord of Wales, admitting feudal obligations in their own N. Wales principality.
	Jun. 13	Richard of Cornwall given contract to reform coinage: old silver coin is called in and replaced by new; Richard finances operation with loan of 10,000 marks (£6,666 13s 4d), repayable in new coin, and establishes 17 local mints; he and Henry III share profits (6 pennies per pound).
1248	*Mar.* 11	Richard of Cornwall presides at first 'trial of the Pyx' (testing coinage by assay).
	Spring	Simon de Montfort sent as Governor to pacify turbulent Gascony; his harsh rule provokes opposition.

1249 *Jul.* 8   Alexander II, K. of Scots, dies, succeeded by Alexander III.

LITERATURE AND SCHOLARSHIP

1250   *Genesis and Exodus*, Middle English narrative poem from Norfolk.

MUSIC AND DRAMA

1250   *Sumer is icumen in*, one of earliest English lyrics, appears in Reading Abbey commonplace book, with music and instructions for singers.

RECREATION AND FASHION

by 1250   Surcoat (long, slit-sided gown adapted from crusader's tabard and worn over tunic) is main top garment for men and (later) women. Women wear pill-box hat and net, often of gold thread, encasing back hair.

RELIGION AND EDUCATION

1246   Cistercian abbey of Hailes, Gloucestershire, founded by Richard of Cornwall.

1247   Adam Marsh is first friar to be professor of theology and master of Franciscan school at Oxford.

SCIENCE AND INVENTION

1250   Roger Bacon returns to Oxford.

Events Elsewhere

1248   Louis IX of France goes on 7th Crusade.

1250   Louis IX taken prisoner during Crusade.

AD 1251–1255

1251 *Dec.* 26   Alexander III of Scots marries Henry III's daughter Margaret.

1252 *Jan.*   Gascon opposition leaders in England put case against Simon de Montfort's governorship.

     May–Jun.   Simon de Montfort defends self against Gascon charges, but gives up office and withdraws to France.

1253 *Aug.* 6   Henry III leads expedition to defend Gascony against rumoured invasion by K. Alfonso of Castile; Q. Eleanor and Richard of Cornwall left as Regents to raise army and funds.

1254 *Feb.* 11   Regents summon 2 knights elected from each shire to meet Council: first instance of elected representatives meeting to discuss taxation.

     Mar.   Henry III accepts Pope's offer to make his second son Edmund K. of Sicily; Henry to pay expenses of Sicilian campaign.

Apr. 1	Ty of Toledo between England and Castile: K. Alfonso to renounce claim on Gascony; Henry to consult Alfonso in dealing with Gascons.
Oct.	Henry's elder son Edward marries Eleanor of Castile; he is granted Chester, Ireland, Gascony and royal castles in Wales.
Dec. 27	Henry returns to England after visiting Louis IX in Paris.
1255	Llewelyn makes self sole ruler of N. Wales.
Aug.	Henry III meets K. and Q. of Scots at Roxburgh; he arranges dismissal of Scottish Regency Council and replacement by own supporters.
	Jews in Lincoln accused of boy's murder; 19 Jews executed, but others saved by Franciscans and Richard of Cornwall.

FINE ARTS AND ARCHITECTURE

1255	'Angel' Choir of Lincoln Cathedral begun.

LITERATURE AND SCHOLARSHIP

by 1253	Robert Grosseteste translates Aristotle's *Ethics*, develops studies in natural sciences and philosophy at Oxford and writes metaphysical work *De Luce* (On Light).

RECREATION AND FASHION

1252 *Sep.*	Henry III is given polar bear from Norway: he orders it a muzzle and chain long enough to allow it to swim and fish in R. Thames.
1255	Henry III instals elephant, gift of Louis IX of France, in special building in Tower; it dies by 1258.

AD 1256–1260

1256	Richard of Cornwall has himself elected King of the Romans (heir to Holy Roman Empire), by paying large subsidies in Germany.
1257 *May 17*	Richard of Cornwall crowned K. of Romans at Aachen.
Aug.	Henry III issues gold penny, worth 20 silver pennies, later withdrawn as too valuable to be of use and depressing price of gold.
Aug.–Sep.	Llewelyn, having subdued most of Wales, resists English attacks.
1258 *Mar.*	Llewelyn calls himself 'Prince of Wales'. Rebel Scots barons, having seized K. Alexander III, make alliance with Llewelyn.
Apr. 30	Simon de Montfort and 6 other barons demand that Henry III reform his administration and free himself from Pope's Sicilian campaign.
May 2	Henry accepts proposals for reform.
Jun. 12	Council at Oxford appoints Committee of 24 to produce 'Provisions of Oxford': elected Council of barons to control administration jointly with King; King and Council to summon 3 Parliaments a year. Henry and barons take oath to observe Provisions.

	17	Truce with Llewelyn of Wales.
Jul.	*14*	Poitevins in royal administration refuse oath to observe Provisions and leave England; P. Edward agrees to Provisions.
Nov.		Henry and Council make compromise agreement with Scots barons over guardianship of Alexander III.
		Pope releases Henry from obligations in Sicily.
		O'Donnells resist English advance westwards in N. Ireland with help of 'gallowglasses' (Scottish mercenaries from Western Isles). Brian O'Neill acclaimed High K. of Ireland but killed in battle.

1259	*Oct.*	*13*	Provisions of Westminster: embody permanent changes in legal system, as proposed by barons.
		15	P. Edward swears friendship with Simon de Montfort.
	Dec.	*4*	Ty of Paris: Henry III gives up claim to Normandy, Maine, Anjou, Poitou, and pays homage to Louis IX for Gascony and Aquitaine.

1260		Llewelyn renews war, attacking S. Wales.
		Henry III remains in France, fearing rebellion from P. Edward and de Montfort, and so prevents holding of Parliament.
	Apr. 23	Henry returns to England and is reconciled to Edward and (apparently) de Montfort; Edward settles in Gascony.
	Aug. 22	Truce with Llewelyn of Wales renewed.
	Oct.	Richard of Cornwall, after helping Henry to agree with barons, fails to reach Rome in time to be chosen Holy Roman Emperor, but remains K. of Romans.

FINE ARTS AND ARCHITECTURE

| 1258 | Salisbury Cathedral, rebuilt in Early English Gothic style, consecrated. |

LITERATURE AND SCHOLARSHIP

| by 1259 | Matthew Paris, monk of St Albans, completes *Chronica Maiora* (1235–59). |
| 1260 | Chained Library of Hereford Cathedral built, at first used as muniment room. |

AD 1261–1265

1261	*May*		Henry III imports mercenaries and retreats to Tower of London.
	Jun.	*12*	Papal bull absolving Henry from oath to maintain reforms published.
	Jul.		Henry dismisses baronial officials and appoints royal sheriffs; he regains control of government. Simon de Montfort leaves England.

| 1262 | | Henry III fails to make agreement with Simon de Montfort in Paris. |
| | | Llewelyn of Wales attacks P. Edward's castles, meeting little resistance from disaffected Marcher lords. |

1263	Jan.		Henry III reissues Provisions of Westminster (v. 1259).
	Apr.		Simon de Montfort returns to England. Barons meet to demand Henry's adherence to Provisions of Oxford (v. 1258). On Henry's refusal, de Montfort's party take arms and subdue S. England.
	Jul.	16	Henry accepts barons' terms; de Montfort occupies London.
	Oct.	2	Ψ Largs, W. Scotland: Alexander III, K. of Scots, defeats K. Haakon IV of Norway and takes Hebrides.
			Henry III, de Montfort and barons meet royalist exiles and Louis IX at Boulogne for Louis' arbitration; barons refuse to accept it.
	Dec.		Henry affirms support for Provisions of Oxford and goes to France.
1264	Jan.	23	Mise of Amiens: judgment of Louis IX in favour of Henry III and against barons.
	Feb.		Henry and P. Edward land in England; war against barons begins.
	Apr.–May		Edward takes Northampton. Simon de Montfort's force besieges Rochester. Royal army secures rest of Kent and advances to Lewes.
	May	14	Ψ Lewes: de Montfort defeats royalists, captures Henry and Richard of Cornwall and dictates peace terms, keeping Edward and Richard's son, Henry of Almain, as hostages.
	Aug.	12	Peace of Canterbury: reform of government confirmed. Barons condemned by Louis IX and papal legate, and later excommunicated.
	Dec.	12	Simon de Montfort imposes terms on royalists, led by Roger Mortimer, who are still resisting in Welsh Marches; de Montfort now controls W. England.
1265	Jan.	20	Parliament in London: 2 knights from each shire and, for first time, 2 burgesses from selected boroughs are summoned to attend.
	May	28	P. Edward escapes from custody and joins E. of Gloucester and Roger Mortimer, who lead opposition to Simon de Montfort.
	Jun.	22	Simon de Montfort comes to terms with Llewelyn, recognizing his conquests in Wales; Henry III, now a prisoner, ratifies treaty.
	Aug.	4	Ψ Evesham: de Montfort defeated and killed, Henry rescued.
	Sep.	16	All who fought against Henry are disinherited; rebels hold out in Kenilworth and isles of Axholme and Ely.
	Dec.		Rebels in Axholme surrender to Edward.

LITERATURE AND SCHOLARSHIP

1264 *Song of Lewes*, verse narrative of battle, written in Latin.

RELIGION AND EDUCATION

1264 Walter de Merton grants funds for support of students at Oxford University: beginning of Merton College (v. 1274).

AD 1266–1270

1266		Simon de Montfort's sons escape from England.
	Jun.	Henry III and P. Edward besiege rebels in Kenilworth Castle.
	Jul. 2	Ty of Perth between Alexander III, K. of Scots, and K. Magnus of Norway: grants Hebrides and I. of Man to Scotland.
	Oct. *31*	Dictum of Kenilworth, produced by committee under papal legate and Henry of Almain: defines legal means for rebels to recover estates.
	Dec. *14*	Kenilworth surrenders.
1267	*Apr.* 9	E. of Gloucester, quarrelling with other royalists, occupies London with some of rebels.
	Jun.	Henry III reconciled to E. of Gloucester; P. Edward subdues I. of Ely and remaining rebels surrender.
	Sep. 29	Ty of Montgomery: Llewelyn recognized as P. of Wales and pays homage to Henry.
	Nov. *18*	Statute of Marlborough: confirms laws in Provisions of Westminster and imposes legal obligation to observe Magna Carta.
1269	*Apr.*	Richard of Cornwall pays last visit to Germany.
1270	*Apr.*	Parliament agrees tax of 1/20 of personal property, to be levied from clergy as well as laymen, to finance P. Edward on Crusade.
	Aug. 20	Edward leaves for Crusade.
		K. of Connaught routs English army near Carrick-on-Shannon, Ireland.

FINE ARTS AND ARCHITECTURE

| 1269 *Oct.* *13* | New Westminster Abbey dedicated (*v.* 1245). |

LITERATURE AND SCHOLARSHIP

| by 1268 | Henry de Bracton, judge, writes *De Legibus et Consuetudinibus Angliae* (On Laws and Customs of England), first complete work on England law, and *Notebook* of over 2,000 cases. |

RELIGION AND EDUCATION

| by 1266 | Balliol College, Oxford, exists as community (*v.* 1282) |

SCIENCE AND INVENTION

| 1266 | Roger Bacon writes *Opus Maius*, first part of account of his philosophical and scientific studies. |
| by 1268 | Roger Bacon describes gunpowder in *Opus Tertium*. |

Events Elsewhere

| 1270 | | 8th Crusade begins. |
| | *Aug.* 25 | Louis IX of France dies in Tunis on Crusade, succeeded by son Philip III. |

1272	*Apr.* 2	Richard of Cornwall dies.
	Nov. 16	Henry III dies.
	20	Edward I proclaimed King in absence.
		Court of Common Pleas recognized as permanent court by appointment of its own chief justice.
1273	*Aug.*	Edward I does homage for French lands to Philip III of France and visits Gascony.
1274	*Aug.* 2	Edward I returns to England.
	19	Edward I crowned at Westminster.
		David, brother of P. Llewelyn of Wales, rebels against Llewelyn and flees to England.
		Edward orders 'inquests', enquiry into rights and liberties of all landowners in England.
1275	*Apr.* 25	First Parliament of Edward I's reign.
	May	First regular customs duty imposed on exports of wool and leather.
		Statute of Westminster (I), based on results of inquests (*v.* 1274): defines legal privileges.
		Llewelyn of Wales refuses homage to Edward I. Edward detains de Montfort's daughter Eleanor, betrothed to Llewelyn, as hostage.
	Sep.	Statute forbidding Jews to lend money at interest.

LITERATURE AND SCHOLARSHIP

by 1272	*Lay of Havelock the Dane*, Middle English verse romance, written.
	Walter of Henley writes *Husbandry*, treatise on agriculture and estate management.

RECREATION AND FASHION

1274	Edward I begins reconstruction of royal mews at Charing (later Charing Cross) for falcons and hounds; falconry is his favourite field sport.

RELIGION AND EDUCATION

1274	Merton College, Oxford (*v.* 1264), is first to receive statutes.
1276	Reinterment of 'Arthur's bones' at Glastonbury Abbey in presence of Edward I and Q. Eleanor (*v.* 1191).

Events Elsewhere

1271	*Mar.* 13	Richard of Cornwall's son Henry murdered in Italy by sons of Simon de Montfort.
	May 9	Edward (I) reaches Acre on Crusade.
		Venetian Marco Polo begins travels to Far East.

after 1271	St Thomas Aquinas completes *Summa Theologica*, reconciling Aristotelianism with Christianity.
1272 *Sep.* 22	Edward (I) leaves Palestine.

AD 1276–1280

1276 *Nov.*	Edward I begins successful campaign against Llewelyn of Wales.
1277 *Nov.* 9	Ty of Conway: Llewelyn pays homage to Edward I for Gwynedd; rest of Wales held by Edward, either directly or through Welsh vassals.
1278 *Aug.* 7	Statute of Gloucester: requires claimants to privileges to prove right to them in court and fixes competence of local courts.
Oct. 13	Llewelyn of Wales, reconciled to Edward I, marries Eleanor de Montfort at Worcester.
1279	Statute of Mortmain: limits right to grant land to Church.
Dec.	New coinage ordered: groat (fourpenny piece), round farthing and (1280) halfpenny introduced, all silver coins. Many, especially Jews, are prosecuted for debasing old coinage; penalty is usually hanging.

RELIGION AND EDUCATION

1279	Franciscan scholar John Pecham made Archbp of Canterbury.
1280	University College, Oxford, receives statutes.

AD 1281–1285

1282 *Mar.* 21	David of Wales starts Welsh revolt, joined by brother Llewelyn.
Mar.–Aug.	Edward I leads large army into Wales for successful campaign.
Dec. 11	English defeat and kill Llewelyn near Builth; first recorded use of archers armed with longbow in English army.
1283 *Apr.* 25	Welsh finally defeated at Bere Castle, Merionethshire.
Oct. 3	David of Wales, surrendered by own men, is condemned and executed.
	Statute of Acton Burnell: enables merchants to recover debts quickly.
1284 *Mar.* 19	Statute of Rhuddlan: settles laws and administration in Wales.
Apr. 25	P. Edward born at Caernarvon.
1285 *Easter*	Statute of Westminster (II): defines rights of heirs and limits on alienation of property; introduces idea of entail.
	Statute of Merchants: restates Statute of Acton Burnell (*v.* 1283); prison or confiscation of property for obdurate debtors.

Sep.	Statute of Winchester: measures against crime: towns to be guarded, strangers questioned and curfews imposed; right of property-holders between 15 and 60 to bear arms redefined.

FINE ARTS AND ARCHITECTURE

1284 Edward I begins building new town at Winchelsea, Sussex.

RECREATION AND FASHION

1284 Edward I is first King to organize 'Round Table' tournament, at Nefyn, Wales.

Events Elsewhere

1285 Philip III of France dies, succeeded by Philip IV, 'the Fair'.

AD 1286–1290

1286	*Mar. 19*	Alexander III, K. of Scots, dies, leaving as heir his granddaughter Margaret, 'Maid of Norway'.
	Jun. 5	Edward I pays homage to Philip IV in Paris.
	Jul.	Edward visits Gascony, staying 3 years.
1287	*Jun. 8*	Revolt in S. Wales.
1288	*Jan.*	Welsh revolt suppressed.
1289	*Aug. 12*	Edward I returns to England from Gascony and Aquitaine.
	Nov. 6	Ty of Salisbury: Edward I agrees to assist Margaret of Norway to Scottish throne.
1290	*May 21*	Statute *Quo Warranto*, referring back to inquests of 1274: rights may be established by long usage as well as by royal charter.
	Jul. 8	Statute *Quia Emptores*: limits new feudal obligations resulting from alienation of land.
	18	Edict expelling Jews from England.
		Ty of Birgham: Margaret of Norway to marry P. Edward; Scotland to remain separate kingdom, but K. of England's rights to be preserved.
	Sep. 26	Margaret dies on board ship to England; dispute over claims to Scottish throne begins.
	Nov. 28	Q. Eleanor dies at Harby, Northants.

FINE ARTS AND ARCHITECTURE

1290 *Mappa Mundi* drawn by prebendary of Hereford Cathedral, Richard of Haldingham.

1290   Osman I becomes first Ottoman ruler in Turkey.

AD 1291–1295

1291 *May 10*	Edward I meets Scottish magnates at Norham Castle (to Jul.); they recognize his right as overlord to decide succession to Scottish throne.
Aug. 3	12 claimants to Scottish throne submit claims to Edward at Berwick.
1292 *Nov. 17*	Edward I declares John Balliol, distant cousin of previous king, K. of Scots. Balliol pays homage to Edward.
1293 *May 15*	Fleet from Cinque Ports defeats Norman fleet and sacks La Rochelle.
1294 *May 19*	Philip IV of France declares Gascony confiscated.
Jun.	Edward I takes control of wool trade until 1297, exporting some himself and imposing heavy duty on export of remainder.
Aug. 24	Ty of Nuremberg between Edward and Emperor-elect Adolf of Nassau: alliance against France.
Sep. 30	Welsh revolt interrupts preparation for French campaign.
Oct. 9	English force leaves for Gascony.
1295 *Mar. 5*	Ψ Maes Moydog, Montgomery: Welsh are defeated; revolt collapses.
Oct. 22	Scots, resenting summons from Edward I to join French campaign, make alliance with France ('Auld Alliance').
Nov.	'Model' Parliament includes heads of monastic houses and representatives of clergy as well as prelates, barons, knights and burgesses; it grants 1/10 tax on clergy as well as laity.

FINE ARTS AND ARCHITECTURE

1291   Edward I erects 9 carved stone 'Eleanor' crosses to mark resting-places of wife's coffin between Harby and Westminster (*v.* 1290). Eleanor's tomb in Westminster Abbey is made of Purbeck marble with gilded bronze image of queen.
Nave of York Minster begun.

by 1295   Edward I builds castles in Wales: Flint, Rhuddlan, Builth, Conway, Caernarvon, Criccieth, Harlech, Denbigh, Beaumaris.

RELIGION AND EDUCATION

1292   Edward I limits right to practise in law courts to those chosen by judges; legal education given by practitioners to their apprentices becomes standardized; Inns of Chancery and Court grow up as hostels and centres of teaching; first is Strand Inn (1294).

1294   Robert Winchelsey appointed Archbp of Canterbury.

SCIENCE AND INVENTION

by 1292   Roger Bacon invents spectacles and discovers possibility of telescope; he may have made gunpowder.

AD 1296–1300

1296	Mar. 28	Edward I invades Scotland and sacks Berwick.
	Apr. 27	Ψ Dunbar: Edward defeats Scottish army.
	Jul. 10	Balliol abdicates Scottish throne. Edward makes triumphal progress to Elgin, taking coronation stone of Scone on way back.
	Aug. 28	Edward receives homage of Scots in assembly at Berwick and organizes government under English officials.
1297	Jan.	Edward I makes alliance with Count of Flanders against France. Archbp Winchelsey and bishops refuse to let clergy pay tax to King without Pope's consent.
	May	William Wallace kills English sheriff of Lanarkshire; general rebellion in Scotland follows.
	Aug. 22	Edward I leads army to fight French in Flanders. Barons send remonstrance (list of grievances) to Edward and forbid collection of tax without their consent.
	Sep. 11	Ψ Stirling Bridge: Scots under Wallace defeat English army.
	Oct. 9	Truce between England and France. Scots invade Northumberland and Cumberland.
	Nov. 5	Edward agrees to confirmation of the Charters (Magna Carta and Forest Charter), with added clause promising no taxation without consent of whole kingdom.
1298	Mar.–Jun.	Edward I returns to England, moves administration to York and invades Scotland.
	Jul. 22	Ψ Falkirk: Edward's army defeats Scots under Wallace; archers armed with longbow decide battle. Wallace leaves Scotland, but Scots continue to resist.
1299	Sep. 4	Edward I marries Margaret, sister of Philip IV of France.
	Dec.	Scots take Stirling Castle.
1300	Mar. 28	Edward I confirms Charters and issues 20 'Articles on the Charters', at Parliament's request: punishments for infringing Charters established, but rights of King exempted.
	Apr.	Edward condemns all 'bad' (foreign or debased) coin: only sterling to be current. London mint moved from Westminster to Tower.
	Jun.–Oct.	Edward campaigns unsuccessfully in Scotland.
	Aug.	Edward receives Pope's demand that he withdraw from Scotland.
	Oct. 30	Edward makes truce with Scots.

1298   Rebuilding of St Stephen's Chapel, Westminster begun.

LITERATURE AND SCHOLARSHIP

1300   *Sir Tristrem*, narrative poem written in N. England; first English version of Tristan and Isolde story.

MUSIC AND DRAMA

1300   Earliest surviving secular entertainments in English: *Interludium de Clerico et Puella* (The Cleric and the Girl), comic dialogue; *Dame Sirith*, comic monologue, possibly with performing dog.

RECREATION AND FASHION

by 1299   Old Green, Southampton, is used for recreation and possibly first bowling-green in England.

1300 *Mar.*   'Creag' (?cricket) first mentioned, in P. Edward's wardrobe accounts.

by 1300   Hood is most common head-covering; point (liripipe), later very long, hangs from top of hood down back.

AD 1301–1305

1301 *Feb.* 7   At Nettleham, Lincoln, Edward I invests son P. Edward with all royal lands in Wales and title 'Prince of Wales'.

Jul.–Oct.   English campaign in Scotland: Edward advances from Berwick, P. Edward from Carlisle; Scotland south of Forth secured and administered from York.

1302 *Jan.* 26   Edward I makes truce with Scots.

1303 *Feb.* 1   *Carta Mercatoria*: gives privileges to foreign merchants.

May   Edward I's last Scottish campaign begins with military progress through N. Scotland; he winters at Dunfermline Abbey.

20   Ty of Paris with France: England recovers Gascony; P. Edward to marry Isabella, daughter of Philip IV of France.

1304 *Mar.*   Parliament at St Andrews. Scottish barons submit to Edward I, except for William Wallace, now outlawed, and garrison of Stirling.

Apr.   Edward begins to besiege Stirling Castle.

Jul. 20   Scots surrender Stirling Castle.

1305   William Wallace captured.

Aug. 23   Wallace tried and executed.

Sep.   Edward I issues ordinances for laws and government of Scotland. New Council includes Robert Bruce, grandson of claimant to Scottish throne (*v.* 1291).

1303   Robert Mannyng, canon of Sempringham, begins *Handling Synne*, English verse translation of *Manuel des Péchés*; he condemns outdoor performances of 'miracle' plays.

Events Elsewhere

1303 *Sep.* 7   French arrest Pope Boniface VIII.

AD 1306–1310

1306 *Feb.* 10   Robert Bruce murders rival John Comyn and seizes Dumfries.
        12   Archbp Winchelsey suspended and summoned to Rome by Pope.
   Mar. 25   Bruce crowned Robert I, K. of Scots, at Scone.
   Jul.   English army led by P. Edward invades Scotland.
   Aug. 23   After second defeat Bruce disappears for 4 months.
   Sep. 29   Edward I, now very ill, goes north to Lanercost, near Carlisle.

1307 *Jan.*   Statute of Carlisle: forbids religious foundations to send money to mother houses abroad.
   Feb.   Bruce returns to Scotland.
   May 10   Ψ Loudoun Hill: Bruce defeats English army.
   Jul. 7   Edward I dies at Burgh-upon-Sands, Solway.
   Aug. 6   Edward II, leaving Scotland after short campaign, makes favourite Piers Gaveston, a Gascon, E. of Cornwall.

1308 *Jan.*   Edward II complies with Pope's order to dissolve Order of Knights Templar; property of arrested Templars confiscated for King's use.
        25   Edward marries Isabella at Boulogne; Gaveston left as Regent.
   Feb. 25   Edward crowned; new coronation oath binds King to keep future laws and customs passed by consent of realm.
   Apr.   Parliament forces Edward to banish Gaveston.
   May 9   Edward appoints cousin Thomas, E. of Lancaster, Steward of England.
   Jun. 16   Gaveston leaves to become King's Lieutenant in Ireland.
          Bruce defeats remaining Scottish enemies.

1309 *Jul.* 27   Parliament at Stamford: Gaveston allowed back in return for Edward II's promise to reform administration.
          Scots hold most of Scotland north of Forth-Clyde line.

1310 *Mar.* 16   Edward II agrees to election of 21 Lords Ordainers to reform his household and government.
   Oct.   Edward II and Gaveston lead army through S. Scotland but fail to penetrate north.

1306   Wells Cathedral chapter house completed in Decorated Gothic style.

LITERATURE AND SCHOLARSHIP

by 1308   Duns Scotus, Scottish Franciscan and philosopher, writes on theology and philosophy.

RECREATION AND FASHION

1306 May   Great festival at Westminster to celebrate P. Edward's knighthood: 175 'minstrels' (musicians, dancers, acrobats and jugglers) are employed, paid from 40d to 5s each; they include 1 girl dancer.

Events Elsewhere

1307   Dante Alighieri, Italian poet, begins *Divina Commedia*.

1309   Popes begin to reside at Avignon ('Babylonian Captivity').

AD 1311–1315

1311 *Jul.*   Edward II returns from Scotland.

Aug.   Ordinances published in Parliament: King's advisers, including Gaveston, to be dismissed and barons to control his affairs.

Bruce invades Northumberland and burns Corbridge.

Nov. 3   Gaveston apparently exiled.

Dec. 25   Gaveston and Edward spend Christmas together at Windsor.

1312 *Jan.*   Edward II removes government to York and prepares to fight barons, led by E. of Lancaster.

Jun. 19   Gaveston, captured at Scarborough, is killed near Kenilworth by order of Lancaster and 3 other earls.

Bruce invades as far as Durham; he is paid by northern counties of England to stop attacks.

Dec. 22   Edward agrees to pardon Lancaster and his party, but they refuse to apologize for actions.

1313 *Spring*   Scots take Perth, Roxburgh, Edinburgh and I. of Man.

May 20   Ordinance of the Staple: establishes compulsory 'staple' (depot) through which all wool exports to Europe must pass; first (1314) is at St Omer.

Summer   Bruce and brother Edward begin siege of Stirling Castle.

Oct.   Barons apologize publicly to Edward II and accept his pardon.

1314 *May–Jun.*   Edward II collects large army and invades Scotland.

Jun. 24   Ψ Bannockburn, Stirling: Scots heavily defeat English; Edward flees with survivors to Berwick and York. Scots raid N. England as far as Richmond, Yorks.

1315	*Feb.*	Last of Edward II's supporters removed from Council; E. of Lancaster and party control government.
	May 25	Edward Bruce, offered High Kingship of Ireland, lands at Larne with 200 ships and 6,000 soldiers.
	Jun.	Edward Bruce takes Dundalk.
	Sep. 10	Edward Bruce defeats E. of Ulster near Connor.
1315–1317		Heavy rain ruins harvest: widespread famine.

LITERATURE AND SCHOLARSHIP

1312   Walter of Guisborough writes *Cronica*, English history 1066–1312.

RECREATION AND FASHION

1314   First law against playing violent ball games, precursors of football, in city streets; ban is generally ignored.

SCIENCE AND INVENTION

1311   John Maudit, mathematician and astronomer, is bursar of Merton College, Oxford; he writes on trigonometry, *De Chorda et Umbris* (On Chord and Tangents), and composes astronomical tables. 'Merton school' of mathematics begins to flourish.

AD 1316–1320

1316	*Feb.*	Edward II confirms Ordinances and accepts E. of Lancaster as Chief Councillor.
	May	Edward Bruce crowned High K. of Ireland at Faughart, nr Dundalk.
	Sep.	Edward Bruce takes Carrickfergus.
		Robert Bruce, with force of 'gallowglasses', joins brother in Ireland.
1317		Scots army ravages central Ireland, already suffering from famine; Scots lose support outside Ulster and abandon siege of Dublin.
	Apr.	Roger Mortimer made Justiciar of Ireland and drives Scots back to north.
	by July	Edward II, now openly hostile to E. of Lancaster, reinstates favourites.
	Nov.	E. of Pembroke forms new (Middle) party, pledged to maintain Ordinances and support Edward II.
		Irish princes send Pope complaint against English rule.
1318	*Spring*	Scots take Berwick and raid as far south as Ripon, Yorks.
	Aug. 9	Ty of Leake: E. of Lancaster and Middle party agree on control of administration; Edward II reconciled to Lancaster. Edward's new favourite, Hugh Despenser, made Chamberlain.

Oct. 14	Ψ Faughart, Ireland: Edward Bruce defeated and killed.
1319 *Jul.*	Edward II besieges Berwick. Scottish raiding-party aims for York, to attack Q. Isabella, Exchequer and courts; Queen escapes.
Sep. 20	Ψ Myton-in-Swaledale, Yorks: Scots defeat Archbp of York and march towards Pontefract. E. of Lancaster and northern earls force Edward to abandon siege of Berwick. Truce made with Scots.
1320 *Jan.*	E. of Lancaster refuses to attend Parliament.
Apr. 26	Declaration of Arbroath: letter of Scottish barons to Pope declaring loyalty to Bruce as King despite papal opposition.

LITERATURE AND SCHOLARSHIP

by 1320	*Cursor Mundi*, religious poem, written in N. England.
	Guy of Warwick, popular verse romance, written.

RELIGION AND EDUCATION

1318	Feast of Corpus Christi celebrated in England with processions.
1320	Archbp of Dublin founds first Dublin University.

SCIENCE AND INVENTION

1316	John of Gaddesden, Black Prince's doctor, writes *Rosa Medicina (Anglica)*, medical treatise based partly on observation in practice, anticipating some later treatments; he includes diet, cookery. He is named in Chaucer's *Canterbury Tales*.

AD 1321–1325

1321 *Mar.*	Marcher lords, resenting aggrandizement of Hugh Despenser, form confederation and seize Despenser lands in S. Wales.
May 24	Lancaster summons assembly of northern barons at Pontefract.
Jun. 28	Lancaster holds assembly at Sherburn-in-Elmet to demand reforms of administration and denounce Hugh Despenser and his father.
Jul.	Parliament forces Edward II to banish Despensers.
by Dec.	Edward raises army and recalls Despensers.
1322 *Jan.*	Most of Marcher lords submit to Edward II, but others join Lancaster at Pontefract; Edward leads army north.
Mar. 12	Lancaster proclaimed rebel.
16	Ψ Boroughbridge, Yorks: royal army defeats Lancaster.
22	Lancaster executed.
May 2	Parliament at York includes representatives of Wales: Ordinances repealed; Mortimer and other enemies of King punished; Despensers given new lands; elder Despenser made E. of Winchester.

	Sep.	Scots raid NW England; Edward's invasion of Lowlands fails.
	Oct. 14	Scots defeat and almost capture Edward near Byland, Yorks.
1323	*Mar.*	Edward II makes 13-year truce with Scots.
		Walter Stapledon, Bp of Exeter and Treasurer, begins to reorganize Exchequer rolls and all government records.
		Mortimer escapes from Tower to exile in France.
1324	*Aug.*	Charles IV of France invades Gascony.
1325	*Mar.* 9	Q. Isabella goes to France to negotiate truce with Charles IV; she and Mortimer become lovers.
	Sep. 21	P. Edward goes to France to pay homage for Gascony; Isabella refuses to return with son unless Despensers are removed from power.

FINE ARTS AND ARCHITECTURE

1322   Ely Cathedral tower collapses; rebuilding of choir and Lady Chapel in Decorated style begins.

LITERATURE AND SCHOLARSHIP

1324   William of Ockham, Franciscan theologian disagreeing with synthesis of Aristotelianism and Christianity, summoned by Pope to Avignon on heresy charges.

by 1324   *Modus Tenendi Parliamentum*, anonymous treatise apparently describing parliamentary procedure, but with reforming elements unknown to period.

SCIENCE AND INVENTION

1321   First recorded tower clock in England begun for Norwich Cathedral, with astronomical dial made in London.

AD 1326–1330

1326		Q. Isabella betrothes son P. Edward to Philippa, Count of Hainault's daughter, in return for mercenaries and use of ports to invade England.
	Sep. 23	Isabella and Mortimer land at Orwell, Suffolk; barons join them.
	Oct.	London favours rebels; Edward II and friends flee to west.
	15	London mob kills Treasurer Bp Stapeldon.
	26	Assembly of barons at Bristol proclaim P. Edward Keeper of the Realm in place of King.
	27	Elder Despenser, captured at Bristol, is executed.
	Nov. 16	Edward II and younger Despenser captured at Neath Abbey.
	24	Younger Despenser executed.
1327	*Jan.* 7	Parliament meets: deposition of Edward II eventually agreed. Edward, imprisoned in Kenilworth Castle, abdicates.

Feb.	*1*	Edward III crowned; Regency Council appointed.
		Mortimer's lands restored with additions; he becomes Justice of Wales and most powerful man in Wales and Marches.
Sep.		Edward II murdered in Berkeley Castle.
		Mortimer and Q. Isabella control administration, disregarding Regency Council.
		Scots invade Northumberland and force retreat of English army.
1328 *Jan.*	*24*	Edward III marries Philippa of Hainault.
May	*4*	Ty of Northampton: England ratifies treaty drawn up by Scots in Edinburgh; Robert Bruce recognized as K. of Scots.
Jul.	*12*	Edward's sister Joan marries Bruce's son David.
Oct.		Pope recognizes Bruce as King. Mortimer makes self E. of March.
1329 *Jun.*		Edward III pays homage for Gascony to Philip VI of France.
	7	Robert Bruce dies, succeeded by David II, with E. of Moray as Regent.
1330 *Mar.*	*19*	Edmund, E. of Kent, son of Edward I, executed for opposing Mortimer and Q. Isabella.
Oct.		Edward III and friends arrest Mortimer.
Nov.	*29*	Mortimer executed. Isabella allowed to live in retirement. John Stratford, Bp of Winchester, appointed Chancellor.

SCIENCE AND INVENTION

1326	Richard of Wallingford, Fellow of Merton, later abbot of St Albans, begins construction of great public clock at St Albans. His works include: instructions for clock's operation; specifications for astronomical instrument and instrument to measure altitudes; 2 treatises on trigonometry.
1327	Cannon first depicted in *De Officiis Regum* (On Duties of Kings), dedicated to Edward III by author Walter de Millinate.

Events Elsewhere

1328 *Apr.*	*1*	Philip VI of Valois chosen K. of France, as nearest heir in male line.

AD 1331–1335

1331 *Mar.*		Edward III confirms homage to Philip VI of France (*v.* 1329).
1332 *Aug.*	*6*	Edward Balliol and 'Disinherited', exiled supporters of his father, invade Scotland from England.
	12	Ψ Dupplin Moor: Balliol defeats loyal Scots forces.
		Edward III moves administration to York (until 1337).
Sep.	*24*	Balliol crowned K. of Scots.
Dec.	*12*	Balliol defeated by loyalists and flees to England.

1333	*May*		Balliol and Edward III besiege Berwick.
	Jul.	19	Ψ Halidon Hill: English defeat Scottish force attempting to relieve Berwick. Berwick falls.
			England seizes I. of Man from Scotland and retains it.
			Bp John Stratford, Chancellor, becomes Archbp of Canterbury.
			Last E. of Ulster murdered by tenants in Ireland; his infant daughter Elizabeth de Burgh taken to England.
1334	*Feb.*		In Parliament at Edinburgh Balliol cedes Berwick to England.
	May		David II, K. of Scots, escapes to France and is supported by French.
	Jun.		At Newcastle Balliol recognizes Edward III as overlord, ceding all counties of S. Scotland to England.
	Sep.		Scots rebel. Edward campaigns in Scottish lowlands.
1335	*Summer*		Edward III and Balliol campaign as far as Perth.
	Nov.		Edward makes truce with Scots.

RELIGION AND EDUCATION

1334	After riot between northern and southern students at Oxford, some masters secede to start university at Stamford, Lincs.

AD 1336–1340

1336	*Jul.*		Edward III campaigns in N. Scotland as far as Elgin.
	Aug.		Attempting to detach Flanders from French alliance, Edward bans wool exports to Flanders and invites Flemish weavers to settle in England; English cloth manufacturing industry begins to expand.
			French fleet, diverted to Channel ports, threatens to help Scots.
	Sep.		Parliament at Nottingham votes taxes for war with France.
1337	*May*		English embassy in Valenciennes, Hainault, buys alliance of German princes and all Low Countries except Flanders.
		24	Philip VI confiscates Gascony.
	Aug.		English embassy buys support of Emperor Lewis against France.
			Edward III's last Scottish campaign; he relieves Stirling Castle.
	Oct.		Edward formally rejects Philip VI's right to French throne (start of 100 Years' War).
1338			French fleet raids Portsmouth and Southampton and attacks shipping.
	Jul.		Before embarking for Antwerp, Edward III issues Walton Ordinances at Walton-on-Naze, Essex: emergency powers given to royal officials; tax-collection for war effort to be expedited; King's eldest son Edward, 'Black Prince', to be nominal Regent.
	Sep.	5	Edward meets Emperor Lewis at Coblenz and is named imperial Vicar-General west of R. Rhine.

1339		French fleet attacks Dover and Folkestone.
	Sep.–Oct.	Edward III campaigns indecisively in Hainault and N. France.
	Sep. 29	Archbp Stratford made chief of Regency Council and sent to England to speed funds.
	Dec. 3	Edward makes alliance with new government in Flanders.
1340	Jan. 25	Edward III assumes title K. of France in Ghent, Flanders, and is recognized as such by Flemings.
	Mar.	Edward returns to England and persuades Parliament to grant taxes in return for modification of Walton Ordinances. Archbp Stratford resigns; his brother Robert becomes Chancellor.
	Jun. 24	Ψ Sluys, Flanders: Edward III, directing English fleet, destroys large French fleet and gains control of Channel.
		Edward's siege of Tournai fails; funds from England insufficient.
	Sep. 25	Truce of Espléchin made with French.
	Nov. 30	Edward returns to England, dismisses Chancellor Robert Stratford, arrests government officials and begins verbal conflict with Archbp Stratford.

FINE ARTS AND ARCHITECTURE

| 1337 | Rebuilding of Gloucester Abbey (later Cathedral) in Perpendicular style begins. |

RECREATION AND FASHION

| by 1340 | Brightly coloured, patterned materials are worn. Men's clothes are trimmed with jagged edges (dagged) and women's with fur. Women's gowns are close fitting, necessitating a corset; men's outer garment is a very short fitted tunic (cotehardie) with the newly fashionable buttons down the front and a belt on the hips. |

AD 1341–1345

1341	Apr.	Parliament supports Archbp Stratford; Edward III is reconciled to him and drops charges.
	Jun.	K. David II returns to Scotland. Balliol withdraws to England.
	Jul.–Sep.	England and France support rival claimants to Brittany.
1342	Sep.	English army defeats French at Morlaix in Brittany.
	Oct. 23	Edward III embarks for Brittany and conquers most of duchy.
		Edward's second son Lionel marries Elizabeth de Burgh and so becomes E. of Ulster.
1343	Jan. 19	Truce of Malestroit between England and France.
	Apr.	Black Prince made Prince of Wales.

1344		Noble, gold coin worth 6s 8d, is first coined in England; it shows Edward III on ship.
	Oct.–Dec.	Anglo-French peace talks, held by Pope at Avignon, fail.
1345	Jul.	Edward III goes to Flanders to repair alliance.
		English armies wage successful campaigns against French in Brittany and Gascony.

LITERATURE AND SCHOLARSHIP

| 1345 | | Richard de Bury, Bp of Durham, bibliophile, once Edward III's tutor, writes *Philobiblon*, Latin autobiography. |

RECREATION AND FASHION

| 1341 | | Two 'Jousts of war', real combats between English and Scottish knights, held in Border country. |
| 1344 | Jan. 19 | Edward III holds 3-day 'Round Table' tournament at Windsor, last of series begun in 1341. |

SCIENCE AND INVENTION

| 1345 | Mar. 20 | Total eclipse of moon and conjunction of 3 major planets recorded by John of Ashendon, Oxford astronomer, who claims to have predicted Black Death (*v.* 1348) from astronomical observations. |

AD 1346–1350

1346	Apr.	New French army, led by king's son John, invades Gascony.
	Jul. 12	Edward III lands in Cotentin, Normandy, with army of 15,000.
	26	Edward takes and sacks Caen.
	Aug. 26	Ψ Crécy: Edward defeats and destroys French army; Philip VI escapes.
	Sep. 4	Edward begins siege of Calais.
	Oct. 17	Ψ Neville's Cross, Durham: David II of Scots, invading England at request of French, is defeated and captured; his nephew Robert the Steward escapes to become Regent.
		Italian bankers Bardi bankrupted, mainly by Edward's failure to pay debts; he turns to English financiers.
1347	Jun.	In Brittany English defeat and capture French claimant to duchy.
	Aug. 4	Calais surrenders. Edward III expels inhabitants and fills town with English colonists.
	Sep. 28	Truce with French.
1348	Apr. 23	Most likely date for Edward III's institution of Order of Garter.
	Summer	Black Death reaches S. England from France.
	Nov.	Black Death reaches London.

1349		Black Death reaches N. England, Scotland and Ireland; estimated over 20% of population have died.
	Oct.	Edward III and Black Prince lead small force to Calais to prevent betrayal of town to France.
1350	Aug. 29	Les Espagnols-sur-Mer, naval battle: Edward III defeats Castilian fleet off Winchelsea.

FINE ARTS AND ARCHITECTURE

1348 *Aug.* Plans drawn up for completion of St George's Chapel, Windsor.

LITERATURE AND SCHOLARSHIP

1347 Adam of Murimuth, canon of St Paul's, London, writes *Continuatio Chronicarum*, continuing Walter of Guisborough's work to 1347.

by 1349 Richard Rolle of Hampton, hermit and poet, most read English writer of the age, writes *Meditations on the Passion*.

MUSIC AND DRAMA

1350 *Pride of Life*, earliest surviving fragment of morality play in English.

RELIGION AND EDUCATION

1349 *Aug. 25* Archbp Thomas Bradwardine, Oxford mathematician and theologian, dies shortly after appointment to Canterbury; mathematical works include *Tract on Proportions* (on relation of force and velocity); mentioned by Chaucer in *Canterbury Tales*.

1350 'Gough' map of Britain produced; first map showing shape of country; roads plotted and distances given accurately.

SCIENCE AND INVENTION

1348 *Dec.* John of Ashendon completes treatise on world-wide natural disasters; claims again to have predicted Black Death.

Events Elsewhere

1350 *Aug. 22* Philip VI of France dies; succeeded by son John II.

AD 1351–1355

1351 *Spring* Ψ Taillebourg: English defeat French army invading Gascony.
Statute of Labourers: wages fixed at pre-Black Death rates and movement of labour restricted.
Statute of Provisors: forbids papal appointment of clergy to English benefices.

1352 *Aug.*	Ψ Mauron, Brittany: English heavily defeat French.
	Statute of Treasons: defines high treason as attack on king, his family or his officials.
1353	Peace negotiations begin with France.
	Statute of *Praemunire*: forbids appeals to foreign courts from jurisdiction of royal courts in England.
1354	Statute of Staples: 15 wool staple towns in England, Wales and Ireland replace foreign staple.
	Ransom for David II, K. of Scots, agreed, but French send force to persuade Scots to renew war. Scots take Berwick.
1355 *Feb. 10*	Beginning of St Scholastica's Day riots at Oxford, 3-day battle between 'town and gown': many students killed and town made to take annual oath to uphold University privileges.
Spring	Negotiations with France abandoned. Edward III makes alliance with Charles 'the Bad', K. of Navarre.
Sep. 9	Black Prince sails to Gascony as King's Lieutenant.
Oct. 5	Black Prince raids S. France from Bordeaux, burning towns and ravaging countryside.

Events Elsewhere

1353	Giovanni Boccacio writes *Decameron*.
1355	Ottoman Turks conquer Gallipoli; first European possession.

AD 1356–1360

1356 *Jan.*	Edward Balliol surrenders Scotland to Edward III permanently.
Jan.–Feb.	Edward retakes Berwick and burns countryside of Lothian.
Jul.–Aug.	Black Prince raids France as far as R. Loire.
Sep. 19	Ψ Poitiers: Black Prince defeats French army and captures John II of France.
1357 *Mar. 22*	2-year truce made between England and France at Bordeaux.
Nov. 6	Ty of Berwick, agreeing release of David II, K. of Scots, for ransom, is ratified by Scottish General Council at Scone; representatives of burghs attend; 'Three Estates' first mentioned.
1358 *Jan.*	Proposed treaty with French fixes ransom for John II and territorial concessions to England; France refuses ransom.
1359 *Mar. 24*	Second proposed treaty, with increased territorial concessions, rejected by France.
Oct. 27	Edward III and Black Prince embark for France.
Dec.	English blockade Rheims without success.

1360	Jan.		Edward III abandons siege of Rheims and marches towards Paris.
	Apr.		Edward leaves Paris region after ravaging countryside; violent storm hits English army near Chartres.
	May	8	Ty of Brétigny: John II's ransom reduced; France to grant England sovereignty over enlarged Aquitaine from R. Loire to Pyrenees, with Calais and part of N. France; Edward to abandon claim to French throne, Brittany and Normandy.
	Oct.	24	Ty of Calais: Edward and John ratify Ty of Brétigny, omitting renunciation of sovereignty on either side.

FINE ARTS AND ARCHITECTURE

| 1360 | Jun. | 25 | Henry Yevele becomes master mason of Westminster; under Edward III he rebuilds Clock and Jewel towers in Palace of Westminster. |

LITERATURE AND SCHOLARSHIP

| 1360 | | | *Le Morte Arthur*, alliterative English poem, written in Midlands. |

RECREATION AND FASHION

| 1358 | Jan. | | Edward III holds night-time tournament at Bristol. |
| | Apr. | | 'Round Table' tournament at Windsor costs £32 to proclaim through Europe and attracts foreign contestants. |

RELIGION AND EDUCATION

| by 1357 | | | Richard fitzRalph, Chancellor of Oxford University, Archbp of Armagh, writes *De Pauperie Salvatoris* (On Saviour's Poverty), treatise against mendicant friars. |

Events Elsewhere

| 1358 | May | 28 | Beginning of peasants' revolt in France (*Jacquerie*). |

AD 1361–1365

1361	Spring		Plague breaks out again.
	Sep.	15	Edward III's son Lionel, E. of Ulster and Connaught (*v.* 1342), arrives in Dublin as Lieutenant in Ireland.
	Oct.	10	Black Prince marries Joan of Kent.
1362	Jun.	22	Alliance between England and Castile.
	Jul.	19	Black Prince appointed ruler of Aquitaine.
			P. Lionel becomes D. of Clarence, and Edward III's fourth son, John of Gaunt, D. of Lancaster.
			Use of English in law-courts ordered.

1363		Wool staple established at Calais.
	Jun. 29	Black Prince arrives at Bordeaux to govern Aquitaine.
	Nov.	David II, K. of Scots, makes agreement for Edward III to succeed him.
		Parliament first opened in English.

1363

Jun. 29   Black Prince arrives at Bordeaux to govern Aquitaine.

Nov.   David II, K. of Scots, makes agreement for Edward III to succeed him.
          Parliament first opened in English.

1364 Mar. 4   Scottish Parliament repudiates David II's agreement with Edward III over
              succession to throne.

     Apr. 8   John II of France dies in England, having returned to captivity as ransom
              unpaid; son Charles V succeeds him.

1365   Parliament repudiates Pope's overlordship of England (v. 1213) and passes
              Statute of *Praemunire* (II) specifically forbidding appeals to papal court (v.
              1353).

LITERATURE AND SCHOLARSHIP

1362   William Langland begins *Piers Plowman*, poem has first mention in literature
              of 'Robin Hood'.

by 1364   Ranulf Higden, Benedictine monk of Chester, writes *Polychronicon*, world
              history to 1327 (v. 1387).

RECREATION AND FASHION

1362 Apr.   5-day tournament at Smithfield; Spanish, Cypriot and Armenian knights take
              part.

AD 1366–1370

1366   Statutes of Kilkenny attempt to keep English-controlled area free from Irish
              influence: most contacts between 'obedient English' and 'Irish enemies'
              forbidden.

     Nov.   Clarence leaves Ireland without extending English rule there.

1367 Feb.   Black Prince crosses Pyrenees to invade Castile in support of K. Pedro 'the
              Cruel', driven out by French-backed rival.

     Apr. 3   Ψ Nájera: Black Prince defeats Castilian and French forces.
              William of Wykeham, Bp of Winchester, made Chancellor.

1368 Jun. 30 Gascon barons, resenting new taxes, appeal to Charles V of France.
              Powers of justices of peace in each shire legally established.

1369 May 2   French assembly approves war against England.
     Jun. 3   Edward III resumes title K. of France.
     Aug.   Q. Philippa dies; Alice Perrers gains influence at court.
     Sep.   John of Gaunt raids Picardy and Normandy from Calais.
     Nov. 30 Charles V confiscates English lands in France.
              Harvest fails.

14-year truce made between England and Scotland.
Sir William of Windsor, later husband of King's mistress Alice Perrers, sent as deputy to Ireland to raise taxes.

1370 Sep. 19   Black Prince sacks Limoges, recently surrendered to French.

FINE ARTS AND ARCHITECTURE
from 1367   Nave of Winchester Cathedral rebuilt in Perpendicular style.

LITERATURE AND SCHOLARSHIP
1370   Geoffrey Chaucer, poet and royal official, writes *The Book of the Duchess*, poem in memory of Blanche, 1st wife of John of Gaunt.

Events Elsewhere

1369   Tamburlane of Samarkand establishes Mongol empire in central Asia.
Jean Froissart begins *Chronicles*.

AD 1371–1375

1371 Feb. 22   David II of Scotland dies, succeeded by Robert II, first Stewart.
Mar.   Anti-clerical Parliament secures replacement of bishops by laymen as Chancellor and Treasurer. John Wyclif, Oxford theologian and opponent of papal domination, attends Parliament.

1372 Mar.   John of Gaunt marries Castilian princess and claims throne of Castile.
Jun.   Owain Lawgoch ('of the Red Hand'), great-nephew of Llewelyn, assumes title Prince of Wales; planning to invade Wales, he raids Guernsey with Welsh exiles and French support.
23   Naval battle off La Rochelle: Castilians destroy English fleet.
Aug. 7   Poitiers surrenders to French.
Owain Lawgoch's force and French fleet defeat English reinforcements at La Rochelle; La Rochelle surrenders.
Dec. 1   French take control of Poitou.

1373 Apr. 28   French take all Brittany except Brest.
Aug.   John of Gaunt raids from Calais to Champagne and Burgundy.

1374 Jan.   John of Gaunt reaches Bordeaux.

1375 Jun. 27   General truce made at Bruges: England retains: Calais; Gascony around Bordeaux and Bayonne; Brest and 3 other forts in Brittany.

LITERATURE AND SCHOLARSHIP
1375   Narrative of travels attributed to 'Sir John Mandeville' first appears in English.

Pearl and *Sir Gawain and the Green Knight* written: alliterative poems from
NW Midlands, often considered to be by same author.
Cloud of Unknowing written: mystical prose work from Midlands.

MUSIC AND DRAMA

1375 Cornish sequence of mystery plays, *Origin of World, Passion, Resurrection*,
performed in round, open-air theatres, as at St Just in Penwith.

RECREATION AND FASHION

1375 7-day tournament, last recorded under Edward III; Alice Perrers as 'Lady of
the Sun' leads contestants in procession at start.

AD 1376–1380

1376 *Apr.* 28		'Good' Parliament meets, John of Gaunt presiding: Sir Peter de la Mare, Hereford knight, chosen 'to speak' for Commons in full Parliament; King's Chamberlain and other royal officials tried by Parliament for embezzlement, first use of impeachment process; Alice Perrers dismissed; new Council appointed.
	Jun. 8	Black Prince dies.
	Oct.	Acts of 'Good' Parliament annulled, de la Mare imprisoned and old councillors reinstated, through John of Gaunt's influence.
1377 *Jan.* 27		Parliament meets and grants poll tax of 4d per head. Sir Thomas Hungerford, John of Gaunt's steward, is first spokesman for Commons to hold title of Speaker.
	Feb. 19	John of Gaunt attacks privileges of City of London; he defends Wyclif against charges brought by Bp Courtenay of London and insults Courtenay.
	20	Londoners riot and attack John of Gaunt's palace of Savoy.
	Jun. 21	Edward III dies, succeeded by grandson Richard II with permanent Council; London reconciled to John of Gaunt.
	Jul. 16	Richard II crowned. French burn Rye and Hastings, raid I. of Wight, sail into R. Thames and burn Gravesend.
1378		Castilian fleet raids Cornwall and burns Fowey.
	Oct. 20	Parliament meets at Gloucester: refuses taxation; agrees to support Roman Pope against Avignon Pope in schism.
1379		French lose control in Brittany, but English fail to take St Malo. Edmund Mortimer, E. of March, made lieutenant of Ireland.
1380 *Jan.* 16		Parliament meets: declares king of age to rule.
	Jul.–Sep.	Edward III's youngest son, Thomas of Woodstock, raids France from Calais to Champagne, Loire valley and Brittany.

Nov.	Parliament imposes new poll tax on all aged over 15.
	Absentee landlords commanded to return to Ireland or forfeit ⅔ of revenues to Irish Justiciar.

FINE ARTS AND ARCHITECTURE

1378	Henry Yevele begins to rebuild nave of Westminster Abbey.

LITERATURE AND SCHOLARSHIP

1376	Thomas Walsingham, monk of St Albans, begins *Historia Anglicana*, English history 1272–1422.
by *1380*	Chaucer writes *House of Fame*.

MUSIC AND DRAMA

1376	Earliest record of Corpus Christi pageants at York.
1377	Corpus Christi play first mentioned at Beverley, Yorks.

RELIGION AND EDUCATION

1376–1379	Wyclif writes: *De Dominio Civili* (On Human Authority); *De Dominio Divino* (On Divine Authority); *De Ecclesia* (On the Church); *De Potestate Papae* (On Pope's Power). Pope condemns his views.
1379 Nov. 26	William of Wykeham founds New College, Oxford (*v.* 1382).
1380	Wyclif and followers begin to translate Bible into English.

SCIENCE AND INVENTION

1376	John Arderne, surgeon, writes treatise on own secret technique for operating on haemorrhoids and anal fistulae.

Events Elsewhere

1378	Papal schism begins between Pope in Rome and Pope in Avignon.
1380	Charles V of France dies, succeeded by son Charles VI.

AD 1381–1385

1381 Jan.	Brittany submits to France, but English remain in Brest.
May	Peasants' Revolt against collection of poll tax begins in Essex and spreads to Kent; Kentishmen choose Wat Tyler as leader.
Jun. 13	Tyler and excommunicated priest John Ball lead Kentishmen to Blackheath; Essex men encamp at Mile End. Rebels burn property and kill enemies in London; John of Gaunt's palace of Savoy destroyed.
14	Richard II meets rebels at Mile End and promises justice and freedom for all; mob storms Tower and executes Chancellor Archbp Sudbury and others on Tower Hill; king and his mother escape.

	15	Richard meets Kentishmen at Smithfield; Wat Tyler is killed, king takes command and promises concessions; rebels leave London.
	until 24	Peasant risings occur outside London, especially at St Albans and in E. Anglia. Richard revokes promise of freedom.
	Jul.	John Ball and other rebel leaders executed; rising suppressed.
1382	*Jan.* 14	Richard II marries Anne of Bohemia.
		Edmund of Langley, Edward III's 5th son, fails in expedition to help K. of Portugal against Castile.
1383	*May* 16	Bp of Norwich leads 'Norwich Crusade' to Flanders, ostensibly in support of Roman Pope against Avignon rival, but fails to take Ypres from French army.
	Oct.	Chancellor Michael de la Pole impeaches Bp of Norwich; Parliament attacks Richard II's counsellors, especially Robert de Vere, E. of Oxford, and Pole.
1384	*Jan.*	John of Gaunt makes truce with France.
	Apr.	John of Gaunt and Thomas of Woodstock quarrel with Richard II.
1385		French send force to Scotland and raid Northumberland with Scots. Richard II leads large army north. He makes his uncles dukes, Edmund of York and Thomas of Gloucester, and Pole E. of Suffolk.
	Aug.	English burn Melrose and Dryburgh abbeys, Holyrood and Edinburgh, but return home without bringing enemy to battle.

LITERATURE AND SCHOLARSHIP

1381	John Gower, poet, writes *Vox Clamantis*, Latin poem on political subjects including Peasants' Revolt.
1382	Chaucer writes *Parliament of Fowls* for Richard II's wedding.
by 1383	John Fordun, priest of Aberdeen, writes *Scoticronicon*, Scottish history from Noah to 1383 (*v.* 1449).
1385	Chaucer writes *Troilus and Cressida*.

RELIGION AND EDUCATION

1381	Wyclif's theology in *De Eucharistia* condemned at Oxford; he reasserts views in *Confessio*.
1382	Wyclif barred from teaching in Oxford.
	William of Wykeham founds Winchester College as grammar school to provide scholars for New College, Oxford (*v.* 1379).
from 1384	After Wyclif's death supporters of his views are known as 'Lollards'; group includes poor preachers and knights.

SCIENCE AND INVENTION

1384	John Dombleday writes *Stella Alchimiae*, treatise on alchemy.

AD 1386–1390

1386	*Mar. 8*	Richard II recognizes John of Gaunt as K. of Castile; he grants de Vere, now Marquis of Dublin, all royal lands in Ireland.
	Apr. 12	England makes perpetual Ty of Windsor with Portugal.
	Jul.	John of Gaunt sails to Corunna on expedition to Castile.
		French apparently prepare to invade England, but abandon plans.
	Oct.	Richard makes de Vere D. of Ireland. Parliament, led by Gloucester, forces Richard to dismiss Chancellor, E. of Suffolk, and Treasurer; Suffolk impeached and imprisoned; commission appointed to oversee government and court.
1387	*Feb. 9*	Richard II begins tour of Midlands and North to win support; he recruits bodyguard in Cheshire and Wales.
	Aug.	Richard consults judges at Shrewsbury and Nottingham, who declare royal prerogatives infringed by commission of 1386.
	Autumn	John of Gaunt abandons claim to Castile in return for payment and withdraws to Gascony.
	Nov. 14	D. of Gloucester, EE of Arundel and Warwick ('Lords Appellant') take arms and demand arrest of King's friends.
	Dec.	Army under John of Gaunt's son Henry Bolingbroke and Thomas Mowbray sent to intercept royalist army.
	20	Ψ Radcot Bridge, Oxon: Gloucester and Bolingbroke defeat royalists under de Vere; de Vere and E. of Suffolk escape to Europe.
1388	*Feb. 3*	'Merciless' Parliament meets: king's friends convicted of treason; Lords Appellant control government.
	Aug. 5	Ψ Otterburn (Chevy Chase), Northumberland: Scots under E. of Douglas defeat and capture Henry Percy ('Hotspur') son of E. of Northumberland.
		Agreement with Hanseatic League allows English merchants to trade in Hanse territory.
1389	*May 3*	Richard II resumes control of government.
	Nov.	John of Gaunt returns home and reconciles Richard to other uncles; Richard makes him governor of Aquitaine for life.
1390	*Apr. 19*	Robert II, K. of Scots, dies, succeeded by son Robert III.
		Statute against livery and maintenance: limits employment of retainers and forbids them to wear livery off duty.
		Statute of Provisors (II) (*v.* 1351) imposes penalties on clergy accepting nominations to benefices from Pope.
	Autumn	Richard II presses for Edward II's canonization.

FINE ARTS AND ARCHITECTURE

from 1390   Nave and transepts of Canterbury Cathedral rebuilt to design of Henry Yevele, now king's chief mason.

1387 | John Trevisa translates Ranulf Higden's *Polychronicon* (*v.* 1364) into English with introduction.
Chaucer begins *Canterbury Tales.*
1390 | Gower writes *Confessio Amantis*, English poem.

Events Elsewhere

1389 *Jun.* 15 | Ψ Kossovo: Turks defeat Serbs and control Balkans for 500 years.

AD 1391–1395

1391 *Nov.* | Parliament reasserts royal prerogatives.

1392 | Richard II takes control of London, removing mayor and sheriffs; liberties restored only on payment of £10,000 to king.
D. of Gloucester appointed Lieutenant of Ireland but forbidden to go.

1393 | Statute of *Praemunire* (III) (*v.* 1353, 1365): increased penalties for appealing to Rome; new offence of promoting papal bulls or excommunications added.
Spring | D. of Gloucester and John of Gaunt in Calais for peace talks with France.
Summer | Rebellion in north against peace negotiations suppressed by return of Gloucester and John of Gaunt.

1394 *Jun.* 7 | Q. Anne dies.
Oct. 2 | Richard II lands at Waterford, Ireland, at head of army including his cousin and heir presumptive Roger Mortimer, E. of March, and D. of Gloucester.
Christmas | Richard, in Dublin, decrees: English territory to be east of line from Dundalk to R. Boyne and down R. Barrow to Waterford (later called 'English Pale'); Irish to be expelled from Leinster, but Irish chiefs who swear allegiance to be confirmed in ancestral lands.

1395 *May* 15 | Richard II leaves Dublin after receiving submission of 80 Irish chiefs.

FINE ARTS AND ARCHITECTURE

1393–1394 | Richard II begins rebuilding Westminster Hall to design by Henry Yevele; porch and great oak hammer-beam roof added, widest unsupported span in England.

LITERATURE AND SCHOLARSHIP

1392 | Chaucer writes *Treatise on Astrolabe* for small son.

MUSIC AND DRAMA

1392 | Corpus Christi play at Coventry first mentioned.

1393	Julian of Norwich, mystic, writes *Sixteen Revelations of Divine Love*, reflections on her visions of 1373.
1395	*The Twelve Conclusions* of the Lollards, manifesto, published and fixed to doors of St Paul's Cathedral and Westminster Abbey.

Events Elsewhere

1392 *Aug.* 5	Charles VI of France has first attack of insanity.

AD 1396–1400

1396	*Mar.* 9	28-year truce with France. Richard II marries Isabella, Charles VI's daughter, by proxy.
	Oct. 27	Richard and Charles meet near Calais and swear friendship: English to leave Brittany; Richard to support French policy, but not to abandon claim to French throne.
1397	*Feb.*	D. of Gloucester and E. of Arundel quarrel with Richard II.
	Jul.	Richard arrests Arundel, E. of Warwick and Gloucester; Gloucester taken to Calais.
	Sep.	Parliament condemns acts of Lords Appellant; Arundel, Warwick and Gloucester impeached; Arundel executed, Warwick banished to I. of Man, Gloucester already murdered in Calais.
1398	*Jan.* 27	Parliament meets at Shrewsbury: Acts of 1388 Parliament annulled.
	Sep. 16	Duel at Coventry to settle dispute between Bolingbroke and Mowbray, now D. of Norfolk. Richard stops duel and exiles both.
1399	*Feb.* 3	John of Gaunt dies, leaving exiled son Bolingbroke as heir.
	Mar. 18	Richard II confiscates Bolingbroke's inheritance.
	Jun. 1	Richard returns to Ireland to suppress new Irish revolt.
	Jul.	Bolingbroke lands at Ravenspur, Yorks, and is joined by northern lords; he marches to south-west; Richard returns from Ireland.
	29	Bolingbroke reaches Bristol, captures and executes King's friends.
	Aug.	Richard arrives at Conway Castle and is tricked into surrender.
	Sep. 30	Parliament meets: accepts Richard's abdication and declares Bolingbroke K. Henry IV.
	Oct. 13	Henry IV crowned.
	15	Henry's son, P. Henry of Monmouth, made P. of Wales.
1400	*Jan.* 6	Conspiracy by supporters of Richard II fails.
	by 31	Richard murdered in Pontefract Castle.
	Aug.	Henry IV invades Scotland and holds Edinburgh. Robert III, K. of Scots, refuses to pay homage and Scots conduct guerrilla warfare.

Sep.	*16*	Owen Glendower, richest landowner in Wales, begins revolt by attacking Lord Grey of Ruthin.
	17	Glendower proclaimed P. of Wales, burns Ruthin and ravages other English settlements in N. Wales; he is joined by his cousins Gwilym and Rhys ap Tudor; revolt spreads to Anglesey.
	24	Glendower raids England and is defeated at Welshpool.
Oct.		Henry conducts punitive campaign in N. Wales.

1400 Hops, and possibly onions and cabbages, first introduced into England from Flanders (but *v. 1525*).

FINE ARTS AND ARCHITECTURE

1397 *Wilton Diptych*: painting depicting Richard II.

RECREATION AND FASHION

by 1399 Male fashions outshine female: men wear voluminous robe in rich material, usually buttoned down front ('houppelande'), and hose joined together at top to form tights, with exaggeratedly long toes; tights are fastened up by laces ('points') and codpiece is worn at front; hats begin to replace hoods for men.

RELIGION AND EDUCATION

by 1396 Walter Hilton, Augustinian canon of Newark, mystic, writes *Scale of Perfection*.

AD 1401–1405

1401		Statute *De Heretico Comburendo*, imposing death penalty by burning for obdurate heretics, passed at request of bishops.
	Mar. 2	Lollard William Sawtrey is first man burned at Smithfield.
		Hotspur (*v. 1388*), now Justiciar of Chester, made military governor to P. Henry of Wales and in charge of campaign against Glendower.
	Jun.	Hotspur resigns post, alleging arrears of pay.
		Henry IV's second son Thomas made Governor of Ireland; English Pale reduced to Louth, Meath, Kildare and Dublin; Irish and Anglo-Irish control rest of country.
	by Dec.	Glendower controls N. Wales and appeals for support to Scotland.
1402	*Jun. 22*	Ψ Pilleth, Radnorshire: Glendower defeats and captures Edmund Mortimer, whom Henry IV refuses to ransom.
	Aug.	Glendower campaigns in S. Wales; Glamorgan joins revolt.
	Sep. 14	Ψ Homildon Hill: E. of Northumberland and his son (Hotspur) defeat Scots, capture E. of Douglas but refuse to yield him to Henry IV.
	Nov.	Mortimer marries Glendower's daughter; Glendower agrees to support Mortimer's nephew Edmund, E. of March, as K. of England.

1403	Feb.	7	Henry IV marries Joan, widow of D. of Brittany.
	Mar.		P. Henry takes command in Wales and Marches.
	Jul.		E. of Northumberland and son rebel against Henry IV.
		13	Hotspur leads rebel army to Shrewsbury.
		21	Ψ Shrewsbury: Henry IV and P. Henry defeat rebels; Hotspur is killed; his uncle, E. of Worcester, is captured and executed.
	Aug.		Northumberland submits to King and is kept under guard.
	Nov.		Glendower allied with French. French fleet attacks Welsh coast.
1404	Jan.	14	Parliament meets: Henry IV agrees to nominate councillors in Parliament; Council to account to Parliament for expenditure.
	May	10	Glendower holds Parliament at Dolgellau.
	Jul.	14	Glendower makes formal treaty with French; French fleet ravages south coast towns of England.
	Oct.	6	Parliament at Coventry: new tax on revenue from land and personal property granted; Henry regains power over Council.
	by Dec.		Glendower controls most of Wales.
1405	Feb.	28	Compact made dividing England and Wales between Glendower, E. of Northumberland and Mortimer.
	Mar.	11	Ψ Grosmont: Sir John Talbot defeats Glendower.
	Apr.		Richard Scrope, Archbp of York, leads new revolt in North.
	May	5	Ψ Usk: P. Henry defeats Glendower.
		29	Scrope rebellion collapses.
	Jun.	8	Archbp Scrope and other rebels executed outside York.
	Aug.		French force lands at Milford Haven; together with Welsh they advance almost to Worcester. French attack Aquitaine.

FINE ARTS AND ARCHITECTURE

| 1405 | | | John Thornton of Coventry makes east window of York Minster, largest mediaeval window in England (78ft × 31ft). |

AD 1406–1410

1406	Mar.	1	'Long' Parliament meets and sits until December.
		30	P. James of Scotland captured by English at sea.
	Apr.	4	Robert III, K. of Scots, dies; his brother Robert, D. of Albany, is Regent during James's captivity in England.
	Dec.	22	Parliament is dissolved after achieving aims: king's Council is nominated in and accountable to Parliament; councillors are paid.
1407	Jan.		Thomas Arundel, Archbp of Canterbury, made Chancellor.
	Oct.		P. Henry begins siege of Aberystwyth Castle.

1408	*Feb.*	*19*	Ψ Bramham Moor: Sheriff of Yorkshire defeats remaining rebels; E. of Northumberland killed.
	Sep.		P. Henry takes Aberystwyth Castle.
1409	*Jan.*		Henry IV is seriously ill.
	Feb.	*28*	P. Henry appointed Constable of Dover and Warden of Cinque Ports.
	Mar.		Welsh surrender Harlech Castle; Mortimer killed; revolt ends.
	Dec.		P. Henry opposes Archbp. Arundel over taxation; Arundel resigns as Chancellor.
1410	*Jan.*		P. Henry controls Council: friends appointed include king's half-brothers, Thomas Beaufort, later D. of Exeter, as Chancellor, and Henry Beaufort, Bp of Winchester.
	Mar.		P. Henry becomes Captain of Calais. Glendower makes final, unsuccessful attempt at revolt.

RECREATION AND FASHION

| 1410 | | Edward, D. of York, translates *The Master of Game*, hunting manual, from French. |
| | | Crowds skate on frozen 'fin' (fen) at Finsbury Park, where ice lasts 14 weeks; skates are made of sharpened bones. |

Events Elsewhere

| 1407 | *Nov.* | John 'the Fearless', D. of Burgundy, has Charles VI's brother, D. of Orleans, murdered: start of feud between Burgundians and Orleanists. |
| 1410 | *May 17* | Third Pope, John XXIII, elected in Rome. |

AD 1411–1415

1411	*Oct.*		Small English force sent to help D. of Burgundy defend Paris against Armagnacs (Orleanist party).
	Nov.	*30*	Henry IV dismisses P. Henry and friends from Council.
	Dec.	*19*	Archbp Arundel becomes Chancellor again.
1412	*May*		Henry IV allied to Armagnacs, who promise to restore all Aquitaine to England.
	Jun.	*17*	P. Henry defends himself against imputations of treason; he is eventually reconciled to King.
	Autumn		P. Thomas, now D. of Clarence, leads force to France, but finds both parties renounce English alliance; he winters in Bordeaux. Thomas Beaufort is first permanent Admiral of England.
1413	*Mar.*	*20*	Henry IV dies, succeeded by son Henry V.
	Apr.	*9*	Henry V crowned during heavy snow-storm.

			Bp Beaufort replaces Archbp Arundel as Chancellor.
	Sep.	23	Sir John Oldcastle arrested on charge of Lollardy.
	Oct.	19	Oldcastle escapes from Tower of London and plans revolt.
	Dec.		Henry has Richard II's body reinterred in Westminster Abbey.
1414	Jan.	9	Henry V breaks up Lollard rising in London, arresting and hanging leaders; Oldcastle escapes; risings in Midlands and South fail.
	Aug.		English embassy in Paris to negotiate Henry's marriage to Catherine, Charles VI's daughter; Henry claims French throne.
1415	Mar.	12	Second English embassy in Paris fails in negotiations.
	Jul.	6	Henry V joins expeditionary force at Southampton.
	Aug.	5	Henry's cousin Richard, E. of Cambridge, and Lord Scrope are executed after failure of plot to kill King.
		11	Henry, with army of c.9,000 men, sails for France.
	Sep.	22	Harfleur surrenders to Henry; he expels citizens and sends for English colonists.
	Oct.	8	Henry begins march to Calais.
		25	Ψ Agincourt: English defeat French and inflict heavy casualties on nobility; D. of York killed.
	Nov.	16	Henry returns to England.

FINE ARTS AND ARCHITECTURE

1411   Rebuilding of Guildhall, London, begun; finished 1426.

LITERATURE AND SCHOLARSHIP

1411–1412   Thomas Hoccleve, royal official, poet, translates *De Regimine Principum* (Direction of Princes) for P. Henry.

1412   John Lydgate, monk of Bury St Edmunds and poet, begins *The Troy Book*, story of Trojan War translated from Italian.

MUSIC AND DRAMA

1415   *Agincourt Song* composed.

RELIGION AND EDUCATION

1413   Bp Henry Wardlaw, of St Andrew's, founds and is first Chancellor of St Andrew's University.

1414   Bp Henry Chichele, of St David's, becomes Archbp of Canterbury.

1415   Henry V founds last new monastery of Middle Ages at Twickenham.

Events Elsewhere

1414   General Council of Church opens at Constance.

1415   Council of Constance declares General Councils to be supreme authority in Church, deposes John XXIII and condemns teachings of Wyclif and Bohemian John Huss.

         Jul.   6   Huss burned at Constance.

AD 1416–1420

1416	*May*	*1*	Emperor Sigismund arrives in England.
			Franco-Genoese fleet begins to blockade Harfleur.
	Aug.	*15*	Henry V's brother John, D. of Bedford, wins naval battle in Seine estuary and relieves Harfleur. Ty of Canterbury between Henry and Sigismund, for mutual defence and support.
	Sep.–Oct.		Henry negotiates at Calais: truce made with French and secret pact with D. of Burgundy.
1417	*Jul.*	*23*	Henry V embarks for Normandy with army of *c*.12,000.
	Sep.	*8*	English take and sack Caen.
	Dec.		Oldcastle recaptured and burned.
1418	*Feb.*	*16*	Falaise surrenders to Henry V.
	Jul.	*30*	Henry begins siege of Rouen.
	Aug.	*22*	Cherbourg surrenders to Henry.
	Nov.		Henry resumes negotiations with Dauphin Charles.
1419	*Jan.*	*19*	Rouen surrenders to Henry V; English control Normandy.
	May	*30*	Henry V meets Charles VI and D. of Burgundy at Meulan; Burgundy breaks off peace negotiations.
	Jul.	*30*	English take Pontoise.
	Dec.	*25*	Philip 'the Good', new D. of Burgundy, makes alliance with Henry.
1420	*May*	*21*	Ty of Troyes: Henry V to be D. of Normandy, Regent of France and heir to French throne; he promises to defeat Dauphin's party.
	Jun.	*2*	Henry marries Charles VI's daughter Catherine.
	Sep.	*3*	D. of Albany dies, succeeded as Regent of Scotland by son Murdoch.
	Nov.	*17*	Melun surrenders to Henry.
	Dec.	*1*	Henry, Charles and D. of Burgundy enter Paris together.

LITERATURE AND SCHOLARSHIP

1416	*Gesta Henrici Quinti* (Deeds of Henry V, to 1416) written.
1417	John Capgrave, friar of King's Lynn, writes *Chronicle*, English history from creation to 1417.
1420	Paston family letters begin; continue till 1504.
1420	Lydgate translates *Siege of Thebes* from French.

MUSIC AND DRAMA

1419	Lionel Power is instructor of choristers in household chapel of D. of Clarence; he is one of inventors of 'cyclic mass', where all 5 main items are linked in theme.

1417   End of papal schism (*v.* 1378); Pope Martin V is elected.
1418   Henry the Navigator of Portugal sends expedition which discovers Madeira.
1419 *Sep.* 10   Dauphin Charles of France has D. of Burgundy murdered.

AD 1421–1425

1421 *Feb.* 23   Q. Catherine crowned at Westminster. Henry V begins tour of England.
      Mar. 22   Ψ Baugé: Dauphin defeats English army; D. of Clarence killed.
      May 12   Parliament meets and ratifies Ty of Troyes.
      Jun.   Henry returns to France.
      Oct. 6   Henry begins siege of Meaux.

1422 *May* 2   Meaux surrenders to English.
      Aug. 31   Henry V dies, succeeded by son Henry VI, with Council to rule in minority; Henry V's brothers made protectors of realm, Humphrey, D. of Gloucester, to act only when D. of Bedford in France.
      Oct. 21   Charles VI of France dies; Bedford proclaims Henry VI K. of France, but Dauphin declares himself Charles VII.

1423 *Feb.*   Jacqueline, Countess of Hainault, has marriage to John of Brabant annulled and marries D. of Gloucester.
      Apr.   D. of Bedford makes triple alliance with Burgundy and Brittany.
      Dec. 4   Ty of London: James I, K. of Scots, to be ransomed.

1424 *Feb.*   James I, K. of Scots, marries Joan Beaufort, Bp Beaufort's niece.
      Apr.   James I returns to Scotland.
      Aug. 17   Ψ Verneuil: English defeat Charles VII and Scottish mercenaries.
      Oct. 16   D. of Gloucester invades Hainault to recover wife's inheritance from Burgundy; in his absence Bp Beaufort controls government.

1425 *Apr.*   D. of Gloucester abandons unsuccessful campaign in Hainault and leaves Jacqueline for Eleanor Cobham (*v.* 1442).
      May   James I, K. of Scots, executes D. of Albany, his sons and father-in-law.
      Aug. 10   Le Mans surrenders to English.
      Oct. 30   Bp Beaufort's followers try to occupy London; Gloucester prevents their entry.

LITERATURE AND SCHOLARSHIP

1424   James I, K. of Scots, writes *The King's Quair*, (King's Book), love poem.
by 1425   Last manuscript of *The Mabinogion*, 4 Welsh legends, completed.

1422 First mention of Corpus Christi play at Chester.

1424 Lydgate writes 'mumming', dumb-show presented by solo speaker, for royal Christmas feast at Eltham Palace.

RECREATION AND FASHION

by 1422 Men's hair is worn short and curled under; women begin to wear wide headdresses, heart shaped or with horns, from which veils hang.

AD 1426–1430

1426 *Mar.* 12	At Leicester Parliament, D. of Bedford reconciles D. of Gloucester to Bp Beaufort; Beaufort resigns as Chancellor and leaves England.
1427 *Mar.* 25	At Calais D. of Bedford grants Beaufort cardinal's hat, offered by Pope in 1418 but withheld by Henry V.
1428 *Oct.* 7–12	English begin siege of Orléans.
Nov.	Cardinal Beaufort returns to England to preach Crusade against Hussites in Bohemia, but is not admitted as papal legate.
1429 *Feb.* 12	Ψ Rouvray ('Battle of Herrings'): failure of French attempt to divert supplies from English army besieging Orléans.
Apr. 30	Joan of Arc enters Orléans, followed in 3 days by relieving force.
May 8	English abandon siege of Orléans.
Jun. 18	Ψ Patay: French, led by Joan, defeat English and capture John Talbot.
Jul. 1	Cardinal Beaufort's force raised for Bohemian Crusade diverted to France as reinforcement.
Nov. 6	Henry VI crowned at Westminster by Archbp Chichele.
	Statute restricts right to elect knights to Parliament to those with property over 40s freehold.
by 1429	Dowager Q. Catherine secretly marries Owen Tudor, son of Glendower's cousin.
1430 *May* 23	Joan of Arc is captured by Burgundians at Compiègne and sold to English.
Apr.	Council, led by Cardinal Beaufort, embarks for Calais, taking Henry VI to be crowned K. of France (*v.* 1431); D. of Gloucester made King's Lieutenant in England.
Jun.	Henry and Council established at Rouen.

LITERATURE AND SCHOLARSHIP

by 1430 Adam of Usk writes *Chronicon*, English history 1377–1421, as seen by himself.

1426   John Awdelay, monastic chaplain, compiles collection of carols, introduced by line 'Synge these caroles in Cristemas'.

RELIGION AND EDUCATION

by 1430   Thomas Netter, Carmelite theologian, writes *Doctrinale Fidei Catholicae* (Theory of Catholic Faith), standard defence of Church against Lollards and Hussites.

Events Elsewhere

1428   German Johann Gutenberg begins experiments in printing with individual cast metal letters and a press.

1429 *Mar. 8*   Joan of Arc first meets Dauphin at Chinon.
    Jul. 18   Dauphin crowned Charles VII at Rheims.

AD 1431–1435

1431 *May*   D. of Gloucester crushes Lollard conspiracy centred on Abingdon, Oxon., and led by 'Jack Sharp'.
    30   Joan of Arc, convicted of heresy, burned by English at Rouen.
   Dec. 16   Henry VI crowned K. of France in Paris, by Cardinal Beaufort.

1432 *Feb. 9*   Henry VI returns to England; expense of 2 coronations results in financial crisis.

1433 *Jun.*   D. of Bedford in England tries to obtain subsidies for French campaigns.
   Dec. 24   Henry VI begins 4-month stay in Bury St Edmunds Abbey.

1434   English suppress revolts in Normandy.
   Jul.   D. of Bedford leaves England for France, having secured finance for further French campaign, while initiating peace talks with French.

1435 *Jul.–Aug.*   Congress of Arras: English, French and Burgundian embassies meet.
   Sep. 6   English embassy, led by Cardinal Beaufort, leaves Arras, abandoning negotiations.
    14   D. of Bedford dies in Rouen.

RELIGION AND EDUCATION

from 1435   Humphrey, D. of Gloucester, gives over 281 books, as well as money to provide lectures, to Oxford University; he promises £100 to build new library there.

AD 1436–1440

1436	Apr. 13	Paris surrenders to French.
	May 1	Richard, D. of York, appointed Lieutenant in France.
1437	Feb. 12	Talbot takes Pontoise.
	21	James I, K. of Scots, murdered in Perth, succeeded by son James II.
	Mar. 25	James II is first K. of Scots crowned at Holyrood, Edinburgh.
	Nov. 13	Henry VI declared of age to rule.
1439	Jul. 6	English and French embassies meet at Gravelines, near Calais, but negotiations fail as Henry VI insists on claim to French throne.
	Sep. 13	English surrender Meaux to French.
1440	Jul. 2	D. of York appointed Lieutenant in France for 5 years, but remains in England for year to organize army.
	Oct.	Harfleur surrenders to English army.
	Nov. 28	Guardians of James II, K. of Scots, murder E. of Douglas and start civil war in Scotland.

LITERATURE AND SCHOLARSHIP

1436	*Libelle [little book] of English Policy*, political poem on trade and sea-power.
1438	Margery Kempe of King's Lynn, mystic, writes *Book of Margery Kempe*, first English autobiography.

MUSIC AND DRAMA

1440	*Castle of Perseverance*, earliest surviving complete morality play.

RELIGION AND EDUCATION

1438	Archbp Chichele founds All Souls' College, Oxford, for graduate students in theology and law, who are to pray for souls of Henry V and English soldiers fallen in France.
1440 Oct. 11	Henry VI founds Eton College, for 25 poor scholars and 25 paupers.

AD 1441–1445

1441	Sep. 19	French take Pontoise and hold all Île-de-France.
1442	Jan. 19	Eleanor Cobham, Duchess of Gloucester, convicted of attempting to kill Henry VI by sorcery, is divorced and imprisoned for life.
	Jun. 11	Charles VII begins conquest of Gascony.
1443	Apr. 23	D. of York agrees perpetual truce with Burgundy.

	Aug.	John Beaufort, D. of Somerset, lands at Cherbourg with new expeditionary force of *c*.8,000 men.
	Dec.	Somerset raids Anjou and retires to Rouen.
1444	*Mar.* 15	William de la Pole, E. of Suffolk, arrives in France at head of English embassy to negotiate with Charles VII at Tours.
	May 22	Suffolk concludes treaty with René of Anjou, K. of Sicily, for marriage of daughter Margaret of Anjou to Henry VI.
	May 28	Truce of Tours between Henry and Charles VII.
1445	*Apr.* 22	Henry VI marries Margaret of Anjou at Titchfield Abbey, Hants.
	Jul. 14	French embassy arrives in London to negotiate final peace.
	Dec. 22	Henry promises to cede Maine to France.

FINE ARTS AND ARCHITECTURE

1441   Work on Eton College begun under Henry VI's master mason Robert Westerley.

MUSIC AND DRAMA

1444   English composer John Plummer is appointed Master of Chapel Royal, by now well-established choir of men (clerks) and boys chosen to sing services in King's own chapels.

RELIGION AND EDUCATION

1441 *Apr.* 2   Henry VI lays foundation stone of King's College, Cambridge.

AD 1446–1450

1446		Peace negotiations with France continue through Suffolk and Q. Margaret; Henry VI fails to surrender Maine (*v.* 1445).
	Jun. 26	Henry reasserts claim to be overlord of Brittany.
	Dec. 24	Edmund Beaufort, E. (later D.) of Somerset, appointed Lieutenant in France, but remains in England until 1448.
1447	*Feb.* 18	D. of Gloucester, coming to Parliament at Bury St Edmunds, is arrested.
	23	Gloucester dies in captivity.
	Dec. 9	D. of York appointed king's Lieutenant in Ireland, but remains in England for 2 years.
1448	*Mar.* 11	Ty of Lavardin: English finally agree to cede Maine to French.
	16	English surrender Le Mans and rest of Maine. English and French embassies attempt again to negotiate final peace, but negotiations break down over Henry VI's rights in Brittany.
1449	*Mar.* 24	English army seizes Fougères, Brittany.

	Jul.	French and Breton armies invade Normandy.
	Oct. 29	D. of Somerset surrenders Rouen to French.
1450 *Jan.*	28	D. of Suffolk impeached in Parliament and sent to Tower of London.
Apr.	15	Ψ Formigny: French defeat last English army sent to Normandy.
May	2	Suffolk murdered on board ship on way to exile.
	24	Jack Cade, Irish ex-soldier calling himself 'John Mortimer', begins revolt in Kent; men from Middlesex, Surrey and Sussex join.
Jun.	15	Rebels encamped on Blackheath disperse before Henry VI, but defeat section of pursuing royal army; Henry flees north.
Jul.	1	D. of Somerset surrenders Caen to French and leaves Normandy.
	2–5	Rebels occupy Southwark, pillage London and kill Treasurer, Lord Say, and William Crowmer, Sheriff of Kent.
	7	Henry takes refuge in Kenilworth Castle, Warwicks; rebels disperse after pardons are granted them; Cade later killed in Kent.
1450 *Aug.*		Commissioners appointed to inquire into grievances in Kent.
	12	English surrender Cherbourg to French; French hold all Normandy.
Sep.		D. of York returns from Ireland, marches to London with army and attacks 'traitors' on Council, especially D. of Somerset. York included in Council and Somerset lodged briefly in Tower 'for safety'.

FINE ARTS AND ARCHITECTURE

1446	King's College Chapel, Cambridge, begun; chief mason, Reginald Ely.
1450	Priory Church, Great Malvern, begun, with fine stained glass.

LITERATURE AND SCHOLARSHIP

by 1449	Walter Bower, abbot of Inchcolm, continues Fordun's *Scotichronicon* to 1437 (*v.* 1383).

MUSIC AND DRAMA

1450	Earliest date for MS of Wakefield mystery plays; comic Nativity play, *Second Shepherd's Play*, is most famous.

RELIGION AND EDUCATION

1448	Q. Margaret of Anjou founds Queens' College, Cambridge (*v.* 1465). William Waynflete, Bp of Winchester, founds Magdalen College, Oxford, together with Magdalen College School; College statutes (1486) are first to provide for 20 fee-paying students (commoners) as well as free scholars.

AD 1451–1453

1451 *Jan.*	28	Henry VI begins judicial progress through Kent.
Jun.		Henry accepts Parliament's demand that he cancel all previous land grants of

		his reign; subsequent grants are mainly to own family.
	22	Henry makes judicial progress through Surrey, Sussex, Hampshire and Wiltshire.
	30	Bordeaux surrenders to French.
Aug.	21	Bayonne surrenders to French: end of English rule in Gascony.
Sep.		D. of York intervenes to stop faction fighting in W. England. Henry summons all participants for breaking peace; York refuses summons.
1452 Feb.		D. of York appeals for armed support to defend himself and remove D. of Somerset from Council; Henry VI commands all loyal men to resist York.
	22	James II, K. of Scots, murders E. of Douglas at Stirling.
Mar.	1–3	Yorkist and royal armies confront each other at Dartford; York yields and is pardoned.
Jun.	23	Henry begins judicial progress through West, Welsh Marches and Midlands; many Yorkist rebels are condemned.
Sep.	6	Henry begins judicial progress through E. Anglia.
Oct.	22	John Talbot, now E. of Shrewsbury, leads expedition to Gascony and enters Bordeaux; English recover most of Gascony.
1453 Jan.		Henry VI makes his Tudor half-brothers earls: Edmund of Richmond and Jasper of Pembroke.
Mar.		Pro-royal Parliament grants Henry all taxes needed and calls for past rebels to forfeit lands.
Jul.	17	Ψ Castillon, last of 100 Years' War; Talbot is killed and French win decisive victory.
	21	Council meets to settle dispute over possession of Glamorgan between D. of Somerset and Richard Neville, E. of Warwick ('the Kingmaker').
Aug.		Henry suffers first mental breakdown.
	24	Fighting breaks out in north between Neville and Percy families.
Oct.	13	P. Edward born.
	19	Bordeaux surrenders to French; England retains only Calais.
Nov.	23	D. of Somerset sent to Tower.

RELIGION AND EDUCATION

1451		Bp William Turnbull founds Glasgow University.

MUSIC AND DRAMA

1453 Dec.	24	Death of John Dunstable, one of greatest liturgical composers of age, enjoying European reputation; he was a master of isorhythmic motet and votive antiphon.

Events Elsewhere

1453 May	29	Ottoman Turks under Mohammed II take Constantinople.

AD 1454–1455

1454	Mar. 15	Henry VI's son Edward created P. of Wales.
	27	Council appoints D. of York Protector and Defender of Realm.
	Jun.	York suppresses northern revolt of Henry Holland, D. of Exeter, and Percy family.
1455	Jan.	Henry VI recovers senses; York deprived of protectorship.
	Feb. 4	Somerset is released from Tower.
	Mar.	D. of York and E. of Warwick leave London for north to raise army.
	May	Calais garrison mutinies and seizes wool in warehouses of Staple, demanding arrears of pay or licence to sell wool.
	22	1st Ψ St Albans: Yorkists attack royal army and capture Henry VI; D. of Somerset killed. D. of York becomes Constable of England; E. of Warwick is made Captain of Calais, but mutinous garrison refuses him entry.
	Nov. 19	York made Protector for second time (v. 1454); rioting and civil war in Devon.
	Dec.	York pacifies south-west.

LITERATURE AND SCHOLARSHIP

1455   Reginald Pecock, Welsh Bp of Chichester, writes *Repressor of Overmuch Blaming of the Clergy*, anti-Lollard prose work containing many new English words.

RECREATION AND FASHION

by 1456   First written reference to knitting ('one knyt gyrdll') in accounts of chapter of SS Peter and Wilfrid church, Ripon, Yorks.

AD 1456–1460

1456	Feb. 25	D. of York is deprived of protectorship, but remains on Council.
	Apr.	Mutiny of Calais garrison ends; wool merchants guarantee soldiers' pay and E. of Warwick takes up command as Captain of Calais.
	Aug. 17	Q. Margaret moves Henry VI to Kenilworth Castle, strengthening its defences with cannon; court now based at Coventry.
1457	Aug. 28	French force lands in Kent and sacks Sandwich.
1458	Mar. 25	Day known as 'Loveday', when Henry VI forces reconciliation between Yorkists and their enemies; they go hand in hand in procession to St Paul's Cathedral, and Yorkists agree to compensate heirs of those defeated at St Albans (v. 1455).

May		E. of Warwick raises own fleet, defeats Spanish fleet in English Channel and attacks ships of Hanseatic League.
1459	*Sep.* 23	Ψ Blore Heath: Yorkist force defeats royal army. E. of Warwick with force from Calais meets D. of York and allies at Ludlow.
	Oct. 12	Ψ Ludford Bridge: royal army routs Yorkists, Warwick's force deserting to Henry VI. York flees to Ireland; Warwick and York's eldest son Edward, E. of March, escape to Calais.
	Nov. 20	Parliament at Coventry condemns York and allies as traitors.
	Dec.	Irish Parliament at Drogheda supports York as Governor of Ireland.
1460	*Jan.* 15	Force from Calais raids Sandwich and captures royal fleet.
	Jun. 26	EE. of Warwick and March land at Sandwich.
	Jul. 10	Ψ Northampton: Yorkists defeat and capture Henry VI.
	Aug. 3	James II, K. of Scots, accidentally blown up at siege of English-held Roxburgh, is succeeded by son James III.
	Oct. 10	D. of York returns from Ireland to London and claims throne.
	24	Act of Accord, passed in Parliament, makes York heir to throne. Q. Margaret organizes Lancastrian opposition.
	Dec. 30	Ψ Wakefield: Lancastrian army under Henry, D. of Somerset, defeats Yorkists. D. of York is killed.

MUSIC AND DRAMA

1457	*Jun.* 16	Q. Margaret visits Coventry to see Corpus Christi mystery plays.
	Sep. 14	Coventry greets Q. Margaret with pageants of saints and heroes.

RECREATION AND FASHION

1457	Name 'golf' is first applied to game; it is banned in Scotland.
by 1459	London livery companies build (real) tennis courts in London and play each other in matches.
1460	*Hennin*, high pointed headdress for women, often with veil attached, becomes popular in England.

Events Elsewhere

1456	Turks take Athens but are defeated at Belgrade.
1459	Turks conquer Serbia.

AD 1461–1465

1461	*Feb.* 2	Ψ Mortimer's Cross, Herefordshire: Edward of York defeats Welsh royalist army; he executes Owen Tudor and other prisoners.
	17	2nd Ψ St Albans: Q. Margaret's army defeats E. of Warwick, rescues Henry VI, but retires to Dunstable.

		26	Edward and Warwick enter London.
	Mar.	4	Edward is proclaimed K. Edward IV.
		29	Ψ Towton: Edward defeats Lancastrians, killing most of leaders; Henry, Margaret and P. of Wales flee to Scotland.
	Apr.	25	Henry cedes Berwick to Scots.
	Jun.	28	Edward IV is crowned.
	Aug.		Edward makes judicial progress through S. and W. England, Welsh Marches and W. midlands.

1462 *Jun.*   Q. Margaret seeks help in France, offering Calais to Louis XI.

Oct. 25   Margaret invades Northumberland with small French force, but fails to gain support.

Ψ Pilltown, Ireland. Thomas Fitzgerald, later E. of Desmond, defeats Butlers of Ormond, Lancastrian supporters.

1463 *Mar.*   E. of Desmond is made Governor of Ireland.

Aug.   Q. Margaret and P. of Wales sail for Flanders, leaving Henry VI.

Oct. 8   Truce of Hesdin between England, France and Burgundy ends Franco-Lancastrian alliance.

Dec. 9   Truce at York between England and Scotland.

1464 *Apr.* 25   Ψ Hedgeley Moor, Northumberland: Lancastrian army, led by D. of Somerset, is defeated.

May 1   Edward IV secretly marries Elizabeth Woodville.

15   Ψ Hexham: Lancastrian army is heavily defeated; Yorkists gradually gain control of N. England.

Jun. 11   Edward ratifies 15-year truce with Scotland.

Sep. 14   Edward reveals marriage to Royal Council at Reading.

1465 *May*   Elizabeth Woodville is crowned Queen at Westminster.

Jun. 24   Henry VI, captured in Ribblesdale, is brought to London and imprisoned in Tower.

Edward IV reforms currency; more gold coins are minted and angel and rose noble replace noble (*v.* 1344).

LITERATURE AND SCHOLARSHIP

1461–1463   Sir John Fortescue, Chief Justice under Henry VI, writes *De Natura Legis Naturae*, on constitutional monarchy.

RECREATION AND FASHION

1463   Playing-cards are popular; Edward IV prohibits import of foreign cards to protect English manufacturers.

RELIGION AND EDUCATION

1465   Q. Elizabeth (Woodville) refounds Queens' College, Cambridge (*v.* 1448).

1466	James III, K. of Scots, is kidnapped by Robert, Lord Boyd, who thus becomes Governor of Scotland.
1467 *May*	E. of Warwick is sent to France to negotiate with Louis XI.
Jun. 8	Edward IV dismisses Warwick's brother George Neville, Archbp of York, as Chancellor.
1468	James III, K. of Scots, marries Margaret, daughter of K. Christian of Denmark, who pledges Orkneys and Shetlands as security for her dowry (*v.* 1472).
	Edward IV makes alliances with Burgundy and Brittany.
	Rack, imported into England by D. of Exeter, is first used to extract information from prisoner in Tower.
Feb. 14	E. of Desmond is convicted of treason and executed at Drogheda; Irish and Anglo-Irish rise in revolt.
May	Edward's sister Margaret marries Charles 'the Bold', D. of Burgundy.
Jul. 29	Hansa merchants are expelled from London; war breaks out at sea between English and Hanseatic fleets.
1469 *Spring*	'Robin of Redesdale' (?Sir William Conyers, ally of E. of Warwick) raises revolt in Yorkshire, denouncing power of Queen's family.
Jun.	Rebellion spreads to Lancashire.
Jul. 11	E. of Warwick's daughter Isabel marries Edward IV's brother George, D. of Clarence, at Calais, against Edward's wish.
by 20	Warwick and Clarence land in Kent; Warwick joins northern rebels.
26	Ψ Edgecote: rebel army defeats Yorkist army.
29	Edward's army deserts him at Olney; he is arrested and imprisoned.
Aug. 12	Q. Elizabeth's father and brother, E. Rivers and Sir John Woodville, are captured and executed.
Sep.	Riots and revolts break out throughout England. Edward, released, returns to London and seeks agreement with Clarence and Warwick.
1470 *Mar.*	Rebels in Lincolnshire claim support of D. of Clarence and E. of Warwick.
12	Ψ Empingham, Lincs: Edward IV defeats rebels.
May 1	Warwick and Clarence escape from England to France.
Jul. 22	Warwick is reconciled to Q. Margaret of Anjou, betrothes daughter Anne to P. of Wales and promises to restore Henry VI.
Aug.–Sep.	Edward suppresses rebellion in N. England.
Sep. 13	Warwick's army lands in Devon. Edward, deserted by supporters at Doncaster, flees to Burgundy.
Oct. 13	Warwick restores Henry VI to throne.
	E. of Kildare made Governor of Ireland.

1468   Sir John Fortescue writes *De Laudibus Legum Angliae* (In Praise of the Laws of England).

by 1470   *Historiae Croylandensis Continuatio* (Continuation of the Croyland Abbey Chronicle) is written to Jan. 1470, possibly by former prior.

MUSIC AND DRAMA

1469   Edward IV grants charter to own minstrels, putting them at head of gild which all other minstrels in England must join.

AD 1471–1475

1471	*Mar.* 14	Edward IV lands at Ravenspur, Yorks, with small force.
	Apr. 3	D. of Clarence deserts E. of Warwick for Edward.
	11	London submits to Edward.
	14	Ψ Barnet: on foggy morning, Edward defeats Warwick, who is killed. Q. Margaret of Anjou and son Edward land at Weymouth.
	May 4	Ψ Tewkesbury: Edward defeats Lancastrians; P. Edward and many other Lancastrians are killed fleeing battle.
	12	Kentish and Essex rebels attack London, but disperse before arrival of Edward (21 May).
	21/22	Henry VI is murdered in Tower. Margaret is imprisoned in Tower.
	Jul. 3	Council recognizes king's son Edward as P. of Wales.
		Edward IV makes youngest brother Richard, D. of Gloucester, Constable and Admiral of England, with authority over N. England.
	Sep.	Henry, E. of Richmond, now sole Lancastrian claimant to throne, escapes from Pembroke to Brittany.
1472		Scotland annexes Orkney and Shetland islands (*v.* 1468).
	Apr.	D. of Gloucester marries Anne, widow of P. Edward of Lancaster.
1473	*May* 28	Lancastrian E. of Oxford attacks Essex coast.
	Sep. 30	Oxford seizes St Michael's Mount, Cornwall.
		Edward IV raises money for French war by new method of taking 'gifts' (benevolences), mainly from merchant class.
1474	*Feb.*	Oxford surrenders St Michael's Mount, is pardoned but imprisoned.
	Jul.	Ty of London: Edward IV and D. Charles of Burgundy agree to attack and divide France; Edward is to be crowned K. of France.
	Sep.	Peace of Utrecht ends conflict with Hanseatic League; Hansa merchants regain privileges in England, including freehold of Steelyard, London; Englishmen may trade in Hanseatic territories.
	Nov. 3	Ty with Scots includes betrothal of Edward's daughter Cicely to James III's son James.

1475	Jul.	4	Edward IV lands at Calais to invade France; D. of Burgundy fails to join him with army.
	Aug.	29	Ty of Picquigny: 7-year truce with Louis XI; Edward to receive £18,750 to leave France and £12,500 a year thereafter; French to pay ransom of £12,500 for Margaret of Anjou.

FINE ARTS AND ARCHITECTURE

1474	Rebuilding of St George's Chapel, Windsor, with Edward IV's tomb, is begun.
1475	New hall of Eltham Palace is begun.

LITERATURE AND SCHOLARSHIP

by 1471	Sir Thomas Malory writes *Morte d'Arthur*.
1475	William Worcester rewrites his *Book of Noblesse* urging war on France, addressing Edward IV instead of Henry VI.
1474	William Caxton prints own English translation of *Recuyell of Historyes of Troye* in Bruges.

AD 1476–1480

1476	Dec.		Edward IV forbids D. of Clarence to marry Mary of Burgundy. Council of P. of Wales is given judicial powers.
1477	Jun.		Clarence, implicated in E. Anglian rising, is imprisoned in Tower.
1478	Feb.	7	Clarence is condemned in Parliament for high treason.
		14	Clarence is murdered in Tower. Garrett Fitzgerald, 'Great Earl' of Kildare, is confirmed as Governor of Ireland in succession to his father.
1479			James III, K. of Scots, arrests his brother Alexander, D. of Albany, who escapes to France.
1480			Scots burn Bamburgh; D. of Gloucester leads army to raid Scotland.
	Aug.	1	Edward IV confirms treaty of perpetual friendship with Mary of Burgundy and her husband, Archduke Maximilian.

FINE ARTS AND ARCHITECTURE

1478	William Orchard, mason and owner of Headington stone-quarry, Oxford, completes chapel and cloister of Magdalen College.
1480	Orchard begins vault of Oxford Divinity Schools (completed 1483) and Duke Humphrey's Library on floor above (completed 1488).

AD 1481–1485

	Sep. 8	Richard's son Edward is invested as P. of Wales at York.
	Oct.	D. of Buckingham rebels and sends to Brittany for Henry Tudor, who fails in attempted landings at Poole, Dorset, and at Plymouth.
	Nov. 2	D. of Buckingham is executed at Salisbury.
1484	Apr. 9	P. Edward of Wales dies at Middleham, Yorks.
		Richard III establishes Council of North with judicial powers, based on York; 1st president is Richard's nephew, now his heir, John de la Pole, E. of Lincoln.
	Sep.	3-year truce made between Richard and James III, K. of Scots.
		Richard grants charter to College of Arms of royal heralds.
1485	Mar. 16	Q. Anne dies.
	Aug. 7	Henry Tudor lands at Milford Haven and marches unopposed through Wales to Midlands.
	22	Ψ Bosworth: Richard III is defeated and killed. Henry Tudor is proclaimed king. D. of Clarence's son, Edward, E. of Warwick, is arrested and sent to Tower.
	Oct. 30	Henry Tudor is crowned Henry VII at Westminster.

LITERATURE AND SCHOLARSHIP

1481	Caxton translates and prints *Reynard the Fox*, collection of traditional fables.
1482	Caxton prints Trevisa's translation of *Polychronicon* (v. 1387), adding punctuation and continuation to 1460.
1483	Caxton prints English translation of *Golden Legend*, collection of religious works, his most frequently reprinted book.
1485	Caxton prints version of Malory's *Morte d'Arthur*.

VOYAGES AND EXPLORATION

1481	Bristol seamen explore Atlantic and discover 'isle of Brasile' (?Newfoundland).

AD 1486–1490

1486	Jan. 18	Henry VII marries Elizabeth, daughter of Edward IV.
	Mar. 6	Henry appoints Bp Morton of Ely, later Archbp of Canterbury, as Chancellor.
	Apr.	Lord Lovell leads revolt in Yorkshire; after failure he escapes to Flanders.
1487	May 24	Lambert Simnel, claiming to be E. of Warwick, is crowned in Dublin as Edward VI of England.
	Jun. 4	Simnel and Irish force, supported by Lovell and E. of Lincoln with army of 2,000 German mercenaries, land at Furness, Lancs.

	16	Ψ Stoke, nr Newark: Simnel is defeated, captured and sent to royal kitchens; Lincoln is killed; Lovell escapes, possibly to die later in hiding at Minster Lovell, Oxon.
		New tribunal to deal with offences against public order is set up by law mistakenly called 'Star Chamber Act'.
1488 *Jun.*	*11*	James III, K. of Scots, is murdered after battle near Stirling, succeeded by son James IV.
Nov.	*25*	Q. Elizabeth is crowned.
1489 *Feb.*	*14*	Ty of Redon: Henry VII to aid Brittany against France.
Mar.	*27*	Ty of Medina del Campo with Spain: Henry's son Arthur to marry P. Catherine of Aragon.
Apr.		Henry sends force of 6,000 to support Brittany and Archduke Maximilian against French.
	28	Murder of E. of Northumberland by Yorkshire mob objecting to war tax starts revolt in north, quickly suppressed.
Jun.	*13*	Ψ Dixmude: Maximilian and English force defeat French.
Nov.	*29*	P. Arthur is made P. of Wales.
		Henry VII reforms coinage; first gold pound coin (sovereign) is minted, worth 20s or 240d.

FINE ARTS AND ARCHITECTURE

1490	Tower of Magdalen College, Oxford (by Orchard) and Bell Harry tower of Canterbury Cathedral (by John Wastell) are begun.

LITERATURE AND SCHOLARSHIP

after *1486*	2nd Continuation of Croyland Chronicle (Oct. 1459–1486) is written, possibly by John Russell, Bp of Lincoln and Chancellor under Edward IV and Richard III (*v.* 1470).
	John Rous writes history of Earls of Warwick (2 versions, 2nd revised after 1485) and *Historia Regum Angliae* (History of the Kings of England, to 1486).
1490	Robert Henryson, Scottish poet from Dunfermline, writes *Testament of Cresseid*, sequel to Chaucer's poem.

RECREATION AND FASHION

1486	Word 'football' is first used for game where ball is kicked.
1488	Law fixes price of knitted woollen hats (1s 8d) and caps (2s).

Events Elsewhere

1488	Portuguese explorer Bartholomew Diaz rounds Cape of Good Hope.

1491	*Jun.* 28	Future Henry VIII born at Greenwich; created D. of York, Oct. 1494.
	Jul.	Benevolence for war against France creates legend of Chancellor Morton's 'fork': tax commissioners told to assume that people who spent little have savings and those who spent much must be wealthy.
	Nov.	Perkin Warbeck, claiming to be Edward IV's son Richard (*v.* 1483), arrives in Cork and receives some Irish support.
	Dec. 21	Truce of Coldstream: 5-year peace with Scotland.
1492	*Oct.*	Henry VII invades France because of Charles VIII's support of Warbeck in Brittany; Boulogne besieged.
	Nov. 3	Peace Ty of Etaples: Charles VIII to expel Warbeck and pay Henry VII £159,000 compensation for incorporating Brittany in France.
1493	*Jun.*	James IV, K. of Scots, secures submission of rebellious clans in Western Isles.
	Jul.	Henry VII denounces Margaret of Burgundy's support for Warbeck.
	Sep. 18	Sanctions imposed on Burgundy hit cloth trade with Netherlands.
1494	*May*	Emperor Maximilian I recognizes Warbeck as K. of England.
	Oct. 13	Edward Poynings sent to Ireland as Deputy to tighten links with England.
	Dec. 1	Irish Parliament at Drogheda passes 'Poyning's Law': Irish legislation only valid if confirmed by English Privy Council.
1495	*Feb.* 16	Lord Chamberlain Sir William Stanley executed for treasonable links with Warbeck.
	Feb. 27	Poynings has E. of Kildare (*v.* 1478) attainted of treason and imprisoned in Tower of London.
	Jul. 3	Abortive attempt by Warbeck to land at Deal.
	23	Warbeck in Ireland; his supporters besiege Waterford, but town relieved by Poynings on 3 Aug.
	Oct.	Statute of Treason (so-called De Facto Act): loyalty to the reigning king could not be treated as treason by a successor, thus retrospectively justifying allegiance to Richard III.
		Beggars Act: vagabonds to be punished and returned to their parishes.
	Nov. 27	James IV, K. of Scots, receives Warbeck at Stirling.

RELIGION AND EDUCATION

1493	William Grocyn, having studied in renaissance Italy, gives first public lectures in Greek in Britain at Oxford.
1495	University of Aberdeen established, with foundation of King's College, under auspices of Bp William Elphinstone.

Events Elsewhere

1491	*Dec.* 6	Charles VIII of France marries Duchess Anne of Brittany and incorporates

		duchy in France.
1492	*Oct.*	Christopher Columbus discovers 'the New World': Bahamas, Cuba, Haiti.
1494		Charles VIII of France invades Italy and takes Rome.

AD 1496–1500

1496	*Feb.*	24	*Intercursus Magnus* Ty with Burgundy: favourable terms for English to resume trade in Netherlands through Antwerp.
	Mar.	5	Henry VII gives patronage to John Cabot for voyages of discovery.
	Jul.	18	England joins anti-French Holy League.
	Aug.	6	E. of Kildare reappointed Deputy of Ireland.
	Sep.		Scots invade Northumberland in support of Warbeck.
1497	*Jan.*		Parliament grants high taxes to raise troops against Scots.
	May		Cornish rebellion against taxation; rebels win support in Somerset from Lord Audley.
	Jun.	17	Ψ Blackheath: Audley and Cornish rebels defeated by King's troops.
	Aug.	10	Scots besiege Norham Castle.
	Sep.	7	Warbeck lands in Cornwall, having come from Scotland by way of Ireland.
		10	Warbeck proclaimed as Richard IV in Bodmin.
		30	Truce of Ayton: 7-year peace with Scotland.
	Oct.	5	Warbeck brought as prisoner to Henry VII at Taunton.
	Dec.	29	Sheen Palace, Richmond, destroyed by fire while king in residence.
1498	*May*		Monopoly of trade with Netherlands given to the Merchant Adventurers, based on Antwerp.
1499	*Nov.*	21	Perkin Warbeck executed after alleged conspiracy with Edward, E. of Warwick, in Tower of London.
		23	Execution of E. of Warwick.
1500	*Jun.*	9	Henry VII confers with Archduke Philip of Burgundy outside Calais to improve relations with Netherlands.

RELIGION AND EDUCATION

1496	Lectures on the Pauline epistles by John Colet at Oxford bring Christian humanism to England.
	Bp John Alcock founds Jesus College, Cambridge.
	Scottish Parliament passes Schools Act: barons and substantial freeholders to send eldest sons to school at age of 8 to be grounded in Latin and law.
1499	First visit of Desiderius Erasmus to England.

VOYAGES AND EXPLORATION

1497	*May* 2	John Cabot, having been forced back to England in 1496, sails from Bristol across Atlantic to Cape Breton Island (Jun.); back in Bristol, 6 Aug.

| 1498 *May* | Cabot sails for the Americas again with 5 ships; nothing known of their fate. |

Events Elsewhere

| 1495–1498 | Leonardo da Vinci paints *The Last Supper* on conventual refectory wall in Milan. |

AD 1501–1505

1501 *Oct.* 2	Catherine of Aragon arrives at Plymouth from Spain.
Nov. 14	Marriage of Arthur, P. of Wales, and Catherine at St Paul's Cathedral.
1502 *Jan.*	Prince and Princess of Wales receive homage of Welsh at Ludlow Castle.
Apr. 2	P. Arthur dies at Ludlow.
May 6	Sir William Tyrell beheaded, having allegedly confessed to murder of 'Princes in the Tower'.
1503 *Feb.* 11	Death of the Queen, Elizabeth of York, in childbirth.
Jun. 24	Formal betrothal of widowed Catherine of Aragon to 12-year-old P. Henry.
Aug. 8	Henry VII's eldest daughter, P. Margaret, marries James IV, K. of Scots.
1504	Shilling coin worth 12 pence minted: first English coin to carry recognizable portrait of a king.
Feb.	Corporations Act: provides for state supervision of gild ordinances.
15	P. Henry invested as P. of Wales, Westminster.
Mar.	Statute of Liveries: bans private liveried retainers.
	Parliament compromises on £30,000 grant to King in lieu of traditional feudal aids due on knighting of eldest son and marriage of eldest daughter.
Aug. 14	Ψ Knockdoe, Ireland: E. of Kildare defeats hostile confederacy in Galway.
1505 *Jun.* 28	Non-arrival from Spain of second instalment of dowry for Catherine postpones planned nuptials of P. Henry.

FINE ARTS AND ARCHITECTURE

1501	Work starts on palace of Holyrood House, Edinburgh.
Mar.	Henry VII holds court at new Richmond Palace.
1503 *Jan.* 24	Work begins on Henry VII's Chapel, Westminster Abbey; completed 1519.

LITERATURE AND SCHOLARSHIP

| 1501 | William Dunbar, Scottish diplomat-poet, receives gift of 10 marks from Henry VII for poem of which each stanza ends 'London thou art the floure of Cities all'. |
| 1503 | Dunbar writes *The Thristill and the Rois*, poem to celebrate marriage of James IV, K. of Scots, and Margaret Tudor. |

1504	MUSIC AND DRAMA Robert Fayrfax composes *Missa, O quam glorifica.*

1503 *Nov. 19*	RELIGION AND EDUCATION William Wareham becomes Archbp of Canterbury.

Events Elsewhere

1501	First transhipment of African slaves, to Hispaniola (Haiti).
1504	Ty of Lyons: French accept cession of Naples to Aragon (until 1713).

AD 1506–1510

1506 *Jan. 16*	Emperor Maximilian's son, Philip of Burgundy, and his wife Joanna, Q. of Castile, shipwrecked near Weymouth in 'Great Storm' of 15-26 Jan.; in England until 23 Apr.
Feb. 9 and Mar. 20	Treaties of Windsor: associate England with Burgundy and the Habsburgs against France, including an (abortive) marriage contract between Henry VII and Emperor Maximilian's widowed daughter, Margaret, prospective Governor of the Netherlands.
Apr. 24	Chief Yorkist claimant, Edmund de la Pole, E. of Suffolk, imprisoned in Tower of London.
30	*Intercursus Malus*: trade treaty enabling English to sell cloth freely in the Netherlands but not in Flanders.
1507 *Dec. 21*	Marriage diplomacy: Henry VII's youngest daughter Mary formally betrothed to Habsburg Archduke Charles, future Emperor Charles V.
1508 *Dec.*	Reconciliation of French and Habsburg rulers in League of Cambrai frustrates Henry's marriage diplomacy.
1509 *Apr. 21*	Death of Henry VII at Richmond Palace; P. of Wales accedes as Henry VIII.
25	Henry VIII offers reparations to those who had suffered from the fiscal extortion of his father's ministers, of whom Richard Empson and Edmund Dudley served as scapegoats.
Jun. 11	Henry VIII marries Catherine of Aragon at Greenwich.
24	Coronation of Henry VIII at Westminster; followed by banquet in Westminster Hall 'greater than any Caesar had known'.
Nov.	Thomas Wolsey, a court chaplain since 1507, becomes royal almoner and virtual royal secretary.
1510 *Jan. 21*	First Parliament of Henry VIII (to 21 Feb.) grants him generous subsidies, including tonnage, poundage and wool duties for life.
Aug. 17	Execution of Empson and Dudley for 'constructive treason'.

LITERATURE AND SCHOLARSHIP

1506   Henry VII gives patronage to Polydore Vergil to write a history of England.

1509   Erasmus publishes *Moriae Encomium* (The Praise of Folly), a satire critical of contemporary society, especially the Church hierarchy; 7 printed editions in a few months.

RECREATION AND FASHION

1506   Philip of Burgundy, visiting Windsor, plays real tennis with a racket.

by 1509   Men wear doublets as main garment, with low, square neck to show white undershirt; heads are covered by velvet bonnet. Chief female headdress is the gable hood.

RELIGION AND EDUCATION

1505   Lady Margaret Beaufort founds Christ's College, Cambridge.

1509   Dean John Colet founds St Paul's School, London, with 153 free scholars, more than at any other school in England.

Foundation of St John's College, Cambridge, and Brasenose College, Oxford.

Erasmus at Queens' College, Cambridge, lectures on theology and Greek.

SCIENCE AND INVENTION

1506   James IV, K. of Scots, grants charter to newly founded College of Surgeons, Edinburgh.

1507   Walter Chepman and Andrew Myllar set up first Scottish printing press in Edinburgh.

AD 1511–1515

1511	*Jan.*	*1*	Son born to Henry VIII and Catherine; lives only 52 days.
	Nov.		Alliances with papacy, Venice and Aragon for war against France.
1512	*Feb.*		Richard Strode MP secures Act of Parliament condemning his imprisonment by a stannary court for introducing a bill regulating privileges of tin-miners.
	Mar.		Parliament approves supplementary poll tax for war against France, but it fails to yield a third of the expected revenue.
		16	Franco-Scottish Ty of Edinburgh: renews the 'Auld Alliance'.
	Apr.		Anglo-French war begins with raids on Brittany.
1513	*Jun.*	*4*	Edmund de la Pole, E. of Suffolk, executed for alleged treason.
		30	Henry VIII takes personal command of army in France.
	Aug.	*16*	Ψ 'of the Spurs': Emperor Maximilian and Henry defeat the French at Guinegate.
		22	James IV invades Northumbria, capturing Norham (29 Aug.).
	Sep.	*9*	Ψ Flodden: English army, led by Thomas Howard, E. of Surrey, defeats Scots; James IV is killed and succeeded by James V.

	24	Henry VIII's army captures Tournai.

1514	Jun.		*Henry Grace à Dieu* (the 'Great Harry') launched at Erith; at over 1,000 tons largest warship in the world until accidentally destroyed by fire in 1553.
	Aug.	6	Peace between England and France.
	Sep.		Wolsey becomes Archbp of York.
	Oct.		P. Mary Tudor marries K. Louis XII of France, but is widowed 11 weeks later; she secretly marries Charles Brandon, D. of Suffolk, soon afterwards.
	Dec.	4	Richard Hunne, wealthy merchant tailor, dies mysteriously when in custody of Bp of London; death provokes widespread anti-clericalism.

1515	Jul.		Scottish Parliament proclaims D. of Albany as Regent of the realm, forcing Queen-Mother Margaret Tudor into exile.
	Sep.	10	Wolsey created a cardinal.
	Dec.	24	Wolsey made Lord Chancellor.

FINE ARTS AND ARCHITECTURE

1514 Building work starts for Wolsey on: York House (future Whitehall Palace), finished 1515; and Hampton Court, finished 1520.

LITERATURE AND SCHOLARSHIP

1514 (?1513) Thomas More writes his *History of King Richard the Thirde*, anonymously.

MUSIC AND DRAMA

1513 William Cornysh accompanies Henry VIII to France with choristers of Chapel Royal.

Sep. Henry VIII sings and plays flute, lute and cornet to entertain Archduchess Margaret at Lisle Castle.

VOYAGES AND EXPLORATION

1514 Royal charter granted to Trinity Fraternity, Deptford ('Trinity House') for the 'relief, increase and augmentation' of English shipping.

Events Elsewhere

1513 The Spaniard, Vasco de Balboa, explores Isthmus of Panama and (on 26 Sep.) becomes first European to sight the Pacific.

AD 1516–1520

1516	Feb.	8	Birth of P. Mary, future Q. Mary I.
1517	May	1	Evil May Day riots in London: artisans attack foreign workers and their property.
		27	Wolsey sends out 17 commissioners to investigate enclosures in 35 counties.

1518	Oct.		Peace of London: Wolsey negotiates settlement between England, France, Spain, the papacy and Emperor Maximilian.
1519	May		After Maximilian's death in Jan., Henry VIII makes compromise bid for election as Holy Roman Emperor, but Charles (V) is elected in June.
1520	May	26–31	Henry VIII and Charles V meet at Dover and Canterbury.
	Jun.	7–24	Wolsey stage-manages meetings between Henry and Francis I of France at Balinghen, 8 miles south of Calais, the 'Field of Cloth of Gold'; diplomacy largely abortive.
	Jul.	11–14	Henry and Charles V confer in Calais and conclude treaty of friendship, benefiting English commerce.

FINE ARTS AND ARCHITECTURE

1516		Jean Perreal's portrait of Henry VIII.
1519		Completion of Henry VII's Chapel, Westminster Abbey (begun 1503): Robert Vertue is chief mason; Pietro Torrigiano responsible for the sculptured tomb of Henry VII, finished in 1518.
	May 15–18	Protracted Garter ceremonies at Windsor mark completion of St George's Chapel (begun 1473).

LITERATURE AND SCHOLARSHIP

1516	First edition (in Latin) of Thomas More's *Utopia*, printed and published in Louvain.

MUSIC AND DRAMA

1516		Richard Sampson introduces Renaissance-style choral music to Chapel Royal.
1517	Jul.	Henry VIII listens to recital of Renaissance music by Dionisio Memo, Venetian organist, for 4 hours.

RECREATION AND FASHION

1520	Jun.	Much jousting and tilting at Field of Cloth of Gold.

RELIGION AND EDUCATION

1517		Richard Fox of Winchester founds Corpus Christi College, Oxford.
1518	May	Wolsey created papal legate a latere, giving him supreme authority over Church in England.

SCIENCE AND INVENTION

1518	Royal College of Physicians founded, London; Thomas Linacre as 1st president.

Events Elsewhere

1516	Oct. 23	At Wittenberg Martin Luther's 95 Theses condemning papal indulgences mark start of Reformation.

AD 1521–1525

1521	*May 17*	Execution of Edward Stafford, D. of Buckingham, for treason.
	Aug.	Wolsey presides over abortive Calais Conference seeking to arbitrate between Charles V and Francis I.
1522	*Jan.*	Wolsey fails to be elected Pope, the conclave choosing a Spaniard, Adrian VI.
	May	Henry VIII declares war on France and Scotland.
	22	Charles V a guest of Henry at Greenwich and Windsor (to 6 Jul.); concludes anti-French alliance.
	Jul.–Oct.	Charles Brandon, D. of Suffolk, leads raids on Picardy and Normandy.
1523	*Apr.*	Parliament resists Wolsey's appeal for higher taxation to pay for war; Thomas More elected speaker.
	Apr.–Sep.	Thomas Howard, D. of Norfolk from 1524, attacks Scottish border towns, destroying Kelso and Jedburgh.
	Sep.–Oct.	D. of Suffolk leads inconclusive expedition in Picardy.
	Nov.	On death of Adrian VI, Wolsey again disappointed in papal election; conclave chooses Cardinal de Medici as Clement VII.
1524	*Jul.* 26	James V becomes K. of Scotland in his own right, backed by his mother and uncle (Henry VIII) to check pro-French faction led by Bp David Beaton.
	Sep.	Henry unable to raise funds for attack on France.
1525	*Jun.*	Wolsey abandons levying of the 'Amicable Loan', a poll tax imposed without parliamentary consent.
		Wolsey gives Henry VIII the lease of Hampton Court.
	Aug. 30	Peace signed with France: Henry accepts annual pension for not asserting claims to French throne.

LITERATURE AND SCHOLARSHIP

1523	John Skelton writes poem, *The Garlande of Laurell*, dedicated to Wolsey.

RELIGION AND EDUCATION

1521	*Oct. 11*	Pope Leo X confers title 'Defender of the Faith' on Henry VIII for his 'Assertion of the Seven Sacraments', a Latin study refuting Lutheranism.
1525		Wolsey founds school at Ipswich and Cardinal College (later Christ Church), Oxford, using funds from 21 small monastic foundations suppressed in 1518.

SCIENCE AND INVENTION

1523	Anthony Fitzherbert's *Book of Husbandry* is first practical English manual of agricultural technique.
1525	First known cultivation of hops in Kent, brought from Artois (but *v.* 1400).

1524 *Jun.*   Peasants' Revolt in S. Germany, chiefly against enclosures and feudal
              obligations.
1525 *Feb.* 25   Habsburg defeat of French at Pavia gives Emperor Charles V control over
              Italy.

AD 1526–1530

1526   Wolsey begins debasement of coinage: upward revaluation of gold
              sovereigns, reduction in weight of silver coins.
     Apr.   Henry VIII's diplomatic revolution: supports France against Emperor Charles V.

1527 *Apr.* 30   Ty of Westminster: consolidates Anglo-French alliance.
     May 17–31   At Greenwich Archbp Warham holds first secret inquiry into validity of
              Henry VIII's marriage with his brother's widow.
     Aug. 18   Wolsey and Francis I ratify alliance treaty at Amiens.

1528 *Feb.*   Wolsey's secretary, Stephen Gardiner, and King's almoner, Edward Fox, go
              to Rome to seek papal consent to Henry VIII's divorce.
     Jul.   'Sweating sickness' (plague) severe in London.
     Oct.   Cardinal Campeggio arrives in England to settle validity of Henry's marriage.

1529 *May–Jul.*   Campeggio and Wolsey preside over legatine court at Blackfriars to test
              validity of Henry VIII's marriage.
     Jul. 13   Pope orders divorce question to be settled at Rome.
     Oct. 18   Wolsey falls from power; presents York Place (Whitehall Palace) to Henry as
              placatory gesture.
        26   Sir Thomas More is first layman to be appointed Lord Chancellor.
     Nov. 4   First session (to 17 Dec.) of Reformation Parliament (ends 1536): Henry
              rejects petition for action against Wolsey, but allows attacks on clerical
              abuses.

1530 *Jan.* 26   Thomas Boleyn, E. of Wiltshire, appointed Keeper of the Privy Seal.
     Feb. 6   Charles Brandon, D. of Suffolk, becomes Lord President of the Council (to
              1545).
     Nov. 4   Wolsey arrested at York; dies at Leicester while under escort to London, 29
              Nov.
     Dec.   Clergy accused of breaking Statute of *Praemunire* (*v.* 1353) in recognizing
              Wolsey as legate.

              FINE ARTS AND ARCHITECTURE
1526   Hans Holbein the Younger visits England and (1527) paints portraits of
              More's family.

1526–1530 John Taverner becomes first organist at Wolsey's Cardinal College, Oxford; composes three masses, three magnificats and several antiphons.
1530 Wynkyn de Worde's *Song Book* published.

RECREATION AND FASHION
1530 Organized horse-racing at York.

RELIGION AND EDUCATION
1526 German-printed English translation of the Bible by William Tyndale reaches London; in Scotland by 1530.
1527 *Dec.* Thomas Bilney, a Cambridge priest, having preached sermons in London against idolatry, is tried before Cuthbert Tunstal, Bp of London, who encourages him to recant.
1529 Bp John Fisher of Rochester upholds traditional doctrines in his *De Veritate Corporis et Sanguinis Christi in Eucharistia*.
1530 *May* Alleged heretical books, including Tyndale's Bible, burnt in London.

Events Elsewhere

1526 *May* Emperor Barbar establishes Mogul dynasty in Delhi.
  Aug. 29 Turks decisively defeat Hungarians at Mohacs.
1527 *May* 6 Mutinous troops in Emperor Charles V's army sack Rome.

AD 1531–1535

1531 *Feb.* Convocation recognizes Henry VIII as 'Supreme Head' of English Church 'as far as Law of Christ allows'; clergy pay £100,000 to purge breach of *praemunire*.
  Mar. Statute against Vagabonds: impotent beggars licensed by JPs; sturdy beggars pilloried or whipped.
  Jul. 11 Henry orders Q. Catherine to leave Windsor.
  Aug. 19 Bilney burnt at the stake in Norwich for heresy.
1532 *Mar.* 18 'Supplication against the Ordinaries': address from the Commons to Henry VIII against authority of Church courts.
  Apr. 15 Formal Submission of the Clergy: no ecclesiastical laws without royal approval.
  May 13 James V, K. of Scots, receives papal consent to use Church funds to endow College of Justice, a permanent judicature with 15 nominated judges.
  16 More resigns office; succeeded by Sir Thomas Audley, 20 May.
  Aug. 23 Death of William Warham, Archbp of Canterbury.
  Sep. 1 Anne Boleyn created Marquis of Pembroke.
  Oct. Henry and Anne Boleyn received by Francis I at Boulogne.

1533	Jan.	25	Henry VIII secretly marries Anne Boleyn.
	Feb.	6	Act in Restraint of Appeals: claims legal independence of 'realm of England' as 'an empire'.
	Mar.	28	John Fisher of Rochester only bishop in Convocation to insist on legality of Henry's marriage to Catherine.
		30	Thomas Cranmer becomes Archbp of Canterbury.
	Apr.	12	Thomas Cromwell made Secretary of State.
	May	23	Cranmer pronounces Henry's marriage to Catherine void.
	Jun.	1	Coronation of Anne Boleyn.
	Jul.	11	Henry excommunicated by Pope Clement VII.
	Sep.	7	Birth of P. Elizabeth, future Q. Elizabeth I.
1534	Mar.	30	Succession Act: oath required from peers, MPs and clergy; slandering of Boleyn marriage is treason.
	Apr.	13	More refuses to take succession oath.
		20	Elizabeth Barton ('Nun of Kent') executed at Tyburn for prophesying against the King.
	Jun.	11	Thomas Fitzgerald, 10th E. of Kildare, leads Irish rebellion (to spring 1535).
	Nov.		Act of Supremacy: confirms Henry VIII as Supreme Head of Church.
			Acts of Attainder against More and Bp John Fisher for misprision.
1535	Jan.	21	Thomas Cromwell appointed Vicar-General to hold visitation of English and Welsh religious houses.
	Jun.	22	Bp John Fisher beheaded on Tower Hill.
	Jul.	6	Thomas More beheaded on Tower Hill.

FINE ARTS AND ARCHITECTURE

1531	Works begins on Great Hall of Hampton Court (to 1536).
1532	Holbein settles in England (portrait of Henry VIII, 1535).
	Building of St James's Palace begins (completed 1540).

LITERATURE AND SCHOLARSHIP

1531	Sir Thomas Eliot's Boke of the Governour published.

RECREATION AND FASHION

1532 Oct.	Henry VIII loses £42 betting on his own skill at real tennis.

RELIGION AND EDUCATION

1535	T. Cromwell forbids study of canon law at English universities.
Jan.–Sep.	Official returns made of value of all Church property: Valor Ecclesiasticus.

Events Elsewhere

1532–1534	Francisco Pizzaro undertakes conquest of Peru.
1533	Accession of Ivan IV ('the Terrible'); Tsar until 1584.

1536	*Jan.*	7	Catherine of Aragon dies at Kimbolton.
	Apr.		Wales legally incorporated in England.
		14	Act to dissolve smaller monasteries passed.
	May	2	Q. Anne, accused of treasonable adultery, imprisoned.
		17	Cranmer declares Henry VIII's marriage to Anne null and void.
		19	Anne Boleyn beheaded with a sword on Tower Green.
		30	Henry marries Jane Seymour.
	Jun.		Act of Succession: excludes PP Mary and Elizabeth.
	Oct.	1	Riot at Louth, Lincs, against social changes imposed by dissolution of monasteries.
		13	Name 'Pilgrimage of Grace' assumed by York rioters.
	Dec.		Exiled Reginald Pole, great-nephew of Edward IV, made a cardinal.
		6	Thomas Howard, D. of Norfolk, at Doncaster, promises pardon to Yorkshire rebels, who disperse.
1537	*Jan.*	2	Yorkshire rebel leader, Robert Aske, received by Henry VIII and Cromwell.
	Feb.	3	Kildare and 5 of his uncles executed at Tyburn for treason in Ireland.
	Jul.		Over 200 rebels executed, including Aske.
	Oct.	12	Birth of P. Edward, future K. Edward VI.
		15	New 'Council of the North' meets, in York.
		24	Death of Q. Jane Seymour.
1538	*Jan.*		Visitation of greater monasteries begins.
	Jun.		James V, K. of Scots, marries Mary of Guise.
	Dec.	20	Archbp Beaton of St Andrews made a cardinal; soon afterwards, becomes James V's chief counsellor.
1539	*Mar.–May*		Invasion scare following reports of collaboration between Spain, France and Scotland.
	Apr.		Dissolution of the greater monasteries begins.
	May		Act imposing neo-Catholic Six Articles of Religion passed.
	Jul.	1	Protestant Bps of Exeter and Worcester (Nicholas Shaxton and Hugh Latimer) resign sees.
	Oct.	4	Cromwell negotiates King's marriage with Anne of Cleves, linking England with German Lutheran princes.
	Nov.		Abbots of Reading, Colchester and Glastonbury executed.
1540	*Jan.*	6	Henry VIII marries Anne of Cleves; annulled on 9 Jul.
	Mar.		Waltham Abbey, last of the monasteries, dissolved.
	Apr.	17	Cromwell made E. of Essex.
	Jun.	18	Cromwell arrested, charged with treason in supporting Lutheran alliance; D. of Norfolk becomes chief minister.
	Jul.	28	Execution of Cromwell; Henry marries Catherine Howard, niece of D. of Norfolk.

1540 *Jan.* 6   *Pleasant Satyr of the Three Estates*, by David Lyndsay, performed before Scottish court, Linlithgow.

RECREATION AND FASHION

1539   James V, K. of Scots, builds real tennis court at Falkland Palace.

1540 *Feb.* 9   Horse racecourse opened on the Roodee at Chester, for an annual meeting.

RELIGION AND EDUCATION

1536 *Jul.*   Ten Articles: against 'usurped power and jurisdiction' of papacy; make some Lutheran concessions on doctrine.

1537   Cranmer's 'Bishops' Book' (*Institute of a Christian Man*) issued to help clergy interpret Ten Articles.

1539   English 'Great Bible', based on translations by Tyndale and Miles Coverdale, circulated to parishes.

1539   Six Articles: anti-papal, but reaffirm Catholic doctrines.

1540   Henry VIII endows Regius professorships at Cambridge.

AD 1541–1545

1541 *May* 27   Countess Margaret of Salisbury beheaded for treasonable links with her son, Cardinal Pole.

Jul.–Nov.   Impressive royal progress to York.

Jun. 23   Irish Parliament passes statutes acknowledging Henry VIII as 'King of Ireland' and Head of the Irish Church.

1542 *Feb.* 13   Q. Catherine Howard beheaded for alleged adultery.

Jul. 12   Henry VIII marries Catherine Parr.

Oct. 6–12   D. of Norfolk raids Scotland and burns Kelso.

Nov. 24   Ψ Solway Moss: James V, raiding Cumberland, is defeated with heavy losses.

Dec. 8   Princess born at Linlithgow.

14   James V dies at Falkland; infant princess accedes as Mary, 'Q. of Scots'.

1543 *Jan.* 10   James Hamilton, E. of Arran, ousts Beaton from control of Scottish Regency Council.

Feb. 11   Alliance of Henry VIII and Charles V against France.

Mar.   Consolidating Act of Welsh Union: removes anomalies in parliamentary representation, establishes 12 counties and gives statutory basis to a Council of Wales.

Jul. 1   Peace of Greenwich: settles disputes with Scotland; proposes marriage for P. Edward and Q. Mary.

Sep. 3   Beaton recovers control of Scottish Council.

Dec. 11   Scottish Parliament repudiates Greenwich treaty.

1544(–1547)		Further debasement of the coinage: weights of gold and silver coins reduced.
Mar.		Revised Succession Act: reinstates claims of Mary and Elizabeth after Edward.
May	3	Edward Seymour, E. of Hertford, invades Scotland; captures Leith and Edinburgh.
Jul.	14	Henry VIII goes to Calais with largest army yet sent to France.
Sep.		Henry captures Boulogne, but returns to England as Emperor Charles V makes separate peace with France.
1545 Feb.	25	Scots defeat English at Ψ Ancrum Moor.
Jul.	19	*Mary Rose* sinks off Portsmouth when about to oppose French landing on I. of Wight.
Sep.	8	E. of Hertford raids Scottish borders.

LITERATURE AND SCHOLARSHIP

| 1544 | Roger Ascham presents to Henry VIII his *Toxophilus*, an English-language treatise on archery, in dialogue form. |

MUSIC AND DRAMA

| 1545 | Sir Thomas Cawarden appointed first permanent Master of the Revels, with responsibility for playhouses. |

RECREATION AND FASHION

| by 1545 | Men's dress has become square cut, with short, wide gowns and skirted doublets; women encase their bodies in corsets, with padded metal bands. |

RELIGION AND EDUCATION

1541–1542	New dioceses created at Westminster (until 1550), Bristol, Gloucester, Chester (revived; v. 1075), Peterborough and Oxford.
1543	'King's Book' (*Necessary Doctrine and Erudition for any Christian Man*) revises Bishop's Book of 1537, affirming royal supremacy but restating traditional Catholic doctrines.
1544	Henry VIII refounds St Bartholomew's Hospital, London, suppressed with priory in 1537.

Events Elsewhere

| 1544 | Discovery of silver mines of Potosi, Peru. |
| 1545 Dec. 13 | Opening of Council of Trent (to 1563) marks start of Counter-Reformation. |

AD 1546–1550

| 1546 Mar. | 1 | Scottish reformer, George Wishart, burnt at stake in St Andrews. |
| May | 29 | Cardinal Beaton murdered at St Andrews as religious reformers seize the city. |

	Jun. 7	Peace Ty of Ardres: Boulogne to be held by England for 8 years.
1547	*Jan.* 28	Henry VIII dies at Whitehall Palace; 9-year-old son accedes as Edward VI.
	Jan. 31	E. of Hertford, King's uncle, becomes Lord Protector and (16 Feb.) D. of Somerset.
	Feb. 20	Coronation of Edward VI.
	Apr.	John Knox at St Andrews as chaplain to reformers.
	Jul. 21	French intervene in Scotland, suppressing Protestant revolt in St Andrews.
	Sep. 4	Protector Somerset invades Scotland.
	10	Ψ Pinkie: Somerset and John Dudley, E. of Warwick, defeat Scots.
1548	*Aug.* 15	Mary, Q. of Scots, arrives in France, where she lives for 13 years.
	Nov.	Act for dissolution of chantries.
1549	*Jan.* 15	Act of Uniformity: imposes Book of Common Prayer.
	Mar. 20	Thomas Seymour, Protector's brother, executed for treason.
	Jun. 9	First Prayer Book in use in English churches.
	Jun.–Aug.	Risings in Devon and Cornwall against Prayer Book religion.
	Jul.	Robert Kett leads Norfolk anti-enclosure rising.
	Aug. 9	England declares war on France, but French take the initiative and besiege Boulogne.
	26	Ψ Dussindale: E. of Warwick defeats Kett's rebels outside Norwich.
	Oct. 10	Protector Somerset deposed, power passing to E. of Warwick.
1550	*Jan.*	Act against Books and Images: encourages iconoclasm.
	Mar. 24	Peace Ty of Boulogne: ends English wars with France and Scotland and returns Boulogne to France.
	Jul. 2	Mary refuses chance to escape in Flemish ships from Essex coast.

FINE ARTS AND ARCHITECTURE

1547–1550	Lord Protector builds Somerset House, a Renaissance palace on the Strand.

MUSIC AND DRAMA

1548	John Bale, Bp of Ossory, writes *King John*, earliest English historical drama.
1550	John Marbeck completes his *Book of Common Prayer Noted*, first musical setting of the prayer book.

RELIGION AND EDUCATION

1546 *Dec.*	Henry VIII endows Trinity College, Cambridge.
1547	Repeal of the Six Articles.
1548	Swiss Protestant scholar, Peter Martyr Vermigli, appointed Professor of Divinity at Oxford.
1548	German Lutheran, Martin Bucer, appointed Professor of Divinity at Cambridge.

VOYAGES AND EXPLORATION

1546	Henry VIII establishes Navy Board, responsible for supply and administration of English fleet.

1551			Further debasement of English coinage.
	Feb.	14	Bp Stephen Gardiner deprived of see of Winchester.
	Oct.	11	E. of Warwick created D. of Northumberland.
1552	Jan.		Act of Uniformity: imposes Second Book of Common Prayer.
		22	D. of Somerset executed.
	Oct.		Bp Tunstall of Durham deprived of his see; D. of Northumberland seeks to acquire see's revenue.
1553	May	21	Northumberland's son marries Lady Jane Grey, Protestant great-niece of Henry VIII.
	Jun.	21	Edward VI 'devises' (nominates) Lady Jane Grey as his successor.
	Jul.	6	Edward dies at Greenwich.
		10	Accession of 'Queen Jane' proclaimed in London.
		19	P. Mary proclaimed Queen; Lady Jane Grey sent to Tower.
	Aug.	9	Q. Mary welcomed in London on arrival from Framlingham.
		13	Mary hears Latin mass in Chapel Royal; Archbp Cranmer detained in Tower of London.
		22	D. of Northumberland executed on Tower Hill.
		23	Gardiner, reinstated as Bp of Winchester, becomes chief minister as Lord Chancellor.
1554	Jan.	25	Sir Thomas Wyatt leads Kentish rebels to London, opposing Q. Mary's proposed Spanish marriage.
	Feb.	9	Rebellion crushed, Wyatt executed on 11 Apr.
		12	Lady Jane Grey and her husband executed.
	Mar.	18	P. Elizabeth imprisoned in Tower of London.
	Apr.	12	Scottish Parliament approves transfer of Regency from E. of Arran to Queen-Mother, Mary of Guise.
	May	19	P. Elizabeth moved from Tower to Woodstock.
	Jul.	25	Q. Mary marries Philip of Spain at Winchester.
	Nov.	20	Cardinal Pole lands at Dover as papal legate.
	Dec.		Parliament revives statutes for punishment of heresy.
1555	Feb.	4	Prebendary John Rogers is first Protestant burnt at Smithfield.
	Oct.	16	Bps Latimer and Ridley burnt at stake in Oxford.
	Nov.	12	Chancellor Stephen Gardiner dies.

FINE ARTS AND ARCHITECTURE

| 1554 | | | Antonio Moro welcomed to London as court painter. |

1552	Second Book of Common Prayer is basically Protestant; eucharist a purely commemorative act.
1552–1553	36 grammar schools founded in K. Edward VI's name.
1553 Jun. 26	Edward VI founds Christ's Hospital for orphans of City of London.
Aug.	Deprived Catholic bishops reinstated.
Dec. 20	Church services return to form used in Dec. 1546.
1554 Apr. 16–18	Cranmer, Ridley and Latimer in disputation at Oxford over nature of the Mass.
1554 Nov. 30	Formal reconciliation of England and papacy.
1555 May	Knox in Scotland preaching Calvinism (returns to Geneva, Jul. 1556).

VOYAGES AND EXPLORATION

1553–1554	Hugh Willoughby and Richard Chancellor explore northern coast of Russia, Chancellor travelling south to Moscow.
1555 Nov.	Chancellor drowned returning from second Russian voyage.
1555	English seaman John Locke challenges Portuguese monopoly with voyage to Guinea.

Events Elsewhere

| 1555 | First tobacco brought from America to Europe (Spain). |

AD 1556–1560

1556	Rapid inflation: price of basic commodities doubles within 12 months.
Jan. 1	Archbp Heath of York becomes Lord Chancellor.
Mar. 21	Archbp Cranmer burnt at the stake in Oxford.
22	Cardinal Pole, ordained a priest on 20 Mar., consecrated Archbp of Canterbury.
1557 Feb. 28	First Anglo-Russian commercial treaty signed with Russian envoy in London.
Jun.	England, as an ally of Spain, declares war on France.
Aug. 10	English army, under William Herbert, E. of Pembroke, threatens Paris.
1558 Jan. 7	Calais, English base for 220 years, taken by French.
Nov. 17	Q. Mary dies at St James's Palace; accession of P. Elizabeth.
	Cardinal Pole, Archbp of Canterbury, dies 12 hours after Q. Mary.
20	Sir William Cecil becomes chief Secretary of State.
1559 Jan. 15	Coronation of Elizabeth.
Feb. 10	'Loyal address' from Commons urging Queen to marry.
Apr. 2	Ty of Cateau-Cambresis: cedes Calais for 8 years to France; Anglo-French truce over Scotland.
May 8	Act of Supremacy: restores anti-papal laws of Henry VIII and reasserts

Crown's power over Church.

Act of Uniformity: imposes revised Book of Common Prayer.

May 10   Sermon by Knox at Perth incites Protestant Lords of the Congregation to seize Edinburgh and attack religious houses.

Oct. 21   Regent Mary of Guise deposed by Lords of the Congregation for allowing French to fortify Leith.

Dec. 17   Matthew Parker consecrated Archbp of Canterbury.

18   Q. Elizabeth sends help to Scottish Lords to expel French.

1560 *Feb. 27*   Anti-French Ty of Berwick between England and Scottish Lords.

Jun. 10   Scottish Regent Mary of Guise dies.

Jul. 6   Anglo-Scottish Ty of Edinburgh: French troops to leave Scotland; Protestant Regency Council appointed.

Aug.   Scottish Parliament abolishes papal jurisdiction and approves Knox's Calvinistic Confession of Faith.

Sep. 8   Amy Robsart, wife of Q. Elizabeth's favourite, Robert Dudley, dies after falling down the stairs of Cumnor Place, Oxon.

LITERATURE AND SCHOLARSHIP

1557   Royal charter gives Stationers' Company printing monopoly.

Richard Tottel publishes pioneer anthology of songs and sonnets, *Tottel's Miscellany*.

1558   John Knox publishes *First Blast of the Trumpet against the Monstrous Regiment of Women*.

1559   William Baldwin's *Mirror for Magistrates* recounts in verse the fate of famous historical characters.

RELIGION AND EDUCATION

1557 *May*   Benedictine monks restored to Westminster Abbey (until 1559).

Dec. 3   In Scotland 4 prominent nobles sign Covenant ('First Bond') to seek overthrow of Roman Catholicism.

1559 *Jun. 24*   Elizabethan Prayer Book used in English churches.

Nov. 26   Bishop Jewel of Salisbury preaches at Paul's Cross, London, and formulates a theory of Anglicanism.

1560   Q. Elizabeth refounds Westminster School.

VOYAGES AND EXPLORATION

1558–1560   Anthony Jenkinson travels to Bokhara, Astrakhan and Moscow.

AD 1561–1565

1561   Cecil reforms coinage to check debasement and increase trading confidence.

May   Lightning strikes St Paul's Cathedral, London, destroying spire and setting

		roof ablaze.
	Aug. 19	Widowed Mary, Q. of Scots, lands at Leith on returning from France.
1562	Jan. 6	Shane O'Neill, rebellious Irish E. of Tyrone, takes oath of allegiance to Elizabeth, but rebels in May.
	Sep. 20	Ty of Hampton Court with French Huguenots: provides for help in Normandy.
	Oct.	English force occupies Le Havre (to July 1563).
		Q. Elizabeth gravely ill from smallpox at Hampton Court.
	28	Ψ Corrichie: rebellion by George Gordon, E. of Huntly, crushed by royal army led by James Stewart, E. of Moray.
1563	Jan.–Apr.	Q. Elizabeth gives evasive response to petitions from Lords and Commons urging her to marry.
	Mar.	Poor Relief Act: compels rich parishes to help poorer ones.
	Apr.	Statute of Labour ('Apprentices'): JPs to settle wage levels, labour and apprenticeship disputes.
	Jun.–Oct.	Severe outbreak of plague: over 20,000 die in London.
	Sep.	Cecil begins royal marriage negotiations, favouring Archduke Charles, brother of Emperor Maximilian II; project not abandoned until Nov. 1567.
1564	Apr. 11	Peace Ty of Troyes with France: Q. Elizabeth receives 222,000 crowns to renounce claims to Calais.
	Jul. 18	Q. Elizabeth grants new charter to Merchant Adventurers.
1565	Jul. 29	Mary, Q. of Scots, marries first cousin Henry Stewart, Lord Darnley, at Holyrood.

LITERATURE AND SCHOLARSHIP

1563 — John Shute publishes *First and Chief Grounds of Architecture*, pioneer textbook.

John Foxe's *Book of Martyres* first printed in English.

MUSIC AND DRAMA

1561 Jan. 6 — *Gorboduc* by Thomas Norton and Thomas Sackville performed at Inner Temple Hall; first English blank verse tragedy.

1563 Feb. 27 — William Byrd becomes organist of Lincoln Cathedral (to 1572).

RELIGION AND EDUCATION

1562 — Bishop Jewel publishes his *Apologia Ecclesiae Anglicanae*. Convocation approves Articles of Religion (39 Articles).

SCIENCE AND INVENTION

1561 — Lead and copper mining begins, under German engineers.

1564–(1566) — Building of Exeter canal; first in Britain; under 2 miles long; improves navigation of R. Exe at Countess Wear.

1565 — German craftsmen teach ironmasters in the Weald of Kent to produce steel.

First blacklead pencils made in England.

Royal College of Physicians authorized to carry out human dissection.

VOYAGES AND EXPLORATION

1562 *Oct.*   John Hawkins begins African slave trade from Sierra Leone to Hispaniola.

1564–1565   Hawkins's second voyage to S. America; he introduces tobacco to England.

Events Elsewhere

1562 *Mar.* 2   Outbreak of French Wars of Religion (to 1598) with massacre of Huguenots at Vassy.

AD 1566–1570

1566 *Mar.* 9   Murder at Holyrood of David Rizzio, secretary and adviser to Mary, Q. of Scots.

Jun. 19   Son born to Mary and Darnley at Edinburgh, the future K. James VI and I.

Sep.–Oct.   Henry Sidney leads punitive expedition through Ulster.

1567 *Jan.* 2   Parliament dissolved; Q. Elizabeth refuses to name successor.

Feb. 10   Darnley killed in explosion at Kirk o'Field, Edinburgh.

May 15   Mary, Q. of Scots, marries James Hepburn, E. of Bothwell, whom she creates D. of Orkney.

Jun. 2   Rebel E. of Tyrone murdered in Ireland.

17   Lords of Covenant imprison Q. Mary in Lochleven Castle.

Jul. 24   Q. Mary abdicates; Moray becomes Regent for James VI.

1568 *May* 2   Q. Mary escapes from Lochleven; raises army against Regent Moray, but is defeated at Langside, 13 May.

16   Q. Mary sails across Solway Firth to exile in England.

Sep. 26   Spanish capture English ships after fight with Hawkins off San Juan de Ulloa, Mexico, and confiscate their treasure cargoes.

Oct.   Conference of York: Anglo-Scottish inquiry into Q. Mary's alleged complicity in Darnley's murder; Elizabeth transfers inquiry to Westminster in late Nov.

Dec.   Bullion aboard Spanish ships at Plymouth seized.

1569 *Jan.* 10   Q. Elizabeth declares murder complicity of Mary, Q. of Scots, not proven.

20   Q. Elizabeth orders Mary's detention at Tutbury Castle.

Mar. 22   E. of Leicester and Thomas Howard, D. of Norfolk, fail to induce Q. Elizabeth to dismiss Cecil.

Oct. 1   D. of Norfolk imprisoned in Tower of London for seeking to marry Mary, Q. of Scots.

Nov. 15   Seizure of Durham by Catholic northern earls (EE of Northumberland and Westmorland).

Dec. 20		Counter-measures by Q. Elizabeth's cousin, Henry Carey, Baron Hunsdon, force northern earls to flee across Scottish border.
1570 *Jan.*	23	Scottish Regent Moray assassinated; succeeded (27 Jan.) by Matthew Stewart, E. of Lennox.
Feb.	20	Hunsdon defeats Lord Dacre's attempt to revive rebellion at Hexham.
May		Papal bull of 25 Feb., *Regnans in Excelsis*, excommunicating Q. Elizabeth, made public in London.
Aug.		D. of Norfolk released from the Tower.

FINE ARTS AND ARCHITECTURE
1568 (–1575) Robert Smythson becomes architect at Longleat.

LITERATURE AND SCHOLARSHIP
1570 Roger Ascham's *The Schoolmaster* published posthumously.

MUSIC AND DRAMA
1566 Comedy *Gammer Gurton's Needle* performed at Christ's College, Cambridge.
1568 Welsh bards granted licence to hold Eisteddfod at Caerwys.

RELIGION AND EDUCATION
1567 New Testament in Welsh.
1569 Archbp Parker supervises publication of the Bishops' Bible to counter Calvinist translations.

SCIENCE AND INVENTION
1566 Pioneer manual of veterinary science printed: G. Blundeville, *Four Chief Offices belonging to Horsemanship*.

VOYAGES AND EXPLORATION
1567–1568 Hawkins's third voyage, to Guinea and Caribbean.

Events Elsewhere

1570 Potatoes introduced into Spain from America.

AD 1571–1575

1571 *Jan.*	2	Talks over royal marriage with Henri, D. of Anjou, begin.
	23	Royal Exchange, founded by Sir Thomas Gresham, opened in London.
Feb.	21	William Cecil made Baron Burghley.
Mar.–May		Roberto di Ridolfi, Florentine banker in London, visits Spanish Netherlands hoping to co-ordinate plots to free Mary, Q. of Scots, depose Elizabeth and

		restore Catholicism.
Apr.		Parliament passes Acts to promote export of grain and forbid export of wool.
		Treason Act: makes conspiracy to attempt Queen's death a capital offence.
May		Act against papal bulls: declares all instructions from Pope treasonable.
Sep.	5	John Erskine, E. of Mar, becomes Scottish Regent on murder of Lennox at Stirling.
	7	D. of Norfolk sent back to Tower for allegedly subsidizing Scottish conspirators.
Sep.	28	Burghley's agents reveal Ridolfi plots.

1572 *Jan.*	16	D. of Norfolk sentenced to death for treason; Elizabeth delays execution until 2 Jun.
Apr.	21	Ty of Blois: Anglo-French co-operation against Spain; projected royal marriage with François, D. of Alençon.
May		Elizabeth rejects Commons' pleas to execute Q. Mary.
Jul.	11	Sir Humphrey Gilbert lands 1,500 volunteers at Flushing to help Dutch rebels against Spain.
Nov.	24	James, E. of Morton, becomes Scottish Regent on death of Mar.

1573 *Jan.–Feb.*		Drake intercepts Spanish mule-trains carrying treasure across the Isthmus of Panama.
Feb.		Sir John Perrot subdues rebellion in Munster.
	23	Pacification of Perth: most supporters of Q. Mary recognize James VI's sovereignty.
Apr.	17	English troops capture Edinburgh Castle from Marians.
Dec.	18	Francis Walsingham becomes Secretary of State.

1574 *Aug.*	18	Ty of Bristol: compromise settlement of Anglo-Spanish commercial disputes.

1575 *Mar.*		Q. Elizabeth agrees to stop aiding Dutch rebels in return for Spanish opening of Antwerp to English traders.
Aug.	13–23	Q. Elizabeth extravagantly entertained by E. of Leicester at Kenilworth during her summer progress.
Nov.	14	Elizabeth declines offer of sovereignty of Netherlands.
Dec.	29	Edmund Grindal, Archbp of York since 1580, transferred to Canterbury, succeeding Matthew Parker.

FINE ARTS AND ARCHITECTURE

1572	Nicholas Hilliard recognized as official limner ('miniaturist') to the Queen.
1574	Smythson completes Longleat House.
	Gate of Honour, Caius College, Cambridge.

LITERATURE AND SCHOLARSHIP

1572	Foundation of the Society of Antiquaries in London.
1575	Christopher Saxton's *County Atlas of England and Wales* published.

MUSIC AND DRAMA

1572   Byrd and Thomas Tallis become joint organists of the Chapel Royal.

1575   Byrd and Tallis publish their *Cantiones Sacrae* and receive monopoly from the Queen for printing of music.

RECREATION AND FASHION

1575   Men's clothing at court is highly decorative: padded doublets and jerkins, embroidered ruffs at neck; trunk hose with full breeches and coloured stockings; velvet caps with high crowns and feathers. Women's gowns shaped around Spanish farthingale; ruffs and ruffles follow men's fashion.

RELIGION AND EDUCATION

1571   Foundation of Harrow School.

1574   First Roman Catholic priests from Douai seminary reach England.

VOYAGES AND EXPLORATION

1572   Francis Drake leads privateering expedition which sacks Nombre de Dios in the Spanish Main (Panama).

1573 *Feb.* 11   Drake becomes first Englishman to see Pacific Ocean.

1575   Sir Humphrey Gilbert publishes *Discourse*, advocating colonization.

Events Elsewhere

1571 *Oct.* 7   Ψ Lepanto: Turkish naval power destroyed.

1572 *Aug.* 24   St Bartholomew's Day massacre of Huguenots in Paris.

   Dutch revolt against Spain begins.

AD 1576–1580

1576 *Feb.–Mar.*   Agitation for Church reform by Puritan MPs.

    Mar. 12   Peter Wentworth MP imprisoned for accusing Q. Elizabeth of denying the Commons free speech.

1577 *Jun.*   Archbp Grindal 'sequestered' (suspended) for refusing to suppress Puritan agitation.

    Nov. 29   Cuthbert Maine is first seminarist priest executed at Tyburn for treason.

1578 *Sep.*   E. of Leicester marries Lettice Knollys; kept secret from Q. Elizabeth for 14 months.

1579 *Jan.* 7   Ty of alliance with Dutch, under William of Orange.

    Jun.   Rebellion of E. of Desmond (Gerald Fitzgerald) and James Fitzmaurice Fitzgerald in Munster, aided by Spanish and Portuguese troops.

    Jul.–Dec.   Ruthless suppression of Irish rebellion.

    Aug.   D. of Alençon visits Q. Elizabeth at Greenwich as a suitor.

	Oct.	John Stubbs has right hand cut off for writing pamphlet against Alençon marriage.
	Nov.	Opposition from Commons postpones Alençon marriage.
1580	*Apr.* 6	Earthquake in London damages St Paul's Cathedral.
	Jul. 5	Ban on new building within 3 miles of City of London.

FINE ARTS AND ARCHITECTURE

1580   Smythson begins work on Wollaton Hall, near Nottingham.

LITERATURE AND SCHOLARSHIP

1576   William Lambarde publishes *A Perambulation of Kent*, pioneer antiquarian survey of the county as observed in 1570.

1577   John Dee publishes *General and Rare Memorials Pertaining to the Perfect Art of Navigation*; first use of the words 'British Empire'.

First edition of Raphael Holinshed's *History of England* published.

1579   Edmund Spenser publishes *The Shepheardes Calendar*.

Thomas North completes *Lives of the Noble Grecians and Romans*, a translation of Plutarch.

1580   John Stow prints *The Chronicles of England*.

MUSIC AND DRAMA

1576 *Dec.*   James Burbage opens The Theatre, London's first playhouse, in Holywell St, Shoreditch.

1579   Stephen Gosson's pamphlet, *The School of Abuse*, denounces the morality of plays and poetry.

1580   First mention of 'Greensleeves' as a traditional English song.

RELIGION AND EDUCATION

1580   Robert Browne leads austere Protestant group in Norwich, the 'Brownists' (pioneer Congregationalists).

late Jul.   Robert Parsons and Edmund Campion land secretly at Dover to head Jesuit mission.

VOYAGES AND EXPLORATION

1576		Frobisher seeks North-West Passage, giving his name to bay in Baffin Island.
1577	*Dec.* 13	Francis Drake leaves Plymouth aboard *Pelican* to sail around the world.
1578	*Aug.* 21	Drake sails through Magellan Strait to Pacific (to 5 Sep.).
	Nov. 19	H. Gilbert and Walter Ralegh sail from Plymouth with 7 ships in abortive attempt to set up English colony in North America; forced back to Devon by May 1579.
1579	*Jun.* 17	Drake, ashore north of San Francisco, declares the Pacific coast annexed to England as 'New Albion'.
1580	*Sep.* 26	Drake completes circumnavigation of world when *Golden Hind* (ex-*Pelican*) reaches Plymouth.

1576 *Nov. 4*   'The Spanish Fury': Antwerp sacked by Spanish troops.

AD 1581–1585

1581 *Mar.*   Act against Reconciliation to Rome: heavy fines for hearing mass and for recusancy (non-attendance at parish church).

Apr. 4   Q. Elizabeth knights Drake aboard *Golden Hind* at Deptford.

Jul. 17   Edmund Campion seized at Lydford, Berkshire.

Oct.   Alençon comes to Whitehall Palace to sign marriage treaty (10 Nov.) with Elizabeth, 20 years his senior in age.

Nov.   Renewed Commons opposition to Alençon marriage.

Dec. 1   Campion executed at Tyburn.

1582 *Feb. 5*   Q. Elizabeth escorts Alençon to the Kentish coast on his way to Antwerp (dies, aged 30, in 1584).

Aug. 22   James VI taken hostage at Ruthven Castle by pro-English faction; held until escape in June 1583.

1583 *Aug. 14*   John Whitgift, Bp of Worcester, becomes Archbp of Canterbury in succession to Grindal.

Nov.   Francis Throckmorton arrested in London for conspiring in the 'Catholic Enterprise' with D. of Guise and Spanish ambassador: Mary, Q. of Scots, to accede.

Dec. 20   John Somerville, awaiting execution for threat to kill Elizabeth, found strangled in his Newgate cell.

1584 *Jan. 9*   Spanish ambassador, Mendoza, expelled.

Jul. 10   Throckmorton executed.

Oct. 19   Q. Elizabeth receives Bond of Association: thousands pledge to defend her and avenge her murder should she be assassinated.

Dec.   Act banishing Jesuits and seminary priests.

1585 *Mar. 2*   William Parry, MP for Queenborough and doctor of laws, executed for plotting Elizabeth's death.

29   Act for Queen's Safety: legalizes in advance the levying of war against 'a pretended successor'.

May 19   English ships in Spanish ports seized.

Aug. 14   Q. Elizabeth takes Netherlands under her protection.

Sep. 3   Ty of Nonsuch: promises Dutch an expeditionary force; sent under E. of Leicester, 17 Dec.

1581–82 *Christmas*	At Whitehall Palace, 5 plays and a masque are presented to entertain Q. Elizabeth and Alençon.
1583	Companies of players formed: Queen's Men, under Master of Revels; Lord Chamberlain's Men, under Lord Hunsdon.
1585	The comic actor Richard Tarlton writes *Seven Deadly Sins*, popular comedy at court.

SCIENCE AND INVENTION

1582 *Dec.* 24	Water-wheel installed by Pieter Morice in London Bridge pumps supply to Cornhill.

VOYAGES AND EXPLORATION

1581	English Levant Company founded, to trade with Ottoman empire.
1583 *Aug.* 5	H. Gilbert founds colonial settlement in Newfoundland, calling it St Johns.
Sep. 9	Gilbert drowned when *Squirrel* sinks off Azores.
1584 *Sep.*	John Newbery travels to Agra and presents letter from Q. Elizabeth to Moghul Emperor Akbar.
1585 *Jul.* 7	Roanoak colony established in Virginia.
Jul.–Sep.	John Davis explores coast of Greenland.

Events Elsewhere

1584 *Jul.* 10	William the Silent assassinated at Delft.

AD 1586–1590

1586 *Jul.* 1	Ty of Berwick: promises James VI, K. of Scots, annual grant.
Sep. 20	Sir Anthony Babington and 2 other conspirators executed at Tyburn.
22	Sir Philip Sidney wounded fighting at Zutphen (dies 17 Oct.).
26	Mary, Q. of Scots, brought as a state prisoner to Fotheringay Castle, near Peterborough.
Oct. 15–16	Q. Mary on trial at Fotheringay for treasonable correspondence with Babington.
25	Court of Star Chamber sentences Q. Mary to death.
Nov.	E. of Leicester returns from Netherlands, leaving Sir John Norris in command.
1587 *Feb.* 1	Elizabeth signs, but retains, Q. Mary's death warrant.
8	Q. Mary executed at Fotheringhay.
9	Elizabeth, angry at despatch of warrant by councillors, ostracizes Burghley for 5 months.
Mar. 1	Peter Wentworth MP again imprisoned for urging greater freedom of speech.
Apr. 19	Drake raids Cadiz, 'singeing King of Spain's beard' by taking booty and

		destroying ships.
	29	Sir Christopher Hatton made Lord Chancellor.
	Aug. 6	E. of Leicester again commands in Netherlands (to Mar. 1588).
	Dec. 21	Lord Howard of Effingham given command of navy and army against Spain.

1588 May 31   Spanish Armada leaves Tagus estuary; sighted off Cornwall (19 Jul.); running fights up Channel; anchors off Calais (27 Jul.) and is attacked by fire-ships; defeated off Gravelines; scatters northwards (30 Jul.).

        Aug. 9   Elizabeth addresses troops encamped at Tilbury.

        Sep. 4   E. of Leicester dies at Cornbury Park, Oxon.

1589

        Apr.–Jul.   Drake and Norris raid Portugal and destroy Corunna.

        Sep. 30   Lord Willoughby commands expedition to assist Henri IV against Catholics in Normandy.

        Nov. 24   James VI marries Anne of Denmark in Oslo.

FINE ARTS AND ARCHITECTURE

1588   Isaac Oliver produces earliest miniature, *A Man aged 59*.

LITERATURE AND SCHOLARSHIP

1586   William Camden publishes *Britannia*, pioneer antiquarian study.
Timothy Bright, in *A Treatise of Melancholy*, distinguishes mental from physical causes of sorrow.

1588   Thomas Hariot prints *Brief and True Report of the new found land of Virginia*, first book on American colonization.
T. Bright publishes *Characterie*, early form of shorthand.

1590   Thomas Lodge's euphuistic novel *Rosalynde* published.

MUSIC AND DRAMA

1587–1588   Christopher Marlowe's *Tamburlaine* performed.

1588   William Byrd composes *Psalms, Sonnets and Songs of Sadness and Piety*.

1590   First production of 2 plays by William Shakespeare: *Henry VI*, Part 1 and *Titus Andronicus*.

RELIGION AND EDUCATION

1587 Aug. 7   William Allen, founder of the college at Douai for training priests to convert England, is made a cardinal.

1588–1589   *Martin Marprelate Tracts*, secretly printed, advocate Presbyterianism rather than episcopacy.

SCIENCE AND INVENTION

1589   William Lee, Nottinghamshire clergyman, invents knitting machine; it fails because products are coarse compared to hand-knitted silk stockings now popular, especially with Q. Elizabeth.

1586 *Jul.* Thomas Cavendish becomes second English circumnavigator (to Sep. 1588).

28 Hariot lands first potatoes in Britain at Plymouth in cargo from Colombia.

AD 1591–1595

1591 *Aug.* Queen's favourite, Robert Devereux, E. of Essex, commands English force helping Henri IV against Catholic League in Normandy (to Jan. 1592).

30–31 Grenville's flagship *Revenge* fights Spanish squadron for 15 hours off Flores, Azores, before capture.

Sep. 3 Wounded Grenville dies aboard Spanish flagship.

1592 *Aug.* Spanish treasure worth over £800,000 seized in the capture of the galleon *Madre de Dios* at Flores.

Dec. Plague comes to London: 17,000 deaths in 12 months.

1593 *Feb. 23* Peter Wentworth MP imprisoned for raising the succession question in Parliament.

May 29 John Penry, probable author of *Martin Marprelate Tracts*, executed for denying Q. Elizabeth's Church supremacy.

30 Christopher Marlowe killed in tavern brawl at Deptford.

1594 *May–Jul. and Sep.* Heavy rainstorms lead to poor harvest.

Jun. 7 Q. Elizabeth's physician Roderigo Lopez, a Portuguese Jew, executed at Tyburn for allegedly planning to poison her.

Aug. Hugh O'Neill, E. of Tyrone, leads Catholic rising in Ulster and seeks Spanish help.

1595 *Feb. 2* Jesuit priest and poet Robert Southwell executed at Tyburn after being tortured on 13 occasions.

May 4 Norris sent to Ireland to suppress Tyrone's revolt.

Jul. 23 Spaniards raid Cornwall, burning Penzance and Mousehole.

Aug. 28 Drake and Hawkins leave Plymouth to raid Panama Isthmus.

LITERATURE AND SCHOLARSHIP

1592 Anonymous play, *Arden of Faversham*, published.

Robert Greene writes *A Groatsworth of Wit bought with a Million of Repentance*, pamphlet attacking several playwrights, including Shakespeare ('an upstart crow').

1593 *Jan.* John Norden authorized to make 'perfect descriptions, charts and maps' of the English counties; his first volume (on Middlesex) published later in the year.

1594 Thomas Nashe publishes *The Unfortunate Traveller*, earliest English adventure novel.

Richard Barnfield prints *The Affectionate Shepherd*, poetic variations on Vergil's *Eclogues*.

1595   Spenser's epithalamion, *Amoretti*, and also his allegoric pastoral, *Colin Clout's Come Home Again*, published.

MUSIC AND DRAMA

1592   William Alabaster writes *Roxana*, Latin tragedy, for Trinity College, Cambridge.

1592   1st production of Shakespeare's *Richard III*.

Lord Admiral's Company perform Marlowe's *The Jew of Malta*; also his *Faustus* and *Edward II*, 1593.

1593   Long closure of London theatres because of plague.

1593/1594   First productions of Shakespeare's *The Comedy of Errors, Two Gentlemen of Verona, Love's Labour's Lost* and *The Taming of the Shrew*.

Lord Chamberlain's Men (*v.* 1583) reconstituted under leadership of James Burbage and his son Richard Burbage, with Shakespeare in the company.

1595   First productions of Shakespeare's *Midsummer Night's Dream, Richard II* and *Romeo and Juliet*.

SCIENCE AND INVENTION

1594   Bevis Bulmer sets up experimental pumping system at Blackfriars, London, to give water supply to parts of City of London.

VOYAGES AND EXPLORATION

1591 *Apr.* 10   James Lancaster leaves Plymouth on first English voyage to E. Indies (returns May 1594).

1595 *Feb.*   Ralegh heads expedition to Orinoco Basin.

AD 1596–1600

1596 *Jun.–Jul.*   Cadiz raid by Effingham and E. of Essex prevents fitting out of new Armada.
Dec.   Spanish expedition to aid Tyrone wrecked off Finisterre.

1597 *Jul.–Oct.*   'The Islands Voyage': abortive attempt by Ralegh and Essex to seize Spanish treasure fleet off Azores.

1598 *Mar.*   Poor Relief Act: local poor rate, workhouses set up.
Aug. 14   Tyrone annihilates English force on Blackwater R.

1599 *Apr.* 15   E. of Essex arrives in Ireland as Lord Lieutenant.
Sep.   Essex signs unauthorized truce with Tyrone, returns to England; Queen orders his arrest.
Oct. 2   Charles Blount, Baron Mountjoy, succeeds Essex as Lord Lieutenant in Ireland.

1600	*Jun.*	Essex sentenced to lose his titles for his misdemeanours.
	Aug. 5	James VI, K. of Scots, held in Gowrie House, Perth; rescued by guards, who kill 3rd E. of Gowrie in skirmish.
	Dec. 31	Founding charter of East India Company sealed.

LITERATURE AND SCHOLARSHIP

1597		Francis Bacon's first 10 *Essays* published.
1598		The diplomat and bibliophile Sir Thomas Bodley offers to restore Oxford's 15th-century library.
		First edition of John Stow's *A Survey of London* published.
		Francis Meres publishes *Palladis Tamis, Wit's Treasury*, anthology and critical assessment of 125 English writers, musicians and artists.
1599		James VI writes *Basilikon Doron*, doctrine of divine right of kings.
1600		Robert Allott edits *England's Parnassus*.
		Edward Coke's first *Law Reports* published.

MUSIC AND DRAMA

1596		First production of Shakespeare's *King John* and *Merchant of Venice*.
1597		The lutenist John Dowland publishes *First Book of Songs* (harmonized tunes, not madrigals).
		George Carey, 2nd Lord Hunsdon, becomes Lord Chamberlain and patron of the Lord Chamberlain's Men.
	Jul.	*Isle of Dogs* by Thomas Nashe and Ben Jonson presented at Swan Theatre, Bankside, London.
1597		First production of Shakespeare's *Henry IV*, Part 1.
1598		Ben Jonson's *Every Man in His Humour* staged.
	Dec. 28	Richard Burbage and his nephew Cuthbert demolish The Theatre in Shoreditch, transporting its fabric across R. Thames to Bankside, Southwark.
1597		First productions of *Henry IV*, Part 2, and *Much Ado about Nothing*.
1599		Thomas Dekker's *A Shoemaker's Holiday* performed.
1599		First production of *Henry V, As You Like It* and *Julius Caesar*.
1600		First productions of *Merry Wives of Windsor* and *Twelfth Night*.

RECREATION AND FASHION

| 1600 | *Feb. 11* | Comic actor, William Kempe, leaves London on his Morris dance to Norwich (reached 11 Mar.); 9 days dancing between 19 days of rest; *Kempe's Nine Days Wonder* published later in the year. |

RELIGION AND EDUCATION

| 1596 | | Gresham College, Bishopsgate, London, opened. |

SCIENCE AND INVENTION

| 1599 | | Edward Wright publishes pioneer studies in navigation: *Certain Errors in Navigation . . . Detected and Corrected*; and *The Haven Finding Art*. |

Events Elsewhere

1598 Apr. 15 Huguenot privileges recognized by Edict of Nantes.
     Sep. 13   Death of K. Philip II of Spain.

AD 1601–1605

1601 Jan. 7–8 E. of Essex leads abortive revolt in London against Q. Elizabeth's advisers.
     Feb. 25   Essex executed for treason.
     Sep.   3,000 Spanish troops land at Kinsale, Ireland, to support Tyrone, but are besieged by Mountjoy.

1602 Jan. 2   Mountjoy accepts surrender of Spaniards in Kinsale.

1603 Mar. 24 Death of Elizabeth I at Richmond Palace; accession of James VI of Scotland as James I.
          30 Tyrone submits to Mountjoy, but benefits from a general amnesty.
     May 7   James VI and I enters London.
     Jul. 17 Ralegh arrested for planning to change succession.
          25 Coronation of James I at Westminster.
     Nov. 12 Ralegh found guilty of treason; imprisoned in Tower.

1604 Jan. 14–16 James I presides over Hampton Court Conference between Anglicans and Puritans.
     Apr. 11   James accepts Commons' complaint that he had no right to declare null and void the election of an outlaw, Francis Goodwin, as MP for Buckinghamshire.
     May 15   'Shirley's Case': James accepts that MPs cannot be denied seats in Commons by arrest for minor offences.
     Jun.   The 'Form of Apology': clarification by Commons for King of alleged privileges (claiming more rights over religious settlement than Elizabeth had conceded).
     Aug. 18   Anglo-Spanish Peace Ty: James to cease aiding Dutch rebels in return for trade concessions with Spain in Europe (but not in the Americas).
     Dec. 10   Richard Bancroft, Bp of London since 1597, succeeds Whitgift as Archbp of Canterbury.

1605 Nov. 4   Guy Fawkes arrested in cellar of Palace of Westminster while preparing explosives for the following day's royal opening of Parliament.
          8   Fawkes's co-conspirator Robert Catesby shot while resisting arrest at Holbeach Hall, Staffs.

LITERATURE AND SCHOLARSHIP
1602   Richard Carew publishes *A Survey of Cornwall*.

T. Campion publishes *Observations in Art of English Poesie*.

Samuel Daniel publishes *A Defence of Rhyme*.

Nov. 8   Bodley opens his library in Oxford.

MUSIC AND DRAMA

1601   Richard Carlton publishes book of madrigals.

1601   First production of *Hamlet*.

1602 *Feb. 2*   Diary of John Manningham notes performance of *Twelfth Night* at the Middle Temple.

1603   First production of Shakespeare's *Othello*.

1604   Paul's Boys produce George Chapman's *Bussy d'Ambois*.

1604   First productions of Shakespeare's *All's Well That Ends Well* and *Measure for Measure*.

1605   John Dowland composes *Lachrymae*, 5-part instrumental music for dances.

1605   First production of *King Lear*.

Ben Jonson and George Chapman briefly imprisoned for anti-Scottish remarks in their comedy *Eastwood Ho!*

RELIGION AND EDUCATION

1603 *Apr.*   Thomas Cartwright's Millenary Petition, anti-ritualist appeal to King from 1000 Puritan ministers.

1604   Hampton Court Conference agrees on need for newly 'authorized' translation of the Bible.

VOYAGES AND EXPLORATION

1601 *Feb. 13*   First 5 ships of East India Company sail for Sumatra.

AD 1606–1610

1606 *Jan. 27*   Trial of Guy Fawkes; executed 31 Jan.

Mar.   Parliament passes anti-Catholic legislation: convicted recusants barred from public office.

Apr. 10   Charter granted to Virginia Companies in London and Plymouth to encourage colonization.

12   James I proclaims a national flag ('Union Jack') combining St. George's cross and St Andrew's saltire.

1607 *May*   Anti-enclosure riots in Northants and Leics.

Jul.   James I angered by English parliamentary rejection of proposed union with Scotland.

Sep. 14   Ireland, the 'flight of the earls': rebel EE Tyrone and Tyrconnel flee to Spain.

1608 *Jun.*   'Calvin's Case': English judges rule that a Scot born after March 1603 is a natural subject of the K. of England.

1609	Plantation of Ulster begins: settlement of English and Scot Protestants on forfeited estates of rebel leaders.
1610 Feb.–Jul.	James I in conflict with Commons over his levying of impositions, taxes on foreign trade not authorized by Parliament.
Jun. 26	James accepts from Parliament the Great Contract: a grant of £200,000 if he abolishes feudal tenures and wardship; final negotiations break down, Feb. 1611.
Jul. 9	Arbella Stuart, claimant to throne, imprisoned at Lambeth for secretly marrying another claimant, William Seymour.

LITERATURE AND SCHOLARSHIP

1606 Dec.	Michael Drayton publishes Ode to the Virginia Voyage.
1609	Thomas Thorpe publishes first edition of Shakespeare's sonnets, dedicated 'to Mr W.H.'.
	Thomas Dekker writes The Guls Horne-booke, satirical attack on the fops and gallants of fashionable London.

MUSIC AND DRAMA

1606	King's Men perform Jonson's Volpone.
1606	First production of Shakespeare's Macbeth.
1607	The Revenger's Tragedy published; traditionally ascribed to Cyril Tourneur. George Chapman's Bussy d'Ambois published.
1607	First productions of Shakespeare's Antony and Cleopatra, Coriolanus and Timon of Athens.
1608	Thomas Middleton's satirical comedy A Mad World My Masters performed.
1608	First production of Shakespeare's Pericles.
1609	Jonson's Epicoene, or The Silent Woman performed.
1610	Jonson's The Alchemist performed by the King's Men.
1610	First production of Shakespeare's Cymbeline.

RECREATION AND FASHION

1610 Jun. 4	Investiture of P. Henry as P. of Wales is followed by week of festivity in London.

RELIGION AND EDUCATION

1610	Scottish Parliament formally re-establishes episcopacy.

VOYAGES AND EXPLORATION

1606 Dec.	Christopher Newport leaves London with 3 ships of Virginia Company and 120 colonists.
1607 May 13	Newport reaches Virginia; English settle at Jamestown, under John Smith.
1608 May–Oct.	Thomas Coryat walks London-Venice and back.
1610 May 10	George Somers and Thomas Gates reach Jamestown, after 10 months as castaways in the Bermudas.
Aug. 3	Henry Hudson leads expedition into the huge bay named after him.

AD 1611–1615

1611	*Jan.–Feb.*	Attacks in Commons on prerogative powers of Court of High Commission anger James I.
	Mar.	James's chief favourite, Robert Carr, created Viscount Rochester.
	Jun.	Arbella Stuart seeks to escape to Holland; her ship is overtaken and she is sent to the Tower.
1612	*Mar. 24*	Robert Cecil, E. of Salisbury (Secretary of State since James I's accession), dies.
	Sep.	Elector Palatine, Frederick V, arrives in London as suitor for James's daughter, Elizabeth.
	Nov. 6	Henry, P. of Wales, dies at St James's Palace from typhoid contracted when swimming at Windsor.
1613	*Feb. 14*	Marriage of Elector Palatine and P. Elizabeth; they leave for the Rhineland, 21 Apr.
	Apr.	Carr (Rochester) quarrels publicly with his secretary, Sir Thomas Overbury, who is imprisoned in the Tower; dies of poison there, Sep.
	Dec. 24	Carr (made E. of Somerset on 3 Nov.) marries Frances Howard, the recently divorced Countess of Essex.
1614	*Apr. 5*	The 'Addled Parliament' (to 7 Jun.): refuses to vote taxes unless James I ceases to raise money through impositions.
	Jun.	James seeks funds through a Benevolence; non-contributors arraigned before Court of Star Chamber.
	Sep.	George Villiers becomes James's favourite.
1615	*Feb. 21*	William Cokayne appointed Controller of King's Merchant Adventurers, with monopoly to export cloth.
	Sep. 27	Arbella Stuart starves herself to death in the Tower.

LITERATURE AND SCHOLARSHIP

1612		Samuel Purchas writes *Purchas his Pilgrimage, or Relations of the World and the Religions observed in all Ages and Places*.
1612–1613		Many elegiacs published in honour of P. Henry.
1613		Sir Anthony Shirley publishes account of his 10 years in the service of the Shah of Persia.
	Feb.	John Donne writes *Epithalamium*, for royal wedding.

MUSIC AND DRAMA

1611		First productions of Shakespeare's *Winter's Tale* and *The Tempest*.
1612		John Dowland publishes final collection of songs, *A Pilgrim's Solace*.
		First collection of madrigals by Orlando Gibbons.

1613	Elizabeth Cary's *Miriam the Fair, Queen of Jewry* published; Cary (née Tanfield) is first known English woman dramatist.
Feb.	Shakespeare's company present 14 plays at court during royal wedding festivities.
Jun. 29	Globe Theatre destroyed when faulty discharge of cannon in *Henry VIII* fires thatch; reopens following summer.
1614	Jonson's *Bartholomew's Fair* performed.

RECREATION AND FASHION
| c.1612–1613 | Robert Dover revives traditional annual 'Cotswold Games' at Whitsun, near Chipping Camden. |

RELIGION AND EDUCATION
| 1611 | Authorized Version of the Bible published: 25s loose sheets; 30s bound. |

SCIENCE AND INVENTION
| 1613 | 'New River', 39-mile canal to springs near Ware, augments London's water supply; constructed over 4 years to plan by Hugh Middleton MP. |

VOYAGES AND EXPLORATION
| 1611 *Jun.* 23 | Mutineers aboard *Discoverie* cast off Henry Hudson and 8 other seamen in open boat in James Bay. |

AD 1616–1620

1616 *Mar.* 20	Ralegh released from Tower after 13 years; to undertake expedition to Guiana in search of gold, provided no attacks made on Spanish possessions.
May 25	Robert Carr, E. of Somerset, and his wife condemned to death for poisoning Overbury, but pardoned by James.
Jul.	James I begins to raise revenue by sale of peerages.
Nov. 1	James dismisses Chief Justice Sir Edward Coke for resisting royal prerogative.
4	P. Charles invested P. of Wales at Westminster; no further investitures until 1911.
1617 *Jan.*	Villiers made E. of Buckingham (Duke in 1623).
	Pocahontas (native American princess married to colonist, John Rolfe) received by James I at court; she dies in March 1617 when about to return to Virginia.
May 13– *Aug.* 4	James in Scotland.
1618 *Jan.* 8	Francis Bacon becomes Lord Chancellor and Sir Robert Naunton, a Puritan, Secretary of State.

Jul.		Thomas Howard, E. of Suffolk, dismissed as Lord Treasurer; imprisoned for embezzling state funds.
Sep.		Spanish ambassador protests at attacks by Ralegh's expedition on Spanish outposts.
Oct.	29	Ralegh, having been arrested on his return to England, is executed for treason.
1619 *Jul.*	30	Jamestown, Virginia: first colonial assembly meets.
Sep.	26	James I urges Elector Palatine to refuse Bohemian Crown offered him by Prague Protestants; advice ignored.
1620 *Apr.*	27	Secret Anglo-Spanish Ty: P. of Wales and Infanta Maria to marry if laws against Roman Catholics are relaxed.
Sep.	16	Pilgrim Fathers (101 Puritans) sail from Plymouth aboard *Mayflower*; reach Cape Cod, 11 Nov.; land in Massachusetts, 21 Dec.
Dec.	24	James I condemns 'excess of lavish speech in matters of state'; warning against criticizing pro-Spanish policy.

FINE ARTS AND ARCHITECTURE

1616	Inigo Jones designs the Queen's House, Greenwich (first stage built 1618; completed 1635).
1618	Jones begins Banqueting House, Whitehall (completed 1622).

LITERATURE AND SCHOLARSHIP

1616	Jonson's plays, masques and poems published in first collected folio edition of an English dramatist.
	John Smith publishes *A Description of New England*.
	Robert Fludd's *Apologia Compendiaria Fraternitatem de Rosea Cruce Afluens* spreads Rosicrucian medico-theosophic ideas and revives interest in alchemy.
1617	John Selden publishes *Analecton Anglo-Britannicon*, antiquarian study of pre-Conquest records.
1618	John Tradescant prints *A Voyage of Ambassad* study of flora and fauna of N. Russia as observed on his travels.

MUSIC AND DRAMA

1616		T. Middleton and William Rowley write *A Fair Quarrel*, tragi-comedy on the ethics of duelling.
Apr.	23	Shakespeare dies at Stratford-upon-Avon.
1619		Beaumont and Fletcher's play *A King and No King* printed.

RECREATION AND FASHION

1618	K. James's 'Book of Sports' distinguishes between Sunday 'lawful recreations' (dancing, archery, athletic contests) and 'unlawful games' (animal baiting, bowls, etc.).

1616   Privy Council orders a school in each Scottish parish.

1618 *Aug.*   Five Articles of Perth: General Assembly of Scottish Church accepts rites practised by Anglican Church.

SCIENCE AND INVENTION

1616   William Barlow writes *Magnetical Advertisements concerning the Nature and Property of the Lodestone.*

1617   Mark Ridley writes *Magnetical Animadversions.*

1619   William Harvey, lecturing in London, first postulates his belief in the circulation of the blood.

VOYAGES AND EXPLORATION

1617   William Baffin, in search for North-West Passage, discovers Baffin Bay and Lancaster, Smith and Jones Sounds.

    Jun. 12   Ralegh sails from Plymouth; reaches mouth of R. Orinoco, 31 Dec.

1618   English West Africa Company founded; trading stations set up in Gambia and Gold Coast.

1619   Jamestown: Dutch vessel lands first African slaves.

Events Elsewhere

1618 *May 23*   Defenestration of Prague: start of Thirty Years War.

1620 *Nov. 8*   Ψ of the White Mountain: Elector Palatine's army defeated near Prague.

AD 1621–1625

1621 *Jan. 30*   Parliament meets: Commons revive impeachment (not used since 1449) to arraign Giles Mompesson and Francis Mitchell before H. of Lords for profiting from monopolies.

    May 3   Impeachment of Lord Chancellor Bacon for corruption; fined and declared incapable of holding public office.

    Sep. 29   Lionel Cranfield made Lord Treasurer.

    Dec. 1   Commons petition James I to defend German Protestantism and find Protestant wife for P. of Wales.

    3   James tells Commons 'not to meddle with anything concerning our Government or deep affairs of state'.

    18   Commons Protestation: Parliament's privileges are 'the ancient and undoubted birthright and inheritance of the people of England'.

    30   James tears out Protestation from Commons Journal.

1622 *Jan. 7*   John Pym MP placed under house arrest by James I for hostile remarks in Commons.

1623	Feb.	Dutch massacre English traders and settlers at Amboyna island in the Moluccas (Indonesia).
	19	Buckingham and P. of Wales leave Dover incognito for Spain; arrive in Madrid, 7 Mar.
	Aug. 31	Buckingham and P. of Wales leave Madrid after failing to agree on marriage terms; reach Portsmouth, 5 Oct.
	Dec. 14	James I abrogates Anglo-Spanish Marriage Ty of 1620.
1624	Feb. 24	James I's fourth Parliament meets: passes act declaring monopolies illegal.
	Mar.	Commons grant James funds specifically for war against Spain.
	10	James agrees to declare war on Spain.
	Apr. 24	Count Mansfeld reaches London to raise volunteer army to fight for Elector Palatine in Germany.
	May	Commons impeach Lord Treasurer Cranfield for alleged bribery; he is fined and suspended from office.
	Jun. 24	Virginia constituted a crown colony.
	Dec. 12	Anglo-French treaty provides for marriage of P. of Wales and P. Henrietta Maria, daughter of Henri IV.
1625	Jan.–Mar.	Mansfeld's expedition with English troops proves abortive; disease and shortage of food leads to high death toll and much desertion.
	Mar. 27	James VI and I dies at Theobalds; P. of Wales accedes as K. Charles I.
	May 1	Proxy wedding of Charles I and Henrietta Maria in Notre Dame, Paris.
	Jun. 12	Henrietta Maria, escorted by Buckingham and with many French attendants, lands in Dover as Charles's bride.
	18	Charles's 1st Parliament (to 12 Aug.): grants tunnage and poundage for a year rather than for life; no additional war funds so long as Buckingham determines policy.
	Aug.	Plague in London sends court and Parliament to Oxford.
	Oct.–Nov.	Abortive Cadiz expedition: 5,000 seamen and 10,000 soldiers, inadequately supplied and poorly led.
	Dec. 9	Ty of the Hague: Dutch and English to subsidize Danish support for German Protestants.

FINE ARTS AND ARCHITECTURE

1625		Daniel Mytens appointed official royal painter.

LITERATURE AND SCHOLARSHIP

1621		Robert Burton's *The Anatomy of Melancholy*, satire on human behaviour, written as a medical work.
	Jun. 6	*Corante*, earliest newsbook in English, printed in Amsterdam; from Sep. available in London.
1623		First folio, earliest collected edition of Shakespeare's plays.
1624		Henry Briggs publishes *Arithmetica Logarithmica*.
1625		Completed third edition of 58 of Bacon's *Essays* published.

1622   Orlando Gibbons' anthem 'O Clap Your Hands' celebrates Oxford's bestowal on him of a doctorate in music.

1623   Philip Massinger's tragedy *Duke of Milan* printed.

SCIENCE AND INVENTION

1621   Oxford Physic Garden (earliest in Britain) founded.

AD 1626–1630

1626 Feb. 6   Charles I's second Parliament meets: refuses to grant funds without redress of grievances.

23   Commons begin impeachment of D. of Buckingham.

May 10   John Eliot and Dudley Digges sent to the Tower for seeking to impeach Buckingham.

Jun. 15   Charles dissolves Parliament; orders a forced loan.

26   Charles expels Henrietta Maria's French attendants.

1627 Jan.–Feb.   Seizure of French ships and cargoes in the Channel leads to an undeclared Anglo-French war.

Jul. 12   Buckingham lands 6,000 men on I. of Ré in attempt to relieve Huguenots besieged in La Rochelle.

Nov. 8   Buckingham's force leaves Ré, having lost 3,000 men.

28   'Darnel's Case': Sir Thomas Darnel and 4 other knights unsuccessfully appeal against their imprisonment without trial for opposing forced loan.

1628 Jan. 2   Charles I frees 76 opponents of forced loan, of whom 27 are elected to new Parliament.

Mar. 17   Charles opens third Parliament: MPs include Oliver Cromwell, elected for Huntingdon.

Jun. 7   Charles accepts the Petition of Right: a bill declaring forced loans, forced billeting of troops, imprisonment without trial and martial law to be illegal.

11   Commons vainly seek dismissal of Buckingham.

Jul. 20   Charles gives a viscountcy to Thomas Wentworth, Leader of the Commons.

Aug. 23   Buckingham, about to sail again for La Rochelle, is stabbed to death at Portsmouth by John Felton, an officer with a grievance.

Dec. 16   Wentworth is made President of the Council of the North.

1629 Mar. 2   Commons defy Speaker Finch to pass resolutions condemning ritualistic innovations in religion and the levying and payment of unauthorized tunnage and poundage.

5   John Eliot and 8 other MPs imprisoned.

10   Charles I dissolves Parliament.

1630 May 29   Future Charles II born at St James's Palace.

Sep. 17	John Winthrop, Puritan lawyer from Suffolk, lands in Massachusetts as Governor of new colony and founds city of Boston.

LITERATURE AND SCHOLARSHIP

1627	F. Bacon's *New Atlantis* published posthumously.
1628	Edward Coke completes *Institutes*, first of his 4 law commentaries.
	William Harvey publishes *Exercitatio Anatomica de Motu Cordis et Sanguinis*.
1630	*All the Workes of John Taylor, the Water Poet* published, the verse and prose of an eccentric, well-travelled Thames waterman.

MUSIC AND DRAMA

1627 *Feb.*	William Heather founds Professorship of Music at Oxford.
1630	T. Middleton's *A Chaste Mayde in Cheapside*, satirical comedy, published posthumously (written 1613).

RELIGION AND EDUCATION

1628	William Laud becomes Bp of London, and Richard Montagu Bp of Chichester; both are 'Arminian' High Churchmen, opposed by Puritan Parliamentarians for their ritualistic traditionalism.

SCIENCE AND INVENTION

1626 *Apr. 9*	Bacon dies at Highgate after catching a cold while conducting an experiment on a stuffed fowl, using snow as a means to preserve flesh.

AD 1631–1635

1631	Social distress caused by poor harvest for second year running.
1632 *Apr.*	Charles I issues charter for colony of Maryland with Lord Baltimore, a Roman Catholic, as first Governor.
1633 *May*	Charles I revives antiquated forest laws to raise funds by new fines.
Jun. 18	Charles I's Scottish coronation at Edinburgh.
Jul. 3	Wentworth goes to Ireland as Lord Deputy.
Aug. 6	Laud becomes Archbp of Canterbury; succeeded as Bp of London by William Juxon in October.
Sep. 9	Laud writes to Wentworth advocating, 'for the State', a policy 'of Thorough'.
1634 *May 7*	Puritan pamphleteer William Prynne is pilloried and has ears amputated after trial by Court of Star Chamber for libelling Henrietta Maria in *Histrio-Mastix, the Players Scourge* (1633), an attack on acting.
Oct. 20	Writs issued to levy ship money from London and coastal ports, allegedly to protect merchant shipping.

1635 *Aug. 4*   New writs extend ship money to inland towns.

FINE ARTS AND ARCHITECTURE
1631–1641   Charles I is an outstanding patron of the fine arts.
1632   Anthony Van Dyck arrives in London from Netherlands and is knighted by
                Charles.
1633   Daniel Mytens's final portrait of Charles I.
1634   Van Dyck's equestrian portrait of Charles I.
1635   Peter Paul Rubens paints panels representing the apotheosis of James I for
                the ceiling of the Banqueting Hall, Whitehall.

LITERATURE AND SCHOLARSHIP
1632   Selden dedicates to Charles I his *Mare Clausum*, antiquarian study asserting
                England's claim to sovereignty over the seas.
1633   *Collected Poems* of John Donne published by his son.

MUSIC AND DRAMA
1633   John Ford publishes 3 plays: *Love's Sacrifice; 'Tis Pity She's a Whore; The
                Broken Heart.*
1634   Massinger's *A New Way to Pay Old Debts* published (acted 1625?), a
                comedy satirizing greed of merchant class.

RECREATION AND FASHION
1634   Newmarket Gold Cup horse-race instituted.
1630s   Fashion favours 'Cavalier' style for men: jerkins, fitted to waistline, replace
                doublets; much lace on shirts and cuffs; long, decorated breeches; pointed
                beards; hair, full and curly; hat, cocked on side, trimmed with feathers.
                French style for women, favours high-waisted bodice cut low, with much
                lace; a full skirt falling in natural folds to the ground.

RELIGION AND EDUCATION
1635   Charles I authorizes new book of canons for Scottish Church.
                The English High and Latin School, Boston, Massachusetts, is established;
                first colonial secondary school.

SCIENCE AND INVENTION
1631   Thomas Hariot's algebraic studies posthumously published as *Artis
                Analyticae Praxis.*
1634   Cornelius Vermuyden begins work to reclaim East Anglian fens, for company
                founded by E. of Bedford.
1635   First General Post Office open to the public, Bishopsgate, London.

VOYAGES AND EXPLORATION
1635   Settlers from Massachusetts begin colonization of Connecticut.

Events Elsewhere

1631–1632   Intervention of Gustavus Adolphus of Sweden in Thirty Years War.

AD 1636–1640

1636 *Mar.* 6   Bp Juxon of London appointed Lord Treasurer.

Oct. 9   Third ship money writ; payment refused by John Hampden, former MP for Wendover.

1637 *Apr.* 30   Royal proclamation seeks to check emigration to America.

Jun. 30   Second Star Chamber trial of Prynne: condemned to pillory and further mutilation for seditious writings.

Jul. 23   Riot in St Giles's Cathedral, Edinburgh, when Laudian prayer book first used.

Nov.   'Hampden's Case' against legality of ship money: 7 judges support Charles I; 5 agree with Hampden.

1638 *Mar.*   National Covenant, favouring Presbyterianism rather than episcopacy, circulated and signed throughout Scotland.

Jul.   Charles I withdraws Laud's Scottish liturgy and appoints Marquis of Hamilton Commissioner in Scotland.

Nov.–Dec.   Glasgow Assembly defies Hamilton: rejects episcopacy and repudiates Charles's church innovations.

1639 *Mar.*   Covenanters take control of Edinburgh and Stirling.

May–Jun.   First Bishops War: border skirmishes between Covenanters, under Alexander Leslie, and royal army raised by Charles I in York.

Jun. 18   Pacification of Berwick: Leslie's army disbanded; Charles allows Scots a General Assembly and Parliament.

Sep. 22   Wentworth returns from Ireland to serve as Charles's chief adviser.

Oct. 31   Scottish Parliament dissolved in royal change of policy.

1640 *Jan.* 12   Wentworth created E. of Strafford.

Apr. 13   'Short Parliament' at Westminster (to 5 May): attacks Laud's and Strafford's policies and refuses to authorize taxes.

Aug. 20   Second Bishops War; Scots cross the Tweed.

28   Scottish army wins skirmish at Newburn.

30   Scots enter Newcastle-on-Tyne.

Sep. 24   Charles opens abortive Great Council of Peers in York, which concludes armistice (Ty of Ripon) with Scots but insists on need to summon a Parliament.

Nov. 3   'Long Parliament' meets, under leadership of Pym.

11   Strafford impeached; on 25 Nov. sent to the Tower.

Dec.	7	Commons unanimously declare ship money illegal.
	11	Commons petition Charles to abolish episcopacy 'root and branch'.
	18	Archbp Laud impeached.

FINE ARTS AND ARCHITECTURE

1637   Van Dyck paints *The Children of Charles I* and *Charles I in Three Positions*.

LITERATURE AND SCHOLARSHIP

1637   John Milton's *Comus* published anonymously.

1638   J. Milton's *Lycidas* published; written in 1637 when his Cambridge contemporary Edward King was drowned while sailing to Dublin.

1640   Thomas Carew's *Poems* published; Carew is archetypal Cavalier poet.

MUSIC AND DRAMA

1638 Jan.   Lavish staging at author's expense of *Aglaura* a 5-act play by the wealthy courtier Sir John Suckling; alternative last acts, one tragic, one 'happy'.

RELIGION AND EDUCATION

1636   College founded at Cambridge, Massachusetts; named Harvard in 1639 after legacy from John Harvard.

VOYAGES AND EXPLORATION

1637   English traders establish first 'factory' (trading settlement) in China, at Canton.

1640   East India Company traders establish Fort St George (Madras).

AD 1641–1642

1641 Feb.	16	Triennial Act: provides for minimum 50-day session of Parliament at least every 3 years.
Apr.	21	Bill of Attainder for Strafford's execution.
May	2	P. Mary marries P. William of Orange quietly at Whitehall, but remains in England.
	10	Charles I accepts attainder of Strafford.
		Act against dissolution 'of this present Parliament' without its own consent.
	11	P. of Wales sent by his father to H. of Lords in vain plea for Strafford's life.
	12	Strafford executed.
Jun.	22	Tunnage and Poundage Act: grants Charles the revenue from customs and excise for only 2 months.
Jul.	5	Parliamentary acts abolish Court of Star Chamber and High Commission.
Aug.	7	Act against levying of ship money.
Oct.	23	Rebellion of Irish Catholics.
Nov.	8	Pym vainly seeks parliamentary control of army sent to suppress Irish rebellion.

27	'Grand Remonstrance': Pym's manifesto of reforms carried out and grievances still requiring settlement; carried in Commons by only 11 votes.
1642 *Jan.* 4	Charles I enters H. of Commons to arrest 5 MPs (including Pym and Hampden) for alleged treason; but they find refuge in City of London.
10	Charles and his family leave London.
Feb. 23	Q. Henrietta Maria sails for Holland from Dover, escorting P. Mary to her husband and entrusted with the crown jewels.
Jun. 2	The Nineteen Propositions, seeking Parliament's control of State, Church and royal family – presented to Charles at York and rejected.
Aug. 9	Proclamation 'for Suppressing the Present Rebellion'.
22	Charles raises his standard at Nottingham.
Sep. 23	First skirmish of the Civil War: Charles's nephew, P. Rupert of the Rhine, defeats Parliamentarians under E. of Essex at Ψ Powick Bridge, Worcester.
Oct. 23	Ψ Edgehill: Rupert again defeats Essex.
29	Charles enters Oxford, his headquarters until June 1646.
Nov. 12	Charles watches Rupert's successful attack on Brentford, 5 miles from Westminster, but retreats on Essex's approach with reinforcements.

LITERATURE AND SCHOLARSHIP

1642	John Denham's *Cooper's Hill* piratically published; earliest topographical poem, reflections on the landscape around Runnymede.
	Thomas Hobbes's *De Cive*, treatise on government, published in Paris; expanded English edition, 1651.
	J. Milton writes *The Reason of Church Government*, anti-episcopalian pamphlet.
	Jeremy Taylor publishes *Of the Sacred Order and Offices of Episcopacy*.

MUSIC AND DRAMA

1641	John Barnard compiles *First Book of Selected Church Music*, earliest printed collection of cathedral music.
	J. Denham stages his *The Sophy*, tragedy set in Ottoman Turkey.
1642 *Jan.* 6	Last Christmas entertainment at court: P. of Wales sees King's Players in Beaumont and Fletcher's *The Scornful Lady*.
Sep. 2	Parliamentary Ordinance bans all public stage plays; theatres closed until 1660.

AD 1643–1644

1643 *Jan.* 6	*Mercurius Aulicus*, Royalist weekly newspaper, goes on sale in Oxford.
23	Thomas Fairfax takes Leeds for Parliament.
Feb.	'Eastern Association', new Parliamentarian army, organized.

May	13	Ψ Grantham: first victory for Cromwell and Eastern Association.
Jun.	18	J. Hampden defeated and killed at Ψ Chalgrove Field, Oxon.
	30	Fairfax defeated at Ψ Adwalton Moor, Yorkshire.
Jul.	13	Royalist cavalry gain victory at Ψ Roundway Down, Wilts.
	14	Q. Henrietta Maria joins Charles I at Oxford.
	26	P. Rupert takes Bristol (England's 2nd port).
	28	Cromwell wins Ψ Gainsborough.
Aug.	3	Charles unsuccessfully besieges Gloucester (to 6 Sep.).
Sep.	15	Charles concludes truce with Irish rebels so as to free his troops for service in England.
	20	P. Rupert defeated at 1st Ψ Newbury.
Oct.	10	Fairfax, supported by Cromwell's cavalry, routs royalists at Ψ Winceby, Lincs.
Dec.	8	John Pym dies of cancer, leaving more conservative Parliamentarians without a leader.
1644 *Jan.*		E. of Leven (Alexander Leslie) leads Scottish Covenanters into England as allies of Parliamentarians.
	22	Charles opens a 'parliament' of 44 peers and 118 commoners at Christ Church, Oxford.
Apr.	17	Q. Henrietta Maria leaves Oxford (sails for France from Falmouth, 14 Jul.).
Jun.	29	Charles wins skirmishes at Cropredy Bridge, Oxon.
Jul.	2	Cromwell defeats P. Rupert at Ψ Marston Moor.
	16	Cromwell takes city of York.
Sep.	1	James Graham, Marquess of Montrose, rallies Scottish Royalists to defeat Covenanters at Ψ Tibbermore and capture Perth.
	3	Charles takes Fowey, Cornwall, after brief siege; E. of Essex narrowly escapes capture there.
Oct.	27	2nd Ψ Newbury (indecisive).
Dec.	19	H. of Commons passes Self-Denying Ordinance, requiring members of either House to give up army commands within 40 days; passage of Ordinance delayed by H. of Lords.

LITERATURE AND SCHOLARSHIP

1643	J. Milton's pamphlet, *The Doctrine and Discipline of Divorce*, published.
1644	J. Milton's *Areopagitica* published, 'a speech . . . for the liberty of the unlicensed printing, to the Parliament of England'.

RECREATION AND FASHION

1643–1644	The Royalist court at Oxford retains Cavalier fashion and social habits, encouraging plays and musical entertainments banned by the parliamentary Puritans. Parliamentarians tend to wear high crowned hats, stiff brimmed and with plain bands, over straight hair cropped near the ears; they favour plain cloth suits or sleeveless buff coats. Their womenfolk wear severe dark dresses with deep, closed collars. Both men and women abhor jewellery.

RELIGION AND EDUCATION

1643 *Sep.* *25* Westminster Assembly, convened by Parliament, accepts Scottish Solemn League and Covenant, and gives pledge to set up a Presbyterian system of church government.

1644 *Feb.* Book of Common Prayer replaced by the Directory of Public Worship, which prints rubrics and biddings but no prayers.

Apr. Parliament orders a strict observance of Sunday.

Dec. Parliament forbids celebration of Christmas.

AD 1645–1646

1645 *Jan.* *10* Archbp Laud executed on Tower Hill.

14 Commons appoint Fairfax as Commander-in-Chief in succession to E. of Essex; Cromwell emerges as leader of the Puritan Independents against the Presbyterian majority in the Commons.

29 Armistice talks open at Uxbridge.

Feb. *2* Montrose defeats Covenanters at Ψ Inverlochy.

22 Uxbridge talks fail.

Mar.–Apr. Cromwell prominent in organizing and training the New Model Army.

Mar. *4* P. of Wales leaves Oxford for Bristol as nominal C.-in-C. in the West Country.

Apr. *3* H. of Lords approves the Self-Denying Ordinance.

May *9* Montrose again defeats Covenanters, at Ψ Auldearn.

Jun. *1* P. Rupert's army captures and sacks Leicester.

10 Cromwell confirmed as Lieutenant-General of Cavalry despite the Ordinance.

14 Fairfax and Cromwell inflict heavy defeat on Charles I and P. Rupert at Ψ Naseby.

Jul. *10* Cromwell victorious at Ψ Langport, Somerset.

Sep. *10* P. Rupert shocks Charles by surrendering Bristol.

13 Covenanters, under David Leslie, surprise and rout Montrose's Royalists at Ψ Philiphaugh, near Selkirk.

24 Ψ Rowton Heath, Chester: Charles sees cavalry defeated.

Oct. *8* Cromwell orders bombardment of Basing House, Hants, to end 2-year siege.

1646 *Mar.* *13* Royalists in Cornwall capitulate to Fairfax at Truro.

21 Sir Jacob Astley, commanding last Royalist army in the field, surrenders at Stow-on-the-Wold.

Apr. *13* City of Exeter surrenders to Fairfax.

15 P. of Wales escapes from Scilly Isles to Jersey.

27 Charles I leaves Oxford in disguise.

May *5* Charles surrenders to the Scottish Covenanter army at Southwell, Notts.

9 Scots escort Charles to Newcastle.

Jun.	24	Oxford surrenders, effectively ending the Civil War.
Jul.	30	Charles receives Parliamentary Commissioners at Newcastle with proposals for a settlement: he must accept abolition of episcopacy and other church reforms and allow Parliament to control army for 20 years.
Oct.	17	Charles offers compromise over church reform and control of army; rejected by Parliament.
Dec.	24	With French help, Charles tries to elude his Scottish guards; escape is frustrated.

LITERATURE AND SCHOLARSHIP

| 1645 | Leveller ideas publicized in pamphlet by John Lilburne, *England's Birthright*. Edmund Waller *Poems* printed (showing early use of heroic couplets). |
| 1646 | Sir Thomas Browne publishes *Pseudoxia Epidemica* (often called *Vulgar Errors*), learned study of common misconceptions. J. Suckling's *Fragmenta Aurea* published (posthumous collected writings). Publication of Henry Vaughan's *Poems with the Tenth Satire of Juvenal Englished*. |

RELIGION AND EDUCATION

| 1646 | Puritan soldiers sack and burn manor-house and church at Little Gidding, Huntingdonshire, where in 1621 Nicholas Ferrar had set up an Anglican community of prayer. |
| Oct. | Episcopacy formally abolished. |

AD 1647–1648

1647 Jan.	30	Scots agree to hand over Charles I to Parliamentary Commissioners in return for £400,000 army back pay.
Feb.	14	Parliament interns Charles at Holdenby House, Northants.
Mar.	15	Harlech is last royalist fortress to capitulate.
May	15–18	Presbyterians in Commons wish to disband army, thus widening breach with Independents.
Jun.	3	Cornet George Joyce seizes Charles at Holdenby House and escorts him to Newmarket as prisoner of the army.
	6	Charles receives Cromwell, Henry Ireton and Fairfax for talks at Childerley Hall, Cambridge.
Jul.	23	Charles shown Cromwell's compromise settlement, the Heads of the Proposals.
Aug.		Matthew Hopkins, 'Witch-Finder General' of East Anglia, having supervised over 200 executions in 2 years, is found guilty of witchcraft by his own test of floating, when bound, in water; hanged at Bury St Edmunds.
	6	Cromwell's army enters London to control Parliament.
	13–14	Charles, prevaricating over acceptance of Proposals, is moved to Hampton Court.

Oct.		Levellers draw up the Agreement of the People: radical parliamentary reform; tolerance of Protestant sects.
	28	Cromwell presides over the early 'Putney Debates' (to 5 Nov.): army discussions of the Leveller proposals at meetings in St Mary's Church, Putney.
Nov. 11		Charles escapes to Carisbrooke, I. of Wight.
Dec. 26		The Engagement: Charles and Scots agree on Presbyterianism for 3 years and joint action against Independents.
1648 *Jan. 3*		Vote of No Addresses: Commons pledge not to negotiate with Charles I.
Mar. 8		Welsh rebellion; Royalists seize Pembroke.
Apr. 30		Capture of Berwick and Carlisle by Royalists, with Scottish support, marks coming of Second Civil War.
May and Jun.		Risings in Kent and Essex and pro-Royalist mutiny in the fleet.
Jun.–Jul.		Cromwell besieges Pembroke Castle for 6 weeks.
Aug. 17–19		Cromwell defeats Scottish invaders at Ψ Preston, effectively ending Second Civil War.
Nov. 20		Ireton issues 'Remonstrance of the Army' to Parliament demanding the king's trial.
Dec. 6		Colonel Thomas Pride purges the Commons of dissidents so as to facilitate the king's trial.

FINE ARTS AND ARCHITECTURE

1647 Peter Lely paints Charles I and the D. of York.

LITERATURE AND SCHOLARSHIP

1648 Thomas Gage's *The English American, His Travail by Sea and Land* stimulates Cromwell's imperialism.

Robert Herrick publishes *Hesperides* (secular poems) and *Noble Numbers* (religious).

MUSIC AND DRAMA

1648 *Feb.* New ordinances against plays: fines on actors; theatres to be pulled down.

RECREATION AND FASHION

1647 *Mar.* Ordinances ban bear-baiting and folk dancing.

Dec. Youths charged at Canterbury with playing football 'and brawling thereafter' on Christmas Day.

Events Elsewhere

1648 *Jul.*	*26*	Riots in Paris, the first 'Fronde'.
Oct.	*24*	Peace Ty of Westphalia: ends Thirty Years War.

AD 1649–1650

1649	Jan.	20–27	Trial of Charles I in Westminster Hall.
		30	Charles beheaded outside Banqueting House, Whitehall.
	Feb.	5	Charles II proclaimed King in Edinburgh; in Jersey, 16 Feb.
	Mar.	17	Parliament abolishes 'the office of a king'.
		19	Parliament abolishes H. of Lords.
		28	Lilburne accused of sedition by Commons.
	Apr.	19	The Diggers (a splinter group of Levellers) dispersed by troops after taking communal possession of land at St George's Hill, Weybridge.
	May	13	Cromwell suppresses Leveller mutiny at Burford, Oxon.
		14	Treason Act transfers to Parliament the status hitherto possessed by Crown.
		17	Leveller mutiny ringleaders shot in Burford churchyard.
		29	'England' proclaimed 'a Commonwealth, or a Free State'.
	Aug.	15	Cromwell lands in Ireland to suppress widespread Royalist rebellion.
	Sep.	11	Cromwell's troops capture and sack Drogheda.
	Oct.	11	Sack of Wexford.
1650	Apr.	26	Premature Scottish rising suppressed when Montrose is defeated at Ψ Carbisdale.
	May	20	Cromwell returns to England from Ireland.
		21	Montrose hanged in Edinburgh.
	Jun.	28	Cromwell leaves London for Scotland.
	Jul.	3	Charles II arrives at Speymouth from Holland and pledges himself to uphold the Covenants and Presbyterianism.
	Sep.	3	Cromwell defeats Scots under David Leslie at Ψ Dunbar and occupies the lowlands.
	Dec.	24	Edinburgh Castle surrenders to Cromwell after 108-day siege.

LITERATURE AND SCHOLARSHIP

1649		J. Milton defends deposition of tyrants in *The Tenure of Kings and Magistrates*; hostile to Presbyters.
		J. Lilburne publishes *An Agreement of the Free People of England*.
		Richard Lovelace's *Lucasta; Epodes, Odes, Sonnets, Songs* published; prepared by him for publication while imprisoned.
	Feb.	Anon.: *Eikon Basilike*, 'A Portrait of His Sacred Majesty in his Solitudes and Sufferings'; regarded as Charles I's final meditations; Bp John Gauden of Worcester probable author; 47 editions.
	Mar.	J. Milton refutes *Eikon Basilike* in *Eikonoklastes*.
	Apr. 20	Gerard Winstanley publishes *The True Levellers' Standard Advance*, communistic manifesto.
1650		Richard Baxter publishes *The Saints Everlasting Rest*, the devotional classic of Puritanism.
		J. Lilburne writes *England's Chains*, allegedly seditious pamphlet.

| 1650 (−1654) | James Ussher, former Archbp of Dublin, publishes *Annales Veteris et Novi Testamenti*, scriptural chronology dating the Creation at 4004 BC. |

MUSIC AND DRAMA

| 1649 | Despite Puritan restraints, Sir Balthazar Gerbier opens an academy in Bethnal Green in 1649 to teach music, dancing and 'declamation'. |
| 1650 | John Playford publishes *The English Dancing Master*. |

RELIGION AND EDUCATION

1649	Maryland colonial assembly grants religious toleration to all believers in the Trinity.
Feb.–Mar.	Fifth Monarchy sectarians active in Norfolk.
1650	'Friends of the Truth', followers of the preacher George Fox for about 3 years, first described as Quakers.

AD 1651–1655

1651	Jan.	1	Charles II crowned at Scone.
	Aug.	5	Charles and Scottish army cross the border.
	Sep.	3	Cromwell defeats Charles at Ψ Worcester.
		6	Charles hides from Cromwellian troops in oak tree at Boscobel House, Shifnal, Shropshire.
		21	Charles narrowly escapes capture at Bridport, Dorset.
	Oct.	9	First Navigation Act gives monopoly in foreign trade to English shipping, causing friction with Dutch.
		15	Charles smuggled out of Southwick, West Sussex, in brig sailing to Normandy.
		21	Limerick surrenders to Ireton after 146-day siege.
1652	Feb.	10	Act of Pardon and Oblivion: favours reconciliation.
	May	19	Admiral Robert Blake defeats Dutch squadron under Tromp off Dover.
	Jun.	30	England declares war on Netherlands.
	Nov.	30	Blake defeated by Dutch off Dungeness.
1653	Apr.	20	Cromwell's 'expulsion of the Rump' dissolves Long Parliament, which was seeking to perpetuate itself.
	Jun.	3	Blake defeats Tromp at sea off North Foreland in running battle begun on 2 Jun. off Suffolk coast.
	Jul.	4	Unsuccessful experiment with nominated assembly: 'Barebones Parliament' (to 12 Dec.).
	Dec.	16	Instrument of Government, a written constitution for England, Wales, Scotland and Ireland: Cromwell becomes Protector, with triennial unicameral Parliament.

1654	Apr.	5	Peace Ty of Westminster ends first Dutch War: Dutch to respect Navigation Act.
	Aug.		Cromwell approves the 'Western Design': an anti-Spanish expedition to the Caribbean.
	Sep.	3	First Parliament of the Protectorate meets.
		12–15	Staunch republicans criticize Cromwell's ambitions.
1655	Jan.	22	Cromwell dissolves first Protectorate Parliament.
	Mar.	11–14	Rising in Wiltshire under Col. Penruddock suppressed.
	Apr.	28	Blake routs Barbary pirates of Algiers.
	May		Western Design: Jamaica captured.
	Aug.	9	Administrative division of England into 11 districts, each governed by a Major-General.
	Oct.	24	Ty with France: provides for joint action against Spain and exclusion of Charles II.
	Dec.	4	Cromwell convinces his Council of the justice of readmitting Jews to England.

LITERATURE AND SCHOLARSHIP

1651	T. Hobbes publishes *Leviathan*.
1653	Izaak Walton publishes first edition of *The Compleat Angler*.
1655	John Wallis publishes *Arithmetica Infinitorum*, starting-point for differential calculus.

MUSIC AND DRAMA

1652	John Hilton prints his *Catch That Catch Can* (rounds, etc.).

RECREATION AND FASHION

1651	England's first coffee house opened: High Street, Oxford.

RELIGION AND EDUCATION

1654	Commission of Triers: fills vacant Anglican benefices with Puritan ministers.

SCIENCE AND INVENTION

1651	William Harvey publishes *Exercitationes de Generatione Animalium*, pioneer study of the development of the embryo.

VOYAGES AND EXPLORATION

1654	Commercial treaties with Sweden (Apr.) and Denmark (Jul.) open up the Baltic to British ships.

AD 1656–1660

1656 *Feb.* 24 Spain declares war on Britain.
Sep. 9 Blake captures Spanish treasure ships off Cadiz.
17 Second Protectorate Parliament summoned.

1657 *Jan.* Regional authority of Major-Generals abolished.
23 Thanksgiving services held for Cromwell's preservation from alleged assassination plot.
Mar. 13 Ty with France for attack on Spanish Netherlands.
Apr. 20 Blake destroys Spanish treasure fleet in harbour at Santa Cruz, Tenerife.
May 8 Cromwell rejects offer of the Crown.
25 Humble Petition and Advice: enhances Cromwell's power and provides H. of Lords with nominated life peers.
Jun. 26 Cromwell invested as Lord Protector of England, Scotland and Ireland in Westminster Hall.

1658 *Feb.* 4 Second Protectorate Parliament dissolved.
Apr. Stage-coach service first advertised: London to Exeter, York and Chester, each in 4 days.
Jun. 4 Anglo-French victory over Spanish in Ψ of the Dunes leads to British acquisition of Dunkirk.
Aug. 30 Hurricane winds sweep S. England; worst storms for centuries.
Sep. 3 Cromwell dies at Whitehall after fortnight's illness; his son Richard named as successor.

1659 *May* 25 Richard Cromwell resigns; subsequent conflict between army and survivors of Long Parliament.
Dec. 16 George Monk, commanding general in Scotland, urges summoning of free Parliament to check mounting anarchy.

1660 *Jan.* 1 Monk leads army across the Tweed; enters London, 3 Feb.
Apr. 4 Declaration of Breda: Charles II promises amnesty, liberty of conscience, settlement of land claims and army back pay.
25 Convention Parliament (two Houses) meets.
May 1 Parliament votes for Restoration.
25 Charles welcomed at Dover; enters London, 29 May.
Oct. 13 26 surviving regicides hanged in Whitehall.

LITERATURE AND SCHOLARSHIP

1656 James Harington publishes *The Commonwealth of Oceana*, Utopian constitutional study, with historical analysis.
Abraham Cowley's *Poems* introduce new ode style.

1660 J. Milton publishes *Ready and Easy Way to Establish a Free Commonwealth*.
John Dryden celebrates Charles II's return in *Astraea Redux*.

	Jan. 1	First entry in diary of Samuel Pepys.

MUSIC AND DRAMA

1656	*Sep.*	First English opera, *The Siege of Rhodes*, performed at Rutland House, London; Henry Lawes among 5 composers of the music; William Davenant's libretto.

RECREATION AND FASHION

1657	*Jun.*	A chocolate house (cocoa) and coffee houses known to flourish in St James's parish, Westminster.
1658		Tea introduced into England, from China by way of Holland.

RELIGION AND EDUCATION

1657		Cromwell establishes Durham College (suppressed 1660).
1660	*Oct.* 25	Charles II's abortive proposal of a modified episcopacy, with some Presbyterian ministers becoming bishops.

SCIENCE AND INVENTION

1656–1659		Robert Boyle and Robert Hooke conduct experiments on air pump and combustion at Oxford.
1660	*Nov.*	The Royal Society for the Improvement of Natural Knowledge founded at Gresham College, London.

AD 1661–1665

1661	*Jan.* 30	Corpses of Cromwell and Ireton hanged at Tyburn.
	Apr. 20	Chancellor Edward Hyde made E. of Clarendon.
	23	Charles II's Westminster coronation.
	May 8	Charles opens Cavalier Parliament (to 1679).
	Jun. 23	Ty of alliance with Portugal: Tangier and Bombay ceded as dowry for Charles to marry K. of Portugal's daughter.
	Dec. 20	Corporation Act: English and Welsh magistrates must renounce the Covenant and accept Anglican sacraments.
1662	*Apr.*	Hearth tax of 2s for each fireplace.
	May 19	Act of Uniformity: enforces revised Anglican Prayer Book.
	21	Charles II marries Catherine of Braganza at Portsmouth.
	Oct. 27	Dunkirk sold to France for £400,000.
	Nov. 10	Charles creates James Crofts, his illegitimate son by Lucy Walter, D. of Monmouth.
1663		Charles II encourages colonialism by charters to Royal Africa Company (Jan.), Carolina (March), Rhode Island (July).
	Feb.	Pressure from Commons makes Charles withdraw proposed Declaration

of Indulgence.

1664	May		Conventicle Act: bans unauthorized religious meetings of more than 5 people.
	Aug.	18	English squadron seizes New Amsterdam from Dutch; renamed New York.
		22	Order in Council assures Jews of royal protection so long as they 'demean themselves peaceably and quietly'.
	Nov.		Severe frost; R. Thames frozen (to Mar. 1665).
1665	Feb.		Second Anglo-Dutch War begins, after skirmishes at sea and in colonies.
	Apr.	15	Great Plague of London (to Dec.); 70,000 deaths.
	Jul.	3	Naval victory over Dutch off Lowestoft.
	Oct.	1	Court and Parliament move to Oxford because of plague.
		18	Five Mile Act: keeps nonconformist ex-ministers from vicinity of towns where they formerly held benefices.

FINE ARTS AND ARCHITECTURE

| 1661 | Peter Lely appointed court painter. |
| 1664 | Christopher Wren begins his first major work, the Sheldonian Theatre, Oxford (completed 1669). |

LITERATURE AND SCHOLARSHIP

| 1662–1663 | Samuel Butler publishes satire, *Hudibras*, Parts 1 and 2. |

MUSIC AND DRAMA

1661		Matthew Locke appointed Composer in Ordinary to the King.
	Aug. 28	Davenant produces first *Hamlet* with scenery, at his Lincoln's Inn Theatre, Portugal Street.
1662		Royal Letters Patent give London theatre monopoly to Davenant and Thomas Killigrew.
1663	May 7	Killigrew opens Theatre Royal, Drury Lane, with *The Humorous Lieutenant*.

RECREATION AND FASHION

| 1661 | Oct. 1 | Race from Greenwich to Gravesend and back between yachts of Charles II and D. of York makes the sport fashionable. |

RELIGION AND EDUCATION

1661	Apr. 15	Savoy Conference (12 bishops and 12 Presbyterians) fails to agree on Prayer Book revision (to 21 Jul.).
	Dec.	Convocations of Canterbury and York complete revision of the Prayer Book.
1662	Aug. 24	Revised Prayer Book imposed on England and Wales; 2,000 nonconforming ministers ejected from their livings.

SCIENCE AND INVENTION

1661		R. Boyle's *The Sceptical Chemist* questions accepted theories.
1662		Boyle's Law on pressure of gas formulated.
	Apr. 22	Charles II extends his patronage to the Royal Society with grant of

1665   foundation charter.
        R. Hooke's *Micrographia* describes a microscope.

AD 1666–1670

1666 *Jan.* 16   France joins Holland in war against England.
     Feb. 1   Charles II and his court return to London after the Plague.
     Jun. 1–4   The Four Days' Battle: inconclusive naval action in southern North Sea in
                  which the Dutch admiral Ruyter engages a smaller English fleet under the D.
                  of Albemarle (formerly G. Monk), who is saved from defeat by the coming of
                  P. Rupert's squadron.
     Jul. 25   Albemarle victorious over Dutch off Orfordness.
     Sep. 2   Great Fire of London begins in Pudding Lane.
            4   Great Fire destroys St Paul's Cathedral.
            6   Great Fire ends: 460 acres ravaged; 9 deaths; 13,300 buildings destroyed.
     Nov. 28   Pentland Rising, of Scottish Covenanters, defeated by Sir Thomas Dalyel at
                  Rullion Green.

1667 *Jun.* 12   'The Black Day': Dutch fleet, under Ruyter, attacks Sheerness, sails up the
                 Medway to Chatham, sinks 3 'first-raters' and tows flagship back to
                 Holland.
     Jul. 21   Peace Ty of Breda: England confirmed in possession of New York (taken
                 from the Dutch in 1665).
     Aug. 30   Clarendon, blamed for Medway defeat, resigns.
     Aug. 31   The Cabal administration (to Jun. 1673): Charles II's chief ministers are Sir
                 Thomas Clifford, E. of Arlington, the 2nd D. of Buckingham, Lord Ashley,
                 D. of Lauderdale.
     Nov. 29   Clarendon, threatened with impeachment, flees to France.

1667 *Dec.*   Probable first meeting of Charles II and Nell Gwynne.

1668 *Jan.* 28   English ambassador Sir William Temple negotiates anti-French Triple
                 Alliance treaty with Dutch and Swedes.
     May 2   Louis XIV accepts a general peace: Ty of Aix-la-Chapelle.

1670 *May* 22   Secret Anglo-French Ty of Dover: Charles to receive subsidies from Louis
                 XIV, declare himself a Roman Catholic at a suitable moment; the 2
                 kingdoms to collaborate in war on Holland.

                 FINE ARTS AND ARCHITECTURE
1666–1667   Lely paints portraits of the Admirals, Greenwich.

                 LITERATURE AND SCHOLARSHIP
1667   J. Dryden publishes long poem *Annus Mirabilis*.
                 J. Milton's *Paradise Lost* published (written 1658–63).

1668	Mrs Aphra Behn writes *Oroonoko, or the History of the Royal Slave*, novel based on a visit to Surinam in 1663; published in 1688.
Apr. 13	Charles appoints Dryden as the Poet Laureate, making him Historiographer Royal in 1670.
1669 *May 31*	Failing eyesight forces Pepys to cease writing his diary.

MUSIC AND DRAMA

| 1668 | John Blow, composer of over 100 anthems, appointed organist at Westminster Abbey. |
| 1670 | Thomas Betterton has the lead in Aphra Behn's first play, *The Forced Marriage*, at Lincoln's Inn Theatre. |

RELIGION AND EDUCATION

| 1668 | William Penn is imprisoned for *The Sandy Foundation Shaken*, a pamphlet attacking Trinitarian beliefs. In the Tower he writes *No Cross, No Crown* (1669), a Quaker classic. |

RECREATION AND FASHION

| 1666–1669 | Charles II popularizes wearing of coat, waistcoat and curled periwig; men and women favour colour, with ribbons, bows and silk ruffles. |

SCIENCE AND INVENTION

| 1669 *Oct. 29* | Isaac Newton appointed Lucasian Professor of Mathematics at Cambridge. |

AD 1671–1675

1671 *Apr.*	Charles II prorogues English Parliament.
1672 *Jan.* 2	Imminent threat of national bankruptcy leads to suspension of Exchequer cash payments for a year.
Mar. 15	Charles II issues Declaration of Indulgence: penal laws against Catholics and dissenters lifted.
17	Third Anglo-Dutch War begins; Charles allied to France.
May 28	Anglo-Dutch naval Ψ Southwold Bay indecisive.
Jun.	Scottish Parliament refuses to grant taxes for the war against Protestant Holland.
Nov. 17	Ashley made E. of Shaftesbury and Lord Chancellor.
1673 *Feb.*	English Parliament reassembles, will not vote funds until Declaration of Indulgence is withdrawn.
Mar. 8	Charles II revokes Declaration of Indulgence.
29	Parliament prorogued, having granted subsidy and passed Test Act requiring all office-holders to declare their rejection of Catholic doctrines of the mass and to certify that they recently received Anglican communion.

Jun.	*12*	Test Act forces James, D. of York, as a Roman Catholic, to retire as Lord High Admiral.
	19	Thomas Osborne made Lord Treasurer.
Nov. 9		Charles dismisses Shaftesbury for hostility to D. of York; end of Cabal; Osborne is chief minister.
	23	D. of York marries Mary of Modena, despite Parliament's opposition to an Italian marriage.
1674 *Feb.* 9		Under pressure from Parliament, Charles II accepts peace Ty of Westminster with the Dutch.
Jun.		Thomas Osborne becomes E. of Danby.
1675 *Apr.* *13*		Charles II opens a 9-week Parliament: Commons refuse to vote further funds; Shaftesbury leads the Opposition.

FINE ARTS AND ARCHITECTURE

1672	John Dwight establishes Fulham pottery, earliest salt-glazed domestic ware.
1672–1679	Wren rebuilds St Stephen's, Walbrook, regarded by contemporaries as his masterpiece.
1675 *Jun.*	Foundation stone of Wren's new St Paul's Cathedral laid.

LITERATURE AND SCHOLARSHIP

1671	J. Milton's *Paradise Regained*, epic poem in 4 books, published in same volume as the tragedy *Samson Agonistes*.

MUSIC AND DRAMA

1672		First public concerts organized by the royal violinist John Banister at Whitefriars, off Fleet Street.
Jun.	*25*	Theatre Royal, Drury Lane, destroyed by fire.
1673		J. Dryden publishes comedy *Marriage à la Mode*; performed 1672.
1674 *Mar.*	*26*	Wren's rebuilt Theatre Royal opens in Drury Lane.
1675		William Wycherley's *The Country Wife*, satirical comedy, performed and published.

RECREATION AND FASHION

1671 *Oct.* *14*	Charles II wins 4-mile Plate Race at Newmarket.
1675	Earliest political club: Green Ribbon Club at King's Head Tavern, Fleet Street, home for Shaftesbury's supporters.

RELIGION AND EDUCATION

1672	John Bunyan, released from Bedford gaol after serving 12 years for preaching without a licence, publishes *A Confession of My Faith and a Reason of My Practice*.

SCIENCE AND INVENTION

1675	John Flamsteed appointed first Astronomer Royal.

Events Elsewhere

1672 *Jul.*   William of Orange, future K. William III, elected Stadtholder of Zeeland and Holland.

AD 1676–1680

1676 *May* 26   Fire of Southwark: burns 625 houses south of R. Thames.
   Sep.–Nov.   First recorded influenza epidemic.

1677 *Feb.* 15   Parliament in session (to 28 May): conflict with Danby and Charles II over attempts by the Commons to dictate foreign policy, especially a Dutch alliance against France.
   Nov. 4   P. Mary of York marries her cousin William of Orange at St James's Palace.

1678 *Aug.* 13   Charles II learns from intermediary of Titus Oates about Roman Catholic plot to kill him; discounts it.
   Sep. 6   Oates tells London magistrate, Sir Edmund Berry Godfrey, of plot to massacre Protestants and put D. of York on throne.
   Oct. 17   Berry Godfrey found murdered on Primrose Hill, London.
      21   Charles opens Parliament, which strongly supports Oates, voting him £1,200 a year pension from the Crown.
   Nov.–Dec.   The height of the 'Popish Plot' mania: arrests of priests, exclusion of Catholics from Parliament, etc.
   Dec. (to   First use of the terms 'Whigs' (for the Country party, an Opposition group
   Feb. 1679)   led by Shaftesbury) and 'Tories' (for the Court party, led by Danby).
      23   Commons seek to impeach Danby.

1679 *Jan.* 24   Cavalier Parliament at last dissolved.
   Feb. (3rd   General election won by Shaftesbury's Whigs.
   week)
   May 3   Archbp James Sharp of St Andrews murdered at Magus Muir by Covenanter supporters.
      26   Habeas Corpus Amendment Act: upholds civic rights of political prisoners.
      27   Charles II prorogues (later dissolves) Parliament after Exclusion Bill denies D. of York's right to succeed.
   Jun. 22   Covenanter rising defeated by Monmouth at Bothwell Brig.
   Aug. 23–29   Charles feverishly ill at Windsor (recurs May 1680).
   Oct.   General election returns Parliament favouring Exclusion; prorogued by Charles for 12 months before it meets.

1680 *Nov.* 4   In H. of Commons, Shaftesbury secures passage of 2nd Exclusion Bill, keeping York in permanent exile.

| | 15 | H. of Lords rejects Exclusion Bill. |
| | Dec. 4 | P. George Ludwig, future K. George I, reaches London from Hanover in vain attempt to woo his second cousin, P. Anne, future Q. Anne. |

FINE ARTS AND ARCHITECTURE

| 1676(–1684) | Wren's Trinity College Library, Cambridge, built. |

LITERATURE AND SCHOLARSHIP

1677	Andrew Marvell publishes *Account of the Growth of Popery and Arbitrary Government in England*.
1678	S. Butler completes *Hudibras*.
Feb.	First part of Bunyan's *Pilgrim's Progress* published.
1680	Sir Robert Filmer's *Patriarcha, the Natural Power of Kings*, defence of divine right, published (written *c*.1638).

MUSIC AND DRAMA

1677	W. Wycherley publishes *The Plain Dealer*.
1678	J. Dryden stages and publishes *All for Love*, blank verse tragedy.
	Weekly concerts begun by London coal merchant Thomas Britton above stables in Jerusalem Passage, Clerkenwell.
1679	Henry Purcell becomes organist of Westminster Abbey.

RELIGION AND EDUCATION

| 1676 | First Greek Orthodox church in England: at Hog Lane, Soho. |

SCIENCE AND INVENTION

| 1676–1677 | Edmond Halley visits St Helena and makes catalogue of stars in southern hemisphere; published 1679. |

AD 1681–1685

1681	Mar. 14	Charles II grants charter to William Penn for sectarian colony.
	19–28	Parliament at Oxford: dissolved by Charles when it reintroduces Exclusion Bill.
	Jul. 2	Shaftesbury sent to the Tower on treason charge.
	Nov. 24	Shaftesbury acquitted amid wild celebrations.
1682	Feb.	Charles II lays foundation stone of the Chelsea Hospital for wounded and discharged soldiers.
	Nov. 19	Fire of Wapping: 1,500 families made homeless.
	20	Shaftesbury, having planned unsuccessful coup, flees to Holland; dies there 2 months later.

1683	Jun.	21	Rye House Plot to murder Charles II and D. of York discovered.
	Jul.	21	Lord William Russell executed for his part in the plot.
		28	P. Anne marries P. George of Denmark at St James's Palace.
	Aug.		Charles rescinds Titus Oates's annual pension.
	Dec.	7	Algernon Sidney executed for his role in Rye House Plot.
		10	'The Great Frost' (to 4 Feb. 1684); Frost Fair held on R. Thames throughout January.
1684	Jan.		D. of Monmouth goes into exile in Holland.
	Mar.	15	John Nevison, highwayman and crime 'king' of West Riding, hanged for murder at York.
	May		Revision of city charters (including London) begins, to check control of corporations by Whig factions.
1685	Feb.	6	Charles II dies at Whitehall; succeeded by D. of York.
	Apr.	23	Coronation of James II and Mary of Modena with Anglican rites in Westminster Abbey.
	May	20/22	Titus Oates whipped through streets of London.
	Jun.	11	D. of Monmouth lands at Lyme Regis to lead Protestant rising against James II.
	Jul.	6	Monmouth defeated at Sedgemoor by royalist army, effective commander John Churchill.
		15	Monmouth executed on Tower Hill.
	Sep.	2–24	Judge Jeffreys conducts Bloody Assize in the West Country against alleged supporters of Monmouth.
		28	Jeffreys made Lord Chancellor.

FINE ARTS AND ARCHITECTURE

1681–1682	Tom Tower, Christ Church, Oxford, built; designed by Wren.
1682–1692	Wren's Chelsea Hospital built.

LITERATURE AND SCHOLARSHIP

1681–1682	J. Dryden publishes *Absalom and Achitophel*.
1682	Sir William Petty publishes *Quantulumcumque, or A Tract concerning Money*.
	Advocates Library, Edinburgh, founded by Sir George Mackenzie of Rosehaugh.
1683 May	D. of York opens Ashmolean Museum, Broad Street, Oxford; first in England.

MUSIC AND DRAMA

1682	Thomas Otway's tragedy *Venice Preserved* produced.

SCIENCE AND INVENTION

1683–1684	Newton demonstrates his theory of gravitation at meetings of the Royal Society.

1684		Hooke invents optical telegraph.
1685		Charles II appoints John Rose as first English Royal Gardener.
	Sep.	First organized street lighting: Edward Hemming authorized to light main London streets with oil lamps outside every tenth house on moonless winter nights.

Events Elsewhere

| 1685 | *Oct.* | *18* | Louis XIV revokes Edict of Nantes, prompting mass migration of Huguenots. |

AD 1686–1688

1686	*Jun.*	*20*	Judgment in *Godden* v. *Hales*, a collusive court action, affirms James II's dispensing rights over the Test Act.
	Jul.	*10*	James creates a new Court of Ecclesiastical Commission.
		17	James makes 4 Catholic peers Privy Councillors.
	Aug.–Sep.		James forms a military camp on Hounslow Heath, mainly under Catholic officers.
1687	*Feb.*	*17*	Catholic army commander Richard Talbot, E. of Tyrconnell, becomes Lord Deputy in Ireland.
	Apr.	*2*	Declaration of Indulgence: suspends penal laws against Catholics and dissenters.
	Jul.	*3*	James II receives papal nuncio, who comes to Windsor in state with a cavalcade of 36 carriages.
	Sep.	*4*	James in Oxford, seeking to expel the Fellows of Magdalen for refusing to catholicize their college.
1688	*May*	*4*	Order in Council requires revised Declaration of Indulgence to be read in all Anglican churches on two successive Sundays.
	May	*18*	Archbp William Sancroft of Canterbury and 6 other bishops protest at Order in Council.
	Jun.	*8*	Archbp Sancroft and bishops imprisoned in the Tower.
		10	Q. Mary of Modena gives birth to P. James Francis Edward ('The Old Pretender'); created P. of Wales in first week of July.
		30	7 bishops, tried for seditious libel, acquitted.
			7 Whig and Tory peers send secret letter inviting William of Orange 'to defend the liberties of England'.
	Nov.	*5*	William of Orange lands at Torbay with army which includes 3,000 Swiss mercenaries and 200 Surinamese.
		9–27	William in Exeter, gathering support.
		24	John Churchill, Lieutenant-General of James I's army, defects and joins William of Orange.

Dec.	*9*	Mary of Modena and her baby cross to France.
	12	James detained by magistrates at Faversham when seeking to reach France.
	18	William enters London, welcomed by the aldermen and sheriffs.
	25	James lands at Ambleteuse to begin his exile.
	27	William agrees to a request from members of Charles II's last Parliament that he should take over the provisional government and issue writs for a Convention Parliament.

LITERATURE AND SCHOLARSHIP

1687	J. Dryden publishes *The Hind and the Panther* and *Song for St Cecilia's Day*.
1688 *Dec.*	Dryden dismissed as Poet Laureate and Historiographer Royal; succeeded in 1689 by Whig dramatist Thomas Shadwell.

SCIENCE AND INVENTION

1686 *Jul.*	*5*	Pepys, as President of the Royal Society, orders printing of Newton's *Philosophiae Naturalis Principia Mathematica*, on gravitation; published 1687.

Events Elsewhere

1687 *Sep.*	*26*	Parthenon at Athens wrecked by explosion during Venetian bombardment of Turkish positions on Acropolis.

AD 1689–1690

1689 *Jan.*	*22*	Convention Parliament meets.
	28	H. of Commons' Resolution that James II 'has abdicated the Government and that the throne is thereby vacant'.
Feb.	*12*	Declaration of Rights: declares James II's constitutional practices illegal. P. Mary arrives in London from Holland.
	13	Accession of K. William III and Q. Mary II proclaimed in Whitehall.
Mar.	*12*	James II lands at Kinsale, Ireland.
Apr.	*11*	Joint coronation of William and Mary at Westminster. John Churchill created E. of Marlborough.
	20	Start of 17-weeks siege of Ulster Protestants in Londonderry.
May	*7*	James II opens a Parliament in Dublin.
	12	England and Holland enter War of League of Augsburg against France.
	24	Toleration Act: grants freedom of worship to most Protestants; excludes Catholics and Unitarians.
Jul.	*27*	Jacobite supporters of K. James in Scottish Highlands defeat Covenanter army at Killicrankie.
Aug.	*21*	Jacobite rising repulsed at Dunkeld.
	23	Count Schomberg lands in County Down with mercenary army to uphold

			William and Mary's authority.
	Dec.		William and Mary make Kensington Palace their principal London residence.
1690	Jun.	24	William III lands at Carrickfergus.
		30	French defeat Anglo-Dutch fleet off Beachy Head, but fail to exploit victory.
	Jul.	1	William III defeats James II at Ψ of the Boyne.
		20	James II arrives back in France.
		25	French raid and burn Teignmouth, Devon.
	Sep.	6	William returns to England, having summoned Marlborough to take command in Ireland.
		27	Marlborough captures Cork (Corcaigh); also Kinsale, 15 Oct.
	Oct.		Ty with the Moghul Emperor: allows English to found a trading settlement at Calcutta.
	Oct.–Dec.		Much land confiscation in Ireland, encouraging settlement of Scottish Protestant farmers.

LITERATURE AND SCHOLARSHIP

1689   John Locke publishes *On Civil Government*, and his *Letter on Toleration*.

1690   Locke's *Essay concerning Human Understanding* pioneers the English analytical philosophy of the mind.

MUSIC AND DRAMA

1689 Dec.   Purcell's opera *Dido and Aeneas* first performed at 'gentlewomen's boarding school' in Chelsea.

RELIGION AND EDUCATION

1689	Jul.	1	Presbyterianism again replaces episcopacy in Scotland.
	Aug.	1	Archbp Sancroft, 8 bishops and 400 clergy suspended for refusing to take oath of allegiance, considering their oath sworn to James II was still valid.
1690	Feb.	1	The suspended 'Non-Jurors' deprived of their livings by Act of Parliament.

Events Elsewhere

1689 Sep. 12   Peter the Great (aged 17) overturns regency of his half-sister Sophia and becomes effective Tsar of Russia.

AD 1691–1695

1691	Jul.	12	Decisive defeat of Irish Jacobites at Ψ Aughrim.
	Aug.		William III offers pardon to all rebellious Highlanders who swear allegiance by end of year.
	Oct.	3	Ty of Limerick seeks pacification of Ireland: Catholics promised liberties possessed under Charles II.

1692	Jan.	10	Marlborough dismissed for suspected treasonable contacts with James II.
		16	William III signs generalized order for disciplining Highlanders who have not sworn allegiance.
	Feb.	13	MacDonald clan massacred at Glencoe by troops commanded by Captain Robert Campbell of Glenlyon.
		19	P. Anne withdraws from court after quarrels with her sister Q. Mary, who resents her close friendship with Sarah, Lady Marlborough.
	Mar.	4	William begins campaign against French in Netherlands (to 20 Oct.).
	May	5	Q. Mary sends Marlborough to the Tower for alleged treason; released 15 Jun.
		24	English naval victory off La Hogue frustrates French and Jacobite invasion plans.
	Aug.	3	William's Anglo-Dutch army defeated at Ψ Steenkerk.
	by Dec.		Lloyd's coffee house in Tower St, London, has become recognized as main office for marine insurance.
1693	Mar.	14	William III vetoes Triennial Parliament Bill.
1694	May		First mainly Whig government ('junta'): John Somers and E. of Shrewsbury chief ministers.
	Jul.	27	Bank of England established, with William Patterson founder director.
	Dec.	3	Triennial Act: elections at least every 3 years.
		28	Q. Mary II dies from smallpox at Kensington.
1695	Jan.	13	P. Anne returns to court and acts as royal hostess on state occasions over the next 7 years.
	Apr.		Parliament refuses to renew statute requiring the licensing of printed material: effective end of press censorship.
	May	6	D. of Leeds (Danby), last remaining Tory in government, resigns because of alleged taking of bribes.
	May–Oct.		William III serves with army in Netherlands; captures Namur in September.
	Jul.	17	Edinburgh Parliament passes Act creating Bank of Scotland.
	Nov.		General election returns overwhelmingly Whig H. of Commons.

FINE ARTS AND ARCHITECTURE

1694–1695	Sir Godfrey Kneller paints his series of Hampton Court 'beauties'.
1695	William III orders Wren to proceed with Mary II's plan to turn Greenwich Palace into the naval equivalent of Chelsea Hospital.

LITERATURE AND SCHOLARSHIP

1693	William Penn proposes federation of Europe in his *Essay on the Present and Future Peace of Europe*.

MUSIC AND DRAMA

1691	H. Purcell composes opera *King Arthur*.
1693	William Congreve's *Double Dealer* first performed.
1695	Congreve's *Love for Love* reopens Lincoln's Inn Theatre, London.

RECREATION AND FASHION
Tricorne hats become fashionable for men.

RELIGION AND EDUCATION
1693
J. Locke publishes *Ideas on Education*.

VOYAGES AND EXPLORATION
1695
Company of Scotland Trading to the Indies and Africa set up in Edinburgh; supports specifically Scottish expeditions.

AD 1696–1700

1696	Feb.	24	Parliament told of plot to murder William III at Turnham Green.
		27	Commons propose nationwide Oath of Association to defend King and Protestant succession.
	Mar.		Habeas Corpus Act suspended during Jacobite invasion scare.
	Apr.		Window tax introduced in England.
	May		Reminting of silver coinage causes specie shortage before currency is stabilized; value of a guinea reassessed at 21s instead of 30s.
1697	Apr.		Whig government with Somers as Lord Chancellor.
	Sep.	20	Peace Ty of Ryswick: provides truce in war with France; Louis XIV recognizes William III as K. of England.
	Nov.	10	Robert Harley leads Commons Opposition in seeking reduction in size of army.
1698	Jan.	4	Whitehall Palace destroyed by fire.
		10	Peter the Great in England, studying shipbuilding (to 23 Apr.)
	Jun.	16	Marlborough reinstated in army and Privy Council.
	Jul.–Aug.		General election favours 'New Country Party' (Tory).
1699	Jan.	19	Commons resolve that home army should not exceed 7,000 men, all native-born.
	Dec.	1	Affair of Captain Kidd: Commons attempt to censure Whig leaders and William III for having unwittingly helped the pirate fit out his vessel *Adventure* in 1695-6 narrowly fails.
1700	Feb.	3	Fire destroys much of central Edinburgh.
	Apr.	2	Resumption Bill debates: William III attacked for large grants of Irish lands to Dutch favourites.
		10	Parliament asks William to exclude from his Council all foreigners except P. George.
		17	William dismisses Somers in hope of placating Tories.
	Jul.	4	William goes to Holland, threatening to abdicate.
		30	William, D. of Gloucester, last surviving child of P. Anne, dies from smallpox

soon after 11th birthday.

Oct. 18   William returns from Holland; to end political deadlock, agrees to dissolve Parliament.

LITERATURE AND SCHOLARSHIP

1697   Daniel Defoe publishes *An Essay upon Projects*, a stimulating first work; favours income tax and women's education.

MUSIC AND DRAMA

1696   John Vanbrugh's *The Relapse, or Virtue in Danger* is an outstanding success at Drury Lane.

1697   Vanbrugh's *The Provoked Wife* first performed.

1699   George Farquhar's comedy *The Constant Couple* is produced.

1700   Congreve's comedy *The Way of the World* produced but poorly received.

RECREATION AND FASHION

1700   Popularity of Indian printed calicoes leads to a law seeking to ban their importation.

RELIGION AND EDUCATION

1696   John Toland publishes *Christianity not Mysterious*, the seminal work of Deism.

1697 Dec. 2   Wren's St Paul's Cathedral consecrated.

1698   SPCK (Society for Promoting Christian Knowledge) founded by the Revd Thomas Bray.

SCIENCE AND INVENTION

1699   Eddystone Rock, first high-seas lighthouse, completed.

VOYAGES AND EXPLORATION

1698–1699   Abortive attempt to found Scottish colony in Darien Isthmus.

1699–1700   William Dampier explores north-western coast of Australia.

AD 1701–1702

1701 Feb. 23   Captain Kidd hanged as a pirate at Wapping.

May 8   Parliament petitioned by Kentish freeholders to grant funds to William III for war against France.

31   Marlborough made C.-in-C. of English army in Holland.

Jun. 12   Act of Settlement provides for a Protestant succession: Crown to pass, after P. Anne, to James I's granddaughter, Electress Sophia of Hanover.

Aug. 27   Grand Alliance signed at The Hague: Britain, Holland and Habsburg Emperor ally against Louis XIV's attempts to unify France and Spain.

	Sep. 6	James II dies at St Germain; Louis XIV recognizes his son as James III.
1702	Feb.	2 parliamentary Acts make support for the Pretender ('James III') treasonable.
	21	William's horse stumbles on mole-hill near Hampton Court; King breaks collar-bone.
	Mar. 8	K. William III dies at Kensington; accession of Q. Anne.
	11	*Daily Courant*, single sheet newspaper, begins publication in London.
	14	Anne makes Marlborough Captain-General of her army.
	Apr. 23	Q. Anne crowned at Westminster.
	May 4	War declared on France and Spain.
		Sidney Godolphin made Lord Treasurer, serving as chief minister until 1710.
	Jun.–Jul.	General election gives Tories majority of 113 MPs.
	Aug.	Chronic asthma incapacitates P. George (Anne's husband).
	Sep.	Victories for Marlborough from Venlo to Liège (to 12 Oct.).
	Oct. 1	The 'Tory Admiral', Sir George Rooke, destroys or captures Spanish treasure fleet in Vigo Bay.
	24	Q. Anne first shows anger at the anti-Tory prejudice of her confidante, Sarah Marlborough.
	Nov. 12	In Marlborough's honour, Q. Anne revives Elizabethan practice of victory procession through City of London to St Paul's for thanksgiving service.
	Dec. 2	Q. Anne creates Marlborough a duke.

FINE ARTS AND ARCHITECTURE

1702   G. Kneller begins painting 42 Kit-Cat portraits of members of a Whig Club (to 1717).

Completion of main buildings of Castle Howard, Yorkshire; first house of which John Vanbrugh was the architect, collaborating with Nicholas Hawksmoor.

LITERATURE AND SCHOLARSHIP

1701   Jonathan Swift publishes *A Discourse of the Contests and Dissentions between the Nobles and the Commons in Athens and Rome*, pamphlet against the Irish land policy of William and his Dutch favourites.

1702   D. Defoe writes *The True-Born Englishman*, poem satirizing xenophobic prejudice.

MUSIC AND DRAMA

1702   G. Farquhar writes *The Twin Rivals*, melodrama.

RELIGION AND EDUCATION

1702   SPG (Society for the Propagation of the Gospel in Foreign Parts) founded in London to work with SPCK.

SCIENCE AND INVENTION

1701   Jethro Tull, Berkshire farmer, invents sowing drill.

Events Elsewhere

1702 *Feb.*   War of Spanish Succession begins when Louis XIV's grandson Philip of Anjou is received in Madrid as K. Philip V of Spain.

AD 1703–1704

1703 *Apr.–May*   Marlborough, advancing down Rhine, ejects French from Cologne and Bonn.
Apr. 21   Portugal, as ally of Britain, joins Grand Alliance against Louis XIV.
26   The Great Storm: hurricane sweeps S. England.
Sep.   Scottish Parliament's Act of Security asserts right to choose Anne's Protestant successor unless England satisfies 'Scotland as to her conditions of government and of complete freedom and equality of trade'.
Dec. 16   Methuen Ty with Portuguese: Portugal to import all its woollen goods from England and Scotland; Portuguese wine to be admitted at one-third less duty than French wine.

1704 *Apr. 20*   Henry St John, a Tory, joins Godolphin's government as Secretary for War.
May 8   Marlborough inspects army of 19,000 men at Bedburg (north-west of Cologne) before beginning march to R. Danube.
18   Harley made a Secretary of State, strengthening Tory influence in government.
30   Marlborough encamps at Mundelsheim (east of Heilbronn) where he meets chief allied commander, Prince Eugene.
Jun. 21   Marlborough's troops storm the Schellenberg, outside Donauworth on R. Danube.
Jul. 24   Admiral Rooke (politically a Tory) captures Gibraltar after 3-day fleet bombardment.
Aug. 2
(Aug. 13 NS)   Marlborough and P. Eugene defeat the French, led by Marshal Tallard, at Ψ Blenheim.
5   Q. Anne reluctantly signs Scottish Act of Security.
10   News of Blenheim reaches England.
13   Rooke defeats Franco-Spanish fleet seeking to recover Gibraltar in Ψ Velez Malaga, off Marbella.
Nov. 28   Godolphin and Whigs defeat 'the Tack', a Tory attempt in Commons to pass an Occasional Conformity Bill, requiring civil, naval and military office-holders to be practising Anglicans.
29   Q. Anne breaks precedent by attending debates in H. of Lords (to 16 Dec.).

FINE ARTS AND ARCHITECTURE
1704   Thomas Archer designs North Front, Chatsworth.

1703 *May*   D. Defoe, a Dissenter, pilloried and imprisoned for 6 months for his ironical pamphlet, *The Shortest Way with Dissenters*.

1704   'Q. Anne's Bounty': Q. Anne sets up fund to use money confiscated by Henry VIII to augment livings of poorer Anglican clergy.

Irish 'Act to prevent the further growth of popery' imposes greater restraints on Catholics.

J. Swift's *A Tale of a Tub* satirizes theological disputes.

RECREATION AND FASHION

1703   Celia Fiennes completes 18 years of riding side-saddle through England; her comprehensive travel journal not published until 1888.

1703–1704   Taking of snuff becomes fashionable after capture of large quantities in Spanish ships at Vigo.

1704   Richard Nash ('Beau Nash') becomes master of ceremonies at Bath; arbiter of fashion there for 50 years.

Following the Methuen Ty, port wine rapidly becomes fashionable because of low excise duty.

Events Elsewhere

1703 *May 16*   Peter the Great founds St Petersburg (Leningrad).

AD 1705–1706

1705 *Jan. 3*   Blenheim victory parade in London.
Feb. 17   Act of Parliament assigns royal manor of Woodstock to D. of Marlborough.
Apr. 18   Q. Anne visits Cambridge and knights Newton.
May–Jun.   Marlborough at Trier prepares to advance up R. Moselle, but fails to penetrate into France.
May   Indecisive general election, with neither Tories nor Whigs having absolute majority.
Sep. 25   Anne appoints commissioners to negotiate political union with Scotland.
Oct. 4   Charles Mordaunt, E. of Peterborough, leads Anglo-Dutch expedition which captures Barcelona.

1706 *Jan.–Feb.*   Peterborough's army advances through Catalonia on Valencia.
Feb.   Regency Act: provides for transition to Hanoverian rule when Q. Anne dies.
Act of Naturalization: makes all Protestant members of Hanoverian royal family British citizens.
May 11   Peterborough defeats French force besieging Barcelona.
12
(May 23 NS)   Ψ Ramillies: Marlborough's 2nd major victory virtually clears the French from modern Belgium.

Jun.	27	Anglo-Portuguese army under Henri, E. of Galway (a Huguenot refugee, originally Marquis de Ruvigny), enters Madrid (retaken by French in August).
Jul.	23	Ty of Union ceremonially presented to Q. Anne by English and Scottish commissioners at St James's Palace.
Aug.	21	Franco-Spanish assault on colonial settlement at Charleston, S. Carolina, defeated.
Dec.	3	Anne reluctantly makes a leading Whig, Charles Spencer, E. of Sunderland, a Secretary of State.
	31	Anne, accompanied by Marlborough, celebrates a year of victory at thanksgiving service in St Paul's.

FINE ARTS AND ARCHITECTURE

1705		Kensington Palace Orangery completed for Q. Anne, probably to Hawksmoor's design.
Jun.	18	Foundation-stone of Vanbrugh's Blenheim Palace laid at Woodstock, Oxon.

MUSIC AND DRAMA

1705 *Sep.*	Vanbrugh's comedy *The Confederacy* performed at Queen's Theatre in the Haymarket, a new building of which he was the architect.
1706	George Farquhar's *The Recruiting Officer* first performed.

RELIGION AND EDUCATION

1705–1706	Samuel Clarke delivers Boyle lectures defending rational theology against deism and Lockean empiricism.

SCIENCE AND INVENTION

1705	E. Halley publishes his research on the orbit of comets; he identifies sighting in 1682 with sightings in 1607, 1531, etc. and predicts comet's return in 1758.
1706	Newton's *Opticks* published in a Latin translation (*Opticae*) by Samuel Clarke so as to make his research on the emission of light known abroad.

Events Elsewhere

1706 *Sep.* 7	P. Eugene wins Ψ Turin.

AD 1707–1708

1707	*Jan.* 16	Scottish Parliament accepts Act of Union.
	Apr. 14	
	(Apr. 25 NS)	Anglo-Portuguese army under E. of Galway defeated at Ψ Almanza by French army led by D. of Berwick (James II's natural son by Marlborough's sister).

May 1		Proclamation of the Union of England and Scotland, providing for one Parliament and accepting the Hanoverian succession.
Jun.?		Q. Anne encourages her close friend Abigail Hill secretly to marry Colonel Samuel Masham; Mrs Masham replaces her cousin Sarah, Duchess of Marlborough, as Q's favourite and increases the influence at court of her kinsman Harley.
Oct. 23		Anne opens first Parliament of the United Kingdom (Commons elected in 1705 supplemented by 45 Scottish MPs; 16 Scottish peers in H. of Lords).
1708	*Feb. 13*	Harley, mistrusted by Marlborough, dismissed as Secretary of State.
	25	Robert Walpole becomes Secretary at War, strengthening Whig hold on government.
	Mar. 23–24	A French naval squadron brings the Old Pretender to Firth of Forth from Dunkirk to encourage a Jacobite rising, but is unable to land him.
	Apr. 15	Parliament dissolved; subsequent general election gives Whigs 69-seat majority in H. of Commons.
	Jun. 30 (Jul. 11 NS)	French defeated at Ψ Oudenarde; Marlborough's 3rd major victory.
	Aug. 1	Marlborough begins siege of Lille, strongest fortified town in Europe.
	18	British naval force seizes Minorca and garrisons Port Mahon (until 1756).
	19	Bitter dispute between Q. Anne and Duchess of Marlborough as they ride to St Paul's for the thanksgiving service for Oudenarde.
	Oct. 12	Marlborough captures Lille (France's second city), but not the citadel.
	28	Death of Q. Anne's husband, P. George of Denmark.
	Nov. 29 (Dec. 9 NS)	Citadel of Lille surrenders.

FINE ARTS AND ARCHITECTURE

1707	Vanbrugh completes remodelling of 16th-century Kimbolton House, Cambridgeshire.

MUSIC AND DRAMA

1707	G. Farquhar's *The Beaux Stratagem* performed at Drury Lane.

RELIGION AND EDUCATION

1707	Isaac Watts, dissenting pastor in London, publishes his *Hymns and Spiritual Songs*; collection includes 'O God, our help in ages past' and 'When I survey the wondrous Cross'.
	Thomas Wilson, Bp of Sodor and Man from 1698 to 1755, publishes his personal catechism, *Principles and Duties of Christianity*, the first book printed in the Manx language; he later translated many of the great works of Christian literature into Manx.
1708	Henry Birkhead founds first Professorship of Poetry, at Oxford; limited in time of tenure and elected by votes of Masters of Arts.

AD 1709–1710

1709	Jan. 6	Extraordinarily cold weather in W. Europe; floating ice in North Sea (to 6 Mar.)
	Mar. 22	Louis XIV turns down peace proposals.
	Jul. 19	Marlborough and P. Eugene capture Tournai.
	Aug. 31 (Sep. 11 NS)	Ψ Malplaquet: won by Marlborough at very heavy cost.
	Oct. 9	Marlborough's army captures Mons.
	18	Charles, Viscount Townshend, negotiates the first Barrier Ty with Holland: Dutch may garrison 9 forts in Belgium and 10 others if taken from the French.
	Nov. 5	Dr Henry Sacheverell preaches sermon at St Paul's on 'The Perils of False Brethren in Church and State', an attack on the Whig government and the idea of the Hanoverian succession.
	Dec.	Whigs in Commons resolve to impeach Sacheverell.
1710	Jan.	War weariness intensified by food shortage caused by previous harsh winter: price of grain in London and bigger English cities higher than ever before.
	Feb. 27	Trial of Dr Sacheverell before H. of Lords begins in Westminster Hall.
	Mar. 1	Anti-Whig riots in London in support of Sacheverell.
	23	Sacheverell's mild sentence (3 years suspension from preaching) is regarded as a defeat for the Whigs.
	Apr. 6	Q. Anne receives Duchess of Marlborough for the last time.
	Jun. 14	E. of Sunderland dismissed as Secretary of State.
	Jul. 16	Cavalry victory of James, Viscount Stanhope, at Ψ Almenara revitalizes war in Spain.
	Aug. 3	H. St John founds a Tory periodical, *The Examiner*; William King first editor.
	8	Godolphin dismissed; new Tory minister headed by Harley and H. St John retains the moderate Whig, Somers.
	9	Stanhope victorious at Ψ Saragossa.
	Sep. 21	Q. Anne dissolves Parliament after Somers leaves government.
	Oct.–Nov.	General election gives Tories 151 majority.
	Nov. 29	British defeated at Ψ Brihuega; Stanhope taken prisoner.

FINE ARTS AND ARCHITECTURE

1709	Wren begins building Marlborough House; but in 1710 is dismissed by Duchess of Marlborough who supervises its completion.

LITERATURE AND SCHOLARSHIP

1709		George Berkeley writes *A New Theory of Vision*.
	Apr. 12	*The Tatler*, a thrice-weekly magazine offering 'accounts of gallantry, pleasure and entertainment' published by Richard Steele, with assistance from his

boyhood friend, Joseph Addison.

| 1710 | | G. Berkeley writes *Principles of Human Knowledge*. |
| | *Apr. 10* | Copyright becomes effective throughout United Kingdom, having been established by the 1709 'Act for the Encouragement of Learning'. |

MUSIC AND DRAMA

| 1711 | First visit to London of Georg Friedrich Handel. |

RECREATION AND FASHION

| 1710 | Hoop petticoats worn; fashionable until about 1785; at court until 1818. |

RELIGION AND EDUCATION

| 1709 *Aug. 15* | Sacheverell preaches Assize Sermon at Derby denouncing Whig government's acceptance of religious toleration. |

SCIENCE AND INVENTION

| 1709 | Abraham Darby of Coalbrookdale in Shropshire uses coke in a blast-furnace for iron smelting. |

AD 1711–1714

1711	*Mar. 29*	Harley (E. of Oxford from 23 May) made Lord Treasurer.
	May 4	Harley outlines to the H. of Commons his project for setting up the South Seas Company.
	Sep. 12	Marlborough takes Bouchain; threatens Paris.
	27	Secret preliminaries for peace talks agreed in London.
	Dec. 15	Occasional Conformity Act: excludes Dissenters from civil or military office.
	31	Marlborough dismissed from his army commands.
1712	*Jan. 1*	Peace Congress opens at Utrecht.
	May 10	Q. Anne approves 'restraining orders' virtually imposing Anglo-French truce.
	Jul. 7	H. St John made Viscount Bolingbroke.
	Dec. 1	Marlborough goes into voluntary exile.
1713	*Mar. 16*	1st Ty of Utrecht: Spain recognizes cession to Britain of Gibraltar and Minorca and concedes the Asiento (monopoly to import slaves into Spain's colonies).
	31	2nd Ty of Utrecht: includes French recognition of the Protestant succession.
	Jul. 16	Parliament dissolved; in ensuing general election Tories secure majority of about 150.
1714	*Jan. 15*	E. of Oxford in contact with the Pretender.
	Feb. 6	Bolingbroke secretly corresponds with the Pretender.
	May 19	Q. Anne refuses to allow any member of the House of Hanover to settle in

		Britain in her lifetime.
	30	Electress Sophia dies in Hanover; her son, the Elector George Ludwig, becomes heir to British Crown.
Jul.	27	E. of Oxford dismissed.
	30	Ailing Q. Anne appoints veteran Whig E. of Shrewsbury as Lord Treasurer.
Aug.	1	Q. Anne dies at Kensington; Elector of Hanover proclaimed K. George I 8 hours later.
Sep.	18	George I and his son P. George Augustus, the future George II, land at Greenwich.
	19	Marlborough reinstated in commands under Whig government; Townshend and Stanhope as Secretaries of State.
	27	George Augustus created P. of Wales.
Oct.	20	Coronation of George I.

LITERATURE AND SCHOLARSHIP

1711	Alexander Pope's *Essay on Criticism*, didactic poem, published anonymously.
Mar. 1	*The Spectator*, periodical concerned mainly with life and literature, and edited by J. Addison and R. Steele, first published; appears daily until 6 Dec. 1712.
1712	Barnaby Lintot's *Miscellaneous Poems* published; includes first version of Pope's *The Rape of the Lock*.
1713	G. Berkeley writes *Hylas and Philonous*.
1714 Jan.–Jul.	Scriblerus Club of anti-Whig writers patronized by E. of Oxford meets; members include Swift and Pope.

MUSIC AND DRAMA

1711 Feb. 24	Handel's first London opera *Rinaldo* produced at Queen's Theatre, Haymarket.
1713	Handel's *Te Deum* and *Jubilate* to celebrate peace earn him life pension of £200 from Q. Anne.

RECREATION AND FASHION

1711	Ascot racecourse laid out under the patronage of Q. Anne.
1711–1712	First sedan chairs come to London.

RELIGION AND EDUCATION

1711	Parliament passes Act for building 50 new churches in London and Westminster with funds raised from a tax on seaborne coal.

AD 1715–1720

1715 Feb.–Mar.	General election gives majority of about 150 to Whigs.

Mar. 27	Bolingbroke flees to France; is impeached, 10 Jun.
Jul. 9	Fear of Jacobite rising leads to the Riot Act.
Sep. 6	'The Fifteen', a Jacobite rebellion, begins at Braemar, led by 11th E. of Mar.
Oct. 12	Walpole forms his first government.
Nov. 13	D. of Argyll scatters Mar's Jacobites at Ψ Sheriffmuir.
14	Jacobite incursion defeated at Ψ Preston.
Dec. 22	The Pretender, James III, lands at Peterhead and joins Jacobites at Perth.

1716 Feb. 4	Pretender sails back to France.
Apr. 26	Septennial Act: extends life of Parliament to 7 years.
Dec. 15	Townshend resigns as Secretary of State; Stanhope in charge of foreign affairs.
24	Anglo-French Ty: French will curb Jacobite intrigues.

| 1717 Apr. 10 | Fall of 1st Walpole Government; Stanhope succeeds Walpole as Lord Treasurer and Chancellor of Exchequer. |
| May | Stanhope's budget establishes Sinking Fund to reduce national debt by annual instalments. |

1718 Jan. 7	Occasional Conformity Act repealed.
Mar. 21	John Aislabie becomes Chancellor of Exchequer.
Dec. 17	Britain declares war on Spain.

| 1719 Jun. 10 | Spanish-backed Jacobite rising crushed at Glenshiel. |
| Jun.–Jul. | Riots in Spitalfields against Indian calico imports. |

1720 Jan.	South Sea Company's offer to take over national debt welcomed by Aislabie.
Jul.–Aug.	Feverish speculation in South Sea stock.
Sep.	Rumours of instability end South Sea boom.
Oct.–Dec.	Panic selling makes 'South Sea bubble' burst; thousands ruined.
Dec. 31	P. Charles Edward ('the Young Pretender') born in Rome.

FINE ARTS AND ARCHITECTURE

| 1715–1720 | Continuous work on 3 new London churches designed by N. Hawksmoor: St Anne's, Limehouse; Christ Church, Spitalfields; St George's-in-the-East; also on Thomas Archer's St John, Smith Square, Westminster. |

LITERATURE AND SCHOLARSHIP

| 1719 | D. Defoe writes *Robinson Crusoe*. |

MUSIC AND DRAMA

1716	James Quin begins 14 years as leading actor at Lincoln's Inn Fields Theatre.
1717	Handel's *Water Music* first performed, serenading George I's royal barge at concert on R. Thames.
Mar. 2	First ballet in England, *The Loves of Mars and Venus* (libretto and choreography, John Weaver) presented at Theatre Royal, Drury Lane.

1715   Stephen Switzer writes *The Nobleman, Gentleman and Gardener's Recreation*, seminal book on landscape gardening.

1715–1718   Grey powdered wigs and lace cravats in fashion for men.

1718–1719   John Aislabie, Chancellor of Exchequer, pioneers landscape gardening at Studley Royal, Yorkshire.

RELIGION AND EDUCATION

1717 *Mar. 31*   Benjamin Hoadly, absentee Bp of Bangor, preaches controversial sermon hostile to sacramentalism; becomes 'Broad Church' leader, supported by George I.

AD 1721–1725

1721 *Jan.*   Aislabie dismissed as Chancellor for fraud over South Sea Company; sent to the Tower in March.

Feb. 5   Sudden death of Stanhope worsens government crisis.

Apr. 3   Political life stabilized when George I appoints Walpole as Prime Minister and Chancellor of Exchequer; his brother-in-law Townshend and John Carteret are Secretaries of State.

1722 *Jun. 16*   Death of D. of Marlborough.

Sep. 24   Francis Atterbury, Bp of Rochester, sent to the Tower for alleged contacts with the Pretender.

Oct. 17   Habeas Corpus Act suspended; Jacobite rising expected.

Oct.–Nov.   Affair of 'Wood's Halfpence': deep resentment caused in Dublin at the sale by George I's mistress to an enterprising manufacturer, William Wood, of the right to issue a new copper coinage for Ireland.

1723 *May*   H. of Commons passes Bill of Pains and Penalties depriving Atterbury of his see and sending him into exile.

Waltham Black Act: creates 50 new capital offences.

Jun.   Bolingbroke allowed back from exile, but forbidden to sit in H. of Lords.

Sep. 29   Ty of Charlottenburg: provides for Anglo-Prussian alliance and dynastic links.

1724 *Apr. 3*   Carteret dismissed after dispute with Walpole.

6   Walpole appoints the skilful Whig political manager Thomas, D. of Newcastle, as successor to Carteret; makes Newcastle's brother Henry Pelham Secretary at War.

Nov. 16   Highwayman Jack Sheppard hanged at Tyburn before an estimated 200,000 onlookers.

1725 *May 24*   'Thief-Taker General' Jonathan Wild executed at Tyburn as master of criminal underworld.

Sep. 3	Ty of Hanover: allies Britain, Prussia and France against Austria and Spain.

FINE ARTS AND ARCHITECTURE

| 1722–1724 | James Gibbs rebuilds St Martin-in-the-Fields. |
| 1725 | E. of Burlington designs Chiswick House, inspired by Palladio's Villa Rotonda at Vicenza. |

LITERATURE AND SCHOLARSHIP

1721	J. Weaver's *Anatomical and Mechanical Lectures on Dancing* published.
1722	D. Defoe publishes *Moll Flanders*.
1724	First volume of Defoe's *Tour through the Whole Island of Great Britain* published; other volumes, 1725-6.
1725	J. Swift's *Drapier Letters* ridicule Wood's Halfpence and prompt Walpole to have the patent withdrawn.

MUSIC AND DRAMA

| 1724 *Sep.* | Three Choirs Festival founded, uniting choirs of Gloucester, Hereford and Worcester. |

RECREATION AND FASHION

| 1723 | Reduction of duty on imported tea and coffee makes their drinking more widespread. |

RELIGION AND EDUCATION

| 1722 | Ashkenazim 'Great Synagogue' opens in Duke's Place, Aldgate. |
| 1725 | Opening of Guy's Hospital (first clinical hospital in London since Reformation) advances medical education. |

SCIENCE AND INVENTION

| 1721 | Willingness of Caroline of Ansbach, P. of Wales, to be inoculated against smallpox helps to make a new practice socially acceptable. |

AD 1726–1730

1726	General George Wade uses Highlanders to begin 11 years of metalled road construction in Scotland, with the building of 40 bridges.
May	Voltaire begins 3-year exile in England.
Dec.	*The Craftsman*, an Opposition periodical depicting Walpole as a 'man of craft', begins publication; Bolingbroke a leading contributor.
1727 *Feb.*	Spanish besiege Gibraltar, without formally going to war with Britain.
Jun. 3	George I leaves London for visit to Hanover.
11	George I dies at Osnabruck.

	15	P. of Wales's accession, as K. George II, proclaimed in London.
	Oct. 11	Coronation of George II at Westminster Abbey.
1728	Jan. 24	Arthur Onslow elected Speaker of H. of Commons; in office for 33 years.
	Feb. 24	Convention of the Prado: provides a truce in Anglo-Spanish fighting; Spaniards raise siege of Gibraltar 10 days later.
	May 6	Roman Catholics disfranchised in Ireland.
	Dec. 7	George II's son, P. Frederick Louis ('Poor Fred'), who had continued to live in Hanover after 1714, arrives in London.
1729	Jan. 8	P. Frederick Louis made P. of Wales.
1730	May 15	Townshend leaves Walpole's government after the two men disagree; subsequently concentrates on agriculture.

FINE ARTS AND ARCHITECTURE

1727	John Wood 'the Elder' outlines town plans for Bath.
1728	James Gibbs's *Book of Architecture* favours Palladian style.
1729	J. Wood begins work on Queen's Square, Bath (completed 1736).
1730	J. Gibbs's Senate House at Cambridge completed.

LITERATURE AND SCHOLARSHIP

| 1726 | J. Swift's satire *Gulliver's Travels* published. |
| 1728 | A. Pope publishes *The Dunciad*, first 3 books. |

MUSIC AND DRAMA

1726		Handel naturalized as a British citizen.
	Mar. 12	Handel's opera *Scipio* performed at King's Theatre, Haymarket.
1728	Jan. 29	*The Beggar's Opera*, play with songs by John Gay, first performed at Lincoln's Inn Fields Theatre.
1729		Gay's ballad opera sequel *Polly* published, but not allowed to be performed until 1777.

RECREATION AND FASHION

| 1726 | Allan Ramsay opens Britain's first circulating library, in Edinburgh. |

RELIGION AND EDUCATION

| 1729 | Charles Wesley founds Holy Club at Oxford; members include John Wesley and George Whitefield; the group, systematic in its religious observance, derisively named 'Methodists' in 1733. |

SCIENCE AND INVENTION

| 1727 | Stephen Hales publishes *Vegetable Staticks*, pioneering study of plant physiology. |
| 1730 | Retired statesman C. Townshend improves rotation of crops husbandry at Raynham Hall, Norfolk, specializing in turnips. |

Events Elsewhere

1730 *Aug.* Crown Prince Frederick (later 'the Great') imprisoned at Kustrin by his father and threatened with execution for attempting to flee to England.

AD 1731–1735

1731 *Jul.* 11 Ty of Vienna: end of Anglo-French *entente*; Walpole gives Emperor Charles VI assurance that Britain will support the 'Pragmatic Sanction', the succession of his daughter Maria Theresa to all his titles.

1723 *Jun.* James Oglethorpe obtains royal charter to establish American colony where emigrants from debtors' prisons could start a new life.

1733 *Apr.* 11 Parliamentary hostility induces Walpole to withdraw his Excise scheme, which would have imposed internal taxation rather than customs duties on tobacco and wine, so as to destroy need for smuggling.

1734 *Nov.* Walpole fights off Opposition to win his third general election victory.

FINE ARTS AND ARCHITECTURE

1731 E. of Burlington designs Assembly Rooms, York.

1731–1732 Edward Shepherd builds theatres at Covent Garden and at Goodman's Fields, Whitechapel.

1733–1735 William Hogarth paints his 8-picture series, *The Rake's Progress*.

1734 William Kent begins work on Holkham Hall, Norfolk.

1735 Hawksmoor's North Quadrangle and Codrington Library of All Souls College, Oxford, completed after 19 years of work.

LITERATURE AND SCHOLARSHIP

1731 *Apr.* 26 Edward Cave founds *The Gentleman's Magazine* as a monthly digest of news, with critical literary comment; first periodical called a 'magazine'.

1733 J. Tull publishes *The Horse-Hoeing Husbandry*, scientific treatise to serve as guide for the agricultural revolution.

MUSIC AND DRAMA

1731 *Mar.* 13 Handel's *Acis and Galatea* (libretto, J. Gay) performed at Lincoln's Inn Fields Theatre, London.

1732 *May* 2 *Esther*, Handel's 1st English oratorio, performed at King's Theatre, Haymarket.

1732 *Dec.* 7 Congreve's *The Way of the World* opens Theatre Royal, Covent Garden.

1734 *Nov.* 9 Handel's opera *Il Pasto Fido* and a ballet, *Terpsichore*, performed at Covent Garden.

1735   Full-bottomed wigs for men out of fashion; perukes tied above nape of neck coming into favour. Coats become more richly decorated. Hoops beneath women's petticoats become oval rather than round, making skirts look wider.

RELIGION AND EDUCATION

1735   The brothers Charles and John Wesley accompany Oglethorpe to Georgia, but their preaching against the slave trade and alcohol alienates the settlers.

SCIENCE AND INVENTION

1731   John Hadley invents a reflecting quadrant, soon used by the Admiralty to improve navigation.

1732   Stephen Gray elected to Royal Society for his experiments on conduction and static electricity.

1733 *May*   John Kay increases speed of weaving by inventing a flying shuttle.

1735   John Harrison perfects a chronometer, after 7 years of working on it.

VOYAGES AND EXPLORATION

1733   Oglethorpe's first voyage to Savannah, with 120 settlers; he makes further voyages in 1735 and 1738.

AD 1736–1740

1736 *May* 8   P. of Wales marries Augusta of Saxe-Coburg-Altenburg at Chapel Royal, St James's Palace.

        18   Repeal of statutes against witchcraft.

    Jul. *27–30*   Anti-Irish riots in E. London; immigrants blamed for accepting work at low wages.

    Sep. 7   Porteous Riots in Edinburgh.

1737 *Feb.*   William Pitt ('the Elder') supports P. of Wales in attacks on Walpole's government.

    Mar.   Dr Samuel Johnson settles in London.

    Oct. *10*   George II expels P. and Princess of Wales from court in anger at his collaboration with Opposition.

    Nov. *20*   Q. Caroline dies at St James's Palace.

1738 *Mar.* *28*   Commons debate Spanish naval affronts; anger over treatment of Captain Robert Jenkins, who asserts he had an ear cut off by Spanish coastguards while trading in the Caribbean in 1731.

    May 9   Against Walpole's wishes, Parliament insists on strengthening naval squadrons to threaten Spain.

	(Jun. 4 NS)	Future K. George III born at Norfolk House, St James's Square, London.
1739	*Jan.* 3	Convention of the Prado: compromise settlement of commercial disputes with Spain.
	Apr. 10	Dick Turpin, highwayman, hanged at York for murder committed near Epping, Essex.
	Oct. 19	Complaints in H. of Commons of breaches of Prado Convention terms lead Walpole reluctantly to declare war on Spain.
	Nov. 22	Admiral Edward Vernon MP begins 'War of Jenkin's Ear' with seizure of Spanish stronghold of Porto Bello, Panama.
	Dec. 25	'Great Frost' in S. England (to 8 Feb.).
1740	*Jul.*	False alarms over Franco-Spanish invasion emphasize Walpole's weaknesses as a possible war leader.

FINE ARTS AND ARCHITECTURE

1736	Town-planning in Mayfair, London, by E. Shepherd.
1737	Work begins on Radcliffe Camera round library, Oxford, to designs by James Gibbs; completed 1748.
1739	W. Kent house and gardens of Rousham, Oxfordshire.

LITERATURE AND SCHOLARSHIP

1738	S. Johnson contributes poem 'London' to *Gentleman's Magazine*.
1739	David Hume's *A Treatise on Human Nature* published anonymously.
1740	Samuel Richardson writes *Pamela*, a novel.

MUSIC AND DRAMA

1737		Licensing Act: Lord Chamberlain recognizes only Covent Garden, Drury Lane and King's Theatre, Haymarket, as patent theatres.
1739	*Jan.* 16	Handel's oratorio *Saul* presented at King's, Haymarket.
1740	*Aug.* 1	'Rule Britannia', composed by Thomas Arne, sung in his masque *Alfred* at P. of Wales's home, Cliveden, Bucks.

RELIGION AND EDUCATION

1736		Joseph Butler publishes *Analogy of Religion Natural and Revealed*.
1738	*May* 24	John Wesley experiences vocational call to evangelism while at religious meeting at Aldersgate Street, London.

SCIENCE AND INVENTION

1737	Thomas Simpson publishes *Treatise on Fluxions*.

VOYAGES AND EXPLORATION

1740	*Sep.* 18	George Anson sails in HMS *Centurion* to raid Spanish possessions in voyage of circumnavigation.

Events Elsewhere

1740 May 31   Accession of Frederick II ('the Great') of Prussia.
     Dec. 16   Prussians invade Austrian-held Silesia.

AD 1741–1745

1741
    Mar.–Apr.   Vernon fails to take Cartagena (Colombia).

1742 Jan. 11   Walpole resigns after 21 years as Prime Minister; succeeded by E. of Wilmington, with Carteret, as Secretary of State, determining policy.
     Feb. 18   George II and P. of Wales formally reconciled after over 4 years of ostracism.
     Nov. 7   Carteret concludes Ty of Westminster with Prussia, safeguarding Hanover from attack.
     Dec. 10   William Pitt, attacking Carteret's war policy in H. of Commons, complains that Britain 'is considered only as a province of a despicable Electorate'.

1743 Jun. 16
    (Jun. 27 NS)   George II's multinational Pragmatic Army defeats French at Ψ Dettingen on R. Main.
         20   Anson in *Centurion* captures over £500,000 of treasure in taking the Spanish ship *Nuestra Senora de Covadonga* off the Philippines.
     Aug. 27   Pelham succeeds Wilmington as Prime Minister.

1744 Mar. 4   France belatedly declares war on Britain.
     Nov. 23   Carteret resigns as Secretary of State.
     Dec. 28   Britain allies with Austria and Holland against Prussia.

1745 Apr. 30   Ψ Fontenoy: George II's 4th son William, D. of Cumberland, defeated by French under Marshal Saxe.
     Jul. 23   P. Charles Edward, 'the Young Pretender', lands on Eriskay Island.
     Aug. 19   Jacobite royal standard raised at Glenfinnan.
     Sep. 11   Jacobites capture Edinburgh.
         21   Jacobites rout General Cope's dragoons at Ψ Prestonpans.
     Dec. 4   Jacobites reach Derby, but find no support from English.
         6   Panic in London, but Jacobites begin retreat northwards.

FINE ARTS AND ARCHITECTURE

1743–1745   William Hogarth paints his *Marriage à la Mode* series.
1745   Hawksmoor completes west towers, Westminster Abbey.
    Porcelain works established at Chelsea; best work, 1752-8.

1741–1742   David Hume publishes *Essays Moral and Political*.
1742   Henry Fielding publishes *Joseph Andrews*.
1745   Fielding edits propaganda journal *The True Patriot*.

MUSIC AND DRAMA

1741 Oct. 19   David Garrick makes sensational London debut as Richard III at Goodmans
                 Fields Theatre, Whitechapel.
1742 Apr. 13   Handel's oratorio *Messiah* performed in Dublin.
1743 Mar. 23   *Messiah* at Covent Garden: George II originates custom of standing for the
                 'Hallelujah Chorus'.
     Nov. 27   Handel's *Dettingen Te Deum* performed at Chapel Royal, St James.
1744   *Thesaurus Musicus* includes 'God Save the King'; first known to be sung at
                 Drury Lane, 28 Sep. 1745.

RECREATION AND FASHION

1743 Aug. 16   Jack Broughton codifies boxing rules.
1744 Jun. 18   First fully documented cricket match, Kent v. All England, at Finsbury,
                 coincides with printing of code of laws.
1745 Jun. 26   Earliest women's cricket match: Bramley v. Hambleton, Gosden Common,
                 Surrey.

SCIENCE AND INVENTION

1745   Robert Bakewell begins scientific reform of stockbreeding, Leicestershire.

VOYAGES AND EXPLORATION

1744 Jun. 15   Anson completes circumnavigation of the world.

Events Elsewhere

1741 Aug.   War of the Austrian Succession begins (to 1748).

AD 1746–1750

1746 Jan. 16   Jacobites gain victory at Falkirk against small royalist force.
     Feb. 10–22 Political crisis caused by George II's reluctance to accept Pitt in Pelham's
                 cabinet.
     Apr. 16   Jacobite army defeated by Cumberland at Ψ Culloden.
     May   Pitt becomes Paymaster-General and Henry Fox Secretary of War.
     May–Jun.   Cumberland's summary executions and burning of homes in the Highlands
                 earns him nickname 'Butcher'.
     Jun.   Flora MacDonald of South Uist helps the Young Pretender escape from
                 Benbecula to Portree, Skye.

	Sep.	20	Young Pretender sails from Hebrides for France.
1747	*Apr.*	9	Lord Lovat beheaded for Jacobitism; last execution on Tower Hill; 12 onlookers killed when spectators' stand collapses.
	May		Abolition of Hereditable Jurisdictions Act ends the power of heads of Scottish clans.
		3	Anson defeats two French squadrons off Cape Finisterre.
	Jun.	21	Cumberland, commanding large allied army in Netherlands, defeated by Saxe at Ψ Laffeldt.
	Jul.		Pelham safeguards his position by winning snap election.
1748	*Oct.*	17	Ty of Aix-la-Chapelle (Aachen): accepts a stalemate peace; British rivalry with France and Spain unresolved.

1749 *Feb.* Anson, at the Admiralty, reforms command structure of fleet and issues new *Fighting Instructions*.

May ? Henry Fielding becomes Bow Street magistrate; enlists help of 6 mobile 'thief-takers'; succeeded in 1754 by half-brother John, who further develops system of 'runners'.

1750 *Sep.* 24 Anglo-Spanish Commercial Ty: settles trading disputes.

FINE ARTS AND ARCHITECTURE

1746 Antonio Canaletto paints in England (to 1755), occasionally returning to Venice.

1748 Thomas Gainsborough paints *Cornard Wood*, his earliest Suffolk landscape.

LITERATURE AND SCHOLARSHIP

1747 Thomas Gray's *Ode on a Distant Prospect of Eton College*, his first work in print.

1748 D. Hume publishes *Enquiry concerning Human Understanding*.
S. Richardson publishes first part of *Clarissa* (completed 1749).
Tobias Smollett's first novel *Adventures of Roderick Random*.

1749 Viscount Bolingbroke's *Idea of a Patriot King* published (written 1738).
H. Fielding publishes *Tom Jones*.
John Cleland writes *Fanny Hill, Memoirs of a Woman of Pleasure*.

MUSIC AND DRAMA

1747 *Apr.* 1 Handel's oratorio *Judas Maccabeus* performed at Covent Garden.
Sep. 15 Garrick begins 29 years as actor-manager at Drury Lane.
1749 *Apr.* 27 Handel's *Music for the Royal Fireworks* performed at peace celebrations, Green Park, London.

RECREATION AND FASHION

1750 Jockey Club founded at Star and Garter coffee house, Pall Mall.

RELIGION AND EDUCATION

1748 The widowed Selina, Countess of Huntingdon, appoints G. Whitefield as her personal chaplain, establishing a personal ascendancy over his group of Methodists.

1747   Benjamin Robins, mathematician and specialist in the principles of gunnery, delivers pioneer paper on ballistics to the Royal Society.

AD 1751–1755

1751	Mar. 20	P. of Wales dies from pneumonia at Leicester House.
	Apr.	Gin Act: imposes government inspection on distillation and sale of spirits.
	Aug. 31	During skirmishing for commercial dominance between British and French East India Companies, Robert Clive seizes citadel of Arcot and holds it for 11 weeks against Governor-General Dupleix's soldiery.
1752	Sep. 3–13 incl.	11 days omitted from the calendar when United Kingdom abandons the 'Old Style' Julian calendar in favour of the 'New Style' Gregorian calendar.
1753	Jul.	Marriage Act: ends marriage by unlicensed ministers and regularizes calling of banns.
	7	Jewish Naturalization Act: seeks to remove disabilities; repealed later in year because of widespread hostility shown towards Jews.
1754	Mar. 6	Henry Pelham dies; succeeded as Prime Minister by his elder brother, D. of Newcastle.
	May	General election gives Newcastle substantial Whig majority.
	Jun.–Jul.	Skirmishing with French colonists in America around Fort Duquesne (Pittsburgh).
	Aug.–Dec.	Abortive Anglo-French talks in Paris over colonial boundary disputes.
1755	Jun.	Admiral Edward Boscawen, obeying orders to prevent reinforcements reaching Canada, captures 2 French vessels off mouth of R. St Lawrence.
	Jul. 9	Ψ of the Wilderness, near Fort Duquesne: General Braddock defeated and killed; Col. George Washington leads survivors back to Maryland.
	Nov. 12–20	Government crisis in London; Pitt leaves cabinet; H. Fox becomes Secretary of State and Leader of Commons.

FINE ARTS AND ARCHITECTURE
1751	W. Hogarth paints *Gin Lane; Beer Street; The Four Stages of Cruelty*.
1753	Thomas Chippendale opens furniture workshop in St Martin's Lane, London.
	Joshua Reynolds paints portrait *Commodore Keppel*.
1754	T. Chippendale publishes *The Gentleman and Cabinet Maker's Director*.

1751   T. Gray's *Elegy written in a Country Churchyard* published (completed at Stoke Poges in 1750).
T. Smollett publishes *Adventures of Peregrine Pickle*.

1753 *Apr.* 5   Foundation charter for establishment of the British Museum.

1755   S. Johnson's *Dictionary of the English Language* published.

c. 1754–1755   'Blue Stockings', an informal circle of intelligent women, begin holding receptions aimed at promoting good, rational conversation between women and men of London society; flourished for about 40 years; chief founder-hostesses were Mrs Elizabeth Vesey, Mrs Elizabeth Montagu, Mrs Mary Delany.

RECREATION AND FASHION

1754   First written rules for golf agreed at St Andrews, at the foundation of the Royal and Ancient Club.

SCIENCE AND INVENTION

1754   Mungo Murray completes *Treatise on Shipbuilding and Navigation*.

Events Elsewhere

1755 *Nov.* 1   Lisbon earthquake.

AD 1756–1760

1756 *Jan.* 16   Anglo-Prussian Ty of Westminster: Frederick II guarantees protection of Hanover.

May 17   Britain at war with France; conflict becomes general ('Seven Years War') when Prussia goes to war with France's new ally, Austria, over Saxony in August.

20   Admiral John Byng breaks off naval action against French off Minorca; island surrenders, 26 Jun.

Jun. 20   Siraj-ud-Daula, allied to French in Bengal, seizes Calcutta; over 120 captives die in 'Black Hole'.

Aug. 12–24   Montcalm drives British from Canadian Great Lakes.

Oct.   Charles O'Conor founds Catholic Association in Dublin.

Nov. 16   D. of Newcastle succeeded as Prime Minister by D. of Devonshire.

Dec. 4   Pitt enters government as a Secretary of State.

1757 *Jan.* 2   Clive recovers Calcutta.

Mar. 14   Byng shot at Portsmouth for cowardice.

Apr. 6   Pitt resigns after dispute with Cumberland over command in Germany.

Jun. 23   Clive defeats Siraj-ud-Daula at Ψ Plassey.

29   D. of Newcastle returns as Prime Minister, with Pitt (Secretary of State

			again) as effective war leader.
	Jul.	26	D. of Cumberland routed by French at Ψ Hastenbeck.
	Sep.	8	Convention of Klosterzeven: Cumberland surrenders Hanover to French.
1758	*Apr.*	11	Ty of London: Britain to pay subsidy of £670,000 to Prussia and maintain troops in Germany.
	Jul.	26	Jeffrey Amherst and James Wolfe capture Louisburg fortress, Canada.
	Aug.	15	8,500 British augment D. of Brunswick's army.
	Nov.	25	Fort Duquesne captured and renamed Pittsburgh.
1759	*May*	1	British capture French island of Guadeloupe.
	Aug.	1	Brunswick's Anglo-German army defeats French at Ψ Minden.
		17	Boscawen pursues French squadron into Lagos Bay, capturing 2 large warships.
	Sep.	13	Wolfe's troops scale Heights of Abraham, Quebec.
		18	British capture Quebec; both Wolfe and Montcalm killed.
	Nov.	20	Admiral Edward Hawke destroys French squadron off Quiberon, despite westerly gale.
1760	*May*	5	Earl Ferrers, last peer executed in Britain, hanged for murder at Tyburn.
	Sep.	8	Amherst's capture of Montreal secures control of Canada.
	Oct.	25	George II dies at Kensington; succeeded by his grandson, K. George III.

LITERATURE AND SCHOLARSHIP

1759			S. Johnson publishes *Rasselas, Prince of Abyssinia*, didactic novel.
			Laurence Sterne's *Tristram Shandy*, vols 1 and 2, published in York after being rejected in London.

RECREATION AND FASHION

1759	*Jan.*	16	Public first admitted to British Museum.

SCIENCE AND INVENTION

1758			John Dollond, English Huguenot optician, invents achromatic telescope.
1759			Eminent chemist John Roebuck establishes Carron ironworks in Stirlingshire.
			Jebediah Strutt patents machine for making ribbed cotton goods.
1760			John Wyatt perfects system of spinning by rollers begun by Lewis Paul.

AD 1761–1765

1761	*Jan.*	16	Eyre Coote takes Pondicherry after 4-month siege, ending French dominance in Madras.
	Mar.	25	George III's ex-tutor, E. of Bute, made a Secretary of State.
	Sep.	8	George III marries Charlotte of Mecklenburg-Strelitz at St James's Palace.
		22	George III and Q. Charlotte crowned.

	Oct. 5	Pitt resigns as a Secretary of State because of anti-war policies favoured by George III and Bute.
1762	*Mar. 10*	Britain seizes French West Indian island of Grenada.
	May 22	King and Queen first take up residence at 'Buckingham House'.
	26	Bute succeeds Newcastle as Prime Minister.
	Jun. 18	John Wilkes MP and the Revd Charles Churchill launch the *North Briton*, a satirical weekly savagely hostile to Bute.
	Aug. 12	Future George IV born; made P. of Wales 5 days later.
	Nov. 1	Peace preliminaries signed at Fontainebleau.
1763	*Feb. 10*	Peace Ty of Paris ends Seven Years War: Canada, Nova Scotia, Dominica, Grenada and Tobago ceded to Britain.
	Mar.	Proposed cider tax increases Bute's unpopularity.
	Apr. 16	George Grenville succeeds Bute as Prime Minister.
	23	*North Briton*, no. 45: Wilkes hostile to George III.
	30	Wilkes imprisoned in the Tower on a 'general warrant'.
	May 6	LCJ Pratt rules that Wilkes's detention under a general warrant breaks parliamentary privilege.
	Nov. 23	Commons vote to deprive Wilkes of parliamentary privileges because of *North Briton* article and for printing an obscene poem, *Essay on Woman*.
	Dec.	Wilkes takes refuge in France.
1764	*Feb. 21*	Wilkes found guilty of seditious libel and obscenity.
	May 18	Sugar tax to be levied from American colonists.
1765	*Feb.–May*	George III ill; alleged nervous breakdown unproven.
	Mar. 23	Stamp Act: imposes taxation on American colonists.
	May 7	HMS *Victory* (Nelson's flagship) launched at Chatham.
	29	Patrick Henry denounces Stamp Act in Virginia.
	Jul. 16	Grenville succeeded as Prime Minister by Marquis of Rockingham.

FINE ARTS AND ARCHITECTURE

1764	Robert Adam remodels Kenwood House, Highgate.
1765	Lancelot ('Capability') Brown designs landscape gardens at Blenheim, Hampton Court and Broadlands.

LITERATURE AND SCHOLARSHIP

1762	Oliver Goldsmith publishes *The Traveller*, poem.
1763 *May 16*	James Boswell first meets Johnson, at 8 Russell St, Covent Garden, a bookshop.
1764 *Mar.*	Johnson founds 'The Club' on Reynolds's suggestion.

MUSIC AND DRAMA

1763 *Feb. 19*	J.C. Bach attends performance of his opera *Orion* at King's, Haymarket.
1764	W.A. Mozart (aged 8) performs before George III.

AD 1766–1770

1768 *Dec. 10*	Foundation of the Royal Academy of Arts, under presidency of Reynolds.
1770	T. Gainsborough paints *The Blue Boy*.

LITERATURE AND SCHOLARSHIP

1766	Oliver Goldsmith's novel *The Vicar of Wakefield* published.
1767	L. Sterne completes final vols of *Tristram Shandy*.
1768	L. Sterne publishes *A Sentimental Journey*.
1770	Edmund Burke writes *Thoughts on the Cause of the Present Discontents*.
	O. Goldsmith's poem *The Deserted Village* published.

MUSIC AND DRAMA

1768	Bath's Orchard St Theatre (built 1750) patented as first Theatre Royal in provinces.

RECREATION AND FASHION

1766	Golf club opened at Blackheath, Kent; first outside Scotland.

SCIENCE AND INVENTION

1767	Joseph Priestley publishes *History of Electricity*.
1769	Richard Arkwright sets up spinning frame at Preston.
	James Watt patents steam engine.
	Josiah Wedgwood opens Etruria pottery works.

VOYAGES AND EXPLORATION

1767	Nevil Maskelyne, newly appointed Astronomer Royal, publishes first annual *Nautical Almanac*.
1768 *May 25*	James Cook sails on first Pacific voyage.
1769 *Oct. 7*	Cook reaches New Zealand.
1770 *Apr. 28*	Cook discovers and names Botany Bay.
Nov. 14	James Bruce, exploring N. Ethiopia, discovers source of Blue Nile.

AD 1771–1775

1771 *Jan.*	Spain recognizes British rights in Falklands.
1772 *Mar. 24*	George III, angered at conduct of 2 of his brothers, secures passage of Royal Marriages Act: Crown's consent needed for marriage of all British descendants of George II.
Jun.	Financial crisis: Scottish banker Alexander Fordyce fails; bankruptcy threatens East India Co.
22	Ruling of LCJ Mansfield in 'Somerset's Case': slaves automatically free on reaching England.
Sep. 14	Birmingham linked by canal to R. Severn.

1773		Spitalfields Act: protects silk-weavers over pay and number of apprentices and imposes import duty.
		First informal Stock Exchange opens, Threadneedle St, London.
	Mar.	General Turnpike Act: regularizes road toll system.
	May	North's Regulating Act reforms East India Co.: Warren Hastings made first Governor-General; Co. given monopoly of tea trade with America.
	Dec. 16	Boston Tea Party protest: 343 chests thrown into sea.
1774	*Mar.–Apr.*	North responds to Boston protests by Coercive Acts against Massachusetts, including closure of Boston port.
	Apr.	Quebec Act: gives Roman Catholics in Canada full rights and sets up strong Canadian executive.
	Sep.–Oct.	Continental Congress of colonists at Philadelphia.
	Oct. 4	Highwayman robs Lord North at Gunnersbury Lane, Chiswick.
	13	Wilkes returned unopposed as MP for Middlesex (and becomes Lord Mayor in November).
1775	*Jan. 20*	Chatham, in H. of Lords, supports American cause.
	Mar. 22	Edmund Burke speaks in H. of Commons on need for conciliation with America.
	Apr. 19	War of Independence starts with shooting at Lexington.
	May 10	American colonists take Ticonderoga fort.
	Jun. 17	Colonial militia defeated by British at Bunker Hill.
	Nov. 13	Americans take Montreal.

FINE ARTS AND ARCHITECTURE

1775	George Romney begins portrait painting in London.
	Wedgwood employs John Flaxman to design classical models for his jasper ware.

LITERATURE AND SCHOLARSHIP

1771	T. Smollett publishes *The Expedition of Humphry Clinker*.

MUSIC AND DRAMA

1773 *Mar. 15*	O. Goldsmith's *She Stoops to Conquer* performed at Covent Garden.
1775 *Jan. 17*	R.B. Sheridan's *The Rivals* performed at Covent Garden.
Dec. 29	Sarah Siddons, as Portia, makes London debut at Drury Lane; fails to impress.

RECREATION AND FASHION

1773	James Weatherby publishes first *Racing Calendar* for Jockey Club.

RELIGION AND EDUCATION

1775	'Rock of Ages', hymn by Augustus Toplady, published.

Events Elsewhere

AD 1776–1780

FINE ARTS AND ARCHITECTURE

1780   J. Reynolds paints *Mary Robinson as Perdita*.

LITERATURE AND SCHOLARSHIP

1776 *Jan.* 9   Tom Paine writes *Common Sense*, pamphlet.
     Adam Smith publishes *The Wealth of Nations*.
     Edward Gibbon publishes *The Decline and Fall of the Roman Empire*, vol. 1;
     further vols in 1781 and 1788.
1777   E. Burke's *Letter to the Sheriffs of Bristol* is published
1778   Fanny Burney's anonymous novel *Evelina* published.
1779   S. Johnson publishes *The Lives of the Poets*.

MUSIC AND DRAMA

1776 *Jun.* 10   Garrick's farewell performance at Drury Lane, as Don Felix in *The Wonder, a Woman never Vexed*.
1777 *May* 8   Sheridan's *School for Scandal* opens at Drury Lane.
1779 *Oct.* 29   Sheridan's *The Critic* opens at Drury Lane.

RECREATION AND FASHION

1778 *Sep.*   Col. St Leger establishes horse race at Doncaster.
     Jonas Hanway sets London fashion for carrying umbrellas.
1779 *May* 14   The Oaks first run at Epsom.
1780 *May* 4   Sir Charles Bunbury's 'Diomed' wins the first Derby.

RELIGION AND EDUCATION

1779   Countess of Huntingdon's dissenting chapel opens at Spa Fields, Clerkenwell.
1780   Robert Raikes opens a Sunday school, Gloucester.

SCIENCE AND INVENTION

1779   Samuel Crompton perfects his spinning mule after 5 years of work.

VOYAGES AND EXPLORATION

1778 *Jan.* 18   Cook, on third Pacific voyage, discovers and names Sandwich Islands.
1779 *Feb.* 14   Cook killed by natives, Kealakelua Bay, Hawaii.

AD 1781–1785

1781 *Sep.* 30   Washington's army, supported by French under Lafayette, cuts Cornwallis's communications, Virginia.
     Oct. 19   Cornwallis surrenders at Yorktown.

1782	Mar.		North resigns (19 Mar.); K. drafts abdication message (28 Mar.).
	Apr.	1	George III reluctantly accepts Rockingham Whig ministry; Foreign Secretary (Charles James Fox) and Home Secretary (E. of Shelburne) first appointed.
		12	Admiral Rodney defeats French at Ψ The Saints, off Dominica.
	Jun.	21	Ireland given greater legislative independence; Dublin Parliament led by Henry Grattan.
	Jul.	1	Rockingham dies; succeeded by Shelburne; the younger William Pitt becomes Chancellor of Exchequer.
1783	Feb.	24	Shelburne resigns over proposed peace terms.
	Apr.	1	George III accepts Fox-North coalition; D. of Portland nominal Prime Minister.
	Sep.	3	Ty of Versailles: peace with France and Spain; recognition of American independence.
	Dec.	17	Fox's India Bill defeated in Lords; government falls.
		19	Pitt made Prime Minister of minority Tory government.
1784	Apr.		Pitt wins general election; 160 Foxite Whigs lose seats.
	May	14	Foster's Corn Law: encourages Irish arable farming.
	Jun.	21	Commutation Act: Pitt reduces duties on tea and spirits, makes window tax effective.
	Jul.	24	P. of Wales 'commutes' from Brighton to London and back: 180 miles, 10 hours in saddle.
	Aug.	2	John Palmer establishes first mail-coach service, Bristol to London: 17 hours overnight.
		13	India Act: puts East India Co. under government control.
	Sep.		First flight over England: Vincenzo Lunardi in balloon from Moorfields, London to Ware.
1785	Jan.	1	John Walter founds *Daily Universal Register*.
		7	Frenchman J.-P. Blanchard and American John Jeffries cross Channel, Dover to Calais, in balloon.
	Apr.	4	Fast mail-coach service spreads to Norwich.
		18	Pitt's proposed Reform Bill defeated in Commons.
	Dec.	21	P. of Wales secretly weds widow, Maria Fitzherbert; ceremony contravenes Royal Marriage Act.

FINE ARTS AND ARCHITECTURE

1783–1784	Henry Holland converts Carlton House into a palace for P. of Wales.
1784	J. Reynolds paints *Mrs Siddons as the Tragic Muse*.

LITERATURE AND SCHOLARSHIP

1783	George Crabbe writes *The Village*, botanically precise and realistic poem in heroic couplets.
1785	William Cowper publishes poems *John Gilpin* and *The Task*. Horace Walpole publishes *Essay on Modern Gardening*.

MUSIC AND DRAMA

1782 *Oct.* *10* Sarah Siddons's first London triumph, in *Isabella* at Theatre Royal, Drury Lane; her brother, John Kemble, played his first Hamlet there on 30 Sep.

RELIGION AND EDUCATION

1783 Charles Simeon becomes vicar of Holy Trinity, Cambridge, and leads evangelical movement there.

1784 John Wesley provides for continuance of the 'Yearly Conference of the People called Methodists' and names 100 ministers.

SCIENCE AND INVENTION

1781 James Watt perfects his steam-engine, using a cog-wheel to give it a rotary movement.

1783 Henry Cort perfects method for 'puddling' iron.

1785 Edmund Cartwright invents power loom for weaving.

AD 1786–1790

1786 *Mar.* *29* Pitt establishes a Sinking Fund in order to reduce the national debt.

Apr. Anglo-Irish Trade Bill abandoned in face of protests from English commercial interests.

Aug. *11* East India Co. sets up base on Penang island.

Sep. *26* William Eden signs commercial treaty with France.

1787 *May* *10* In H. of Commons Burke impeaches Warren Hastings for maladministration and corruption in Bengal.

1788 *Jan.* *1* *Daily Universal Register* renamed *The Times* (*v.* 1785).

26 Penal settlement at Botany Bay, near new town of Sydney.

Jan. *30* P. Charles Edward ('the Young Pretender') dies in Rome.

Feb. *13* Trial of Warren Hastings begins in Westminster Hall.

Apr. *15* Ty of alliance with Holland; with Prussia, 13 Aug.

May *9* Proposal to abolish slave trade fails in H. of Commons.

Nov. *5* George III suffers mental collapse.

1789 *Feb.* *3* Pitt introduces Regency Bill, imposing a strictly limited authority on P. of Wales (a Foxite Whig).

19 George III recovers health; Regency Bill dropped.

Apr. *23* Thanksgiving service at St Paul's for George III's recovery.

28 Mutiny aboard HMS *Bounty* off Tonga.

Jun.–Jul. Crisis with Spain over attack on British fishing vessels at Nootka Sound (Vancouver island).

Nov. *19* Thames-Severn canal opens.

1790 *Jan.* *1* Opening of 91-mile canal from Coventry to Oxford (begun 1770) gives

		Midlands industry outlet to Thames valley.
Feb.		In Commons debate on the army estimates Fox praises changes in France; Burke denounces them.
Jun.–Jul.		Cornwallis (Governor-General of India 1786-93) makes alliances with Mahrattas and Nizam of Hyderabad.
Jun.	*28*	Forth and Clyde canal opens.
Jul.	*5*	Twice-weekly London-Birmingham canal barge service advertised.
Oct.	*28*	Spain abandons claim to Nootka Sound and Vancouver.
Nov.		General election gives Pitt increased majority.

FINE ARTS AND ARCHITECTURE

1786	John Hoppner paints *Portrait of a Lady*.
1787	H. Holland's pavilion at Brighton first used by P. of Wales.
1788	George Hepplewhite's *Cabinet-maker's and Upholsterer's Guide* published posthumously.

LITERATURE AND SCHOLARSHIP

1786	Robert Burns's *Poems, chiefly in the Scottish Dialect* printed.
1788 *Dec.*	Gilbert White publishes *Natural History of Selborne*.
1789	William Blake publishes *Songs of Innocence* (with his engravings).
1790	E. Burke publishes *Reflections on the Revolution in France*.
	Archibald Alison writes *Essays on the Nature and Principles of Taste*.

MUSIC AND DRAMA

1786	General Burgoyne's comedy *The Heiress* a success at Drury Lane.

RECREATION AND FASHION

1787	Thomas Lord opens his first cricket ground in London (site now covered by Dorset Square).
	Marylebone Cricket Club (MCC) founded.
1788 *May 30*	MCC issues revised Laws of Cricket.

VOYAGES AND EXPLORATION

1788 *Jan. 9*	Association for Promoting the Discovery of the Interior Parts of Africa founded in London.

Events Elsewhere

1787 *Sep.*	*17*	Final signature of US Constitution.
1789 *Jul.*	*14*	Fall of the Bastille in Paris; traditional date for start of French Revolution.

AD 1791–1792

1791 *Mar. 13*   Part of T. Paine's political manifesto *The Rights of Man* printed and widely circulated.

28   Pitt asks for increased naval spending: crisis over Russian acquisition from Turkey of Ochakov, wrongly assumed to possess strategic importance in Black Sea.

May 6   Canada Constitution Act: provides for separate legislatures for Upper Canada in Ontario and Lower Canada in Quebec.

Jun. 14–17   Anti-Dissenter 'Church and King' riots in Birmingham; Joseph Priestley's house destroyed.

Oct. 14   United Irish Society, led by Theobald Wolfe Tone, founded in Belfast.

Nov. 9   First Dublin meeting of United Irishmen.

Dec. 4   Sunday newspaper, *The Observer*, begins publication.

1792 *Jan.*   London Corresponding Society for Parliamentary and Social Reform founded by radical shoemaker Thomas Hardy at Bell Tavern, Exeter St.

4   *Northern Star* founded in Belfast as a United Irish radical newspaper.

Feb. 5   Sultan Tippoo of Mysore, defeated by Cornwallis at Ψ Seringapatam and forced to cede half of Mysore.

8   Paine's 'seditious' *Rights of Man*, part 2, published.

Apr.   Whigs found Society of Friends of the People.

18   Relief Act: allows Irish Catholics to practise law.

May   Royal Proclamation against Seditious Publications.

Sep. 14   To escape prosecution, Paine flees to France.

Dec. 18   Paine tried *in absentia* and outlawed.

LITERATURE AND SCHOLARSHIP

1791   J. Boswell publishes *The Life of Samuel Johnson*.

1792   Arthur Young's *Travels in France* appear.

Mary Wollstonecraft, in *A Vindication of the Rights of Woman*, attacks inadequacies of women's education for perpetuating their 'ignorance and slavish dependence'.

MUSIC AND DRAMA

1791 *Jul.*   F.J. Haydn receives honorary music doctorate at Oxford; conducts performance in Sheldonian Theatre of his Symphony no. 92 in G major (composed 1788), renamed the 'Oxford Symphony'.

RECREATION AND FASHION

*c.*1792   Men begin to favour a frock coat in place of cut-away tails, common since mid-1780s. Women's huge 'Gainsborough' hats, ornamented with plumes and ribbons, are succeeded by simpler and smaller felt or straw hats.

1792 *Oct.* 2   Baptist Missionary Society founded at Kettering, Northants.

VOYAGES AND EXPLORATION
1791 *Apr.* 1   Captain George Vancouver sails on 4-year expedition to explore Pacific islands and western coast of Canada.

Events Elsewhere

1792   France declares war on Austria (Apr.) and Prussia (Jul.).
    Sep.   Prison massacres in Paris; French Republic proclaimed.

AD 1793–1794

1793 *Feb.* 1   France declares war on Britain and Holland.
          13   First Coalition of allies constituted: Britain, Austria, Netherlands, Prussia, Sardinia-Piemont, Spain.
    Mar. 1   Frederick, D. of York, arrives in Netherlands, commanding vanguard of 2,000 Guardsmen.
          15   Habeas Corpus Act suspended as war emergency.
    Apr. 9   Further Relief Act: enfranchises Irish Catholics and grants some civil and military rights.
          15   Bank of England issues first £5 notes.
    May   Cornwallis Code: reforms Indian administration and settlement of Bengal.
    Jul.   British force occupies Corsica.
    Aug.   Advocate Thomas Muir sentenced in Edinburgh to 14 years' transportation for promoting sedition.
          28   British occupy and hold Toulon (to 19 Dec.)
    Sep.   Pitt establishes Board of Agriculture, with Arthur Young as first Secretary.
    Nov. 18 British Convention meets in Edinburgh (to 3 Dec.); organizers subsequently transported to Australia for sedition.

1794 *Jan.*   King Kamehameha of Polynesia receives Capt. Vancouver and cedes Hawaii to George III; cession not ratified.
    Apr. 19 Pitt agrees to subsidize Prussian and Dutch troops against France.
    May 12   T. Hardy charged with high treason; acquitted, 5 Nov.
          23   United Irishmen outlawed.
    Jun. 1   'Glorious First of June' naval victory of Admiral Lord Howe in N. Atlantic: 6 French ships captured; no British vessel lost.
    Dec.   D. of York recalled after failure to besiege Dunkirk.

LITERATURE AND SCHOLARSHIP
1793   T. Paine publishes *The Age of Reason*; book condemned as blasphemous because of its flippancy, reflects a Quaker deism; did not circulate in Britain

		until 1795.
1794		New interest in classical studies, marked by the teaching of Richard Porson as Regius Professor of Greek at Cambridge from 1792 and by publication in March of James Stuart and Nicholas Revett's *The Antiquities of Rome, Measured and Delineated.*

RECREATION AND FASHION

1794	George 'Beau' Brummell, protégé of P. of Wales, establishes himself as the arbiter of elegance (to 1813); emphasizes need for cleanliness of clothing, perfectly tied and starched cravat, exquisite style of taking snuff; encourages transition by 1800 from breeches to light-coloured trousers, with socks replacing men's stockings.

RELIGION AND EDUCATION

1794	French Revolution forces Jesuit school for English boys, established at St Omer in 1592, to migrate to Stonyhurst Hall, Lancs.
	William Paley publishes *View of the Evidences of Christianity*; clarity of style makes it theological best-seller.

Events Elsewhere

1793	*Jan.* 21	K. Louis XVI of France executed.
1794	*Jul.* 28	French 'Terror' ends with execution of Robespierre and leading Jacobins.

AD 1795–1796

1795	*Apr.* 8	P. of Wales marries his first cousin, Caroline of Brunswick, at St James's Palace.
	23	Acquittal of Warren Hastings after 7-year trial.
	May	Magistrates at Speenhamland, Berkshire, devise sliding scale for outdoor poor relief, based on price of bread and size of the family; system soon in general use in central and S. England.
	Jul. 3	British force captures Quiberon to support rising by Breton Chouans, but is unable to consolidate gains.
	Aug. 25	British seize Trincomalee in bid to take control of Ceylon from the Dutch as Holland becomes a French dependency.
	Sep. 16	General Sir James Craig captures Cape Town from the Dutch.
	21	Affray between Catholics and Protestants in Armagh followed by founding of the first Orange lodge.
	Sep.–Oct.	Acute food shortage; bread riots in several towns.
	Oct. 2	English occupy Île d'Yeu, off Brittany.
	29	George III, on way to open Parliament, is stoned by angry crowd demanding peace and bread.

Nov.		Treasonable Practices Act and Seditious Meetings Act: limit rights of protest.
1796 *Jan.*	7	P. Charlotte, daughter of P. and Princess of Wales, born at Carlton House.
Feb.	*1*	Q. Charlotte hit by a stone as protesters over price of bread pelt King and Queen returning from theatre.
	16	British occupation of Colombo is followed by treaty with K. of Kandy giving East India Co. all rights previously held in Ceylon by the Dutch.
Mar.	*24*	Insurrection Act in Ireland: provides for curfews and the death penalty for secret oath-taking.
Oct.	*5*	Spain declares war on Britain.
Dec.	*22–27*	French fleet, with Wolfe Tone aboard, lands 15,000 troops in Bantry Bay.
Dec.	*23*	Invasion rumours lead to a run on the banks in the English provincial cities.

FINE ARTS AND ARCHITECTURE

1795 Humphrey Repton's *Sketches of History on Landscape Gardens* encourages growth of 'picturesque' landscaping.
Sir John Soane begins building Bank of England.

LITERATURE AND SCHOLARSHIP

1796 E. Burke's *Letters on a Regicide Peace* printed.
Fanny Burney's novel *Camilla* published.

RECREATION AND FASHION

1795 Pitt's imposition of a tax on hair-powder speedily brings the fashion to an end.

RELIGION AND EDUCATION

1795 Maynooth Seminary endowed from public funds; opens in October.
London Missionary Society founded.
1796 Glasgow Missionary Society founded.
Richard Watson writes *Apology for the Bible*.

SCIENCE AND INVENTION

1796 *May 14* Edward Jenner discovers vaccine against smallpox from cows.

VOYAGES AND EXPLORATION

1795(–1797) Mungo Park reaches Segu and R. Niger.

Events Elsewhere

1795 *Aug.* Executive Directory governs French Republic (to 1799).
1796 *Apr.* Start of Bonaparte's Italian campaign.

1797	Feb.	British take Trinidad and Santa Lucia.
	14	Admiral Jervis defeats Spaniards off Cape St Vincent.
	Feb. 26	Bank of England suspends cash payments and makes first issue of £1 bank notes.
	Mar.–Oct.	Lord Lake undertakes campaign to disarm rebellious Ulster.
	Apr. 16	Easter Sunday mutiny of fleet at Spithead over food and conditions.
	May 10	Admiral Howe pacifies and reassures Channel fleet; puts to sea again, 17 May.
	12	More serious mutiny at the Nore, spreads to squadron based on Yarmouth.
	Jun. 30	Nore mutiny suppressed; ringleader Richard Parker and 24 seamen hanged at the yardarm.
	Jul. 21	Rear-Admiral Horatio Nelson has arm amputated after unsuccessful attempt to capture Spanish treasure ship at Santa Cruz, Panama.
	Oct. 11	Admiral Duncan defeats Franco-Dutch fleet at Ψ Camperdown.
	Dec.	Ralph Abercromby appointed C.in-C. Ireland.
1798	Jan. 9	Last session of independent Irish Parliament.
	May	Pitt's budget proposes an income tax at 2s in £1; prohibits import of foreign newspapers; imposes additional 1d stamp duty on all British newspapers. Marquess of Wellesley goes to India as Governor-General.
	23	Irish rebellion in Wexford (to 21 Jun.).
	Aug. 1	Ψ of the Nile: Nelson destroys French fleet at anchor in Aboukir Bay.
	22	1000 French troops land at Killala; forced to surrender at Ballinamuck, 8 Sep.
	Nov. 3	Wolfe Tone arrested after landing in Lough Swilly; commits suicide in prison, 19 Nov.
	Dec. 24	Anglo-Russian alliance treaty.

FINE ARTS AND ARCHITECTURE

1797   J.M.W. Turner paints *Millbank, Moonlight*.

LITERATURE AND SCHOLARSHIP

1798   Wordsworth and Coleridge publish *Lyrical Ballads*.

Thomas Malthus writes *Essay on the Principle of Population as it affects the Future Improvement of Society*; argues that growth of population outstrips food supplies; wages should not exceed subsistence level to check labouring classes' natural profligacy.

RECREATION AND FASHION

1797 Jan. 15   Top-hat introduced to London society by haberdasher, James Hetherington; gains rapid popularity.

RELIGION AND EDUCATION

William Wilberforce writes *A Practical View of the Prevailing Religious System of Professed Christians.*
Andrew Bell explains his 'Madras System' of monitorial teaching in *An Experiment in Education.*

SCIENCE AND INVENTION

1797   Henry Maudslay invents a metal carriage lathe.
1798   Henry Cavendish experiments on density of the earth.

VOYAGES AND EXPLORATION

1798   George Bass and Matthew Flinders discover Bass Strait, confirming Tasmania is an island.

Events Elsewhere

1797 Oct.   Bonaparte imposes Peace of Campo-Formio on Austria.
1798 May 19   Bonaparte leaves Toulon for Egyptian campaign.

AD 1799–1800

1799 Mar. 19   Sir Sidney Smith defies Bonaparte at siege of Acre (to 20 May).
May 4   Sultan Tippoo of Mysore killed at Ψ Seringapatam; East India Co. and Nizam of Hyderabad share his kingdom.
Jun. 1   Pitt completes Second Coalition against France: Britain, Russia, Austria, Portugal, Turkey, Naples.
Jul. 12   Combination Act: gives a magistrate right to ban political associations of workers.
Sep.   Abortive Anglo-Russian expedition to the Netherlands.
1800 Jan. 8   First soup kitchens to relieve hungry poor, London.
Mar. 28   Irish Parliament passes Act of Union with England; passed by Westminster Parliament, 2 Jul.
May 15   James Hadfield fires shots at George III, Theatre Royal, Drury Lane.
Jun.   Combination Act modified: 2 magistrates to assess, not 1; includes arbitration clause.
Sep. 5   French occupation troops on Malta surrender to British.
Autumn   Robert Owen begins philanthropic reforms for workers employed in his mills at New Lanark.

FINE ARTS AND ARCHITECTURE

1800   Josiah Spode of Stoke-on-Trent uses bone as well as felspar to perfect his porcelain.

LITERATURE AND SCHOLARSHIP

W. Wordsworth, in Preface to second edition of *Lyrical Ballads*, defines poetic romanticism.

Robert Bloomfield's long poem *The Farmer's Boy* becomes bestseller.

Maria Edgeworth publishes *Castle Rackrent*, one of the earliest historical novels.

RELIGION AND EDUCATION

1799   John Venn founds Church Missionary Society to serve in 'Africa and the East'.

SCIENCE AND INVENTION

1800   Royal Institution (for encouraging applied science) established in London; Humphry Davy lectures there, 1801-23.

William Herschel's astronomical research at Slough reveals existence of infra-red solar rays.

H. Davy publishes his *Researches, Chemical and Philosophical, Chiefly Concerning Nitrous Oxide*.

Charles Hatchett discovers metallic element niobium.

Events Elsewhere

1799 Oct. 9   Bonaparte returns from Egypt; overthrows Directory and establishes Consulate, 9 Nov. ('18 Brumaire').

1800 Jun. 14   Bonaparte defeats Austrians at Ψ Marengo.

AD 1801–1802

1801   First British census, supervised by John Rickman: 8.3 million in England; 1.6 Scotland; 0.5 Wales; 5.2 Ireland.

Jan.   Act of Union with Ireland becomes effective.

   14   Britain threatens to seize Russian, Swedish and Danish vessels trading with France.

Feb. 5   Pitt resigns as Prime Minister over George III's hostility to Catholic Emancipation; stays in office until 14 Mar. because of King's illness; succeeded by Henry Addington (later Viscount Sidmouth).

Apr. 2   Ψ Copenhagen: Admirals Hyde Parker and Nelson attack Danish fleet.

   14   Habeas Corpus Act suspended to allow political suspects to be detained without trial.

Jun.   General Enclosure Act: cheapens enclosing of common land for tillage.

   17   St Petersburg Convention: Russia acknowledges British naval right of search in Baltic.

   23   Clergy Disqualification Act: clergy excluded from Commons, but Revd John

		Horne Tooke, radical MP for Old Sarum, allowed to stay until end of session.
	27	French garrison at Cairo capitulates to British force.
Oct.	1	Peace preliminaries between Britain and France signed in London.
1802 Jan.		William Cobbett's *Weekly Political Register* begins publication; runs until 1835, with 13-week gap in 1817.
Mar.	27	Peace Ty of Amiens: begins 14-month interlude in the conflict between Britain and France.
Jun.	22	Health and Morals of Apprentices Act, first protective factory legislation: no children under 9 in mills; maximum 12-hour day for children.
Aug.		West India Import Dock opens, Isle of Dogs; first commercial dock in London.
Oct.		*Edinburgh Review*, Whig quarterly, begins publication; editor Francis Jeffrey; published until 1929.

LITERATURE AND SCHOLARSHIP

1802(–1803)   Walter Scott's ballads *Minstrelsy of the Scottish Border* published in 3 vols.

RECREATION AND FASHION

1802   Racecourse laid out for D. of Richmond at Goodwood, Sussex.

Mme Marie Tussaud mounts first waxworks exhibition, Lyceum Hall, London.

SCIENCE AND INVENTION

1801   'Dalton's Law': law on partial pressure in gases, formulated by John Dalton after research in Manchester.

Jul.	24	Iron horse-tram road links Croydon and Wandsworth.
Dec.	24	Steam-carriage of Richard Trevithick carries road passengers at Camborne, Cornwall.
1802		*Charlotte Dundas*, a wooden ship with a single paddle-wheel, designed by William Symington, covers 20 miles of the Forth and Clyde canal with lighters in tow; world's first steam vessel.

Events Elsewhere

1801 Jul. 16   Concordat between French Republic and Papacy.

AD 1803–1804

1803 May	17	Britain imposes embargo on French and Dutch ships in British ports.
	18	War resumed between Britain and France because of disputes over Malta, Switzerland and Italy.
Jun.		British take St Lucia and Tobago from the French.

Jul. 23	Irish rising led by Robert Emmet fails to receive expected French aid; Emmet captured (25 Aug.) and hanged (20 Sep.).
Aug. 6	Second Mahratta War: Arthur Wellesley victorious at Assaye (23 Sep.) and Argaum (29 Nov.); war ends when mountain fastness of Gawilghur stormed (15 Dec.).
1804 *Apr. 25*	Pitt and C.J. Fox attack Addington's muddled plans for raising militia, forcing his resignation (29 Apr.).
May 16	Pitt heads new government; Fox excluded on insistence of George III.

FINE ARTS AND ARCHITECTURE

1803 *Feb. 19*	John Crome presides at first meeting of Norwich school of artists.
	J.M.W. Turner exhibits *Calais Pier*.
	Martello Towers built; defensive forts on Kent and Sussex coasts.
1804	J.M.W. Turner prominent in foundation of English Water Colour Society.

LITERATURE AND SCHOLARSHIP

1804	William Blake's *Milton*, Book I, published, with prefatory poem known as 'Jerusalem'; Book II published 1808.

RECREATION AND FASHION

1803	First book on cricketing technique published: Thomas Boxall, *Rules and Instructions for Playing at the Game of Cricket, as Practised by the Most Eminent Players*.

RELIGION AND EDUCATION

1803	Interdenominational Sunday School Union established in London.
	Joseph Lancaster's *Improvements in Education as it Respects the Industrious Classes* advocates monitorial system of teaching.
1804	British and Foreign Bible Society established.

SCIENCE AND INVENTION

1803	John Dalton completes his tables of atomic weights.
	Major Henry Shrapnel perfects his explosive shell; first fired on French at Vimeiro, 1808.
	Thomas Telford begins work on Scottish roads and on Caledonian canal as chief engineer to Commissioners for Highland Roads and Bridges.
1804 *Feb. 21*	Trevithick demonstrates steam-locomotive in Glamorgan.

Events Elsewhere

1803 *Apr.*	Louisiana Purchase by USA from France.
1804 *May 16*	Bonaparte proclaimed Emperor of the French; coronation in Notre Dame, Paris, 2 Dec.

1805	*Jan.*	*30*	*London Packet*, a brig with wine from Oporto, is first ship to use London Docks.
	Apr.	*11*	Ty of St Petersburg: Anglo-Russian alliance to create Third Coalition against France: Austria joins, 9 Aug.
	Sep.	*3*	Napoleon finally abandons invasion plans and leaves camp at Boulogne.
	Oct.	*21*	Ψ Trafalgar: Nelson defeats Franco-Spanish fleet, but is mortally wounded.
1806	*Jan.*		Invasion and seizure of Dutch colony at Cape of Good Hope.
		23	Pitt dies, leaving no clear successor among Tories.
	Feb.	*10*	Lord Grenville (William Wyndham Grenville; Foreign Secretary, 1791-1801) forms coalition 'Ministry of All the Talents', with C.J. Fox at the Foreign Office.
	Jun.	*27*	Buenos Aires captured from Spanish colonists in surprise attack; lost in Aug.; military operations in R. Plate estuary continue for next 18 months.
	Sep.	*9*	P. of Wales visits Llandrinio, Powys: first visit by a P. of Wales to the Principality since 1642.
		13	Fox dies, leaving Charles Grey (Earl, 1807) as leader of Foxite Whigs.
	Nov.		Indecisive general election brings gains to Grenvillites and losses to former Pittite Tories.
		21	Napoleon's 'Berlin Decree' bans trade with British possessions through any port under French control, thus establishing the 'Continental System'.

FINE ARTS AND ARCHITECTURE

1805	David Wilkie's painting *Village Politicians* creates great impression when exhibited at Royal Academy.
1806	Dartmoor prison built for French captives.

LITERATURE AND SCHOLARSHIP

1805	W. Scott publishes *The Lay of the Last Minstrel*.
	Robert Southey's narrative poem *Madoc* published.
	W. Wordsworth completes his autobiographical *The Prelude*; not published until 1850.
1806	Ann and Jane Taylor publish *Rhymes for the Nursery*; includes 'Twinkle, twinkle little star'.

MUSIC AND DRAMA

1806 *Dec.*	Joseph Grimaldi is pantomine clown ('Joey') for first time, Covent Garden Theatre.

SCIENCE AND INVENTION

1806	H. Davy uses electrolysis to isolate sodium and potassium; delivers his Bakerian lecture, 'On Some Chemical Agencies of Electricity'.
	Ralph Wedgwood pioneers 'ink' paper (carbon).

Horse-drawn passenger railway at Oystermouth, Swansea; carries passengers from 25 Mar. 1807 (continuing intermittently until, as an electric tramway, it closes on 5 Jan. 1960).

VOYAGES AND EXPLORATION

1805 *Jan.* 30   Mungo Park leaves Portsmouth with expedition to upper Niger; killed, 1806.

RECREATION AND FASHION

1806   First Gentlemen v. Players match played, at Lord's Ground, Dorset Square; regular cricket fixture until 1963.

Events Elsewhere

1805 *Dec.* 2   Napoleon defeats Russians and Austrians at Austerlitz.

1806 *Aug.* 6   Formal ending of Holy Roman Empire; ruler in Vienna becomes Emperor of Austria.

AD 1807–1808

1807 *Feb.* 19   British warships force the Dardanelles to help Russian ally at war with Turkey.

Mar. 24   Grenville's ministry resigns over George III's veto on (non-Irish) Roman Catholics holding army commissions.

25   Slave trade abolished in all British possessions.

31   Duke of Portland (*v.* 1783) forms Tory government: George Canning Foreign Secretary; Castlereagh Secretary of War and Colonies.

Jun.   'No-Popery' general election increases Tory majority.

4   Frederick Winsor illuminates part of Pall Mall with gas lighting.

22   HMS *Leopard*, seeking recovery of deserters, attacks US frigate *Chesapeake* off Virginian coast; threatens Anglo-American war.

Sep. 2–5   Naval bombardment of Copenhagen in support of military expedition to require handing over of Danish fleet so as to prevent it passing into French hands.

Nov. 7   Anglo-Russian diplomatic relations severed because of Tilsit alliances.

1808 *Jan.* 1   Sierra Leone (settled by British, 1788) becomes crown colony for Africans rescued from slave-ships.

3   *The Examiner*, a radical weekly, founded; Leigh Hunt editor; published until 1881.

Jul. 1   Start of British involvement in the Peninsular War; base set up at Corunna to support Spanish rebellion.

8   Hottest shade temperature recorded in London: 98°F, 36.6°C.

Jul. 20   First despatch from a specialist war reporter: Henry Crabb Robinson in Corunna to *The Times*.

Aug.	*1*	Wellesley lands near Oporto with expeditionary force to help Portuguese against French.
	21	Wellesley defeats Junot at Ψ Vimeiro.
	30	Sir Hew Dalrymple, having superseded Wellesley, concludes much-criticized Convention of Cintra, allowing French to evacuate Portugal.
Oct.	*27*	Sir John Moore sets out from Lisbon with 30,000 men to help Spanish against French.
Nov.	*13*	Moore reaches Salamanca.
Dec.	*21*	Moore wins cavalry action at Sahagun but, at approach of Napoleon with main army, orders retreat on Corunna.

LITERATURE AND SCHOLARSHIP

1807	Charles and Mary Lamb publish their *Tales from Shakespeare*.
	First published poetry collection by Lord Byron, *Hours of Idleness*.
1808	W. Scott's *Marmion; A Tale of Flodden Field* published.

MUSIC AND DRAMA

1807	First lyrics by Thomas Moore for collection of *Irish Melodies*; publication continues until 1834.
1808 *Sep.* 20	Theatre Royal, Covent Garden, destroyed by fire.

RELIGION AND EDUCATION

1808	Royal Lancasterian Institution founded to promote education of the poor on Joseph Lancaster's monitorial principles.

RECREATION AND FASHION

1807 *Jun.*	Ascot Gold Cup first run.

Events Elsewhere

1807 *Jul.* 8	Treaties of Tilsit: Franco-Russian alliance.
1808 *May* 2	Insurrection in Madrid against French occupation of Spain.

AD 1809–1810

1809 *Jan.*	*11*	Moore defends Corunna during British evacuation; is mortally wounded, 16 Jan.
	Feb.	*Quarterly Review* founded by John Murray; William Gifford editor; a Tory periodical, published until 1967.
	Apr. *22*	Wellesley returns to Lisbon as commanding general.
	May *12*	Wellesley defeats Soult at Ψ Oporto; enters Spain, 4 Jul.
	Jun. *19*	'Curwen's Act' passed: a private member's Bill to curb blatant sale of parliamentary seats to supporters.

Jul.	*27–28*	Wellesley defeats Joseph Bonaparte and Jourdan at Ψ Talavera; made Viscount Wellington of Talavera, 4 Sep.
Aug.	*11*	British troops land on Dutch island of Walcheren.
Sep.	*21*	Canning slightly wounded in duel with Castlereagh on Putney Heath; both men resign office.
	30	British evacuate Walcheren, leaving 4,000 soldiers dead from fever, probably malarial.
Oct.	*4*	Spencer Perceval succeeds ailing Portland as Prime Minister.
1810 *Apr.*	*5*	Speaker orders detention of Sir Francis Burdett MP in the Tower for libelling the Commons in an article in the *Weekly Register* advocating parliamentary reform; arrest leads to riots in London.
Jul.	*9*	Cobbett fined £1,000 and jailed for 2 years for denouncing flogging of militiamen at Norwich by German mercenaries.
Oct.	*8*	Wellington falls back on Torres Vedras defensive lines, Portugal; holds them for 5 months.

LITERATURE AND SCHOLARSHIP

1809	Hannah More publishes *Coelebs in Search of a Wife*, novel.
1810	W. Scott's *The Lady of the Lake* published, a narrative poem.

MUSIC AND DRAMA

1809 *Feb.*	*24*	Theatre Royal, Drury Lane, destroyed by fire.
Sep.–Nov.		The OP ('Old Prices') riots for 61 nights at new Covent Garden, until cost of a seat restored to pre-fire level (6s rather than 7s).

RECREATION AND FASHION

1809 *May*		2000 Guineas established at Newmarket.
1810 *Dec.*	*18*	First international prize-fight: Tom Cribb beats black American, Tom Molineaux.

Events Elsewhere

1809 *Aug.*	After Austria's defeat by Napoleon at Ψ Wagram, Metternich begins 39 years as Austrian Foreign Minister.
1810 *Feb.* *11*	Napoleon marries Archduchess Marie Louise.

AD 1811–1812

1811 *Feb.*	*5*	Regency Act in favour of P. of Wales because of George III's senile porphyria.
Mar.		Organized machine-breaking ('Luddism') in Nottingham.
Jun.	*19*	Prince Regent's Grand Fête at Carlton House, ostensibly to honour French Bourbon exiles.

1812	*Jan.*		Major John Cartwright forms first radical Hampden Club in London to campaign for parliamentary reform and a wider franchise.
		8–19	Wellington's siege and capture of Ciudad Rodrigo.
	Feb.		Framebreaking Act: imposes death penalty for Luddism.
	Mar.	4	Castlereagh becomes Foreign Secretary in succession to Lord Wellesley (Foreign Secretary since 1809), who resigned because he thought the government lukewarm in support of his brother, Wellington, in the Peninsula.
	May		Unlawful Oaths Act against Luddites and radical societies.
		11	Spencer Perceval assassinated in lobby of Commons by a bankrupt Liverpool broker, John Bellingham.
	Jun.	9	Lord Liverpool becomes Prime Minister after 4 weeks of parliamentary confusion.
		18	US Congress declares war on Britain over naval interference with American shipping in blockading France.
	Jul.	18	Ty of Örebrö: confirms peace and friendship between Britain, Russia and Sweden.
		22	Wellington defeats Marmont at Ψ Salamanca.
	Aug.	12	Wellington enters Madrid.
	Sep.	19	Unsuccessful siege of Burgos begins (to 22 Oct.).

FINE ARTS AND ARCHITECTURE

| 1811 | John Nash begins 14-year development of London's West End with building of Regent St. |

LITERATURE AND SCHOLARSHIP

| 1811 | | Jane Austen writes *Sense and Sensibility*. |
| 1812 | *Mar.* | Publication of first 2 cantos of Byron's *Childe Harold's Pilgrimage* causes sensation: 'I woke one morning and found myself famous'. |

MUSIC AND DRAMA

| 1812 | *Jun.* 29 | Sarah Siddons makes last appearance at Covent Garden Theatre, as Lady Macbeth. |

RELIGION AND EDUCATION

| 1811 | *Jun.* | National Society set up to spread Anglican Church schools. Ordination of 8 Calvinistic Methodist ministers at Bala marks major Welsh secession from Established Church. |
| 1812 | | Prototype National School set up in Baldwin's Gardens, a criminal rookery in the City of London. |

RECREATION AND FASHION

| 1811 | | Fashionable women reject tight corsets and petticoats. |
| 1812 | *Autumn* | Countess Lieven, wife of Russian ambassador, introduces the waltz to London. |

1812   Henry Bell installs single-cylinder steam-engine in his vessel, *Comet*, and begins passenger and cargo steamship service on R. Clyde.

Events Elsewhere

1812 *Jun.* 24   Napoleon invades Russia; enters Moscow, 14 Sep.; last retreating troops leave Russia, 14 Dec.

AD 1813–1814

1813 *May* 24   Catholic Relief Bill fails because Speaker denies Catholics any right to sit in the Commons.

Jun. 1   HMS *Shannon* captures USS *Chesapeake*.

21   Wellington defeats Jourdan at Ψ Vitoria, destroying Napoleonic hold on Spain.

Jul. 1   East India Co. loses monopoly of trade with the Indies, but retains it for the China trade.

23   'Dandy Ball' at Argyle Rooms, off Oxford Street, London; Prince Regent insulted by Brummel.

Aug. 13   Cape of Good Hope becomes British colony.

Sep. 1   British troops loot and sack San Sebastian.

Oct. 7   Wellington crosses R. Bidassoa to invade SW France.

Dec. 29   British troops seize and fire the town of Buffalo in retaliation for American burning of Newark (10 Dec.).

1814 *Jan.*   Statute of Apprentices 1563 repealed.

14   Ty of Kiel: Denmark cedes Heligoland to Britain.

Apr. 10   Wellington's victory at Ψ Toulouse ends Peninsular War.

May 30   1st Peace Ty of Paris between Allies and France: recognizes British sovereignty over Malta, Tobago, St Lucia, Mauritius.

Jun. 6–27   Tsar Alexander I, King Frederick William III of Prussia, Metternich, Blücher and other allied leaders make state visit to England to celebrate victorious peace.

Aug. 24   British raiding-party occupies Washington DC and sets fire to public buildings, including White House.

Nov. 1   Congress of Vienna officially opens, with Castlereagh as chief British representative.

Dec. 24   Ty of Ghent: ends Anglo-American War.

FINE ARTS AND ARCHITECTURE
1813   J.M.W. Turner paints *Frosty Morning*.

1814	Sir Thomas Lawrence commissioned by Regent to paint the Allied sovereigns and leading public figures; works completed in 1818 and hung in the Waterloo Gallery, Windsor.
	Dulwich Picture Gallery (designed by Sir John Soane) open to public 1 day a week; England's first public art gallery.

LITERATURE AND SCHOLARSHIP

1813	Jane Austen's *Pride and Prejudice* (written 1796–97) at last published.
	R. Owen publishes *A New View of Society*.
	Percy Bysshe Shelley's *Queen Mab*, a visionary poem, published privately.
	Robert Southey appointed Poet Laureate; publishes his *Life of Nelson*.
1814	Jane Austen's *Mansfield Park* (begun 1811) published.
	Lord Byron's poem *The Corsair* published.
	W. Scott publishes *Waverley*, his first novel.
	W. Wordsworth writes *The Excursion*.

MUSIC AND DRAMA

1813	London Philharmonic Society founded; establishes regular series of concerts at Argyll Rooms, until 1830.
1814 *Jan.* 26	Edmund Kean makes sensational debut at Drury Lane as Shylock.

RECREATION AND FASHION

1814 *Jun.* 22	First cricket match on present Lord's ground: MCC beat Hertfordshire.

RELIGION AND EDUCATION

1813	Baptist General Union established, for Britain and Ireland.

SCIENCE AND INVENTION

1813	Smooth-wheeled steam-locomotive *Puffing Billy*, invented by William Hedley, hauls wagons at Wylam colliery, Durham.
1814 *Jul.* 25	George Stephenson's *My Lord*, a steam-locomotive, hauls carts at 6 m.p.h. on Killingworth colliery tram road, Northumberland.
Nov. 29	Steam-press first used to print *The Times*.

Events Elsewhere

1813 *Oct.* 16–19	Napoleon defeated in Ψ 'of the Nations' at Leipzig.
1814 *Apr.* 11	Napoleon abdicates; exiled to Elba.

AD 1815–1816

1815 *Jan.* 8	British defeated by Americans at Ψ New Orleans, news of Ty of Ghent not reaching USA until 11 Feb.

Feb.	20	Budget drops income tax as a source of revenue.
Mar.	7	Wellington, at Congress of Vienna, hears that Napoleon landed in France on 1 Mar.
	15	Corn Law permits free importation of foreign corn only when price of wheat reaches 80s a quarter; troops have to protect Parliament from angry demonstrators.
Jun.	9	Britain a signatory of Final Act of Congress of Vienna.
	18	Wellington and Blücher defeat Napoleon at Ψ Waterloo.
Jul.	10	Apothecaries Act: bans unqualified medical practitioners.
	24	HMS *Bellerophon*, with Napoleon aboard, anchors off Devon coast for 12 days before he is sent to St Helena.
Nov.	5	British given protectorate over Ionian Islands.
	20	2nd Peace Ty of Paris between allies and France.
1816 Jun.		Price of Cobbett's *Political Register* (v. 1802) cut to 2d; circulation rises above 40,000.
	20	G. Canning returns to Cabinet as President of Board of Control for India.
Dec.	2	Spa Fields Riot at Clerkenwell over political reform.

FINE ARTS AND ARCHITECTURE

1816	British Museum purchases Parthenon Marbles from Lord Elgin.
1816(–1819)	John Nash rebuilds the Regent's Marine Pavilion at Brighton in Indian style.

LITERATURE AND SCHOLARSHIP

1815	W. Scott publishes *Guy Mannering*.
1816	J. Austen publishes *Emma*.
	W. Scott publishes *The Antiquary*.
	S.T. Coleridge publishes *Christabel and Other Poems*; includes *Kubla Khan; a Vision in a Dream*.
	Thomas Love Peacock's first satirical novel *Headlong Hall* published.
	Thomas Evans writes *Christian Polity the Salvation of the Empire*, pioneer agrarian Christian socialist tract.

MUSIC AND DRAMA

1815		First London season by a French ballet company, King's Theatre, Haymarket.
1816 Sep.	16	William Macready makes debut at Covent Garden Theatre, as Orestes.

SCIENCE AND INVENTION

1815	Sir Humphry Davy, having investigated fire damp, invents miner's safety lamp.
1816	Leeds-Liverpool canal, across Pennines, finally completed.

Events Elsewhere

1815 Mar.	20	Napoleon's 'Hundred Days' begin (to 22 Jun.).
1816 Jul.	9	Argentina declares independence from Spain.

1817	Jan.	28	Shot allegedly fired at Prince Regent returning from opening Parliament.
	Feb.		Lace machines at Heathcote & Boden's works, Loughborough, destroyed in last major Luddite attack.
	Mar.	4	Fear of imminent insurrection leads to suspension of Habeas Corpus Act.
		10	'Blanketeers' begin protest hunger march from Manchester to London; 160 arrested at Stockport next day.
		17	Repressive emergency measures: magistrates 'advised' to suppress seditious publications; Act making physical attacks on King or Regent treasonable.
		31	Act to prevent seditious meetings.
	Apr.		William Blackwood publishes *The Edinburgh Monthly Magazine*, a Tory periodical; from Oct. 1817 until 1980 uses the publisher's name in its title.
	Jun.	9	Some 200 labourers from Pentridge district, Derbyshire, march on Nottingham, but checked by cavalry; similar rising by clothing workers near Huddersfield.
	Aug.–Sep.		Good harvest temporarily improves living conditions.
	Nov.	6	Death in childbirth of P. Charlotte, only child of Prince Regent, leaves George III with no grandchildren in line of succession.
1818	Jan.	6	Ty of Mundosir: annexation of Rajput states and Indore, India, is completed.
		31	Act suspending Habeas Corpus repealed.
	May	19	Commons motion by Burdett in favour of parliamentary reform defeated.
	Jul.	1–25	General election: Tories keep safe majority.
	Sep.	27	Castlereagh at Aachen (to 21 Nov.) for first assembly in Congress System ('Congress of Aix-la-Chapelle').
	Oct.	20	Agreement with USA settles Canadian border west of Great Lakes along 49th parallel.

FINE ARTS AND ARCHITECTURE

| 1817 | | John Constable paints *Flatford Mill*. |
| | Jun. 18 | Waterloo Bridge opened; built, over 6 years, by John Rennie. |

LITERATURE AND SCHOLARSHIP

1817	Lord Byron's poetic drama *Manfred* printed.
	David Ricardo publishes *Principles of Political Economy and Taxation*.
1818	J. Austen's *Persuasion* and *Northanger Abbey* published posthumously.
	W. Scott writes *The Heart of Midlothian*.
	T.L. Peacock writes *Nightmare Abbey*.
	Mary Wollstonecraft Shelley publishes *Frankenstein, or the Modern Prometheus*.
	John Keats' *Endymion*, poem in 4 books, published.
	Thomas Bowdler publishes *Family Shakespeare*, expurgating any passage unsuitable 'to be read aloud in a family'.

MUSIC AND DRAMA

1817 *Jun.* 23   John Kemble's farewell, as Coriolanus at Covent Garden Theatre.

RELIGION AND EDUCATION

1818   Newly founded Church Building Society receives £1 million from Government as thanksgiving for Waterloo.

SCIENCE AND INVENTION

1817–1818   Gas used to light Covent Garden Theatre (1817) and the Regent's Marine Pavilion, Brighton (1818).

VOYAGES AND EXPLORATION

1818 *Aug.* 30   John Ross, seeking North-West Passage, turns back in Lancaster Bay.

AD 1819–1820

1819 *Feb.* 6   Singapore settlement founded for East India Co. by Stamford Raffles.

May 24   Birth to Duke and Duchess of Kent of P. (Alexandrina) Victoria eases dynastic problem caused in Nov. 1817.

Jun. 2   Poona and Maharatta lands, India, put under rule from Bombay.

Jul. 2   'Peel's Act' passed: finance committee under Robert Peel secures Act pledging return to gold standard by 1823.

Aug. 16   'Peterloo Massacre': 11 people killed by yeomanry at St Peter's Fields, Manchester, during political reform meeting addressed by Henry Hunt.

Dec.   The Six Acts passed: impose curbs on disorder by preventing illegal military training, regularizing public meetings, strengthening press laws and penalties for seditious libel.

1820 *Jan.* 29   George III dies at Windsor; accession of Prince Regent as George IV.

Feb. 28   Plan to blow up the Cabinet discovered; conspirators, led by Arthur Thistlewood, arrested in Cato St, London.

Mar.–Apr.   General election increases Tory majority.

May 1   Thistlewood and 4 associates executed outside Newgate prison; the last beheadings in Britain.

Jun. 5   Princess Caroline, George IV's wife, arrives in Dover after 6 years abroad and claims her rights as Queen.

Jul. 5   Bill of Pains and Penalties, accusing Caroline of 'licentious behaviour' and proposing to dissolve her marriage, introduced in H. of Lords.

Oct. 23   Foreign policy increasingly isolationist; Castlereagh sends only an observer to Congress of Troppau.

Nov. 10   Popular support for Caroline makes government withdraw Pains and Penalties Bill.

FINE ARTS AND ARCHITECTURE

1819   Samuel Ware completes Burlington Arcade of fashionable shops, Piccadilly,
        London, patrolled by beadles.

LITERATURE AND SCHOLARSHIP

1820   J. Keats publishes *Lamia and Other Poems*; includes 'Eve of St Agnes' and
        his main odes ('Grecian Urn'; 'Nightingale'; 'Autumn').
        P.B. Shelley publishes *Prometheus Unbound*, 4-act lyrical drama; also
        published are his 'Ode to the West Wind'; 'To a Skylark'.

SCIENCE AND INVENTION

1820   The *Aaron Manby*, an iron vessel fitted with an H. Bell steam-engine, makes
        several voyages from London to Paris and back, averaging 8.5 knots.

Events Elsewhere

1819 *Sep.* 20   Carlsbad Decrees: impose restrictions on liberal movement in German
                  Confederation after student unrest.
1820 *May* 6   Missouri Compromise on slavery decided by US Congress.

AD 1821–1822

1821 *Apr.* 17   Bill to remove Roman Catholic disabilities defeated in H. of Lords on 2nd
                  reading.
     May 7   Bank of England resumes cash payments; on gold standard 2 years earlier
                  than Act of 1819 requires.
          9   Lord John Russell unsuccessfully moves motion for parliamentary reform in
                  H. of Commons.
     Jul. 19   George IV's coronation; Caroline excluded from Abbey.
     Aug. 8   Queen Caroline dies.
          12   George IV on state visit to Dublin.
     Oct. 31   William Cobbett sets out on his Rural Rides.
     Oct.–Nov. Wellington represents Britain at Congress of Verona.

1822 *Jan.* 17   Robert Peel becomes a reforming Home Secretary in the Liverpool
                  government.
     Jun. 22   Navigation Acts modified to allow foreign ships to bring goods from
                  European ports into Britain.
     Aug. 12   Castlereagh cuts his throat; succeeded as Foreign Secretary by Canning, 15
                  Sep.
     Oct. 20   *Sunday Times* first appears under that title.
     Nov. 6   'Bottle Riot': Protestant Orangemen attack Wellesley (Lord-Lieutenant of
                  Ireland) in Dublin theatre for banning celebrations of William III's birthday.

FINE ARTS AND ARCHITECTURE

1821   J. Constable paints *Hay Wain*.
1822   Thomas Cubitt completes Woburn Walk, Bloomsbury; first London street
        planned as a shopping centre.

LITERATURE AND SCHOLARSHIP

1821   W. Scott publishes *Kenilworth*.
        P.B. Shelley writes *Adonais*, elegy for Keats (died Rome, 23 Feb.)
        Pierce Egan, sen. writes *Life in London; or the Day and Night Scenes of Jerry
        Hawthorn Esq. and Corinthian Tom.*
1822   Thomas de Quincey publishes *Confessions of an English Opium Eater*.

MUSIC AND DRAMA

1821 *Jul.* 4   John Nash's redesigned Haymarket Theatre, London, opens with *The Rivals*.

SCIENCE AND INVENTION

1821   Sir Humphry Davy, as President of the Royal Society, reports to members on
        his research into electromagnetism.

Events Elsewhere

1821 *Apr.*   Greek War of Independence begins.
     May 5   Napoleon I dies on St Helena.

AD 1823–1824

1823 *Jan.* 31   William Huskisson enters cabinet as a reforming President of the Board of
                  Trade, encouraging freer trade to stimulate exports.
     Mar. 25   Canning, as Foreign Secretary, announces British recognition of Greeks as
                  belligerents rather than rebels.
     May 10   Huskisson's Warehousing of Goods Act: allows foreigners to put imports
                  into bond free of duty.
          12   Daniel O'Connell establishes Catholic Association in Ireland.
     Jul.   Peel secures rapid passage of 5 legal reform Acts abolishing death penalty for
                  over 100 offences.
          4   Transportation Act: conditions of convicts shipped to colonies eased by
                  allowing them to be employed on public works.
          10   Peel's Gaol Act: asserts Home Office responsibility for prison conditions and
                  discipline.
          18   Foreign ships to enter British harbours on equal terms with British vessels,
                  provided their home governments offered reciprocal concessions.

1824 *Mar.* 4   Sir William Hillary founds Royal National Institution for the Preservation of
                  Life from Shipwreck to establish lifeboats around the coast.

Apr. 19	Byron, having crossed from Corfu to Greece in Jan. to encourage resistance to the Turks, dies at Mesolongion.
Jun. 21	Combination Law: lifts ban on unions of workers but prohibits intimidation.
Dec. 15	British cabinet recognizes independence of Mexico, Columbia and Buenos Aires.

FINE ARTS AND ARCHITECTURE

1823	Robert Smirke begins work on new British Museum (to 1849), with building of the King's Library (completed 1826).
1824	George IV induces government to purchase the Angerstein Collection of old masters as nucleus of the National Gallery; housed in Pall Mall until 1838.

LITERATURE AND SCHOLARSHIP

1823	The 'King's Library' – 120,800 volumes of George III – presented to the British Museum.
	Royal Society of Literature founded.
	C. Lamb publishes *Essays of Elia*.
1824	W. Scott publishes *Redgauntlet*.

MUSIC AND DRAMA

1823 *Mar.*	Royal Academy of Music opens, Hanover Square, London.
1824 *May 14*	Gioacchino Rossini conducts fashionable concert at Almacks'.

RECREATION AND FASHION

1823 *Nov.*	Traditional date when William Webb Ellis originated the football game at Rugby School.

RELIGION AND EDUCATION

1823	Mechanics' Institutes founded in Glasgow and London on the initiative of George Birkbeck.
1824	Royal Society for the Prevention of Cruelty to Animals set up.

SCIENCE AND INVENTION

1823	Charles Macintosh patents waterproofing of fabrics.
	The Lancet first published.
	'Cabs' introduced from Paris into London streets.

Events Elsewhere

1823 *Dec. 2*	Monroe Doctrine: presidential message to Congress.

AD 1825–1826

1825	*May* 17	H. of Lords rejects Roman Catholic Relief Bill.
	Jun. 22	Cotton Mills Regulation Act: limits children under 16 to 12-hour working day.
	Jul. 5	Navigation Laws modified: British and foreign ships to trade in the United Kingdom on equal terms.
	6	Revised Combination Act to check violence during a strike.
	Sep. 27	First steam-locomotive railway opens: Stockton to Darlington.
1826	*Feb.* 24	Ty of Yandabo: Burma cedes Arakan peninsula to Britain.
	Apr. 4	St Petersburg Protocol: Anglo-Russian recognition of Greek autonomy.
	Jun. 20	Ty of Bangkok: British influence increased in S. Siam.
	Dec. 12	Canning tells H. of Commons British troops will go to Portugal to back liberal government against possible Spanish invasion: 'I call in the New World to redress the balance of the Old.'

FINE ARTS AND ARCHITECTURE

1825–1826	J. Nash converts Buckingham House into Buckingham Palace.
	Sir Jeffry Wyatville rebuilds Windsor Castle.

LITERATURE AND SCHOLARSHIP

1825	Lord Braybrooke edits first edition of *Diary of Samuel Pepys*.
	William Hazlitt publishes *The Spirit of the Age*.
1826	Benjamin Disraeli publishes *Vivian Grey*, his first novel.
	W. Scott publishes *Woodstock*.

MUSIC AND DRAMA

1826 *Apr.* 12	C.M. von Weber conducts première of his opera *Oberon* at Covent Garden.

RELIGION AND EDUCATION

1825 *Dec.*	Oxford Union Society founded.
1826	University College, London, founded in Gower St, to provide non-sectarian higher education.

SCIENCE AND INVENTION

1826 *Apr.* 29	Foundation of the Zoological Society of London, under the presidency of Sir Stamford Raffles and with support from the Royal Society.

Events Elsewhere

1825 *Dec.* 24	Abortive Decembrist uprising in St Petersburg after death of Tsar Alexander I.

1827	Jan.	5	D. of York dies; Wellington succeeds him as C.-in-C. of the army.
	Feb.	16	Lord Liverpool suffers stroke; resigns after premiership of 14 years 41 weeks, 28 Mar.
	Apr.	10	George Canning becomes Prime Minister.
	Jul.	6	Ty of London: Britain, France and Russia agree to coerce Turks into granting Greek autonomy.
	Aug.	8	Canning dies; succeeded by Viscount Goderich, 31 Aug.
	Oct.	20	Allied naval squadron (British, French, Russian) destroys Turkish and Egyptian fleet at Ψ Navarino.
1828	Jan.	8	Goderich, unable to keep Tories united, resigns; Wellington becomes Prime Minister, 9 Jan.
	May	20	Huskisson and liberal Tory 'Canningites' resign from government.
	Jul.	4	Daniel O'Connell elected MP at County Clare by-election but cannot sit in Commons because of his Roman Catholicism.
	Oct.	28	Opening of St Katherine's Dock, London.

FINE ARTS AND ARCHITECTURE

| 1827 | | J. Constable paints *The Cornfield* (1827) and *Dedham Vale* (1828). |
| | Dec. | George IV receives keys of Windsor Castle as reconstructed by Sir Jeffry Wyatville. |

LITERATURE AND SCHOLARSHIP

1827	John Clare publishes *The Shepherd's Calendar*.
	W. Scott publishes *The Life of Napoleon Buonaparte*.
1828	W. Hazlitt publishes *Life of Napoleon*, vols. 1 and 2; vols 3 and 4 follow in 1830.
	William Napier publishes *History of the War in the Peninsula*, vol. 1; not completed until 1840.

MUSIC AND DRAMA

| 1828 Mar. 17 | Grimaldi's final stage appearance, Sadler's Wells. |

RELIGION AND EDUCATION

1827	John Keble's *The Christian Year*, sacred verses, published anonymously.
	Henry Brougham founds Society for the Diffusion of Useful Knowledge.
1828	King's College, London, founded as an Anglican rival to University College.
	Thomas Arnold becomes headmaster of Rugby School.

SCIENCE AND INVENTION

| 1827 | Michael Faraday succeeds Davy as professor of chemistry at the Royal Institution. |

| Apr. 1828 | John Walker, Stockton pharmacist, invents his 'Lucifer' first friction match. James Neilson uses hot-air blast to smelt iron. |

Events Elsewhere

| 1828 Apr. | Russia at war with Turkey (to Sep. 1829). |

AD 1829–1830

1829 Mar. 5	Catholic Emancipation (Roman Catholic Relief Bill) passes H. of Commons; becomes law, 16 Apr.
21	Wellington fights pistol duel at Battersea with E. of Winchilsea; neither man aims at the other.
Jun. 19	Metropolitan Police Act passed: first 'Peelers' go on the beat in London, 29 Sep.
Jul. 4	George Shillibeer introduces 3-horse omnibus, Paddington to the Bank: 20 passengers, fare 1s.
Nov.	Thomas Attwood founds Birmingham Political Union to press for parliamentary reform.
Dec.	Grand General Union of Operative Spinners set up at I. of Man conference by John Doherty.
1830 Feb. 3	London Protocol: establishes a Greek kingdom, its independence guaranteed by Britain, France and Russia.
Jun. 4	Death of George IV; his brother, D. of Clarence, accedes as William IV.
Aug.	General election leaves Wellingtonian Tories with a majority, but Whigs make considerable gains.
Aug.–Oct.	'Captain Swing' agrarian riots in S. England against enclosures and threshing machines.
Sep. 15	William Huskisson killed by Stephenson's *Rocket* at opening of Liverpool-Manchester railway.
20	Doherty sets up National Association for the Protection of Labour, at Manchester.
Nov. 4	Conference on Belgian independence opens in London.
16	Wellington resigns as Prime Minister; succeeded by E. Grey.
22	Lord Palmerston appointed Foreign Secretary.
Dec. 25	Yeomanry kill farm worker in fight with 400 destructive labourers at Pyt House, nr Salisbury.

LITERATURE AND SCHOLARSHIP

1829	James Mill publishes *Analysis of the Phenomena of the Human Mind*.
1830	Alfred Tennyson publishes *Poems, Chiefly Lyrical*.
	W. Cobbett completes *Rural Rides* (essays from his *Political Register*).
	Charles Lyell publishes *Principles of Geology*.

MUSIC AND DRAMA

1829 *Aug.* 7   Mendelssohn's rough crossing to Staffa, Inner Hebrides, inspires 'Fingal's Cave' overture; performed London, 1832.

RECREATION AND FASHION

1829 *Jun.* 10   First University Boat Race: Oxford beat Cambridge at Henley.

RELIGION AND EDUCATION

1830   John Darby establishes his Pietistic Calvinist 'Brethren Movement' in Plymouth.

SCIENCE AND INVENTION

1829 *Oct.*   Rainhill Locomotive Speed Trials, nr Liverpool, won by Stephenson's *Rocket* at 29 m.p.h.

1830   Thomas Graham formulates his law on the molecular diffusion of gases.

VOYAGES AND EXPLORATION

1828–1829   Charles Sturt, penetrating inland from Sydney, discovers the rivers which he names Darling and Murray.

1829   Gibbon Wakefield publishes *A Letter from Sydney*; encourages voyages for settlement and colonization.

Events Elsewhere

1830 *Jul.* 26–29   Revolution in Paris leads to election of Louis Philippe as King of the French and to liberal revolts in Belgium, Italy, Germany and Poland.

AD 1831–1832

1831	*Mar.* 23	First Parliamentary Reform Bill for England and Wales steered through H. of Commons by Lord John Russell; but defeated in Committee.
	Apr. 22	Parliament dissolved; general election gives majority to the Whig reformers.
	Sep. 21	Second Reform Bill approved in Commons.
	Oct. 8	Second Reform Bill defeated in Lords by 41 votes; bishops' opposition decisive.
	29	Mob fires bishop's palace and city gaol, Bristol.
	Nov. 5–7	Bp of Exeter's palace protected by Yeomanry cavalry.
	15	Ty of London: separates Belgium from the Netherlands.
	Dec. 12	Russell introduces 3rd Reform Bill in Commons.
1832	*Feb.* 13	Cholera comes to London (Rotherhithe, Limehouse).
	Mar. 21	National Day of Fasting and Humiliation, because of cholera.
	23	Third Reform Bill passes Commons.
	Apr. 13	Third Reform Bill passes Lords: 12 bishops for, 16 against.

May	*7*	Lords amendment seeks to safeguard pocket boroughs.
	8	Grey resigns but Wellington cannot form a government.
	18	William IV reluctantly accepts Grey's request that he should threaten to create enough peers to defeat opponents of reform in the Lords.
Jun.	*4*	Reform Bill approved: constituencies created in new towns; rotten and pocket boroughs abolished; franchise extended to include all upper middle class.
Jul.	*11*	Scottish Parliamentary Reform Bill passed.
Aug.	*7*	Irish Parliamentary Reform Bill passed.
Dec.		General election on the reformed franchise gives Grey 300 majority in 658-seat H. of Commons.

FINE ARTS AND ARCHITECTURE

1831 · New London Bridge designed by John Rennie.
Travellers' Club, Pall Mall, designed by Charles Barry.

LITERATURE AND SCHOLARSHIP

1831 · T.L. Peacock publishes *Crotchet Castle*.
1832 · Frances Trollope writes *Domestic Manners of the Americans*.
A. Tennyson publishes *Poems*, including 'The Lady of Shalott'.

MUSIC AND DRAMA

1831 *Jun.–Aug.* · Nicolo Paganini, violin virtuoso, earns £7,500 from 1st London season, 15 concerts.
1832 *May 14* · Felix Mendelssohn conducts 'Fingal's Cave' ('Hebrides') overture, Covent Garden.
Sacred Harmonic Society founded, London.

RELIGION AND EDUCATION

1831 · Congregational Union of England and Wales established.
John Wade writes *The Extraordinary Black Book*, best-selling exposure of alleged wealth of Church.
1832 · More than 30 pamphlets favouring disestablishment published.

SCIENCE AND INVENTION

1831 · M. Faraday's experiments discover electromagnetic current.
British Association for the Advancement of Science founded.

VOYAGES AND EXPLORATION

1831 · Thomas Mitchell, Surveyor of New South Wales, sets out on first of 4 expeditions to explore NE Australia.
Jun. 1 · James Clark Ross discovers magnetic North Pole during Arctic expedition of John Ross.
Dec. 27 · Charles Darwin sails aboard HMS *Beagle* for scientific survey of S. American waters (to Oct. 1836).

Events Elsewhere

1831 *Feb.–Dec.*   Revolt in Russian Poland.

AD 1833–1834

1833 *Jan.*	1	Falkland Islands formally annexed.
Jul.	12	Irish Church Temporalities Act: abolishes 10 bishoprics.
Apr.		Factory commission set up; reports in June.
Aug.	23	East India Co. monopoly of trade with China abolished.
		Parliament approves Bill to end slavery within a year.
	29	Factory Act (Lord Althorp): no labour for children under 9; 9-hour day for under-13s; inspectors appointed.
		Bank Charter Act: joint-stock banks may be set up in London.
1834 *Jan.–Dec.*		Grand National Consolidated Trade Union experiment.
Feb.	24	6 farm workers at Tolpuddle, Dorset, arrested for taking 'unlawful oaths' in initiation ceremony of a labourers' union.
Mar.		Report of Royal Commission on Poor Law, drafted by Edwin Chadwick, published.
	18	'Tolpuddle Martyrs' sentenced to 7 years' transportation.
Apr.	21	30,000 trade unionists at Tolpuddle protest meeting in Copenhagen Fields, London.
	22	Palmerston's Quadruple Alliance Ty (Britain, France, Spain, Portugal) to uphold constitutionalism in Iberian peninsula, forms counter-weight to the 'Holy Alliance' powers (Russia, Austria, Prussia).
Jul.		Grey resigns, succeeded by Viscount Melbourne.
Aug.	1	Slaves throughout British empire become legally free.
	14	Poor Law Amendment Act: curbs outdoor poor relief and sets up workhouses.
	15	South Australia Act: for founding a new colony.
Oct.	16	Houses of Parliament burnt down.
Nov.	13	William IV dismisses Melbourne for proposing more Church reforms; Wellington forms interim administration.
Dec.	9	Peel reaches London from Italian holiday; becomes Prime Minister next day.
	17	Peel issues Tamworth Manifesto, outlining principles of a liberal conservatism.

LITERATURE AND SCHOLARSHIP

1833	Robert Browning writes *Pauline*, first poem, blank verse, published anonymously.
1833–1834	Thomas Carlyle writes *Sartor Resartus*, published in *Fraser's Magazine*.
1834	Edward Bulwer-Lytton publishes *The Last Days of Pompeii*.

Frederick Marryat publishes *Peter Simple*.

MUSIC AND DRAMA

1833 *Mar. 23*   Kean's farewell at Covent Garden Theatre, playing Othello; dies 6 weeks later.

RELIGION AND EDUCATION

1833   Durham University refounded (*v.* 1657); surplus funds of dean and chapter of cathedral used.

Jul. 14   John Keble preaches Oxford Assize Sermon on 'National Apostasy' over Irish Church Act, accusing government of 'sacrilegious' attitude towards Church funds.

Sep. 9   John Henry Newman, vicar of St Mary's, Oxford, publishes first of the *Tracts for the Times*; with Keble's sermon, these tracts inaugurate the Oxford Movement.

SCIENCE AND INVENTION

1834   Charles Babbage designs 'analytical engine', a digital computer; proves too complex to manufacture.
Pedal tricycle invented by Kirkpatrick MacMillan, blacksmith at Keir, Dumfriesshire.
Architect Joseph Aloysius Hansom brings patent safety cab ('hansom') to London streets.

AD 1835–1836

1835 *Jan.*   General election: Conservatives 273; Whigs and others 380; but William IV asks Peel to stay in office.

Feb. 18   Lichfield House Compact: Whigs, Radicals and Irish agree on joint Opposition.

Apr. 18   Peel resigns; Melbourne forms second ministry.

Sep. 9   Municipal Corporations Act: gives 178 cities and boroughs uniform pattern of local government.

1836 *Jan.*   3,300 stage-coaches and 700 mail-coaches in service on British roads; but over following 2 years 44 railway companies are established.

May 23   Irish Constabulary Act: centralizes police in Ireland and establishes a salaried magistracy.

Jun. 9   William Lovett founds London Working Men's Association at Tavistock St, Covent Garden.

Aug. 13   Tithe Commutation Act: provides for money, variable according to price of corn, to be paid to a parish incumbent in lieu of the traditional tithe.

17   Marriage Act: licences may be issued for weddings in nonconformist chapels.

Registrar-General of Births, Marriages and Deaths appointed; registration becomes compulsory in England and Wales 1837, Scotland 1855, Ireland 1864.

Sep. 15 Reduction in stamp duties from 4d to 1d increases sale of newspapers.

Dec. 14 Steam-trains come to London when 4-mile railway opens between London Bridge and Deptford.

LITERATURE AND SCHOLARSHIP

1835 R. Browning publishes *Paracelsus*.

E. Bulwer-Lytton publishes *Rienzi*.

W. Wordsworth writes *Yarrow Revisited*.

Connop Thirlwall begins *History of Greece*; completed 1845.

1836 Charles Dickens publishes *Sketches by Boz*.

C. Dickens begins *Pickwick Papers*; 20 monthly instalments.

B. Disraeli publishes *Henrietta Temple*.

F. Marryat publishes *Mr Midshipman Easy*.

RECREATION AND FASHION

1836 Mar. 2 Point-to-point horse-racing begins, at Madresfield, Worcs.

RELIGION AND EDUCATION

1835 Government sets up 2 commissions to report on state of Church of England. Dr Gentili, an Italian priest placed in charge of a seminary at Prior Park, Bath, introduces the clerical 'dog collar' to England.

Nov. 15 First solemn public consecration of Roman Catholic chapel in England since Reformation, Weobley, Herefordshire.

1836 Melbourne's government establishes University of London, to examine 'persons who have acquired proficiency in Literature, Science and Art' for degrees.

Established Church Act: authorizes ecclesiastical commissioners (of 1835) to continue administering the estates and revenues of the Church of England; stipends of bishops equalized; new sees created at Manchester and Ripon; many anomalies removed.

VOYAGES AND EXPLORATION

1835 Dec. First major movement of ox-wagons cross Orange river as Boers begin their 'Great Trek' northwards from Cape Colony.

AD 1837–1838

1837 Feb. 28 London Working Men's Association proposes 'Charter' petition to Parliament for 6 democratic reforms.

Mar. New Australian city named after Prime Minister, Melbourne.

Apr.	18	Attwood revives Birmingham Political Union.
Jun.	20	William IV dies; his niece Victoria learns of her accession at Kensington Palace. Her uncle, D. of Cumberland, accedes in Hanover.
Jul.		General election: Liberals 348; Conservatives 310; Disraeli elected for Maidstone.
	13	Q. Victoria takes up residence in Buckingham Palace.
	20	Euston station, London's first railway terminus, opens.
Oct.		British seize Aden from Sultan of Lajeh.
Nov.		Feargus O'Connor refounds radical *Northern Star*, in Leeds; soon sells widely as Chartist newspaper.
	22–24	Louis Papineau rebels in Lower Canada.
Dec.	5	Rebellion begins in Upper Canada, led by William Lyon Mackenzie (to 12 Jan.).
	7	Disraeli makes disastrous maiden speech in Commons.
1838 May	8	'People's Charter' printed and published.
	29	Lord Durham arrives in Quebec as Governor-General of British North America.
Jun.	28	Coronation of Q. Victoria, Westminster.
Jul.	31	Irish Poor Law, based on 1834 English Act.
Sep.		Tolpuddle labourers (pardoned 1836) return to England.
	7	Grace Darling becomes national heroine for her rescues from wrecked ship *Forfarshire* on Farne Islands.
	17	First train service linking London (Euston) to Birmingham; 112 miles in 5 hours.
	18	Richard Cobden establishes Anti-Corn Law League, Manchester.
Oct.	1	First Afghan War (to 1842) to check Russian infiltration.
	9	Lord Durham resigns over criticism of his leniency towards Canadian rebels.
Dec.	16	Boers on 'Great Trek' defeat Zulus at Blood River.

FINE ARTS AND ARCHITECTURE

1837		Charles Barry completes Reform Club, London.
		George Basevi builds Fitzwilliam Museum, Cambridge.
		E. Henry Landseer paints *Chief Mourner*.
Apr.	9	National Gallery opens.
1838		Philip Hardwick builds Euston Arch, portico of 4 Doric columns, 72ft high.

LITERATURE AND SCHOLARSHIP

1837	T. Carlyle publishes *The French Revolution*.
	C. Dickens begins *Oliver Twist* as a serial in *Bentley's Miscellany*.
	B. Disraeli publishes *Venetia, or the Poet's Daughter*.
	Isaac Pitman issues *Stenographic Sound-Hand*, the 4d primer of shorthand.
1837–1838	J.G. Lockhart publishes *Life of Sir Walter Scott*.
1838	C. Dickens writes *Nicholas Nickleby*.
	Robert Smith Surtees' *Jorrocks's Jaunts and Jollities*, sporting comic sketches appearing in magazines for 7 years, published in book form.

1837   Charles Wheatstone and William Cooke patent electric telegraph.

1838 *Dec.*   William Fox Talbot experiments with photographic prints on silver chloride paper (to Jan. 1839).

VOYAGES AND EXPLORATION

1838 *Apr.* 4–22   First crossing of the Atlantic fully under steam: SS *Sirius*, from Queenstown (Cobh) to New York.

AD 1839–1840

1839	*Feb.* 4	Chartist National Convention, London.
	11	H. of Lords debates Durham's report on Canada.
	Mar. 9	Anti-Corn Law League becomes organized on a national basis after London meeting.
	Apr. 19	Ty of London: Belgium as 'independent and perpetually neutral state' guaranteed by 5 powers including Britain.
	May 7–11	'Bedchamber Crisis': Melbourne resigns; Peel unable to form government as Q. Victoria declines to change Whig ladies of bedchamber for Tories; Melbourne stays in office.
	May 13 and	Protests against turnpike trusts at Efailwen, Carmarthenshire, mark first
	Jun. 6	'Rebecca Riots' in Wales.
	Jun. 14	First Chartist petition presented to Parliament.
	Jul.	Opium War begins with China when authorities at Canton seek to check smuggling.
	4 and 15	Chartist riots in Birmingham.
	5	Lady Flora Hastings, bedchamber lady treated uncharitably by Q. Victoria, dies of cancer; London society hostile to Queen.
	11	Q. Victoria, with Melbourne, hissed in Ascot carriage drive.
	12	H. of Commons rejects Chartist petition.
	Nov. 3–4	Chartist insurrection at Newport, Mon: 24 killed.
1840	*Jan.* 10	Penny Post introduced by Rowland Hill.
	Feb. 5	Ty of Waitangi: Maori chiefs surrender New Zealand sovereignty to Q. Victoria.
	10	Q. Victoria marries her first cousin, P. Albert of Saxe-Coburg-Gotha, at Chapel Royal, St James's.
	Jun. 10	Narrow escape for Q. Victoria as insane potboy Edward Oxford fires 2 shots at her carriage on Constitution Hill.
	Jul. 23	Union Act: Canadian provinces to have single legislature.
	Aug. 10	Irish Municipal Reform Act: 48 old boroughs lose status.
	Aug.	Chimney Sweeps Act: bans 'climbing boys'; evaded.
	Sep. 11	British warships bombard Egyptian army in Beirut.

| Oct. 25 | Bradshaw's *Railway Companion* provides first timetables. |
| Nov. 3–4 | British bombard Acre and seize it from Mehemet Ali's army. |

FINE ARTS AND ARCHITECTURE

1839	J.M.W. Turner exhibits his *Fighting Téméraire*.
1840	C. Barry paves and levels Trafalgar Square.
	C. Barry begins rebuilding Houses of Parliament; completed 1860.

LITERATURE AND SCHOLARSHIP

| 1839 | C. Darwin publishes *Journal of Researches into the Geology and Natural History of the Various Countries Visited by HMS Beagle*. |
| 1840 | Richard Harris Barham's *The Ingoldsby Legends* published in book form; includes 'Jackdaw of Rheims'. |

RECREATION AND FASHION

1839 Feb. 26	First Grand National steeplechase, Aintree.
Jun. 14	First Henley Regatta, with Grand Challenge Cup.
Aug.	Mock tournament revived by historical Romantics for high society at Eglinton Castle; ruined by rain.

RELIGION AND EDUCATION

| 1839 | Committee of Privy Council to assign public money for education. |
| May | Cambridge Camden Society set up to improve Anglican art. |

SCIENCE AND INVENTION

| 1839 | Kirkpatrick Macmillan perfects pedal bicycle (*v.* 1834). |

VOYAGES AND EXPLORATION

| 1840 | Paddle-steamer mail services open from Falmouth to Alexandria (P. & O.) and Liverpool to Boston (Cunard). |

Events Elsewhere

| 1839–1840 | Britain backs Turkey in Eastern Question crisis caused by conflict between the Turkish Sultan Abd-el-Medjid and his vassal, Mehemet Ali, ruler over Egypt, Syria and Crete. |

AD 1841–1842

1841 Jan. 26	Naval landing-party raises British flag at Possession Point, Hong Kong.
May 3	Proclamation of New Zealand as British colony.
Jul. 13	Palmerston sponsors the Straits Convention, closing Dardanelles and Bosphorus to warships in time of peace.

	17	First issue of *Punch* on sale.
Aug.	28	Melbourne resigns; Peel forms Conservative government; E. of Aberdeen succeeds Palmerston as Foreign Secretary.
Nov.	2	Anti-British uprising in Kabul.
	9	Future K. Edward VII born; made P. of Wales, 7 Dec.
1842		Fourth successive year of bad harvests.
Jan.	1	Kabul capitulates; 4,000 troops and 12,000 camp-followers seek to retreat to India; only 1 survivor reaches Jellahabad.
Mar.–Apr.		Renewed anti-turnpike gate Rebecca Riots spread in S. Wales.
May	3	Parliament rejects second Chartist petition.
	11	Peel introduces first peacetime income tax: 7d in pound on annual incomes above £150.
	14	*The Illustrated London News* published.
Jun.	13	Q. Victoria's first train journey.
	19	Dragoons used against Rebecca Rioters in Carmarthen.
Jul.		Edwin Chadwick's Report on the Sanitary Condition of the Labouring Population of Great Britain presented to H. of Lords.
Aug.		Ashley's Mines Act: children under 10 and women not to work underground.
Aug.	7–27	'Plug Riots': Chartists and Anti-Corn Law protesters seek general strike in Lancashire and N. midlands.
	9	Frontier in Canada defined by Webster-Ashburton Ty.
	16	Manchester garrisoned by 2,000 troops with 6 field guns in anticipation of Chartist riot.
	29	Ty of Nanking ends Opium War: China gives rights to British traders in 5 ports and cedes Hong Kong island.
Aug.–Oct.		2nd Afghan War, to avenge Kabul killings.

FINE ARTS AND ARCHITECTURE

| 1841 | Sculptor Sir Francis Chantrey bequeathes fortune to Royal Academy. |

LITERATURE AND SCHOLARSHIP

1841	C. Dickens publishes *The Old Curiosity Shop* and *Barnaby Rudge*.
	London Library founded in Pall Mall on initiative of Carlyle; moved to present site in St James's Square in 1845.
1842	Thomas Babington Macaulay publishes *Lays of Ancient Rome*, narrative poems based mainly on Livy; includes 'Horatius'.
	A. Tennyson's *Collected Poems* published; include 'Locksley Hall'.

RECREATION AND FASHION

| 1841 | | Royal Botanic Gardens at Kew open to public. |
| Jul. | 5 | Thomas Cook pioneers railway excursions: temperance outing from Leicester to Loughborough. |

RELIGION AND EDUCATION

| 1841 | Feb. | 27 | Newman's *Tract XC* causes controversy for interpreting the Thirty-Nine |

Articles in a Catholic context.

Jul. *31*   David Livingstone begins missionary work in Bechuanaland.

Oct.   British and Prussian governments approve creation of a joint Protestant bishopric in Jerusalem.

VOYAGES AND EXPLORATION

1841   Edward John Eyre crosses Nullarbor Plain to link S. and W. Australia.

Jan.   James Ross discovers and claims Victoria Land, Antarctica.

AD 1843–1844

1843 *Jan.*   General Charles Napier conquers Sind.

Jan. 20   Peel's secretary, Edward Drummond, shot dead in Whitehall by Daniel Macnaghten in mistake for Peel.

Mar. 3   Macnaghten acquitted of murder on grounds of insanity; Law Lords subsequently explain the 'Macnaghten Rules' on the criminal responsibility of the mentally abnormal.

25   Opening of Thames Tunnel, completed by Isambard Brunel; Wapping-Rotherhithe pedestrian link.

Apr. 11 *and*

May 4   Gambia and Natal become colonies.

Sep. 2–7   Victoria and Albert guests of K. Louis Philippe at Eu; first courtesy visit to French sovereign since 1520.

Oct. 7   Repeal rally at Clontarf banned.

Dec. 13   Basutoland made British protectorate.

1844 *May* 30   D. O'Connell sentenced to 12 months for conspiracy; sentence quashed on appeal to the Lords, 4 Sep.

Jun. 1   Tsar Nicholas I unexpectedly arrives in London for 8-day visit; in 'Windsor Conversations' with Peel and Aberdeen he discusses possible break-up of Ottoman Empire.

15   Factory Act: 12-hour day for women; 6-hour day for children 8-13; proposal they should attend Church-maintained school dropped through sectarian hostility.

Jul. 19   Bank Charter Act: regulates issue of bank notes.

Oct. 15–21   Q. Victoria and P. Albert visit Osborne (I. of Wight) preparatory to purchasing it (Mar. 1845).

Dec. 21   Rochdale Equitable Pioneers open the first co-operative retail shop, Toad Lane.

FINE ARTS AND ARCHITECTURE

1843   John Ruskin publishes *Modern Painters*, vol. 1.

1844   Decimus Burton builds Palm House, Kew.

J.M.W. Turner paints *Rain, Steam and Speed*.

LITERATURE AND SCHOLARSHIP

1843   C. Dickens writes *A Christmas Carol*.

T. Carlyle publishes *Past and Present*.

George Borrow publishes *The Bible in Spain*.

John Stuart Mill's *System of Logic* defines the canons of inductive reasoning in philosophy.

Wordsworth succeeds Southey as Poet Laureate.

1844   B. Disraeli publishes *Coningsby*.

A(lexander) W(illiam) Kinglake anonymously publishes *Eothen: or Traces of Travel Brought Home from the East*.

MUSIC AND FASHION

1843   Theatre Act: ends patent monopoly; all theatres free to present legitimate drama, subject to Lord Chamberlain's supervision.

RECREATION AND DRAMA

1844   Royal Commission on Health of Towns set up.

1843–1844   Men's evening dress assumes basic white tie and tails form; women's headdresses dependent on some form of bonnet.

RELIGION AND EDUCATION

1843 *Feb.*   Ashley extends his philanthropic work to 'ragged schools'.

May 18   'The Disruption' in Church of Scotland: 451 out of 1,203 ministers form 'Free Church' over patronage rights.

1844   George Williams founds interdenominational Young Men's Christian Association in London.

SCIENCE AND INVENTION

1843   John Lawes, pioneer of artificial fertilizer industry with Henry Gilbert, founds Rothamsted experimental station to stimulate agricultural science.

Jul. 19   Isambard Brunel's *Great Britain* launched, first screw-propelled iron transatlantic liner; maiden voyage, 26 Jul. 1845.

AD 1845–1846

1845 *Mar.*   Maori risings against British settlers in New Zealand.

Apr.   Peel's budget favours free trade by cutting export duties.

Jun. 30   Maynooth College Act provokes controversy by grant of funds towards rebuilding the 'Royal Catholic College'.

Sep. 9   Potato blight first noticed in Ireland.

Oct. 18   Peel learns of total failure of Irish potato crop.

Nov.		To ease Irish famine Peel orders import of Indian corn.
	12–16	Railway investment fever so speculative that it excites press comment.
	22	Russell, Opposition leader, publishes his 'Edinburgh Letter', committing Whig liberals to free trade.
Dec.	*4*	*The Times* reports that Peel will repeal Corn Laws.
	6	Party split over Corn Laws forces Peel to resign.
	11	Sikhs launch surprise attack on British at Mudki.
	20	Peel resumes as Prime Minister, Russell having been unable to form an administration because of feuds among veteran Whigs.

1846 *Jan.–Mar.*		Peel's Public Health Acts: provide state-aided palliatives for Irish famine.
Jan.	*21*	*Daily News*, a Liberal paper, founded by C. Dickens.
	22	Disraeli's attack on Peel's proposed repeal of Corn Laws makes him effective leader of the Protectionists.
Feb.	*9*	Commons begin to debate repeal of Corn Laws.
	10	Sikhs defeated in Ψ Sobrahan.
Mar.	*9*	Ty of Lahore ends first Sikh War.
May	*16*	Repeal of Corn Laws approved by Commons; Lords approve, 25 Jun.; royal assent, 26 Jun.
Jun.	*15*	Dispute over Oregon-Canada border settled by Ty of Washington: boundary follows 49th parallel.
	25	Protectionists under Lord George Bentinck and Disraeli defeat Peel's Irish Coercion Bill by 73 votes.
	27	Peel travels to Osborne to resign premiership.
Jul.	*5*	Russell becomes Prime Minister; Palmerston Foreign Secretary.
Sep.–Oct.		Anglo-French tension over marriage links between French and Spanish dynasties.
Dec.	*31*	Enactment of the year's 272nd railway construction Bill; a record.

LITERATURE AND SCHOLARSHIP

1845	B. Disraeli publishes *Sybil, or The Two Nations*.
	Henry Layard begins excavations at Nimrud and Nineveh.
1846	Edward Lear writes *Book of Nonsense*.

MUSIC AND DRAMA

1845 *Jul.*	*12*	*Pas de Quatre* (chor. Perrot) danced by Taglioni, Grissi, Cerrito and Grahn at Her Majesty's Theatre; peak of English enthusiasm for the Romantic ballerina.
1846 *Sep.*	*26*	Mendelssohn conducts his oratorio *Elijah* at Birmingham.

RECREATION AND FASHION

1845		First University Boat Race over Putney-Mortlake course.
May	*1*	Cricket first played at Kennington Oval.
		Victoria Park, created to serve London's overcrowded East End, opens to the public.
1846 *Jun.*		3 public parks open in Manchester; first in a provincial city.

RELIGION AND EDUCATION

1845 Oct. 9   Newman becomes Roman Catholic.

1846   Evangelical Alliance founded to combat Tractarianism.

VOYAGES AND EXPLORATION

1845 May 19   Abortive expedition of Sir John Franklin to search for North-West Passage; last sighted, 26 Jul.

AD 1847–1848

1847 Apr.   Anti-Jewish mob wreck Athens home of Don David Pacifico, a Gibraltar-born moneylender who is a British citizen.

Jun. 8   John Fielden responsible for a 'Ten Hours' Factory Act, for which Ashley had campaigned since 1831: 10-hour day for women and both sexes from 13 to 18.

Jul.   General election: Liberals 325; Protectionist Tories 226; Peelites 105; Lionel de Rothschild elected for City of London, cannot take seat because of oath, sworn 'on the true faith of a Christian'.

Dec.   Protectionist Tories force Bentinck off front bench because of his support for a Bill removing Jewish disabilities.

1848 Jan. 12   E. of Dalhousie arrives in India as Governor-General.

Feb. 8 and 22   Attempts by Radicals to impeach the Foreign Secretary as a Russian agent induce Palmerston (1 Mar.) to give masterly speech justifying his policy as the championship 'of justice and right'.

12   John Mitchel publishes *United Irishman*; seeks a crusade to force the English out of Ireland.

Apr. 10   Wellington organizes defence of London against Chartist demonstration at Kennington; 170,000 special constables enlisted; 15,000 Chartists disperse peacefully; a third Chartist petition taken by cab to Downing St.

20   Metternich reaches London; joins many refugees from revolution, including K. Louis Philippe, his chief minister Guizot and the future Emperor Wilhelm I.

Jul.   Public Health Act: sets up Board of Health.

29   William Smith O'Brien leads rising at Ballingary, Co. Tipperary, after suspension of Habeas Corpus Act.

Sep. 8   Q. Victoria visits Balmoral for first time.

Oct.   Direct train route from London to Edinburgh opened.

FINE ARTS AND ARCHITECTURE

1848   Pre-Raphaelite Brotherhood founded, led by Henry Holman Hunt, John Millais, Dante Gabriel Rossetti.

1847   Charlotte Brontë's *Jane Eyre*, Anne Brontë's *Agnes Grey* and Emily Brontë's *Wuthering Heights* are published.
B. Disraeli publishes *Tancred, or the New Crusade.*
William Makepeace Thackeray begins *Vanity Fair*; in monthly instalments.

1848   T.B. Macaulay begins *History of England*; completed 1861.
J.S. Mill publishes *Principles of Public Economy.*
A. Brontë writes *The Tenant of Wildfell Hall.*
(Mrs) Elizabeth Gaskell publishes *Mary Barton.*
W.M. Thackeray begins *Pendennis*; in instalments.
James Anthony Froude writes *The Nemesis of Faith*, novel which loses him his Oxford Fellowship.

MUSIC AND DRAMA

1847 *May* 4   Jenny Lind's London debut, in *Roberto il Diavolo* at Her Majesty's Theatre.

RECREATION AND FASHION

1848 *Nov.* 1   As part of expansion of Euston station (completed May 1849) the first railway bookstall is opened.

Events Elsewhere

1848   German and French editions of Marx and Engels, *Communist Manifesto*; first English translation, 1850.

Jan. 24   Gold discovered at Sutter's Creek, California.

Feb. 22   Republican revolution in Paris; followed in March by revolutions in Italy, Austria, Hungary and Germany.

AD 1849–1850

1849 *Feb.* 22   Disraeli becomes Conservative leader in Commons.

Mar. 29   Dalhousie annexes Punjab after pitched battles with Sikhs at Chillianwalla (13 Jan.) and Gujerat (21 Feb.)

Jun.–Oct.   14,000 die in London cholera epidemic.

Sep.–Oct.   British fleet in Aegean supports Turkish refusal to hand back Hungarian and Polish refugees.

Oct. 14   Tenant Protection Society set up at Callen, Kilkenny.

1850 *Jan.* 15   British fleet blockades port of Piraeus to obtain compensation from Greece for Don Pacifico (*v.* 1847).

Jun. 25–26   Palmerston defends himself over Don Pacifico in his '*Civis Romanus sum*' dusk-to-dawn speech.

29   Government has majority of 46, despite Peel, Disraeli, Gladstone all voting against Palmerston.

30	Peel thrown from his horse in Hyde Park; dies 2 Jul.; leadership of 'Peelites' passes to E. of Aberdeen.
Aug. 5	Australia Government Act: representative government given to South Australia, Victoria and Tasmania.
5–13	Complaints to Russell by Q. Victoria and P. Albert about Palmerston's irresponsibility as Foreign Secretary.
9	Irish Tenant League established.
14	Irish Franchise Act, with stricter registration, increases rural electorate and reduces urban.
Sep. 4	Austrian General Haynau, loathed for his cruelty in Lombardy and Hungary, beaten up by draymen while visiting Barclay & Perkins brewery, Southwark.
Dec. 16	Foundation of city of Christchurch, New Zealand.

FINE ARTS AND ARCHITECTURE

1849	J. Ruskin publishes *The Seven Lamps of Architecture*.
1850	J. Millais paints *Christ in the House of His Parents*.

LITERATURE AND SCHOLARSHIP

1849	Matthew Arnold publishes *The Strayed Reveller and Other Poems*.
1849–1850	C. Dickens publishes *David Copperfield* in monthly instalments.
1850	Charles Kingsley publishes 2 novels, *Yeast* and *Alton Locke*.
	Elizabeth Barrett Browning publishes *Sonnets from the Portuguese*.
	A. Tennyson writes *In Memoriam*; succeeds Wordsworth as Poet Laureate.
	Herbert Spencer publishes *Social Statics*.
Jan. 1	*The Germ*, periodical of the Pre-Raphaelite Brotherhood (to 30 Apr.); contains Rossetti's 'Blessed Damozel'.

RECREATION AND FASHION

1849 Jun.	First modern organized athletics competition, Woolwich.
Dec. 17	First bowler hat sold; made by T. and W. Bowler of Southwark, for Norfolk gamekeepers.

RELIGION AND EDUCATION

1850 Mar. 9	Committee of Privy Council clears Revd G.C. Gorham of unsound views on baptism attributed to him by Bp of Exeter; ruling by a lay body induces more Tractarians to become Roman Catholics, notably (6 Apr. 1851) Henry Manning.
Oct. 7	Fr. Nicholas Wiseman, in Rome, issues pastoral letter: Roman Catholic hierarchy to be created in England, with himself as Cardinal Archbp of Westminster.

SCIENCE AND INVENTION

1849	Robert Stephenson builds cast-iron bridge over Tyne at Newcastle.
1850 Mar. 5	Stephenson's tubular bridge across Menai Straits opens for rail traffic to Holyhead.

1849 *Aug.*   Hungarian revolution jointly suppressed by Russians and Austrians.

AD 1851–1852

1851 *Feb.*	12	Australian Gold Rush begins with discovery of gold at Summerhill Creek, 20 miles north of Bathurst, New South Wales.
May	1	Q. Victoria opens Great Exhibition in Hyde Park.
Jul.	24	Window tax abolished.
Aug.	1	Ecclesiastical Titles Act: seeks to prevent Roman Catholic bishops assuming territorial titles within Britain; never effective, repealed 1871.
Oct.	13	Exiled Hungarian leader Lajos Kossuth arrives at Southampton; much fêted for 4 weeks in England.
	15	Great Exhibition closes.
Dec.	19	Palmerston dismissed as Foreign Secretary for having sent personal congratulations to Louis Napoleon on his coup.
1852 *Jan.*	17	Sand River Convention recognizes Transvaal republic.
Feb.	21	Russell resigns after Palmerston, backed by Conservatives, moves amendment to his Militia Bill.
	23	E. of Derby forms minority Conservative government with Disraeli as Chancellor of Exchequer.
Jun.	30	New Zealand Constitution Act: representative government for the colony.
Jul.		General election: Conservatives 310; Liberals 270; Peelites 40; Irish Nationalists 40.
Nov.	18	State funeral of D. of Wellington (d. 14 Sep.).
Dec.	17	Derby resigns, after defeat of Disraeli's budget.
	28	E. of Aberdeen becomes Prime Minister of Whig-Peelite coalition: Gladstone as Chancellor; Palmerston Home Secretary.

FINE ARTS AND ARCHITECTURE

1851	Joseph Paxton completes 600-yard-long glass Crystal Palace for Great Exhibition.
	John Tenniel begins 63 years of drawing for *Punch*.
1852	Lewis Cubitt completes King's Cross station; biggest in Europe when opened.
	I.K. Brunel begins enlarged Paddington station; opens 1854.

LITERATURE AND SCHOLARSHIP

1851	G. Borrow publishes *Lavengro*.
1852	W.M. Thackeray publishes *The History of Henry Esmond*.

1851 Feb. 26   William Macready's last performance at Drury Lane, as Macbeth.

RECREATION AND FASHION
1852   Samuel Orchard Beeton publishes *The Englishwoman's Domestic Magazine*; each issue contains a dress pattern; stimulates spread of home dressmaking.

RELIGION AND EDUCATION
1851   Foundation of Owen's College, Manchester.
1852 Nov.   Convocation of Church of England becomes active for first time since 1717.

SCIENCE AND INVENTION
1851   William Thomson (Lord Kelvin from 1892) publishes research on the laws of conservation of energy.
1852   James Joseph Sylvester develops the theory of calculus.

VOYAGES AND EXPLORATION
1852   D. Livingstone begins 4-year expedition up R. Zambesi.

Events Elsewhere

1851 Dec. 2   President Louis Napoleon carries out *coup d'état* strengthening his executive authority.
1852 Dec. 2   Second Empire established in France, the President becoming Emperor Napoleon III.

AD 1853–1854

1853 Jan. 9   Tsar Nicholas I tells British ambassador that he wishes for closer Anglo-Russian relations over Turkey, where 'we have a sick man on our hands'.
     Feb.–Mar. Russian proposals for agreement over future partition of Ottoman empire mistrusted in London.
     Apr. 18   Gladstone's first Free Trade budget.
     Jun. 5   Mediterranean Fleet ordered to Besika Bay, south of Dardanelles, because of Russian threats to Turkey.
     Jul. 1   Cape Colony receives a constitution, providing for elected Legislative Council.
     Sep. 23   British squadron ordered to sail through Dardanelles and be prepared to defend Constantinople.
     Oct. 4   British attempts to restrain Turkey from declaring war on Russia fail.
     Dec. 10   Split in Aberdeen's cabinet; Palmerston hostile to Russell's campaign for a new Reform Bill.
          12   News reaches London of the Russian destruction of the Turkish fleet at

		Sinope (30 Nov.); widespread demands for war against Russia.
	14	Palmerston resigns, ostensibly over reform agitation; changes his mind, 23 Dec.
1854 *Jan.*	*4–5*	Anglo-French fleet enters Black Sea.
Feb.	*13*	Russell introduces Parliamentary Reform Bill; withdrawn in Apr. because of war.
	23	First troopships leave Southampton for Turkey.
Mar.	*12*	Ty of Constantinople: Britain, France and Turkey ally.
	31	Britain declares war on Russia.
Apr.–May		Cholera in London: 10,000 die; epidemic identified for first time as water-borne.
Jun.	*10*	Q. Victoria opens Crystal Palace at Sydenham.
	20	Baltic fleet active off Finland (to 4 Jul.); on 21 Jun. Lt Charles Lucas of HMS *Hecla* throws live shell overboard, earliest deed for which Victoria Cross awarded.
Jun.	*21*	British expeditionary force at Varna, Bulgaria (to 4 Sep.).
Aug.	*16*	Baltic fleet captures Bomarsund in Aland Islands.
Sep.	*14*	Anglo-French force makes landing in the Crimea.
	20	Russians defeated at Ψ R. Alma.
Oct.	*12–13*	*The Times* exposes army medical service inadequacies.
	17	Siege of Sebastopol begins.
	21	Florence Nightingale in London engages nurses for Turkey.
	25	Ψ Balaclava: costly allied victory; a day of 4 cavalry charges, including that of Light Brigade.
Nov.	*4*	Florence Nightingale and her nurses reach Scutari.
	5	Ψ Inkerman: allies repulse Russians.
	18	Gale hits British anchorage in Crimea, destroying ships and equipment.
Dec.	*2*	Eureka Stockade, Ballarat: 23 diggers, defending their rights against suspected corruption, killed in clash with troops.

LITERATURE AND SCHOLARSHIP

1853		M. Arnold publishes *Poems*; includes 'Scholar Gypsy' and 'Sohrab and Rustam'.
		Mrs E. Gaskell's novel *Cranford* published.
1854 *Dec.*	*9*	Tennyson's 'Charge of Light Brigade' published in *The Examiner* weekly.

RELIGION AND EDUCATION

1854 *Apr.*	*26*	'National Day of Fast and Humiliation' for the war.

AD 1855

Jan.	*23*	Arthur Roebuck, Radical MP for Sheffield, seeks appointment of a select committee to investigate 'the condition of the army before Sebastopol'.

	26	Britain and France conclude the Ty of Turin with Cavour: provides for Piedmontese participation in the Crimean War.
	29	Roebuck's motion is carried, the government being defeated by 157 votes; Aberdeen resigns next day.
Feb.	6	Palmerston becomes Prime Minister of a coalition.
	8	Single secretaryship of war created; first War Secretary is Lord Panmure.
	23	John Bright urges H. of Commons to seek peace in his great 'angel of death' speech.
Mar.	15	Lord John Russell in Vienna to explore, with Russian and French delegates, the possibilities of making peace; attempt is abandoned 5 weeks later.
Apr.	9–18	Heavy bombardment of Sebastopol.
	11	The first 6 experimental pillar boxes installed by the Post Office in London.
	15	Headquarters at Balaclava linked by electric telegraph to London.
	16	Napoleon III and Empress Eugenie arrive at Windsor on a state visit.
May	5	Foundation of the Administrative Reform Association to combat bureaucratic mismanagement.
	25	Anglo-French expedition secures control of the Sea of Azov.
Jun.		Demonstrations in Hyde Park on 4 successive Sundays against proposals 'to prevent Sunday trading in the metropolis'.
	8	British attack on the outer Mamelon defences of Sebastopol is beaten off with heavy losses.
	15	Stamp duty abolished on newspapers.
	18	British and French suffer heavy losses in attack on the Malakoff fort.
	29	*Daily Telegraph* is first published.
Jul.	16	Australian colonies accorded responsible government (except Western Australia).
	31	Limited Liability Act: safeguards investors from individual responsibility in case of company failure.
Aug.	18–27	Q. Victoria makes a state visit to Paris.
Sep.	9	British and French troops force their way into Sebastopol.

FINE ARTS AND ARCHITECTURE
F. Madox Brown paints *The Last of England*.

LITERATURE AND SCHOLARSHIP
Charles Kingsley publishes *Westward Ho!*
Anthony Trollope's first Barchester novel, *The Warden*, is published.
Mrs E. Gaskell publishes *North and South*.
W.M. Thackeray writes *The Rose and the Ring*.
A. Tennyson publishes *Maud and Other Poems*.

MUSIC AND DRAMA
Regular Crystal Palace weekend concerts are first given.

Feb.

RELIGION AND EDUCATION
Convocation of Canterbury meets for 3 days; vainly seeks Crown permission to modernize its constitution.

SCIENCE AND INVENTION
Henry Bessemer patents a process for turning molten pig-iron into steel.

Nov.

VOYAGES AND EXPLORATION
David Livingstone discovers and names the Victoria Falls.

Events Elsewhere

Mar. 2   Tsar Nicholas I dies; succeeded by his son, Alexander II.

AD 1856

Jan. 17   *The Times* breaks the news in London that the Russians are seeking peace rather than risk Austria's entry into the war on the side of the allies.
     29   Victoria Cross instituted for acts of conspicuous valour.
Feb. 13   Oudh annexed.
     16   Clarendon arrives in Paris as chief British delegate to a peace conference.
     28   Armistice with the Russians concluded in Paris; fighting in the Crimea ends next day.
Mar. 30   Peace Treaties of Paris signed: Russia accepts neutralization of Black Sea and surrenders territory at mouth of R. Danube for a future Romanian state.
Apr. 15   Britain, together with France and Austria, concludes a further Ty of Paris guaranteeing independence and integrity of the Ottoman empire.
May   5 regiments sail directly from Sebastopol to Canada because of mounting tension with USA over alleged enticement of American citizens to serve in British army and navy.
Jul. 9   Natal becomes a crown colony with an elected assembly.
     12   Last British troops leave the Crimea.
Aug. 1   Colonial Office approves grant of self-government to Tasmania and accepts responsible government in New Zealand.
Oct. 8   *Arrow* incident: Chinese board a Hong Kong-registered vessel off Canton and imprison crew for suspected piracy; great indignation in London.
Nov. 1   East India Co. settles mounting tension with the Persians after their occupation of Herat, in Afghanistan.
     3–4   British warships bombard forts protecting Canton over the *Arrow* incident.

FINE ARTS AND ARCHITECTURE
J. Millais paints *Autumn Leaves* and *The Blind Girl*.

Apr. 28   Ellen Terry makes her stage debut as Mamillius in *The Winter's Tale* at the Princess Theatre, London.

Events Elsewhere

Dec.   An independent Transvaal republic is organized under the leadership of Marthinius Pretorius.

AD 1857

Mar. 3   Cobden moves censure of Palmerston's aggressive China policy; carried by 263 to 247; Palmerston asks Q. Victoria to dissolve Parliament.

Apr. (early)   General election gives Palmerston clear majority of 85.

May 10   Sepoys in Meerut revolt; start of Indian Mutiny.

May 11   Delhi seized; Bahadur Shah proclaimed Moghul Emperor.

Jun. 6–26   Cawnpore resists siege by mutineers.

26   Albert created Prince Consort by Letters Patent.
Q. Victoria distributes first 62 VCs in Hyde Park.

27   Cawnpore garrison treacherously killed after surrender.

Jul. 15   Cawnpore women and children, held hostage, murdered on approach of relief force; atrocities committed in reprisal.

Aug. 28   Matrimonial Causes Act: sets up divorce courts for England and Wales.

Sep. 20   Delhi recaptured by British.

25   Lucknow, besieged for 4 months, is reinforced; but the siege is resumed.

Nov. 12   Financial crisis in the City because of failure of US banks over railway speculation; Bank of England authorized to raise bank rate to 10% to check run on funds.

17   Lucknow finally relieved by Sir Colin Campbell.

Dec. 6   Cawnpore recaptured.

29   British and French troops enter Canton to avenge insults to their nationals.

FINE ARTS AND ARCHITECTURE

Mar.   Edward Middleton Barry publishes design for Royal Opera House, Covent Garden, the previous theatre having been destroyed by fire on 5 Mar. 1856.

May 5   P. Albert opens Manchester Art Treasures Exhibition; 1st to be held in the provinces.

Robert Michael Ballantyne publishes *The Coral Island*.
G. Borrow publishes *Romany Rye*.
Elizabeth B. Browning publishes her 'novel-in-verse', *Aurora Leigh*.
C. Dickens completes *Little Dorritt*.
Thomas Hughes publishes *Tom Brown's Schooldays*.
A. Trollope publishes *Barchester Towers*.
W.M. Thackeray writes *The Virginians*; in instalments.
Mrs Caraik (Dinah Maria Mulock) publishes *John Halifax, Gentleman*.

May 18   Reading Room of British Museum opens.

RECREATION AND FASHION
Cage-crinoline comes to England from Paris in 1857, making women's skirts increasingly bell-shaped over next 10 years. Masculine dress very sombre; moustaches and side-whiskers favoured; Macassar oil accepted on the hair.

RELIGION AND EDUCATION

Oct. 7   (Wed.) At Q. Victoria's request a 'Day of Solemn Fast, Humiliation and Prayer' occasioned by the Indian Mutiny; churches packed; over 23,600 people at Crystal Palace for 35-minute sermon by the Baptist preacher, Charles Spurgeon.

VOYAGES AND EXPLORATION
Richard Burton and John Speke sent by the Geographical Society in search of the equatorial lakes of Africa.

AD 1858

Jan. 25   Princess Royal (Victoria Adelaide) marries P. Frederick of Prussia at St James's Palace.

Feb. 19   H. of Commons rejects anti-terrorist Conspiracy to Murder Bill.

21   Palmerston resigns as Prime Minister.

26   E. of Derby forms Conservative government with Disraeli as Chancellor of Exchequer.

Mar. 17   Irish Republican Brotherhood established in Dublin by James Stephens; associated with Fenian Brotherhood, founded in America, Apr. 1859.

Jun. 26   Ty of Tientsin offers peace in Anglo-Chinese dispute: Britain obtains commercial concessions and acquires Kowloon and Stonecutter's Island; not ratified by China.

Jul. 2   The 'Great Stink' of R. Thames in a hot summer makes both Disraeli and Gladstone unwell in H. of Commons.

8   Proclamation of Peace in India: formal end of Mutiny.

23   Jewish Disabilities Act: enables L.N. de Rothschild to take his Commons

	seat, 26 Jul. (*v.* 1847).
Aug.	Property Qualification of MPs Act: removes need for MPs to be men of financial substance.
Aug. 2	India Act: East India Co. powers surrendered to the Crown; Governor-General becomes a Viceroy.
17	Completion of Atlantic telegraph cable linking Ireland and Newfoundland; Q. Victoria and President Buchanan exchange greetings.
26	Trade treaty opens up Japan to British commerce.
Sep. 7	Q. Victoria opens Leeds town hall, amid an intense celebration of local civic pride.

FINE ARTS AND ARCHITECTURE
William Powell Frith paints *Derby Day*.

LITERATURE AND SCHOLARSHIP
T. Carlyle publishes *Frederick the Great*.
William Morris publishes *The Defence of Guinevre and Other Poems*.
Charles Darwin and Alfred Wallace present papers to Linnean Society (of biologists) on problems of evolution.
Thomas Henry Huxley addresses Royal Society on vertebrate skulls.

MUSIC AND DRAMA
May 15	New Royal Opera House, Covent Garden, opens with Meyerbeer's *Les Huguenots*.

RELIGION AND EDUCATION
Oxford and Cambridge 'Locals' begin; first university-sponsored secondary school examinations in England.

SCIENCE AND INVENTION
Jan. 31	Brunel's *Great Eastern* – at 18,900 tons 3 times the displacement of most ships – finally launched at Millwall after 10 weeks of problems in getting her off the slipway.

Events Elsewhere

Feb. 11	Bernadette Soubirous experiences miraculous vision on 16 occasions at Lourdes (to 16 Jul.), which becomes Europe's principal pilgrimage centre.

AD 1859

Jan. 27	Q. Victoria becomes a grandmother with birth, in Berlin, of the future Kaiser William II.
Feb. 28	Disraeli introduces Reform Bill in Commons; defeated by 39 votes, 31 Mar.

Apr. and May	General election gives Conservatives 30 more seats, but they remain a minority party.
Jun. 6	'Willis's Rooms Meeting' of 300 Whigs, Liberals and Radicals: Palmerston and Russell agree to work together against Derby and Disraeli.
10	Derby resigns as Prime Minister after his government is defeated in Commons by 13 votes.
11–12	Q. Victoria invites E. Granville, as Liberal leader in Lords, to form a government, which proves impossible.
13	Palmerston returns as Prime Minister; Russell Foreign Secretary; Gladstone Chancellor of the Exchequer.
25	Chinese refuse passage of British envoys to Peking; British ships and marines attack Taku forts on Peiho river, but suffer heavy casualties.
Dec.	Queensland made a colony independent of New South Wales.

FINE ARTS AND ARCHITECTURE

| Jan. 15 | National Portrait Gallery, London, opens. |

LITERATURE AND SCHOLARSHIP

Charles Darwin's *The Origin of Species by Natural Selection* published.

J.S. Mill publishes *On Liberty*.

C. Dickens publishes *A Tale of Two Cities*.

'George Eliot' (Mary Ann Evans) publishes *Adam Bede*.

Edward Fitzgerald's translation of *Rubaiyat of Omar Khayyam* published anonymously.

A. Tennyson publishes *Idylls of the King*.

George Meredith publishes *The Ordeal of Richard Feverel*.

RECREATION AND FASHION

S.O. Beeton (v. 1852) publishes, in parts, *A Book of Household Management* by his wife, Isabella Beeton; popularly called a 'cookery-book'.

| Sep. 6 | First overseas tour by 'twelve Cricketers of England', to Canada and the United States (to 29 Oct.) organized by Fred Lillywhite. |

RELIGION AND EDUCATION

| Jun. | Violent anti-ritualistic demonstrations at St George's-in-the-East, Wapping, E. London (to May 1860). |

Events Elsewhere

| Jun. 4/24 | French defeat the Austrians at Ψs Magenta and Solferino. |
| Oct. 16–18 | John Brown leads abolitionist raid on Harper's Ferry; he is captured and hanged, 2 Dec. |

AD 1860

Jan. 23 Cobden negotiates free trade treaty with the French.
Mar. First Food and Drugs Act: seeks to check adulteration of basic cheap foods.
17 Taranaki War of Maoris and colonists begins in New Zealand.
May 11 British warships give unofficial cover to Garibaldi's Thousand as they land in Sicily to promote Italian unification.
Jul. Q. Victoria reviews 21,000 soldiers of the Volunteers movement, at a time of apprehension over the strengthening of the French army and navy.
Aug. 1 Anglo-French force, seeking observance of treaties from the Chinese, occupies Taku forts and advances on Tientsin and Peking.
Sep. 1 P. of Wales, undertaking first royal tour of imperial territories, lays foundation stone of Federal Parliament building in Ottawa.
5 Britain joins Austria, France, Russia, Prussia and Turkey in agreeing to police Syria after a massacre of Christians by the Druse.
21 Anglo-French force defeats Chinese army at Pa-li-chiao.
Oct. 3–8 P. of Wales is a guest of President Buchanan in Washington DC.
17 As a reprisal for cruelty to captives, British troops burn the Emperor's Summer Palace at Peking.
Oct. 24 Ty of Peking: China ratifies Ty of Tientsin of 1858 and gives further commercial concessions, including the opening of 11 new ports to British commerce.

LITERATURE AND SCHOLARSHIP
J.S. Mill's *Treatise on Representative Government* published.
Wilkie Collins publishes *The Woman in White*.
George Eliot publishes *The Mill on the Floss*.
Tennyson writes patriotic poem, 'Riflemen form!', in support of Volunteer movement.

RECREATION AND FASHION
Apr. Last major bare-fists boxing contest in England: Tom Sayers and American John Heenan over 42 rounds for £200 each at Farnborough, Hants; a drawn fight.
Jun. First golf championship, held at Prestwich; although limited to professionals it is reckoned as the first 'Open' (which it became, technically, in 1861).

RELIGION AND EDUCATION
English Church Union founded, by amalgamation of the 'Church of England Protection Society' (set up in 1859) and other groups established to defend High Church principles and practice.
The 'Broad Church' *Essays and Reviews*, collection of theological studies seeking to reconcile traditional beliefs with current scholarship, is widely attacked as being too liberal.

Joseph Swan invents electric lamp.

VOYAGES AND EXPLORATION
Jul. Robert Burke and William Wills leave Melbourne with expedition seeking to cross Australia from south to north.

Events Elsewhere

Oct. 26 Garibaldi and Cavour make possible the proclamation of united Kingdom of Italy.
Nov. 6 Abraham Lincoln elected President of USA.

AD 1861

Mar. 19 Pacification of the Maoris in New Zealand.
May 13 British government announces determination to remain neutral in American Civil War.
Jun. 21–26 Much of Southwark destroyed in great riverside fire.
Jul. 31 Bankruptcy and Insolvency Act: provides basic codification of company law.
Sep. 16 Post Office Savings Bank opens.
Oct. 31 Britain agrees with Spain and France on need to enforce payment of foreign debts refused by radical Mexican government.
Nov. 8 *Trent* incident: 2 Confederate supporters are removed by US vessel from the British ship *Trent* while travelling to Europe; threat of Anglo-American war until they are released, Dec.
Dec. 14 P. Consort dies from typhoid fever at Windsor.

FINE ARTS AND ARCHITECTURE
William Morris founds a company to produce artistically designed wallpaper and tapestries.

LITERATURE AND SCHOLARSHIP
C. Dickens's *Great Expectations* appears in book form.
A. Trollope publishes *Framley Parsonage*.
G. Eliot writes *Silas Marner*.
Charles Reade writes *The Cloister and the Hearth*.
F.T. Palgrave edits *The Golden Treasury of Best Songs and Lyrical Poems in the English Language*.

RECREATION AND FASHION
May 17–24 Thomas Cook's first continental holiday tour: 6 days in Paris.

RELIGION AND EDUCATION
Parochial and Burgh Schoolmasters Act: removes imposition of Presbyterian
religious tests on applicants for teaching posts in Scotland.

SCIENCE AND INVENTION
Australian engineer, Thomas Mort, designs first machine-cooled refrigerated
store, Sydney.

Oct.   Completion of first all-iron warship, HMS *Warrior*.

VOYAGES AND EXPLORATION
John McDouall crosses from Adelaide to Van Diemen's Gulf, Australia,
pioneering the route followed by a telegraph line to Darwin 10 years later.

Events Elsewhere

Mar. 3   Emancipation of serfs in Russia.
Apr. 12 Outbreak of American Civil War.

AD 1862–1863

1862 Jan.	10–20	Small British naval force in token anti-Mexican protest at Vera Cruz.
Jan.	14–25	Q. Victoria in a state of nervous collapse; royal duties are exercised by her uncle, K. Leopold I of the Belgians, in residence at Buckingham Palace.
Mar.	15	Stalybridge, Lancs.: riots over cotton recession.
	20	H. of Commons resolution approves the raising of defensive forces by the self-governing colonies.
Jul.	29	The *Alabama*, fitted out as a sea-raider for the Confederate Navy, sails from Birkenhead.
Oct.	24	British warship evacuates King Otho of Greece after army revolt declares Greek throne vacant.
Nov.		'Garroter's Act': amends criminal law to make robbery with violence punishable by flogging.
1863 Jan.	10	World's first Underground Railway open to public: Paddington to Farringdon Street.
Feb.	3	Greeks offer throne to Q. Victoria's second son, Alfred, D. of Edinburgh; Government insists on rejecting the offer as the Great Powers were pledged not to put their nationals on the Greek throne.
Mar.	10	P. of Wales marries P. Alexandra of Denmark at Windsor.
May		William Whiteley opens his Universal Provider department store, Westbourne Grove, Bayswater.
May	4	Second Maori War begins with fresh risings against colonists.
Jul.		Palmerston encourages Denmark to resist German pressure in the Schleswig-Holstein dispute.

1862   C. Frith paints *Railway Station*.

Joseph Bazalgette begins construction of Thames Embankment; completed 1874.

1863   James Whistler paints *Symphony in White*.

LITERATURE AND SCHOLARSHIP

1862   G. Meredith publishes *Modern Love*.

H. Spencer publishes *First Principles*.

Mary Elizabeth Braddon writes *Lady Audley's Secret*, first of 75 luridly sensational novels, serialized.

1863   J.S. Mill publishes *Utilitarianism*.

C. Kingsley publishes *The Water Babies*.

RECREATION AND FASHION

1863 Oct.   Football Association established, London.

RELIGION AND EDUCATION

1862   Alleged heretical views of Bp John Colenso of Natal on the Pentateuch cause divisions in Anglican Church.

'Revised Code' of education introduces government grants to individual schools on a 'payment by results' basis, dependent on tests by official inspectors to assess progress in the 'three Rs'.

SCIENCE AND INVENTION

1862 May 1   International Exhibition of Industry and Science opens in S. Kensington; attracts over 5 million visitors.

VOYAGES AND EXPLORATION

1862   Richard Burton explores Benin.

William Gifford Palgrave explores central Arabia.

Events Elsewhere

1862 Sep. 22   Bismarck becomes chief minister of Prussia.

1863 Jul. 1–3   Ψ Gettysburg.

AD 1864

Mar. 24   Ty with Greece: cedes the Ionian Islands.

Apr. 21   Garibaldi ends an English visit in which he was enthusiastically received in London.

25   London Conference of great powers seeks solution of Schleswig-Holstein problem; fails 25 Jun.

May 11	Gladstone supports parliamentary reform, with universal suffrage, in speech in H. of Commons; confirms his natural leadership of progressive Liberals.
24	Complaints in H. of Lords about Q. Victoria's excessive partiality towards Prussia in Schleswig-Holstein dispute.
Sep. 5–6	Royal Navy bombards Kagoshima after Japan closes ports and expels foreign traders.
Oct. 10	Quebec Conference opens: plans proposed for a federated Dominion of Canada.
20	Palmerston, on his 80th birthday, inspects new forts protecting Portsmouth.
22	Japan reopens ports and agrees to pay indemnity.

FINE ARTS AND ARCHITECTURE
W.H. Barlow designs St Pancras station arched roof.

LITERATURE AND SCHOLARSHIP
G. Meredith publishes *Emilia in England*; title changed to *Sandra Belloni*, 1886.
A. Trollope writes *The Small House at Alington* and *Can You Forgive Her?*, first of the Palliser novels.
Tennyson completes narrative poem, *Enoch Arden*.

Nov. 25	Public debate on Darwinian theory of evolution at Sheldonian Theatre, Oxford. Disraeli declares himself 'on the side of the angels'.

RECREATION AND FASHION
First county cricket championship held.

Jul. 21	W.G. Grace scores 50 in his first match at Lords, playing for MCC against New South Wales, 3 days after his 16th birthday,.

RELIGION AND EDUCATION
J.H. Newman publishes *Apologia Pro Vita Sua*.

SCIENCE AND INVENTION
J. Swan patents carbon process for photographic printing.
James Slater patents driving chain for textile industry, later developed for bicycles.

VOYAGES AND EXPLORATION

Mar. 14	Samuel White Baker, with expedition, seeking source of R. Nile, discovers and names Lake Albert Nyanza.

Events Elsewhere

Feb. 1	Prussian and Austrian troops invade Schleswig-Holstein.

AD 1865

Feb.–Mar.   Hurried enactment of a New Poor Law Bill to improve conditions in workhouses.

May 2   Colonial Laws Validity Act: legislatures have a right to pass their own laws, but must not contravene statutes of Westminster Parliament.

30   Commercial treaty between Britain and German Customs Union (*Zollverein*).

Jul.   General election increases overall majority of Liberals from 46 to 82.

Oct. 9–20   Rebellion in Morant Bay area of Jamaica; put down with great brutality; over 400 executions, excessive floggings and burning of 1,000 homes.

29   E. ('Lord John') Russell becomes Prime Minister, following Palmerston's death in office (18 Oct.).

Nov. 3   E. of Clarendon becomes Foreign Secretary.

Dec. 16   Edward J. Eyre (*v.* 1841), Governor of Jamaica, is recalled to London; is subsequently censured and dismissed for way in which rising was suppressed.

LITERATURE AND SCHOLARSHIP

Lewis Carroll (C.L. Dodgson) publishes *Alice's Adventures in Wonderland*.
C. Dickens publishes *Our Mutual Friend*.
M. Arnold's *Essays in Criticism*, first series, published.
J. Ruskin publishes *Sesame and Lilies*.

MUSIC AND DRAMA

Apr. 15   Squire Bancroft and his future wife Marie Wilton begin 20-year actor-manager partnership at Prince of Wales Theatre (Scala), London.

RELIGION AND EDUCATION

Jul. 2   William Booth leads his first evangelical Christian Mission meeting, Whitechapel, London; not yet called 'Salvation Army'.

SCIENCE AND INVENTION

Road Locomotion Act: imposes 4 m.p.h. speed limit on any form of mechanical road transport; road 'locomotives' require 3 attendants, one of whom must walk in front with a red warning flag.
Benjamin Maugham patents first gas-fired 'geyser' boiler for domestic use.
William Crookes, conducting chemical research at Chester, discovers the sodium amalgamation process.

Events Elsewhere

Apr. 9   Confederate states capitulate at Appomatox.

14   Abraham Lincoln fatally wounded.

AD 1866

Feb. 17 Habeas Corpus Act again suspended in Ireland because of Fenian campaign of violence.

Mar. 12 Gladstone introduces a Parliamentary Reform Bill, which subsequently proves unacceptable to Whig 'Adullamites' among Liberals.

Apr. 10 Q. Victoria, without consulting her government, sends personal appeal to K. William of Prussia to keep peace; her message is very hostile to his chief minister, Bismarck.

May 11 First 'Black Friday' City panic as bankers Overend, Gurney and Co. fail; financial instability leads to many bankruptcies over following 3 months.

Jun. 18–19 In reform debate, 48 Liberals support Opposition.

26 Russell resigns because of party split over reform.

28 E. of Derby becomes Prime Minister, heading a minority Conservative government.

Jul. 6 Derby appoints his son and successor Lord Stanley (succeeds in 1869) as Foreign Secretary; Disraeli appointed as Chancellor of Exchequer and Leader of the Commons.

23, 24 and 25 Violent demonstrations for parliamentary reform in Hyde Park.

Oct. 'Sheffield Outrages': intimidation of non-union workers, including dynamiting of a worker's home.

LITERATURE AND SCHOLARSHIP
Mrs E. Gaskell's *Wives and Daughters* published, posthumously and unfinished.
C. Kingsley publishes *Hereward the Wake*.
J.H. Newman's poem *The Dream of Gerontius* in book form.
C. Reade publishes *Griffith Gaunt*.

RECREATION AND FASHION
John Graham Chambers, walker and oarsman, founds Amateur Athletic Club and draws up basic rules for athletic competitions.

RELIGION AND EDUCATION
Considerable controversy aroused by *Ecce Homo*, 'popular' life of Christ by historian John Robert Seeley.

SCIENCE AND INVENTION

Dr Elizabeth Garrett Anderson, first woman to qualify as medical practitioner (1865), establishes medical dispensary for women in London; she institutes medical courses for women there.

HMS *Albert* is first warship to have guns mounted in an iron turret.

Mancunian engineer Robert Whitehead constructs first self-propelling torpedo at Fiume (Rijeka), Austria.

Events Elsewhere

Jul.   3   Prussian defeat of Austria at Ψ Sadowa (Königgrätz) ensures victory in Seven Weeks War and primacy of Prussia in new North German Confederation.

AD 1867

Feb. 12   Disraeli tells H. of Commons that Conservatives will introduce a Parliamentary Reform Bill.

      13   Fenian attempt to seize city of Chester thwarted by battalion of Guardsmen sent by overnight train from London.

Mar. 5   Fenian risings in several Irish towns.

      15   'Conference of Trades' meets in London to discuss joint trade union policy.

      18   Disraeli introduces a Reform Bill in H. of Commons based upon a 'fancy franchise'.

Apr. 1   Colonial Office succeeds India Office as government department responsible for the Straits Settlements (Malaya).

May   2–17 Amendments in Commons debates on Reform replace 'fancy franchise' by proposals for uniform male household suffrage in boroughs.

      11   London Conference to safeguard neutrality of Luxembourg.

      18   John Stuart Mill introduces motion to give women the vote; defeated by 196 votes to 73, with 290 abstentions.

Jul. 1   British North America Act: unites Quebec, Ontario, New Brunswick and Nova Scotia in the Dominion of Canada, a confederation with provincial governments and a bicameral parliament to which other colonial settlements could accede.

Aug. 15   Second Parliamentary Reform Act: enfranchises virtually all men in towns and extends franchise in country, but excludes poorer agricultural labourers; size of electorate in England and Wales almost doubled (from 1,056,000 to 1,994,000 voters).

            Redistribution Act: 25 new seats in counties, 15 in towns, 4 in older cities; 7 new Scottish seats.

            Factory Act: extends earlier laws to smaller premises.

      21   Workshop Hours Act: to protect women and young children.

Sep. 18   Policeman killed in escape of Fenians in Manchester; 3 of 5 rescuers later hanged.

Oct.	Dr Thomas Barnardo opens children's shelter in Stepney. (His first permanent Home for Destitute Boys built in 1870.) Sailing of last convict ship for Western Australia marks end of transportation as a punishment.
Nov. 12	National Union of Conservative and Constitution Associations inaugural meeting, Freemasons Tavern, Westminster.
Dec. 13	Clerkenwell gaol explosion: 12 people killed during Fenian escape attempt.

LITERATURE AND SCHOLARSHIP
Walter Bagehot's *The English Constitution* published.
G. Meredith publishes *Vittoria*.
A. Trollope writes *The Last Chronicle of Barset*.

RECREATION AND FASHION
Marquis of Queensberry, in collaboration with J.G. Chambers, draws up rules to govern boxing.

RELIGION AND EDUCATION
Sep. First 'Lambeth Conference' of Anglican bishops worldwide is held under presidency of Archbp Archibald Tait.

SCIENCE AND INVENTION
Joseph Lister, professor of surgery at Glasgow, introduces an antiseptic system based on phenol.

Events Elsewhere

Jun. 12	Compromise (*Ausgleich*) establishes Dual Monarchy of Austria-Hungary.
19	Emperor Maximilian of Mexico executed at Queretaro.

AD 1868

Jan. 2	British expedition led by Sir Robert Napier enters Ethiopia to release hostages held by K. Theodore.
Feb. 27	Disraeli becomes Prime Minister on retirement of Lord Derby.
Mar. 12	Basutoland annexed.
Apr. 2 and *May 26*	Last public hangings: Frances Kidder at Maidstone; Michael Barrett at Newgate, London.
Apr. 13	Napier's troops storm Magdala, Ethiopian capital, and free hostages.
May 25–29	First Trades Union Congress meets, at Manchester; attended by 34 representatives, mostly from N. England and Birmingham area.
Jul.	3rd Maori War in New Zealand; continues for 2 years.
13	Irish Reform Act: increases borough franchise and introduces for first time in

Ireland a lodger franchise.
31 Parliament is prorogued; general election announced for mid-November.
Nov. 15–24 General election gives Liberals overall majority of 112 seats with over half a million more votes than Conservatives.
Dec. 1 Gladstone, at Hawarden in Cheshire, is invited to Windsor to form government; he declares, 'My mission is to pacify Ireland'.
3 Gladstone becomes Prime Minister.
9 Lord Clarendon returns to Foreign Office; Robert Lowe succeeds Gladstone as Chancellor of the Exchequer.

FINE ARTS AND ARCHITECTURE
Sir G. Gilbert Scott completes St Pancras Hotel (designed in 1865).

LITERATURE AND SCHOLARSHIP
Q. Victoria's *Leaves from the Journal of Our Life in the Highlands* published.
Wilkie Collins publishes *The Moonstone*.

RELIGION AND EDUCATION
Cambridge Higher Local Examination is open to girls as well as to boys.

Events Elsewhere

Sep. Liberal revolution in Spain deposes Q. Isabella II.

AD 1869

Mar. 1 Gladstone introduces Church Disestablishment Bill as his first gesture towards pacifying Ireland.
Jun. 24 Corn Importation Act repealed.
Aug. Second TUC meets, at Birmingham; attended by 40 delegates representing a quarter of a million trade unionists.
Oct. 11 Louis Riel's Red River Rebellion begins near Winnipeg, Canada; order restored, May 1870.
30 Gladstone convinces his cabinet of need for land reform in Ireland.
Nov. 17 P. of Wales attends opening of Suez Canal by Empress Eugenie.
19 Hudson Bay Co. surrenders rights to Dominion of Canada.
22 By-election in Tipperary is won by Jeremiah O'Donovan, an imprisoned Fenian; as 'a convicted felon' his election is declared null and void.

FINE ARTS AND ARCHITECTURE
Royal Academy is established in Burlington House.

LITERATURE AND SCHOLARSHIP
J.S. Mill's *The Subjection of Women* published.
M. Arnold publishes *Culture and Anarchy*.
W. Morris publishes *The Earthly Paradise*.
R.D. Blackmore publishes *Lorna Doone*.
A. Trollope publishes *Phineas Finn*.

RECREATION AND FASHION
Inverness capes, plaid or check cloth, come into fashion for men when travelling and, with 'Dundreary side-whiskers', suggest a Scottish influence. Women's skirts begin to be bunched up at the back; light coloured parasols are popular.

RELIGION AND EDUCATION

Jul.   Endowed Schools Act: creates commissioners with powers to review and revise all educational endowments.
          Emily Davies founds a women's college at Hitchin; she moves it to Girton, Cambridge, in 1872.

Jul. 26 Irish Church Act: disestablishes (Protestant) Church of Ireland.

VOYAGES AND EXPLORATION
Diamond rush begins in S. Africa after discovery of great mineral wealth some 540 miles north of Cape Town; 3 main mining camps form town of Kimberley, 1870.

Events Elsewhere

Jul.   Napoleon III introduces a parliamentary system, 'the Liberal Empire'.

AD 1870

May 10–13 2 Fenian raids on Quebec from Vermont thwarted by Canadian militia.
      19   Isaac Butt founds Home Government Association, a constitutional movement for Irish Home Rule.
Jun. 4   Civil service reforms promulgated: competitive examination for entry into most departments (not into Foreign Office).
      20   Army Enlistment Act, first of reforms of Edward Cardwell as War Secretary: introduces short-service enlistment.
      28   Cardwell induces Q. Victoria to sign, reluctantly, order-in-council confirming authority of War Secretary over Commander-in-Chief.
Jul. 6   E. Granville becomes Foreign Secretary on death of Lord Clarendon.
Aug. 1   Irish Land Act: loans to peasants to purchase land; compensation for eviction and improvement.
      9   Married Women's Property Act: acknowledges principle that wives may have

property of their own; not extended to Scotland until 1877.

9 and 11 Treaties concluded in London with Prussia and France: reaffirm respect for Belgian neutrality.

Oct. 31 Granville denounces Russian abrogation of clauses in Ty of Paris demilitarizing Black Sea (*v.* 1856).

FINE ARTS AND ARCHITECTURE
J. Millais paints *The Boyhood of Raleigh*.

LITERATURE AND SCHOLARSHIP
C. Dickens begins *Mystery of Edwin Drood*; unfinished at his death, 9 Jun.
B. Disraeli publishes *Lothair*.
John Lubbock completes his *Origin of Civilisation*.
D.G. Rossetti writes *Poems*.

RECREATION AND FASHION
Growing concern for uniform excellence of playing conditions in competitive sport is shown by innovative use of heavy roller at Lord's cricket ground.

RELIGION AND EDUCATION
William Edward Forster responsible for Education Act which accepts that basic schooling is a government responsibility: locally elected boards to establish schools; existing Church schools to receive government backing.
Frances Buss hands over North London Collegiate School (which she founded in 1850) to a trust which, as the Girls' Public Day-Schools Company, establishes similar schools nationwide.
Pioneer programme of extension lectures at Cambridge.
Keble College, Oxford, founded.

SCIENCE AND INVENTION
T.H. Huxley presents paper to British Association on spontaneous generation.
London and Australia linked by telegraph.

VOYAGES AND EXPLORATION
New York Herald commissions Welsh explorer-journalist Henry Stanley to search for Livingstone in Tanganyika.

Events Elsewhere

Jul. 18 Vatican Council affirms papal infallibility in questions of faith and morals.

19 France declares war on Prussia.

Sep. 3 Third French Republic proclaimed following capture of Napoleon III at Sedan.

20 Italian army enters Rome; Italy's capital from 2 Oct.

AD 1871

Jan.	*17*	London Conference on revision of Ty of Paris opens.
Mar.	*17*	Convention of London: repudiates Black Sea clauses of Ty of Paris.
	29	Q. Victoria opens Royal Albert Hall.
May	*8*	Arbitration Ty signed in Washington: settles boundary and fishery problems; refers *Alabama* claims to international tribunal.
Jun.	*16*	University Test Act: removes requirement of religious tests for students entering Oxford and Cambridge universities.
	29	Trade Union Act: legalizes unions by recognizing their status as 'friendly societies'.
Jul.	*20*	Q. Victoria's assent given to royal warrant abolishing purchase of army commissions.
		British Columbia becomes a province of Canada.
Aug.	*17*	Army Regulation Act: centralized control; regiments constituted according to geographical districts and with a linked battalion system for home and overseas service.

FINE ARTS AND ARCHITECTURE
James Whistler paints *The Artist's Mother*.
Slade School of Fine Art established at University College, London.

LITERATURE AND SCHOLARSHIP
C. Darwin publishes *The Descent of Man*.
L. Carroll publishes *Through the Looking Glass*.
J. Ruskin publishes *Fors Clavigera*.
Col. G. Chesney writes novel *The Battle of Dorking*, propaganda for army modernization, published anonymously; a German invasion is first envisaged.

RECREATION AND FASHION

		W.G. Grace's greatest cricket season; scores 2,739 runs.
Jan.	*26*	Rugby Football Union founded, London; Scotland defeat England in first international, Raeburn Park, Edinburgh, 7 Mar.
Aug.	*7*	First Bank Holiday, resulting from recent enactment of John Lubbock's Bank Holiday Bill, giving three leisure breaks between Spring and autumn each year.

RELIGION AND EDUCATION
Ecclesiastical Titles Act of 1851 repealed.
First hall of residence for women in Cambridge opens; called Newnham College in 1880.

SCIENCE AND INVENTION
Cambridge University establishes a chair of experimental physics.

Nov. 10   Stanley finds Livingstone at Ujiji.

Events Elsewhere

Jan. 18   K. Wilhelm I of Prussia proclaimed German Emperor at Versailles.
Mar. 18   Paris Commune begins (to 28 May).
May 10   Franco-German Peace Ty of Frankfurt.

AD 1872

Feb.   Joseph Arch founds National Agricultural Labourers' Union.
   2   Dutch government sells a number of forts along Gold Coast to Britain.
   8   Viceroy of India, E. Mayo, murdered by convict while inspecting penal settlement in Andaman Islands.
Mar. 18   In H. of Commons, Charles Dilke, claiming to be a republican by conviction, seeks an official inquiry into Q. Victoria's expenditure.
Apr. 3   Disraeli describes government as being 'a range of exhausted volcanoes'.
Jun. 24   Disraeli's Crystal Palace speech advocates building up a greater 'colonial empire'.
Jul. 18   Ballot Act: ensures secrecy at elections; first secret ballot is at Pontefract by-election, 15 Aug.
   31   Licensing Act, associated with Home Secretary Henry Bruce: limits hours and places at which alcoholic liquor may be consumed; more moderate measure than a licensing bill withdrawn, under pressure from H. of Lords, in previous session.
Sep. 14   Tribunal in Geneva finds Britain responsible for depredations caused by the *Alabama*; Britain must pay USA £3 million compensation.
Nov. 5   Revised commercial treaty between Britain and France.

FINE ARTS AND ARCHITECTURE
J. Whistler paints *Old Battersea Bridge*.
Jul. 1   Q. Victoria inspects Albert Memorial and knights the designer, George Gilbert Scott; statue not added until 1876.

LITERATURE AND SCHOLARSHIP
C.P. Scott begins 57 years as editor of *Manchester Guardian*.
Samuel Butler publishes *Erewhon*.
George Eliot publishes *Middlemarch*.
Thomas Hardy publishes *Under the Greenwood Tree*.

RECREATION, SPORT AND FASHION

Earliest lawn tennis club founded, Manor House Hotel, Leamington.

Mar. 16   First FA Cup Final, at Kennington Oval: Wanderers beat R. Engineers 1-0; only 16 clubs entered for the competition.

Nov. 1   First international football match in the world: goalless draw between Scotland and England at Partick.

RELIGION AND EDUCATION

Scottish Education Department is created.

SCIENCE AND INVENTION

William Thomson perfects Kelvin sounding-machine for determining depth of the sea.

VOYAGES AND EXPLORATION

HMS *Challenger*, a screw steam corvette commanded by George Nares, begins 4-year oceanographic survey voyage on behalf of Royal Society.

AD 1873

Jan. 9   Napoleon III dies in exile in England, at Chislehurst.

Mar. 13   Gladstone resigns after government is defeated over Irish University Bill, with 43 Liberals in opposition.

14–15   Disraeli declines to form a government and Gladstone remains Prime Minister.

31   Judicature Act: central court structure in England reformed; Supreme Court established, with separate divisions; Court of Appeal instituted.

Apr.   Ashanti War begins with attacks on British troops in Gold Coast forts taken over in 1872 from the Dutch.

May   Joseph Chamberlain begins 3 years of civic reform as mayor of Birmingham.

Jun. 18   Shah of Persia arrives in London, entertained mainly by P. of Wales; commercial interests with Persia are strengthened.

Aug. 30   Gladstone reforms government, becoming his own Chancellor of Exchequer; Robert Lowe replaces Bruce as Home Secretary.

Nov. 26   British troops begin march into Ashanti interior.

Dec.   General Sir Garnet Wolseley arrives on Gold Coast with 2,400 men for a campaign against the Ashanti.

FINE ARTS AND ARCHITECTURE

Alfred Waterhouse completes Natural History Museum, South Kensington.

Walter Pater, in *Studies in the History of the Renaissance*, preaches 'the love of art for art's sake'.

LITERATURE AND SCHOLARSHIP
J.S. Mill completes his *Autobiography*.
H. Spencer publishes *The Study of Sociology*.

RECREATION AND FASHION
Women's fashion favours long sleeves and draperies, a bustle, small hats with a veil, gloves, high necks; men of elegance wear frock coats, black top hats, lightly striped trousers, spats, light gloves, silver-topped canes.

RELIGION AND EDUCATION
American evangelists, Dwight Moody and Ira David Sankey, undertake a 2-year revivalist mission throughout Britain using their own *Sankey and Moody Hymnbook*.

SCIENCE AND INVENTION
J. Clerk-Maxwell's *Treatise on Electricity and Magnetism* develops mathematical theory of electromagnetic radiation.
William Crookes first observes cathode rays.

Apr. 2   Sleeping car introduced on Glasgow to London night express; first in Britain.

VOYAGES AND EXPLORATION
Livingstone continues his exploration of central Africa, dying on 1 May beside Lake Bangweulu (now in Zambia).

Events Elsewhere

May   Financial crisis in central Europe, centred on Vienna.

AD 1874

Jan. 23   Q. Victoria's second son, P. Alfred marries Tsar Alexander II's daughter, Grand Duchess Marie, in St Petersburg; first marriage link between British and Russian royal families.

31   Ashanti defeated at Ψ Amoafo.

Feb. 2   General election: rioting in several towns in the Midlands, particularly against the Licensing Act (*v.* 1872).

4   Wolseley enters Kumasi, Ashanti tribal capital, which he burns.

17   Gladstone resigns when final election count gives Conservatives overall majority despite Liberal pledge to abolish income tax: Conservatives 350; Liberals 245; Irish Home Rule 57.

20   Disraeli returns as Prime Minister.
First organized strike of agricultural labourers begins (to 10 Aug.); spreads from Suffolk to much of E. England.

21   Lord Derby becomes Foreign Secretary; Sir Stafford Northcote Chancellor of

Exchequer; Richard Cross Home Secretary.

28   Arthur Orton given sentence of 14 years' hard labour for perjury as an impostor; since 1866 he had claimed the Tichborne baronetcy and estates.

Mar. 14   Wolseley makes peace with the Ashanti, who promise an end to human sacrifices and freedom of movement for British Gold Coast traders.

May   State visit of Tsar Alexander II to London.

Aug. 30   Factory Act: 56-hour working week; further safeguards to protect children from employment as chimney sweeps.

Sep. 15   P. of Wales makes first royal visit to a French republic.

FINE ARTS AND ARCHITECTURE
George Street is architect of Law Courts, London.

LITERATURE AND SCHOLARSHIP
John Richard Green publishes *A Short History of the English People*.
Henry Sidgwick publishes *Methods of Ethics*.
T. Hardy writes *Far from the Madding Crowd*.

RELIGION AND EDUCATION
W.E. Gladstone writes pamphlet, *The Vatican Decrees*.

Aug. 7   Public Worship Regulation Act: seeks to curb alleged ritualism in Church of England services.

Sep.   Foundation of Yorkshire College, Leeds; becomes University of Leeds, 1904.

SCIENCE AND INVENTION
South Eastern Railway sinks experimental shafts to examine feasibility of a Channel Tunnel.

Apr. 1   First weather map is printed in a British newspaper, *The Times*.

VOYAGES AND EXPLORATION
H.M. Stanley continues exploration of the Congo basin begun by Livingstone.
General Charles Gordon establishes outposts on upper R. Nile and completes navigational survey of Lake Albert.

Events Elsewhere

Feb.   First Impressionist exhibition, Paris.

AD 1875

Jan. 13   Gladstone resigns Liberal leadership; succeeded by Lord Hartington (later D. of Devonshire), 3 Feb.

May 8   Derby co-operates with Russia in easing Franco-German war crisis.

Jul.	*31*	Public Health Act: consolidates over 100 local Acts into a national code of sanitation.
Aug.		Colonial Secretary Lord Carnarvon holds conversations in London over a possible South African federation.
	13	Artisans Dwellings Act: gives local authorities power to purchase and replace insanitary buildings.
		Agricultural Holdings Act: displaced tenants to receive compensation for improvements.
		Sale of Food and Drugs Act: provides basic protection against adulteration.
		Conspiracy and Protection of Property Act: legalizes peaceful picketing by trade unions.
Sep.		Main sewerage system for London is completed after 30 years' work by Sir Joseph Bazalgette.
Nov.	*8*	P. of Wales makes first royal state visit to India and Ceylon, on behalf of Q. Victoria (to 13 Mar. 1876).
	25	Disraeli purchases 176,602 Suez Canal shares (40%) from the Khedive of Egypt for £4 million, making Britain the largest single shareholder in the Canal Company.

FINE ARTS AND ARCHITECTURE
Edward Burne-Jones paints *The Mirror of Venus*.

LITERATURE AND SCHOLARSHIP
G. Meredith publishes *Beauchamp's Career*.

MUSIC AND DRAMA
Mar. 25	W.S. Gilbert and Arthur Sullivan present *Trial by Jury* at Royalty Theatre, under management of Rupert D'Oyly Carte.

RECREATION AND FASHION
Marylebone Cricket Club drafts first laws for lawn tennis.
Apr. 16	English Hockey Association founded, London.
Aug. 25	Matthew Webb becomes first swimmer of the English Channel: Dover to Calais in 21 hrs 45 mins.

RELIGION AND EDUCATION
London Medical School for Women established.

Events Elsewhere

Apr.–May	'Is War In Sight?' crisis between Germany and France.
Jul.–Aug.	Rising in Bosnia-Herzegovina against Turkish rule begins the Great Eastern Crisis (to 1878).

AD 1876

Mar.	Merchant Shipping Act, for which Samuel Plimsoll MP had campaigned for 8 years: establishes safety measures, notably the Plimsoll mark to guard against overloading of vessels.
Mar. 26	Cave Report on Egypt's finances indicates that the country is near bankruptcy.
Apr.	Royal Titles Act: Q. Victoria to be Empress of India.
May 19	Disraeli refuses to co-operate with Germany, Austria-Hungary and Russia in putting pressure on Turkey for reform in the Balkans.
24	British fleet ordered to Besika Bay, off the Dardanelles, in case of a crisis at Constantinople.
Jun. 8	Reports in *Daily News* describe Turkish atrocities in suppressing an insurrection in Bulgaria; further reports, 23 and 30 Jun.
Jul. 31	Disraeli tells H. of Commons that press reports are based on 'coffee-house babble'.
Aug. 11–23	Widespread indignation at further reports from Bulgaria.
12	Disraeli is created E. of Beaconsfield; goes to H. of Lords, remaining Prime Minister.
Sep. 6	Gladstone's pamphlet, *The Bulgarian Horrors and the Question of the East*, published; 40,000 copies sell in a week.
9	Gladstone's speech at Blackheath on Bulgarian atrocities marks his return to active politics.
Oct.	Britain and France set up dual control of Egypt's finances.
Nov. 1	Appellate Jurisdiction Act: confirms historic juridical status of H. of Lords and Judicial Committee of Privy Council.
2	Beaconsfield seeks to co-operate with Russia and proposes conference in Constantinople.
Dec. 5	Lord Salisbury, India Secretary, arrives in Constantinople for conference.
8	'National Convention on the Eastern Question', London, chaired by Shaftesbury, addressed by Gladstone.
12	Constantinople Conference opens.

FINE ARTS AND ARCHITECTURE
Chapel of Keble College, Oxford, begun in 1873, is completed; designed by William Butterfield.

LITERATURE AND SCHOLARSHIP
Francis Herbert Bradley publishes *Ethical Studies*.
George Eliot publishes *Daniel Deronda*.

Aug. W.G. Grace scores 1,209 runs during the month, including triple centuries against Kent and Yorkshire; average 134.33.

Oct. 7 Greyhound racing with an artificial hare staged experimentally at Hendon.

RELIGION AND EDUCATION
Presbyterian churches south of the Cheviots unite to form Presbyterian Church of England.

Events Elsewhere

Jun. 2 Serbia declares war on Turkey.

Aug. 31 Sultan Murad V deposed as insane; succeeded by Abdul Hamid II, who grants Turkey a constitution, 23 Dec.

AD 1877

Jan. 1 Q. Victoria is proclaimed Empress of India at Delhi.

22 Salisbury, highly critical of the Turks, leaves for London immediately after breakdown of Constantinople Conference.

Mar. 31 London Protocol: on Derby's initiative, great powers demand effective reforms within Turkish empire; rejected by Sultan, 12 Apr.

Sir Bartle Frere appointed High Commissioner in S. Africa with orders to seek federation.

Apr. 12 Sir Theophilus Shepstone, administrator in Natal, annexes Transvaal, which is close to bankruptcy and threatened by Zulus.

Jul. 21 Beaconsfield secures cabinet backing for declaration of war on Russia if Tsar's army occupies Constantinople.

31 Irish Home Rule MPs begin obstructionist tactics in H. of Commons to publicize their cause.

Aug.–Dec. Gaika campaign: Frere's troops suppress Kaffirs in Transkei.

Aug. 28 Charles Stewart Parnell, MP for Co. Neath since 1875, becomes President of Home Rule Confederation of Great Britain.

FINE ARTS AND ARCHITECTURE
Grosvenor Gallery, New Bond Street, provides fashionable London with exhibitions to rival Royal Academy throughout the decade.

William Morris begins high-quality tapestry weaving.

A. Waterhouse builds Manchester town hall; with 12 frescos by Ford Madox Brown, not finished until 1893.

LITERATURE AND SCHOLARSHIP

William Hurrell Mallock writes *The New Republic*, satire on 'culture, faith and philosophy in an English country house'.
Grant Allen writes *Physiological Aesthetics*.

MUSIC AND DRAMA

May 7–9   3-day festival at Albert Hall to familiarize public with Wagner's music; conducted partly by Wagner himself, but mainly by Hans Richter.

Nov. 17   Gilbert and Sullivan's *The Sorcerer* performed at Opera Comique, Strand.

Dec.   'We don't want to fight but, by Jingo, if we do . . .', patriotic music-hall song, by G.W. Hunt, popularized in London by 'The Great Macdermott' (Gilbert H. Farrell).

RECREATION AND FASHION

All England Croquet and Lawn Tennis Club holds first championship at Worple Road, Wimbledon; Spencer Gore wins singles title, 9 Jul.

Mar. 17   Australia beat England in the inaugural Test Match, Melbourne.

VOYAGES AND EXPLORATION

Oct. 17   Stanley completes 1,000-day trek across Africa from Dar es Salaam to Boma, at mouth of Congo river.

Events Elsewhere

Apr. 24   Russia declares war on Turkey, but Tsar's armies are halted by the defence of Plevna.

AD 1878

Jan.   'Cleopatra's Needle' reaches London from Alexandria after 4-month voyage.

23   British fleet anchors off Constantinople.

Mar. 12   Walvis Bay, SW Africa, annexed.

27   Troopships sail for Malta.

Apr. 2   Salisbury succeeds Derby as Foreign Secretary.

May 30–31   Anglo-Russian agreements signed in London on acceptable frontiers in Bulgaria and the Caucasus.

Jun. 4   Cyprus Convention: Turkey retains sovereignty but hands over the administration of the island to Britain.
Defensive alliance treaty with Turkey to protect Asiatic provinces from Russia.

11–12   Beaconsfield and Salisbury arrive in Berlin for the Congress over the Eastern Question.

Jul. 11–12   Anglo-Russian Declarations respecting Bosphorus and Dardanelles.

13   Ty of Berlin signed; Beaconsfield is chief British signatory.

16	Beaconsfield arrives home at Dover declaring he has brought 'peace with honour'.
Oct. 16	British troops enter Afghanistan after Amir Yakub refuses to receive envoy at Kabul.
Dec. 11	Bartle Frere sends ultimatum to K. Cetewayo of Zululand.

FINE ARTS AND ARCHITECTURE

The 'Glasgow Boys' school of painters come together: Stuart Park, James Paterson, James Guthrie and others; group opposes allegedly conformist and parochial outlook of the Royal Scottish Academy in Edinburgh.

J. Millais paints *The Yeoman of the Guard*.

Whistler sues Ruskin for libel over comments on his *Nocturne in Black and Gold*; awarded a farthing's damages.

LITERATURE AND SCHOLARSHIP

T. Hardy writes *The Return of the Native*.

A.C. Swinburne publishes *Poems and Ballads*, second series (contains 'A Forsaken Garden', etc.).

MUSIC AND DRAMA

May 25	Gilbert and Sullivan's *HMS Pinafore* performed at Opera Comique, Strand.
Dec. 30	Henry Irving becomes manager of the Lyceum Theatre and begins a 24-year stage partnership there with Ellen Terry.

RECREATION AND FASHION

Cyclists' Touring Club set up.

RELIGION AND EDUCATION

William Booth organizes his Christian Mission (*v.* 1865) as the Salvation Army; he is styled 'General', 1880.

Roman Catholic hierarchy is restored in Scotland.

SCIENCE AND INVENTION

Feb. 11	Meteorological Office issues first weekly weather report.
Dec. 18	Joseph Swan demonstrates his incandescent electric lamp in Newcastle.

Events Elsewhere

Mar. 3	Russo-Turkish Peace Ty of San Stefano creates a big Bulgaria; invalidated by Ty of Berlin, which accepts a small Bulgarian principality and recognizes independence of Serbia.

AD 1879

Jan.	8	British force in Afghanistan occupies Kandahar.
	12	British advance into Zululand.
	22	Zulus defeat British at Ψ Isandhlwana, massacring 826 whites and about 800 black soldiers.
	22–23	Ψ Rorke's Drift: small force successfully resists Zulu attacks; 11 VCs awarded for the action.
May	26	Ty of Gandamak: Britain pays Amir of Afghanistan annual subsidy for occupying Khyber Pass; and has right to have an agent (envoy) at Kabul.
Jun.	*1*	The Prince Imperial, Napoleon III's only son, is killed by the Zulus at Itelezi, while serving with the British army.
Jul.	4	Zulus defeated at Ψ Ulundi.
	24	Sir Louis Cavagnari reaches Kabul as agent.
Aug.	28	British capture K. Cetewayo; deported.
Sep.	*1*	Zulu War formally ends.
	3	Cavagnari and his staff massacred in Kabul.
	4	Anglo-French financial control of Egypt reasserted after 9 months of dispute.
Oct.	4	General Sir Frederick Roberts defeats Afghans at Charasia.
	12	Roberts's troops enter Kabul.
	21	Foundation of Irish National Land League.
Nov.	*25*	Gladstone makes first speech in his Midlothian campaign; at Edinburgh.
	27	West Calder speech: Gladstone defines governing principles which should determine foreign policy.
Dec.	*23*	Afghan attack on Kabul beaten off by Roberts.
	28	Tay Bridge disaster: collapses in a gale while train crossing; 78 lives lost.

FINE ARTS AND ARCHITECTURE
J. Millais paints *Mrs Jopling*.

LITERATURE AND SCHOLARSHIP
A(rthur) J(ames) Balfour publishes *A Defence of Philosophic Doubt*.
G. Meredith publishes *The Egoist*.
Robert Louis Stevenson's *Travels with a Donkey* published.

RELIGION AND EDUCATION

Oct. First women students at Oxford: Lady Margaret Hall (Church of England), founded 1878, and Somerville College (undenominational).

SCIENCE AND INVENTION
Electric street lighting in London, on north side of Embankment and Waterloo Bridge.

Nov. 1 A 'restaurant car' serves meals on the King's Cross to Leeds express.

VOYAGES AND EXPLORATION
Lady Annabel Blunt explores Nejd, in S. Arabia.

Events Elsewhere

Oct. 7   Alliance treaty between Germany and Austria-Hungary (to 1918).

AD 1880

Apr. 18   General election results give Liberals overall majority of 54: Liberals 353;
          Conservatives 238; Irish Home Rulers 61.
      23   Gladstone returns as Prime Minister; also serves as Chancellor of Exchequer.
      28   E. Granville becomes Foreign Secretary; William Harcourt, Home Secretary;
          Forster, Chief Secretary for Ireland; J. Chamberlain becomes a cabinet
          minister as President of Board of Trade.
May 3   The free-thinker Charles Bradlaugh, elected MP for Northampton, refuses to
          take oath, seeking instead to affirm; acrimonious dispute continues for 5
          years, with Bradlaugh unable to take his seat.
     17   Parnell elected Chairman of Irish Party in Commons.
Jun. 25   Plans for S. African federation rejected by Cape Colony Parliament.
Jul. 27   Afghan force attacks British troops at Maiwand, forcing them to retire on
          Kandahar.
Aug. 8–23 Roberts marches 10,000 troops 313 miles across Afghanistan from Kabul to
          relieve Kandahar.
Sep. 19   Parnell, speaking at Ennis, urges Irish tenants to ostracize possessors of an
          evicted farmer's land.
Oct.   Captain Charles Boycott, agent for Lord Erne in Co. Mayo, is ostracized by
          tenants, as urged by Parnell at Ennis.
     16   First Boer War between Britain and restored Transvaal republic begins.
Nov.   Boycott's harvest garnered by 50 Ulstermen, protected by several hundred
          police.
     11   Ned Kelly hanged in Melbourne after 2 years of notoriety as a bushranger.
Dec. 13   Parnell and 13 Land Leaguers on trial for conspiracy; jury fail to agree.

FINE ARTS AND ARCHITECTURE
Work begins on Truro Cathedral (designed by J.L. Pearson); consecrated
1887.
E. Burne-Jones paints *Golden Stairs*.

LITERATURE AND SCHOLARSHIP
American millionaire, Andrew Carnegie, presents his native town of
Dunfermline with a free library; first of several hundred founded in Britain
over the following 30 years.
T. Hardy publishes *The Trumpet Major*.
Henry George's *Progress and Poverty*, published in America in 1879,
becomes available in England; his single tax proposal influences radical
thought.

MUSIC AND DRAMA
Guildhall School of Music founded, London.

Apr. 3 Gilbert and Sullivan's *The Pirates of Penzance* performed at Opera Comique,
Strand.

Dec. 15 First Ibsen production in Britain: abridged version of *The Pillars of Society*,
entitled *Quicksands*, at Gaiety Theatre, London.

RECREATION AND FASHION

Sep. 6–8 First Test Match played in England: Australia lose to England at Kennington
Oval.

SCIENCE AND INVENTION
Cragside, Rothbury, Northumberland, becomes first English mansion lit by
electricity; installed by J. Swan.

Feb. 2 Refrigerated meat from New South Wales first reaches England, aboard SS
Strathleven; first frozen meat from New Zealand arrives, March 1882.

AD 1881

Jan. Bessborough Commission's report on Irish land problem recommends reform
based on the 'three Fs': fair rents; free sale; fixity of tenure.

1 First issue of postal orders in Britain.

28 Boers check advance of British troops at Laing's Neck, Transvaal.

31 Irish Party MPs obstruct business of H. of Commons for 41 continuous hours
(to 2 Feb.).

Feb. 27 Boers inflict defeat on the British at Ψ Majuba.

Mar. 2 Habeas Corpus Act is suspended in Ireland following mounting agrarian
unrest.

21 Peace Preservation Act: authorizes coercive measures in Ireland.

Apr. 5 Convention of Pretoria: British recognize an independent Boer Republic of
the Transvaal, under presidency of Kruger.

20 Following Beaconsfield's death, Conservative Party leadership is shared
between Salisbury in H. of Lords and Sir Stafford Northcote in H. of
Commons.

27	British troops withdrawn from Afghanistan.
Jul. 26	First issue of a London evening paper, *Evening News*.
Aug. 22	Irish Land Act: seeks to implement Bessborough Report.
Sep. 9	British and other foreigners attacked in Egyptian nationalist revolt under Arabi Pasha.
Oct. 1	Land Commission Court opens in Ireland.
13	Parnell arrested for inciting defiance of land courts.
20	Irish Land League declared illegal.

LITERATURE AND SCHOLARSHIP

R.L. Stevenson publishes *Virginibus Puerisque*.
D.G. Rossetti's final *Ballads and Sonnets* published.
Oscar Wilde's *Poems* published.

MUSIC AND DRAMA

Apr. 23	Gilbert and Sullivan's *Patience* performed at Opera Comique, Strand; transfers in October to the new Savoy Theatre, first to be lit by electricity.

RELIGION AND EDUCATION

Revised Version of New Testament, encouraged by Convocation of Canterbury, is published.
University College, Liverpool, established.

Events Elsewhere

Mar. 13	Assassination of Tsar Alexander II in St Petersburg.
May	Tunisia becomes a French protectorate.
Jun. 18	League of the Three Emperors Alliance: Germany, Austria-Hungary, Russia.

AD 1882

Jan. 25	Foundation of a London Chamber of Commerce.
May 2	Kilmainham Agreement between government and Parnell: an amnesty in return for his aid in ending Irish terrorism.
6	Extreme Fenians ('Invincibles') murder Lord Frederick Cavendish (Chief Secretary for Ireland) and his deputy (Thomas Burke) in Phoenix Park, Dublin.
Jun. 12	Anti-British and anti-French riots in Alexandria.
28	Anglo-French agreement settles disputed boundaries of French Guinea and Sierra Leone.
Jul. 9	Royal Navy bombards Alexandria.
12	Irish Crime Prevention Act: trial by jury abolished; police given exceptional powers of arrest.
Aug.	Married Women's Property Act: further safeguards rights.

	17	Irish family massacred by Fenian Invincibles at Maamtrasna.
Sep.	*13*	Sir Garnet Wolseley lands troops in Egypt and defeats Arabi Pasha at Ψ Tel-el-Kebir.
	15	Wolseley's troops occupy Cairo; Arabi exiled.

LITERATURE AND SCHOLARSHIP

Leslie Stephen begins compiling and editing *Dictionary of National Biography*.

Sir Walter Besant publishes *All Sorts and Conditions of Men*; 3-volume fantasy about an idealized East End.

R.L. Stevenson publishes *The New Arabian Nights*.

MUSIC AND DRAMA

Nov.	*16*	Henry Arthur Jones's *The Silver King* performed at Princess Theatre, London.
	25	Gilbert and Sullivan's *Iolanthe* performed at Savoy Theatre, London.

RECREATION AND FASHION

Aug.	*29*	*Sporting Times* refers to 'the ashes' in printing a mock obituary for English cricket, following first home Test defeat by Australia.

RELIGION AND EDUCATION

Polytechnic movement in London begins with opening of Regent Street Polytechnic, founded by sugar merchant and philanthropist Quintin Hogg.

Wilson Carlile founds voluntary Anglican evangelistic Church Army in slum tenements of W. London.

SCIENCE AND INVENTION

Society for Psychical Research founded under presidency of ethical philosopher Henry Sidgwick.

General Augustus H. L.-F. Pitt-Rivers becomes first Inspector of Ancient Monuments and evolves a scientific method of excavation.

Mar.	*4*	Electric trams come to London area: Leytonstone, Essex.

Events Elsewhere

May	*20*	Italy joins Austro-German alliance, transforming it into the Triple Alliance.

AD 1883

Jan.	*3*	Granville informs great powers that Britain will withdraw from Egypt as soon as order is restored.
	18	Khedive Mohammed Tewfik of Egypt signs decree appointing a British adviser (agent), without whose concurrence no financial administrative

	decisions will be taken.
Feb. 6	Dufferin Report on Egypt accepts retention of nominal Turkish sovereignty delegated to the Khedive, but urges establishment of a Legislative Council, assisted by a British adviser (agent).
Apr.	Premier of Queensland orders annexation of Port Moresby (New Guinea) to forestall Germans; repudiated by Colonial Secretary in London.
24	Britain warns German colonists to respect existing claims in SW Africa.
May 1	Organic Law imposed on Egypt by Khedive: implements Dufferin Report and establishes Legislative Council.
Jun.	'How the Poor Live', an influential series of articles by George Sims in *Pictorial World*.
	Eventual union of Australian colonies is advanced by opening of railway between Melbourne and Sydney.
Aug. 18	Corrupt and Illegal Practices Act: imposes limits on spending by a candidate in a particular constituency and by a political party in a general election.
Sep. 11	Evelyn Baring (Lord Cromer from 1892) arrives in Egypt as British agent; holds the post until 1907.
Oct. 18	Anonymous pamphlet (by Andrew Mearns), *The Bitter Cry of Outcast London*, rapidly stirs many social consciences.
Nov. 5	Ψ El Obeid: Anglo-Egyptian force in Sudan is defeated by followers of Islamic nationalist insurgent El-Mahdi.

LITERATURE AND SCHOLARSHIP

J.R. Seeley publishes *The Expansion of England*.
George Moore publishes *A Modern Lover*.
R.L. Stevenson publishes *Treasure Island*.
G. Meredith publishes *Poems and Lyrics of the Joy of Earth*.

MUSIC AND DRAMA

Foundation of Royal College of Music, London.

RELIGION AND EDUCATION

Boy's Brigade established.

SCIENCE AND INVENTION

Aug. 4	Electric traction comes to British railways with opening of Volk's electric railway at Brighton.
	William Thomson delivers paper to Royal Institution on size and nature of the atom.

Events Elsewhere

Aug. 24	Ty of Hue: places Annam and Tonkin under French protection.

AD 1884

Jan.	Fabian Society established, to educate public in socialist ideas and to work out application of socialist principles to British conditions.
Feb. 18	General Gordon reaches Khartoum to evacuate Anglo-Egyptian residents, but negotiates abortively with the Mahdi.
22	Royal Commission on the Housing of the Working Classes set up; Dilke as chairman; P. of Wales, Lords Salisbury and Shaftesbury and Cardinal Manning among its members.
26	Anglo-Portuguese Ty: seeks to check German colonial pretensions.
27	Convention of London: settles relations with Transvaal.
Apr. 22	4 killed by East Anglican earthquake.
May	Capture of Berber by Mahdi's dervishes cuts off Gordon in Khartoum.
11	Bismarck indirectly offers Britain German support over African issues, including Egypt, in return for cession of Heligoland.
Jun.	Toynbee Hall, first of the universities' settlements, founded in Whitechapel.
28	London Conference of the Powers over Egyptian Finance (to 2 Aug.): France and Germany oppose British attempt to use Egyptian funds for suppressing Mahdi's insurgency.
Jul.	India Office establishes protectorate over Somali coast of E. Africa, hitherto administered by Egyptians.
Oct. 1	Parnell assures Irish Roman Catholic hierarchy of support in education issues.
5	Wolseley, sent out from England in August, leaves Wadi Halfa with relief army for Khartoum.
13	Mahdi captures Omdurman, closely investing Khartoum.
Nov. 10	Britain annexes St Lucia Bay, incorporating it in Natal so as to deny Transvaal Boers a sea-coast.
15	Berlin Conference on West Africa (to 26 Feb.): Britain agrees with other powers over Congo question, colonial boundaries and need to suppress Congo slavery.
Dec. 10	Third Parliamentary Reform Act: uniform male suffrage in town and country; some 2 million farm workers get the vote.

LITERATURE AND SCHOLARSHIP

Work begins on the *New English Dictionary*, later known as *Oxford English Dictionary*, under editorship of lexicographer James Murray.

G(eorge) A(lfred) Henty writes *With Clive in India*, boys' adventure story.

MUSIC AND DRAMA

Charles Stanford completes his opera *Savonarola* for production in April at Hamburg.

Jan. 5	Gilbert and Sullivan's *Princess Ida* performed at Savoy Theatre, London.

RECREATION AND FASHION

Straw boaters have come into general use for men's summer casual wear (having until 1880 been associated with sailing).

Women's bustles are at fullest extent; disappear by 1890.

SCIENCE AND INVENTION

At Liverpool University, Oliver Lodge completes his researches into electrical precipitation.

Edward Butler fits a jet carburettor to a tricycle; first British petrol-driven vehicle.

Charles Parsons perfects a practical steam-turbine to drive a dynamo for electric light in Durham.

Events Elsewhere

Jul.–Aug.   German colonies in Cameroons and SW Africa.

AD 1885

Jan. 17	British relief column defeats Dervishes at Ψ Abu Klea.
24	Irish 'dynamiters' damage Westminster Hall and Tower of London.
26	Mahdi's troops storm Khartoum; Gordon killed.
28	British relief force approaches Khartoum too late; withdraws.
Feb. 5	News of Gordon's death reaches England.
	Gladstone considers resignation on receipt of telegram from Q. Victoria critical of government's slowness in seeking relief of Khartoum.
Mar. 3	New South Wales infantry leave Sydney for service in Sudan; first Australian contingent sent overseas 'in the defence of the Empire'.
31	Protectorate over N. Bechuanaland proclaimed.
Apr. 26	Port Hamilton in Korea occupied; retained for 2 years.
Jun. 5	Protectorate established over whole of Niger river basin.
7	Hostile demonstration in Hyde Park at budget's proposed increases on spirits and beer duties.
9	Gladstone defeated by Irish Party's vote on budget.
23	Lord Salisbury becomes Prime Minister and Foreign Secretary.
24	Lord Randolph Churchill, regarded as leader of the 'Tory Democrats', attains cabinet rank as India Secretary.
25	Redistribution of Seats Bill (proposed in Feb.) is enacted: gives additional seats to industrial towns in Yorkshire and Lancashire and to outer London, while merging smaller boroughs in surrounding 'county' constituencies.
Aug. 14	Salisbury's nephew A.J. Balfour becomes Scottish Secretary; enters cabinet in November.
	Irish Land Purchase Act: proposes loans to help tenants buy holdings cheaply.

	21	Criminal Law Amendment Act to protect women and girls: age of consent raised to 16; child prostitution outlawed.
Sep.	10	Anglo-Russian agreement delineating Afghan frontiers.
Oct.		Chamberlain begins campaign speeches on his Unauthorized Programme; 'three acres and a cow' to encourage small farming.
	7	Salisbury's Newport speech shows sympathy for the Irish.
	22	Ultimatum delivered to King Theebaw of Upper Burma for having confiscated property of Bombay traders.
Nov.	1	Expeditionary force leaves Calcutta for Rangoon.
	7	Transcontinental Canadian Pacific Railway completed.
	16–30	Campaign in Upper Burma.
	21	Parnell advises Home Rule supporters in English constituencies to vote Conservative in next election.
	23	General election: Liberals 335; Conservatives 249; Irish Party 86; Salisbury remains Prime Minister, dependent on Irish vote.
	28	British occupy Mandalay; King Theebaw exiled.
Dec.	17	Newspapers quote Gladstone's son as saying his father is converted to support of Home Rule.

LITERATURE AND SCHOLARSHIP

G. Meredith publishes *Diana of the Crossways*.
G. Moore publishes *A Mummer's Wife*.
Walter Pater publishes *Marius the Epicurean*.

MUSIC AND DRAMA

Mar.	14	Gilbert and Sullivan's *The Mikado* performed at Savoy Theatre, London.
	21	Arthur Wing Pinero's *The Magistrate* performed at Belgravia (Royal Court) Theatre, London.

RECREATION AND FASHION

Mar.	10	Cruft's Dog Show first held, London.

Events Elsewhere

Sep.		Rising in Phillipolis (Plovdiv) secures union of E. Rumelia with Bulgaria.

AD 1886

Jan.	1	Upper Burma annexed.
	27	Salisbury resigns having lost Irish Party support.
Feb.	1	Gladstone forms his third government; Chamberlain, hostile to Home Rule and not offered a major post, refuses to serve in cabinet.
	2	Lord Rosebery becomes Foreign Secretary.
	7–8	Demonstrations by unemployed in the coldest February weather for 30 years

		lead to window-smashing in London's West End.
	10	Army on stand-by in case of unemployed riot in London.
	12	Dilke discredited after appearing as co-respondent in sensationally reported divorce suit.
	16	Irish hierarchy gives formal backing to Home Rule movement.
	22	Lord R. Churchill gives militant speech to encourage Ulster Protestants, Belfast.
Apr.	8	Gladstone introduces his Irish Home Rule Bill.
May	8	British ships join French and Russian vessels in blockading Greece to discourage invasion of Turkish-held Epirus.
Jun.	8	Home Rule Bill defeated in H. of Commons: 93 elected Liberals, including Chamberlain, vote against it.
Jul.	24	General election: Conservatives 316; Liberals 191; Irish Party 85; Chamberlainite Liberal Unionists 78.
	25	Salisbury returns as Prime Minister.
Aug.	3	Lord R. Churchill becomes Chancellor of Exchequer.
Oct.	2	Churchill's Dartford speech promises wide-ranging reforms.
	23	Irish militants' 'Plan of Campaign': rents to be withheld on certain estates.
Nov.	1	Anglo-German treaty over spheres of interest in E. Africa.
Dec.	18	Irish Plan of Campaign declared illegal.
	23	Churchill unexpectedly resigns when cabinet will not support defence economies he wishes to include in budget.

FINE ARTS AND ARCHITECTURE

New English Art Club founded, sponsored by J. Whistler, Walter Sickert, Wilson Steer.

J. Millais paints *Bubbles*, a commercial for Pear's soap.

LITERATURE AND SCHOLARSHIP

George Gissing publishes *Demos*.

H. Rider Haggard writes *King Solomon's Mines*.

R.L. Stevenson publishes *Kidnapped* and *Dr Jekyll and Mr Hyde*.

Rudyard Kipling's *Departmental Ditties* published.

Nov.	British School of Archaeology opens in Athens.

RECREATION AND FASHION

Colonial and Indian Exhibition in London attracts visitors from all classes and encourages spread of imperial pride.

Jan.	18	Hockey Association formed.

RELIGION AND EDUCATION

Jun.	3	Massacre of converts to both Anglicanism and Roman Catholicism in Buganda.

Feb. *1* Mersey railway opens, linking Liverpool and Birkenhead; steam locomotion until 1903.

Sep. *1* Severn Tunnel, at 4 miles 628 yards the longest railway tunnel in Britain, is opened after 14 years of engineering, supervised by Sir John Hawkshaw.

Events Elsewhere

Jan. *8* General Boulanger becomes War Minister in France; leads right-wing nationalists for 2 years.

AD 1887

Jan. *14* Liberal Unionist George Goschen succeeds Churchill as Chancellor of the Exchequer.

Feb. *12* Salisbury concludes Mediterranean Agreement with Italy: accepts need to maintain status quo.

Mar. *7* Balfour appointed Chief Secretary for Ireland; holds office until Nov. 1891; mingles firm policy of coercion and reform.

   23 Q. Victoria entertained by Chamberlain when she lays foundation-stone of Birmingham Law Courts.

   24 Austria-Hungary accedes to the Mediterranean Agreement.

   28 Balfour introduces drastic Irish Crimes Bill: trial by jury suspended; strong powers to resident magistrates; Bill enacted in September after intense opposition in Commons.

Apr. *4* First Colonial Conference of imperial prime ministers is held in London; strong support from Australian colonial leaders for federation.

   18 *The Times* prints facsimile letter linking Parnell and Phoenix Park murders (*v.* 1882); denounced as a forgery by Parnell.

May *22* Drummond Wolff Convention with Egypt: British military withdrawal by 1890 if no further disorders; Convention not subsequently observed.

Jun. *21* Q. Victoria's Golden Jubilee celebrated.

   22 Britain annexes Zululand, further impeding Transvaal's attempt to reach the coast.

   25 Washington Conference (to 26 Jul.): British envoys confer with Germans and Americans over rival claims on Samoa.

Jul. 35 warships at the first Spithead Naval Review.

Aug. *23* Balfour's Irish Land Act: courts may revise unjust rents.

Nov. *13* 'Bloody Sunday' in Trafalgar Square: clashes between police and demonstrators.

Nov. *20* Further unrest in London; demonstrator fatally injured in Northumberland Avenue by mounted police.

H. Rider Haggard publishes *She*.
T. Hardy writes *The Woodlanders*.

MUSIC AND DRAMA

Jan. 22   Gilbert and Sullivan's *Ruddigore* performed at Savoy Theatre, London.
Mar.   John Stainer's *The Crucifixion* performed at St Paul's, London.
May 14   Q. Victoria opens People's Palace for music and entertainment in East End of London.
Sep. 5   187 killed when Theatre Royal, Exeter, burns down for second time in 2 years.

RELIGION AND EDUCATION

Pope Leo XIII beatifies Sir Thomas More, Bp John Fisher and others martyred in the Tudor period.

Events Elsewhere

Jun.   Secret 3-year 'Reinsurance Ty' between Germany and Russia.

AD 1888

Jan. 17   *The Star*, London evening paper, goes on sale.
Feb. 11   Cecil Rhodes, as chairman of De Beers Consolidated Mines Company, encourages K. of Matabeleland to accept British protection.
13   First issue of the *Financial Times*.
Mar. 19   Protectorates established over Sarawak and (12 May) Borneo and Brunei.
Apr. 15   Goschen's budget cuts the interest on Britain's national debt.
Jul. 5   First strike by unorganized women workers: match girls in Bow, E. London.
Aug. 8   6 'Jack the Ripper' murders of prostitutes in Whitechapel, London (to 9 Nov.).
9   Local Government Act: elected county councils to be established in England and Wales, with single women enjoying equal voting rights with men; large counties such as Yorkshire and Lincolnshire administratively divided; London to be an administrative county; 60 towns with more than 50,000 inhabitants to have status of 'county borough', carrying greater independence.
13   Special commission appointed to investigate alleged Parnell involvement with Phoenix Park murders.
Oct. 30   All mining rights in Matabeleland conceded to Cecil Rhodes.

FINE ARTS AND ARCHITECTURE

1st exhibition of Arts and Crafts Guild.

LITERATURE AND SCHOLARSHIP
Bernard Bosanquet publishes *Logic*.
Ralph Boldrewood writes *Robbery Under Arms*; first Australian adventure to become popular in Britain.
Kipling's short stories *Plain Tales from the Hills* published.
Q (Arthur Quiller-Couch) publishes *The Astonishing History of Troy Town*.

MUSIC AND DRAMA
Oct. 3   Gilbert and Sullivan's *The Yeoman of the Guard* performed at Savoy Theatre, London.

RECREATION AND FASHION
Lawn Tennis Association formed; takes over responsibilities for the sport from MCC.
Apr. 17   Football League meets for first time, in Manchester; 12 professional clubs compete in following, inaugural, season (won by Preston North End).

RELIGION AND EDUCATION
Lambeth Conference (of Pan-Anglican bishops) approves the 'Lambeth Quadrilateral' guidelines of basic principles for a re-united Church: the Scriptures; Creeds; Sacraments of baptism and communion; Episcopate.

SCIENCE AND INVENTION
John Boyd Dunlop patents a pneumatic tyre; fitted to 'safety bicycles' from 1891.
Aug. 13 and 31   'Railway race' between rival companies to speed up London-Scotland routes; won by East Coast route (average speed 57.7 m.p.h.).

VOYAGES AND EXPLORATION
C.M. Doughty publishes his *Travels in Arabia Deserta*, austerely literary narrative of journeys undertaken 1875-7.

Events Elsewhere
Jun. 15   Accession of Kaiser Wilhelm II in Germany, following deaths of his father, Frederick III, and (9 Mar.) of his grandfather Wilhelm I.
Aug. 12   First through railway train links Paris and Constantinople (last 'direct Orient Express' run, 19 May 1977).

AD 1889

Jan.–Mar.   Intermittent Anglo-German talks of a possible alliance; opposed by Salisbury as inopportune.
Feb. 12   Lord Rosebery is elected chairman of the newly formed London County Council.

28	*The Times* concedes that its Parnell facsimile letter was forged by Richard Pigott.
May 31	Naval Defence Act: establishes principle of the Two-Power Standard; fleet to be 'at least equal to the naval strength of any two other countries'; shapes naval policy until 1912.
Jul.	Local Government (Scotland) Act: sets up a similar structure to previous year's England and Wales Act.
Aug. 12	Start of London dock strike: Ben Tillett and John Burns lead campaign for 'the dockers' tanner', 6d an hour; widespread sympathy for dockers.
Sep. 16	London dockers return to work having won their 'tanner'.
Oct.	Newly established Board of Agriculture begins functioning as a government department.
29	Cecil Rhodes's British South Africa Company receives royal charter; expands in present-day Zimbabwe, developing resources of Mashonaland.
Nov. 23	Parnell Commission clears his name after 129 sessions.
Dec. 24	Parnell cited in O'Shea divorce suit.

LITERATURE AND SCHOLARSHIP
George Bernard Shaw edits *Fabian Essays in Socialism*.
T.H. Huxley publishes *Agnosticism*.
R. Kipling publishes *Soldiers Three*, short stories.
Arthur Conan Doyle writes *Micah Clarke*.
Jerome K. Jerome's *Three Men in a Boat* published.
A. Tennyson's last poem, 'Crossing the Bar', appears.

MUSIC, ENTERTAINMENT AND DRAMA

Nov.	Americans Phineas Barnum and James Bailey bring their circus to London's Olympia.
Dec. 7	Gilbert and Sullivan's *The Gondoliers* performed at Savoy Theatre, London.

RECREATION AND FASHION
Day-trips to seaside become popular with construction of Southend Pier in Essex and Blackpool Tower.

RELIGION AND EDUCATION
Welsh Intermediate Education Act: provides secondary education in Wales.
Technical Instruction Act: encourages local authorities to provide basic structure for national system of technological education.
Charles Gore edits *Lux Mundi*, Anglican essays seeking to update Tractarian tradition.
First 'purpose built' mosque in Britain is completed at Woking, Surrey.

SCIENCE AND INVENTION
Institution of Electrical Engineers founded.

AD 1890

Jan.	*4*	*Daily Graphic* goes on sale; first British 'picture paper'.
Mar.	*4*	Forth Railway Bridge opened by P. of Wales.
May	*24*	Private treaty with K. Leopold II of Belgium, who cedes land near Lake Tanganyika to British East Africa Co.
Jul.	*1*	Heligoland Ty: Britain cedes Heligoland in the North Sea to Germany in return for Zanzibar and Pemba.
Aug.	*5*	Anglo-French treaty defines spheres of interest in Nigeria, Zanzibar and Madagascar.
Sep.		Tithe Bill enacted after 3-year delay: responsibility for payment depends on landlord not tenant.
	12	Rhodes's British South Africa Co. founds city of Salisbury (Harare) in Basutoland.
Oct.	*22*	Western Australia given responsible government.
Nov.	*14*	Ty with Portugal consolidates British hold on land between lower Zambesi and Congo rivers.
	15–17	O'Shea divorce case discredits Parnell with Roman Catholics.
Dec.	*6*	Parliamentary Irish Party rejects Parnell as leader; he resigns, 12 Dec.
	18	British East Africa Co. authority established in Uganda.

FINE ARTS AND ARCHITECTURE
Whitworth Institute in Manchester and the Irish Art Museum, Dublin, open.
William Morris founds the Kelmscott Press at Hammersmith, for which he designs founts of type and ornamental borders.

LITERATURE AND SCHOLARSHIP
James G. Frazer begins *The Golden Bough*, vol. 1; study in comparative religion in 12 vols, completed in 1915.
H.M. Stanley publishes *In Darkest Africa*.
Salvation Army General William Booth writes *In Darkest England and the Way Out*.

MUSIC AND DRAMA
Sep.   Edward Elgar's *Froissart* overture performed at the Three Choirs Festival in his native Worcester.

RELIGION AND EDUCATION
Education Code promulgated: phases out discredited payment-by-results system of teaching.

SCIENCE AND INVENTION

First electrical power station is constructed, at Deptford, SE London.

Dec. 18 City and South London railway, from the Mansion House to Stockwell, opens; first underground electric railway in the world; locomotives built in Salford, Lancs.

Events Elsewhere

Mar. 20 Kaiser Wilhelm II dismisses Bismarck ('dropping the pilot').

AD 1891

Mar. 24 and
Apr. 15 Treaties with Italy settle Somaliland boundary.

Mar.–Jul. Sydney Constitutional Convention: draws up federal plan for Australia; shelved because of opposition from New South Wales.

Jun. 2 P. of Wales gives evidence as witness in libel action brought by Guards officer accused of cheating at baccarat at Tranby Croft, nr Hull.

10 Dr Leander Starr Jameson is appointed administrator of South Africa Co. based on Salisbury.

Aug. 5 Balfour's Irish Land Act: Congested Districts Board set up to ease housing problems.

Oct. 2 Gladstone attends Liberal Party meeting at Newcastle and approves the 'Newcastle Programme': Home Rule; triennial Parliaments; reform of H. of Lords; abolition of double franchise; Welsh disestablishment; local right of veto on sales of liquor.

Nov. 13 Salisbury and Chamberlain emphasize Unionist alliance at a public dinner in Birmingham town hall.

LITERATURE AND SCHOLARSHIP

The Strand Magazine published; it includes, serialized in its first numbers, Conan Doyle's *The Adventures of Sherlock Holmes*.
G. Gissing publishes *New Grub Street*.
W. Morris publishes *News from Nowhere*.
T. Hardy publishes *Tess of the d'Urbervilles*.
Oscar Wilde's *The Picture of Dorian Grey* published.

MUSIC AND DRAMA

Jacob Thomas Grein founds the Independent Theatre Society to produce 'plays of literary merit rather than of commercial value'.

Mar. 13 Grein presents single performance of Ibsen's *Ghosts* at Royalty Theatre, Soho; the play, and Ibsen, are virulently attacked in several hundred English press articles for remainder of year.

Education Act: abolishes all fees for elementary schooling in England and Wales.

Pastor John Clifford, as president of the Baptist Union, brings about a reconciliation between the 2 main Baptist sects of England and Wales.

SCIENCE AND INVENTION

Apr. 1   Public telephone links London and Paris.

Events Elsewhere

May 15   Papal encyclical *Rerum Novarum* rejects socialism but stresses importance of the social question in industrialized states.

AD 1892

Jan. 7   Khedive Abbas, aged 18, accedes to Egyptian throne on death of his father, Tewfik; he remains hostile to the British Agent.

Mar. 28   George Curzon, as Under-Secretary for India, introduces India Councils Bill, which is enacted within 10 weeks: nominated Indian members to be admitted to Legislative Councils of the Viceroy and provincial administrations.

May   Small Holdings Act: designed to protect small farmers during an agricultural recession.

Jun.   Cabinet meetings discuss evident Franco-Russian joint threat in Mediterranean; Salisbury insists on continued friendship with Italy and its alliance partners.

23   Parliament dissolved.

Jul.   General election is fought by Liberals on Newcastle Programme and by Salisbury on imperialism and hostility to Home Rule.

Aug. 4   Salisbury stays in office when Commons reassemble: Conservatives and Unionists 314 seats; Liberals 272; Irish Party 81.

11   Irish vote with Liberals at first important division and defeat government; Salisbury resigns.

15   Gladstone (aged 82) forms his fourth government.

18   Rosebery returns to Foreign Office and Herbert Asquith becomes Home Secretary.

Sep.   Opening of railway from Cape Town to Johannesburg leads to rapid increase in foreign workers on goldfield of Witwatersrand.

Oct. 15   Treaty with Germany over boundaries of Cameroons.

LITERATURE AND SCHOLARSHIP

Israel Zangwill publishes *Children of the Ghetto*.

R. Kipling's *Barrack Room Ballads* published.

Feb. 20   Oscar Wilde's *Lady Windermere's Fan* performed at St James's Theatre, London.

Dec. 9   J.T. Grein stages, for first time, a play by G. Bernard Shaw: *Widowers' Houses* at Royalty Theatre, London.

RELIGION AND EDUCATION

Charles Gore founds Anglican Community of the Resurrection at Oxford; moves to Mirfield, Yorkshire, 1898.

SCIENCE AND INVENTION

HMS *Royal Sovereign*, first warship to cost over £1 million, joins fleet; invention of quick-firing guns enables her to fire 15 100lb shells a minute.

Events Elsewhere

Nov.   Panama Scandal in France intensifies peasant mistrust of capitalism, implicates radical politicians and leads to wave of anti-semitism.

AD 1893

Jan. 13   Independent Labour Party founded in Bradford; led by James Keir Hardie, elected MP for West Ham South in 1892.

Mar. 10   Colonial Office takes over responsibility for Uganda from East Africa Co.

May 10   Natal given responsible self-government.

Jun. 22   HMS *Victoria*, flagship of Mediterranean fleet, rammed and sunk by HMS *Camperdown* as a result of dangerous turn ordered by C.-in-C.; 361 lives lost.

Jul.   Rising in Matabeleland against British South Africa Co.

    31   Strained relations with France over French penetration of Siam (Thailand).

Sep. 2   Gladstone's second Irish Home Rule Bill approved in H. of Commons.

    9   H. of Lords rejects Home Rule Bill.

Nov. 15   Anglo-German West Africa Agreement over Shari district: transfers region east of Lake Chad to Germany.

    16   Jameson occupies Bulawayo in suppressing Matabele revolt.

Dec. 4   Anglo-French agreement respects the 2 nations' differing interests in Siam.

FINE ARTS AND ARCHITECTURE

Jul.   Imperial Institute, S. Kensington (designed by Thomas Colcutt), to encourage knowledge of arts and culture of the empire, is opened by Q. Victoria.

LITERATURE AND SCHOLARSHIP
F.H. Bradley publishes *Appearance and Reality*.
Francis Thompson's *Poems* published; they include 'The Hound of Heaven'.
R.L. Stevenson publishes *Catriona*.

MUSIC AND DRAMA

May   A.W. Pinero's *The Second Mrs Tanqueray*, with Mrs Patrick Campbell, performed at St James's Theatre, London.

Oct. 7   Gilbert and Sullivan's *Utopia Limited* performed at Savoy Theatre, London.

RELIGION AND EDUCATION

Nov. 30   Royal charter incorporates colleges at Aberystwyth (1872), Cardiff (1883) and Bangor (1884) to create University of Wales.

SCIENCE AND INVENTION

Yarrow shipyard on London's Isle of Dogs builds world's first destroyers, HMS *Havock* and HMS *Hornet*.

Feb. 4   Lord Salisbury opens 1st section of Liverpool's overhead railway.

Events Elsewhere

Oct. 13–29 Visit of Russian fleet to Toulon marks beginning of secret Franco-Russian Alliance.

AD 1894

Jan. 1   Vessels first use Manchester Ship Canal; officially opened by Q. Victoria, 21 May.

Feb. 11   Gladstone withdraws Employers' Liability Bill when Lords amendments change it beyond recognition.

Mar. 1   Local Government Act: establishes parish councils and gives women equality with men as voters and candidates for council election.

     3   Gladstone, critical of high navy estimates, resigns office and retires.

     5   E. of Rosebery becomes Prime Minister.

    11   E. of Kimberley becomes Foreign Secretary.

Apr. 11   British protectorate established over Uganda.

    12   Budget of the Chancellor, Sir William Harcourt, includes death duties.

May 12   Germans are unresponsive to tentative approaches from Rosebery for closer co-operation with Triple Alliance.

Jul. 16   Anglo-Japanese Ty: Britain agrees to abolish privileged consular status by 1899, thus becoming first European power to acknowledge Japan's full national sovereignty.

FINE ARTS AND ARCHITECTURE
Aubrey Beardsley designs and illustrates the *Yellow Book* magazine.

LITERATURE AND SCHOLARSHIP
Sidney and Beatrice Webb publish *History of Trade Unionism*.
Robert Blatchford's *Merrie England* preaches an undoctrinaire socialism and sells a million copies.
A. Conan Doyle publishes *The Memoirs of Sherlock Holmes*.
Anthony Hope (A.H. Hawkins) publishes *The Prisoner of Zenda*.
George du Maurier writes and illustrates *Trilby*.
R. Kipling's first *Jungle Book* published.
G. Moore publishes *Esther Waters*.

MUSIC AND DRAMA
Apr. 21   G.B. Shaw's *Arms and the Man* performed at Avenue Theatre, London.

RECREATION AND FASHION
Lord Rosebery is first Prime Minister to own the Derby winner (Ladas).

RELIGION AND EDUCATION
Informal talks in Rome by Viscount Halifax on possible reconciliation between papacy and Church of England continue intermittently for 2 years.

SCIENCE AND INVENTION
Joint research by Lord (John) Rayleigh and William Ramsay identifies the colourless gas argon.

Events Elsewhere

Oct. 15   Arrest of Captain Alfred Dreyfus in Paris, on false charge of spying.

AD 1895

Jan.   Kimberley takes initiative in securing Great Power pressure on the Sultan to stop Armenian massacres.
Mar. 11   Ty with Russia settles Afghan frontier in the Pamirs.
   28   Britain warns France that occupation of the Upper Nile would be regarded as an unfriendly act.
May 2   The name 'Rhodesia' given to British South Africa Co. territory south of R. Zambezi.
   25   Oscar Wilde sentenced to 2 years' hard labour for homosexuality.
Jun. 20   The War Secretary, Sir Henry Campbell-Bannerman, secures Q. Victoria's assent to resignation of her cousin D. of Cambridge as C.-in-C. of the British army, after 39 years.

21	Rosebery resigns after adverse vote in H. of Commons on supply of cordite to the army.
22	Lord Salisbury forms third ministry; is also Foreign Secretary.
28	J. Chamberlain joins cabinet, becoming, at his own request, Colonial Secretary.
Jul. 1	Rosebery government's decision to transfer responsibility for British East Africa to the Foreign Office is implemented (until Apr. 1905).
10	Salisbury warns Sultan of urgent need for reform.
Aug. 5–6	Misunderstanding between Kaiser Wilhelm II and Salisbury over talks during Cowes regatta week.
10	General election gives Salisbury overall majority of 152 seats: Conservatives 340; Liberal Unionists 71; Liberals 177; Irish Party 82.
Sep. 26	British naval squadron off the Dardanelles (to 28 Oct.).
Nov. 26	Mounting tension in Anglo-American relations over Venezuelan affairs (to 28 Dec.).
Dec. 29	Jameson Raid: invasion of Transvaal from Bechuanaland.

LITERATURE AND SCHOLARSHIP

Grant Allen's novel *The Woman Who Did* champions feminism.

T. Hardy publishes *Jude the Obscure*.

R. Kipling's second *Jungle Book*.

G. Meredith publishes *The Amazing Marriage*.

Arthur Morrison's novel of the London slums, *A Child of the Jago*, published.

H(erbert) G(eorge) Wells publishes *The Time Machine* (pioneer science fiction).

Hilaire Belloc's *Verses and Sonnets* published.

MUSIC, ENTERTAINMENT AND DRAMA

Henry Arthur Jones publishes *The Renaissance of the English Drama*.

Jan. 3	O. Wilde's *An Ideal Husband* performed at Haymarket Theatre, London.
Feb. 14	O. Wilde's *The Importance of Being Earnest* performed St James's Theatre, London.
Mar. 30	G.B. Shaw's *Candida* performed at Theatre Royal, South Shields; not in London until 1904.
Oct. 6	Henry Wood conducts first Promenade Concert at Queen's Hall, London.

RECREATION AND FASHION

National Trust founded.

Jan. 25	First hockey international, Rhyl: Wales 0, Ireland 3.
Aug. 29	21 Rugby clubs in Yorkshire and Lancashire form Northern Union; accept professionalism, 1898; change name to Rugby Football League, 1922.
Oct. 15	Britain's first Motor Car Show, Tunbridge Wells, Kent.

RELIGION AND EDUCATION

Foundation of London School of Economics and Political Science.

SCIENCE AND INVENTION

William Ramsay uses spectroscope to identify helium.

Events Elsewhere

Apr. *17*   Peace Ty of Shimonoseki: Japan victorious over China.

AD 1896

Jan. 2	Jameson and his raiders surrender to Boers at Doornkop.
3	Kruger Telegram from Kaiser Wilhelm II congratulates Transvaal President on suppression of raid.
4–5	Anti-German demonstrations in Britain.
6	Rhodes resigns as premier of Cape Colony pending enquiries into Jameson Raid.
17	Ashanti township of Kumasi captured in new campaign to suppress unrest in Gold Coast hinterland.
26	Naval 'flying squadron' of 2 battleships, 4 cruisers and 6 destroyers kept on alert at Spithead (to Oct.).
29	1st contingency plans completed for military landing on the Gallipoli peninsula should Russia seize the Bosphorus forts.
Mar. 12	Suspicion of French ambitions on the Upper Nile leads Salisbury to order campaign from Egypt to reoccupy the Sudan.
May	*Daily Mail* goes on sale, at ½d.
29	James Connolly founds Irish Socialist Republican Party.
Jul.	Jameson on trial at Old Bailey for a breach of the Foreign Enlistment Act; sentenced to 15 months' imprisonment.
	Light Locomotives on Highways Act: repeals red warning flag legislation of 1865.
Aug. 27	Protectorate over Ashanti established.
Sep. 2	Chamberlain arrives in USA on extended visit; has talks over Venezuelan problem in Washington, 8 Sep.
22	Tsar Nicholas II and his family at Balmoral (to 3 Oct.); Tsar and Salisbury hold talks over Eastern Question.
23	General Horatio Herbert Kitchener begins advance into Sudan by capturing Dongola.
24	Gladstone's final political speech, at Hengler's Circus, Liverpool; urges British action against Turkey following 3-day massacre of Armenians in Constantinople.
Oct. 4	Rosebery resigns as Liberal leader; successor in the Lords is Kimberley; in the Commons, Harcourt.
Nov. 29	Q. Victoria successfully intercedes for release of Jameson on medical grounds.

FINE ARTS AND ARCHITECTURE
National Portrait Gallery opens in Westminster.

LITERATURE AND SCHOLARSHIP
Alfred Edward Housman publishes *A Shropshire Lad.*

MUSIC, ENTERTAINMENT AND DRAMA

Jan. 15   Henry Arthur Jones's *Michael and His Lost Angel* performed at Lyceum Theatre, London; withdrawn after 10 performances; audience shocked as it concerns a priest who committed adultery.

Mar. 7   Gilbert and Sullivan's last operetta *The Grand Duke* performed at Savoy Theatre, London.

Dec.   Albert Christian sings newly composed 'Soldiers of the Queen' at Pavilion Theatre, Whitechapel.

RELIGION AND EDUCATION

Sep. 13   Pope Leo XIII's encyclical *Apostolicae Curae* denies validity of Anglican orders; halts progress towards Anglican and Roman Catholic reconciliation.

SCIENCE AND INVENTION

Oct. 3   Q. Victoria and Tsar's family filmed at Balmoral by William Downey in first royal 'moving cinematograph photographs'.

Events Elsewhere

Mar. 1   Italian army defeated by Ethiopians in Ψ Adowa.

Oct.   1st Olympiad of modern era, Athens.

AD 1897

Jan.   Hobart Federal Constitutional Convention: discusses structure of proposed Australian Commonwealth; Queensland sends no delegates.

Feb. 15   British detachments are among international force landed in Crete during Greek insurrection against Turkish authorities.

May 5   Sir Alfred Milner arrives at Cape Town as British High Commissioner.

Jun. 22   Celebrations of Q. Victoria's Golden Jubilee.

Jul. 7   15 colonial premiers, attending Imperial Conference, are sworn of the Privy Council, at Chamberlain's suggestion.

19   Curzon, in Commons, warns Russia not to seek a base in Korea.

26   Chamberlain cleared when H. of Commons debates report on responsibility for Jameson raid; C. Rhodes heavily criticized.

29   Salisbury successfully steers through H. of Lords first Workmen's Compensation Bill, proposed in Commons by Chamberlain.

Aug.–Sep.   Campaign against Afghans along India's north-west frontier; Lieutenant

Winston Churchill mentioned in despatches while serving with the Malakand field force.

Dec. 23   Salisbury and Foreign Office officials assess reports from Kiaochow and Port Arthur, and agree to seek preservation of China from partition.

FINE ARTS AND ARCHITECTURE

Jul. 21   National Gallery of British Art opens; takes the name of its benefactor, sugar magnate Sir Henry Tate.

LITERATURE AND SCHOLARSHIP

R. Kipling's poem 'Recessional' written for Diamond Jubilee Day; also his *Captains Courageous*.
H.G. Wells publishes *The Invisible Man*.

MUSIC AND DRAMA

Johnston Forbes Robertson plays Hamlet at Lyceum Theatre, London.
Apr. 17   G.B. Shaw's *The Devil's Disciple* performed at Bayswater Bijou Theatre.

RELIGION AND EDUCATION

Mar. 29   Joint encyclical of Archbps of Canterbury and York replies to Leo XIII's *Apostolicae Curiae* (*v.* 1896) and asserts the validity of Anglican orders.

SCIENCE AND INVENTION

Joseph John Thomson delivers paper to Royal Institution describing his discovery of electrons in cathode rays; revolutionary research basic to nuclear physics.
Henry Havelock Ellis publishes first volume of his *Studies in the Psychology of Sex*; final (seventh) volume, 1928.
Ronald Ross, practising in the Indian medical service since 1881, discovers the malaria bacillus.

Events Elsewhere

Apr.–May   'Thirty Days War': Turks defeat Greek invasion of Thessaly.
Nov. 28   Germany occupies Chinese port of Kiaochow.
Dec. 13   Russian fleet winters at Port Arthur (Lu-ta).

AD 1898

Jan. 1   Kitchener seeks reinforcements for further advance up R. Nile.
     17   Salisbury takes a diplomatic initiative in seeking Anglo-Russian collaboration in Far East.
     25   Abortive attempt at Anglo-Russian *entente* (to 3 Mar.); fails when Russians lease Port Arthur from China.

Apr. 2	Britain leases naval anchorage of Wei-hai-wei, 'for such period as Russia shall hold Port Arthur'.
8	Kitchener's Anglo-Egyptian army defeats the Khalifa's dervishes on Atbara river.
May 4	Salisbury's Albert Hall speech: divides world into 'living and dying' nations and emphasizes 'England's . . . Imperial instincts'.
13	Chamberlain's Birmingham speech: urges better Anglo-American relations; supports need for Britain to find allies and emerge from isolation.
Jun. 9	Peking Convention: Britain obtains for 99 years a lease of 376 square miles of Chinese territory north of Kowloon.
14	Anglo-French treaty settles frontiers of French colonies with Nigeria and the Gold Coast in Britain's favour.
Jul. 25	British cabinet meets (attended by Lord Cromer) and resolves to establish an Anglo-Egyptian condominium in the Sudan.
Aug. 2	Kitchener ordered to proceed as soon as possible to Fashoda and oppose French claims of sovereignty there.
11	Curzon appointed Viceroy of India.
12	Irish Local Government Act: elective county and district councils set up.
30	Anglo-German agreement over possible purchase and partition of Portuguese colonies.
Sep. 2	Kitchener defeats the Khalifa's army at Ψ Omdurman.
5	Kitchener enters Khartoum.
19	Kitchener reaches Fashoda to find Colonel Marchand there, claiming the region for France.
Oct. 27	Salisbury rejects compromise talks with France until troops withdrawn from Fashoda.
	Royal Navy put on war alert.
Nov. 4	Fashoda crisis ends; French announce recall of Marchand.

FINE ARTS AND ARCHITECTURE
John Sargent paints portrait *Asher Wertheimer*.
Ebenezer Howard writes *Tomorrow; the Peaceful Path to Real Reform*, primer of garden city planning.

LITERATURE AND SCHOLARSHIP
G.A. Henty writes *With Moore at Corunna*.
H.G. Wells writes *The War of the Worlds*.

Mar. Winston Churchill's first book, *The Story of the Malakand Field Force*, is published.

MUSIC AND DRAMA
Jan. 20 A.W. Pinero's *Trelawny of the Wells* performed at Royal Court Theatre, London.

SCIENCE AND INVENTION
John Philip Holland builds first successful submarine for Royal Navy.

Events Elsewhere

Apr.–Dec.   Spanish-American War over Cuba and the Philippines.

AD 1899

Jan. *3*   Ceremonial reception of Curzon as Viceroy in Calcutta, India's administrative capital.

19   Campbell-Bannerman becomes Liberal leader in the Commons.

Mar. *20*   Chamberlain advises Kruger to give civil rights to foreign workers ('Uitlanders') in Transvaal.

21   Anglo-French agreement over boundaries of French colonial Africa and the Sudan.

Apr. *15*   Salisbury warns of need to protect Persian Gulf ports from foreign control.

16   Petition to Q. Victoria from more than 21,000 British Uitlanders reaches London; seeks British protection.

May *31*   Abortive Bloemfontein Conference over Uitlander grievances between Kruger and Milner (to 5 Jun.).

Jul. *18*   Transvaal offers rights to Uitlanders of 7 years' residence.

27   Chamberlain demands fuller concessions by Kruger.

Aug.   Bill establishing borough councils within London enacted.

12   Jan Smuts, Transvaal's Attorney-General, offers a compromise which is acceptable to Chamberlain.

23   Kruger stiffens proposed terms, convincing Chamberlain that the Boers wish to provoke war.

Sep. *4*   Kruger formally repudiates the Smuts offer.

5   Cabinet warned by War Office that troops in S. Africa are too few to withstand initial Boer attacks.

21   'Curzon Despatch': Viceroy's memorandum on Persia and the Gulf as outposts of the Indian empire.

29   Cabinet decides to call up army reservists.

Oct. *9*   Transvaal declares war on Britain.

11   Boers in Orange Free State enter war as Transvaal's ally.

15–16   Towns of Kimberley and Mafeking are besieged by Boers.

Nov. *2*   British column cut off and besieged in Ladysmith.

20–25   Kaiser Wilhelm II makes state visit to Windsor.

28   British check the Boers with heavy losses at crossing of the Modder River.

30   Chamberlain's Leicester speech: advocates an alliance of Britain, Germany and USA.

Dec. *10*   Start of 'Black Week': British defeated at Ψ Stormberg.

11   Boer victory at Ψ Magersfontein.

15   At Colenso Boers defeat British force seeking to relieve Ladysmith.

LITERATURE AND SCHOLARSHIP
Lord Acton becomes founder editor of the *Cambridge Modern History*.
Opening of the John Rylands Library, Manchester.
R. Kipling publishes *Stalky and Co..*
Edith Nesbit publishes *The Story of the Treasure Seekers*.
H.G. Wells publishes *When the Sleeper Wakes*.

MUSIC AND DRAMA
May 15   G.B. Shaw's *Caesar and Cleopatra*, with Mrs Patrick Campbell, performed at Theatre Royal, Newcastle; not in London until 1907.

Jun. 19   Elgar's *Enigma Variations* performed in London.

RECREATION AND FASHION
Sussex cricket captain, Jam Sahib Ranjitsinhji, is first batsman to score 3,000 runs in a season.

RELIGION AND EDUCATION
Board of Education for England and Wales set up.

SCIENCE AND INVENTION
Oct. 9   First motor-bus in London.

Events Elsewhere

May 13–
Jul. 29   First Hague Peace Conference.

AD 1900

Jan. 10   Lord Roberts arrives in S. Africa as Commander-in-Chief; Kitchener is his chief of staff.

24–25   Ψ Spion Kop: Boers repulse troops under General Sir Redvers Buller, inflicting heavy losses.

Feb. 15   Sir John French relieves Kimberley.

18   Boer General Cronje surrenders at Paardeberg.

27   Labour Representation Committee (embryonic Labour Party) set up, with Ramsey Macdonald as secretary.

28   Buller enters Ladysmith after 118-day siege.

Mar. 13   Roberts captures Bloemfontein.

Apr. 4   Q. Victoria lands in Dublin for 3-week visit to Ireland.

24   *Daily Express* published; first English paper to carry news on front page.

May 16   Mafeking relieved after 7 months of stubborn resistance by Col. Robert Baden-Powell.

18–19   Wildly excited celebrations of Mafeking's relief.

22	Mines Act: no children under 13 in the pits.
28	Orange Free State becomes the Orange River Colony.
31	Roberts occupies Johannesburg; also occupies Pretoria, 4 Jun.
Jun. 10	British force leaves Tientsin for Peking to help suppress Boxer Rising.
20	British envoy, Sir Claude MacDonald, organizes defence of Peking Legations, besieged by Boxers (to 13 Aug.).
Jul. 9	Q. Victoria signs the Commonwealth of Australia Act, federating the 6 colonies.
Aug. 14–24	Taff Vale railway strike, S. Wales.
Oct. 16	The 'Khaki' election gives Conservatives majority of 134: Conservatives 334; Liberal Unionists 68; Liberals 186; Irish Nationalists 82; Labour Representation Committee 2; Winston Churchill enters Commons as MP for Oldham.
Oct. 25	Transvaal formally annexed, in ceremony at Pretoria.
Nov. 12	Salisbury remains Prime Minister but gives the Foreign Office to Lord Lansdowne.

FINE ARTS AND ARCHITECTURE

	John Sargent paints *The Sitwell Family*.
Jan. 22	P. of Wales opens the Wallace Collection in Hertford House, Manchester Square, London.

LITERATURE AND SCHOLARSHIP

Arthur Evans begins excavating Knossos, Crete.
Bertrand Russell publishes *The Philosophy of Leibnitz*.
G.B. Shaw's *Three Plays for Puritans* published, with prefaces.
Sir Leslie Stephen's *The Utilitarians* published in 3 vols.
Winston S. Churchill publishes his only novel *Savrola*.
Joseph Conrad writes *Lord Jim*.

MUSIC, ENTERTAINMENT AND DRAMA

	The cakewalk, an American dance, becomes popular.
Oct. 3	Elgar's oratorio *The Dream of Gerontius* performed in Birmingham.

RECREATION AND FASHION

Great Britain loses to USA in first Davis Cup tennis competition, Boston, Mass.

RELIGION AND EDUCATION

Feb.	New constitution for London University; restructured so as to accommodate 23 colleges or institutions.

SCIENCE AND INVENTION

Jun. 27	Opening of the 'Tuppeny Tube': the central London railway underground from Shepherd's Bush to the Bank at a flat rate charge of 2d.

AD 1901

Jan. 1   Commonwealth of Australia inaugurated.
22   Q. Victoria dies at Osborne House; P. of Wales accedes as K. Edward VII.
30   Kitchener plans system of block houses and enforced evacuation of Boer farms so as to check mounting guerrilla warfare.
Feb. 2   Funeral of Q. Victoria.
May 2   International Exhibition opens at Glasgow.
29   Salisbury drafts cabinet memorandum strongly opposing an alliance with Germany and Austria-Hungary.
Jul. 22   Law Lords give ruling in the Taff Vale case: a union may be sued corporately for the damage caused by its members during a strike.
Oct. 25   J. Chamberlain delivers speech on world affairs at Edinburgh which is considered hostile by the Germans.
Dec. 18   Angry crowd at Birmingham town hall prevents speech by allegedly pro-Boer Liberal, David Lloyd George.

FINE ARTS AND ARCHITECTURE
Mar. 12   Whitechapel Art Gallery opens.

LITERATURE AND SCHOLARSHIP
British Academy founded, a learned society concerned with the humanities.
R. Kipling publishes *Kim*.
H.G. Wells publishes *The First Men in the Moon*.
Beatrix Potter writes *Peter Rabbit*.

MUSIC AND DRAMA
Elgar composes first of a planned set of 6 military marches, *Pomp and Circumstance*.
Jun. 30   Elgar's *Cockaigne Overture* performed in London.

RECREATION AND FASHION
Excessive femininity in women's dress: full-bosomed, wasp-waisted, light fabrics with much lace; floral hats, often with veils. Men accept lounge suits for informal wear; high collars to shirts; trilby hats; boots rather than shoes; moustaches for younger generation.

Electric tramways laid in several British cities, notably London, Glasgow and Portsmouth.

Oct. 2   Experimental petrol-driven submarine launched for the Admiralty at Barrow-in-Furness.

Dec. 11   Guglielmo Marconi sends wireless message from Poldhu, Cornwall, to Newfoundland.

VOYAGES AND EXPLORATION

Aug.   Cmdr. Robert Scott, in the polar vessel *Discovery*, sails on the first National Antarctic Expedition.

Events Elsewhere

Sep. 14   Theodore Roosevelt becomes America's youngest President on death of President McKinley, shot and wounded 8 days before.

AD 1902

Jan. 30   Anglo-Japanese Alliance Ty.

May 31   Peace Ty of Vereeniging ends South African War: Boers accept British sovereignty in return for aid to restock arms.

Jun. 24   Edward VII has appendicitis operation.

30   London Colonial Conference (to 11 Aug.): favours imperial preference over trade.

Jul. 12   Salisbury retires as Prime Minister; succeeded by Balfour.

Aug. 9   Coronation of Edward VII, postponed from 26 Jun.; Order of Merit instituted.

Sep. 5   Favourable commercial treaty with China.

27   East African Crown Lands ordinance encourages white settlement on Kenyan uplands.

Oct.   Russian exiles Lenin and Trotsky meet for first time, Holford Square, London.

Nov. 8–20 Kaiser Wilhelm II visits Britain.

Dec. 18   First session of Committee of Imperial Defence.

19   Britain joins Germany and Italy in blockading Venezuela, where the government refuses to pay compensation to foreign nationals for losses during revolutionary disturbances.

LITERATURE AND SCHOLARSHIP
J.A. Hobson publishes *Imperialism, A Study.*
H. Belloc publishes *The Path to Rome.*
John Masefield publishes *Salt Water Ballads.*
Arnold Bennett publishes *Anna of the Five Towns.*
J. Conrad publishes *Heart of Darkness.*
A. Conan Doyle publishes *The Hound of the Baskervilles.*
R. Kipling's *Just So Stories* published.
P.G. Wodehouse publishes *The Pothunters*, his first book, a school story.

MUSIC AND DRAMA
Irish National Theatre Movement founded in Dublin, led by the actor brothers Frank and William Fay and by the dramatists, Yeats and Lady (Augusta) Gregory.

Apr. 2 Edward German's *Merrie England* operetta performed at Savoy Theatre, London.
W.B. Yeats's *Cathleen ni Houlihan* performed at Abbey Theatre, Dublin.
Nov. 4 James Barrie's *The Admirable Crichton* performed at Criterion Theatre, London.

RECREATION AND FASHION
Apr. An unprecedented 110,000 spectators attend the FA Cup Final at Crystal Palace; Southampton and Sheffield United draw 1-1; playing as an amateur for Southampton is England's leading batsman and world record long-jumper, C.B. Fry.

RELIGION AND EDUCATION
Publication of the Gifford lectures by the Harvard professor, William James, *The Varieties of Religious Experience*, stimulates an interest in psychology.
Dec. Balfour's Education Act: provides basic state secondary education in England and Wales, establishing local education authorities and integrating denominational schools.

SCIENCE AND INVENTION
Ronald Ross receives Nobel prize for physiology for his work on the malaria parasite.
Devonshire telegraphist Oliver Heaviside postulates existence of an upper atmosphere layer, which eventually serves to bounce back radio signals.

VOYAGES AND EXPLORATION
Dec. 30 National Antarctic Expedition: R.F. Scott, Dr Edward Wilson and Ernest Shackleton reach record southerly latitude of 82° 16′.

AD 1903

Feb.	Blockade of Venezuela ends; Britain, Germany and Italy agree on Hague Tribunal arbitration.
Feb.–Mar.	J. Chamberlain tours S. Africa and favours Boer reconciliation.
Mar. 3	Admiralty announces plans to build naval base at Rosyth.
May 1–4	Edward VII's state visit to Paris breaks down traditional French suspicion of Britain.
5	Lansdowne, in H. of Lords, gives further warning to other countries not to seek bases in Persian Gulf.
15	J. Chamberlain publicly asserts need to substitute imperial preference for free trade.
Jul. 6–9	President Loubet and French Foreign Minister (Delcassé) visit London; start of *Entente Cordiale*.
21	Irish Land Purchase Act: government gives increased financial backing to purchase of land from big estates by peasantry.
25	Barnard Castle by-election won for Labour by Arthur Henderson.
Sep. 18	J. Chamberlain leaves Balfour's government to lead Tariff Reform League in favour of imperial preference.
Oct. 9	Austen Chamberlain becomes Chancellor of Exchequer in cabinet reshuffle caused by his father's resignation.
10	Mrs Emmeline Pankhurst founds Women's Social and Political Union at Manchester.
Nov. 7	Esher Committee appointed to examine ways of modernizing the War Office.

FINE ARTS AND ARCHITECTURE
Westminster Cathedral, designed by John Francis Bentley, is completed in 8 years.
Work begins on an Anglican cathedral in Liverpool, designed by Giles Gilbert Scott.

LITERATURE AND SCHOLARSHIP
Erskine Childers publishes *The Riddle of the Sands*, popular thriller about German invasion plans.
G.R. Gissing's novel *The Private Papers of Henry Ryecroft* published.
American novelist and journalist Jack London's *The People of the Abyss* reports on the squalor of the East End.
G.E. Moore publishes *Principia Ethica*, influential study in moral philosophy emphasizing the pleasures of human association and of aesthetics.

MUSIC AND DRAMA
Frederick Delius sets Whitman's poem *Sea Drift* to music for baritone solo and chorus; not performed in England until the Sheffield Festival of 1908.

Dec. 14   Worcestershire's R.E. Foster, on his Test Match debut in Sydney, scores 287, the highest English Test innings in Australia.

Events Elsewhere
Aug.–Sep.   Anti-Turkish uprising in Macedonia is harshly suppressed.

AD 1904

Jan. 1   Licensing of motor cars, and fitting of number plates, introduced; 23,000 registered cars; speed limit of 20 m.p.h.

Apr. 8   Anglo-French Convention signed: settles disputes in W. Africa, Siam, Madagascar, New Hebrides, Egypt and Morocco, and over fishing rights off Newfoundland.

May 6   British expedition to Tibet attacked; 400 Tibetans killed.

Aug. 11   Drink Licensing Act: brewers to be compensated from a trade fund for loss of licences in towns considered by local justices to be overstocked with public houses; Act angers temperance campaigners.

Sep. 7   Ty of Lhasa: safeguards Tibet from Russian penetration.

Oct. 21   Admiral Sir John Fisher becomes First Sea Lord, intent on modernizing training and tactics in the Royal Navy.
Dogger Bank incident: Russian Baltic fleet, sailing to Far East, mistakes Hull trawlers for Japanese torpedo-boats and opens fire; 1 Hull vessel sunk, 2 fishermen killed.

22–28   British threaten Russians with war over Dogger Bank incident, but French mediate.

Dec. 12   Fisher's redistribution of fleet concentrates more battleships in home waters.

FINE ARTS AND ARCHITECTURE
Charles R. Mackintosh builds Scotland Street School, Glasgow; innovative use of glass.

LITERATURE AND SCHOLARSHIP
Thomas Hardy's *The Dynasts*, Part 1, an unstageable epic drama, is published; Parts 2 and 3 follow in 1906 and 1908.
G.K. Chesterton publishes *The Napoleon of Notting Hill*.
W.H. Hudson publishes *Green Mansions*, romantic novel.
M.R. James's *Ghost Stories of an Antiquary* published.

MUSIC AND DRAMA

Mar.   Delius's *Appalachia* suite and opera *Koanga* performed in Germany, at Elberfeld.

Dec. 24   London Coliseum opens; first theatre with revolving stage.

26   J.M. Barrie's *Peter Pan* performed at Duke of York's Theatre, London.

27   Abbey Theatre, Dublin, opens with a double bill: W.B. Yeats's *On Baile's Strand* and Lady Gregory's *Spreading the News*.

RELIGION AND EDUCATION

University of Leeds established as an independent entity.

Oct.   WEA (Workers' Educational Association) set up.

SCIENCE AND INVENTION

Sir William Ramsay wins Nobel prize for chemistry and, working with Frederick Soddy, traces the transformation of radium emanation into helium.

F.G. Heath patents hydraulic braking system for motor vehicles.

John Fleming invents a 2-electrode thermionic valve.

Apr.   Henry Royce of Manchester invents his first 10hp 2-cylinder car; Charles Rolls agrees to market them as 'Rolls-Royce', 4 May.

Events Elsewhere

Feb. 4   Russo-Japanese War begins.

AD 1905

Mar. 8   Dungannon Club set up in Belfast, the germ of the Sinn Fein movement.

Apr. 2–3   Widespread concern in London at visit made (31 Mar.) by Kaiser Wilhelm II to Tangier, at which he emphasized Germany's interest in Morocco.

May 12   Mrs Pankhurst organizes first outdoor protest meeting, Westminster.

17   Britain proposes international discussions on Moroccan crisis; in Sep. France and Germany agree on the summoning of a great-power conference.

Jun. 24   Admiral Fisher requests Admiralty to draft contingency plan in case of German attack on France.

Jul.   Aliens Act: safeguards right of political asylum for immigrants, but from 1 Jan. 1906 authorizes refusal of entry to 'undesirables' without 'decent means' of support.

Aug. 20   Curzon resigns as Viceroy of India over reorganization of Indian army.

Sep. 12   Anglo-Japanese Ty of 1902 extended and modified; Japanese pledge help in defending India against attack.

Nov. 12   Q. Alexandra launches the Queen's Fund for the Unemployed.

Dec. 4   Balfour resigns as Prime Minister owing to Conservative-Unionist Party splits over tariff reform.

5	Sir Henry Campbell-Bannerman becomes Liberal Prime Minister, pending a general election.
11	Herbert Asquith becomes Chancellor of Exchequer; Sir Edward Grey, Foreign Secretary; Richard Haldane, War Secretary, to begin major army reforms.
15	Anglo-French military staff talks begin unofficially.

FINE ARTS AND ARCHITECTURE

Work begins on pioneer garden city at Letchworth, Herts, with houses in Norton Way South and Birds Hill designed by Barry Parker and Raymond Unwin for Ebenezer Howard (*v.* 1898).

Work completed on construction of Aldwych and Kingsway, London; opened by Edward VII, Oct. 18.

LITERATURE AND SCHOLARSHIP

A. Conan Doyle publishes *The Return of Sherlock Holmes*.

E(dward) M(organ) Forster publishes *Where Angels Fear to Tread*.

Baroness Orczy writes *The Scarlet Pimpernel*.

H.G. Wells publishes *Kipps*.

E. Clerihew Bentley writes *Biography for Beginners*, light verse.

	MUSIC, ENTERTAINMENT AND DRAMA
Jan. 5	Private performance of G.B. Shaw's *Mrs Warren's Profession* at New Lyric, London; not publicly in London until 1925.
May 23	G.B. Shaw's *Man and Superman* performed at Royal Court Theatre, London; performance omits Act 3.
Nov. 28	G.B. Shaw's *Major Barbara* performed at Royal Court Theatre, London.

	RECREATION AND FASHION
Jun. 29	Foundation of the AA (Automobile Association).

RELIGION AND EDUCATION

University of Sheffield founded.

	SCIENCE AND INVENTION
Oct.	Construction begins of HMS *Dreadnought*, will outpace and outrange any other warships; to be at sea within 12 months.

Events Elsewhere

	Revolutionary unrest in Russia throughout the year.
Sep. 5	Ty of Portsmouth, New Hampshire: ends Russo-Japanese War.

AD 1906

Jan. *10*	*Daily Mail* invents word 'suffragette' for militant campaigners.
	Grey authorizes Anglo-French General Staff talks.
12	General election gives Liberals a landslide victory, overall majority 84:
	Liberals 377; Conservatives 157; Irish Nationalists 83; Labour 53.
16	Algeciras Conference on Morocco begins, with Sir Arthur Nicolson as chief British delegate.
Feb. *10*	Launch of HMS *Dreadnought* outdates all previous battleships.
12	Parliamentary Labour Party formed; chairman Keir Hardie.
Apr. *7*	'Act of Algeciras' ends Moroccan crisis by providing a compromise settlement safeguarding Morocco's sovereignty.
Aug. *15*	Edward VII and Kaiser meet at Cronberg, hoping to ease worsening Anglo-German relations.
Oct. *23*	Suffragettes disrupt state opening of Parliament; 11 are subsequently jailed, including Sylvia Pankhurst.
Dec. *6*	Transvaal and Orange River Colony granted self-government.
13	Trade Disputes Act: legalizes peaceful picketing.
	Merchant Shipping Act: improves seagoing conditions and restricts use of foreign seamen in British vessels.
	Workmen's Compensation Act: makes 6 million workers entitled to compensation for accidents or 'industrial diseases'.

FINE ARTS AND ARCHITECTURE
Hampstead garden suburb begun, on Ebenezer Howard's principles under the inspired leadership of Henrietta Barnett; with St Jude's Church, a Free Church and the Institute designed by Edwin Lutyens.

LITERATURE AND SCHOLARSHIP
John Galsworthy's *The Man of Property* begins Forsyte saga.

MUSIC AND DRAMA
R. Vaughan Williams becomes musical editor of *The English Hymnal*, co-editor Percy Dearmer.

Sep. *25*	J. Galsworthy's *The Silver Box* performed at Royal Court Theatre, London.
Nov. *20*	G.B. Shaw's *The Doctor's Dilemma* performed at Royal Court Theatre, London.

RECREATION AND FASHION

Mar. *22*	First international Rugby Union match against a foreign country: England beat France in Paris, 35-8.

Jun. 21   Report of Royal Commission on Ecclesiastical Discipline criticizes encroachment of practices contrary to Anglican teaching; recommends Prayer Book revision and the division of dioceses.

Dec. 12   H. of Lords rejects Education Bill sympathetic to non-Anglicans.

SCIENCE AND INVENTION

J.J. Thomson awarded Nobel prize for physics for his work on ions.

Dr Frederick Gowland Hopkins of Guy's Hospital delivers his first paper on vitamins.

Events Elsewhere

May 10   First Duma meets in Russia.

AD 1907

Jan. 1   Haldane issues a special army order on creation of an expeditionary force for service in Europe.

Senior FO official Eyre Crowe completes 15,000-word memorandum for Grey emphasizing the German danger to Britain's world interests.

Feb. 9   3,000 non-militant suffragists in the 'Mud March', a peaceful London demonstration in heavy rain.

Apr. 21   Sinn Fein League formally constituted in Ireland.

Jun. 3   Government drops devolutionary Irish Council Bill because of nationalist opposition.

26   Commons pass resolution on need to limit power of the Lords to reject bills passed by the elected House.

Aug. 12   Rioting in Falls Road district of Belfast; troops open fire; 4 Roman Catholics killed.

31   Anglo-Russian *entente*: St Petersburg Convention settles rivalry in Persia, Afghanistan and Tibet.

Sep. 27   Dominion of New Zealand created.

Nov. 9   Lloyd George, as President of Board of Trade, acts as arbitrator to prevent a major rail strike.

12–18   Kaiser Wilhelm II pays a state visit; he remains privately resting at Highcliffe Castle, Bournemouth, for 3 weeks.

27   Committee of Imperial Defence begins an anti-invasion study.

29   Order of Merit bestowed on 87-year-old Florence Nightingale.

FINE ARTS AND ARCHITECTURE

Central Criminal Court, Old Bailey, designed by Edward Mountford; opened by Edward VII, 27 Feb.

LITERATURE AND SCHOLARSHIP
J. Conrad writes *The Secret Agent*.

Dec.   Kipling is first English Nobel laureate for literature.

MUSIC AND DRAMA
Jan. 26   John Millington Synge's *The Playboy of the Western World* opens at the Abbey Theatre, Dublin, and causes a riot.

Apr.   Elizabeth Robins's *Votes for Women* performed at Royal Court Theatre, London.

RECREATION AND FASHION
R.E. Foster, in successfully leading England's cricketers against S. Africa, becomes the only man to captain his country in both football (6 caps) and cricket (8 caps).

Jul. 6   Brooklands, near Weybridge, Surrey, opens as the world's first motor-racing track; racing there until 1939.

25   Baden-Powell forms Boy Scouts; camp at Brownsea Island.

RELIGION AND EDUCATION
Education (Administrative Provisions) Act: provides for medical inspection in state schools, and encourages provision of medical treatment services.

Sep. 18   First United Methodist Church conference opens, Islington.

Events Elsewhere
Jun.–Oct.   Second Hague Peace Conference.

AD 1908

Feb. 16   Tweedmouth Letter: Kaiser Wilhelm writes to First Lord of Admiralty deploring Anglo-German naval rivalry.

Apr. 1   Territorial Army, authorized by Haldane's Territorial and Reserve Forces Act (1907), is officially constituted.

7   Asquith becomes Prime Minister on resignation of Campbell-Bannerman, terminally ill.

8   Lloyd George becomes Chancellor of Exchequer; Churchill attains cabinet rank as President of Board of Trade.

May 7   Asquith announces his government's intention to introduce old-age pensions.

Jun. 12   Edward VII meets Tsar Nicholas II at Reval.

21   Women's Sunday, London suffragette protest; estimated 200,000 participants.

Oct. 12   Constitutional convention of S. African colonies (to Feb. 1909).

15   Admiralty opens new naval harbour at Dover.

16   Samuel Cody makes first aeroplane flight from English soil at Farnborough, Hampshire.

FINE ARTS AND ARCHITECTURE

Imre Kiralfy prepares 'White City', as London exhibition centre; lake, fountains, Indian-style pavilions.

Augustus John paints *The Lord Mayor of Liverpool*.

Jacob Epstein completes 18 nude figures for façade of the BMA building in the Strand, London.

LITERATURE AND SCHOLARSHIP

A. Bennett publishes *The Old Wives Tale*.

G.K. Chesterton publishes *The Man Who Was Thursday*.

E.M. Forster publishes *A Room with a View*.

Kenneth Grahame publishes *The Wind in the Willows*.

W.H. Davies publishes *The Autobiography of a Super-Tramp*.

MUSIC, ENTERTAINMENT AND DRAMA

First purpose-built cinema in Britain opens at Colne, Lancs.

May 19 Campaign for a National Theatre opens with a mass meeting at Lyceum, London.

Sep. 3 J.M. Barrie's *What Every Woman Knows* performed at Duke of York's Theatre, London.

7 Manchester Repertory Company, founded by Annie Horniman, begins first season at the refurbished Gaiety Theatre, London; earliest provincial repertory company in England.

Dec. 3 E. Elgar's Symphony no. 1 performed at Free Trade Hall, Manchester.

RECREATION AND FASHION

Apr. 20 Last first-class innings of W.G. Grace, for Gentlemen v. Surrey, 12 weeks before his 60th birthday.

May.–Oct. Franco-British Exhibition at White City; largest yet mounted in Britain.

Jul. IVth Olympiad held in London, at White City stadium.

RELIGION AND EDUCATION

Aug. Irish Universities Act: establishes Queen's University, Belfast, and National University, Dublin.

SCIENCE AND INVENTION

Prof. Ernest Rutherford of Manchester asserts that his research shows the atom to possess a nucleus surrounded by electrons; he receives Nobel prize for chemistry in December.

VOYAGES AND DISCOVERY

Jan. Shackleton commands British National Expedition to Antarctica in *Nimrod*.

Events Elsewhere

Jul. 5–24	Young Turk revolution challenges authority of Sultan Abdul Hamid.
Oct. 6	Austria-Hungary annexes Bosnia-Herzegovina.

AD 1909

Jan. 1 First payment of old-age pensions: 5s a week to people over 70.

Mar. 15 Selfridge's, the first American-style department store in England, opens in London's Oxford Street.

Apr. 4 Anglo-Persian Oil Company set up.

29 Lloyd George introduces his 'People's Budget'.

Jul. 25 Louis Blériot is first man to fly the Channel, crossing from Sangatte to Dover in 43 minutes.

Aug. 7 Edward VII complains to Lloyd George that his Limehouse speech on land taxation (30 Jul.) 'set class against class'.

19 Imperial Conference on Defence meets in London.

23 First counter-espionage unit set up secretly; soon to be called MI5.

Sep. 26 Forcible feeding of suffragettes on hunger strike begins at Winson Green prison, Birmingham.

Nov. 14 Churchill attacked by suffragette at Bristol railway station.

30 H. of Lords rejects People's Budget.

Dec. Unofficial Anglo-German talks over Berlin-Baghdad railway project.

Dec. 2 Asquith secures dissolution of Parliament for an election campaign over Lords' right to reject a budget.

3 Irish Land Act: extends facilities for land purchase.

7 Union of South Africa, with dominion status, is proclaimed at ceremony in London.

21 Law Lords give their 'Osborne Judgment': Labour Party's fund-raising from trade unions illegal.

FINE ARTS AND ARCHITECTURE
C.R. Mackintosh completes his Glasgow School of Art.

Jun. 26 Edward VII opens Victoria and Albert Museum, South Kensington (designer, Aston Webb); 10 years in building.

LITERATURE AND SCHOLARSHIP
William Beveridge publishes *Unemployment*, a report on state insurance schemes.
H.G. Wells publishes *Ann Veronica* and *Tono-Bungay*.
P.G. Wodehouse's *Mike* introduces the character Psmith.

MUSIC, ENTERTAINMENT AND DRAMA

Provincial Cinematograph Theatres Co. Ltd founded; company sets up some 3,000 'moving-picture houses' over next 5 years.

Mar. 9 J. Galsworthy's *Strife* performed at Duke of York's Theatre, London.

Jun. 22 Ethel Smyth's opera *The Wreckers* performed at His Majesty's Theatre, London, (first performed Leipzig, 1906).

Aug. 25 G.B. Shaw's *The Showing-Up of Blanco Posset* opens at Abbey Theatre, Dublin, having been banned by the Lord Chamberlain in London.

Nov. Newly established Glasgow Repertory Company stages first British production of Chekhov (*The Seagull*) at Royalty Theatre, Glasgow.

RECREATION AND FASHION

Girl Guides established to complement Boy Scout movement.

May 26 Edward VII sees his horse Minoru win the Derby.

RELIGION AND EDUCATION

University of Bristol founded.

VOYAGES AND DISCOVERY

Jun. Shackleton returns from Antarctica, having come within 100 miles of South Pole; he is knighted.

Events Elsewhere

Jul. Crete asserts its independence of the Ottoman Empire.

AD 1910

Jan. 10 A Juvenile Court opens in London.

15 General election: Liberals 275; Conservative-Unionists 273; Irish Nationalists 82; Labour 40.

Feb. 1 First 80 'job centres' open, authorized by Labour Exchanges Act of 1909.

21 Edward Carson becomes founder leader of the Ulster Unionist Council.

Mar. 3 Asquith tells MPs to 'wait and see' if he persists with Lords reform and People's Budget.

Apr. 4 Parliament Bill abolishing veto of H. of Lords receives first reading in H. of Commons.

May 1 Government establishes Development Commission to advise on loans for developing rural areas.

6 Edward VII dies at Buckingham Palace; P. of Wales accedes as K. George V.

20 Edward VII's funeral cortège is followed by the Kaiser, 8 kings, 5 heirs apparent and some 50 royal princes or dukes.

Jun. 17 Abortive informal constitutional conference discusses proposed Lords reform (to 10 Nov.).

Jul.	*31*	Fugitive murderer Dr Crippen arrested aboard SS *Montrose* off Quebec after ship's ocean radio signal used to alert detectives; Crippen is hanged 23 Nov.
Sep.	*3*	Lock-out in Lancashire cotton industry.
Nov.	*7*	Violence in Welsh coal strike, especially around Tonypandy, Rhondda; troops put on alert at Cardiff and Swindon.
	16	George V confidentially assures Asquith that, if Liberals won a further election and if H. of Lords remained obdurate, he would create enough peers to secure passage through the Lords of a Parliament Bill.
Dec.	*19*	General election narrowly keeps Liberals in power: Conservative-Unionists 273; Liberals 271; Irish Nationalists 84; Labour 42.

FINE ARTS AND ARCHITECTURE

Sir Aston Webb's Admiralty Arch completed; part of a 7-year project transforming the Mall into a processional route (open 1911).

LITERATURE AND SCHOLARSHIP

B. Russell and A.N. Whitehead complete *Principia Mathematica*, the seminal work on mathematical logic.
Norman Angell publishes *The Great Illusion* on the economic futility of war.
A. Bennett writes *Clayhanger*, first of a series of 4 novels.
E.M. Forster publishes *Howards End*.
H.G. Wells publishes *The History of Mr Polly*.
John Masefield's *Ballads and Poems* published; includes 'Cargoes'.

MUSIC, ENTERTAINMENT AND DRAMA

Feb.	*21*	J. Galsworthy's *Justice* performed at Duke of York's Theatre, London.
	22	Delius's opera *A Village Romeo and Juliet* has English première at Covent Garden, London.
Oct.	*12*	R. Vaughan Williams's *A Sea Symphony* performed in Birmingham.
Nov.	*11*	Elgar conducts first performance of his Violin Concerto, with Kreisler as soloist.
Dec.	*26*	London Palladium opens as a music hall.

RECREATION AND FASHION

Daily Mail sponsors a London-Manchester air race.

RELIGION AND EDUCATION

World Missionary Conference held in Edinburgh.

VOYAGES AND DISCOVERY

Jun.	*1*	Scott sails for Antarctica in *Terra Nova*.

Events Elsewhere

Oct.	*5*	Portuguese overthrow the monarchy and accept a republic.

AD 1911

Jan.	*1*	Knighthood for Roger Casement of the consular service for humanitarian work in the Congo and Brazil.
	3	'Siege of Sidney Street', Stepney: troops deployed against alleged Russian anarchists.
Feb.	*6*	Ramsay MacDonald becomes chairman of Labour Party.
	21	Asquith introduces new Parliament Bill in Commons.
May	*4*	Lloyd George introduces National Insurance scheme.
Jun.	*14*	Seamen go on strike.
	22	Coronation of George V.
Jul.	*1*	Many anti-German protests at news of arrival of German gunboat *Panther* at Agadir, Morocco.
	13	Investiture of P. of Wales, Caernarfon; first since 1616 and first held in Wales.
	21	Lloyd George's Mansion House speech warns Germany not to endanger peace over Morocco.
Aug.	*1*	Dock strike against newly established Port of London Authority; open-air protests in an unusually hot summer.
	10	Parliament Bill passes H. of Lords.
		Commons approve payment of MPs (£400 a year).
	14	Welsh miners end strike lasting 10 months.
	18	Official Secrets Act is hurried through H. of Commons in 2 days because of continued international crisis.
	21	Irish Women's Suffrage Federation formed.
	23	Admiralty and War Office begin to co-ordinate strategic planning for possible German war.
Oct.	*24*	Churchill becomes First Lord of the Admiralty.
Nov.	*8*	Balfour resigns as Conservative leader; succeeded by Andrew Bonar Law.
Dec.	*12*	George V, as Emperor of India, holds Delhi Durbar.

FINE ARTS AND ARCHITECTURE

		Camden Town Group flourishes: 16 'modernist' artists led by Walter Sickert.
May	*16*	George V unveils Queen Victoria Memorial and knights the designer Thomas Brock.
Nov.	*6*	Roger Fry's 'Manet and the Post-Impressionists' exhibition, Grafton Galleries, introduces art of Cezanne, Gauguin, Matisse and Picasso to London.

LITERATURE AND SCHOLARSHIP
Max Beerbohm publishes *Zuleika Dobson*, ironical romance.
Hugh Walpole publishes *Mr Perrin and Mr Traill*.
D.H. Lawrence publishes *The White Peacock*.
G.K. Chesterton publishes *The Innocence of Father Brown*.
J. Masefield publishes *The Everlasting Mercy*.
Rupert Brooke's *Poems, 1911* published.

MUSIC, ENTERTAINMENT AND DRAMA
Charles B. Cochran transforms interior of Olympia to look like a cathedral, for Max Reinhardt's production of *The Miracle*.
Cecil Sharp founds English Folk Dance Society.

May 11   Elgar conducts première of his Symphony no. 2, Queen's Hall, London.
Jun. 21   The Ballets Russes de Sergei Diaghilev open at Covent Garden: *Le Pavillon d'Armide* with Karsavina and Nijinsky; *Carnaval*; *Prince Igor*.
Nov. 11   Liverpool (Playhouse) Repertory Company opens.

SCIENCE AND INVENTION
Oct. 4   First electric escalators, Earl's Court underground station, London.

Events Elsewhere

Sep. 28   Italy, seeking to acquire Libya, goes to war with Turkey.

AD 1912

Jan. 3   Ulster Unionists say they will not obey any Irish Home Rule Parliament.
Feb. 8–11   Haldane visits Berlin to seek reduction of tension.
Mar. 1   Suffragettes smash shop windows in London's West End.
    18   Churchill proposes changes in naval dispositions.
    19   To halt a national pit strike Asquith introduces a miners' minimum wage bill.
Apr. 9   Bonar Law pledges Conservative-Unionist support for Ulster resistance to Home Rule proposals.
    11   Irish Home Rule Bill introduced in H. of Commons.
    15   White Star liner *Titanic* strikes iceberg on maiden voyage; over 1,500 drowned.
May 12   Creation of the Royal Flying Corps.
    23   London dock strike (to 31 Aug.); frequent violent clashes with police.
Jul. 15   National Health Insurance Act becomes effective.
Aug.   The Marconi Scandal breaks: alleged share speculation by cabinet ministers in anticipation of contract for British Marconi Co. to construct imperial network of radio stations.
Sep. 6   TUC votes against syndicalism.
    18   Carson leads militant protest against Home Rule at Enniskillen.

28	Solemn League and Covenant signed in Ulster by Unionists pledging opposition to Home Rule.
Nov. 26	George Lansbury (Labour MP until he resigned in Oct.) loses Bow by-election when standing as independent women's suffrage supporter.
Dec. 16	Ambassadorial Conference opens at St James's Palace to seek peace in the Balkans.

FINE ARTS AND ARCHITECTURE

George Frampton sculpts *Peter Pan*, Kensington Gardens.
William Orpen paints *Café Royal*.
W. Sickert paints *Ennui*.

Nov.	Second Post-Impressionist exhibition, Grafton Galleries.

LITERATURE AND SCHOLARSHIP

Edward Marsh edits *Georgian Poetry*, vol. 1.
Ethel M. Dell writes *The Way of an Eagle*, earliest of her romantic novels.

MUSIC, ENTERTAINMENT AND DRAMA

Lilian Baylis in charge of Old Vic music hall, London.
American 'ragtime' popular with the young; revue *Hello Ragtime* at the London Hippodrome.

Jul. 2	George V attends first Royal Command Variety Performance, Palace Theatre, London.
18	Diaghilev Ballet present *Firebird* at Covent Garden, London; first public performance of any Stravinsky music in Britain.

RELIGION AND EDUCATION

Apr. 23	Welsh Disestablishment Bill introduced in Commons.

SCIENCE AND INVENTION

Scottish physicist Charles Rees Wilson devises a cloud chamber to study behaviour of ions.
English engineer Charles Belling perfects an electric cooker with wired fireclay elements.

VOYAGES AND DISCOVERY

Jan. 18	Scott and 4 companions reach South Pole, to find that Amundsen's Norwegian party arrived there on 15 Dec.; all five of Scott's party die in blizzards in March 1913.

Events Elsewhere

Oct. 18	First Balkan War begins.

Jan.	*15*	Sickness, unemployment and maternity benefits introduced.
	30	H. of Lords rejects Home Rule Bill.
	31	Ulster Volunteer Force founded to resist Home Rule.
Mar.	*26*	Churchill proposes an Anglo-German 'naval holiday' to reduce expenditure on armaments.
Apr.		'Cat and Mouse Act': provides for temporary release, on licence, of suffragettes who go on hunger strike.
	3	Mrs Pankhurst imprisoned for inciting suffragettes to bomb Lloyd George's Surrey home.
May	*30*	Peace Ty of London between Balkan allies and Turkey.
Jun.	*5*	Suffragette Emily Davison fatally injured in throwing herself in front of the King's horse during the Derby.
	13	Commons Select Committee Report clears ministers named in Marconi Scandal of speculation.
Jul.	*15*	H. of Lords again rejects Home Rule Bill.
Sep.	*27*	Carson prepares a provisional Ulster 'government'.
Nov.	*25*	Irish Volunteers founded.
Dec.	*5*	Proclamation forbids the sending of weapons or explosives to Ireland.

FINE ARTS AND ARCHITECTURE

Wyndham Lewis founds Vorticist movement, relating the impact of technology to art.

Augustus John paints *Lyric Fantasy*.

J.S. Sargent paints portrait *Henry James*.

Eric Gill sculpts *Stations of the Cross*, Westminster Cathedral.

Jul. 8 Roger Fry opens Omega Workshops, Bloomsbury, to encourage young painters to apply their skills to interior decoration; flourishes until Jun. 1919.

LITERATURE AND SCHOLARSHIP

D.H. Lawrence writes *Sons and Lovers*; also *Love Poems*.

E.C. Bentley's *Trent's Last Case* is the prototype for inter-war detective novels.

Compton Mackenzie publishes *Sinister Street*, first part of novel.

MUSIC, ENTERTAINMENT AND DRAMA

Music-hall artist Florrie Forde popularizes song about an Irish lad in London: 'It's a long way to Tipperary'.

Jan. 1   Film censorship imposed in Britain.

Feb. 4   Diaghilev ballet *Petrushka* performed at Covent Garden.

15   Birmingham Repertory Company, founded by Barry Jackson, opens with *Twelfth Night*.

Sep. 1   G.B. Shaw's *Androcles and the Lion* performed at St James's Theatre, London.

RECREATION AND FASHION

Women's fashion is experimental: frills and lace discarded; hats have wide brims; skirts long but tight and restrictive around the ankles; neck-lines lower; hair waved back to a bun; smart handbags. Men's clothing gradually becoming less formal, but gloves essential for the well-dressed.

RELIGION AND EDUCATION

H. of Commons passes Welsh Disestablishment Bill, 5 Feb. and 8 Jul.; rejected by H. of Lords, 13 Feb. and 22 Jul.

SCIENCE AND INVENTION

Frederick Soddy discovers and names the isotope.

Mar. 28   William Morris (Lord Nuffield) produces 2-seater Morris-Oxford car, selling at £175, at Cowley.

Events Elsewhere

Jun.–Aug.   Second Balkan War.

AD 1914

Mar. 19   Anglo-German treaty over Turkish oil wells.

20   Curragh incident: officers serving in Dublin say they would resign their commissions rather than coerce Ulster.

Apr. 24–26   Large-scale gun-running by Ulster Volunteers.

May 25   Home Rule Bill passes Commons.

Jun. 15   Anglo-German treaty over German construction of Baghdad railway.

23   Amending Bill, allowing temporary exclusion of parts of Ulster, is approved by Commons.

Jul. 8   H. of Lords changes Amending Bill out of all recognition.

21–24   George V convenes Buckingham Palace Conference to seek all-party agreement on Ulster; conference fails.

24   Grey seeks to mediate in mounting Balkan crisis.

26   Gun-running by Irish Volunteers at Howth is intercepted.

	29	Grey warns German ambassador of possible British involvement.
Aug.	2	Cabinet agrees to protect French Channel coast from attack.
	3	Belgium, threatened by Germany, appeals for military support.
		John Redmond, leader of Irish Party in Commons, pledges Irish co-operation in a war.
	4	Following invasion of Belgium, Britain declares war on Germany.
	4–9	Abortive pursuit of German warships *Goeben* and *Breslau* from off Tunisia to the Dardanelles.
	6	Kitchener joins cabinet as War Secretary.
	7	First units of British Expeditionary Force cross to France.
	12	Britain declares war on Austria-Hungary, Germany's ally.
	23	BEF in acton at Mons, beginning retreat into Picardy.
	28	Heligoland Bight: naval victory for Battle Cruiser Squadron (Admiral David Beatty) and lighter cruisers.
Sep.	6–11	BEF participates in 1st Ψ of the Marne.
	16	Home Rule plans postponed for duration of war.
Oct.	3	First charity flag-day: for Belgian war relief.
	9	British naval division helps defend Antwerp.
	19	1st Ψ Ypres; British defend the Menin Road.
Nov.	1	German Pacific Squadron (Admiral von Spee) wins naval Ψ off Coronel, Chile.
	5	Britain (and France) declare war on Turkey.
Dec.	8	Falkland Islands: naval Ψ; Spee's squadron destroyed.
	16	German warships bombard Scarborough, Whitby and Hartlepool.
	17	British proclaim protectorate over Egypt.

FINE ARTS AND ARCHITECTURE
Augustus John paints *G. Bernard Shaw*.
Henry Lamb paints *Lytton Strachey*.

LITERATURE AND SCHOLARSHIP
J. Conrad publishes *Chance*.
James Joyce publishes *Dubliners*.

MUSIC, ENTERTAINMENT AND DRAMA

Feb.	2	First British performance of Wagner's *Parsifal*, Covent Garden.
Apr.	12	G.B. Shaw's *Pygmalion*, with Mrs Patrick Campbell as Eliza Doolittle and Sir Herbert Tree as Henry Higgins, performed at His Majesty's Theatre, Haymarket.
Aug.	26	Rutland Boughton's opera, *The Immortal Hour* performed in Glastonbury.

VOYAGES AND DISCOVERY

May	Shackleton sails on 2-year Imperial Antarctic Expedition.

Jun.	*28*	Austrian Archduke Francis Ferdinand and his wife assassinated at Sarajevo by a Serb.
Jul.	*28*	Austria-Hungary declares war on Serbia.
Aug.	*1*	Germany declares war on Russia, France's ally, converting a Balkan conflict into a world war.

AD 1915

Jan.	*19*	German naval airships bomb Yarmouth and King's Lynn.
	24	Ψ Dogger Bank: German plans for further naval raids on England thwarted.
Feb.	*4*	Turkish attack on Suez Canal beaten off.
Mar.	*9*	Defence of the Realm Act: gives government emergency powers.
	10	Grey accepts post-war Partition Plan for Russia to have Constantinople.
	10–12	BEF and Indian Corps suffer 12,000 casualties in advancing 1,200 yards at Neuve Chapelle.
	18	Naval attempt to force the Dardanelles fails.
Apr.	*22*	2nd Ψ Ypres begins with German use of poison gas.
	25	Landings on Gallipoli peninsula; British at Cape Helles; Australians and New Zealanders (Anzac) further north.
	26	Secret Ty of London for Italy to enter the war.
May	*7*	British liner *Lusitania* torpedoed off Ireland; 128 Americans among 1,152 passengers lost.
	12	General Botha captures Windhoek, German South West Africa.
	25	Asquith forms coalition government: Bonar Law becomes Colonial Secretary; Balfour succeeds Churchill as First Lord of Admiralty; Arthur Henderson, as President of Board of Education, is first Labour MP to have cabinet rank.
	31	First Zeppelin raid on London.
Jun.	*16*	Ministry of Munitions created, under Lloyd George.
Aug.	*6*	Further Gallipoli landings, at Suvla Bay.
Sep.	*25*	Costly British victory at Loos (to 8 Oct.).
	28	British, advancing on Baghdad, take Kut from Turks.
Oct.	*5*	British (and French) troops land at Salonika.
	12	Nurse Edith Cavell shot for alleged spying, Brussels.
	15	Britain declares war on Bulgaria.
	20	Women recruited as bus and tram conductors in London.
Dec.	*7*	Turkish counter-attack isolates Kut.
	16	General Haig becomes C.-in-C., BEF.
	20	Gallipoli evacuation begins, Anzac and Suvla Bay.

LITERATURE AND SCHOLARSHIP

John Buchan publishes *The Thirty Nine Steps*.
Ian Hay writes *The First Hundred Thousand*.
W. Somerset Maugham publishes *Of Human Bondage*.
P.G. Wodehouse writes *Something Fresh*, first Blandings Castle novel; and, in short story for *Saturday Evening Post*, creates Jeeves.
Virginia Woolf publishes her first novel, *The Voyage Out*.
Rupert Brooke's *1914 and Other Poems* published posthumously.
Edith Sitwell writes *The Mother*.

MUSIC, ENTERTAINMENT AND DRAMA

Chu Chin Chow musical is the most popular entertainment in London.

RECREATION AND FASHION

Sep. 11   First British Women's Institute opens, Anglesey.

RELIGION AND EDUCATION

Toc H, interdenominational Christian fellowship, founded as a soldiers' club at Poperinghe, Flanders.

SCIENCE AND INVENTION

First plastic surgery hospital ward opens, Aldershot.
British chemist James Kendall isolates the bacillus that causes dysentery.
Father and son William and Lawrence Bragg share Nobel prize for their work at Leeds University on X-ray crystallography.

Events Elsewhere

May 23   Italy declares war on Austria-Hungary.

AD 1916

Jan. 9   Last troops evacuated from Gallipoli.
     31   9 German naval airships raid the Midlands.
Feb. 9   Military Service Act: conscription for unmarried men between 18 and 41.
     19   National Savings certificates go on sale.
Apr. 21   Roger Casement lands in Ireland from German U-boat; arrested; hanged at Pentonville, 3 Aug.
     24–29 Easter Rising in central Dublin.
     29   Kut garrison surrenders to Turks.
May 3–12   7 leaders of Irish rebellion executed.
     16   Sykes-Picot agreement between British and French proposes post-war partition of Ottoman empire.
     21   Daylight saving (British Summer Time) introduced.

31	Ψ Jutland: tactically indecisive, but confirms British naval supremacy in North Sea.
Jun. 5	Kitchener drowned on voyage to Russia when cruiser HMS *Hampshire* strikes mine off Orkneys.
Jul. 1	Ψ Somme begins; 20,000 British soldiers die in a single day.
Sep. 3	First German airship (SL11) shot down, at Cuffley, during mass attack by 14 airships from R. Humber to R. Thames.
15	Ψ Somme: tanks first used.
Nov. 18	Somme offensive ends without decisive breakthrough.
Dec. 2	British marines killed in Anglo-French clash with Greek royalists in central Athens.
7	Asquith resigns; Lloyd George becomes Prime Minister.
11	Lloyd George forms war cabinet of 5 (himself, Curzon, Bonar Law, Henderson, Milner); Balfour succeeds Grey as Foreign Secretary.
12	Cabinet Secretariat established.

FINE ARTS AND ARCHITECTURE
Mark Gertler paints *The Merry-Go-Round*.

LITERATURE AND SCHOLARSHIP
J. Buchan writes *Greenmantle*.
D.H. Lawrence's *The Rainbow* seized by the police as obscene.
H.G. Wells publishes *Mr Britling Sees It Through*.
Edward Thomas writes *Six Poems*.
Robert Graves writes *Over the Brazier*, poems.

MUSIC, ENTERTAINMENT AND DRAMA
J.M. Barrie's *Dear Brutus* performed at Wyndham's Theatre, London.
Harold Brighouse's *Hobson's Choice* performed at Apollo Theatre, London.
Revue, *The Bing Boys Are Here*, featuring George Robey.

Jan. 28	Ethel Smyth's opera *The Boatswain's Mate* performed at Shaftesbury Theatre, London.
Jun. 13	Beecham's wartime season begins at Covent Garden (to 25 Jul.).

SCIENCE AND INVENTION
A 10-month campaign by the Lankester Committee on the Neglect of Science leads to the setting up of a Board of Scientific Societies and a government Department of Scientific and Industrial Research.
Marie Stopes's *Married Love* disseminates information about birth control.

Events Elsewhere

Feb. 21	Ψ Verdun (to 18 Dec.): 550,000 French casualties; 450,000 German.
Mar.	Germany and Austria-Hungary declare war on Portugal.
Aug. 27–28	Romania enters war against Germany and Austria-Hungary.
Oct. 10	Venizelos sets up pro-allied provisional government in Salonika, Greece, defying the neutral royalists in Athens.

AD 1917

Jan.	*3–4*	Lloyd George in Rome for inter-allied strategic conference.
	19	Silvertown munition works explosion rocks London.
Feb.	*13*	Government agrees to issue taxi licences to women.
	25	British retake Kut; enter Baghdad, 11 Mar.
Mar.	*17–18*	BEF captures Bapaume and Péronne.
	20	Imperial war cabinet meets in London.
	26	2 Ψs Gaza fail to break Turkish defences (to 18 Apr.).
	28	Women's Army Auxiliary Corps founded.
Apr.	*9*	British army advances 4 miles in Ψ Arras (to 4 May).
	9–12	Canadians storm Vimy Ridge, France; 10,000 casualties.
May	*10*	Convoy system instituted to protect merchant ships.
	15–16	On Salonika Front, British gain limited successes against Bulgarians along R. Struma.
Jun.		General Jan Smuts joins war cabinet.
	7	British 2nd Army and Anzacs attack Messines after exploding 19 mines tunnelled under German lines.
	13	Daylight air-raid on London by 17 'Gotha' bombers.
	17	Royal family drops German names; becomes the House of Windsor.
	19	Commons vote for a limited enfranchisement of women.
Jul.	*6*	Rebellious Arabs, co-ordinated by T.E. Lawrence, capture Akaba from Turks.
	31	3rd Ψ Ypres (to 10 Nov.); heavy August rain makes Flanders a quagmire.
Oct.	*22*	Passchendaele phase of 3rd Ψ Ypres (to 9 Nov.); mustard gas.
	31	General Sir Edmund Allenby launches carefully prepared offensive in Palestine at 3rd Ψ Gaza.
Nov.	*2*	Balfour Declaration gives official British support for a Jewish national home in Palestine.
	20	Ψ Cambrai: 381 tanks in first armoured assault.
Nov.	*28*	*Daily Telegraph* letter of Lord Lansdowne appeals for a negotiated peace.
Dec.	*6*	Munitions ship explodes at Halifax, Nova Scotia; 2,000 killed.
	9	Allenby captures Jerusalem.
	18–19	Smuts in Geneva for abortive secret peace talks with an Austrian emissary.

FINE ARTS AND ARCHITECTURE
First official war artists commissioned: Eric Kennington, William Orpen, William Rothenstein.

LITERATURE AND SCHOLARSHIP
Mary Webb publishes novel *Gone to Earth*.
T.S. Eliot publishes *Prufrock and Other Observations*, poems.
R. Graves publishes *Fairies and Fusiliers*, poems.
Siegfried Sassoon publishes *The Old Huntsman*, poems.
The war poetry of Wilfred Owen was mostly written between autumn 1917 and spring 1918; not widely known until collected edition of 1931.

RECREATION AND FASHION
Women factory workers encouraged to have short hair as a safety measure; 'bobbed hair' becomes widely accepted.

RELIGION AND EDUCATION
An Anglican, Maude Royden, becomes Britain's first woman minister, at the (Congregationalist) City Temple, Holborn.

Events Elsewhere

Mar. 16	Tsar Nicholas II abdicates
Apr. 6	USA declares war on Germany.
Nov. 7–8	Lenin leads Bolshevik revolution in Petrograd.

AD 1918

Jan. 5	Lloyd George defines war aims in speech to trade union leaders: 'self-government on true democratic principles'; 'some international organization'.
28–29	Heaviest night bomber-raid on London and south-east.
Feb. 6	Representation of the People Act: gives the vote to women at 30; disfranchises conscientious objectors for 5 years.
25	Meat rationing in Greater London; becomes national in April.
Mar. 21	German offensive breaches British line on the Somme.
Apr. 1	Royal Air Force founded, with amalgamation of RFC and RNAS.
12	Haig urges a 'backs to the wall' resistance to check Germans.
14	British recognize Marshal Foch as allied C.-in-C. in France.
23	Zeebrugge Raid: naval and marine force seeks to seal off U-boat base with blockships; 8 VCs awarded.
Jul. 14	Ration books issued for meat, sugar, margarine, lard, butter.
Aug. 8	Decisive breach of German defences east of Amiens by British, Canadians and Australians using 450 massed tanks.
Sep. 1	British capture Péronne.
18–21	Ψ Lake Doiran: British victory against Bulgarians.
29	Bulgarians sign Salonika Armistice.
Oct. 1–2	Damascus falls to British, Australians and Arabs.

	9	Advancing BEF enters Cambrai; enters Lille, 17 Oct.
Oct.	27	Spanish 'flu epidemic at its height (to 2 Nov.); more than 2,200 die in London alone during the week.
	30	Turks sign Mudros Armistice.
Nov.	3	Padua Armistice with Austria-Hungary.
	11	German Armistice signed, in Forest of Compiègne, ending First World War fighting: total dead for British empire 947,000, of whom 745,000 were from the UK.
	14	Labour Party votes to leave coalition government.
	21	Admiral Beatty receives surrender of German High Seas Fleet.
	27	German warships interned at Scapa Flow.
Dec.	14	General election, first in which women voted: Conservatives and Coalition Liberals 509; Labour 62; Independent Liberals (Asquithites) 36; others 27. 73 Sinn Feiners (including first elected woman, Countess Markievicz) refuse to attend a Westminster Parliament.
	26–31	President Wilson rapturously received on visit to England.

FINE ARTS AND ARCHITECTURE
Paul Nash paints *We Are Making A New World*.

LITERATURE AND SCHOLARSHIP
Lytton Strachey publishes *Eminent Victorians*.
Gerard Manley Hopkins's *Poems* published, edited by his friend, the Poet Laureate Robert Bridges.
Siegfried Sassoon publishes *Counter-Attack*, poems.

MUSIC, ENTERTAINMENT AND DRAMA

Sep.	5	Diaghilev company returns to England for twice-daily performances in music hall at London Coliseum.
Dec.	24	Nigel Playfair opens modernized Lyric Theatre, Hammersmith, with *Make-Believe* by A.A. Milne.

RELIGION AND EDUCATION

Aug.	Education Act, introduced by H.A.L. Fisher: raises school-leaving age to 14, favours part-time education to 18 and authorizes expansion of ancillary services.
Dec.	Festival of Nine Lessons and Carols instituted at King's College, Cambridge; first broadcast in 1928.

Events Elsewhere

Jan.	8	Woodrow Wilson outlines his Fourteen Points.
Mar.	3	Russia makes separate Peace Ty of Brest-Litovsk.
Nov.		Republics founded in Czechoslovakia, Poland, Germany, Austria.

AD 1919

Jan.	*10*	Churchill becomes War and Air Secretary.
	11	Lloyd George and Balfour arrive in Paris to head the delegation to the Peace Conference.
	21	Sinn Fein form their own parliament (Dáil Éireann), Mansion House, Dublin.
Mar.	*21*	Allenby appointed High Commissioner in Egypt.
	25	Lloyd George's Fontainebleau Memorandum seeks to deter France from a punitive policy towards Germany.
Apr.		Peace conference delegation agrees that Covenant of League of Nations shall be written into each peace treaty.
	1	Eamon de Valera elected President of Dáil Éireann, but soon leaves for USA.
	10	379 Indians killed by British troops at Amritsar, Punjab.
May	*3*	Frontier clashes lead to Afghan War; RAF bombs Kabul, 24 May.
	6	Lloyd George accepts mandate for German East Africa; South-West Africa to be S. African mandate.
Jun.	*21*	German fleet scuttled at Scapa Flow.
	23	Sankey Report on coal industry recommends nationalization.
	28	Lloyd George and Balfour sign Peace Ty of Versailles (with Germany) on behalf of Britain.
Jul.	*19*	Victory parades in Britain as peace is celebrated.
Aug.	*8–9*	Treaties of Rawalpindi and Tehran settle relations with Afghanistan and Persia respectively.
	10	British troops, supporting White counter-revolutionaries from Archangel, defeat Bolshevik Red Army on the north Dvina.
Sep.	*10*	Peace Ty of St Germain with Austria signed.
	27	British troops withdrawn from Archangel; withdrawn from Murmansk, 12 Oct.
Oct.	*27*	Curzon succeeds Balfour as Foreign Secretary.
Nov.	*27*	Peace of Neuilly signed with Bulgaria.
	28	Nancy Astor wins by-election at Plymouth, Sutton.
Dec.	*1*	Lady Astor becomes first woman member of H. of Commons.

LITERATURE AND SCHOLARSHIP

W. Somerset Maugham publishes *The Moon and Sixpence*.
P.G. Wodehouse publishes *My Man Jeeves*.
Virginia Woolf publishes *Night and Day*.
John Maynard Keynes writes *The Economic Consequences of the Peace* in 5 months.

MUSIC, ENTERTAINMENT AND DRAMA

Jul.	*22*	Diaghilev company's *The Three Cornered Hat* (décor by Picasso) opens at Alhambra Theatre, London.

Jul. 5 Suzanne Lenglen wins ladies singles at Wimbledon; first non-English-speaking champion; first tennis idol.

RELIGION AND EDUCATION
Church of England Assembly (Powers) Act: sets up 3 partially and indirectly elected Houses (Bishops; Clergy; Laity) to recommend ecclesiastical measures to Parliament.

SCIENCE AND INVENTION
Rutherford bombards atmospheric nitrogen with alpha-rays, liberating hydrogen nuclei.
Francis Aston invents the mass spectrograph.

VOYAGES, PIONEER FLIGHTS AND DISCOVERY
Jun. 14 John Alcock and Arthur Whitten Brown fly the Atlantic: Newfoundland to Co. Galway in 16 hrs, 27 mins.
Dec. 10 Ross and Keith Smith complete flight to Australia in 135 hours.

Events Elsewhere

Nov. 13 US Senate rejects League of Nations Covenant.

AD 1920

Jan. 2 Royal Irish Constabulary ('Black and Tans') accept recruits.
Feb. 11 League of Nations Council first meets, St James's Palace, London.
Mar. 16 British troops prominent in occupation of Constantinople.
Apr. 25 Britain accepts mandates for Mesopotamia and Palestine.
  30 Abolition of conscription.
May 27 Soviet trade delegation reaches England.
Jun. 4 Ty of Trianon with Hungary signed.
Jul. 1 Sir Herbert Samuel becomes first High Commissioner in Palestine.
  6 British troops withdraw from Batum in the Caucasus.
  8 E. African protectorate to be organized as Kenya.
  21–24 Belfast sectarian riots.
  31 Communist Party of Great Britain founded.
Aug. 9 Council of Action organized by Labour movement to plan a general strike should Britain go to war with Soviet Russia.
  10 Ty of Sèvres signed with Ottoman Turkey.
Nov. 11 George V unveils the Cenotaph and attends burial of the Unknown Soldier, Westminster Abbey.
  21 IRA shoots 11 British officers, Dublin; 'Black and Tans' fire on a football crowd, 12 dead.

| Dec. 10 | Martial law in Cork, Limerick and Tipperary. |
| 23 | Government of Ireland Act: Home Rule for both N. and S. Ireland, with Parliaments in Belfast and Dublin. |

FINE ARTS AND ARCHITECTURE
E. Lutyens designs the Cenotaph, Whitehall.
Ebenezer Howard founds a private company to create Welwyn Garden City.
Dora Carrington paints *E.M. Forster*.

LITERATURE AND SCHOLARSHIP
H.G. Wells publishes *Outline of History*.
Agatha Christie's *The Mysterious Affair at Styles* introduces Hercule Poirot.
J. Galsworthy publishes *In Chancery*.
Katherine Mansfield publishes *Bliss*, short stories.

MUSIC, ENTERTAINMENT AND DRAMA
'Sweet' jazz becomes popular through American band tours.

Feb.	Marconi sets up experimental public broadcasting station at Writtle (Chelmsford), Essex.
Jun. 5	John Gay's *The Beggar's Opera* performed at Lyric Theatre, Hammersmith; a highly successful revival.
16	Nellie Melba gives first broadcast song recital.
Nov. 15	Gustav Holst's *The Planets* suite given first public performance, London.

RECREATION AND FASHION
Women's dress conspicuously anti-feminine: tubular, with breasts flattened and a mock waist on the hips.

RELIGION AND EDUCATION
Women at Oxford become full members of the University and are able to receive degrees.

| Mar. 31 | Welsh Church Act of 1914 is implemented; disestablishment. |

SCIENCE AND INVENTION
Rutherford, newly appointed Cavendish professor at Cambridge, reorganizes the laboratory to concentrate on nuclear science; also postulates existence of the neutron.

Events Elsewhere

| Apr. 23 | Turkish revolution; Mustafa Kemal's Grand National Assembly at Ankara. |
| Nov. 2 | USA: Republican Warren Harding wins presidential election. |

AD 1921

Jan.	3	D. of Connaught opens first All-India Parliament in Delhi.
	8	Chequers estate (presented to the nation in Oct. 1917) becomes a country residence for Prime Ministers.
Feb.	12	Churchill appointed Colonial Secretary.
	21	London Conference over Turkish affairs.
Mar.	16	Anglo-Soviet trade agreement signed.
	17	Marie Stopes opens first 'Mothers' Clinic', advocating birth control, Holloway, London.
	21	Austen Chamberlain replaces Bonar Law as Unionist leader.
	24	Reparation Recovery Act: imposes 50% duty on German goods.
Apr.	1	Miners' strike; railwaymen and transport workers threaten to support them from 8 Apr.
	12	Government of Ireland Act becomes effective in Ulster.
May		Palestinian unrest: Samuel halts Jewish immigration following riots and Arab attacks on new settlements.
	24	British Legion founded.
Jun.	20	Imperial Conference in London.
	22	George V opens Belfast Parliament.
		Sir James Craig, first Prime Minister of N. Ireland; holds office until his death in 1940; created Viscount Craigavon in 1927.
Jul.	29	All-India Congress boycotts royal visit of P. of Wales.
Aug.	19	Railways Act: amalgamates 123 companies into 4 groups – GWR, LMS, LNER, SR – from January 1923.
Sep.	1	Poplar borough councillors, including G. Lansbury, imprisoned for seeking proportionally equitable rates between rich and poor boroughs, (to 12 Oct.).
Dec.	6	Treaty with moderates in S. Ireland: 'Free State', with dominion status, to be established.
	13	Britain signs Ty of Washington: joins USA, Japan and France in guaranteeing status quo in the Pacific.
	29	2nd Ty of Washington: accepts an agreed scale of relative size for the navies of the great powers.

LITERATURE AND SCHOLARSHIP

John McTaggart publishes *The Nature of Evidence*, vol. 1; systematic metaphysics.

R.H. Tawney publishes *The Acquisitive Society*.

L. Strachey publishes *Queen Victoria*.

John Galsworthy publishes *To Let*.

Aldous Huxley publishes *Crome Yellow*.

D.H. Lawrence's *Women in Love* published in Britain; published in New York, 1920.

Night clubs become fashionable, especially in London.

Oct. 18 G.B. Shaw's *Heartbreak House* performed at Royal Court Theatre, London.

Nov. 3 Diaghilev Ballet performs Tchaikovsky's *The Sleeping Princess* (décor by Bakst) at Alhambra Theatre, London; unpopular.

RECREATION AND FASHION
Short frocks, cloche hats, bobbed hair and bare arms for women.

Jul. 30 First annual 'Duke of York's Camp' held at New Romsey: seeks integration of boys from different social classes.

RELIGION AND EDUCATION
'First Century Christian Fellowship' is founded by the American evangelist Frank Buchman at Oxford; known as the 'Oxford Group' 1929-38, thereafter as Moral Rearmament.

SCIENCE AND INVENTION
Frederick Soddy awarded Nobel prize for chemistry for his work on isotopes.

Events Elsewhere

Jul. Chinese Communist Party established, Peking.

AD 1922

Jan. 16 Provisional Irish government takes office in Dublin, headed by Michael Collins.

Mar. 16 Protectorate over Egypt ends; British recognize K. Fuad I.

30 Craig and Collins confer; agree on occasional meetings to discuss common Irish problems.

Apr. 14 IRA 'Irregulars', opposed to partition settlement, seize the Four Courts, Dublin.

Jun. 21 IRA shoots FM Sir Henry Wilson in Belgravia.

28 Street-fighting in Dublin between Irish army and IRA Irregulars (to 5 Jul.).

Jul. Separation and Maintenance Orders Act: gives greater security to divorcees.

17 D. of Northumberland denounces Lloyd George's system of awarding honours.

Aug. 22 IRA Irregulars ambush and kill Michael Collins.

24 Palestinian Arabs, at Nablus, denounce British mandate.

Sep. 8–9 Navy helps rescue Greeks from Smyrna on its fall to Kemal.

23 Threat of war with nationalist Turkey as Kemal's troops enter neutralized zone at Chanak.

Oct. 3–11 Mudanya Conference arranges Chanak armistice.

19 At Carlton Club, Conservative MPs vote to end coalition; they back Bonar

Law rather than A. Chamberlain as leader.

Lloyd George resigns as Prime Minister, ending coalition.

23 Bonar Law becomes Prime Minister; Stanley Baldwin, Chancellor of Exchequer.

Nov. 20 Curzon presides over opening of Lausanne Conference to revise peace settlement with Turkey.

Dec. 6 Irish Free State Constitution Act comes into force, with Timothy Healy appointed Governor-General.

FINE ARTS AND ARCHITECTURE

Mar. 21 New Waterloo Station, designed by J.W. Jacomb-Hood, opened.

Jul. 17 LCC's County Hall, architect Ralph Knott, opened.

LITERATURE AND SCHOLARSHIP

J. Joyce's *Ulysses* published in Paris; banned in Britain until 1936.

Richmal Crompton writes *Just William*, first in series.

Bertrand Russell supervises publication of Ludwig Wittgenstein's *Tractatus Logico-Philosophicus*, in German and English.

Oct. *The Criterion*, literary quarterly edited by T.S. Eliot, first published; contains *The Waste Land*.

Sir Leonard Woolley begins excavating Ur.

Nov. Tomb of Tut'ankhamun at Luxor discovered by Howard Carter, under patronage of Lord Carnarvon.

MUSIC, ENTERTAINMENT AND DRAMA

Arthur Bliss composes his *Colour Symphony*.

Mar. 8 J. Galsworthy's *Loyalties* performed at St Martin's Theatre, London.

Jun. 7 A.A. Milne's *Dover Road* performed at Theatre Royal, Haymarket.

Oct. 18 British Broadcasting Company begins transmissions from 2LO (Marconi House, Strand, London).

RECREATION AND FASHION

The cocktail becomes fashionable; motoring becomes widespread among the lower middle class, with sales of £425 Morris-Cowley quadrupling in Feb. and Mar.

SCIENCE AND INVENTION

F. Aston awarded Nobel prize for chemistry for work on isotopic structure.

Herbert Austin produces the 'Baby' Austin 7 at Longbridge, Birmingham.

Events Elsewhere

Oct. 30 Benito Mussolini becomes Italian Prime Minister.

AD 1923

Feb.	*4*	Lausanne Conference breaks down because of Turkish opposition.
Mar.		Neville Chamberlain attains cabinet rank, as Minister of Health.
Apr.	*23*	Lausanne Conference resumes.
	25	Britain declares mandated Transjordan an independent emirate under Abdullah ibn Hussein.
	26	D. of York, future K. George VI, marries Lady Elizabeth Bowes-Lyon.
	27	Irregulars suspend military campaign in Ireland.
May	*20*	Bonar Law resigns because of ill-health.
	21	George V declines to offer premiership to Lord Curzon, believing that head of government should be in Commons.
	22	Baldwin becomes Prime Minister with N. Chamberlain as Chancellor of Exchequer.
Jul.	*18*	Matrimonial Causes Act: equal rights for both sexes in divorce suits; wives can divorce husbands for adultery.
	24	Ty of Lausanne: revises peace settlement with Turkey.
	31	Liquor Act: bans sale of alcohol to under-18s.
Oct.	*2*	Last British troops withdraw from Constantinople.
	26	Imperial Conference in London (to 8 Nov.): acknowledges a dominion's right to make a treaty with foreign power.
Dec.	*6*	General election: Conservatives 258; Liberals 159; Labour 191; Baldwin stays in office though lacking a majority.

FINE ARTS AND ARCHITECTURE

Royal Fine Art Commission sets up committee on the design and siting of public buildings and monuments.

Stanley Spencer begins his 5-year work painting *The Resurrection*, at Cookham.

LITERATURE AND SCHOLARSHIP

W.B. Yeats awarded Nobel prize for literature.

Arnold Bennett publishes *Riceyman Steps*.

Dorothy L. Sayers's *Whose Body?* introduces Lord Peter Wimsey.

MUSIC, ENTERTAINMENT AND DRAMA

Robert Mayer founds his Children's Concerts, London.

May	*14*	G. Holst's opera *The Perfect Fool* performed at Covent Garden; music and words by Holst.
Jun.	*12*	William Walton's *Facade* performed at Aeolian Hall, London; the music accompanied verses by Edith Sitwell, declaimed by her through a megaphone in syncopated rhythm.
Oct.	*9–13*	G.B. Shaw's *Back to Methuselah* performed in Birmingham; performed in London 1924.

Apr. 28 Wembley Stadium opens for FA Cup Final; Bolton Wanderers beat West Ham United 2-1.

SCIENCE AND INVENTION
Edward N. da C. Andrade publishes *The Structure of the Atom*.
Sir Arthur Eddington's *Mathematical Theory of Relativity* helps establish theories of Einstein in English-speaking countries.

Events Elsewhere

Jan. French and Belgian troops occupy the Ruhr because Germany fails to fulfil reparations quotas.

Oct. 29 Turkey is declared a republic, with Kemal as President.

AD 1924

Jan. 22 Baldwin resigns as Prime Minister.

23 Ramsay MacDonald forms minority Labour government, being Foreign Secretary as well as Prime Minister.

Feb. Baldwin sets up Conservative Consultative Committee; first organized 'shadow cabinet'.

1 Britain gives diplomatic recognition to Soviet Russia.

Apr. 23 K. George V opens British Empire Exhibition at Wembley, London.

Jul. Housing Act: encourages planned co-operation between local authorities and building industry; increases central government's subsidy for council house construction.

15 London Convention pleases Mussolini by frontier adjustment which transfers Kismayu port from Kenya to Italian Somaliland.

Aug. 30 London Agreement on reparations signed after conference at St James's Palace: accepts Dawes Plan of scaled annual payments by Germany.

Sep. MacDonald is first Foreign Secretary and only Prime Minister to attend session of League of Nations at Geneva; he proposes the Geneva Protocol for the pacific settlement of international disputes.

20 MacDonald refers Mosul dispute (in which Britain supports Iraq against Turkey) to League of Nations for arbitration.

Oct. 9 Labour government resigns after censure vote over the Campbell case: the dropping of sedition charges against a communist journalist.

25 Newspapers, with Foreign Office backing, publish the Zinoviev letter, which appears to indicate Russian-sponsored attempts to promote revolution in Britain.

29 General election: Conservatives 413; Labour 151; Liberals 40; Labour lose 42 seats but gain 1 million more votes.

Nov. 4 MacDonald resigns; Baldwin returns as Prime Minister.

7 A. Chamberlain becomes Foreign Secretary; N. Chamberlain, Minister of Health; Churchill (having left Liberals in March), Chancellor of Exchequer.

LITERATURE AND SCHOLARSHIP
E.M. Forster publishes *A Passage to India*.
Margaret Kennedy publishes *The Constant Nymph*.

MUSIC, ENTERTAINMENT AND DRAMA

Mar. 8   Sean O'Casey's *Juno and the Paycock*, with Sara Allgood, performed at Abbey Theatre, Dublin.

26   G.B. Shaw's *St Joan*, with Sybil Thorndike, performed at New Theatre, London.

Jun. 4   Sir Edward Elgar is first eminent composer appointed as Master of the King's Music.

Jul. 4   R. Vaughan Williams's opera *Hugh the Drover* performed at Royal College of Music, London.

Nov. 24   Noel Coward's *The Vortex* performed at Everyman Theatre, Hampstead.

RECREATION AND FASHION
VIth Olympiad, Paris: gold medals for Scottish Rugby international Eric Liddell in 400 metres and for Harold Abrahams in 100 metres.
New Zealand All Blacks win all 30 matches of their second Rugby Union tour.

Feb.   Rise in cost of petrol (£1 for 10 gallons) fails to curb mounting popularity of motoring.

Nov 2   *Sunday Express* is first British newspaper with a crossword.

Events Elsewhere

Jan. 21   Death of Lenin; Stalin emerges as Party boss.

AD 1925

Jan. 29   Lloyd George is accepted as leader of Liberals with retirement of Asquith (to become E. of Oxford and Asquith).

Feb. 11   Dáil in Dublin approves legislation making UK divorce laws inoperative in the Irish Free State.

Mar. 12   Austen Chamberlain rejects Geneva Protocol.

Apr. 28   Churchill's budget speech announces return to gold standard, based on pre-war parity of sterling to the dollar ($4.86 to £1).

May 1   Cyprus is proclaimed a Crown Colony.

Jul. 1   Dominions Office, independent of Colonial Office and Foreign Office, is set up to handle relations with 'the autonomous communities within the Empire'.

31	Baldwin avoids threatened coal strike by setting up Royal Commission on Coal Industry under Sir Herbert Samuel.
Dec. 1	Britain is a guarantor of Ty of Locarno.
	British troops withdrawn from Cologne after 7 years of occupation.
3	Frontier demarcation disputes between Irish Free State and N. Ireland settled.
10	Sir Austen Chamberlain shares Nobel peace prize with Charles Dawes of USA for promoting German reconciliation.
16	League of Nations gives ruling over Mosul dispute which favours Iraq and Britain.

FINE ARTS AND ARCHITECTURE

Bird sanctuary honouring W.H. Hudson is opened in Hyde Park, with J. Epstein's sculptured *Rima*.

E. Lutyens completes British Medical Association building, Tavistock Square, London.

Sir Philip Laszlo paints *The Duchess of York*.

Alfred Munnings paints *Their Majesties returning from Ascot*.

LITERATURE AND SCHOLARSHIP

G.B. Shaw awarded Nobel prize for literature.

J.M. Keynes publishes *A Treatise on Money*.

A. Huxley publishes *Those Barren Leaves*.

Virginia Woolf publishes *Mrs Dalloway*.

MUSIC, ENTERTAINMENT AND DRAMA

The Charleston dance becomes popular.

Jun. 8	Noel Coward's *Hay Fever* performed at Ambassadors Theatre, London.
Nov.	Ellen Terry's farewell stage appearance in Walter de la Mare's *Crossings* at Lyric Theatre, Hammersmith.

RECREATION AND FASHION

Men's informal wear favours plus-fours or wide trousers ('Oxford bags') of grey flannel, with sports jackets; everyday dress is striped and double-breasted lounge suits. Women's skirts remain short, narrow and straight; much fur used for outdoor elegance.

AD 1926

Mar. 11	Samuel Report: seeks reorganization of coal industry, end of government subsidy, some pay reductions.
25	Baldwin accepts Samuel Report; miners, led by A.J. Cook, reject it and prepare for strike.
Apr. 21	Birth of P. Elizabeth of York, future Q. Elizabeth II.

May 1		TUC offers full support to miners.
	4	General strike in support of miners.
	12	General strike ends after TUC talks with Samuel; miners stay out, unreconciled.
Oct. 19		4-week Imperial Conference opens in London; accepts that dominions are autonomous and equal in status.
Nov. 8		Indian Statutory Commission under Sir John Simon set up.
	19	Miners call off strike begun on 1 May.

FINE ARTS AND ARCHITECTURE

Royal Academy commemorates J.S. Sargent with special exhibition a year after his death.

Welsh painter Gwen John has one-woman show in London; her brother Augustus John completes his *Lady Ottoline Morrell* portrait.

Stanley Spencer begins 6 years of work on murals for the Burghclere Memorial Chapel, Berkshire.

Roger Fry's study in aesthetics, *Transformations*, published.

LITERATURE AND SCHOLARSHIP

G.M. Trevelyan publishes *History of England*.

R.H. Tawney publishes *Religion and the Rise of Capitalism*.

T.E. Lawrence's *The Seven Pillars of Wisdom*, with portraits by Eric Kennington, is privately printed.

Vita Sackville-West writes *The Lands*, pastoral poem.

A. Christie publishes *The Murder of Roger Ackroyd*.

D.H. Lawrence publishes *The Plumed Serpent*.

Rose Macaulay publishes *Crewe Train*.

A.A. Milne creates *Winnie the Pooh*.

MUSIC, ENTERTAINMENT AND DRAMA

Feb. 26	S. O'Casey's *The Plough and the Stars* performed at Abbey Theatre, London.
Mar. 6	Memorial Theatre, Stratford, destroyed by fire.
Jun. 30	Ben Travers's *Rookery Nook* performed at Aldwych Theatre, London.

RECREATION AND FASHION

Council for the Preservation of Rural England established.

In a cricket season when J.B. Hobbs scores 16 centuries, England regain the Ashes lost to Australia in 1912.

Jul. 24   First British greyhound track opens, Belle Vue, Manchester.

RELIGION AND EDUCATION

Foundation of Reading University.

Traffic lights, manually controlled, are introduced in central London.
Sir James Jeans uses quantum theory to formulate new concept of stellar formation.
Frederick Lindemann (Lord Cherwell) writes *The Physical Significance of the Quantum Theory*.

Jan. 27   Television demonstrated by John Logie Baird in Soho to scientists from the Royal Institution.

VOYAGES, PIONEER FLIGHTS AND DISCOVERY
Scott Polar Research Institute, Cambridge, opens.

Mar. 13   Alan Cobham returns to Croydon after 3-month trip to Cape Town and back, exploring routes for distance airways.

Oct. 1   Cobham lands his seaplane in R. Thames at Westminster after similar 2-month flight to Australia.

AD 1927

Jan. 1   British Broadcasting Company becomes a public corporation.

May 9   D. of York opens Parliament House in Canberra, which formally becomes the federal capital of Australia.

26   Police raid Arcos (Soviet trading company) in Moorgate St, London, in abortive hunt for evidence of communist subversion.

27   Britain breaks off diplomatic relations with Soviet Russia.

Jun. 20   Abortive naval disarmament conference in Washington of Britain, USA and Japan (to 4 Aug.).

Jul.   P. of Wales and Baldwin arrive in Canada for the dominion's Diamond Jubilee celebrations.

28   Trade Disputes and Trade Union Act: sympathetic strikes made illegal; political levy of union members to Labour Party to be on 'contracting in' basis rather than 'contracting out'.

Nov. 22   Baldwin declines to receive 200 unemployed Welsh miners who have walked from Rhondda valley to London.

Dec. 14   Anglo-Iraqi Ty: Britain recognizes independence of Iraq, but mandate will continue until Iraq is admitted to League of Nations.

FINE ARTS AND ARCHITECTURE
E. Lutyens completes the Menin Gate war memorial at Ypres; it is dedicated in July.
Eric Gill designs the 'sans-serif' alphabet.
Rex Whistler paints murals in the Tate Gallery.

LITERATURE AND SCHOLARSHIP
B. Russell publishes *Analysis of Matter*.
Helen Waddell publishes *The Wandering Scholars*.
Henry Williamson publishes *Tarka the Otter*.
V. Woolf publishes *To the Lighthouse*.

MUSIC, ENTERTAINMENT AND DRAMA
Slow foxtrot becomes a popular dance.
Mar.   Gaumont-British Film Corporation established, with studios at Shepherd's
            Bush.
Apr. 7   Sigmund Romberg's American musical *The Desert Song* has English première
            at Theatre Royal, Drury Lane.
Jul. 4   Ben Travers's *Thark* performed at Aldwych Theatre, London.

RECREATION AND FASHION
Fashion for women's hair favours shingling.
Jan. 22   1st radio commentary on a football match (Arsenal v. Sheffield Utd); and on
            the Grand National, 25 Mar.
Apr. 24   English Table Tennis Association set up.

RELIGION AND EDUCATION
Feb. 7   Revised Book of Common Prayer presented to Convocation; approved, 6 Jul.
Dec. 15   H. of Commons rejects revised Prayer Book, 238 votes to 205.

Events Elsewhere

May 21   Charles Lindbergh flies the Atlantic solo from New York to Paris in 33 hrs
            39 mins.

AD 1928

Jan. 12   Joint conference at Burlington House of industrialists, headed by Sir Alfred
            Mond, and trade unionists, headed by TUC chairman Ben Turner and Ernest
            Bevin.
Mar.   2 RAF squadrons sent to Kuwait to protect S. Iraq from raids by Bedouin
            tribesmen.
May 7   Equal Franchise Act: gives the vote to women between the ages of 21 and 30.
    15   Transport House in Smith Square, Westminster opens: headquarters of
            Bevin's union (Transport and General Workers), of TUC and of Labour
            Party.
Jul. 4   Second Mond-Turner conference: eases tension between industrialists and
            trade union movement.
Aug. 27   Britain adheres to the Kellogg-Briand Pact in Paris, renouncing war as an
            instrument of aggression.

FINE ARTS AND ARCHITECTURE
Elizabeth Scott successfully submits plans for a new Shakespeare Memorial Theatre at Stratford-upon-Avon.
Lord Iveagh's art collection at Kenwood opens to the public.

LITERATURE AND SCHOLARSHIP
Edmund Blunden publishes *Undertones of War*.
G.B. Shaw publishes *The Intelligent Woman's Guide to Socialism and Capitalism*.
A. Huxley publishes *Point Counter-Point*.
T.F. Powys publishes *Mr Weston's Good Wine*.
Edgar Wallace publishes *The Squeaker*.
Evelyn Waugh publishes *Decline and Fall*.
V. Woolf publishes *Orlando*.
D.H. Lawrence has *Lady Chatterley's Lover* privately printed in Florence; in London an expurgated edition could not be published until 1932 and the full text only in 1960.

MUSIC, ENTERTAINMENT AND DRAMA
A. Bax composes his Symphony no. 3.
Jun. 26   B. Travers's *Plunder* performed at Aldwych Theatre, London.
Dec. 9   R.C. Sheriff's *Journey's End* performed at Apollo Theatre, London; brings Laurence Olivier to the London stage.

RECREATION AND FASHION
Speedway racing comes to England from Australia and USA; High Beech track, Essex, opens.

RELIGION AND EDUCATION
Jun. 14   Modified revised Prayer Book defeated in H. of Commons by 266 votes to 220; the '1928 Prayer Book' may be used for services if authorized by a diocesan bishop.

SCIENCE AND INVENTION
Alexander Fleming accidentally discovers penicillin at St Mary's Hospital, Paddington.
J.L. Baird successfully experiments with coloured television.
May   *Flying Scotsman* fast steam-train introduced by London and North Eastern Railway on London-Edinburgh run.
Sep.   Oil-fired electric turbines are installed for first time in a liner: P. & O. ship, *Viceroy of India*, under construction on R. Clyde.

VOYAGES, PIONEER FLIGHTS AND DISCOVERY
Queenslander Bert Hinkler makes first solo flight from England to Australia: London to Darwin in 15 days.

Events Elsewhere

Nov.   Stalin announces his first Five-Year Plan.

AD 1929

Mar. *10*   Government in India begins the 'Meerut Conspiracy' trials, against 30
         alleged communist agents.
     30   Imperial Airways inaugurate a London to Karachi commercial air service.
Apr. *22*   First municipal airport opens: Chat Moss, Manchester.
May *30*   General election: Labour 287, Conservatives 262; Liberals 59; others 8.
Jun. *5*   MacDonald returns as Prime Minister of minority Labour government.
     8   Henderson becomes Foreign Secretary, with Philip Snowden as Chancellor of
         Exchequer; Margaret Bondfield, as Minister of Labour, is first woman to
         become a cabinet minister and Privy Councillor.
Aug. *4*   Jews clash with Arabs at the Wailing Wall, Jerusalem.
     23–26 British seek to restore order in Jerusalem following Arab attacks on Jews.
     24   Jewish settlement at Hebron raided by Arabs and destroyed.
Oct.   MacDonald visits USA for talks on naval disarmament.
     3   Anglo-Soviet diplomatic contacts resumed.
     28   Sharp fall in share values on Stock Exchange following start of Wall Street
         'crash' on 24 Oct.
     31   The Viceroy, Lord Irwin (later Lord Halifax), promises India dominion
         status; fails to satisfy independence demands of Congress Party, under
         leadership of Mohandas Gandhi.
Dec. *2*   GPO introduces first public telephone boxes: 22 red-painted boxes put into
         service in London.
     12   British occupation troops leave Wiesbaden headquarters.
     23   First meeting between the Viceroy and Gandhi.

FINE ARTS AND ARCHITECTURE
Charles Holden completes headquarters of London Transport Executive at
55 Broadway, Westminster; externally it carries Epstein's *Night and Day*
together with figures by Eric Gill and Henry Moore.
Jul.   Exhibition of D.H. Lawrence's paintings; 13 seized as obscene.

LITERATURE AND SCHOLARSHIP
R. Graves publishes *Goodbye to All That*.
T.E. Lawrence completes *Revolt in the Desert*, abridged version of *Seven
Pillars of Wisdom*.
V. Woolf writes *A Room of One's Own*, essay in feminism.
Charles Morgan publishes *Portrait in a Mirror*.
J.B. Priestley's first novel *The Good Companions* published.

Barry Jackson founds the Malvern Festival; opens with first production of G.B. Shaw's *The Apple Cart*.

Sep. 12 N. Coward's *Bitter Sweet* performed at Haymarket.

RELIGION AND EDUCATION
The Scottish Presbyterian churches unite, forming the Church of Scotland.

SCIENCE AND INVENTION
Sep. 7 First Schneider Trophy Air Race, above the Solent, tests new aircraft designs; won by Supermarine Rolls-Royce S6 seaplane.

Oct. 14 World's biggest airship, R101, makes flight over London while completing trials at Cardington, Bedfordshire.

Events Elsewhere

Feb. 11 Vatican City State created by Lateran Ty between Pope Pius XI and fascist Italy.

AD 1930

Jan. 21 MacDonald presides at opening of London Conference on Naval Disarmament; Britain, USA, France, Italy, Japan.

Mar. 12 Gandhi begins a peaceful civil disobedience campaign.

Apr. 6 Gandhi symbolically mocks the law by gathering salt illegally on the beach at Dandi.

22 Ty of London on naval disarmament: limitations on submarines and aircraft carriers.

Jun. 24 Simon Report on India published: recommends responsible government in the provinces and talks with Indian rulers on future of central government.

Oct. 1 Wei-hai-wei, leased by Britain in 1898, is restored to China.

2 Imperial Conference in London (to 14 Nov.): agrees on nature of dominion status, but Britain refuses preferential tariff to help Canada's wheat sales.

7 Airship R101 crashes near Beauvais on maiden flight to India, killing 44, including Air Minister, Lord Thomson.

20 Passfield White Paper on Palestine published: emphasizes plight of Arabs – land shortage, work shortage, fear of being swamped by a Jewish majority; recommends temporary ending of Jewish immigration.

Nov. 12 Round Table Conference on India opens in London.

FINE ARTS AND ARCHITECTURE
Painted dining-room with panels by Vanessa Bell and Duncan Grant, Penn-in-the-Rocks, Wythitham, Sussex.

LITERATURE AND SCHOLARSHIP
J.M. Keynes's *Treatise on Money* published.
Leonard Woolley publishes *Digging Up the Past*.
W.C. Sellar and R.J. Yeatman complete book of *1066 and All That*.
A. Christie publishes *Murder at the Vicarage*, first Miss Marple story.
E.M. Delafield writes *Diary of a Provincial Lady*.
J.B. Priestley publishes *Angel Pavement*.
Arthur Ransome writes *Swallows and Amazons*.
H. Walpole's *Rogue Herries* begins Herries chonicles.
E. Waugh publishes *Vile Bodies*.
V. Sackville-West publishes *The Edwardians*.
W.H. Auden publishes *Poems*.
T.S. Eliot publishes *Ash Wednesday*, poem.

MUSIC, ENTERTAINMENT AND DRAMA
BBC establishes a Symphony Orchestra, with Adrian Boult as director of music.
Alfred Hitchcock directs film *Murder*.

Sep. 24	N. Coward's *Private Lives* performed at Phoenix Theatre, London
Oct.	Camargo Society is founded, to encourage British ballet.

RECREATION AND FASHION
Youth Hostels Association established.

Feb. 1	*The Times* prints its first regular crossword.
Summer	Outstanding summer for Donald Bradman: on first visit to England he scores 974 runs in 5 Test matches, including 334 for Australia v. England at Headingley.
Aug.	British Empire games first held, Hamilton, Ontario.

VOYAGES, PIONEER FLIGHTS AND DISCOVERY

May 5	Amy Johnson takes off from Croydon in a Gipsy Moth biplane, seeking to become first woman to fly solo to Australia; reaches Darwin, 24 May; receives triumphant welcome when she returns to London, 4 Aug.

AD 1931

Jan. 10	Mrs Wallis Simpson is introduced to P. of Wales, Burrough Court, Leicestershire.
26	Gandhi released from detention for discussions with Viceroy.
28	Churchill resigns from shadow cabinet over India.
Mar. 4	Delhi Pact: after talks with Viceroy, Gandhi suspends civil disobedience and offers co-operation in the Round Table Conference; political prisoners released.

	10	Sir Oswald Mosley is expelled from Labour Party for seeking to form a new party.
Apr.	*14*	First Highway Code issued by Ministry of Transport.
Jul.	*31*	May Committee Report urges cuts in unemployment relief as budget deficit of £100 million is probable.
Aug.	*11*	Financial crisis in Austria and Germany leads to run on the pound as sterling loans have bolstered several central European economies.
	22–23	MacDonald's cabinet split over need for economy cuts.
	24	MacDonald resigns, but is persuaded to head a coalition National Government to seek means of financial confidence.
	26	Most of Labour Party refuses to support MacDonald and accepts Arthur Henderson as leader.
Sep.	*6*	Philip Snowden, as Chancellor of Exchequer, announces cuts in unemployment relief and in pay for all government employees.
	7	Second India Round Table Conference at St James's Palace (to 1 Dec.); under chairmanship of Sir Samuel Hoare, (later Lord Templewood), attended by Gandhi.
	15	Invergordon Mutiny: seamen in Atlantic fleet refuse to sail in protest at pay cuts.
	21	Snowden takes Britain off the gold standard; value of £1 falls from $4.86 to £3.49.
Oct.	*1–2*	Protest riots in Glasgow.
	27	General election: National Government (predominantly Conservative) 521; Labour 52; Liberals 33; others 5.
Nov.	*9*	MacDonald remains Prime Minister but reforms his cabinet; Baldwin is his deputy as Lord President of Council; N. Chamberlain, Chancellor of Exchequer; Sir John Simon, Foreign Secretary.
Dec.	*11*	Statute of Westminster: defines dominion status.

FINE ARTS AND ARCHITECTURE
E. Lutyens completes his masterpiece, the Viceroy's House, New Delhi.

LITERATURE AND SCHOLARSHIP
V. Woolf publishes *The Waves*.
V. Sackville-West publishes *All Passion Spent*.

MUSIC, ENTERTAINMENT AND DRAMA

Jan.	*6*	Lilian Baylis opens a rebuilt Sadler's Wells Theatre, London, with *Twelfth Night*, John Gielgud as Malvolio; Ninette de Valois introduces ballet there, 15 May.
Jul.	*5*	De Valois's *Job*, music by Vaughan Williams, presented for Camargo Society at Cambridge Theatre, London.
Oct.	*9*	William Walton's choral piece *Belshazzar's Feast* performed in Leeds.
	13	N. Coward's *Cavalcade* performed at Drury Lane.

RECREATION AND FASHION

May 23 Whipsnade Zoo opens; it becomes the great attraction of the year and causes much traffic chaos.

VOYAGES, PIONEER FLIGHTS AND DISCOVERY

Aug. 6 James Mollison flies from Australia to London in 8 days, 19 hrs, 28 mins.

Events Elsewhere

May 11 Failure of the Austrian bank Credit Anstalt leads to mass bankruptcies and unemployment in central Europe and Germany.

Sep. 18 'Manchurian Incident': Japanese troops occupy Manchuria.

AD 1932

Jan. 4 Indian National Congress declared illegal; Gandhi arrested.
Mar. 1 Import Duties Act: Britain returns to protective tariffs.
Apr. 6 Ministry of Health urges local councils to pursue vigorous policy of slum clearance.
19 Chamberlain's budget has low expenditure on defence.
20 Exchange Equalization Fund set up to prevent sudden fluctuations in value of sterling.
27 First airline service, London to Cape Town.
Jul. 21 Ottawa Imperial Economic Conference (to 20 Aug.): attended by Baldwin and N. Chamberlain; decides in favour of limited imperial preference in trade.
Sep. 28 National Liberal free-traders resign from government over moves towards imperial preference.
Oct. Sir Oswald Mosley founds British Union of Fascists.
4 Iraq ceases to be a British mandate.
25 Lansbury elected leader of Labour Party.
30 Series of violent clashes between police and unemployed marchers in London (to 1 Nov.).
Dec. 25 George V begins practice of royal Christmas broadcast.

FINE ARTS AND ARCHITECTURE

Val Myers and Watson Hart architect of Broadcasting House, London, with sculptured Prospero and Ariel by Eric Gill.
Owen Williams, Ellis and Clarke architect of black glass and chrome Daily Express building, Fleet St, London.
Wallis Gilbert and Partners architect of Hoover Factory, Western Avenue, Perivale.
Stanley Spencer paints *May Tree at Cookham*.

LITERATURE AND SCHOLARSHIP

John Galsworthy receives Nobel prize for literature.

John Strachey writes *The Coming Struggle for Power*.

Stella Gibbons publishes *Cold Comfort Farm*.

A. Huxley publishes *Brave New World*.

C. Morgan publishes *The Fountain*.

MUSIC, ENTERTAINMENT AND DRAMA

George Dyson completes choral work *The Canterbury Pilgrims*.

Alexander Korda founds London Film Productions and Denham Studios.

Mar. 15 First transmission from Broadcasting House: Henry Hall conducts his BBC Dance Orchestra.

Apr. 23 Shakespeare Memorial Theatre, Stratford-upon-Avon, opens; *Henry IV*, parts 1 and 2.

May J.B. Priestley's *Dangerous Corner* performed at Lyric Theatre, London.

Oct. Thomas Beecham founds London Philharmonic Orchestra.

Nov. 1 W. Somerset Maugham's *For Services Rendered* performed at Globe Theatre, London.

RECREATION AND FASHION

Jun. 17 Yorkshire score 555-1 against Essex at Leyton.

RELIGION AND EDUCATION

A unified Methodist Church in Great Britain is formally constituted.

SCIENCE AND INVENTION

John Cockcroft and Ernest Walton apply proton bombardment to disintegrate lithium.

Edgar Adrian and Sir Charles Sherrington share Nobel prize for medicine for their research on electrical impulses in the nervous system.

Frederick Bartlett writes *Remembering*, applied psychology.

Events Elsewhere

Mar. 19 Sydney Harbour Bridge, Australia, opened.

Feb.–Jul. Geneva Disarmament Conference.

AD 1933

Feb. 9 Oxford Union Society's debate against fighting 'for King and Country' attracts considerable press publicity.

Apr. 27 Trade agreement signed with Germany.

May 3 Act removing constitutional oath of allegiance to British Crown becomes law in Irish Free State.

Jun.	*12*	George V opens World Economic Conference of 64 countries, Kensington, London.
Jul.	*1*	London Passenger Transport Board created, unifying public services of metropolis.
	4	Gandhi arrested for ignoring court order confining him to Poona area.
	20	Rally in Hyde Park to protest at treatment of Jews in Germany.
	27	Economic Conference fails to agree on methods to check spread of trade barriers.
Aug.	*12*	Churchill's first speech warning of German rearmament.
	23	Gandhi released from prison because of physical weakness.
Oct.		Increasing difficulties for troops in mandated Palestine because of Jewish-Arab clashes.
Dec.	*21*	Newfoundland, a dominion since 1917, reverts to status of crown colony because of financial collapse of administration.

FINE ARTS AND ARCHITECTURE

Designs by Giles Gilbert Scott for Battersea Power Station approved; opens in 1937.
Herbert Read publishes *Art Now*.

LITERATURE AND SCHOLARSHIP

A.N. Whitehead publishes *Adventures and Ideas*.
Walter Greenwood's novel *Love on the Dole* published; later dramatised.
George Orwell writes *Down and Out in Paris and London*.
Helen Waddell publishes *Peter Abelard*.
H.G. Wells publishes *The Shape of Things to Come*.
V. Woolf publishes *Flush*.

MUSIC, ENTERTAINMENT AND DRAMA

A. Korda makes film *The Private Life of Henry VIII*, starring Charles Laughton.

| *Sep.* | | Gordon Daviot's *Richard of Bordeaux*, starring and produced by John Gielgud performed at New Theatre, London. |

RECREATION AND FASHION

National Playing Fields Association established.

| *Jan.* | *18* | Australian Board of Control telegraph to MCC protesting at 'body-line bowling' of English cricket team, captained by Douglas Jardine, in tour of Australia; series ultimately won 4-1 by England, 16 Feb. |

Events Elsewhere

| *Jan.* | *30* | Hitler becomes German Chancellor. |
| *Mar.* | *4* | Inauguration of President Franklin D. Roosevelt. |

AD 1934

Jan. 21	Mosley holds BUF rally in Birmingham, attended by 10,000 people.
Mar. 8	London Labour Party, led by Herbert Morrison, wins clear majority on LCC for first time.
25	Road Traffic Bill: proposes making driving tests compulsory and imposing speed limit of 30 m.p.h.
May 14	N. Chamberlain's Unemployment Act: creates Unemployment Assistance Board to administer aid throughout country at fixed national rate from January 1935.
Jun. 8	Massive rally by Mosley's BUF at Olympia, London.
22	Failing health makes MacDonald assign most of his responsibilities to Baldwin.
25	Bomb attempt on Gandhi's life at Poona.
Jul. 19	Baldwin announces new air defence programme, increasing RAF by 41 squadrons.
Sep. 26	The liner *Queen Mary* is launched at Clydebank; to keep unemployment down, work will start immediately on a sister-ship.
Oct. 23	Naval Disarmament Conference in London fails to reach agreement (to 19 Dec.).
Nov. 20	Government proposes special statutory relief for 'Depressed Areas'.
Dec. 21	Anglo-Irish coal-cattle pact: coal to be sent at beneficial price to Irish Free State and cattle imported.

FINE ARTS AND ARCHITECTURE
Charles Holden designs Arnos Grove underground station for London Transport.
Giles Gilbert Scott completes Cambridge University Library.
John Piper paints *Rye Harbour*.

LITERATURE AND SCHOLARSHIP
Arnold Toynbee writes *A Study in History*, first vols of his meta-historical synthesis of world civilization.
Robert Graves publishes *I, Claudius*.
Dorothy L. Sayers publishes *The Nine Tailors*.
Mortimer Wheeler begins excavating Maiden Castle, Dorset (to 1937).

MUSIC, ENTERTAINMENT AND DRAMA
John Christie founds Glyndebourne Festival of Opera.
Sep. 9   J.B. Priestley's *Eden End* performed at Duchess Theatre, London.

RECREATION AND FASHION

Jul. 7   British wins in both singles finals at Wimbledon: Dorothy Round; Fred
Perry.

Sep.   Jack Hobbs plays his last first-class cricket match.
Stanley Matthews is first capped for England at football.

Events Elsewhere

Jun. 30   Hitler's 'Night of the Long Knives': about 100 rivals or enemies within the
Nazi Party are killed.

AD 1935

Jan.   Imperial Airways and QANTAS inaugurate joint London to Australia
commercial flights.

13   Britain helps to police the Saar during plebiscite by which the Saarlanders
vote for reunion with Germany.

Feb. 28   Irish Free State bans sale or importation of contraceptives.

Mar. 4   Government publishes *Statement Relating to Defence*, White Paper
recognizing need for rearmament.

12   Road Traffic Act operative: speed limit of 30 m.p.h. imposed in built-up
areas.

Apr. 1   LCC establishes protected 'Green Belt' to check ribbon development.

11–14   Stresa Conference: Britain, France and Italy seek agreement on common
front against German rearmament.

May 6   Celebrations of George V's Silver Jubilee.

Jun. 7   Baldwin becomes Prime Minister when Ramsay MacDonald retires; Hoare is
Foreign Secretary, with Anthony Eden entering cabinet as Minister for
League of Nations Affairs.

18   Anglo-German Naval Ty signed: Germany to have navy of up to 35% size of
British.

26–27   Peace Ballot by the League of Nations Union: 90% of people favour
multilateral disarmament.

Oct. 19   Britain supports League of Nations in imposing sanctions on Italy for
invading Ethiopia (2 Oct.).

Aug. 2   India Act: proposes a federation, with 11 provincial assemblies having
considerable autonomy; Burma, Aden, Kuwait and other dependencies no
longer under Viceroy's authority; not operative until Apr. 1937.

Nov. 6   Prototype of Hawker Hurricane fighter begins trials.

15   General election: National Coalition 425 seats (Conservatives 385); Labour
154; Liberals 17; other opposition 9; majority of 245 for Baldwin government.

26   Clement Attlee elected to lead Labour Party.

Dec. 9   Cabinet approves a partition plan for Ethiopia arranged by Hoare and

French Foreign Minister, Laval.
18   Public anger at pact with Laval makes Hoare resign.
23   Eden becomes Foreign Secretary.

FINE ARTS AND ARCHITECTURE
J. Epstein sculpts *Ecce Homo*.

LITERATURE AND SCHOLARSHIP
Allen Lane founds Penguin Books Ltd to begin paperback revolution in publishing.
Christopher Isherwood publishes *Mr Norris Changes Trains*.

MUSIC, ENTERTAINMENT AND DRAMA
Emlyn Williams's *Night Must Fall* performed at Duchess Theatre, London.
May 2   Ivor Novello's *Glamorous Night* performed at Drury Lane.
Jun. 19   T.S. Eliot's *Murder in the Cathedral*, with Robert Speaight as Becket, performed at Chapter House, Canterbury Cathedral.
Nov. 26   Ballet *Le Baiser de la Fée* (chor. Frederick Ashton, music Stravinsky), at Sadler's Wells Theatre, London, gives first leading role to Margot Fonteyn.

SCIENCE AND INVENTION
LNER trains twice set world speed records: 108 m.p.h. on run to Newcastle, 5 Mar.; 112 m.p.h. by new 'Silver Link', 27 Sep.
Feb. 26   Robert Watson-Watt successfully carries out the first experiments with radar.
Apr.   'Cat's-eyes', self-cleaning and reflecting road studs, first used.
Dec.   Sir James Chadwick awarded Nobel prize for Physics for his work in confirming the existence of the neutron.

AD 1936

Jan. 20   George V dies at Sandringham; P. of Wales accedes as K. Edward VIII.
Mar. 5   First test flight of the Spitfire fighter, Eastleigh, Southampton.
Apr. 19   A wave of riots start in Palestine.
May   Victor Gollancz establishes the Left Book Club; choice of monthly books and an issue of *Left News*.
Jun. 21   Arabs ambush British army convoy between Jaffa and Haifa; RAF in action to clear a route for it.
Aug. 26   Anglo-Egyptian Ty: promises an end to British military presence in Egypt, except in Canal Zone.
Sep. 4   Edward VIII, cruising in the yacht *Nahlin*, is received by President Kemal Ataturk at Istanbul.
Oct. 5   Jarrow marchers set out for London; their unemployment protest is backed by their MP, Ellen Wilkinson.

11	'Battle of Cable Street': provocative march into Whitechapel by Mosley's BUF is halted by anti-fascists.
Nov. 10	Public Order Bill introduced into H. of Commons: bans political private armies and controls protest marches; enacted so as to become effective from 1 Jan. 1937.
16	Edward VIII tells Baldwin of his intention to marry Mrs Simpson when her divorce becomes absolute.
18–19	Edward VIII tours distressed areas of S. Wales.
30	Crystal Palace destroyed by fire.
Dec. 2	English press breaks its silence over Edward VIII's alleged matrimonial plans.
10	Edward VIII abdicates in favour of D. of York, who accedes as K. George VI.
11	Ex-King created D. of Windsor.

FINE ARTS AND ARCHITECTURE

Laura Knight paints *Spring in Cornwall* and *Ballet*.

LITERATURE AND SCHOLARSHIP

A.J. Ayer expounds logical positivism in *Language, Truth and Logic*.
A. Huxley publishes *Eyeless in Gaza*.
Dylan Thomas publishes *Twenty Five Poems*.

MUSIC, ENTERTAINMENT AND DRAMA

Terence Rattigan's play *French Without Tears* first performed.
GPO Film Unit's 24-minutes documentary *Night Mail* has music by Benjamin Britten to a 'film-poem' by W.H. Auden.
J. Arthur Rank, taking over Gaumont-British, develops a film-making campus at Pinewood, Bucks.

Nov. 2	BBC opens a regular television service, reaching only London and the Home Counties, from Alexandra Palace, London.

RECREATION AND FASHION

Jun.	William Butlin opens first holiday camp, Skegness, Lincs.

SCIENCE AND INVENTION

Oct. 13	Through trains link London and Paris overnight in 10 hrs, 55 mins using specially constructed Dover-Dunkirk ferries.
Dec.	Sir Henry Dale receives Nobel prize for physiology for his work on the transmission of nerve impulses.

VOYAGES, PIONEER FLIGHTS AND DISCOVERY

May 7	Amy Johnson (Mrs Mollison) reaches England from Cape Town: 3 days, 6 hrs, 25 mins.
Sep. 6	Beryl Markham is first woman to fly solo from England to America.

Events Elsewhere

Mar. 7 German troops occupy the demilitarized Rhineland.
Jul. 18 Spanish Civil War begins.
Aug. Nazis seek to exploit Olympic Games in Berlin.

AD 1937

Jan. 14 Communists and ILP in Britain seek United Front against fascism; Labour unresponsive.
Feb. 2 Naval building programme announced.
Apr. 1 Aden becomes a colony; Burma a 'Governor's province'.
May 12 Coronation of K. George VI.
14 Imperial Conference in London (to 15 Jun.): discusses defence.
28 Baldwin retires; N. Chamberlain becomes Prime Minister; Simon is chancellor of Exchequer.
Jun. 3 D. of Windsor weds Wallis Simpson, Château de Candé, Touraine.
Jul. 7 Peel Commission report proposes partition of Palestine between Arabs and Jews, with British retaining control of Jaffa and Jerusalem.
23 Matrimonial Causes Act: desertion and insanity, as well as adultery, are grounds for divorce.
Sep. 14 Nyon Conference: Eden proposes anti-submarine patrols to protect non-belligerent vessels off Spain.
27 British district commissioner in Galilee murdered by Palestinian terrorists.
Oct. 10 Mosley knocked unconscious at BUF rally in Liverpool.
11–23 Duke and Duchess of Windsor visit Nazi Germany and meet Hitler.
Nov. 17 Lord Halifax sent by Chamberlain to Germany for talks on treaty revision in central Europe.
Dec. 8 Attlee heads Labour delegation visiting British anti-Franco volunteers in the International Brigade at Mondejar.
10 Viscount Cecil of Chelwood receives Nobel peace prize for his work for League of Nations.
29 Constitution of Ireland Act effective: Irish Free State replaced by sovereign state of Eire, within Commonwealth but having no links with Crown.

FINE ARTS AND ARCHITECTURE
Euston Road Group of artists, encouraged by Sir William Coldstream, seek a more naturalistic realism in artistic expression.

LITERATURE AND SCHOLARSHIP
G. Orwell publishes *The Road to Wigan Pier*.
V. Sackvile-West publishes *Pepita*.

MUSIC, ENTERTAINMENT AND DRAMA

Herbert Wilcox directs film *Victoria the Great*, starring Anna Neagle and Anton Walbrook.

A. Korda directs film *Elephant Boy*.

Comedy film *Oh Mr Porter* stars Will Hay.

May 12 W. Walton's march *Crown Imperial* performed for coronation.

Jun. 15 Ballet *Checkmate* (chor. N. de Valois, music A. Bliss) presented by Sadler's Wells company on visit to Paris; presented in London, 15 Oct.

Sep. 26 J.B. Priestley's *Time and the Conways* performed at Duchess Theatre, London.

Dec. 16 Lupino Lane, in the musical play *Me and My Girl* at Victoria Palace, London, creates the dance The Lambeth Walk.

SCIENCE AND INVENTION

Apr. Frank Whittle shows effectiveness of jet engine, in demonstration on the ground.

Dec. George Paget Thomson is a Nobel laureate in physics for his work on electron diffraction.

VOYAGES, PIONEER FLIGHTS AND DISCOVERY

Oct. 24 Jean Batten flies from London to Australia in 5 days, 18 hrs.

Events Elsewhere

Apr. 27 Bombing of Guernica inspires Picasso's masterpiece of protest.

Jul. 7 Japan invades China.

AD 1938

Jan. 4 Peel Report on Palestine shelved; new report sought.

Feb. 20 Eden, critical of Chamberlain's policy towards Italy, resigns as Foreign Secretary; succeeded by Halifax, 25 Feb.

Mar. 14 Warning by Churchill in H. of Commons of Hitler's aggressive plans, following German absorption of Austria.

Apr. 16 Anglo-Italian Ty: Britain recognizes K. of Italy as Emperor of Ethiopia; Italy agrees to withdraw troops from Spain.

25 Anglo-Irish treaty settles trade and financial questions; deprives Royal Navy of Irish bases.

May 3 George VI opens British Empire Exhibition, Bellahouston Park, Glasgow.

22 Britain warns Germany not to attack Czechoslovakia.

Aug. 3 Walter Runciman reaches Prague at head of mission to mediate between Czechs and Sudeten Germans.

Sep. 15 Chamberlain visits Hitler at Berchtesgaden.

16 Runciman recommends transfer to Germany of Sudetenland.

18	Britain and France urge Czechs to transfer Sudeten areas where more than 50% of population is German.
22	Hitler receives Chamberlain at Godesberg; demands immediate cession of all Sudetenland.
27	Royal Navy mobilized.
	Liner *Queen Elizabeth* is launched by the Queen at Clydeside; first ship over 80,000 tons displacement.
28–30	Munich Conference of Chamberlain, Hitler, Mussolini and Daladier (France): Czechoslovakia to be deprived of disputed areas.
Oct. 1	A. Duff Cooper resigns as First Lord of Admiralty in protest at Chamberlain's appeasement.
	Picture Post goes on sale.
19	Woodhead Report on Palestine offers more detailed partition plans than in Peel Report.

FINE ARTS AND ARCHITECTURE

Norwich City Hall completed, designed by C. James and R. Pierce.

LITERATURE AND SCHOLARSHIP

Elizabeth Bowen publishes *The Death of the Heart*.
Graham Greene publishes *Brighton Rock*.

MUSIC, ENTERTAINMENT AND DRAMA

Sep. 21	Emlyn Williams's *The Corn is Green* performed at Duchess Theatre, London.
Oct. 11	J.B. Priestley's *When We Are Married* performed at St Martin's Theatre, London.
	Anthony Asquith directs film *Pygmalion*.
	A. Hitchcock directs film *The Lady Vanishes*.

RECREATION AND FASHION

Jun. 24	Test Match cricket televised for first time from Lords.
Aug. 23	Leonard Hutton scores 364 in fifth Test against Australia at the Oval, where England declare at 903-7 and eventually win by an innings and 579 runs.

SCIENCE AND INVENTION

Jun. 8	Manufacture of Bren-guns begins at Enfield under licence from Brno arms works, Czechoslovakia.
Jul. 3	LNER's newly constructed Mallard engine establishes definitive speed record for steam traction, reaching 125 m.p.h. between Grantham and Peterborough.

Events Elsewhere

Mar. 11	German troops enter Austria; *Anschluss* (union of Germany and Austria) proclaimed, 13 Mar.

| Oct. | 1–10 | German troops enter Sudetenland. |
| Nov. | 2 | First Vienna Award transfers to Hungary the Felvidek region, in S. Slovakia and Ruthenia. |

AD 1939

Jan.	10–11	Chamberlain and Halifax visit Mussolini in Rome.
	16	IRA bombing campaign begins in England: London, Alnwick, Birmingham, Manchester.
Feb.	7	Round Table Conference on Palestine in London (to 17 Mar.).
	27	Britain recognizes Franco's government in Spain.
Mar.	31	Britain (and France) give pledge of support to Poland.
Apr.	13	Anglo-French guarantees to Romania and Greece.
	29	Conscription reintroduced; 6 months' service for men aged 20.
May	17	George VI makes first royal visit to Canada and USA (to 15 Jun.).
Aug.	5	Imperial Airways begin weekly transatlantic flights; suspended, 9 Sep.
	23	Chamberlain warns Hitler that Britain will support Poland in case of attack. London's Civil Defence is put on round-the-clock vigil.
	24	Emergency Powers (Defence) Act: gives full authority of the law to 'defence regulations' issued by government.
	25	IRA bomb in Coventry kills 5 people; 50 injured.
	31	Evacuation of schoolchildren from London begins.
Sep.	1	Britain demands that Hitler halts his invasion of Poland. Blackout imposed throughout Britain.
	2	Eire announces intention to observe strict neutrality.
	3	Britain declares war on Germany at 11 a.m. Churchill returns to cabinet as First Lord of Admiralty. Liner *Athenia* torpedoed by U-boat off the Hebrides at 9 p.m.
	8	Convoy system for all merchant shipping.
	9	British Expeditionary Force begins crossing to France.
	24	Petrol rationing introduced.
	30	Identity cards follow national registration of all people.
Oct.	14	U-boat penetrates Scapa Flow defences; sinks HMS *Royal Oak*.
	16	German planes drop bombs near Rosyth, Scotland.
Nov.	11–18	Magnetic mines sink 50,000 tons of coastal shipping.
	14	To discourage misuse, petrol raised to 1s 9d a gallon.
	23	HMS *Rawalpindi* (converted P. & O. liner) sunk when preventing *Scharnhorst* and *Gneisenau* raiding Atlantic trade routes.
Dec.	13	Cruisers *Exeter*, *Ajax* and *Achilles* engage battleship *Graf Spee* off R. Plate estuary; *Graf Spee* scuttled, 17 Dec.

Burial ship excavated, Sutton Hoo, Suffolk (*v* 621-630).
G. Greene publishes *The Confidential Agent*.
Christopher Isherwood publishes *Goodbye to Berlin*.
Louis Macniece publishes poems *Autumn Journal*.

MUSIC, ENTERTAINMENT AND DRAMA

Mar. 21   T.S. Eliot's *The Family Reunion* performed at Westminster Theatre, London.

27   Ivor Novello's *The Dancing Years* performed at Drury Lane, London.

Sep. 2   All London places of entertainment close in anticipation of heavy bombing; reopen, 14 Sep.

19   BBC radio series *ITMA (It's That Man Again)*, featuring Tommy Handley, gains rapid and lasting popularity.

Oct.   The outstanding Mozart pianist Myra Hess organizes popular lunch-time concerts at National Gallery, London.

SCIENCE AND INVENTION

The cavity magnetron, a thermiotic valve generating microwaves, perfected by John Randall and Henry Boot.

Feb.   'Automatic washing tub' on show at British Industries Fair.

Events Elsewhere

Mar. 16   Germany annexes Bohemia and Moravia.

Apr. 7   Italy annexes Albania.

Aug. 23   Nazi-Soviet Pact.

Sep. 27   Warsaw capitulates to the Germans.

Nov. 30   USSR attacks Finland.

AD 1940

Jan. 8   Rationing of bacon, butter and sugar introduced.

Feb. 16   HMS *Cossack* intercepts German vessel *Altmark* off Bergen and rescues 144 British seamen held captive.

Apr. 15   British units fighting in S. Norway (to 2 May); in response to surprise German invasion (9 Apr.).

May 10   BEF crosses into Belgium to repel German invasion.
Chamberlain resigns; Churchill heads a coalition ministry, with Attlee as Lord Privy Seal.

14   Local Defence Volunteers raised ('Home Guard' from 23 Jul.).

May 27   Dunkirk evacuation begins of cut-off BEF and French troops in 860 vessels (to 3 Jun.).

31   Mosley and 33 fascist sympathizers interned.

Jun. 10   Italy declares war on Britain and France.

	10	Anglo-French force is withdrawn from Narvik, N. Norway, after 8-week campaign.
	18	Churchill declares that Britain and dominions will remain in the war despite French request for separate armistice.
	30	German forces occupy demilitarized Channel Islands.
Jul.	*3*	Royal Navy bombards French naval base at Mers-el-Kebir, Oran, to prevent warships passing under German or Italian control.
Jul.	*10*	Battle of Britain (to 31 Oct.).
Aug.	*15*	Highest German air losses: 75 planes shot down; RAF loses 34.
	24	First bombs on central London.
	25	RAF raids Berlin for first time.
Sep.	*7*	Heavy bombing of London begins; continues for 57 nights.
	17	Hitler postpones invasion after heavy air losses (15 Sep.).
	27	177,000 people shelter from bombing in London's tube system.
Nov.	*3*	British establish base at Suda Bay, Crete, following Italy's invasion of Greece (28 Oct.).
	11	Italian fleet crippled by air attack on Taranto.
	14–15	Bombing devastates Coventry; 1,000 killed.
	18	USA agrees to transfer 50 old destroyers to Britain in return for leasing bases in West Indies.
	20	Birmingham heavily bombed.
	29–30	Long air-raids on Liverpool and Southampton.
Dec.		Heavy attacks on Bristol (2 Dec.), Manchester (22 Dec.) and City of London (29 Dec., with 8 Wren churches destroyed).
	9–15	General Wavell attacks Italians at Sidi Barrani.

FINE ARTS AND ARCHITECTURE
Augustus John Exhibition at Tate Gallery, London.

LITERATURE AND SCHOLARSHIP
G. Greene publishes *The Power and the Glory*.
C.P. Snow publishes *Strangers and Brothers*, first of 10 books centred on the character Lewis Eliot.
W.H. Auden publishes *Another Time*, poems.
C. Day-Lewis publishes *Poems in Wartime*.
T.S. Eliot's poem *East Coker* printed in *New English Weekly*.
A.J. Ayer publishes *Foundations of Empirical Knowledge*.

Dec. J.B. Priestley's *Postscripts* published, book of controversial radio talks broadcast each Sunday evening from 5 Jun. to 20 Oct.

MUSIC, ENTERTAINMENT AND DRAMA
ENSA (Entertainments National Service Association), with headquarters at Theatre Royal, Drury Lane, organizes a service of plays, revues, concert tours and ballets for allied servicemen and factory workers.

SCIENCE AND INVENTION
Practical use of penicillin developed by Howard Florey and Ernest Chain.

Events Elsewhere

Mar. 12   Finland makes peace with USSR.
Jul. 11   Marshal Pétain, at Vichy, becomes head of 'French State'.

AD 1941

Jan.–Nov. Indoor steel table shelters (Morrisons) distributed to 500,000 homes.
21   *Daily Worker* banned as defeatist (to Sep. 1942).
Feb. 6   Wavell's desert army occupies Benghazi, Libya.
Mar. 7   British invade Italian-held Ethiopia from Somaliland.
           British and Commonwealth troops land at Piraeus; help Greece resist
           German invasion from 6 Apr.
11   US Lend-Lease Act: allows President to provide equipment to nations whose
           defence is in America's interest; Britain benefits.
18–19   Over 500 killed in air-raids on Glasgow and Clydeside.
28   Ψ Cape Matapan: Mediterranean fleet, under Admiral Sir Andrew
           Cunningham sinks 5 Italian warships.
31   General Rommel, commanding German Afrika Korps and Italians in Libya,
           launches his first offensive in Cyrenaica.
Apr. 5   British enter Addis Ababa.
7–8   Overnight air-raid on Belfast; also 15-16 Apr., 4-5 May.
18–19   Heaviest air-raid of the year on London.
28   Commonwealth troops evacuate Peloponnese, for Crete.
May 2–8   'The May Week Raids': heavy bombing of Merseyside.
10   H. of Commons chamber destroyed in 550-bomber raid.
           Rudolf Hess, Hitler's deputy, lands by parachute near Glasgow.
20–22   2 nights' heavy bombing of Plymouth.
20–27   Crete falls to German airborne assault.
24   Battleship *Bismarck* sinks HMS *Hood* off Iceland.
27   *Bismarck* sunk off Brest.
Jun. 1   Clothes rationing introduced.
22   Churchill assures USSR of support on news of German invasion.
Aug. 11   Churchill and Roosevelt meet on warships off Newfoundland and sign
           Atlantic Charter.
25   Anglo-Soviet occupation of Iran to check Nazi infiltration.
Dec. 7   Japanese invade Hong Kong and Malaya on same day as attack on Pearl
           Harbour.
8   Britain and USA allied against Japan, Germany and Italy.
10   Japanese aircraft sink capital ships HMS *Prince of Wales* and *Repulse* off
           Malaya.

18   National Service (no. 2) Act: provides for conscription of unmarried women under 30.
22–28   Churchill confers in Washington and Ottawa.
25   Hong Kong surrenders to Japanese invaders.

FINE ARTS AND ARCHITECTURE
H. Moore makes crayon drawings of shelterers from the Blitz.
P. Nash paints air-war pictures, notably *Bombers over Berlin*.
S. Spencer begins painting his *Shipyards* series on R. Clyde.

LITERATURE AND SCHOLARSHIP
T.S. Eliot publishes *The Dry Salvages*, poem.
V. Woolf's *Between the Acts* published posthumously.

MUSIC, ENTERTAINMENT AND DRAMA
Films *The First of the Few* and *49th Parallel* both feature Leslie Howard.
Jul. 2   N. Coward's *Blithe Spirit* performed at Piccadilly Theatre, London.

RELIGION AND EDUCATION
C(live) S(taples) Lewis writes *The Problem of Pain*.
Jan. 7–10   Malvern Anglican Conference, chaired by Archbp William Temple, on Church and economic society.
May 10–11   'Sword of the Spirit' meetings, Kingsway, London; first ecumenical meetings on Church and world affairs, chaired by Cardinal Archbp of Westminster and Archbp of Canterbury.

SCIENCE AND INVENTION
Terylene developed as a synthetic polyester fabric.

AD 1942

Jan. 2   Joint pledge of no separate peace given by Britain, USA, USSR and 23 allies.
21   Rommel launches offensive in Libyan desert.
Feb. 9   Soap rationing begins.
11   German warships *Scharnhorst, Gneisenau* and *Prinz Eugen* evade attacks in dash up Channel from Brest to Wilhelmshaven.
15   Singapore surrenders to Japanese; 70,000 men taken prisoner.
19   Churchill strengthens war cabinet; Sir Stafford Cripps comes in as Lord Privy Seal.
Mar. 11   Cripps Mission to India, offering post-war self-government.
28   British commando raid destroys U-boat base at St Nazaire.
Apr. 15   Malta awarded the George Cross, after sustaining 1,000 air-raids in 4 months.

24	Exeter suffers first of the 'Baedeker' air-raids, ordered by Hitler to avenge bombing of German cities.
26	Further Baedeker raids on Bath, York, Exeter, Norwich, Canterbury (to 6 Jun.).
May 30	1,000 RAF bombers attack Cologne.
Jun. 20	Rommel captures Tobruk.
27	Convoy PQ17 sails from Iceland for N. Russia but 24 of its 35 ships are lost.
Jun. 30	Rommel's advance checked at El Alamein, 60 miles west of Alexandria (to 25 Jul.).
Aug. 6–7	Churchill, visiting Cairo, appoints General Harold Alexander as C.-in-C. Middle East, with General Bernard Montgomery commanding 8th Army.
12–15	Churchill in Moscow, conferring with Stalin.
19	Costly raid on Dieppe by Canadians and commandos; only 2,216 out of 7,000 combatants return to England.
24	George, D. of Kent killed in Scotland flying to Iceland.
Oct. 5	Oxford Committee for Famine Relief (Oxfam) founded.
23	Montgomery's 8th Army attacks Rommel at El Alamein; victorious, 4 Nov.
Nov. 13	British recapture Tobruk as Rommel retreats across Libya.
Dec. 1	Report on Social Insurance by Sir William Beveridge: advocates comprehensive scheme of welfare 'from the cradle to the grave'.

FINE ARTS AND ARCHITECTURE
John Piper paints *Windsor Castle*, water colours commissioned by Q. Elizabeth.
Graham Sutherland paints *Red Landscape*.

LITERATURE AND SCHOLARSHIP
E. Waugh publishes *Put Out More Flags*.
T.S. Eliot writes *Little Gidding*, last poem of his 'Four Quartets'.
Sidney Keyes publishes *The Iron Laurel*.
Alun Lewis publishes *Raider's Dawn*, poems.

MUSIC, ENTERTAINMENT AND DRAMA
| *Oct.* | Noel Coward's film *In Which We Serve* released. |

RELIGION AND EDUCATION
	C.S. Lewis writes *The Screwtape Letters*.
Apr. 23	William Temple, Archbp of York, is enthroned as Archbp of Canterbury; his influential *Christianity and the Social Order* is published.
May 31	George Bell, Bp of Chichester, on Church mission to Sweden, meets Dietrich Bonhoeffer and other German Lutheran dissidents at Sigtuna.

Events Elsewhere

| *Jun.* 3–7 | US naval-air victory at Midway Island ends Japanese expansion in Pacific. |
| *Sep.* 6 | German advance halted at Stalingrad, on lower Volga. |

| Nov. 7 | Allied troops, under Eisenhower's command, land in Algeria. |

AD 1943

Jan. 14–24	Churchill and Roosevelt confer at Casablanca.
23	Tripoli captured by 8th Army.
30	Churchill visits President Inönü of Turkey at Adana.
Feb. 18	In Commons debate on the Beveridge Report, Labour MPs accuse government of indifference to social welfare.
Mar. 3	183 people killed on steps of tube shelter at Bethnal Green, London, in panic rush at sound of new anti-aircraft rockets.
7–27	8th Army overcomes strong German resistance in Tunisia.
23	H. of Lords condemns Nazi persecution of the Jews; Viscount Samuel first uses the word 'holocaust'.
Apr. 8	Common Wealth, independent socialist party, wins by-election at Eddisbury, Cheshire, on pro-Beveridge platform.
May 7	Tunis captured; N. African campaign ends, 12 May.
16	RAF dambusters breach the Möhne and Eder dams, flooding huge areas of the industrialized Ruhr basin.
27–28	British officers parachuted into Yugoslavia to join Tito.
Jun. 1	Airliner from Lisbon to Eire shot down in Bay of Biscay; 13 civilians killed, including actor Leslie Howard.
Jul. 10	Allied invasion of Sicily, with 8th Army taking Syracuse.
Jul. 26	Thousands killed in RAF night bombing of Hamburg (to 3 Aug.).
Aug. 19–24	Quebec Conference: Churchill, Roosevelt and Mackenzie King (Canada) discuss invasion plans for Europe and Burma.
24	Admiral Lord Louis Mountbatten appointed Supreme Allied Commander SE Asia.
Sep. 3	8th Army lands in Calabria as Italy seeks armistice.
10	Admiral Cunningham receives surrender of Italian fleet at Malta. British and Americans land at Salerno.
Nov. 19	Mosley released from prison on health grounds.
22	Cairo Conference: Churchill, Roosevelt, Chiang Kai-shek meet.
28	Tehran Conference: Churchill, Roosevelt, Stalin meet (to 1 Dec.).
Dec. 2	Bevin, as Minister of Labour, announces ballot system by which some conscripts may be sent down the mines.
26	*Scharnhorst* sunk by HMS *Duke of York* and destroyers off N. Norway.

FINE ARTS AND ARCHITECTURE
H. Moore sculpts *Madonna and Child* for St Matthew's Church, Northampton.

LITERATURE AND SCHOLARSHIP

S. Keyes's *The Cruel Solstice*, poems, published posthumously.
Keith Douglas publishes his *Selected Poems*.
T.S. Eliot's *Four Quartets* published as a single volume.

MUSIC, ENTERTAINMENT AND DRAMA

Apr. 29 N. Coward season at Theatre Royal, Haymarket, alternates *Present Laughter* and *This Happy Breed*, both plays having been presented at Bristol, Sep. 1942.

RELIGION AND EDUCATION

Mar.–Apr. Archbp William Temple unsuccessfully seeks to force government to take immediate measures to give asylum to persecuted Jews.
C.E. Raven publishes *Science, Religion and the Future*.
Dorothy L. Sayers's *The Man Born to Be King*, BBC Sunday radio serial of the New Testament, causes controversy because of the representation of Christ as speaking in modern English.

SCIENCE AND INVENTION

Barnes Wallis perfects 'bouncing bomb' for dambusters.

Events Elsewhere

Jan. 31 German 6th Army, under General von Paulus, surrenders to the Russians at Stalingrad.
Jul. 25 Mussolini dismissed; rescued by Germans, 12 Sep.
Oct. 13 Italy declares war on Germany (but north of Naples is under German occupation).

AD 1944

Jan. 9 Common Wealth wins a second by-election, at Skipton, Yorks.
20 RAF drop 2,300 tons of bombs on Berlin.
22 British and allied troops land at Anzio.
Feb. 15 Monte Cassino monastery bombed by Americans as Commonwealth advance is halted by German mountain resistance.
19/26 Last heavy air-raids on London.
25 Indian troops of 14th Army, under General William Slim, defeat Japanese in the Arakan jungle.
Mar. 30–31 RAF loses 96 bombers in raid on Stuttgart area.
Apr. 5 Japanese defeated at Ψ Kohima on Indo-Burman frontier (to 3 Jun.).
Jun. 4 Americans, British and allies enter Rome.
6 D-Day allied landings in Normandy; British at Arromanches, Canadians Ouistreham.

	13	First V-1 (flying bomb) falls in Bow, London.
	22	Japanese defeated at Ψ Imphal, south of Kohima.
Jul.	*9*	British and Canadians take Caen.
Aug.	*9–20*	British and Canadians defeat German 7th Army at Falaise.
Sep.	*1–20*	Lull in flying-bomb attacks as advancing armies capture early sites in Pas-de-Calais.
	8	V-2 rocket bombardment of London begins, with missiles falling at Epping and Chiswick.
	13–16	Second Quebec Conference of Churchill and Roosevelt.
	17 24	Ψ Arnhem, follows airborne landings on lower Rhine.
	21	8th Army captures Rimini.
Oct.	*4*	British troops, landed in the Peloponnese, captures Patras; enables Athens to be liberated, 14 Oct.
	9–18	Churchill in Moscow to confer with Stalin and Molotov.
Nov.	*12*	RAF sink battleship *Tirpitz* in Tromsö fjord.
Dec.	*19*	Montgomery's 21 Army Group plugs gap in defences caused by surprise German counter-offensive in the Ardennes (to 9 Jan. 1945).
	24	Flying bombs aimed at Manchester kill 27 in Oldham.
	25	Churchill and Eden in Athens seeking to check spread of Greek Civil War.

LITERATURE AND SCHOLARSHIP
W. Somerset Maugham's novel *The Razor's Edge*, published.
G.M. Trevelyan publishes *English Social History*.

MUSIC, ENTERTAINMENT AND DRAMA
Laurence Olivier directs and stars in film *Henry V*.
Carol Reed directs *The Way Ahead*.
Old Vic company begins season at New Theatre with Olivier and Ralph Richardson in *Peer Gynt*, *Arms and the Man* and *Richard III*.

RELIGION AND EDUCATION

Feb.	*9*	In H. of Lords Bp Bell of Chichester denounces terror bombing of German cities.
May		Education Bill of R.A. Butler enacted: creates 3-tier system of free secondary state schools, differentiated by 11+ examination – grammar, technical and modern schools.
Oct.	*26*	Archbp Temple of Canterbury dies; succeeded by Geoffrey Fisher, Feb. 1945.

SCIENCE AND INVENTION
Artificial pre-fabricated harbours ('Mulberries') towed across English Channel for use in invasion of Normandy.

Aug.	*2*	PLUTO (Pipeline under the Ocean) becomes operational between Solent and Cherbourg.

Jun.	30	Bretton Woods Economic Conference (to 22 Jul.).
Jul.	20	Anti-Nazi putsch foiled by failure of attempt to kill Hitler.
Aug.	25	General de Gaulle enters liberated Paris.
Oct.	23	De Gaulle's administration is recognized as legitimate French government by the allies.

AD 1945

Jan.	2	Slim opens offensive by 14th Army across R. Irrawaddy, Burma.
Feb.	4–11	Churchill confers at Yalta with Stalin and Roosevelt.
	13–14	Heaviest V-2 rocket attack on London.
		Destruction of Dresden by British and American bombing.
Mar.	20	14th Army captures Mandalay after 12-day battle for the city.
	23–24	British make night crossing of R. Rhine and capture Wesel.
	27	Last V-2 rockets fall, on Bethnal Green and Orpington.
	29	Final air-raid warning (London's 1224th) from last flying-bomb attack.
Apr.	15	British troops deeply shocked on capturing the concentration camp at Belsen.
	29	German army in Italy surrenders to FM Alexander; effective from 2 May.
May	2	British troops enter Lübeck, reach the Baltic and make contact with the Red Army.
	3	14th Army captures Rangoon.
	5	FM Montgomery on Luneberg Heath accepts German surrender in N. Germany, Holland and Denmark.
	8	VE Day celebrations of the end of the war in Europe.
	12	German forces in Channel Islands formally surrender.
	23	Coalition government ends; Churchill forms a caretaker Conservative administration pending an election.
Jun.	15	Family Allowance Act: 5s a week for each child after the first.
	26	San Francisco Conference: Eden, as Foreign Secretary, signs UN Charter for Britain.
Jul.	5	Polling day in most constituencies; count not to be made for 3 weeks so as to allow for the vote of the armed services.
	17	Both Churchill and Attlee attend the Potsdam Conference.
	26	General election gives Labour majority of 146 seats.
	28	Attlee's cabinet has Bevin as Foreign Secretary; Morrison, Lord President of Council; Hugh Dalton, Chancellor of Exchequer; Aneurin Bevan, Minister of Health.
Aug.	15	VJ Day celebrated; Japan's capitulation marks end of war.
Sep.	12	Mountbatten receives surrender of half a million Japanese troops in liberated Singapore.

LITERATURE AND SCHOLARSHIP
A. Koestler publishes *The Yogi and the Commissar*.
Karl Popper publishes *The Open Society and its Enemies*.
Nancy Mitford publishes *The Pursuit of Love*.
G. Orwell publishes *Animal Farm*.
E. Waugh publishes *Brideshead Revisited*.

MUSIC, ENTERTAINMENT AND DRAMA
Film *Brief Encounter* directed by David Lean and starring Celia Johnson and Trevor Howard.

Jun. 7   B. Britten's opera *Peter Grimes* performed at Sadler's Wells Theatre, London.

RECREATION AND FASHION
May 19   Record crowds watch a series of unofficial 'Victory Tests' at Lords, Manchester and Sheffield (to 26 Aug.).

RELIGION AND EDUCATION
Dec.   Christian Action founded by Canon L. John Collins to support politically radical Christianity.

SCIENCE AND INVENTION
Dec.   Nobel prize for medicine shared by Fleming, Florey and Chain for their work on penicillin.

Events Elsewhere

Apr. 12   Sudden death of Franklin D. Roosevelt; succeeded as US President by Harry S. Truman.
Aug. 6   American aircraft drops atomic bomb on Hiroshima.

AD 1946

Jan. 10   First session of UN General Assembly opens, in London.
Feb. 7   World shortage leads to cuts in butter, margarine and cooking fat rations, from 8oz to 7oz a week.
  14   Nationalization of Bank of England effective.
Mar. 5   Churchill's 'Iron Curtain' speech at Fulton, Missouri: urges joint resistance by the West to the Soviet threat.
  22   Britain recognizes independence of former mandated territory of Transjordan, concluding alliance treaty with Emir Abdullah, proclaimed K. of Jordan on 25 May.
  29   Gold Coast granted a new constitution, making it first British colony in Africa to have a majority of Africans in the legislature.
  31   London Airport opens at Heathrow.

May	8	Ministry of Town and Country Planning to supervise building of up to 20 new towns.
	20	H. of Commons approves bill to nationalize coal industry.
	22	Repeal of 1927 Trade Disputes Act; civil service allowed to join TUC.
Jun.	7	Television service resumes for first time since 1939; some 11,500 viewers, all in SE England.
Jul.	21	Shortage of shipping and of wheat worldwide leads to bread and flour rationing.
	22	Jewish terrorists in Irgun Zvai Leumi blow up British GHQ in King David Hotel, Jerusalem; 91 lives lost.
Aug.	*15–16*	British armoured vehicles used to check communal violence between Muslims and Hindus in Calcutta; over 5,000 die.
Sep.	8	London communists encourage 300 homeless families in first 'squat', occupying empty homes in Kensington and Bloomsbury.
Nov.	6	National Health Service Bill enacted.
		Royal Commission reports in favour of equal pay for women.

LITERATURE AND SCHOLARSHIP

L.P. Hartley publishes *The Sixth Heaven*.
Bertraud Russell's *A History of Western Philosophy* published.
D. Thomas publishes *Death and Entrances*, poems.

MUSIC, ENTERTAINMENT AND DRAMA

Feb.	20	Gala reopening of the Royal Opera House, Covent Garden, with Margot Fonteyn and Robert Helpmann leading the Sadler's Wells Ballet in *The Sleeping Beauty*.
Apr.		Sir Barry Jackson reopens Memorial Theatre, Stratford-upon-Avon; Peter Brook produces *Love's Labour's Lost* with Paul Scofield as Don Armado.
	24	Sadlers Wells Ballet perform *Symphonic Variations* (chor. Ashton, music Franck) at Covent Garden.
	25	Christopher Fry's *A Phoenix Too Frequent* performed at Mercury Theatre, London.
May	23	Terence Rattigan's *The Winslow Boy* performed at Globe Theatre, London.
Jul.	12	B. Britten's chamber opera *Rape of Lucretia* performed at Glyndebourne.
Aug.	9	Royal charter incorporates the Arts Council of Great Britain.
Sep.	29	BBC Third Programme begins, with emphasis on culture.
Oct.		J.B. Priestley's *An Inspector Calls* performed at New Theatre, London.

RECREATION AND FASHION

May	4	First-class cricket returns to England; county championship starts 8 May.
Aug.	31	League football resumed for first time since 1939.

RELIGION AND EDUCATION

May	20	Supplementary grants for university students announced.
Nov.	3	Archbp Fisher of Canterbury, preaching at Cambridge, urges the growth of 'full communion' with other churches.

Events Elsewhere

Oct. 16   11 leading Nazis hanged for war crimes, Nuremberg.

AD 1947

Jan. 1   National Coal Board takes over running of mines.

13   Coldest weather since 1883 necessitates rationing of coal to industry and homes.

Feb. 10   Acute fuel crisis as severe cold continues (to 4 Mar.); all newspapers and magazines cut in size.

Mar. 6   Further blizzards cut off 15 towns and block over 300 roads.

11   Exchange Control Bill enacted: supervises movement of capital outside the country.

15   Worst flooding on record follows a general thaw.

23   Mountbatten appointed Viceroy of India, with instructions to negotiate early independence.

May 7   Conscription cut from 18 months to 12 months.

27   Cabinet accepts proposals to partition India, establishing a predominantly Muslim state on the east as well as the west.

Jun. 4   Mountbatten proposes Indian independence within 11 weeks, a year earlier than envisaged in February.

13   Bevin warmly supports European Recovery Programme, proposed (5 Jun.) by US Secretary of State George Marshall.

Jul. 2   Dominions Office renamed Commonwealth Relations Office.

18   Government of India Bill enacted: provides for independence.

31   Bodies of 2 British sergeants, kidnapped by Irgun terrorists, found hanging near Haifa, Palestine.

Aug. 1   Anti-Jewish demonstrations in Lancashire when news of soldiers' execution made public.

6   Attlee announces austerity measures because of financial exchange crisis.

15   India and Pakistan become independent.

Sep. 26   British Colonial Secretary informs UN Assembly of government intention of speedily surrendering Palestine mandate.

29   Stafford Cripps becomes Minister of Economic Affairs; Harold Wilson enters cabinet as President of Board of Trade.

Nov. 13   Cripps succeeds Hugh Dalton as Chancellor of Exchequer, after unintentional autumn budget leak to journalist.

20   P. Elizabeth marries Lt Philip Mountbatten in Westminster Abbey; he is created D. of Edinburgh.

R.B. McCallum and Alison Readman complete *The British General Election of 1945*, pioneering analytical study.
R. Graves publishes *The White Goddess*.
L.P. Hartley publishes *Eustace and Hilda*.
C.P. Snow publishes *The Light and the Dark*.

MUSIC, ENTERTAINMENT AND DRAMA
Main box office hits are American musicals: Irving Berlin, *Annie Get Your Gun*; Rogers and Hammerstein, *Oklahoma*.
Carol Reed directs film *Odd Man Out*.

Jun. 20	B. Britten's opera *Albert Herring* performed at Glyndebourne.
23	J.P. Priestley's *The Linden Tree* performed at Lyceum Theatre, Sheffield; performed later at Duchess Theatre, London.
Aug. 24	First Edinburgh Festival of the Arts opens.

RECREATION AND FASHION

Jun.	Christian Dior's 'New Look', coming to London at midsummer from Paris, brings a smart cut to women's dress after 8 years of austerity.

SCIENCE AND INVENTION

Aug. 15	Britain's first atomic pile comes into operation, at Harwell.
Dec.	Nobel prizes: Sir Edward Appleton, physics, properties of the ionosphere; Sir Robert Robinson, chemistry, structure of biologically active plant extracts.

AD 1948

Jan. 1	Nationalization of British Railways effective.
4	Burma becomes independent republic outside Commonwealth.
12	Britain's first supermarket opens: London Co-operative Society, Manor Park, E. London.
Feb. 4	Ceylon given dominion status.
May 14	British end mandate in Palestine.
Jun. 24	Britain co-operates with USA and France in establishing air lift to W. Berlin after USSR stops all road and rail traffic through E. Germany.
Jul. 5	National Health Service inaugurated.
25	End of bread rationing.
30	British Nationality Act becomes effective: all Commonwealth subjects to have status of British citizens.
	Representation of the People Act: abolishes plural voting; end of university seats.
	Gas industry nationalized.
Sep. 24	Political spokesmen from Britain's African colonies meet in conference in London.

Oct.	*27*	Attlee sets up the Lynskey Tribunal after allegations of corruption at Board of Trade.
	29	Publication of Iron and Steel Bill leads to prolonged campaign against nationalization by Opposition.
Nov.	*14*	Birth of George VI's first grandchild, P. Charles.
Dec.	*1*	Conscription increased from 12 to 18 months.

LITERATURE AND SCHOLARSHIP

G. Greene publishes *The Heart of the Matter*.

A. Huxley publishes *Ape and Essence*.

Harold Acton publishes *Memoirs of an Aesthete*.

T.S. Eliot publishes *Towards the Definition of Culture*.

R. Graves publishes *Collected Poems*.

Oct.	*4*	W.S. Churchill's *The Gathering Story*, first volume of his *The Second World War*, is published.
Dec.	*10*	T.S. Eliot receives Nobel prize for literature.

MUSIC, ENTERTAINMENT AND DRAMA

T. Rattigan's plays *Harlequinade* and *The Browning Version* performed in London.

Powell and Pressburger make ballet drama film *The Red Shoes*.

Apr.	*21*	Vaughan Williams's Symphony no. 6 performed.

RECREATION AND FASHION

Australian cricketers, led by Bradman, outstandingly successful; win 23 first-class matches and lose none; score record 721 runs v. Essex at Southend, 15 May.

Apr.	*14*	The austere XIIth Olympiad opens at Wembley, London.

RELIGION AND EDUCATION

Apr.		Ministry of Education proposes to introduce, in 1951, the General Certificate of Education, at ordinary and advanced levels.
Sep.		Pioneer comprehensives open at Potters Bar and Hillingdon, London.

SCIENCE AND INVENTION

Manchester University operates first stored programme computer.

Oct.		Compact Morris Minor and the Rover's 'Landrover' go on sale at the Motor Show.
Dec.		Nobel prize for physics awarded to Patrick Blackett for his work on cosmic rays and rock magnetism.

VOYAGES AND EXPLORATION

Wilfred Thesiger explores 'empty quarter' of Arabian desert.

Events Elsewhere

Jan. 20   Gandhi assassinated, Delhi.
Feb. 25   Communist coup in Prague.
Jun. 28   Breach between Stalin and Tito over Yugoslavia's increasing independence of USSR.

AD 1949

Jan. 25   Report of Lynskey Tribunal clears Board of Trade but criticizes junior minister, John Belcher, who resigns.
29   Britain recognizes State of Israel.
Mar. 15   End of clothes rationing.
Apr. 1   National Parks Bill enacted.
4   North Atlantic Ty, creating NATO, signed.
18   Republic of Eire formally established.
20   Frigate HMS *Amethyst* disabled by Chinese communist gunfire in R. Yangtze; 17 officers and ratings killed.
21   Commonwealth Prime Ministers meet in London, dropping 'British' from their official reports.
24   End of sweet rationing.
Jun. 7   Dock strikes force government to use troops to unload perishable food (to 25 Jun.).
Jul. 30–31   HMS *Amethyst* escapes from R. Yangtze, sailing at high speed down 120 miles of river to rejoin fleet.
Sep. 18   Pound devalued from $4.03 to $2.80.
Nov. 11   British troops launch major offensive against communist guerillas in Malayan jungle.
24   Iron and Steel Nationalization Bill enacted.
Dec. 16   Parliament Bill, cutting suspensive veto of H. of Lords to 1 year, given royal assent.

FINE ARTS AND ARCHITECTURE
Graham Sutherland paints portrait of Somerset Maugham.

LITERATURE AND SCHOLARSHIP
B. Russell delivers *Authority and the Individual*, first BBC Reith lectures.
G. Orwell completes *Nineteen Eighty Four*; published in Jun.
H.E. Bates publishes *The Jacaranda Tree*.
E. Bowen publishes *The Heat of the Day*.
N. Mitford publishes *Love in a Cold Climate*.
Revd W(ilbert) V(ere) Awdry begins long series of books for younger children with *Thomas the Tank Engine*.

MUSIC, ENTERTAINMENT AND DRAMA

Olivier's *Hamlet* (released 1948) is first British film to receive an Academy Award ('Oscar').

The Goon Show begins on radio.

Mar. 23   James Bridie's *Daphne Laureola* performed at Wyndham's Theatre, London.

May 11   C. Fry's *The Lady's Not for Burning*, with Richard Burton, John Gielgud and Pamela Brown, performed at Globe Theatre, London.

Jun. 14   Britten's opera *Let's Make an Opera!* (text Eric Crozier) has première at Aldeburgh Festival.

Jul. 9   B. Britten's *Spring Symphony*, innovatory song cycle, has première in Amsterdam.

Aug. 22   T.S. Eliot's play *The Cocktail Party* performed at Edinburgh Festival.

Sep. 29   Britten's marriage cantata *Amo Ergo Sum* performed for wedding of Lord Harewood and Marion Stein.

Arthur Bliss's opera *The Olympians* (libretto, J.B. Priestley) performed at Covent Garden.

Oct. 9   Major triumph by Sadler's Wells Ballet at Metropolitan Opera House, New York (to 6 Nov.); Fonteyn highly acclaimed.

RELIGION AND EDUCATION

University College of North Staffordshire founded at Keele.

SCIENCE AND INVENTION

Maiden flights of DH Comet, world's first jet airliner (27 Jul.), and Bristol Brabazon, world's largest passenger aircraft (4 Sep.).

Oct. 12   Scottish biologist Lord Boyd Orr awarded Nobel peace prize for his work on nutrition and famine relief.

Events Elsewhere

Oct. 1   Chinese Communist People's Republic proclaimed.

AD 1950

Feb. 23   General election cuts Labour majority to 5.

24   Hugh Gaitskell enters cabinet as Minister of Economic Affairs to assist Cripps, who is a sick man.

Mar. 1   Harwell scientist, Klaus Fuchs, imprisoned for passing atomic secrets to Soviet agents.

Apr. 19   London dock strike begins (to 1 May); troops called in.

May 26   Petrol rationing ends.

Jun. 27   Attlee pledges support for UN in resisting invasion (25 Jun.) of S. Korea by N. Korea.

Jul. 30   Attlee denounces communist attempts to infiltrate trade unions and paralyse

British industry.

31	J. Sainsbury opens purpose-built supermarket at Croydon, London.
Aug. 7	Government abandons costly project, begun in 1948, by which Overseas Food Corporation sponsored the growing of groundnuts in Tanganyika; plan much criticized by the Opposition since Nov. 1949; terrain too arid.
29	First 2 battalions of British troops reach Korea.
Sep. 6	British troops in action near Pusan.
9	Soap rationing ends.
15	Conscription increased from 18 months to 2 years.
Oct.	Legal aid becomes freely available to men and women of limited means.
19	Gaitskell appointed Chancellor of Exchequer when Cripps's health finally fails.
26	George VI opens restored chamber of H. of Commons.
Dec. 4	Attlee flies to Washington to urge Americans not to use nuclear weapons during Korean War.
25	Scottish Nationalists remove the 'Stone of Destiny' from the Coronation Chair in Westminster Abbey.

FINE ARTS AND ARCHITECTURE
A.J.P. Powell and J.H. Moya design 30-acre estate of flats and maisonettes for 6,500 people, Grosvenor Road, Westminster.

LITERATURE AND SCHOLARSHIP

Dec. 10	Nobel prize for literature awarded to Bertrand Russell.

MUSIC, ENTERTAINMENT AND DRAMA

Jan. 13	Carol Reed's film *The Third Man*, with Orson Welles, has London première (having already been shown at Cannes).
Nov. 14	Old Vic Theatre, Waterloo Road, London (bombed 19 May 1941) reopens with *Twelfth Night*.

RECREATION AND FASHION
West Indies win Test series in England for first time (3-1); victory by 326 runs at Lords (29 Jun.) is especially celebrated in the Caribbean, notably by the calypso 'Cricket, Lovely Cricket'.
Women accept nylon as the basic fabric for stockings, underwear and blouses; corduroy returns to favour for both men and women; men favour informal dress more extensively than before the war – single-breasted lounge suits, sports jackets and no hats.

SCIENCE AND INVENTION

Dec. 10	Professor Cecil Powell of Bristol University awarded Nobel prize for physics for tracking nuclear particles and (1947) discovering the pi-meson.

Events Elsewhere

May 1   First major anti-apartheid demonstration in Johannesburg; 18 killed.
Sep. 15–16   General MacArthur, commanding UN forces from 15 nations, launches counter-offensive against N. Korean invaders.
Nov. 27   China intervenes in Korea with 180,000 'volunteers'.

AD 1951

Jan. 26   Ration for carcass meat cut to 18d a week.
Feb. 15   Vesting day for the nationalized iron and steel industry.
Mar. 9   Bevin, on his 70th birthday, retires as Foreign Secretary; succeeded by H. Morrison.
Apr. 10   Gaitskell's budget imposes prescription charges for NHS dentures and spectacles to help pay for rearmament.
11   Stone of Destiny is discovered at Arbroath and returned to Westminster Abbey.
22   Bevan resigns as Minister of Labour because of prescription charges.
22–25   Ψ Imjin River: first battalion of Gloucestershire Regiment resists successive Chinese assaults.
23   Wilson resigns as President of Board of Trade, protesting at rearmament expenditure.
May 3   George VI opens Festival of Britain from steps of St Paul's Cathedral.
Jun. 7–8   Diplomats Guy Burgess and Donald Maclean defect to USSR while under suspicion of serving as Soviet agents.
19   Mounting tension with Iran over Prime Minister Mussadeq's threats against Anglo-Iranian Oil Company (to 2 Jul.).
Jul. 9   State of war with Germany formally declared at an end.
Sep. 23   Operation on George VI for lung cancer.
Oct. 6   British High Commissioner in Malaya, Sir Henry Gurney, assassinated by communists.
25   General election gives Conservatives majority of 17 seats, although with fewer votes than Labour.
27   Churchill becomes Prime Minister; Eden appointed Foreign Secretary; Butler is Chancellor of Exchequer.

FINE ARTS AND ARCHITECTURE

Robert Matthew designs Royal Festival Hall, Ralph Tubbs the Dome of Discovery.

G. Sutherland paints portrait of Lord Beaverbrook.

May 5   Opening of main Festival of Britain site on South Bank after general planning by Sir Gerald Barry in 27 acres west of Waterloo; architectural supervision by Hugh Casson.

Aug. 15   Basil Spence wins competition for design of a new Coventry Cathedral.

LITERATURE AND SCHOLARSHIP

Anthony Powell publishes *A Question of Upbringing*, first of his 12-book sequence called *A Dance to the Music of Time*.

Nicholas Monsarrat publishes *The Cruel Sea*.

C.P. Snow publishes *The Masters*.

MUSIC, ENTERTAINMENT AND DRAMA

Mar. 13   Ballet *Pineapple Poll* (chor. John Cranko, music Sullivan, arr. Mackerras) performed at Sadler's Wells Theatre, London.

Apr. 19   London stages first 'Miss World' contest at the Lyceum Theatre; won by Sweden.

26   Vaughan Williams's opera *Pilgrim's Progress* performed at Covent Garden.

May 3   Royal Festival Hall opened by George VI.

10–11   Laurence Olivier and Vivien Leigh begin season at St James's Theatre, London, alternating Shaw's *Caesar and Cleopatra* with Shakespeare's *Antony and Cleopatra*.

Jul. 13   Q. Elizabeth lays foundation stone of National Theatre on South Bank.

Dec. 1   B. Britten's opera *Billy Budd* performed at Covent Garden.

SCIENCE AND INVENTION

Mar. 1   Central Coventry becomes Britain's first smokeless zone.

May 28   Festival Exhibition of Industrial Power opens in Glasgow.

Sep. 14   Europe's largest oil refinery opens at Fawley, Southampton.

Dec. 10   Sir John Cockcroft shares Nobel prize for physics with Ernest Walton of Ireland for their atom-splitting experiments.

AD 1952

Jan. 15   General Sir Gerald Templer becomes High Commissioner in Malaya; begins an anti-insurgency campaign against communist guerillas, Mar.

24   British troops kill 41 Egyptians during nationalist rioting at Ismailia, in Suez Canal Zone.

29   Butler, as Chancellor of Exchequer, announces austerity programme; imports cut; NHS prescription charges raised.

Feb. 6	George VI dies in his sleep at Sandringham; Q. Elizabeth II learns of her accession while on royal tour in Kenya and arrives at Heathrow on following day.
21	Identity cards, obligatory since 1939, abolished.
26	Churchill announces that Britain has an atomic bomb.
Apr. 11	Elizabeth II confirms that she wishes her children and grandchildren to bear the name of Windsor.
May 7	Iain Macleod enters cabinet as Minister of Health.
Jun. 18	Proposals for a central African federation, centred on the Rhodesias, announced.
Aug. 16	Freak thunderstorms on Exmoor bring flooding and devastation to Lynmouth.
Oct. 3	British atomic bomb exploded in Monte Bello islands, off NW Australia.
5	Tea rationing ends.
8	Worst railway disaster in England: 112 people killed in triple train crash at Harrow.
20	State of emergency in Kenya over Mau Mau arson and killings.
22	Oil dispute leads Iran to cut diplomatic links with Britain.
Nov. 27	Conservatives introduce bill to denationalize iron and steel.
	Commonwealth Economic Conference in London.
Dec.	Smog in London held responsible for over 2,000 deaths.

LITERATURE AND SCHOLARSHIP

Kathleen Kenyon begins to excavate Jericho.
Michael Ventris deciphers the Cretan 'Linear B'.
Joyce Carey publishes *Prisoner of Grace*, first in his Chester Nimmo trilogy.
A. Powell publishes *A Buyer's Market*.
Barbara Pym publishes *Excellent Women*.
E. Waugh publishes *Men at Arms*.
Angus Wilson publishes *Hemlock and After*.

MUSIC, ENTERTAINMENT AND DRAMA

Apr.	Gielgud directs *Macbeth* at Stratford-upon-Avon, with Ralph Richardson.
Nov. 8	Maria Callas's London debut in *Norma*, at Covent Garden.
25	Agatha Christie's play *The Mousetrap* opens at Ambassadors Theatre, London.

SCIENCE AND INVENTION

Dec. 10	Biochemists Archer Martin and Richard Synge share Nobel prize for chemistry.

Events Elsewhere

Nov. 4	Electoral victory of Eisenhower gives USA first Republican administration since 1932.
6	First hydrogen bomb tested by USA, Enimetok atoll, Pacific.

AD 1953

Jan.	*31*	Heavy loss of life from flooding in Essex and East Anglia caused by gale and high tides.
Feb.	*4*	Sweet rationing ends.
	12	Ty of Cairo: ends Anglo-Egyptian condominium in the Sudan.
Mar.	*16–21*	Marshal Tito visits Britain.
Apr.	*8*	Tougher repressive measures imposed in Kenya; Jomo Kenyatta among 6 politicians jailed for 'managing' Mau Mau.
	17	Road transport denationalized.
	24	Churchill created a Knight of the Garter.
	30	London Conference: proposes a Caribbean Confederation.
Jun.	*2*	Coronation of Q. Elizabeth II.
Jul.	*13*	Steel industry denationalized.
Aug.		Myxomatosis spreads across Britain; millions of rabbits killed.
	24	All-party campaign for a Welsh Parliament is launched.
Sep.	*26*	End of sugar rationing (imposed 1940).
Oct.	*6*	Troops sent to British Guiana to prevent Marxist coup.
	23	Federation of Rhodesia and Nyasaland established.
Nov.	*16*	National Service Act: provides for conscription until 1958.
Dec.	*4*	Bermuda Conference: Churchill is host to President Eisenhower and Joseph Laniel (French Prime Minister).

FINE ARTS AND ARCHITECTURE
J. Epstein sculpts *Madonna and Child* for Convent of the Holy Child, Cavendish Square, London.

LITERATURE AND SCHOLARSHIP
J. Cary publishes *Except the Lord*.
Ian Fleming publishes *Casino Royale*, first James Bond novel.
L.P. Hartley publishes *The Go-Between*.
John Wain publishes *Hurry On Down*.
Churchill awarded Nobel prize for literature for his histories.

MUSIC, ENTERTAINMENT AND DRAMA

May	*4*	Sir T. Beecham produces Delius's 1892 opera *Irmelin* at Oxford.
Jun.	*2*	Ballet *Homage to the Queen* (chor. Ashton, music Arnold) performed at Covent Garden.
	8	B. Britten's opera *Gloriana* performed at Covent Garden.
Aug.	*25*	T.S. Eliot's *The Confidential Clerk* opens in Edinburgh.

May 29   Everest summit reached by Edmund Hillary and a Sherpa, Tenzing Norgay, in expedition led by Sir John Hunt.

Aug. 19   England, led by Hutton, beat Australia at the Oval to regain the Ashes after 20 years.

RELIGION AND EDUCATION

Revd. E. Chad Varah, at St Stephen's Walbrook, London, founds Samaritans to help people in despair; becomes national movement in early 1960s.

SCIENCE AND INVENTION

The Royal Observatory leaves Greenwich for Sussex because of increasing pollution in London skies.

Mar.   Cambridge molecular biologists Francis Crick and James Watson postulate the molecular structure of DNA (deoxyribonucleic acid), 'the code of life'.

Apr. 25   Further research papers on DNA published in the journal *Nature* by Rosalind Franklin, Maurice Wilkins and others.

Events Elsewhere

Mar. 5   Stalin dies; Khrushchev succeeds him as Communist Party secretary.

Jun. 18   Egypt becomes a republic with General Neguib as President and Colonel Nasser as his deputy.

AD 1954

Feb. 3   Elizabeth II, in landing at Sydney, is first reigning sovereign to visit Australia.

8   Successful British drive against communists in Malaya forces their leaders to flee to Indonesia.

Mar. 22   London's foreign exchange gold market (closed 1939) reopens.

Apr. 26   Eden joins foreign ministers of USA, France, USSR and China at Geneva for 3-month conference on Indo-China and Korea.

May 18   Post-war reopening of Liverpool's cotton exchange.

Jun. 29   Churchill in Washington to confer with President Eisenhower.

Jul. 2   Food rationing ends.

27   Royal Commission on Scotland advocates more power to Scottish Office and less English dominance of Scottish affairs.

30   Television Bill enacted: creates an Independent Broadcasting Authority for a commercial channel.

Aug. 5   Dispute with Iran over oil profits settled.

Sep. 8   Britain joins USA, Australia, New Zealand, Pakistan and the Philippines in setting up SEATO.

Oct. 3   Eden presides over conference in London which agrees on W. Germany's admission to NATO.

14	Eden created Knight of the Garter.
18	Harold Macmillan, after 3 years as Minister of Housing, becomes Minister of Defence.
19	Anglo-Egyptian Suez Canal Ty signed: provides for withdrawal of British troops within 20 months.
Nov. 30	Churchill is first octogenarian Prime Minister since Gladstone.
Dec. 18	Anti-British riot at Limassol, Cyprus; demanding *Énosis* (union with Greece).

FINE ARTS AND ARCHITECTURE

John Bratby paints *Dustbin*.

G. Sutherland paints *Churchill*; later destroyed by Lady Churchill.

LITERATURE AND SCHOLARSHIP

Kingsley Amis publishes *Lucky Jim*.

William Golding publishes *Lord of the Flies*.

Iris Murdoch publishes *Under the Net*.

C.P. Snow publishes *The New Men*.

J.R.R. Tolkien publishes *The Fellowship of the Ring*, being part 1 of *The Lord of the Rings*.

John Betjeman publishes *A Few Late Chrysanthemums*, poems.

Prof. William Grimes excavates Temple of Mithras, Queen Victoria St, London.

MUSIC, ENTERTAINMENT AND DRAMA

Jan. 24	D. Thomas's dramatic poem *Under Milk Wood* is broadcast 11 weeks after the author's death.
Oct. 6	B. Britten's opera *The Turn of the Screw* (presented at Venice in September) has London première.
Dec. 3	W. Walton's opera *Troilus and Cressida* performed at Covent Garden.

RECREATION AND FASHION

Apr. 16	Stock-car race introduced into Britain at New Cross, London.
May 6	Roger Bannister runs first 4-minute mile (3mins, 59.4 secs), at Oxford.
30	Diane Leather is first woman to run a mile in under 5 minutes, at Birmingham.

RELIGION AND EDUCATION

Mar. 1	Dr Billy Graham opens his first evangelistic crusade in Britain, at Harringay Stadium, London; crusade lasts 3 months.

SCIENCE AND INVENTION

Feb. 12	British Medical Committee's report suggests links between smoking and lung cancer; findings treated cautiously by Ministry of Health.
Oct.	Mid-air destruction of DH Comet airliners off Italian coast (10 Jan., 8 Apr.) is traced at Farnborough to metal fatigue.

Events Elsewhere

Mar. 1 US hydrogen bomb tested at Bikini atoll.

May 7 French garrison at Dien Bien Phu surrenders to Vietminh.

AD 1955

Jan. 9/23 First ships bringing large influx of Jamaican immigrants reach Plymouth.

Feb. 2 Plans to modernize British roads by building motorways announced.

Apr. 5 Churchill resigns as Prime Minister; succeeded by Eden; Macmillan becomes Foreign Secretary.

May 6 Britain refers right of sovereignty over Falkland Islands to International Court; Argentina and Chile refuse to submit their claims.

15 Macmillan, in Vienna, signs the Austrian State Ty with plenipotentiaries from USSR, France and USA.

26 General election: Conservatives 345; Labour 277; Liberals 6; Sinn Fcin 2 (in prison).

29 Rail strike, together with print strike and dock strike (to 14 Jun.).

Jul. 13 Ruth Ellis hanged in Holloway prison for murdering a lover who ill-treated her; last woman executed in Britain.

18–23 Eden at summit conference in Geneva.

Aug. 13 IRA (inactive since 1939) raids army training camp at Arborsfield, Berks in search of weapons.

29 London Conference on future of Cyprus; ends in deadlock, 7 Sep.

Sep. 7 British commandos sent to Cyprus.

Nov. 26 State of emergency proclaimed in Cyprus.

Dec. 7 Attlee retires as leader of Labour Party.

14 Gaitskell defeats Bevan and Morrison in election to succeed Attlee.

20 Macmillan becomes Chancellor of Exchequer; John Selwyn Lloyd is Foreign Secretary.

FINE ARTS AND ARCHITECTURE
Italian artist Pietro Annigoni attracts record crowds to the RA Summer Exhibition with his portrait *HM The Queen*.
J. Bratby paints *Still Life with Chip Frier*.

LITERATURE AND SCHOLARSHIP
G. Greene publishes *The Quiet American*.
E. Waugh publishes *Officers and Gentlemen*.

MUSIC, ENTERTAINMENT AND DRAMA

Rock music, coming from USA in 1954, gains rapid popularity in Britain.

Jan. 27 Michael Tippett's opera *The Midsummer Marriage* performed at Covent Garden.

Aug. 9 Peter Hall directs first production of Samuel Beckett's *Waiting for Godot* at Arts Theatre, London.

Sep. 22 ITV presents first alternative programmes to BBC television, commercially sponsored.

RECREATION AND FASHION

Fashion for tight-fitting jeans for women spreads from America to Britain; among young men there is a reversion to an older style as 'Teddy Boys'.

Nov. 30 Floodlit international football comes to Wembley Stadium, London: England v. Spain.

RELIGION AND EDUCATION

University College of South-West becomes University of Exeter.
Duke of Edinburgh's Award Scheme instituted, to encourage initiative among young people.

SCIENCE AND INVENTION

Dorothy Hodgkin analyses the composition of vitamin B, helping treatment of pernicious anaemia.

Events Elsewhere

Dec. 1 Martin Luther King begins civil disobedience campaign for black rights in Montgomery, Alabama.

AD 1956

Feb. 1 Coldest day of the century in Britain.

13 Referendum in Malta favours integration within UK.

Mar. 2 General Sir John Glubb is dismissed from command of Jordan's Arab Legion after 17 years.

9 Archbp Makarios and other leaders of *Énosis* movement in Cyprus are deported to the Seychelles.

30 Anti-nuclear protesters make first march from research establishment at Aldermaston, Berks to London (to 2 Apr.).

Apr. 17 Premium bonds introduced in Macmillan's budget.

18–23 Soviet leaders, Bulganin and Khrushchev, visit Britain.

Jun. 13 Last British troops leave Suez Canal Zone.

Jul. 10 H. of Lords throws out bill to abolish the death penalty (passed by Commons, 28 Jun.).

	19	Britain refuses financial aid to help Egypt build Aswan Dam.
	26	Anger in London at Nasser's nationalization of Suez Canal.
Aug.	16	London Conference on Canal boycotted by Egypt; also 19 Sep.
Sep.	3	Abortive mission to Cairo of Australian Prime Minister Robert Menzies.
Oct.	16	Eden and Selwyn Lloyd visit Paris for talks with French over military action against Egypt.
	18	Newly formed Canal Users' Association meets in London.
	30	Following Israel's invasion of the Sinai peninsula on 29 Oct., Britain and France demand an Israeli-Egyptian ceasefire, which Nasser rejects.
	31	British and French bomb Egyptian airfields and bases.
Nov.	4	Mass demonstration in Trafalgar Square against Suez action.
	5	British airborne assault on Port Said.
	6	USA backs United Nations in condemning Anglo-French action; sudden fall in value of £ against $.
	7	Fighting along Canal halted under international pressure.
	15	British transfer captured positions to UN Emergency Force.
	23	Eden, in poor health, flies to Jamaica for 3-week rest cure; Butler acts as his deputy.
Dec.	5	British and French troops start to leave Port Said.
	12	IRA begins 5-year campaign of bombing along Ulster borders.
	17	Petrol rationed because of Middle East crisis.

LITERATURE AND SCHOLARSHIP

S. Beckett's *Malone Dies* published in French, 1951.

W. Golding publishes *Pincher Martin*.

A. Wilson publishes *Anglo-Saxon Attitudes*.

Colin Wilson writes *The Outsider*, study in alleged alienation of men of genius.

MUSIC, ENTERTAINMENT AND DRAMA

May	5	To mark 25th anniversary of Sadler's Wells Ballet the company presents *Birthday Offering* (chor., Ashton), a suite of dances, at Covent Garden.
	8	John Osborne's *Look Back in Anger* performed at Royal Court Theatre, London.
Oct.	3	First visit of a Soviet ballet company, the Bolshoi, to Britain: *Romeo and Juliet* at Covent Garden.
	31	Sadler's Wells Ballet receives charter of incorporation as the Royal Ballet.

RECREATION AND FASHION

Nov.	22	D. of Edinburgh, in Melbourne, opens XVIth Olympiad, first in the overseas Commonwealth.

SCIENCE AND INVENTION

Oct.	17	First large nuclear power station opens at Calder Hall.

Events Elsewhere

Feb. *14–20* Khrushchev denounces Stalinism at 20th Party Congress.
Oct. *23* Hungarian national uprising suppressed by Soviet military intervention in Budapest (to 4 Nov.).

AD 1957

Jan. *9* Eden resigns as Prime Minister.
10 Harold Macmillan becomes Prime Minister after Conservative elder statesmen, in informal discussions, reject R.A. Butler.
13 Cabinet changes: Butler becomes Home Secretary; Peter Thorneycroft, Chancellor of Exchequer.
Mar. *6* Ghana becomes first black African state in Commonwealth.
13 Jordan ends all military links with Britain.
Apr. *21–24* Macmillan meets President Eisenhower in Bermuda, seeking to improve Anglo-American relations after Suez Crisis.
Jul. *25* Macmillan, speaking at Bedford, declares that 'most of our people have never had it so good'.
Aug. *31* Independent Malay Federation; British rule in Malaya ends.
Sep. *4* Report of the Wolfenden Commission recommends legalization of homosexual acts between consenting adults.
Oct. *12–22* Elizabeth II visits Ottawa to open Parliament as Q. of Canada; subsequently visits USA.
22 Hugh Foot made Governor of Cyprus in attempt to end military emergency.
Dec. *5* H. of Lords votes in favour of accepting presence of women peers.

FINE ARTS AND ARCHITECTURE
Kenneth Clark publishes his study *The Nude*.
J. Epstein sculpts *Christ in Majesty* for Llandaff Cathedral.

LITERATURE AND SCHOLARSHIP
John Braine publishes *Room at the Top*.
Ivy Compton-Burnett publishes *A Father and His Fate*.
Muriel Spark publishes *The Comforters*.
Iris Murdoch publishes *The Sandcastle*.
V.S. Naipaul publishes *Things Fall Apart*.
E. Waugh publishes *The Ordeal of Gilbert Pinfold*.
Richard Hoggart's *The Uses of Literacy* studies the vitality of mass culture.
Journalists identify an ill-defined group of 'Angry Young Men' among dramatists and novelists, who are proud of their social alienation from 'the Establishment'.

Jan. 1 *The Prince of the Pagodas* (chor. Cranko, music B. Britten) performed at Covent Garden; first 3-act commissioned ballet score by British composer.

Apr. 10 John Osborne's *The Entertainer*, with Olivier in the title role as Archie Rice, performed at Royal Court Theatre, London.

David Lean directs film *The Bridge on the River Kwai*, with Alec Guinness.

RELIGION AND EDUCATION

Trevor Huddleston publishes *Naught For Your Comfort*, condemnation of apartheid by the former head of the Anglican Community of the Resurrection in S. Africa.

Chief Rabbi Israel Brodie presides over first conference of European rabbis.

SCIENCE AND INVENTION

Radio telescopes used at Jodrell Bank to track Sputnik and installed in Mullard Observatory, Cambridge.

VOYAGES AND EXPLORATION

Nov. 24 As a contribution to International Geophysical Year, Sir Vivian Fuchs sets out from Shackleton Base on first overland crossing of Antarctic.

Events Elsewhere

Mar. 25 Ty of Rome: creates 6-nation EEC, 'Common Market'.

Oct. 4 USSR launches Sputnik into outer space; circles globe in 95 minutes.

AD 1958

Jan. 6 Thorneycroft, Chancellor of Exchequer, and 2 Treasury ministers resign because Macmillan opposes spending cuts.

Feb. 17 CND (Campaign for Nuclear Disarmament), led by Bertrand Russell and Canon L. John Collins, is launched at Westminster.

Apr. 4 4,000 CND protesters complete march from Aldermaston to Trafalgar Square.

30 Royal assent to Life Peerages Act.

May 2 Anti-British unrest leads to state of emergency in Aden.

Jun. 1 Clean Air Act: bans emission of dark factory smoke.

9 Elizabeth II opens modernized Gatwick Airport.

Jul. 17 British troops in Jordan at K. Hussein's request following republican revolution in Iraq (to 2 Nov.).

24 10 men and 4 women made the first life peers.

26 P. Charles created P. of Wales.

Aug. 23/31 Racial violence at Nottingham and Notting Hill.

Oct. 6 Rent Act of June 1957 becomes effective: landlords freed from restraint on

level of rents charged.
21   First women sit in H. of Lords.
28   Queen's state opening of Parliament televised for first time.
31   British confer with Russians and Americans in Geneva on suspension of nuclear tests.

LITERATURE AND SCHOLARSHIP
Lawrence Durrell's novels *Balthazar* and *Mountolive* are added to the 'Alexandrine Quartet' begun by *Justine* in 1957.
G. Greene publishes *Our Man in Havana*.
I. Murdoch publishes *The Bell*.
Mary Renault publishes *The King Must Die*.
Alan Sillitoe publishes *Saturday Night and Sunday Morning*.
J. Wain publishes *The Contenders*.
T.H. White publishes *The Once and Future King*.
J. Betjeman publishes *Collected Poems*.
Roy Fuller publishes poems *Brutus's Orchard*.

MUSIC, ENTERTAINMENT AND DRAMA
Feb. 5   M. Tippett's Symphony no. 2 performed at Royal Festival Hall, London.
Mar. 27   Belgrade Theatre, Coventry, first built since the war, opens with musical version of *The Importance of Being Earnest*.
Apr. 2   R. Vaughan Williams's Symphony no. 9 in E minor has première at Royal Philharmonic Society concert, 4 months before composer's death.
30   London première of *My Fair Lady* at Drury Lane.
May 19   Harold Pinter's *The Birthday Party* performed at Lyric Theatre, Hammersmith.
Jun. 18   B. Britten's *Noye's Fludde* performed at Orford Parish Church, Suffolk.
Jul. 16   Peter Shaffer's *Five Finger Exercise* performed at Comedy Theatre, London.
Aug. 24   T.S. Eliot's *The Elder Statesman* performed at Edinburgh Festival.
Oct. 27   Ballet *Ondine* (chor. Ashton, music Henze), with Fonteyn, performed at Covent Garden.

RECREATION AND FASHION
May 3   Manchester United are finalists in FA Cup despite death of 8 players in Munich air crash (8 Feb.).

SCIENCE AND INVENTION
Sep. 6   Britain's Black Knight ballistic missile fired at Woomera.
Nov. 24   World's first large exhibition of electronic computers held at Earl's Court, London.

VOYAGES AND EXPLORATION
Mar. 2   Vivian Fuchs completes first land crossing of Antarctica: 2,200 miles in 99 days.

Dec. 21   De Gaulle elected first President of Fifth French Republic.

AD 1959

Feb. 19   Macmillan signs treaty with Greeks and Turks for an independent Cyprus within Commonwealth.

21   Macmillan and Selwyn Lloyd visit Moscow.

Mar. 30   20,000 attend CND rally in Trafalgar Square.

Apr. 30   Icelandic gunboat fires on Hull trawlers in 'Cod War' fishing grounds dispute.

Jun. 3   Singapore becomes self-governing state in Commonwealth.

16   H. of Commons debates killing at Hola Camp, Kenya, of 11 Mau Mau detainees (3 Mar.).

26   Elizabeth II, visiting Canada, is joined by President Eisenhower at St Lambert, Quebec, for joint opening of St Lawrence Seaway.

Jul. 29   Obscene Publications Act, sponsored as a private member's bill by Roy Jenkins, becomes law.

Oct. 8   General election increases Macmillan's majority: Conservatives 365; Labour 258; Liberals 6; Independents 1. Among the new MPs is Margaret Thatcher.

14   In cabinet changes, Iain Macleod becomes Colonial Secretary.

Nov. 2   Southern section of M1, Britain's first motorway, is opened.

5   Labour MP and Quaker Philip Noel-Baker awarded Nobel peace prize for championship of arms control.

10   State of emergency in Kenya ended.

20   Britain is founder-member of EFTA, 7-nation European Free Trade Association.

28   Gaitskell urges Labour Party to abandon Clause IV of its constitution, a commitment to public ownership of the means of production, distribution and exchange.

Dec. 1   Formal ending of state of emergency in Cyprus; followed by election of Archbp Makarios as first President, 14 Dec.

LITERATURE AND SCHOLARSHIP

C.P. Snow gives Rede lecture at Cambridge, 'The Two Cultures and the Scientific Revolution'.

Malcolm Bradbury publishes *Eating People is Wrong*.

W. Golding publishes *Free Fall*.

MUSIC, ENTERTAINMENT AND DRAMA

May 28   Bernard Miles opens his Mermaid Theatre, Puddle Dock, London, with the musical *Lock Up Your Daughters*.

Dec. 10   Crowther Report recommends raising school-leaving age to 16.

SCIENCE AND INVENTION

Jul. 17   Louis and Mary Leakey unearth skull of 'nutcracker man' (Zinjanthropus, *c.* 1¾ million years old) in Olduvai Gorge, N. Tanganyika.

25   First crossing of Channel by hovercraft (patented by Christopher Cockerell, 1954).

Aug.   Mini Minor cars, designed by Alec Issigonis for British Motor Corporation, go on sale at £500 taxed.

Events Elsewhere

Jan. 8   Fidel Castro triumphantly enters Havana as leader of Marxist revolution in Cuba.

AD 1960

Jan. 18   Kenya constitutional conference opens in London, but African delegates boycott it until 25 Jan.

Feb. 3   Macmillan, visiting Cape Town, delivers 'wind of change' speech to S. African Parliament.

8   Elizabeth II announces that her descendants shall carry the name Mountbatten-Windsor.

Mar. 21   50 demonstrators arrested outside South Africa House, Westminster, in anti-apartheid protest at death of 67 Africans shot by police at Sharpeville.

Apr. 18   Some 100,000 CND supporters demonstrate in Trafalgar Square after Aldermaston march.

May 16   Macmillan attends abortive summit conference in Paris, ruined by Russian shooting down of an American U-2 'spy plane'.

Jun. 29   H. of Commons rejects call to implement Wolfenden Report's recommendations on homosexuality by 213 to 99 votes.

Jul. 27   Selwyn Lloyd becomes Chancellor of Exchequer; Lord Home is the new Foreign Secretary.

Aug. 16   Cyprus becomes independent.

Sep. 22   Violent disturbances outside St Pancras town hall by tenants suffering from effect of 1958 Rent Act.

30   Bertrand Russell forms Committee of 100 within CND to take non-violent direct action.

Oct. 1   Nigeria becomes independent.

Nov. 3   Harold Wilson unsuccessfully challenges Gaitskell in election for Labour Party leadership.

10   Following death of Bevan (6 Jul.), George Brown is elected deputy leader of Labour Party.

Dec. 31	Conscription ends, with call-up of last men for National Service.

LITERATURE AND SCHOLARSHIP
Stan Barstow publishes *A Kind of Loving*.
Edna O'Brien publishes *The Country Girls*.
M. Spark publishes *The Ballad of Peckham Rye*.
John Betjeman writes autobiography in verse *Summoned by Bells*.

Nov. 2	Penguin Books are cleared in the High Court of publishing an obscene book, D.H. Lawrence's *Lady Chatterley's Lover*.

MUSIC, ENTERTAINMENT AND DRAMA
Royal Shakespeare Company founded, under direction of Peter Hall, to mount productions at Stratford-upon-Avon and Aldwych Theatre, London.

Jan. 28	Ballet *La Fille Mal Gardée* (new chor. Ashton), with Nadia Nerina and David Blair performed at Royal Opera House, Covent Garden.
Apr. 27	Harold Pinter's *The Caretaker* performed at Arts Theatre, London.
28	Olivier performs in E. Ionesco's *Rhinoceros* at Royal Court Theatre, London.
Jun.	Lionel Bart writes *Oliver!*, British musical.
Sep. 13	Keith Waterhouse and Willis Hall's *Billy Liar*, with Albert Finney, performed at Cambridge Theatre, London.

RELIGION AND EDUCATION
Foundation of Churchill College, Cambridge.

Dec. 2	Dr Fisher, in Rome, becomes first Archbp of Canterbury to meet Pope since Reformation.

SCIENCE AND INVENTION

Oct. 21	HMS *Dreadnought*, Britain's first nuclear submarine, launched by Elizabeth II.

Events Elsewhere

Jul. 21	In Ceylon Mrs Sirimavo Bandaranaike becomes world's first woman Prime Minister.
Nov. 9	John F. Kennedy (Dem.) wins US presidential election.

AD 1961

Mar. 7	Macleod's decolonization policy attacked in H. of Lords.
May 4	Anthony Wedgwood Benn, refusing to accept succession to viscountcy of Stansgate, doubles his majority at Bristol by-election; but he is refused admission to H. of Commons because he is a peer, 8 May.
8	George Blake given 42-year sentence for spying.
17	S. African Prime Minister Verwoerd, visiting London, announces that on 31

		May the Union will leave the Commonwealth and become an independent republic.
Jun.	19	Britain relinquishes protectorate over Kuwait (v. 1899).
Jul.	1	British troops and aircraft stationed in Kuwait at Emir's request to counter invasion threat from Iraq (to 19 Sep.).
	25	Anger among teachers and nurses at imposition of 'pay pause' on government employees as deflationary measure.
Aug.	10	Britain formally applies for EEC membership.
Sep.	12	Bertrand Russell OM, in his 90th year, imprisoned in Brixton for inciting breach of the peace at CND protest.
	17	Over 1,300 arrests at CND meeting in Trafalgar Square.
Nov.	8	First talks over Britain's entry into EEC begin in Brussels.
	16	Gaitskell denounces Commonwealth Immigrants Bill in H. of Commons as 'a plain anti-colour measure'.

LITERATURE AND SCHOLARSHIP

Arnold Toynbee publishes vol. 12 of *A Study of History*, begun in 1934.
R. Hughes publishes *The Fox in the Attic*.
I. Murdoch publishes *A Severed Head*.
V.S. Naipaul publishes *A House for Mr Biswas*.
B. Pym publishes *No Fond Return of Love*.
M. Spark publishes *The Prime of Miss Jean Brodie*.
E. Waugh publishes *Sword of Honour*.
A. Wilson publishes *The Old Men at the Zoo*.
James Mellaart begins excavating Çatal Hüyük, Anatolia.

MUSIC, ENTERTAINMENT AND DRAMA

Apr.		BBC radio drops *The Children's Hour* after 39 years of broadcasting.
Jun.	11	B. Britten's opera *A Midsummer Night's Dream* performed at Aldeburgh.
Aug.		*Beyond the Fringe*, irreverent satirical revue, performed at Edinburgh; later moves to London.

RECREATION AND FASHION

May	1	First betting shops open in Britain.
	6	Tottenham Hotspur, captained by Danny Blanchflower, becomes first club to win FA Cup and League Championship since Aston Villa (1897).
Jul.	8	Angela Mortimer defeats Christine Truman in ladies single final to become Britain's first Wimbledon tennis champion for 27 years.

RELIGION AND EDUCATION

Mar.	14	*New English Bible* (New Testament) published.
May	5	Elizabeth II received by Pope John XXII in the Vatican.
	17	Consecration of Guildford Cathedral.
Jun.	27	Bp Michael Ramsey enthroned as 100th Archbp of Canterbury.
Oct.		University of Sussex opens at Stanmer Park, nr Brighton; first campus-landscaped university in Britain.

Events Elsewhere

Aug. *13*   E. Germans begin erecting Berlin Wall.

AD 1962

Mar. *14*   Liberals gain surprise by-election victory at Orpington; Liberal majority of 7,855 replaces Conservative majority of 14,760.

Apr. *1*   Government 'pay pause' officially ends.

18   Commonwealth Immigration Bill enacted: removes, from 30 Jun., the principle of free entry for all Commonwealth citizens.

May *10*   Local elections show loss by Conservatives of 30 councils.

Jun. *2*   Macmillan visits President de Gaulle to discuss British entry to EEC; (also 15-16 Dec.)

Jul. *13*   Macmillan dismisses 7 of his 21 ministers: Lloyd replaced as Chancellor of Exchequer by Reginald Maudling.

Aug. *6*   Independence of Jamaica; followed by independence of Trinidad and Tobago, 31 Aug.; marks end of experimental West Indian Federation.

Sep. *10–19*   Commonwealth Prime Ministers Conference in London: considers implications of Britain's membership of EEC.

Oct. *9*   Uganda becomes independent within Commonwealth.

Dec. *2–7*   Numerous deaths caused by severe smog in London.

8–13   British troops sent from Singapore to quell rebellion in Brunei, Sarawak and N. Borneo.

9   Tanganyika becomes a republic within Commonwealth.

19   Macmillan-Kennedy conference in Nassau over British desire for an independent nuclear missile.

31   British Railways Board set up, headed by Dr Richard Beeching.

FINE ARTS AND ARCHITECTURE

The new Coventry Cathedral (architect Sir Basil Spence) displays G. Sutherland's *Christ in Majesty* as an altar tapestry, J. Piper's stained-glass designs in the baptistry window and J. Epstein's *St Michael and the Devil* at the entrance.

Britain's first open-stage theatre, designed by Philip Powell and Hidalgo Moya, is completed in 12 months at Chichester.

Queen's Gallery, Buckingham Palace, opens to the public to show royal art treasures.

LITERATURE AND SCHOLARSHIP

David Storey publishes *This Sporting Life*.

Anthony Burgess publishes *A Clockwork Orange*.

David Lean makes film *Lawrence of Arabia*, with Peter O'Toole in title role.

May 29 M. Tippett's opera *King Priam* performed in Coventry.

30 B. Britten's *War Requiem*, with poems of Wilfred Owen, performed in Coventry.

Jul. 3 First Chichester Theatre Festival, directed by Olivier, opens with Fletcher's *The Chances* and Chekhov's *Uncle Vanya*.

Aug. 9 Olivier appointed director of new National Theatre company.

Nov. 24 Weekly satirical revue *That Was The Week That Was* brings an anti-Establishment irreverence to BBC.

RECREATION AND FASHION

Amateur first-class cricket status is abolished; last Gentlemen v. Players match, contested at Lords since 1806, ends in a draw.

RELIGION AND EDUCATION

May 25 New Coventry Cathedral consecrated.

Oct. 11 3 Anglican representatives take part in Second Vatican Council (to Dec. 1965).

SCIENCE AND INVENTION

Jul. 11 Telstar beams live TV from USA to England.

Events Elsewhere

Oct. 22–28 Cuban Missile Crisis threatens a US-Soviet nuclear war.

AD 1963

Jan. 14 President de Gaulle vetoes British entry into EEC.

18 Sudden death of Hugh Gaitskell leaves Labour leadership in confusion.

Feb. 14 Harold Wilson elected Labour Party leader with George Brown as his deputy.

Mar. 22 'Profumo Scandal' (to 4 Jun.): media exaggerates importance of association between the War Minister, John Profumo, and a call-girl, Christine Keeler; scandal weakens government's standing.

27 Beeching Report, *The Reshaping of British Railways*, wishes to cut network by 25%, closing over 2,000 stations.

Jul. 1 Kim Philby named as third man in Burgess-Maclean spy cell of 1951.

31 Peerage Bill enacted: peers may renounce inherited titles.

Aug. 8 Glasgow to London Royal Mail express robbed of £2,500,000.

20 Tony Benn, having renounced peerage, is returned for Labour at Bristol South-East by-election without opposition from Conservative or Liberal parties.

Oct.	*10*	Macmillan's resignation, on health grounds, is announced.
	19	Lord Home succeeds Macmillan as Prime Minister; Butler becomes Foreign Secretary.
	23	Home renounces his peerage, becoming Sir Alec Douglas-Home.
Nov. 7		Douglas-Home wins Kinross and West Perthshire by-election.
Dec. *12*		Kenya gains independence within Commonwealth.

FINE ARTS AND ARCHITECTURE
Spread of high buildings in London, notably Hilton Hotel, Park Lane.

LITERATURE AND SCHOLARSHIP
A. Burgess publishes *Inside Mr Enderby*.
Ivy Compton-Burnett publishes *A God and His Gifts*.
Margaret Drabble publishes *A Summer Bird-Cage*.
John Le Carré publishes *The Spy Who Came in From the Cold*.
M. Spark publishes *The Girls of Slender Means*.
L. MacNeice publishes poems *The Burning Perch*.

MUSIC, ENTERTAINMENT AND DRAMA

Feb.		The Beatles make their first recording.
Oct.		Enthusiasm for the Beatles on their first appearance at London Palladium causes massive traffic jams.
	22	National Theatre Company gives its first performance, at Old Vic Theatre, London: Peter O'Toole as *Hamlet*, directed by Olivier.

RECREATION AND FASHION
First one-day knockout competition in cricket; Sussex win the Gillette Cup, 7 Sep.

RELIGION AND EDUCATION
University of East Anglia established at Norwich.
Anglican-Methodist Commission Report, *Conversations between the Church of England and the Methodist Church*, outlines programme for gradual union.

Mar.	John Robinson, Bp of Woolwich, publishes *Honest to God*, best-seller which simplifies modernist, demythologizing theology.
Oct. 23	Robbins Report on Higher Education recommends growth of technological colleges and foundation of 6 new universities.

Events Elsewhere

Nov. 22	President Kennedy assassinated in Dallas.

AD 1964

Feb. 6	Anglo-French agreement on need for Channel railway tunnel.
Mar. 30	Disturbances between rival gangs of young people, 'Mods' and 'Rockers', at several resorts, most seriously at Clacton.
Apr. 1	Unified Ministry of Defence created; the Admiralty, War Office and Air Ministry cease to exist.
13	Ian Smith becomes Prime Minister of S. Rhodesia; seeks independence and continued white supremacy.
Jul. 6	Nyasaland becomes independent as Malawi.
27	Retirement of Churchill as an MP after 64 years in Commons.
Sep. 4	Elizabeth II opens Forth Road Bridge, Europe's longest.
15	The *Sun* replaces the *Daily Herald* as a morning newspaper.
21	Malta becomes independent within Commonwealth.
Oct. 15	General election won by Labour: 317 Labour; 304 Conservatives; 9 Liberals.
16	Harold Wilson becomes Prime Minister; James Callaghan, Chancellor of Exchequer; Patrick Gordon Walker, Foreign Secretary, even though he was defeated in a racist campaign at Smethwick.
18	Welsh Office created as government department; James Griffiths becomes Welsh Secretary.
24	N. Rhodesia gains independence within Commonwealth as Zambia.
Dec. 17	All NHS prescription charges to be free from Feb. 1965.

FINE ARTS AND ARCHITECTURE
Sir Basil Spence completes buildings for University of Sussex.
Bull Ring complex, Birmingham, opens.
Eric Bedford's Post Office Tower (580ft high) completed in London; but not opened until Oct. 1965.

LITERATURE AND SCHOLARSHIP
W. Golding publishes *The Spire*.
C. Isherwood publishes *A Single Man*.
C.P. Snow publishes *The Corridors of Power*.
Philip Larkin publishes poems *The Whitsun Weddings*.

MUSIC, ENTERTAINMENT AND DRAMA

Feb.	National Theatre Company at the Old Vic, London, present *Othello*, with Olivier and Maggie Smith.
Apr. 21	BBC 2 television channel opens.
May	P. Shaffer's *The Royal Hunt of the Sun* performed at Chichester.

RELIGION AND EDUCATION
Universities of Lancaster and Essex established.

SCIENCE AND INVENTION
Leakeys find remains of Homo habilis (*c.* 2 million years old) at Olduvai Gorge.

Oct. Dorothy Hodgkin becomes first Englishwoman awarded a Nobel prize; recognition of her work on X-ray crystallography.

Events Elsewhere

Jul. 2 President Johnson signs Civil Rights Act.

Oct. 15 Khrushchev forced from office; Leonid Brezhnev leads Communist Party; Alexei Kosygin becomes Prime Minister.
China explodes an atomic bomb.

AD 1965

Jan. 14 First meeting of Prime Ministers of N. Ireland and S. Ireland since 1922, Belfast.

21 Gordon Walker fails to retain Leyton for Labour in a by-election.

22 Michael Stewart becomes Foreign Secretary.

30 State funeral of Sir Winston Churchill (died 24 Jan.).

Feb. 4 Confederation of British Industry (CBI) founded.

11 Government sets up Prices and Incomes Board.

Apr. 1 Greater London Council replaces London County Council, assuming responsibility for all Middlesex and metropolitan areas of Essex, Surrey and Kent.

19 150,000 CND demonstrators show hostility to USA over Vietnam.

May 13 Elizabeth II makes first royal visit to Germany since 1913.

Jun. 17 Commonwealth Prime Ministers' Conference in London: establishes a Commonwealth Secretariat.

Jul. 28 Douglas-Home is succeeded as Conservative leader by Edward Heath.

Aug. 5 Trade Disputes Act: gives new safeguards to trade unions against prosecution.
Devlin Committee proposes regular weekly employment for dockers, replacing casual 'call-on' system.

Sep. 30 Dame Elizabeth Lane becomes Britain's first woman High Court judge.

Oct. 25–30 Wilson visits Rhodesia for talks with Ian Smith.

Nov. 8 Murder (Abolition of the Death Penalty) Act becomes law.
Race Relations Act: prohibits public racial discrimination.

11 Unilateral declaration of independence in S. Rhodesia.

16 Southern Rhodesia Bill speedily enacted: gives government power to impose economic sanctions on the colony.

Dec. 8 Rent Act: gives greater security to tenants.

17 Britain imposes oil embargo on Rhodesia.

22 Roy Jenkins becomes Home Secretary.

LITERATURE AND SCHOLARSHIP
M. Spark publishes *The Mandelbaum Gate*.

MUSIC, ENTERTAINMENT AND DRAMA
Jun. 3   H. Pinter's *The Homecoming* performed by RSC, Aldwych Theatre, London.

Nov.   Mrs Mary Whitehouse founds National Viewers and Listeners Association to counter BBC and ITV 'bad taste'.

RECREATION AND FASHION
Miniskirts come to London in the autumn; men's dress is increasingly casual – few hats or ties, hair longer.

Feb. 6   Sir Stanley Matthews, first footballer to be knighted (Jan.), retires after helping Stoke beat Fulham 3-1 in his last First Division match.

RELIGION AND EDUCATION
Universities of Warwick and Kent established.

Post-graduate University College, Cambridge, founded; first for both sexes.

Jul. 12   Ministry of Education asks local authorities to submit plans for establishing comprehensive education within 12 months.

SCIENCE AND INVENTION
Sep. 21   British Petroleum strikes oil in North Sea, 40 miles off Grimsby.

Events Elsewhere

Silicon chip is developed in California.

Mar.   First US marines land in Vietnam.

AD 1966

Jan. 31   Britain bans all trade with Rhodesia.

Mar. 31   General election increases Labour majority to 97 overall: Labour 363; Conservatives 253; Liberals 12; others 2.

May 16   Seamen strike for higher wages and 40-hour week (to 1 Jul.).

26   Colony of British Guiana becomes Guyana, independent within Commonwealth.

Jun. 6   N. Ireland government seeks to curb activities of Ulster Protestant Volunteers, newly refounded by Revd. Ian Paisley, as sectarian rifts deepen.

29   First British credit card is introduced by Barclays Bank.

Jul. 14   Carmarthen by-election returns first Plaid Cymru MP, Gwynfor Evans.

18   Talks begin with Spain over future of Gibraltar.

20   Wilson announces 6-month freeze on prices, wages and salaries.

Aug. 4   Sir Edmund Compton appointed first British Ombudsman.

10   George Brown succeeds Michael Stewart as Foreign Secretary.

18	Tay Road Bridge opens, longest in Britain.
Sep. 5	Selective employment tax, imposed on service industries but not on manufacturing sector, becomes operative.
8	Severn Road Bridge opens.
30	Bechuanaland protectorate becomes Botswana republic.
Oct. 21	Aberfan disaster: coal tip slides down on mining village in S. Wales, killing 116 children and 28 adults.
22	Russian agent George Blake escapes from Wormwood Scrubs.
Nov. 30	Barbados becomes independent within Commonwealth.
Dec. 1–4	Abortive talks on Rhodesia's future between Wilson and Ian Smith aboard cruiser HMS *Tiger* at Gibraltar.

FINE ARTS AND ARCHITECTURE

St Catherine's College, Oxford, completed; planned by Danish architect Arne Jacobsen.

LITERATURE AND SCHOLARSHIP

Jean Rhys publishes *Wide Sargasso Sea*.
Paul Scott's *The Jewel in the Crown* begins his British India series 'The Raj Quartet'.

MUSIC, ENTERTAINMENT AND DRAMA

Joe Orton's play *Loot* performed in London.

RECREATION AND FASHION

Jul. 30 England's footballers, captained by Bobby Moore, defeat W. Germany 4-2 in extra time at Wembley to win the World Cup.
Carnaby Street in London's West End, and King's Road in Chelsea are world centres for wildly uninhibited clothes for young people of both sexes.

RELIGION AND EDUCATION

8 new universities created: Loughborough Univ. of Technology; Univ. of Aston in Birmingham; City Univ., London; Brunel Univ., Uxbridge; Univ. of Bath; Univ. of Bradford; Univ. of Surrey at Guildford; Herriott-Watt Univ., Edinburgh.

Mar. 24 Archbp Ramsey of Canterbury and Pope Paul VI in joint service at St Paul's Basilica, Rome; they call for 'serious dialogue' between their two Churches.

SCIENCE AND INVENTION

May–Dec. 4 finds by different companies of major natural gas fields in North Sea.

VOYAGES AND EXPLORATION

Aug. 27 Francis Chichester, in *Gipsy Moth IV*, sails solo from Plymouth to Sydney in 107 days.

Jan.–Sep.   Cultural Revolution in China at its height.

AD 1967

Jan. 15	Wilson and Brown travel to Rome for new talks on British entry to EEC.
18	Jeremy Thorpe becomes leader of Liberal Party.
Feb. 7	3 main British neo-fascist groups merge to form National Front.
22	Iron and Steel Nationalization Bill enacted.
Apr. 13	Conservatives gain control of Greater London Council.
May 11	Britain again applies to join EEC.
Jun. 8–9 *and*	
23–24	Riots in Hong Kong.
30	Official end to period of economic restraint introduced by wage freeze.
Jul. 14	Decimal Currency Act: provides for currency change by 1971.
27	Defence estimates indicate planned withdrawal of British forces east of Suez within 8 years.
28	Vesting day of new British Steel Corporation.
Aug. 21	Britain again withdrawing troops from Aden and Yemen, having lost 129 men in disturbances over 2 years.
Sep. 10	Referendum in Gibraltar: residents overwhelmingly prefer British sovereignty to Spanish.
Oct. 9	Road Safety Act: provides for penalties for drink-driving offences identified on a breathalyser.
27	Bill legalizing abortion is enacted.
Nov. 2	Scottish Nationalists win Hamilton by-election.
18	Pound is devalued against dollar from $2.80 to $2.40.
27	De Gaulle again vetoes British entry into EEC.
29	Last troops leave Aden; colony gains independence as People's Republic of South Yemen, 30 Nov.
Dec. 19	France again vetoes British application to join EEC.

FINE ARTS AND ARCHITECTURE
Liverpool's cylindrical Roman Catholic Metropolitan Cathedral of Christ the King (planned in 1960 by Sir Frederick Gibberd) is completed with a lantern tower whose windows are designed by John Piper and Patrick Reyntiens. Exhibition of surrealist figures painted by Francis Bacon; conveys a sense of anger.

LITERATURE AND SCHOLARSHIP
V.S. Naipaul publishes *The Mimic Men.*

MUSIC, ENTERTAINMENT AND DRAMA

Popular music still shaped by the Beatles, notably their album *Sergeant Pepper's Lonely Hearts Club Band*.

Apr. 11   National Theatre Company in Tom Stoppard's *Rosencrantz and Guildenstern Are Dead* at Old Vic Theatre, London.

Jul. 1   First coloured TV in Britain; service begins on BBC2.

RECREATION AND FASHION

Aug. 31   'Festival of the Flower Children', Woburn Abbey.

RELIGION AND EDUCATION

University of Salford established.

The 'United Church of Jesus Christ Apostolic', first specifically West Indian immigrant church, opens in Handsworth.

Apr.   National Evangelical Congress, Keele, Staffs.

May 14   Cathedral of Christ the King, Liverpool, consecrated.

VOYAGES AND EXPLORATION

May 28   Francis Chichester reaches Plymouth to complete his solo circumnavigation in *Gipsy Moth IV*, returning from Sydney in 119 days; he is knighted at Greenwich, 7 Jul.

Sep. 27   Liner *Queen Mary* completes her last transatlantic voyage.

Events Elsewhere

Jun. 5–10   Israel defeats Egypt in Six Day War.

AD 1968

Mar. 1   Commonwealth Immigration Act: limits influx of Kenyan Asians by creating voucher system for admission.

14   Rush to buy gold leads to closure of banks and Stock Exchange.

15   Brown resigns as Foreign Secretary; succeeded by Stewart.

17   Mass demonstration in London against US policy in Vietnam.

17–18   Western finance ministers agree on 2-tier system for price of gold to check mounting financial chaos.

Apr. 5   Department of Employment and Productivity set up, with Barbara Castle as Secretary of State.

20   Enoch Powell, speaking in Birmingham, advocates voluntary repatriation of Asians and West Indians to avert bloodshed in inner cities.

23   First decimal coins (5p and 10p) issued.

May 5   Extension of self-government in Gibraltar leads Spaniards to close land frontier.

Jun. 10   NHS prescription charges reintroduced.

Jul.	*10*	New Prices and Incomes Act: tightens control over wages.
Sep.	*16*	Mail differentiation: first- and second-class post created.
	27	France renews veto on British application to join EEC.
Oct.	*5*	Police clash with civil rights marchers in Londonderry; start of new 'Irish Troubles'.
	9	Student demonstrations at Queen's University, Belfast, lead to founding of 'People's Democracy' in which Bernadette Devlin is prominent.
	13	Abortive talks on Rhodesia between Wilson and Smith aboard HMS *Fearless*, Gibraltar.
Dec.	*8*	Royal Navy closes down base and dockyard at Singapore.

FINE ARTS AND ARCHITECTURE

May	*18*	Tower block municipal housing discredited when new high-rise flats at Ronan Point, Newham, collapse after gas explosion.
Jul.	*9*	Elizabeth II opens Hayward Gallery, South Bank, London.

MUSIC, ENTERTAINMENT AND DRAMA

Sep.	*26*	Theatres Act: abolishes dramatic censorship powers exercised by Lord Chamberlain for 400 years.
Oct.	*10*	Alan Bennett's *Beyond the Fringe* performed at Apollo Theatre, London.

RECREATION AND FASHION

First 'Open' Wimbledon tennis championships.

Sep.	*17*	S. African Prime Minister cancels proposed English cricket tour after Cape Coloured Worcestershire player Basil d'Oliveira is included in tour party.

RELIGION AND EDUCATION

Student unrest spreads to British universities from USA and France; protest demonstrations and growth of anarchic societies.

SCIENCE AND INVENTION

May	First British transplant operations at Cambridge and London.

VOYAGES AND EXPLORATION

Jul.	*4*	Alec Rose reaches Portsmouth to complete solo circumnavigation in 354 days.

Events Elsewhere

Apr.	*4*	Martin Luther King assassinated at Memphis, Tenn.
May	*2*	French students protest violently against De Gaulle's policies (to 12 Jun.).
Jun.	*5*	Senator Robert Kennedy fatally wounded in Los Angeles.
Aug.	*20*	Warsaw Pact armies intervene in Czechoslovakia to crush mounting liberalism of Alexander Dubĉek's government.

AD 1969

Jan.	*1*	Baron Constantine of Maraval and Nelson, West Indian cricketer and diplomat, becomes first black peer in H. of Lords.
	1–4	Protestants attack civil rights march from Belfast to Londonderry.
Apr.	*17*	Bernadette Devlin wins by-election as socialist republican Unity candidate at Mid-Ulster; at 21 she is youngest MP since Pitt in 1781.
	19	Riots in Belfast and Londonderry; Catholics erect barricades in Bogside district.
	21	British army units ordered to guard key positions in Ulster.
Jun.	*11*	Redcliffe-Maude Commission proposes radical changes in local government throughout England and Wales.
Jul.	*1*	Investiture of P. of Wales at Caernarvon Castle.
Aug.	*12–15*	3 days of street fighting in Londonderry.
	19	British army assumes responsibility for security and police in N. Ireland.
Oct.	*10*	Hunt Committee Report on Northern Ireland troubles leads to eventual disbandment of B-Special police and creation of Ulster Defence Regiment.
	14	50p piece becomes legal tender at value of 10s.
	22	Divorce Reform Act: makes the breakdown of a marriage adequate grounds for divorce.
Nov.	*25*	Electoral reform within N. Ireland so as to standardize local government franchise.
Dec.	*2*	EEC summit meeting agrees on British negotiations for entry within 6 months.
	16–18	H. of Commons and H. of Lords vote in favour of permanent abolition of death penalty.

FINE ARTS AND ARCHITECTURE

Nov.   Work begins on building National Theatre on London's South Bank; architect Sir Denys Lasdun.

LITERATURE AND SCHOLARSHIP

John Fowles publishes *The French Lieutenant's Woman*.
Irish Murdoch publishes *Bruno's Dream*.
Booker prize for fiction first awarded: won by P.H. Newby, *Something to Answer For*.

Dec.   Samuel Beckett receives Nobel prize for literature.

MUSIC, ENTERTAINMENT AND DRAMA

Aug. 29–31   3-day Isle of Wight Festival of Music attracts 150,000 pop fans.
Sep.   Colour TV is introduced on BBC1 and ITV channels.

RECREATION AND FASHION

In the autumn, women's hemlines are lower, 'maxis' replacing miniskirts.

Feb. London School of Economics closed for a month because of student protests.
Jul. 8 Methodist Conference votes in favour of union with Church of England, but Anglican Convocations give proposal insufficient backing for it to be accepted.

SCIENCE AND INVENTION

Apr. 9 British-built Concorde makes maiden flight; French version had flown on 2 Mar.

Events Elsewhere

Apr. 29 President de Gaulle resigns.
Jul. 21 US astronauts set foot on the moon.

AD 1970

Jan. 1 Legal age of majority and voting age reduced from 21 to 18.
   11 Split in IRA; militant majority become 'Provisionals'.
   30 Leading Conservatives meet at Selsdon Park Hotel, Croydon, to formulate free-market policies hostile to trade unionism.
Feb. 5 Public Order Act for Northern Ireland.
   27 Women's liberation movement uses informal conference at Ruskin College, Oxford, to formulate programme of equal pay and opportunities, with full social benefits.
Mar. 2 White Rhodesians proclaim an independent republic.
Apr. 21 Non-sectarian Alliance Party of moderates formed in Ulster.
May 29 Equal Pay Bill enacted.
Jun. 18 General election unexpectedly gives Conservatives overall majority of 30: Conservatives 330; Labour 287; Liberals 6; among 7 other members is Revd Ian Paisley, Democratic Unionist, North Antrim.
   19 Heath becomes Prime Minister, with Sir Alec Douglas-Home as Foreign Secretary.
   20 Margaret Thatcher attains cabinet rank as Secretary for Education and Science.
   29 Removal of all restrictions on sale of council houses.
      Third British request to join EEC.
Jul. 3 6 killed in Belfast riots.
   20 Sudden death of Chancellor of Exchequer, Iain Macleod; succeeded by Anthony Barber.
Aug. 21 Social Democratic and Labour Party (SDLP) formed in N. Ireland.
   23 Rubber bullets first used by army in Belfast.
Sep. 7–12 PLO hijacks and blows up 3 aircraft in Jordan to secure release of woman Palestinian terrorist held in London.

| 29 | Heath creates Central Policy Review Staff ('Think Tank'), headed by Lord Rothschild, to advise cabinet. |

LITERATURE AND SCHOLARSHIP
C.P. Snow publishes *Last Things*, final Lewis Eliot novel.

MUSIC, ENTERTAINMENT AND DRAMA
Andrew Lloyd Webber composes rock opera *Jesus Christ Superstar*, with lyrics by Tim Rice.

Apr.	Beatles partnership dissolves.
Jun. 15	Sir Laurence Olivier made a life peer; first actor ennobled.
Jul. 17	Uninhibited revue *Oh! Calcutta* devised by Kenneth Tynan, performed at Round House, Chalk Farm, London.

RECREATION AND FASHION

May 22	Under pressure from anti-apartheid groups, MCC cancels proposed cricket tour by S. Africans.

RELIGION AND EDUCATION

Jan.	First meeting of Anglican-Roman Catholic International Commission (ARCIC) at Windsor discusses eventual organic union.
Mar. 16	Complete *New English Bible* published; 1 million copies sold on first day.
Jun. 26	Methodist Conference approves appointment of women ministers.
30	Mrs Thatcher informs local education authorities that they may retain the 1944 Act structure of schools rather than go 'comprehensive'.
Oct. 15	Pope Paul VI canonizes 40 English and Welsh martyrs.
Nov.	A General Synod replaces the Church Assembly as deliberative body of Church of England.

VOYAGES AND EXPLORATION

Jun. 26	SS *Great Britain* arrives back in Bristol after 127 years, towed on a pontoon from the Falklands.

Events Elsewhere

Sep. 28	President Nasser of Egypt dies from heart attack; succeeded by Anwar Sadat.

AD 1971

Jan. 1	Divorce Reform Act of 1969 becomes operative.
2	Barrier collapses at Ibrox Park, Glasgow; 66 football fans are killed.
12	Anarchist group, the 'Angry Brigade', bombs home of Employment Secretary at Hadley Wood, Herts.
Feb. 5	First soldier killed on active service in Ulster.

15	Decimal coinage replaces shillings and pence.
Mar. 6	Women's liberation movement has 4,000 supporters in march from Hyde Park to Downing St.
Feb. 21	140,000 trade unionists protest at proposed Industrial Relations Bill.
May 20–21	Heath meets President Pompidou in Paris for EEC talks.
Jun. 10	Anglo-Maltese tension as Britain declines to pay rent required by Maltese Prime Minister for island bases.
15–29	Widespread protests at Margaret Thatcher's ruling to end free school milk in state schools.
Aug. 6	Industrial Relations Act: only registered unions enjoy legal protection; pre-strike ballots and cooling off periods required before stoppage; fines on members and unions who disobey.
9	Internment without trial imposed in N. Ireland.
Sep. 9	Parliament recalled from recess to discuss Irish problem.
27–28	Prime ministers of United Kingdom, Irish Republic and N. Ireland confer at Chequers.
Oct. 28	H. of Commons and H. of Lords vote in favour of joining EEC. Immigration Act: identical controls for foreign and Commonwealth nationals, but free entry for those whose parents or grandparents were born in UK.
Dec. 7	Colonel Gaddafi nationalizes British Petroleum's oil interests in Libya.
15	British troops and naval personnel begin to pull out of Malta.
20–21	Heath confers with President Nixon in Bermuda.

LITERATURE AND SCHOLARSHIP
V.S. Naipaul publishes *In A Free State*.

RECREATION AND FASHION
Fashion changes favour 'hot pants' for women.

RELIGION AND EDUCATION

Jan. 10	First regular television courses begin for Open University (founded 1969).

SCIENCE AND INVENTION

Autumn	The microprocessor, using a single silicon chip, reaches Britain from USA and speeds up development of computer technology; Sinclair Radionics Ltd pioneers a pocket calculator, using a microchip, which goes on sale at £70 early in 1972.

Events Elsewhere

Dec. 3–16	War between Pakistan and India over secession of E. Pakistan as Bangladesh.

AD 1972

Jan.	9	Miners' strike causes disruption.
	22	Heath, in Brussels, signs Accession to EEC Ty, together with premiers of Denmark, Irish Republic and Norway.
	30	'Bloody Sunday' in Londonderry: 13 demonstrators killed by British troops.
Feb.	2	Angry crowd burns down British Embassy in Dublin.
	4	Britain recognizes former E. Pakistan as republic of Bangladesh; joins Commonwealth, 18 Apr.
	15	1.5 million workers laid off because of power cuts caused by fuel shortage.
	22	IRA bomb at Aldershot barracks kills 7; first Irish terrorist campaign on mainland since 1939 begins.
	28	Miners return to work having had demand for better wages and working conditions recognized by Heath government.
Mar.	24	Direct rule from Westminster imposed on N. Ireland.
	26	Britain and Malta sign defence treaty.
Apr.	1	William Whitelaw is appointed to new post of Northern Ireland Secretary.
Jun.	5	D. of Windsor (K. Edward VIII) buried at Windsor, a week after his death in Paris.
	23	Chancellor of Exchequer adjusts sterling values; minimum lending rate replaces Bank rate.
	26	IRA observes ceasefire in Ulster (to 9 Jul.).
Jul.	18	Maudling resigns as Home Secretary because of alleged contacts with businessman accused of corruption.
	21	5 dockers imprisoned for contempt by National Industrial Relations Court.
	31	'Operation Motorman': army removes barricades in Ulster.
Aug.	4	President Amin of Uganda orders expulsion of 40,000 British Commonwealth Asians.
Sep.	17	Asian refugees from Uganda begin to arrive in Britain.
Oct.	2	Labour Party Conference accepts need to join EEC.
	17	Elizabeth II is Marshal Tito's guest in Yugoslavia; first British royal visit to a communist state.
		European Communities Act: provides for entry into EEC.
	26	Local Government Act: establishes 2-tier system of 44 county councils and 300 district councils.
Nov.	6	Government imposes 90-day freeze on prices, pay, rent and dividends.
Dec.	18	Increasingly dictatorial President Amin nationalizes 34 British farms and tea estates in Uganda.

LITERATURE AND SCHOLARSHIP
Richard Adams publishes *Watership Down*.
M. Drabble publishes *The Needle's Eye*.
Tut'ankhamun Exhibition held in London.

Oct.	10	John Betjeman becomes Poet Laureate.

Aug. 9   A. Lloyd Webber and T. Rice's *Jesus Christ Superstar* (*v.*1970) performed at Palace Theatre, London.

RELIGION AND EDUCATION

May   General Synod of Church of England rejects Anglican-Methodist reunion proposals, although 34 of 40 bishops favour union.

SCIENCE AND INVENTION

Richard Leakey discovers skull of Homo habilis at Koobi Foras, Lake Turkana, Kenya; dated at over 2 million years.

Events Elsewhere

Sep. 5   During XXth Olympiad at Munich, Palestinian guerrillas kill 11 Israeli athletes.

AD 1973

Jan. 1   Britain, together with Denmark and Ireland, joins EEC.

15   Australia ends legal-judicial ties with UK.

Mar. 8   N. Ireland referendum, boycotted by Catholics, gives overwhelming majority in favour of continuing partition.

10   Governor of Bermuda and his aide-de-camp are murdered during unrest in the colony.

Apr. 1   Introduction of value added tax (VAT).

May 19   Royal Navy frigates give protection off Iceland after trawler is fired upon.

Jun. 29   New Ulster Assembly elected; ends in chaos, 31 Jul.

Jul. 5   NHS Reorganization Act: creates 3-tier administrative structure, with area and regional health authorities.

18   Social Security Act: single basic flat-rate pension system.

Sep. 17   Heath goes to Dublin; first visit of a British Prime Minister to Irish Republic.

Oct. 23   Scottish Local Government Act: creates 9 regional and 53 district councils.

Nov. 12   Miners impose overtime ban; drastic cut in production.

Dec. 5   To conserve fuel 50 m.p.h. speed limit is imposed.

5–9   Sunningdale Conference, with politicians from Westminster, Dublin and Belfast participating, agrees to set up Council of Ireland, representing interests of North and South.

6   Stock Exchange, alarmed by strike threats and effects of 'Yom Kippur War' on oil prices, falls 20 points in 3 hours.

13   Heath announces 3-day working week from 31 Dec.

FINE ARTS AND ARCHITECTURE

Tower Hotel, London, completed as part of redevelopment of St Katharine's Dock by Taylow, Woodrow.

Sep.   Exhibition of Chinese art and archaeology, Royal Academy, London.

LITERATURE AND SCHOLARSHIP

Martin Amis publishes *The Rachel Papers*, a novel.
G. Greene publishes *The Honorary Consul*.

MUSIC, ENTERTAINMENT AND DRAMA

Feb. 16   A. Lloyd Webber and T. Rice's 1968 'pop oratorio' *Joseph and the Amazing Technicolour Dreamcoat* performed at Albery Theatre, London.

May 26   M. Tippet's Piano Concerto no. 3 performed in Bath.

Jun.   Alan Ayckbourn's *The Norman Conquests*, 3 linked comedies, performed at Library Theatre, Scarborough.

Sep. 22   Peter Maxwell Davies's *Stone Litany* performed in Glasgow.

Oct. 8   London Broadcasting Company, first commercial radio station in UK, begins service.

Nov. 1   Peter Hall succeeds Lord Olivier as director of National Theatre.

RELIGION AND EDUCATION

Oct. 5   Congregational Church and English Presbyterian Church merge as United Reformed Church.

Events Elsewhere

Jan. 27   Ceasefire in Vietnam agreed at talks in Paris: all US troops to be withdrawn within 60 days.

Oct. 6–24   Abortive Egyptian-Syrian attack on Israel: the 'Yom Kippur War'.

AD 1974

Jan. 1   Power-sharing Executive under Brian Faulkner set up in Belfast.

14   Government-TUC talks over coal dispute break down.

Feb. 7   Grenada becomes independent within Commonwealth.

10   Total miners' strike begins.

17   Harold Wilson concludes a 'Social Contract' with union leaders.

28   General election indecisive: 301 Labour; 296 Conservatives; Liberals 14; Scottish Nationalists 7, Plaid Cymru 2; others 15.

Mar. 2–3   Talks between Heath and Thorpe over possible Conservative-Liberal coalition.

4   Heath resigns; Wilson returns as Prime Minister to form Labour government; Denis Healey, Chancellor of Exchequer; Callaghan, Foreign Secretary; Jenkins, Home Secretary.

11	Miners' strike ends with acceptance of pay offer; normal working week returns.
19	State of emergency declared in N. Ireland as Paisleyites encourage general strike against Executive.
29	Direct rule from Westminster re-established in N. Ireland.
Jun. 1	29 killed in chemical explosion at Flixborough.
Jul. 31	Trade Union and Labour Relations Act: abolishes Industrial Relations Court.
Sep. 7	Devolution White Paper favours elected assemblies for Scotland and Wales.
Oct. 5	IRA Guildford pub bombing kills 5 people.
10	General election gives Labour overall majority of 3: Labour 319; Conservatives 276; Liberals 13; Scottish Nationalists 11; Plaid Cymru 3; others 13.
15	Disturbances begin in the Maze Prison, Belfast.
Nov. 8	Covent Garden Market moves from central London to Nine Elms.
12	Highest VAT (25%) is imposed on petrol.
21	IRA held responsible for 2 Birmingham club bombs which kill 21 and injure 182 people.
29	Prevention of Terrorism Act: gives police wide powers of detention and deportation.
Dec. 17	Conservatives devise new rules for electing a leader.

FINE ARTS AND ARCHITECTURE
Royal Academy mounts exhibition for centenary of Impressionists.

LITERATURE AND SCHOLARSHIP
Beryl Bainbridge publishes *The Bottle Factory Outing*.
M. Spark publishes *The Abbess of Crewe*.

MUSIC, ENTERTAINMENT AND DRAMA

Jun. 17	Alan Ayckbourn's *Absent Friends* performed at Library Theatre, Scarborough; also has 4 plays running concurrently in London.
Oct. 16	English National Opera (formed Jan.) stages first première at the Coliseum, London: Henze's *The Bassarids*.
Nov. 22	First post-war production of *Faust* at Covent Garden, with Kiri Te Kanawa.

Events Elsewhere

Apr. 25	Peaceful revolution in Portugal ends 48 years of veiled dictatorship.
Jul.	Attempted pro-Greek coup in Nicosia provokes Turkish invasion of N. Cyprus, but leads to collapse of Greek ruling junta in Athens after 7 years.
Aug. 8	President Nixon, discredited over Watergate scandal, resigns.

AD 1975

Feb.	*10*	Conservative leadership election is won by Margaret Thatcher, with W. Whitelaw as chief contender; no woman had previously led a major political party in Britain.
May	*8*	Referendum Act institutes Britain's first plebiscite: a single vote to be given for or against continued membership of the EEC.
		Prices Act: gives government power to regulate retail prices through a Prices Commission.
Jun.	*4*	First radio broadcast of proceedings in H. of Commons, members having decided (25 Feb.) against televising debates by 12 votes.
	5	Referendum on membership of EEC, with 64% of electorate voting: for EEC 17,378,581; against EEC 8,470,073.
	16	20-year-old agreement with S. Africa by which Royal Navy uses old base at Simonstown is ended.
Aug.	*7*	Temperature in London reaches 32.3 °C (90 °F), some snow having fallen as recently as 1 Jun.
Nov.	*3*	Elizabeth II formally inaugurates pipeline flow of oil from BP Forties field to Grangemouth, Firth of Forth.
	12	Employment Protection Act: establishes ACAS (Advisory Conciliation and Arbitration Service) to consider industrial disputes; gives protection against unfair dismissal.
		Community Land Act: gives local authority protection to land subject to development.
		Industry Act: establishes National Enterprise Board.
		Petroleum and Submarine Pipelines Act: sets up BNOC (British National Oil Corporation).
		Sex Discrimination Act: ensures equality of opportunity for women and men in applications for jobs.
	27	IRA murders athlete and publisher Ross McWhirter at his home in Enfield, Middlesex.
Dec.	*5*	End of detention without trial in N. Ireland.
	6–12	'Balcombe St. Siege': 4 IRA men hold family hostage in Marylebone, London, before surrendering to police.
	29	Women's Equal Pay Act comes into force.

LITERATURE AND SCHOLARSHIP
M. Bradbury publishes *The History Man*.
David Lodge publishes *Changing Places*.
A. Powell publishes *Hearing Secret Harmonies*.

John McCabe's *The Chagall Windows* performed at Free Trade Hall, Manchester.

Year of great popularity for 'modern dance', with 5-week season at Sadler's Wells Theatre, London, for London Contemporary Dance Co.

Apr. 23 H. Pinter's *No Man's Land* performed by National Theatre Company at Old Vic Theatre, London.

Jun. A. Ayckbourn's *Bedroom Farce* performed at Library Theatre, Scarborough.

RECREATION AND FASHION

Jun. 21 First one-day cricket World Cup is won by West Indies, who beat Australia by 17 runs at Lords.

RELIGION AND EDUCATION

Jan. 24 Archbp Donald Coggan is enthroned at Canterbury; he issues a personal 'Call to the Nation' on moral questions, 15 Oct.

Events Elsewhere

Apr. 30 N. Vietnamese troops enter Saigon to impose unification on country after 30-year struggle.

AD 1976

Jan. 21 British Airways and Air France make inaugural transatlantic Concorde flights.

Feb. 19 Iceland breaks off diplomatic relations with Britain because of fishery dispute.

Mar. 16 Wilson announces his intention to resign as Prime Minister.

Apr. 5 James Callaghan becomes Prime Minister, with Anthony Crosland as Foreign Secretary.

27 Britain becomes an oil-exporting country.

May 10 Jeremy Thorpe resigns Liberal Party leadership.

Jun. 1 Oslo Agreement: settles fishery dispute with Iceland.

Jul. 3 Britain breaks off diplomatic relations with Uganda after murder of a British citizen in a hijacked aircraft.

7 David Steel is elected Liberal Party leader.

10 3 British mercenaries executed by firing squad in Angola.

21 British ambassador in Dublin assassinated by IRA.

Aug. 6 Emergency Drought Act comes into force because of severe water shortage in an unusually hot summer.

14/28 Catholics and Protestants attend Peace Movement rallies in Belfast.

30 Racial rioting at end of annual Notting Hill Carnival.

Sep. 2 Britain condemned by European Commission on Human Rights for ill-treatment of detainees in Ulster.

4   25,000 Protestants and Catholics combine in a peace march in Londonderry, seeking reconciliation and an end to violence.

29   As pound falls in value to $1.64, government announces intention of borrowing £2,300 million from International Monetary Fund.

Nov. 4   Loss of 2 by-elections leaves Callaghan heading a minority government.

22   Race Relations Act: toughens laws against discrimination.

24   Devolution Bill providing for assemblies in Scotland and Wales is introduced in the Commons.

27   Archbps of Canterbury and Westminster support Ulster Peace Movement rally in Trafalgar Square.

Dec. 10   Nobel peace prize is presented to Maired Corrigan and Betty Williams as founders and leaders of Ulster Peace Movement.

MUSIC, ENTERTAINMENT AND DRAMA

Mar. 15   National Theatre Company opens Lyttelton Theatre on South Bank with gala performance of Ben Traver's *Plunder*.

Jun.   Benjamin Britten becomes first ennobled musician when created a life peer; dies on 4 Dec.

Oct. 4   Marlowe's *Tamburlaine the Great*, with Albert Finney, opens Olivier Theatre for National Theatre Company on South Bank.

25   Official opening of completed National Theatre by Elizabeth II.

RELIGION AND EDUCATION

Mar. 25   Installation of the Benedictine Abbot Basil Hume as Cardinal Archbp of Westminster.

Sep.   Labour government begins to phase out direct-grant grammar schools.

SCIENCE AND INVENTION

Oct. 4   British Rail introduces high-speed diesel trains (HS125s) on some express routes.

29   World's most mechanized and largest coal-mining complex opens at Selby, Yorks.

Events Elsewhere

Sep. 9   Mao Tse-tung dies.

AD 1977

Jan. 26   Bullock Report on industrial democracy proposes workers representatives on board of directors of all companies with over 2,000 employees.

Feb. 21   Dr David Owen becomes Foreign Secretary on sudden death of C.A.R. Crosland.

Mar. *17*	Aircraft and Shipbuilding Industries Act: provides for public ownership.
23	Callaghan and David Steel announce a 'Lib-Lab Pact' for limited collaboration over certain issues.
Apr. *15*	Dr Owen visits Rhodesia for abortive talks with Ian Smith on a constitutional settlement.
Jun. *6–13*	Widespread celebrations of Elizabeth II's Silver Jubilee.
24	Mass picketing and frequent clashes at Grunwick Processing Works in N. London because of dismissal of Indian and Pakistani workers (to 14 Nov.).
Aug. *13*	Rioting at an allegedly racist National Front rally in Lewisham.
Oct. *31*	By allowing sterling to float upwards, government effectively revalues the pound.
Dec. *4*	British troops flown to Bermuda after riots over execution of 2 blacks convicted of murdering the Governor in 1972.
13	114 'rebel' Labour MPs join Opposition to vote against proposals in European Assembly Bill for proportional representation in European elections.

FINE ARTS AND ARCHITECTURE
Public sculpture park opens, Bretton Hall, Yorks.

MUSIC, ENTERTAINMENT AND DRAMA
Pop music dominated by punk rock enthusiasm.

Sep.	Malcolm Williamson's incomplete *Mass of Christ the King* performed at Three Choirs Festival, Gloucester.

RECREATION AND FASHION
Young women show liking for blazers and large woollen 'maxi-sweaters'.

Apr. *2*	A woman jockey rides for first time in the Grand National, which is won (as in 1973 and 1974) by Red Rum.
Sep.	Bargain holidays in USA become possible as a 'sky train' service to New York begins.

RELIGION AND EDUCATION

Feb. *17*	Anglican Archbp of Uganda, Dr Janani Luwum, killed while under detention by President Amin's troops.
Jul.	Central London Mosque opens at Islamic Cultural Centre, Regent's Park.

Events Elsewhere

Nov. *19–21*	President Sadat of Egypt goes to Jerusalem and appeals to Israeli Parliament for a Middle East peace settlement.

AD 1978

Jan.	4	London spokesman of PLO is murdered in Mayfair.
	25	Series of defeats for government in Commons over Scottish devolution plans.
Feb.	20	Severe blizzards bring deep snow to West Country.
	21	All-party Speaker's Conference recommends an increase in Ulster representation at Westminster by creation of 5 new seats.
Apr.	11	Free school milk for 7 to 11-year-olds restored by government.
May	1	May Day is celebrated as a Bank Holiday for first time in Britain.
	25	David Steel announces that Lib-Lab Pact will expire at end of July.
Jul.	31	Scottish and Welsh Devolution Acts; never implemented.
Sep.	7	Callaghan, lacking a Commons majority, rejects Opposition proposals for an autumn election.
Oct.	9	Government agrees to accept 346 'boat people' refugees from Vietnam.
Nov.	30	Industrial dispute over new technology and manning levels closes down *The Times* and its associated publications.

FINE ARTS AND ARCHITECTURE

Liverpool Cathedral (C. of E.) is completed after 74 years; a 'Gothic Revival', designed by Sir Giles Gilbert Scott.

Sainsbury Centre for the Visual Arts completed at University of East Anglia; architects, Foster Associates.

LITERATURE AND SCHOLARSHIP

I. Murdoch publishes *The Sea, The Sea*.

MUSIC, ENTERTAINMENT AND DRAMA

Jun. 21 English première of A. Lloyd Webber and T. Rice's *Evita*, Prince Edward Theatre, London.

RECREATION AND FASHION

Protective helmets for batsmen and close fielders become general in first-class cricket matches.

RELIGION AND EDUCATION

Prof. John Hick edits *The Myth of God Incarnate*, theologically sceptical collection of papers.

Jun. 12 Elim Pentecostal Missionaries, based on Cheltenham, are massacred by guerrillas in Rhodesia.

SCIENCE AND INVENTION

Scientists seek to cultivate a stronger strain of elm so as to counter Dutch elm disease, already afflicting 80% of elm trees in S. England.

Jul. 25 Louise Joy Brown, born at Oldham, becomes world's first 'test-tube baby'.

VOYAGES AND EXPLORATION

Jun. 8 Naomi James, aboard *Express Crusader*, is first woman to sail single-handed round the world; she is created DBE in 1979.

Events Elsewhere

Oct. 16 Cardinal Karol Wojtyla becomes Pope John Paul II; he succeeds John Paul I (Cardinal Luciani), who was Pope for only 33 days, having been elected after Paul VI's death on 6 Aug.

AD 1979

Jan. 3–31 Widespread discontent among lower-paid public employees over the restraints of government pay guidelines leads to regional strikes and industrial action by lorry drivers.

4–6 Callaghan attends Western leaders' informal summit conference in Guadeloupe.

Mar. 1 Scottish referendum on devolution: 64.6% of electorate vote; small majority in favour.

Welsh referendum on devolution: 59.8% of electorate vote; large majority oppose it.

28 Callaghan loses no-confidence motion by a single vote and agrees to dissolve Parliament.

30 INLA (Irish National Liberation Army) kills Airey Neave, Conservative spokesman on Ulster, with car bomb which explodes in MPs' car park outside H. of Commons.

May 3 General election gives Conservatives overall majority of 43: Conservatives 339; Labour 268; Liberals 11; Plaid Cymru 2, Scottish Nationalists 2; others 13.

4 Margaret Thatcher becomes Prime Minister; Sir Geoffrey Howe, Chancellor of Exchequer; William Whitelaw, Home Secretary; Lord Carrington, Foreign Secretary.

15 Price Commission abolished.

Jun. 7 First election for European Parliament brings out only a third of electorate but favours Conservatives.

20/26 Scottish and Welsh Devolution Acts repealed.

Aug. 1–8 Thatcher attends Commonwealth Prime Ministers' Conference at Lusaka.

27 E. Mountbatten and 3 companions killed by IRA bomb on holiday in C. Sligo.

IRA kills 18 British soldiers at Warrenpoint, S. Armagh.

Sep. 10 Rhodesia Constitutional Conference at Lancaster House, London (to 18 Oct.).

Oct. 23 Exchange controls on export of capital are removed.

Nov. 13 *The Times* resumes publication

Nov. 21	Sir Anthony Blunt, distinguished art historian, is denounced by Mrs Thatcher as Soviet spy; his knighthood is annulled.
Dec. 4	Immigration rules tightened to deny entry to husbands and fiancés of women resident in Britain but born elsewhere.
11	Rhodesian Parliament formally ends rebellion, as Lord Soames flies out from London as Governor-General.

FINE ARTS AND ARCHITECTURE
Covent Garden piazza: conversion of early 19th-century market buildings into small units completed.

LITERATURE AND SCHOLARSHIP
V.S. Naipaul publishes *A Bend in the River*.

MUSIC, ENTERTAINMENT AND DRAMA

Mar. 8	Tolstoy's play *The Fruits of Englightenment*, adapted by Michael Frayn, performed at Olivier Theatre, London.
May 23	Ballet gala at Covent Garden, for Fonteyn's 60th birthday, an unofficial farewell performance.
Nov. 2	Peter Shaffer's *Amadeus* performed at Olivier Theatre, London.

RELIGION AND EDUCATION

Jun.	Buddhist Peace Pavilion at Milton Keynes; first in Europe.
Jul. 26	Local authorities relieved of requirement to adopt comprehensive systems of education.
Sep. 29–30	Pope John Paul II visits Ireland; at Drogheda condemns terrorism and appeals for an end to violence.

SCIENCE AND INVENTION

Oct. 11	Godfrey Hounsfield receives Nobel prize for medicine for inventing EMI computerized axial tomographic body scanner.

Events Elsewhere

Feb.	Iranian revolution brings Ayatollah Khomeini to power.
Dec. 25–31	Soviet troops occupy Afghanistan.

AD 1980

Feb. 14	Thatcher calls for boycott of Olympic games in Moscow because of Soviet occupation of Afghanistan.
Apr. 1	British authority in Rhodesia ends as the former colony becomes independent republic of Zimbabwe.
2	Rioting by young unemployed in St Paul's area of Bristol.

May	*1*	British Aerospace Act: privatizes the industry.
	5	SAS detachment storms Iranian Embassy in Kensington where 6 Iranian dissidents were holding hostages.
	6	TUC 'Day of Action' in protest against government's policies.
Jun.	*30*	Industry Act: National Enterprise Board to encourage private-sector initiative rather than public corporations.
		Transport Act: reforms system for granting licences to bus companies; Freight Corporation made a limited company.
Aug.	*1*	Employment Act: checks secondary picketing and closed shop.
	8	Housing Act: council house tenants may buy their homes.
Sep.	*13*	Steel works at Consett, Co. Durham, main source of work in the district, closes down.
	21	First CND rally at Greenham Common, Berks, against proposed siting of US Cruise missiles.
Oct.	*27*	7 IRA members at the Maze Prison, Belfast, begin hunger strike, claiming 'political status' (to 18 Dec.).
Nov.	*10*	Michael Foot elected Labour leader after Callaghan's resignation (15 Oct.).
	13	Civil Aviation Act: privatizes British Airways.
		Local Government Planning Act: limits capital expenditure available to local authorities.
Dec.	*8*	British and Irish Prime Ministers meet in Dublin.
	31	2,133,000 unemployed (almost 9% of workforce).

FINE ARTS AND ARCHITECTURE
National Westminster Tower at Bishopsgate, London, designed by R. Seifert and Co. and begun in 1969, is completed; at 600ft and 52 storeys, the tallest building of its kind in Europe.

LITERATURE AND SCHOLARSHIP
M. Drabble publishes *The Middle Ground*.
W. Golding publishes *Rites of Passage*.

RECREATION AND FASHION

Mar.	*21*	British Olympic Association ignores Thatcher's call to boycott Moscow Olympiad.
Jul.	*19*	At Moscow Olympics (to 3 Aug.) Britain wins 6 gold medals.

RELIGION AND EDUCATION

Mar.	*25*	Dr Robert Runcie enthroned as Archbp of Canterbury; most Churches are represented at the service, with Cardinal Hume reading the epistle.
May		National Pastoral Congress of Roman Catholics held at Liverpool.
		Public pilgrimage of Archbps of Canterbury and Westminster to Walsingham, Norfolk.

SCIENCE AND INVENTION

Dec. Biochemist Frederick Sanger, a Nobel laureate in 1958 for his work on insulin, receives Nobel prize for chemistry for his research on DNA.

Events Elsewhere

Apr. 25 US attempt at airborne rescue of Americans held hostage in Tehran Embassy fails.

Aug. 30 Solidarity trade union at Gdansk wins major concessions from Polish government.

Sep. 24 Iraq goes to war with Iran.

AD 1981

Jan. 25 Council for Social Democracy set up by Roy Jenkins, David Owen, Shirley Williams and William Rodgers.

Mar. 1 Hunger strikes spread among IRA prisoners at the Maze Prison, Belfast.

26 Council for Social Democracy forms Social Democratic Party (SDP).

Apr. 9 Bobby Sands, an IRA prisoner on hunger strike at the Maze, is elected MP in by-election at Fermanagh.

May 5 Sands dies after 66-day hunger strike.

7 Labour wins GLC elections; Ken Livingstone becomes GLC leader.

Apr. 11–12 Grave rioting and arson at Brixton.

21 Pound coins replace pound notes in England and Wales.

May Government sets up London Docklands Development Corporation to regenerate 8 square miles on both sides of R. Thames.

Jun. 16 Political pact between Liberals and SDP.

Jul. 2 Representation of the People Act: convicted prisoners disqualified from standing for Parliament.

4–8 Riots and arson at Toxteth, Liverpool, and Moss Side, Manchester.

27 British Telecommunications Act: profit-making British Telecom becomes public corporation separate from Post Office.

28 Further rioting at Toxteth.

29 P. of Wales marries Lady Diana Spencer at St Paul's Cathedral; wedding seen by estimated 700 million world TV viewers.

Sep. 15 Government announces £10 million project to redevelop South Docks area of Liverpool.

Oct. 2 Maze Prison hunger strikes end after 203 days, 10 prisoners having died during the protest.

10 IRA bomb near Chelsea barracks kills 2 people.

20 H. of Lords debates Nationality Bill which limits right to live in UK to British citizens; morality of proposals criticized by Archbp Runcie; bill enacted, 30 Oct.

Dec. 15 Government institutes Youth Opportunities Scheme: 12 months' training for school-leavers without jobs.

Salman Rushdie publishes *Midnight's Children*.

MUSIC, ENTERTAINMENT AND DRAMA

Apr. *1*	Alan Hoddinott's opera *The Trumpet Major* performed in Manchester.
May *14*	A. Lloyd Webber's *Cats* (to T.S. Eliot's words) performed at New London Theatre.
Jul. *30*	Simon Gray's *Quatermaine's Terms* performed at Queen's Theatre, London.
Aug.	John Tavener's *Akhmatova Rékviem* given concert performance at Albert Hall, London.
Sep. *1*	Tom Stoppard's *On the Razzle* performed at Edinburgh Festival; performed at Lyttelton Theatre, London, 22 Sep.

RECREATION AND FASHION

Feb. *15*	Football League games played on a Sunday for first time.
Mar. *29*	First London Marathon run.
Summer	Closely contested series against Australia is won 3-2 by England, with remarkable centuries by Ian Botham at Headingley and Old Trafford.

Events Elsewhere

Jan. *20*	Within minutes of President Reagan's inauguration, Iran releases 52 American hostages detained for 444 days.

AD 1982

Mar. *19*	Argentinian warship lands party of 'scrap dealers' on British island of South Georgia.
Apr. *2*	Argentina invades and annexes Falkland Islands and their dependencies.
5	Carrington and two Foreign Office ministers resign; Francis Pym becomes Foreign Secretary.
	Royal Navy task force sails from Portsmouth.
7	Exclusion Zone of 200 miles around Falklands is announced by Defence Ministry.
25	Marine commandos recapture South Georgia.
May *1*	RAF bombs airfield at Port Stanley, East Falkland.
2	HM submarine *Conqueror* torpedoes Argentinian cruiser *General Belgrano* on outer edge of Exclusion Zone.
4	Destroyer HMS *Sheffield* sunk by Argentinian Exocet missile.
14	Commando raid on West Falkland.
21	British troops land in San Carlos Bay, East Falkland; frigate HMS *Ardent* sunk.

23	Frigate HMS *Antelope* bombed and sunk off East Falkland.
25	Container ship *Atlantic Conveyor* and HMS *Coventry* sunk.
29	Fierce fighting as paratroops secure Goose Green, East Falkland.
Jun. 7	Argentinians bomb 2 landing ships at Bluff Cove causing heavy casualties, particularly among Welsh Guards.
8	President Reagan addresses Parliament in Westminster Hall.
13–14	Pincer attack on Port Stanley leads to Argentinian surrender.
21	Birth of P. William of Wales (3rd in line of succession) at St Mary's Hospital, Paddington.
Jul. 20	IRA bombs in Hyde Park and Regent's Park kill 10 soldiers.
Sep. 22	TUC 'Day of Action' in support of Health Service workers.
Oct. 28	Employment Act: unions may be fined for 'unlawful industrial action'; employer's right to dismiss strikers confirmed; ballots on strike action may be state funded.

FINE ARTS AND ARCHITECTURE

Mar. 3	Elizabeth II opens Barbican Centre for Arts and Conferences, City of London; designed (in 1955) and completed by Chamberlain, Powell and Bon.
Apr.–May	Barbican Art Gallery opens with 'Aftermath' exhibition of post-1945 French art.
May 6	Theatre Royal, Plymouth, completed (architect, Peter Moro).

LITERATURE AND SCHOLARSHIP

J. Le Carré publishes *The Honourable Schoolboy*.

MUSIC, ENTERTAINMENT AND DRAMA

May 7	Barbican Theatre opens with RSC's *Henry IV*, Part 1.
Sep. 1	Caryl Churchill's *Top Girls* performed at Royal Court Theatre, London.
Nov.	Tom Stoppard's *The Real Thing* performed at Strand Theatre, London.
2	ITV's Channel 4 begins transmissions.

RELIGION AND EDUCATION

| May 29 | In first papal visit to Britain, John Paul II joins Archbp Runcie in a Service at Canterbury Cathedral; later he visits London, Coventry, Glasgow and Cardiff. |

SCIENCE AND INVENTION

Oct. 11	*Mary Rose*, sunk in 1545, is lifted from seabed off Portsmouth.
31	Thames Barrier, constructed over 7 years to control water flow and prevent flooding, is raised for first time.
Nov.–Dec.	First Christmas at which home computers and video-recorders are readily available in British shops.

Events Elsewhere

| Jun. | Israel invades Lebanon. |

AD 1983

Jan.	*8–11*	Thatcher visits Falkland Islands.
	31	Wearing of front seat belts in cars becomes compulsory.
Feb.	*28*	Strike begins in S. Wales over proposed pit closures; fails to win support in England or Scotland and collapses, 10 Mar.
Apr.	*1*	CND organizes 14-mile protest of 100,000 people, linking arms between Greenham Common and Aldermaston.
May	*16*	Wheel-clamps introduced for illegal parking in London.
Jun.	*9*	General election increases Conservative majority to 144: Conservatives 397; Labour 209; Liberals 17; SDP 6; others 29.
	11	Sir Geoffrey Howe replaces Pym as Foreign Secretary; Nigel Lawson becomes Chancellor of Exchequer.
Sep.	*25*	Mass escape by 38 IRA prisoners from the Maze Prison, Belfast; prison officer killed.
Oct.	*2*	Neil Kinnock elected Labour leader on resignation of Michael Foot.
	25–26	Widespread criticism in Britain of US invasion of Grenada, a Commonwealth member allegedly infiltrated by Marxist Cubans.
Nov.	*14*	US Cruise missiles arrive at Greenham Common base.
	24	Elizabeth II, visiting India, personally bestows Order of Merit on Mother Teresa at New Delhi.
Dec.	*17*	IRA bomb outside Harrods in Knightsbridge kills 6 and injures 90 Christmas shoppers.

FINE ARTS AND ARCHITECTURE

Jan.	'Post-modernist' TV-AM building, designed by Terry Farrell Partnership, opens at Camden Lock, London.
Sep. 22	Enterprise Zone opened on Isle of Dogs to encourage dockland redevelopment in E. London.

LITERATURE AND SCHOLARSHIP

J. Le Carré publishes *The Little Drummer Girl*.

Dec. 10 William Golding receives Nobel prize for literature.

MUSIC, ENTERTAINMENT AND DRAMA

Breakfast time programmes begin on BBC1 (17 Jan.) and ITV (1 Feb.: TV-AM).

Apr. 12	Sir Richard Attenborough's film *Gandhi* wins 8 Oscars; more awards than any previous British film.
Sep.	Paul Patterson's *Missa Maris* performed at Three Choirs Festival, Gloucester.

Austin Rover add a synthesized voice to their Maestro car to create a 'talking dashboard'.

Sinclair Research puts on sale a pocket television set.

Compact discs marketed in Britain as well as in USA.

Events Elsewhere

Jun.–Dec.   Increasing US involvement in Lebanon's chronic internal conflicts, with naval and air bombardment of Syrian positions.

AD 1984

Jan.	9	Index of share prices tops 800 mark for first time.
	25	Government bans staff of Communications Headquarters (GCHQ) at Cheltenham from belonging to a trade union.
Feb.	9	On his 90th birthday Harold Macmillan is created E. of Stockton.
Mar.	5	Miners' strike against threatened pit closures, begun in Scotland on 21 Feb., spreads to Yorkshire.
	15	140 pits stopped in miners' strike.
	26–30	Elizabeth II makes state visit to Jordan.
Apr.	12	Telecommunications Act: privatizes British Telecom.
	17	WPC Yvonne Fletcher shot dead from within Libyan Embassy while policing St James's Square, London.
	22	Britain cuts diplomatic links with Libya.
May	29	Fighting between police and strikers at Orgreave, S. Yorks; 64 people seriously injured.
Jun.	1	S. African Prime Minister visits Mrs Thatcher at Chequers; many anti-apartheid protests.
	23	Miners march through London, supported by railwaymen.
	26	Rate Act: allows government to limit revenue raised by local authorities through rates.
Jul.	10	Cable and Broadcasting Act: permits cable television.
	16	High Court rules that government ban on unions at GCHQ is illegal; Law Lords reverse ruling, 22 Nov.
	26	Trade Union Act: secret ballot for election of union officers; unions to lose their legal immunity if they strike without a ballot.
Sep.	26	Anglo-Chinese treaty on future of Hong Kong signed in Beijing (Peking): British sovereignty to lapse on 1 Jul. 1997.
Oct.	12	IRA bomb explodes at Grand Hotel, Brighton, during Conservative Party Conference; 4 killed.
	25	High Court orders sequestration of funds of miners' union NUM for not paying fine imposed for striking without a ballot.
Dec.	3	British Telecom shares go public; great gains on first day of trading.

31	184 British people known to be suffering from Acquired Immune Deficiency Syndrome (AIDS), a virus first identified in 1981 in California.

FINE ARTS AND ARCHITECTURE

Jul. 9	York Minster's Rose Window and artistic treasures damaged in fire which destroys south transept.

LITERATURE AND SCHOLARSHIP

A. Brookner publishes *Hotel du Lac*.
D. Lodge publishes *Small World*.

Dec. 19	Ted Hughes appointed Poet Laureate in succession to John Betjeman, who died on 19 May.

MUSIC, ENTERTAINMENT AND DRAMA

Jul. 23	First English performance of Tippett's *The Mask of Time*.
Dec.	Bob Geldof organizes pop stars in 'Band Aid' to record *Do They Know It's Christmas?* for Ethiopian famine relief.

RECREATION AND FASHION

Jayne Torvill and Christopher Dean become 1984 World, European and Olympic ice-dance champions.

RELIGION AND EDUCATION

Mar. 14	Nomination of academically provocative Prof. David Jenkins as Bp of Durham perturbs traditionalists; consecrated 6 Jul.
Nov. 15	Church of England General Synod supports ordination of women as deacons but not as priests.

Events Elsewhere

Great famine in NE Africa, especially severe in Ethiopia.

AD 1985

Jan. 25	Debate in H. of Lords televised for first time.
29	Convocation of Oxford University votes against traditional bestowal of honorary doctorate on Prime Minister Thatcher.
Feb. 4	Spaniards reopen frontier with Gibraltar.
5–6	Troops clear CND protesters from Molesworth missile site.
20	Thatcher addresses joint session of US Congress.
24	Miners rally in central London.
Mar. 5	NUM calls off year-long miners' strike.
Apr. 2	NUM lifts ban on overtime, effective for past 18 months.
May 15	Government announces sale of Sealink subsidiary of British Rail.

Jul.	8	Ban on imports from Argentina, imposed in 1982, is lifted.
	16	Local Government Act: abolishes Greater London Council and 6 metropolitan councils from 1 Apr. 1986.
Sep.	*9–10*	Riots and arson at Handsworth, Birmingham.
	28	Riots in Brixton after accidental shooting of middle-aged black woman during police search of her house.
Oct.	*6–9*	Riots at Broadwater Farm Estate, Tottenham; a police constable is hacked to death.
	16–23	Thatcher attends Nassau Commonwealth Prime Ministers' Conference; she vigorously opposes imposition of sanctions on S. Africa.
	30	Transport Act: denationalizes long-distance bus company.
Nov.	*15*	Hillsborough Accord: an Anglo-Irish treaty providing for no change in Ulster's status without consent of majority of its citizens and for occasional conferences giving the Dublin government a consultative role in N. Ireland's affairs.
Dec.	*5*	Britain leaves UNESCO.

LITERATURE AND SCHOLARSHIP
Peter Ackroyd publishes *Hawksmoor*, novel.
I. Murdoch publishes *The Good Apprentice*.

MUSIC, ENTERTAINMENT AND DRAMA

May	2	Howard Brenton and David Hare's *Pravda* performed at Olivier Theatre, London.
Jul.	*13*	'Live Aid' rock concert at Wembley Stadium (linked by television with USA) raises £40 million worldwide for African famine relief.

RECREATION AND FASHION

May	*11*	55 die in fire at Bradford City's football ground.
	29	38 killed in violence at Liverpool v. Juventus football match at Heysel Stadium, Brussels.
Jun.	6	FIFA bans English football teams from competing abroad.

RELIGION AND EDUCATION

Feb.	26	School teachers begin long campaign of active protests against pay and conditions.
Apr.	30	Canon Wilfred Wood is appointed area Bp of Croydon; Britain's first black bishop.
Dec.	3	*Faith in the City*, report by Church of England commission, urges emergency action by government to relieve plight of inner cities.

SCIENCE AND INVENTION

Jan.		Sir Clive Sinclair puts on sale his C5, light and battery-powered electric tricycle.

Mar. 11 Mikhail Gorbachev becomes Communist Party secretary and effective leader of USSR.

AD 1986

Jan. 3–24 Westland dispute over alternative European or US financial backing for helicopter firm; conflict between Defence Minister (Heseltine) and Trade Secretary (Brittan) leads to eventual resignation of both ministers.

Feb. 12 Ty of Canterbury: provides for construction of twin-tunnel rail link beneath English Channel.

15 Violent clashes in Wapping at protest meeting after media tycoon Rupert Murdoch dismisses 5,000 employees who refuse to sign a no-strike deal when his printing plant moves to Docklands from central London.

17 Britain signs Single European Act: provides for greater EEC economic and social integration from 1992.

Apr. 1 Abolition of GLC; London becomes only metropolis without a co-ordinating authority.

15 US aircraft fly from British bases to bomb Libya in revenge for Gaddafi's support to terrorists; over 100 civilians killed in Tripoli alone.

23 King Juan Carlos of Spain is first foreign sovereign to address both Houses of Parliament, Westminster.

May 3 Renewed violence at Wapping; more than 170 police injured.

8–10 Cattle in parts of Scotland, Cumbria and Wales are found to have high levels of radiation following Chernobyl disaster.

Jun. 26–27 Thatcher attends EEC summit; opposes sanctions against S. Africa.

Jul. 11 High Court injunction against publication of former MI5 officer Peter Wright's memoirs, *Spycatcher*.

31 Three and a quarter million are unemployed, the highest recorded figure; but inflation falls to less than 2.5%.

Sep. 6 Nissan opens car plant at Sunderland; first Japanese company to establish factory in Britain.

Oct. 7 *Independent* newspaper goes on sale.

10 Trustee Savings Bank shares on offer to public.

12 Elizabeth II arrives in Beijing (Peking) at start of 7-day state visit to China.

24 Diplomatic links with Syria cut after convicted terrorist is found to have had links with London Embassy.

27 'Big Bang' Day: London Stock Exchange opens to foreign companies and, with technical problems, is computerized.

Dec. 8 Trading in British Gas shares begins; their value increases by 25% in a day.

J. Le Carré publishes *A Perfect Spy*.

May Final supplementary volume of *Oxford English Dictionary* published, 102 years after project began.

MUSIC, ENTERTAINMENT AND DRAMA

Nov. 3–7 English Shakespeare Co. inaugural performances, *The Henrys*, at Theatre Royal, Plymouth; moves to Old Vic, London, 16-19 Mar. 1987.

RECREATION AND FASHION

Jul. 24 Commonwealth Games in Edinburgh suffer from a boycott by 32 countries alienated by Thatcher's sanctions policy.

RELIGION AND EDUCATION

Jul. 22 H. of Commons votes, by majority of 1, in favour of ban on school corporal punishment.

Aug. School external examination structure is changed: GCSE replaces O Level and CSE.

Events Elsewhere

Feb. 25 Gorbachev introduces *perestroika* reform policy.

Apr. 26 Chernobyl disaster: explosion at Ukrainian nuclear power station releases large quantities of radiation.

AD 1987

Jan. 8 Liberal and SDP Alliance agrees that 327 Liberals and 303 SDP candidates will contest next general election.

12 Severe snowstorms and low temperatures.

20 Archbp of Canterbury's special envoy, Terry Waite, taken hostage in Beirut while seeking release of others.

24 Over 450 people hurt in renewed violence at Wapping.

Feb. 6 Printers' union NGA calls off Wapping strike under threat of sequestration of funds.

11 British Airways share dealings open.

Mar. 7 Dover-bound car ferry, *Herald of Free Enterprise*, capsizes on leaving Zeebrugge; 188 deaths among passengers and crew.

28 Mrs Thatcher visits Soviet Union (to 2 Apr.); warmly received by Russian people.

May 8 8 IRA members killed in SAS ambush at Loughgal, Co. Antrim.

Jun. 11 General election cuts Conservative overall majority to 101: Conservatives 375; Labour 229; Liberals 17; SDP 5; others 24.

15 Alliance pact between Liberals and SDP virtually ends; recriminations over

		poor showing of Alliance in election.
Jul.	22	Ban on publication of *Spycatcher* lifted by High Court judge; but reimposed by Law Lords, 30 Jul.
Aug.	6	Dr Owen resigns as leader of SDP, whose members favour merger with Liberals.
Sep.	17	Liberal Party Conference supports SDP merger.
Oct.	16	Hurricane sweeps across S. England; 19 killed; W. Kent, Sussex and Kew Gardens suffer severely.
	18	Torrential rain brings floods and devastation to Cumbria and much of Wales.
	19	'Black Monday' on London Stock Exchange: shares fall sharply.
Nov.	8	IRA bomb at Enniskillen Remembrance Day parade kills 11 civilians.
	17	Government announces plans for replacing rates by community charge ('poll tax').
	18	Death of 31 people in escalator fire at King's Cross underground station.
	25	New charges announced for NHS dental inspection and eyesight checks.

MUSIC, ENTERTAINMENT AND DRAMA

Oct.	6	P. Shaffer's *Lettice and Lovage* performed at Theatre Royal, Bath.
Dec.	14–16	English Shakespeare Co. begins 2-year tour of historical cycle *The Wars of the Roses* at Theatre Royal, Bath.

SCIENCE AND INVENTION

Jul.	30	E. London's Docklands Light Railway, first driverless computer-run service, is officially opened; use by the public delayed for a month by 'teething troubles'.
Nov.	5	Elizabeth II opens London City Airport, Newham; Britain's first 'Stolport' for short take-off and landing aircraft.

Events Elsewhere

Dec.	8	Missile treaty signed by Gorbachev and Reagan in Washington.

AD 1988

Jan.	4	NHS night nurses in Manchester strike over government plan to cut pay given for anti-social hours; proposed cuts cancelled.
Feb.	3	National 'Day of Action' by nurses to emphasize poor state of National Health Service.
	4	ILEA (Inner London Education Authority) to be abolished.
	25	Government plans to restructure electrical industry announced.
Mar.	3	Liberals and SDP merge as Social and Liberal Democratic Party (SLD).
	6	SAS shoot dead 2 IRA men and a woman activist in Gibraltar.
Apr.	11	Tighter scrutiny of social security claims begins.

	18	Conservative majority after debate on proposed poll tax is cut by 25 by backbench revolt.
Jul.	6	Explosion on North Sea oil-rig Piper Alpha kills 170 and heightens criticism of working conditions in the industry.
	28	Paddy Ashdown elected as leader of SLD.
Sep.	26	SLD Conference votes in favour of being called 'Democrats' rather than using historic term 'Liberals'.
Nov.	10	Britain and Iran agree to resume diplomatic relations.
Dec.	21	Pan Am jumbo jet blown up by bomb above Scottish borders; wreckage falls on Lockerbie; 270 passengers and crew and 11 townsfolk killed.

FINE ARTS AND ARCHITECTURE

Mar.   Canadian developers, Olympia and York, submit architectural plans for Canary Wharf, Isle of Dogs, London, which include building an 800ft high Pyramid Prism Skyscraper.

LITERATURE AND SCHOLARSHIP

D. Lodge publishes *Nice Work*.

S. Rushdie's novel *The Satanic Verses* published.

MUSIC, ENTERTAINMENT AND DRAMA

Feb. 5   First 'Comic Relief' day: raises £6.75 million for charity.

May 16   Government sets up Broadcasting Standards Council as a moral watchdog.

RECREATION AND FASHION

May 5–6   Rhodesian-born cricketer Graeme Hick scores 405 not out for Worcestershire v. Somerset at Taunton; highest score in England this century.

Jun.–Aug.   4 different English cricket captains for a Test series against West Indies in which England won no matches.

Aug. 22   Licensing laws relaxed; public houses allowed to open all day in England and Wales.

Sep.   At Seoul Olympics, S. Korea, Britain wins 12 gold medals.

RELIGION AND EDUCATION

Jul.   Education Act: permits schools to opt out of local authority control; Skegness Grammar School becomes first to make this choice, Nov.

Jul.–Aug.   Largest Lambeth Conference of bishops of the Anglican Communion gathers at Canterbury.

SCIENCE AND INVENTION

Feb.   International conference on the problem of AIDS brings delegates from 150 countries to London.

Dec.   Sir James Black receives Nobel prize for medicine for his work in therapeutic research.

Events Elsewhere

Aug. 20   Ceasefire in Iraq-Iran Gulf War.

AD 1989

Jan. 31   Government publishes *Working for Patients*, White Paper reviewing future of National Health Service.

Feb. 14   Ayatollah Khomeini pronounces death sentence on Salman Rushdie for alleged blasphemy in *The Satanic Verses*.

20   British diplomats summoned home from Tehran.

Mar. 5   UN-sponsored 'Save the Ozone Layer' Conference opens in London; 124 nations represented.

7   Rushdie affair leads Iran to cut diplomatic links with Britain again.

31   British Medical Association launches campaign against proposed reorganization of NHS.

Apr. 1   Mrs Thatcher meets S. African Foreign Minister in Namibia.
Levying of community charge (poll tax) begins in Scotland.

7   Soviet President Gorbachev visits Elizabeth II at Windsor.

15   Hillsborough Stadium disaster, Sheffield: 95 Liverpool fans are crushed to death in FA Cup semi-final against Nottingham Forest.

May 8   Labour Party National Executive drops nationalization as a fundamental objective of policy.

13   SDP decides to cease fighting election campaigns as a national party.

Jun. 4   Thousands of Chinese in Hong Kong demonstrate against Beijing government.

Jul. 3   Foreign Secretary Howe says that Hong Kong residents who are reluctant to remain there under Chinese rule have no automatic right to live in UK.

24   Howe becomes deputy Prime Minister and is replaced as Foreign Secretary by John Major.

Sep. 22   IRA kills 11 bandsmen at Royal Marines School of Music, Dover.

18–24   Commonwealth Conference in Kuala Lumpur, opened by Elizabeth II and attended by Thatcher; Britain differs from its partners over wording of a communiqué condemning S. Africa's apartheid policies.

26   Sudden resignation of Chancellor of Exchequer Nigel Lawson; he is replaced by John Major; Douglas Hurd becomes Foreign Secretary.

Nov. 21   H. of Commons is first televised live.

Dec. 6   Share offers for privatization of water are 5 times oversubscribed.

20   Government announces that 225,000 Hong Kong citizens will be given British citizenship.

John Tavener composes choral work *Akathist of Thanksgiving*.

Feb. 5   Sky Television provides first British satellite service.

RELIGION AND EDUCATION

May 17   Synod of Church of Ireland votes for ordination of women.

Sep. 29   Archbp Runcie visits Vatican for prolonged talks with Pope John Paul II (to 3 Oct.).

Nov. 7   General Assembly of Church of England votes to make provision in canon law for ordination of women as priests.

Events Elsewhere

Jun. 3   Death of Ayatollah Khomeini.

4   Tanks kill thousands of Chinese protesters in vicinity of Tiananmen Square, Beijing (Peking).

Oct.   Rapid withering away of communism in E. Germany, Czechoslovakia and Hungary.

Nov. 9   Demolition of Berlin Wall begins.

Dec. 24–25   Uprising in Romania; N. Ceauşescu, communist President for 22 years, is executed.

AD 1990

Jan. 3   Energy Secretary Norman Fowler resigns, for personal reasons; succeeded by Michael Howard.

Mar. 31   Violent demonstrations against the poll tax in London.

Apr. 10   Customs officials impound steel tubes destined for Iraq, suspecting they are part of a 'super-gun'.

Jun. 3   SDP formally wound up as an independent political party.

Jul. 14   Nicholas Ridley resigns as Trade and Industry Secretary after widespread criticism of anti-German remarks attributed to him in *The Spectator*.

20   IRA bombs London Stock Exchange; little damage.

30   Ian Gow, Conservative MP for Eastbourne, killed by IRA car bomb at his home in E. Sussex.

Aug. 3   Hottest recorded day in Britain: shade temperature of 37.17°C (98.8°F) at Cheltenham.

Sep. 6–7   Parliament recalled from summer recess; MPs back government's anti-Iraqi stand in Gulf crisis.

12   Britain joins wartime allies and E. and W. Germany in signing Moscow Ty of Final Settlement with Germany.

16–19   Mrs Thatcher visits Prague and Budapest.

Oct. 3   Chancellor of Exchequer announces that Britain will participate in European Exchange Rate Mechanism, despite hostility of Prime Minister to monetary

	union projects.
Nov. *1*	Sir Geoffrey Howe resigns as deputy Prime Minister in protest at Mrs Thatcher's attitude to the European Community.
13	Howe's resignation speech criticizes Thatcher's attitude to ERM and her style of cabinet government.
20	Conservative Party leadership election indecisive: Mrs Thatcher 204; Michael Heseltine 152.
22	Mrs Thatcher announces her intention to resign.
27	Conservative Party leadership election won by John Major, 185 votes; Michael Heseltine 131; Douglas Hurd 56.
28	Major succeeds Thatcher as Prime Minister; he is succeeded as Chancellor by Norman Lamont; Heseltine returns to the cabinet as Environment Secretary.

FINE ARTS AND ARCHITECTURE

St Enoch Centre, Glasgow, completed (architect: G.M.W. Partridge).

LITERATURE AND SCHOLARSHIP

A.S. Byatt's novel *Possession* published.

MUSIC, ENTERTAINMENT AND DRAMA

May   'Culture Mayfest' of music, drama and dance celebrated in Glasgow, designated the 'cultural capital of Europe for 1990'.

RECREATION AND FASHION

Jul. *26–30*   Graham Gooch, captaining English cricket team v. India at Lords, scores 333 and 123, highest aggregate in a Test match.

RELIGION AND EDUCATION

Jun.   Dr Penelope Jamieson is consecrated Bp of Dunedin, New Zealand; first women diocesan in the Anglican Communion of churches.

SCIENCE AND INVENTION

Dec. *1*   Channel Tunnel: pilot tunnels from English and French coasts meet; first land route between Britain and the Continent since Mesolithic Age.

Events Elsewhere

Aug. *2*   Iraq invades Kuwait.

Oct. *3*   German reunification completed.

AD 1991

Jan. *16–17*   RAF planes collaborate with UN allies in concentrated bombing of Iraqi airfields and strategic bases.

Feb. 7	IRA mortar bomb attack on 10 Downing Street while cabinet in session.
Feb. 18	IRA bombs explode at Victoria and Paddington railway stations in London.
Feb. 24	British 1st Armoured Division engages Iraqi mechanised troops along the northern Kuwait frontier.
Feb. 28	British advance on Baghdad stops when UN operations are halted by Iraqi acceptance of provisional ceasefire.
Mar. 7	Ribble Valley by-election victory for Liberal Democrats shows 24.7 per cent swing against the Government.
Apr. 23	Government announce that in 1993 poll tax will be replaced by council tax based on capital value of property held.
Jul. 23	Ministry of Defence proposes widespread army reforms, including merging of 22 cavalry and infantry regiments.
Aug. 8	Muslim terrorists free British hostage John McCarthy after five years of imprisonment in Beirut.
Sep. 25	Hostage Jackie Mann freed by Beirut terrorists.
Nov. 5	Publisher and newspaper proprietor Robert Maxwell found dead in sea off Tenerife.
Nov. 18	Hostage Terry Waite is freed (cf. 1987).

FINE ARTS AND ARCHITECTURE

Jun. 10	Sainsbury Wing of National Gallery, London, opens to the public.
	Broadgate re-development at Liverpool Street, London, completed (design by Arup Associates and Skidwell, Owings and Merrill).
	Embankment Place, London (designed by Terry Farrell), completed.

LITERATURE AND SCHOLARSHIP

Oct. 12	Ben Okri's novel *The Famished Road* wins Booker Prize.

RECREATION, SPORT AND FASHION

Oct. 3	Rugby Union World Cup competition opens in Britain for first time.
Nov. 2	Rugby Union World Cup Final at Twickenham won by Australia, defeating England.

RELIGION AND EDUCATION

Apr. 19	George Carey enthroned as 103rd Archbp of Canterbury.
May. 20	Major announces proposed raising of all polytechnics to university level.

Events Elsewhere

Mar. 1	Collapse of federal central government in Yugoslavia.
Aug. 19–22	Abortive attempt by Soviet hardline communists to overthrow Gorbachev.
Dec. 8	Formation of Commonwealth of Independent States leads to disintegration of Soviet Union before end of the month.

AD 1992 TO APRIL

Jan. 15   Britain joins European partners in recognising independence of Croatia and Slovenia and their secession from Yugoslavia.

Feb. 27   Protests by right-wing Conservatives over hostile remarks of Australian prime minister Keating on the Anglo-Australian relationship.

Apr. 9   General election cuts Conservative overall majority to 21: Conservatives 336 seats; Labour 271; Liberal Democrats 20; others 24.

10   2 IRA bombs in London: 3 civilians killed and much of central City devastated; flyover feeding M1 motorway structurally damaged.

RELIGION AND EDUCATION

Mar. 13   Christ the Cornerstone church dedicated at Milton Keynes; the first ecumenical church built in Britain.

Events Elsewhere

Mar. 17   White South African referendum backs government's anti-apartheid reforms.

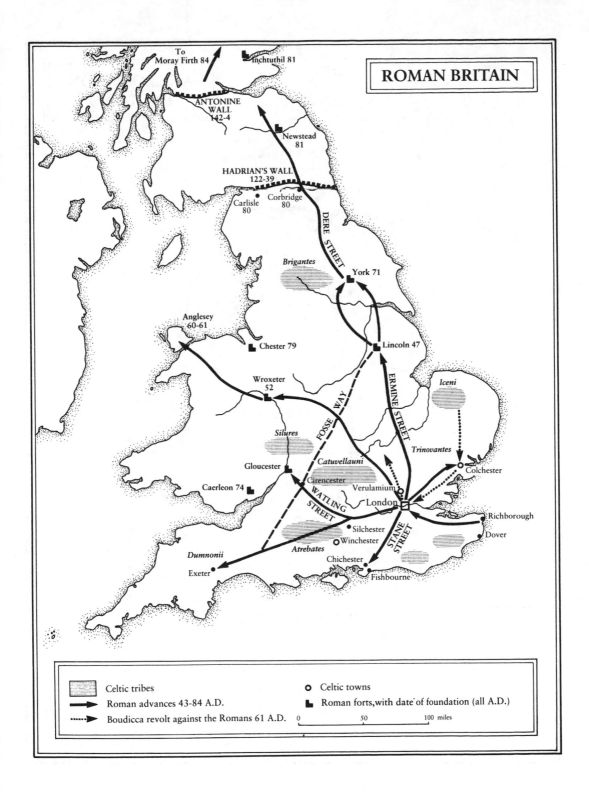

ROMAN BRITAIN

To Moray Firth 84

Inchtuthil 81

ANTONINE WALL 142-4

Newstead 81

HADRIAN'S WALL 122-39

Carlisle 80

Corbridge 80

DERE STREET

Brigantes

York 71

Iceni

Anglesey 60-61

Chester 79

Lincoln 47

ERMINE STREET

Wroxeter 52

FOSSE WAY

Silures

Trinovantes

Catuvellauni

Gloucester

Cirencester

Colchester

Caerleon 74

Verulamium

London

WATLING STREET

Richborough

Dumnonii

Atrebates

Silchester

Winchester

STANE STREET

Dover

Chichester

Exeter

Fishbourne

Celtic tribes	○	Celtic towns
→ Roman advances 43-84 A.D.	🏰	Roman forts, with date of foundation (all A.D.)
⇢ Boudicca revolt against the Romans 61 A.D.		

0   50   100 miles

ANGLO-SAXON
ENGLAND

DAL RIADA

Clyde
Edinburgh
Firth of Forth
BERNICIA
Lindisfarne
Bamburgh
STRATHCLYDE
NORTHUMBRIA
GALLOWAY
Bewcastle
Jarrow
ROMAN WALL
Tyne
Tees
Whitby
Catterick 600
I. of Man
DEIRA
York
Ouse
Mersey
Humber
LINDSEY
Bakewell
Trent
MERCIA
The Wash
Lichfield
Welland
(NORTH FOLK)
Tettenhall 910
EAST ANGLIA
(SOUTH FOLK)
Worcester
Avon
Severn
Ouse
ESSEX
(EAST SAXONS)
OFFA'S DYKE 784
Dee
Wye
Cirencester 628
Thames
Oxford
DYFED
Dyrham 577
Wantage
MID SAXONS
London
Maldon 991
Ellandune 825
Bath
Severn
Thames
I. of Thanet
Glastonbury
WESSEX
(WEST SAXONS)
Canterbury
KENT
(JUTES)
Parret
Winchester
SUSSEX
(SOUTH SAXONS)
DEVON
Corfe
CORNWALL

✕ Battle   Marshland
● Town

0   50   100 miles

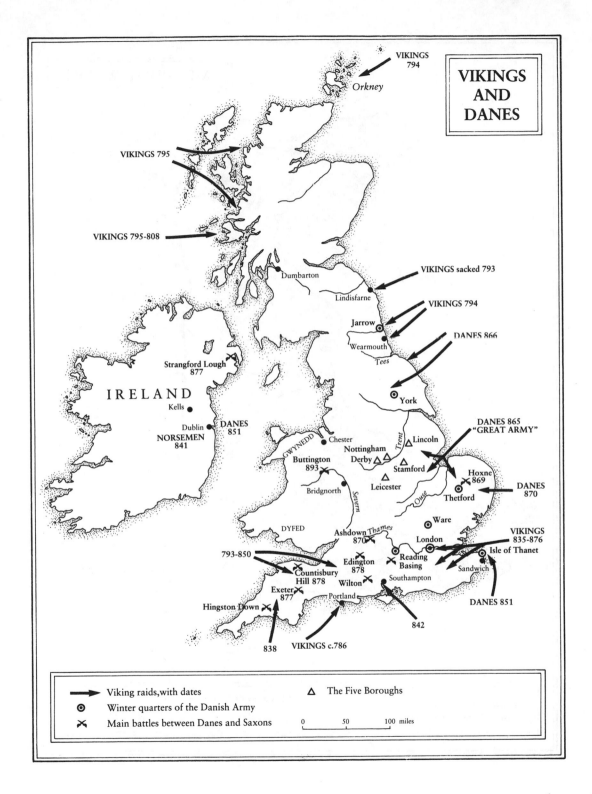

VIKINGS
794

Orkney

VIKINGS
AND
DANES

VIKINGS 795

VIKINGS 795-808

VIKINGS sacked 793

Dumbarton

Lindisfarne

VIKINGS 794

Jarrow

DANES 866

Wearmouth

Tees

Strangford Lough
877

I R E L A N D

Kells

York

Dublin **DANES**
NORSEMEN 851
841

GWYNEDD

Chester

DANES 865
"GREAT ARMY"

Buttington
893

Nottingham Lincoln
Derby

Stamford

Hoxne
869

Bridgnorth

Leicester

DANES
870

Severn

Thetford

DYFED

Ashdown *Thames*
870

Ware

793-850

Edington London
878 Reading

VIKINGS
835-876

Isle of Thanet

Countisbury Basing
Hill 878 Wilton

Sandwich

Exeter
877 Southampton

DANES 851

Hingston Down Portland

842

838 VIKINGS c.786

Viking raids, with dates △ The Five Boroughs

⊙ Winter quarters of the Danish Army

✕ Main battles between Danes and Saxons 0 50 100 miles

463

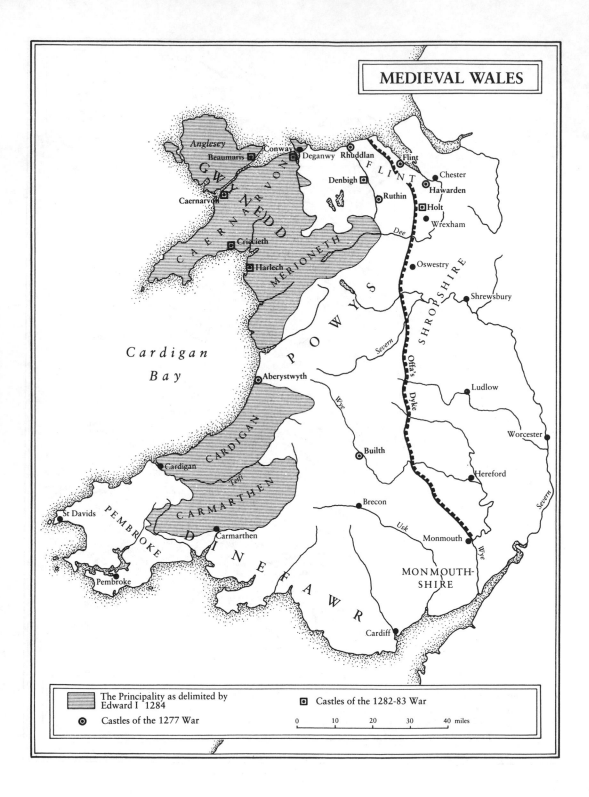

MEDIEVAL WALES

The Principality as delimited by
Edward I 1284

Castles of the 1277 War

Castles of the 1282-83 War

0   10   20   30   40 miles

SCOTLAND AND THE BORDERS

0   20   40   60 miles

Orkney

Skara Brae
Stromness
Kirkwall

Cape Wrath

Thurso
Wick
CAITHNESS

Butt of Lewis

SUTHERLAND

Lewis

Helmsdale
Dunrobin
Dornoch

ROSS

Rosemarkie
Dingwall
BLACK
ISLE
Beauly
Inverness

Moray Firth
Burghead
Elgin
Forres
Nairn
Keith
Pluscarden

Banff
Fraserburgh
BUCHAN
Ruthven

North Uist

Annait
Dunvegan

South Uist

Skye
SLEAT
KINTAIL
Glenelg
GLENELG

Lochindorb
MORAY
STRATHBOGIE

GARIOCH
Kildrummy
Aberdeen
Lumphanan

Barra
Kisimul

Rum
Eigg

Loch Ness

Spey

Dee

MAR

MEARNS

Inverlochy
LOCHABER
ATHOLL

BADENOCH

Tioram
Mingary

Coll

MORVERN

Tiree

Duart
Mull

Oban
GLENORCHY
Tyndrum

Iona

Dunadd

ARGYLL
LORNE

DALRIADA

Brechin
Kirriemuir
Forfar
Montrose

Dunkeld
Tay
Arbroath

Scone
Dundee
STRATHEARN
Perth
Firth of Tay
St Andrews
Balquhidder
STRATHALLAN
Largo
Crail
Cardross
Dunblane
Kinross
Dysart
Stirling
FIFE
Bannockburn
Dunfermline
Dumbarton
Firth of Forth
Falkirk
Leith
Dunbar
Glasgow
Edinburgh
Carberry
Coldingham
PENTLAND
HILLS
Newbattle
Halidon
Berwick-upon-Tweed
Penicuick
Hill
Lanark
Lawder
Coldstream
Flodden
Holy Isle
Peebles
Kelso
Bamburgh
Roxburgh
Homildon
Tweed
Hill
Selkirk
Jedburgh
Alnwick
TEVIOTDALE
Hawick

Colonsay

Tarbert

Rothesay
Largs
Paisley
Bothwell
CUNNINGHAM
Irvine
KYLE
Brodick
Loudon Hill

Islay

Duniveg

KINTYRE

Arran

Ayr

Dunaverty

Turnberry
CARRICK

Clyde

NITHSDALE

LIDDESDALE
Langholm
Otterburn
Lockerbie

Dumfries
Annan
Tyne
Newcastle
Jarrow
Burgh
on Sands
Hexham
Wearmouth
Carlisle
Neville's Cross
Durham

I R E L A N D
Larne

Wigtown
Dundrennan

Carrickfergus
Kirkmadrine

Bangor
Holywood
Belfast

Soluay Firth

E N G L A N D

465

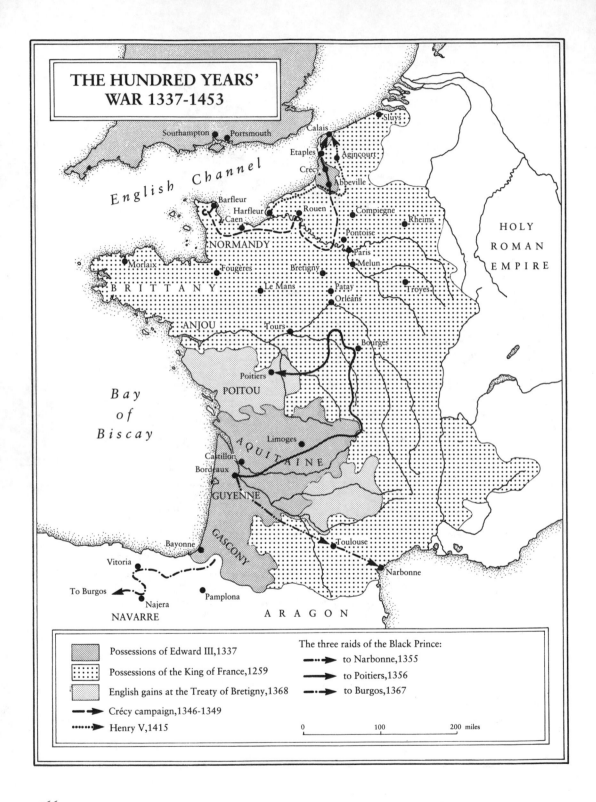

THE HUNDRED YEARS' WAR 1337-1453

Sluys

Southampton • Portsmouth • Calais

Etaples • Agincourt
Crécy •
Abbeville •

English Channel

Barfleur •
Harfleur • Rouen • Compiègne • Rheims
Caen • Pontoise
NORMANDY Paris •
Melun •

HOLY
ROMAN
EMPIRE

Morlaix • Fougères • Bretigny •
B R I T T A N Y Le Mans • Patay • Troyes •
Orléans •
ANJOU Tours •
Bourges •

*Bay
of
Biscay*

POITIERS
POITOU

Limoges •
Castillon •
Bordeaux • A Q U I T A I N E
GUYENNE

Bayonne • GASCONY Toulouse •
Vitoria • Narbonne •
To Burgos ← Pamplona •
Najera •
NAVARRE A R A G O N

		The three raids of the Black Prince:
▨	Possessions of Edward III, 1337	▪▪▪▶ to Narbonne, 1355
⬚	Possessions of the King of France, 1259	──▶ to Poitiers, 1356
▨	English gains at the Treaty of Bretigny, 1368	▬ ▬▶ to Burgos, 1367
─ ─▶	Crécy campaign, 1346-1349	
▪▪▪▶	Henry V, 1415	

0   100   200 miles

PLANTAGENET,
LANCASTRIAN
AND
YORKIST ENGLAND

Berwick

Hedgerley Moor 1464

Alnwick

Hexham 1464

Middleham

Lancaster

York

Towton 1461

Ribblesdale

Wakefield 1460

Pontefract

Ravenspur

Conway Flint   Chester

Bolingbroke

Blore Heath 1459

Shrewsbury

Empingham 1470

Bosworth 1485

Ludlow

Kenilworth

Mortimer's
Cross 1461

Ludford
Bridge
1459

Warwick

Northampton 1460

Edgcote
1469

St Albans
1455   1461

Pleshey

Milford Haven

Tewkesbury
1471

Pembroke

Barnet 1471

Windsor

Cardiff

Bristol

Leeds

Sandwich

Dover

Exeter

Titchfield

Plymouth

St Michael's Mount

✕   Battles of the Wars of the Roses

●   Town

0   50   100 miles

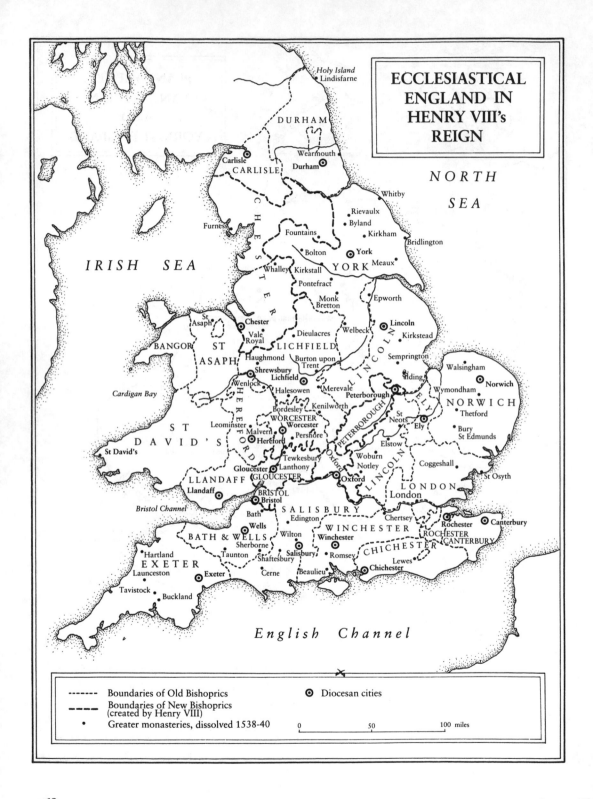

ECCLESIASTICAL
ENGLAND IN
HENRY VIII's
REIGN

NORTH

SEA

IRISH SEA

Cardigan Bay

English Channel

Bristol Channel

------- Boundaries of Old Bishoprics
⊙ Diocesan cities
──── Boundaries of New Bishoprics
(created by Henry VIII)
• Greater monasteries, dissolved 1538-40

0   50   100 miles

Holy Island
• Lindisfarne

DURHAM

• Wearmouth
• Durham
Carlisle
CARLISLE

• Whitby
• Rievaulx
Furness • • Byland
Fountains • Kirkham
• Bridlington
• Bolton • York
Whalley Kirkstall • Meaux
Pontefract

Monk
Bretton • Epworth
St
Asaph • Chester Dieulacres • Lincoln
Vale Welbeck Kirkstead
BANGOR Royal
ST LICHFIELD • Semprington • Walsingham
ASAPH Haughmond Burton upon
• Shrewsbury Trent Tilding • Norwich
Wenlock Lichfield Wymondham
Halesowen • Merevale NORWICH
Bordesley • Kenilworth Peterborough • Thetford
ST WORCESTER St Bury
Leominster • Worcester Neots • St Edmunds
DAVID'S Malvern • Pershore Ely • Coggeshall
• Hereford Elstow
St David's Tewkesbury Woburn
Gloucester Lanthony Notley • St Osyth
LLANDAFF GLOUCESTER Oxford
Llandaff Bristol LONDON
Bath London
SALISBURY
Wells Edington Chertsey
BATH & WELLS Wilton WINCHESTER Rochester • Canterbury
Sherborne Winchester ROCHESTER
Hartland Taunton Shaftesbury Salisbury Romsey CHICHESTER CANTERBURY
EXETER Cerne Beaulieu Lewes
Launceston • Exeter Chichester
Tavistock • Buckland

LINCOLN
ELY
CHESTER
HEREFORD

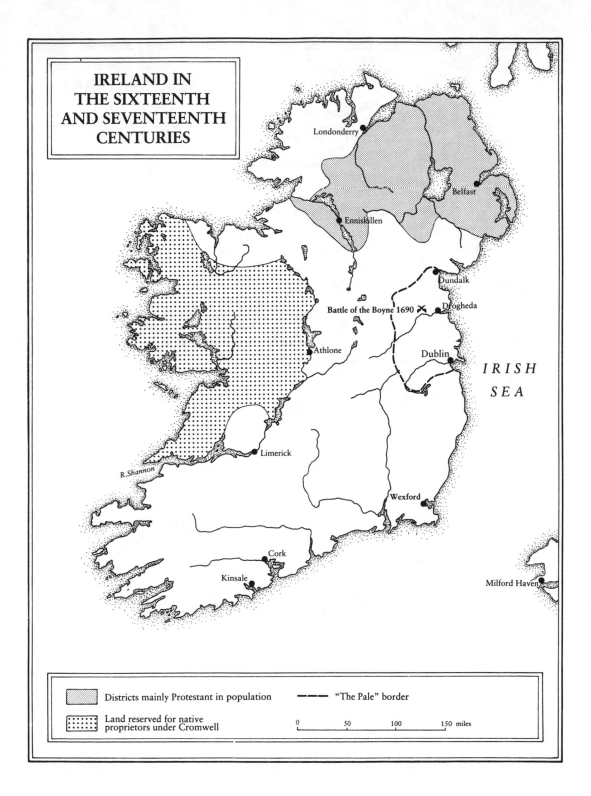

IRELAND IN THE SIXTEENTH AND SEVENTEENTH CENTURIES

Londonderry

Belfast

Enniskillen

Dundalk

Battle of the Boyne 1690 ✕ Drogheda

Athlone

Dublin

IRISH SEA

Limerick

R.Shannon

Wexford

Cork

Kinsale

Milford Haven

Districts mainly Protestant in population

Land reserved for native proprietors under Cromwell

– – – "The Pale" border

0   50   100   150 miles

THE CIVIL WARS
1642-1651

Perth

Edinburgh
Glasgow
Dunbar
Berwick

Philipphaugh

Newcastle

Carlisle

Marston
Moor   York
Preston   Leeds   Hull
Adwalton
Moor
Gainsborough

Rowton Heath

Winceby
Nottingham   Southwell
Shifnal
Leicester   Grantham

Harlech

Newmarket
Worcester   Edgehill   Naseby   Cambridge
Stow-on-the-Wold   Holdenby House
Gloucester   Cropredy Bridge
Oxford   Chalgrove Field
Pembroke   London
Roundway
Bristol   Down
Langport   Newbury
Basing House

Southwick
Exeter   Bridport
Carisbrooke
Fowey   Plymouth
Truro

Scilly Isles

0   50   100 miles

470

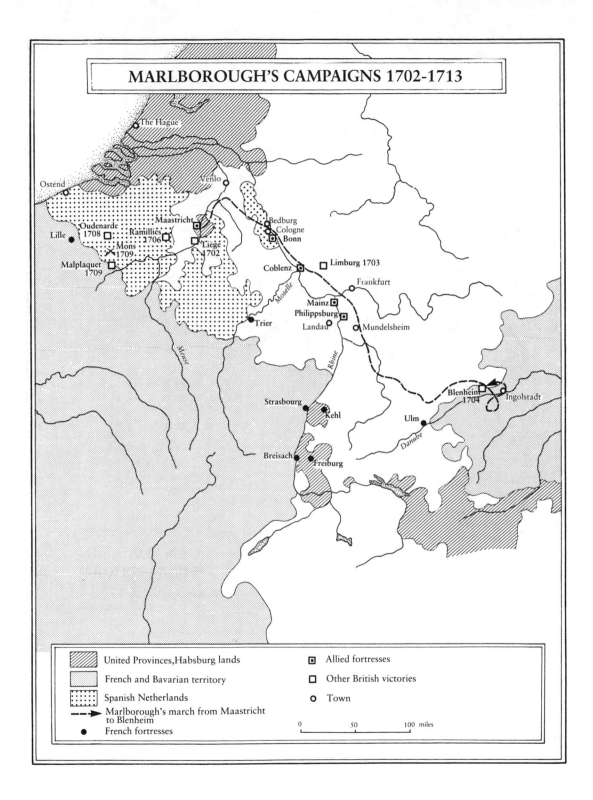

MARLBOROUGH'S CAMPAIGNS 1702-1713

The Hague

Ostend

Lille

Oudenarde
1708

Ramillies
1706

Mons
1709

Malplaquet
1709

Venlo

Maastricht

Liège
1702

Bedburg
Cologne
Bonn

Limburg 1703

Coblenz

Frankfurt

Moselle

Meuse

Mainz
Philippsburg
Landau

Trier

Mundelsheim

Rhine

Blenheim
1704

Ingolstadt

Strasbourg

Kehl

Ulm

Danube

Breisach

Freiburg

	United Provinces, Habsburg lands		Allied fortresses
	French and Bavarian territory		Other British victories
	Spanish Netherlands		Town
	Marlborough's march from Maastricht to Blenheim		
	French fortresses		

0   50   100   miles

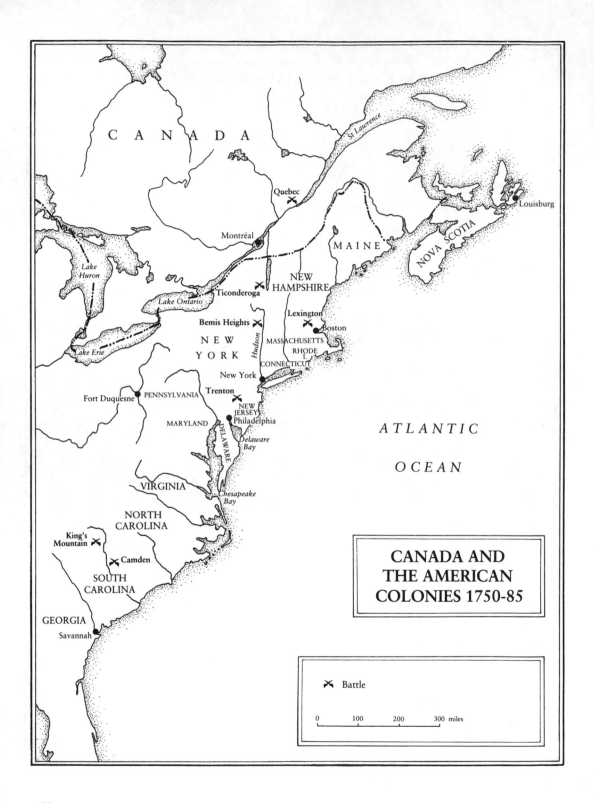

CANADA

St Lawrence

Quebec ✕

Louisburg

Montréal ●

NOVA SCOTIA

MAINE

Lake Huron

Lake Ontario

Ticonderoga ●

NEW HAMPSHIRE

Lexington ✕

Bemis Heights ✕

Boston ●

Lake Erie

NEW YORK

Hudson

MASSACHUSETTS

RHODE I.

CONNECTICUT

New York ●

Trenton ✕

Fort Duquesne ●

PENNSYLVANIA

NEW JERSEY

Philadelphia ●

MARYLAND

DELAWARE

Delaware Bay

ATLANTIC

OCEAN

VIRGINIA

Chesapeake Bay

NORTH CAROLINA

King's Mountain ✕

✕ Camden

SOUTH CAROLINA

GEORGIA

Savannah ●

CANADA AND
THE AMERICAN
COLONIES 1750-85

✕ Battle

0   100   200   300 miles

THE
AGRICULTURAL
AND INDUSTRIAL
REVOLUTIONS

Glasgow
Edinburgh

Newcastle

Belfast

Darlington

Bradford York
Preston Leeds
Halifax
Bolton
Manchester
Sheffield Lincoln
Chester
Stoke
Derby
Shrewsbury Stafford Nottingham
King's Lynn
Leicester
Bridgnorth Birmingham Holkham
Bewdley Coventry

Swansea Oxford
Cardiff London
Bristol
Bath Reading

Southampton

▨ Extent of eighteenth century enclosure   ● Town

⊥⊥⊥⊥⊥ Canal

0   50   100 miles

473

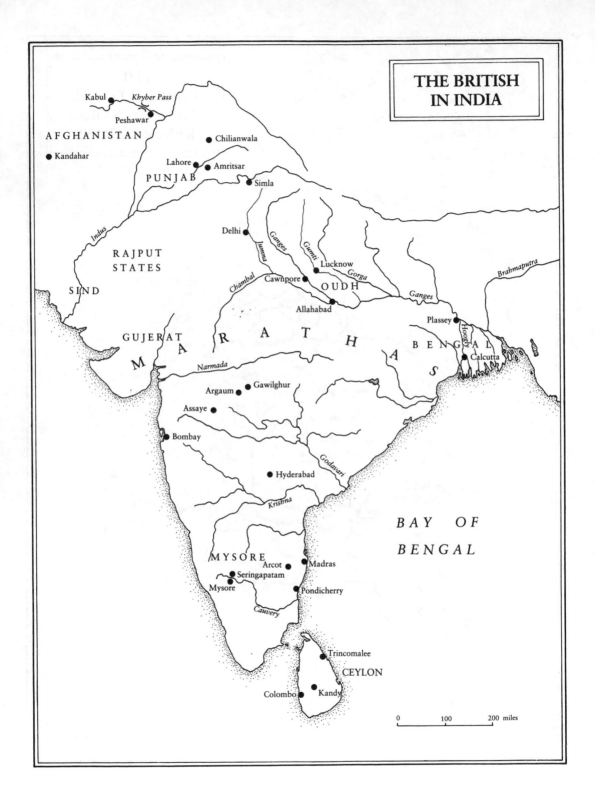

THE BRITISH
IN INDIA

Kabul
Khyber Pass
Peshawar
AFGHANISTAN
Kandahar
Chilianwala
Lahore
Amritsar
PUNJAB
Simla
Delhi
RAJPUT
STATES
SIND
Ganges
Jumna
Gumti
Lucknow
Gorga
Cawnpore
OUDH
Chambal
Allahabad
Ganges
Plassey
Brahmaputra
GUJERAT
M A R A T H A S
BENGAL
Hoogly
Calcutta
Narmada
Argaum
Gawilghur
Assaye
Bombay
Hyderabad
Godavari
Krishna
BAY OF
BENGAL
MYSORE
Arcot
Madras
Seringapatam
Mysore
Pondicherry
Cauvery
Trincomalee
CEYLON
Colombo
Kandy

0   100   200 miles

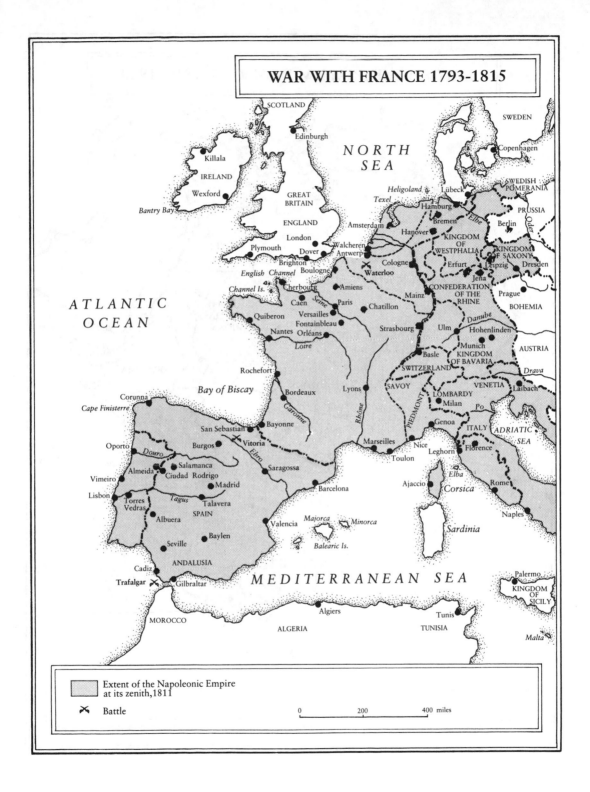

WAR WITH FRANCE 1793-1815

SCOTLAND

SWEDEN

Edinburgh

*NORTH
SEA*

Copenhagen

Killala

IRELAND

SWEDISH
POMERANIA

Heligoland   Lübeck

Texel   Hamburg

PRUSSIA

Wexford

GREAT
BRITAIN

Amsterdam

Bremen

Berlin

Bantry Bay

ENGLAND

Hanover

KINGDOM
OF
WESTPHALIA

KINGDOM
OF SAXONY

Elbe

Oder

London

Walcheren

Plymouth   Dover

Antwerp

Cologne

Erfurt

Leipzig   Dresden

Brighton

Waterloo

Jena

Prague

*ATLANTIC
OCEAN*

English Channel   Boulogne

Cherbourg

Amiens

CONFEDERATION
OF THE
RHINE

BOHEMIA

Channel Is.

Caen   Seine   Paris

Mainz

Quiberon

Versailles
Fontainebleau

Chatillon

Strasbourg

Ulm

Danube

Hohenlinden

Nantes   Orléans

Loire

AUSTRIA

Rochefort

Basle

Munich

KINGDOM
OF BAVARIA

Drava

Bay of Biscay

Bordeaux

Lyons

SWITZERLAND

Cape Finisterre

Garonne

SAVOY

Rhône

VENETIA

LOMBARDY

Laibach

Corunna

Milan

Po

Bayonne

San Sebastian

Vitoria

Ebro

Marseilles

Nice

Genoa

PIEDMONT

ITALY

*ADRIATIC
SEA*

Oporto

Burgos

Douro

Toulon

Leghorn

Florence

Vimeiro

Almeida

Salamanca
Ciudad Rodrigo

Saragossa

Elba

Lisbon

Torres
Vedras

Madrid

Barcelona

Ajaccio

Corsica

Rome

Talavera

Tagus

SPAIN

Albuera

Valencia

Baylen

Majorca   *Minorca*

Naples

Seville

Sardinia

Cadiz

ANDALUSIA

Balearic Is.

MEDITERRANEAN SEA

Palermo

Trafalgar   Gilbraltar

KINGDOM
OF
SICILY

MOROCCO

Algiers

ALGERIA

Tunis

TUNISIA

Malta

	Extent of the Napoleonic Empire at its zenith, 1811
✕	Battle

0   200   400 miles

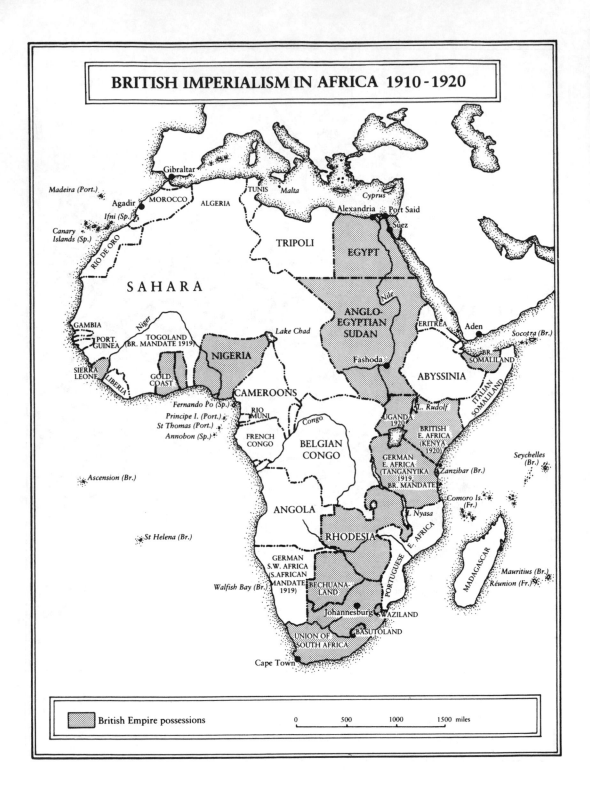

BRITISH IMPERIALISM IN AFRICA 1910-1920

Madeira (Port.)

Gibraltar

TUNIS · *Malta* · *Cyprus*

Agadir · MOROCCO · ALGERIA

Ifni (Sp.)

Alexandria · Port Said

Suez

Canary Islands (Sp.)

RIO DE ORO

TRIPOLI

EGYPT

SAHARA

Nile

GAMBIA

Niger · Lake Chad

PORT. GUINEA

TOGOLAND (BR. MANDATE 1919)

ANGLO-EGYPTIAN SUDAN

ERITREA · Aden

Socotra (Br.)

NIGERIA

BR. SOMALILAND

SIERRA LEONE

LIBERIA

GOLD COAST

Fashoda

ABYSSINIA

ITALIAN SOMALILAND

CAMEROONS

Fernando Po (Sp.)

Principe I. (Port.)

St Thomas (Port.)

Annobon (Sp.)

RIO MUNI

FRENCH CONGO

Congo

L. Rudolf

UGANDA 1920

BELGIAN CONGO

BRITISH E. AFRICA (KENYA 1920)

GERMAN E. AFRICA (TANGANYIKA) 1919 BR. MANDATE

Zanzibar (Br.)

Seychelles (Br.)

Ascension (Br.)

Comoro Is. (Fr.)

ANGOLA

L. Nyasa

St Helena (Br.)

RHODESIA

PORTUGUESE E. AFRICA

MADAGASCAR

GERMAN S.W. AFRICA (S.AFRICAN MANDATE 1919)

Mauritius (Br.)

Réunion (Fr.)

Walfish Bay (Br.)

BECHUANA-LAND

SWAZILAND

Johannesburg

BASUTOLAND

UNION OF SOUTH AFRICA

Cape Town

British Empire possessions

0   500   1000   1500 miles

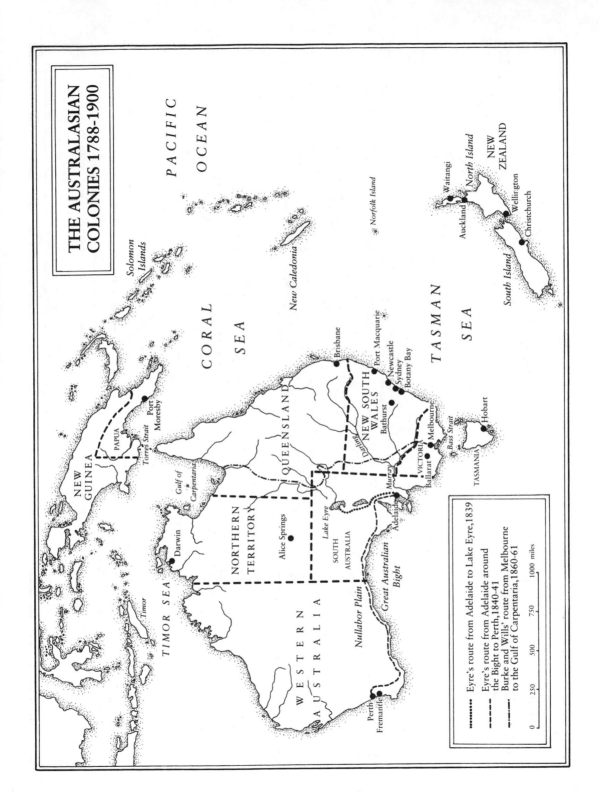

THE AUSTRALASIAN
COLONIES 1788-1900

PACIFIC OCEAN

Solomon Islands

New Caledonia

CORAL SEA

TASMAN SEA

NEW ZEALAND

North Island

Waitangi
Auckland
Wellington
Christchurch

South Island

Norfolk Island

NEW GUINEA

PAPUA

Port Moresby

Torres Strait

Gulf of Carpentaria

Timor

TIMOR SEA

Darwin

NORTHERN TERRITORY

Alice Springs

WESTERN AUSTRALIA

Nullabor Plain

Great Australian Bight

Perth
Fremantle

SOUTH AUSTRALIA

Lake Eyre

Adelaide

QUEENSLAND

Brisbane

NEW SOUTH WALES

Darling

Murray

Bathurst

Port Macquarie
Newcastle
Sydney
Botany Bay

Melbourne

VICTORIA

Ballarat

Bass Strait

TASMANIA

Hobart

Eyre's route from Adelaide to Lake Eyre, 1839
Eyre's route from Adelaide around the Bight to Perth, 1840–41
Burke and Wills' route from Melbourne to the Gulf of Carpentaria, 1860–61

0   250   500   750   1000 miles

477

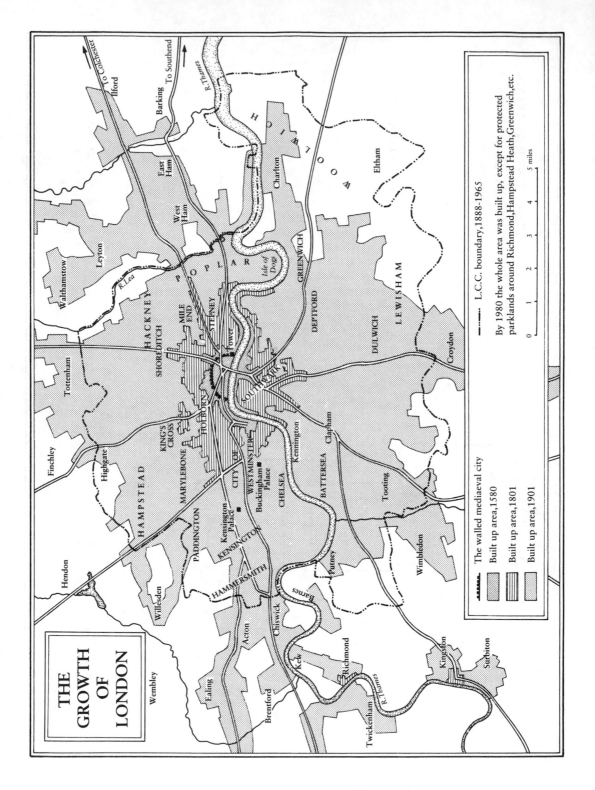

THE
GROWTH
OF
LONDON

L.C.C. boundary, 1888-1965

By 1980 the whole area was built up, except for protected parklands around Richmond, Hampstead Heath, Greenwich, etc.

The walled mediaeval city

Built up area, 1580

Built up area, 1801

Built up area, 1901

0   1   2   3   4   5 miles

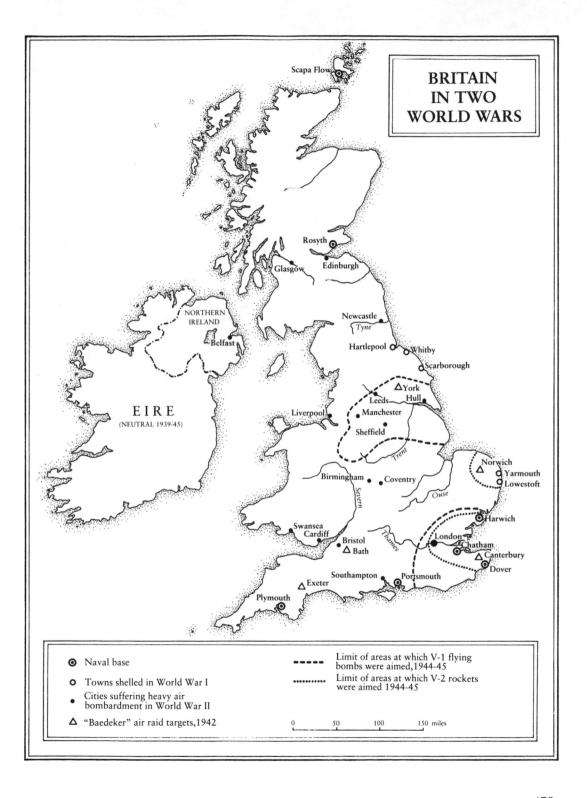

BRITAIN IN TWO WORLD WARS

Scapa Flow

Rosyth
Glasgow Edinburgh

NORTHERN
IRELAND
Belfast

EIRE
(NEUTRAL 1939-45)

Newcastle
Tyne
Hartlepool Whitby
Scarborough

York
Leeds Hull
Liverpool Manchester
Sheffield
Trent

Birmingham Coventry
Severn *Ouse*
Norwich Yarmouth
Lowestoft

Swansea
Cardiff Harwich
Bristol London Chatham
Bath *Thames* Canterbury
Dover

Southampton Portsmouth
Exeter

Plymouth

⊙ Naval base	----- Limit of areas at which V-1 flying bombs were aimed, 1944-45
○ Towns shelled in World War I	·········· Limit of areas at which V-2 rockets were aimed 1944-45
• Cities suffering heavy air bombardment in World War II	
△ "Baedeker" air raid targets,1942	0 50 100 150 miles

479

ROMAN GOVERNORS OF BRITAIN AD 43–208

43–47	A. Plautius	*by 146*	Cn. Papirius Aelianus
47–52	P. Ostorius Scapula	*154/by 158*	Cn. Julius Verus
52–57/8	A. Didius Gallus	*158/9–161*	?anus Longus (or Longinus)
57/8–61	C. Suetonius Paulinus	*161/2*	M. Statius Priscus
61/2–63	P. Petronius Turpilianus	*by 163/4–?166*	S. Calpurnius Agricola
63–69	M. Trebellius Maximus	*by period 168/9–180*	Q. Antistius Adventus
68/9–71	M. Vettius Bolanus	*in period 169–180*	? Caerellius Priscus
71–73/4	Q. Petilius Cerealis	*by 180*	Ulpius Marcellus
74–77/8	S. Julius Frontinus	*185–?187*	P. Helvius Pertinax
78–84/5 *(or 77–83)*	Cn. Julius Agricola	*191/2–?*	Dec. Clodius Albinus
in period 83/4–96	Sallustius Lucullus		(Caesar 193, d. 197)
?by 96	P. Metilius Nepos	*197–?200/2*	Virius Lupus
?97/8–?100–01	T. Avidius Quietus	*?202*	M. Antius Crescens
?100/1–after 103	L. Neratius Marcellus		Calpurnianus (acting
?115–?118	M. Appius (or Atilius)		governor)
	Bradua	*202/3–after 205*	C. Valerius Pudens
118–122	Q. Pompeius Falco	*205/7–?*	L. Alfenus Senecio
122–?125	A. Platorius Nepos	*by 216*	Emperor Caracalla reor-
c.131–132/3	S. Julius Severus		ganizes Britain into 2
?132/3–after 135	P. Mummius Sisenna		provinces; very little is
138/9–?144	Q. Lollius Urbicus		known about subsequent
			governors of either.

ENGLISH RULERS BEFORE 927

Names in capital letters were recognized as overlords of other English rulers.

	EAST ANGLIA (EAST ANGLES)	560	ETHELBERT I; first Christian king
to 627	REDWALD (d. 627)		of Kent
627	Erpwald	616	Edbald
630/1	Sigebert	640	Erconbert
654	Ethelhere	664	Egbert I
655	Ethelwald	673 *Jul.*	Lothere
663/4	Aldwulf	685	Edric
713	Elfwald	688/90	Swefhard and Oswin
749	Kingdom divided	690/2	Witred
855	(St) Edmund; killed by Danes, 20	725	Ethelbert II, Edbert and others
	Nov. 869	765	Egbert II
878/80	Guthrum; first Danish king of E.	784	Elmund
	Anglia	796	Edbert; deposed by Cenwulf, K. of
917	Edward, K. of Wessex, conquered		Mercia, 798
	E. Anglia	798	Cuthred, Mercian prince
		807	Baldred
	KENT	825/7	K. Egbert of Wessex expelled
455	Hengist		Baldred and united thereafter Kent
488	Oeric (Oisc)		with Wessex
?512	Eormenric		

MERCIA

626/32	Penda; killed in Ψ Winwaed against Northumbria, 15 Nov. 655
655–658	Mercia under the rule of Northumbria
658	Wulfhere
675	Ethelred
704	Cenred
709	Ceolred
716	ETHELBALD
757	OFFA; first king to be called 'King of the English', 774
796 *Jul.*	Egfrith
Dec.	Cenwulf
821	Ceolwulf I
823	Beornwulf
825	Ludeca
827	Wiglaf
840	Betwulf
852	Burgred; expelled by Danes, 873/4
873	Ceolwulf II; puppet ruler of part of Mercia under Danes
879	Ethelred II; m. 886/7 Ethelfleda, daughter of ALFRED, K. of Wessex
911	Ethelfleda ('Lady of the Mercians')
918	Elfwyn; taken prisoner by Edward, K. of Wessex, Dec. 918/19; Mercia united with Wessex
924	ATHELSTAN, also K. of Wessex (*q.v.* under Rulers of England)

NORTHUMBRIA

1. Bernicia (northern part of Northumbria)

547	Ida
559	Glappa
560	Adda
568	Ethelric
572	Theodric
579	Frithuwald
585	Hussa
592/3	Ethelfrith; also ruled Deira, becoming first ruler of all Northumbria
633	Eanfrith
634	(St) OSWALD, ruler of all Northumbria
642 *Nov./Dec.*	OSWY; became ruler of all Northumbria, 655/70
655/70–867	Bernicia was part of Northumbria
867	Egbert I, puppet ruler set up by Danes
873	Ricsig
876	Egbert II
878	Eadwulf
913	Aldred
927	ATHELSTAN, K. of Mercia and Wessex (*q.v.* under Rulers of England)

2. Deira (Yorkshire)

560	Aelle
592/3–633	Deira was part of Northumbria
633	Osric
634–642	Deira was part of Northumbria
644	Oswin
651	Ethelwald
655/70–867	Deira was part of Northumbria
867	Deira became Viking kingdom of York

3. Northumbria (592/3–867)

592/3	Ethelfrith, K. of Bernicia; killed in Ψ River Idle, 616
616	EDWIN, K. of Deira; killed in Ψ Hatfield Chase, 12 Oct. 632
634	(St) OSWALD, K. of Bernicia; killed in Ψ Maserfelth, 5 Aug. 642
642 *Nov./Dec.*	OSWY, K. of Bernicia
670 *May/Sep.*	Egfrith
686	Aldfrith
705	*Eadwulf*
705/6	Osred I
716	Cenred
718	Osric
729	Ceolwulf
737	Edbert
758	Oswulf
758/9 *Aug. 5*	Ethelwald Moll
765	Alred
774	Ethelred I; exiled, 778/9
778/9	Elfwald I
788	Osred II; expelled, 790
790	Ethelred I restored
796	Osbald; expelled after 27 days
	Eardwulf
806/8	Elfwald II
808/10	Eanred
840	Ethelred II; expelled, 844
844	Radwulf
	Ethelred II restored
848	Osbert
867	Aelle

	4. Viking Kingdom of York (from 867)		WESSEX (WEST SAXONS)
875/6	Halfdan I; expelled and killed at Ψ Strangford Lough, Ireland, 877	519	Cerdic
		534	Cynric
883	Guthfrith I	560	CEAWLIN
895	Sigfrid and Knut	591	Ceol
899/900	Ethelwald, P. of Wessex, received as king by Vikings	597	Ceolwulf
		611	Cynegils
902	Halfdan II and Eowils; both killed at Ψ Tettenhall, 5 Aug. 910	642	Cenwel
		672	Queen Seaxbur, wife of K. Cenwel
911	Ragnald I; king in York, 919	674	Escwin
921	Sihtric	676	Centwine
927	Guthfrith II	685	Cadwalla; abdicated, baptised and
927	K. ATHELSTAN (*q.v.* under Rulers of England)		died in Rome, 688
		688	Ine
939	Olaf I Guthfrithsson	726	Ethelhard
941	Olaf II Sihtricsson; expelled from York, 943–5	740	Cuthred
		756	Sigebert
943	Ragnald II Guthfrithsson; expelled from York, 944	757	Cynewulf
		786	Britric
944–946	K. Edmund (*q.v.* under Rulers of England)	802	EGBERT; overlord of all English kingdoms, 829–30
946–947	K. Eadred (*q.v.* under Rulers of England)	839	Ethelwulf
		855	Ethelbald
947	Eric 'Bloodaxe'; expelled, 948	860	Ethelbert
949/50	Olaf II Sihtricsson returned to York; expelled again, 952; became K. of Dublin till death, 981	865	Ethelred
		871 *Apr.*	ALFRED
		899 *Oct.*	EDWARD ('the Elder')
952	Eric 'Bloodaxe' returned; expelled and killed at Ψ Stainmore, 954	924 *Jul.*	Elfward
		925 *Sep. 4*	ATHELSTAN, K. of Mercia, crowned king of Wessex (*q.v.* under Rulers of England)
954	K. Eadred (*q.v.* under Rulers of England)		
	SUSSEX (SOUTH SAXONS)		
477	AELLE		

RULERS OF ENGLAND AND THEIR CONSORTS

927	Athelstan of Wessex and Mercia		(Sep. 1013 to Feb. 1014 Swein
939 *Oct.*	Edmund I; m. (1) Elfgifu, (2) Ethelflaed		Forkbeard of Denmark acknowledged as K. of All England.
946 *May*	Eadred		Ethelred resumes his reign in
955 *Nov.*	Eadwig; m. 956 Elfgifu		March 1014)
959 *Oct.*	Edgar I; m. (1) Ethelflaed, (2) Wulfthryth, (3) 965 Elfthryth	1016 *Apr.*	Edmund II Ironside; m. 1015 Eldgyth
975 *Jul.*	Edward 'The Martyr' (assassinated at Corfe, 18 Mar. 978)	*Nov.*	Cnut (d. 12 Nov. 1035); m. (1) Elfgifu of Northampton, (2) Q.
978 *Mar.*	Ethelred 'the Unready'; m. (1) Elfgifu, (2) 1002 Emma of Normandy		Emma, widow of Ethelred
		1037	Harold I 'Harefoot' proclaimed King; widely accepted since 1035

1040 *Jun.*	Harthacnut		1509 *Apr. 22*	Henry VIII; m. (1) 11 Jun. 1509
1042 *Jun.*	Edward 'the Confessor'; m. 23 Jan. 1045, Edith, daughter of E. Godwin of Wessex			Catherine of Aragon, (2) 25 Jan. 1533 Anne Boleyn, (3) 30 May 1536 Jane Seymour, (4) 6 Jan. 1540 Anne of Cleves, (5) 28 Jul. 1540 Catherine Howard, (6) 12 Jul. 1543 Catherine Parr
1066 *Jan. 23*	Harold II 'Godwinson' (killed at Hastings, 14 Oct. 1066); m. Eldgith of Mercia, having had children by his concubine Edith		1547 *Jan. 28*	Edward VI
Dec. 25	William I of Normandy; m. *c.* 1051 Matilda of Flanders		1553 *Jul. 6*	Jane (deposed); m. 21 May 1553 Guildford Dudley
1087 *Sep. 26*	William II 'Rufus'		*19*	Mary I; m. 25 Jul. 1554 Philip of Spain
1100 *Aug. 5*	Henry I; m. (1) 1100 Matilda/ Edith of Scotland, (2) 1121 Adela of Louvain		1558 *Nov. 17*	Elizabeth I
1135 *Dec. 22*	Stephen of Blois; m. 1125 Matilda of Boulogne		1603 *Mar. 24*	James I; m. 20 Aug. 1589 Anne of Denmark
1154 *Dec. 19*	Henry II; m. 18 May 1152 Eleanor of Aquitaine (d. 1204)		1625 *Mar. 27*	Charles I (executed 30 Jan. 1649); m. May 1625 Henrietta Maria of France
1189 *Sep. 3*	Richard I; m. 12 May 1191 Berengaria of Navarre			(Lord Protectors: Oliver Cromwell, 16 Dec. 1653 to 3 Sep. 1658; Richard Cromwell, Sep. 1658 to 24 May 1659)
1199 *May 27*	John m. (1) 29 Aug. 1189 Isabella of Gloucester, (2) 24 Aug. 1200 Isabella of Angouleme		1660 *May 29*	Charles II; m. 21 May 1662 Catherine of Braganza
1216 *Oct. 28*	Henry III; m. 20 Jan. 1236 Eleanor of Provence		1685 *Feb. 6*	James II (d. Sep. 1701); m. (1) 3 Sep. 1660 Anne Hyde, (2) 30 Sep. 1673 Mary of Modena
1272 *Nov. 20*	Edward I; m. (1) Oct. 1254 Eleanor of Castile, (2) 10 Sep. 1299 Margaret of France		1689 *Feb. 13*	William III (d. 8 Mar. 1702) and Mary II (d. 28 Dec. 1694); m. 4 Nov. 1677
1307 *Jul. 8*	Edward II (dep. 1327); m. Jan. 1308 Isabella of France		1702 *Mar. 8*	Anne; m. 28 Jul. 1683 George of Denmark
1327 *Jan. 25*	Edward III; m. 24 Jan. 1328 Philippa of Hainault		1714 *Aug. 1*	George I; m. Nov. 1682 Sophia Dorothea of Celle
1377 *Jun. 23*	Richard II (deposed Sep. 1399, murdered Feb. 1400); m. (1) 20 Jan. 1382 Anne of Bohemia, (2) 12 Mar. 1396 Isabella of France		1727 *Jun. 11*	George II; m. 25 Aug. 1705 Caroline of Anspach
1399 *Sep. 30*	Henry IV; m. (1) *c.* Jul. 1380 Mary of Bohun, (2) 7 Feb. 1403 Joan of Navarre		1760 *Oct. 25*	George III; m. 8 Sep. 1761 Charlotte of Mecklenburg
1413 *Mar. 13*	Henry V; m. 2 Jun. 1420 Catherine of Valois		1820 *Jan. 29*	George IV; m. 8 Apr. 1795 Caroline of Brunswick
1422 *Sep. 1*	Henry VI (deposed Mar. 1461, restored Oct. 1470, deposed Apr. 1471); m. 23 Apr. 1445 Margaret of Anjou (d. 1482)		1830 *Jun. 26*	William IV; m. 11 Jul. 1818 Adelaide of Saxe-Meiningen
1461 *Mar. 4*	Edward IV; m. 1 May 1464 Elizabeth Woodville		1837 *Jun. 20*	Victoria; m. 10 Feb. 1840 Albert of Saxe-Coburg
1483 *Apr. 9*	Edward V (deposed 25 Jun. 1483)		1901 *Jan. 22*	Edward VII; m. 10 Mar. 1863 Alexandra of Denmark
Jun. 26	Richard III; m. 12 Jul. 1472 Anne Neville		1910 *May 6*	George V; m. 6 Jul. 1893 Mary of Teck
1485 *Aug. 22*	Henry VII; m. 18 Jan. 1486 Elizabeth of York		1936 *Jan. 20*	Edward VIII (abdicated); m. 3 Jun. 1937 Wallis Simpson
			Dec. 11	George VI; m. 26 Apr. 1923 Lady Elizabeth Bowes-Lyon
			1952 *Feb. 6*	Elizabeth II; m. 20 Nov. 1947 Philip, D. of Edinburgh

RULERS IN SCOTLAND TO 843

to 584	Brude, son of Maelchon, K. of Picts (d. 584)
574	Aidan, K. of Argyll Scots (Dal Riada)
c.671	Brude, son of Bile, K. of Picts (d. 693)
to 706	Brude, son of Derile, K. of Picts (d. 706)
to 732	Nechtan, K. of Picts (d. 732)
732	Angus, son of Fergus, K. of Picts (d. 761)
to 834	Angus II, K. of Picts (d. 834)
to 843	Brude, son of Feredach, last king of separate Pictish kingdom (d. 843)
840	Kenneth I (MacAlpin), K. of Argyll Scots; K. of Picts, 843; kingdom now known as Alba

KINGS OF ALBA
(sometimes called Kings of Scots)

858	Donald I
862	Constantine I
877	Aed
878	Eochaid and Giric
889	Donald II
900	Constantine II
943	Malcolm I
954	Indulf
962	Dub
971	Kenneth II
995	Constantine III
997	Kenneth III

KINGS OF SCOTS

1005 Mar. 25	Malcolm II, K. of Alba; acquired Lothian and Strathclyde, c.1016
1034 Nov. 25	Duncan I; killed by Macbeth, 14 Aug. 1040
1040 Aug. 14	Macbeth; m. c.1032 Gruoch; killed by Malcolm, son of Duncan I, 15 Aug. 1057
1057 Aug. 15	Lulach (Macbeth's stepson); killed by Malcolm, 17 Mar. 1058

1058 Mar. 17	Malcolm III (Canmore); m. 1069/70 (St) Margaret, daughter of Edward the Atheling of England
1093 Nov. 13	Donalbane, son of Duncan I; deposed, May 1094
1094 May	Duncan II
Nov. 12	Donalbane restored; finally deposed, Oct. 1097
1097	Edgar
1107 Jan. 8	Alexander I
1124 Apr. 25	David I
1153 May 24	Malcolm IV (The Maiden)
1165 Dec. 9	William (The Lion)
1214 Dec. 4	Alexander II
1249 Jul. 8	Alexander III
1286 Mar. 19	Margaret (Maid of Norway); died on way to Scotland, 26 Sep. 1290

FIRST INTERREGNUM (1290–1292)

1292 Nov. 17	John Balliol, chosen by Edward I of England; abdicated, 10 Jul. 1296

SECOND INTERREGNUM (1296–1306)

1296–1306	Edward I of England governed Scotland
1306 Mar. 25	Robert I (Bruce)
1329 Jun. 7	David II; exiled, May 1334–Jun. 1341; imprisoned in England, Oct. 1346–Oct. 1357
1332 Sep. 24	Edward Balliol, expelled Dec. 1332; restored 1333–6; surrendered throne to Edward III of England, 20 Jan. 1356
1371 Feb. 22	Robert II (Stewart)
1390 Apr. 19	Robert III
1406 Apr. 4	James I
1437 Feb. 21	James II
1460 Aug. 3	James III
1488 Jun. 11	James IV
1513 Sep. 9	James V
1542 Dec. 14	Mary; in France, 15 Aug. 1548–19 Aug. 1561; abdicated, 24 Jul. 1567; exiled in England, May 1568; imprisoned, 20 Jan. 1569; executed, 8 Feb. 1587
1567 Jul. 24	James VI; succeeded to English throne as James I, 24 Mar. 1603

RULERS OF GWYNEDD AND PRINCES OF WALES

Names in capital letters were recognized as princes of all Wales.

844	Rhodri the Great (Powys, 855)	1194/5	LLEWELYN AP IORWERTH (E. Gwynedd; W. Gwynedd, 1200; S. Gwynedd 1201/2; S. Powys 1208; overlord in S. Wales, 1216); m. 1205/6 Joan, natural daughter of K. John.
878	Anarawd		
916	Idwal		
942	Hywel Dda (Dyfed c.904; S. Wales, c.920)		
950	Iago ap Idwal	1240	DAVID AP LLEWELYN
979	Hywel ap Ieuaf	1246	LLEWELYN AP GRUFFYDD (part of Gwynedd; all Gwynedd 1255/6; overlord of all Wales and assumes title P. of Wales 1258; recognized as P. of Wales by K. Henry III, 1267); m. 13 Oct. 1278 Eleanor, daughter of Simon de Montfort
985	Cadwallon ap Ieuaf		
986	Mareddud ab Owain (S. Wales, 987)		
999	Cynan ap Hywel		
c.1005	Llewelyn ap Seisyll (S. Wales, c.1018)		
1023	Iago ap Idwal		
1039	GRUFFYDD AP LLEWELYN (Powys, 1039; S. Wales, 1055)	1282	DAVID AP GRUFFYDD, P. of Wales; executed for treason, 3 Oct. 1283
1063	Bleddyn ap Cynfyn (Powys, 1063)		
1075	Trahaern ap Caradog		**RULERS IN SOUTH WALES**
1081	Gruffydd ap Cynan		
1137	Owain Gwynedd	1078	Rhys ap Tudor
c.1170	Cynan ab Owain	1116	Gruffydd ap Rhys
1175	David ab Owain (E. Gwynedd)	1155	Rhys ap Gruffydd (Cardigan by conquest, 1165/7)
1175	Rhodri ab Owain (W. Gwynedd)		

ENGLISH PRINCES OF WALES

Only eleven 'Princes of Wales' were ever formally invested. This list gives the date on which each was created Prince and, where known, the date and place of investiture.

301	*Feb. 7*	Edward, son of K. Edward I, invested Lincoln 1301			invested Westminster 18 Feb. 1504
343	*May 12*	Edward the Black Prince, invested Westminster 1343	1610	*Jun. 4*	Henry, elder son of K. James I, invested Westminster, 4 Jun. 1610
1376	*Nov. 20*	Richard of Bordeaux			
1399	*Oct 15*	Henry of Monmouth, invested Westminster 1399	1616	*Nov. 4*	Charles, sec. son of K. James I, invested Westminster 4 Nov. 1616
1454	*Mar. 14*	Edward of Lancaster, invested Windsor 1454	1640	*date unknown*	Charles, eldest son of K. Charles I
1471	*Jun. 26*	Edward of York			
1483	*Aug. 24*	Edward of Middleham, invested York 8 Sep. 1483	1688	*Jun. 10*	James Francis Edward, son of K. James II
1489	*Nov. 29*	Arthur, elder son of K. Henry VII, invested Westminster 27 Feb. 1490	1714	*Sep. 27*	George Augustus, eldest son of K. George I
1504	*Feb. 18*	Henry, sec. son of K. Henry VII,	1729	*Jan. 8*	Frederick Lewis, eldest son of K. George II

1751	Apr. 20	George William Frederick, eldest grandson of K. George II	1910	Jun. 23	Albert Edward Christian George Andrew Patrick David, son of K. George V, invested at Caernarfon, 13 Jul. 1911
1762	Aug. 17	George Augustus Frederick, eldest son of K. George III			
1841	Dec. 7	Albert Edward, eldest son of Q. Victoria	1958	Jul. 26	Charles Philip Arthur George, eldest son of Q. Elizabeth II, invested at Caernarfon 1 Jul. 1969
1901	Nov. 9	George, D. of York, son of K. Edward VII			

SOME LEADING STATESMEN IN MEDIAEVAL ENGLAND

The following list gives dates of office held and its nature.

1077–1082	Odo of Bayeux; effective Justiciar, but not given the title	1308	Piers de Gaveston, E. of Cornwall; 'Guardian of England'
1087–1099	Ranulf Flambard; officially 'chief agent of the King's will'	1312–1321 & 1322–1326	Hugh Despenser; Chamberlain
1102–1139	Roger, Bp of Salisbury; Justiciar of England	1326–1340	John Stratford, Bp of Winchester, Abp of Canterbury; Treasurer 1326–7, Chancellor 1330–4, 1335–7, 1340
1155–1162	Thomas Becket; Chancellor		
1179–1189	Sir Ranulf de Glanville; Justiciar of England	1344–1363	William Edington, Bp of Winchester; Treasurer 1344–56, Chancellor 1356–63
1189–1191	William Longchamp; Chancellor		
1193–1205	Hubert Walter, Abp of Canterbury; Justiciar until 1198, Chancellor 1199–1205	1363–1391	William of Wykeham, Bp of Winchester; Keeper of the Privy Seal 1363–7, Chancellor 1367–71, 1389–91
1215–1232	Hubert de Burgh; Justiciar of England	1383–1386	Michael de la Pole; Chancellor
1216–1219	William Marshal, E. of Pembroke; Regent	1403–1426	Henry Beaufort, Bp of Winchester; Chancellor 1403–4, 1413–17, 1424–6
1258–1265	(intermittently) Simon de Montfort, E. of Leicester; no formal office of state held	1460–1471	Richard Neville, E. of Warwick; Great Chamberlain
1274–1292	Robert Burnell, Bp of Bath and Wells; Chancellor		

SECRETARIES OF STATE

From the last years of Henry VIII's reign until the loss of the American colonies, two Secretaries of State were, in effect, the departmental chiefs of the administration. After the Restoration it was customary to refer to one of them as 'for the Northern Department' (N) and the other 'for the Southern Department' (S). In 1782 the Northern Department became the Foreign Office and the Southern Department the Home Office.

1540	Sir Thomas Wriothesley	Sir Ralph Sadler
1543 Apr.		William Paget

1544 *Jan.*	Sir William Petre (to 1557)	
1548		Sir Thomas Smith
1549 *Oct.*		Nicholas Wotton
1550 *Sep.*		Sir William Cecil
1553 *Aug.*		Sir John Bourn
1557 *Mar.*	John Boxall	

From Nov. 1558 until July 1572 William Cecil was sole Secretary.

1572 *Jul.*	Sir Thomas Smith	
1573 *Dec.*		Sir Francis Walsingham
1577 *Nov.*	Thomas Wilson	

From May 1581 until Sep. 1586 Walsingham was sole Secretary.

1586 *Sep.*	William Davison	

On Walsingham's death in April 1590 Sir Robert Cecil became acting Secretary.

1596 *Jul.*	Sir Robert Cecil	
1600 *May*		John Herbert
1612 *May*	Robert Carr, Lord Rochester	
1614 *Mar.*	Sir Ralph Winwood	
1616 *Jan.*		Sir Thomas Lake
1618 *Jan.*	Sir Robert Naunton	
1619 *Feb.*		Sir George Calvert
1623 *Jan.*	Sir Edward Conway	
1625 *Sep.*		Sir John Coke
1628 *Dec.*	Dudley Carleton, Lord Dorchester	
1632 *Jun.*	Sir Francis Windebank	
1640 *Feb.*		Sir Harry Vane
1641 *Nov.*	Sir Edward Nicholas	
1642 *Jan.*		Lucius Carey, Lord Falkland
1643 *Oct.*		George Digby

During the Protectorate, John Thurlow was Secretary 1651 to May 1660.

1660 *Jun.*	Sir Edward Nicholas	Sir William Morrice
1662 *Oct.*	H. Bennett (Arlington)	
1668 *Sep.*		Sir John Trevor
1672 *Jul.*		Henry Coventry
1674 *Sep.*	Sir Joseph Wilkinson	
1679 *Feb.*	R. Spencer, E. of Sunderland	
1680 *Apr.*		Sir Leo Jenkins
1681 *Feb.*	E. of Conway	
1683 *Jan.*	E. of Sunderland	
1684 *Apr.*		Sidney, Lord Godolphin
Aug.		E. of Middleton
1688 *Oct.*	Lord Preston	
1689 *Feb.*		E. of Shrewsbury
Mar.	E. of Nottingham	
1690 *Dec.*	Henry, Lord Sydney	E. of Nottingham

1693 *Mar.*	Sir John Trenchard	
1694 *Mar.*	D. of Shrewsbury	Sir John Trenchard
1695 *May*	Sir William Trumbull	D. of Shrewsbury
1697 *Dec.*	James Vernon	
1699 *May*		Edward Villiers, E. of Jersey
1700 *Nov.*	Sir Charles Hedges	
1702 *Jan.*	James Vernon	E. of Manchester
May	Sir Charles Hedges	E. of Nottingham
1704 *May*	Robert Harley	Sir Charles Hedges
1706 *Dec.*		E. of Sunderland
1708 *Feb.*	Henry Bowle	
1710 *Jun.*	Lord Dartmouth	
Sep.	Henry St John (Viscount Bolingbroke 1712)	
1713 *Aug.*	William Bromley	Lord Bolingbroke
1714 *Sep.*	Charles, Lord Townshend	James, Lord Stanhope
1716 *Dec.*	Lord Stanhope	Paul Methuen
1717 *Apr.*	E. of Sunderland	Joseph Addison
1718 *Mar.*		James Craggs
	Lord Stanhope	John, Lord Carteret
1724 *Apr.*		D. of Newcastle
1730 *Jun.*	William, Lord Harrington	
1742 *Feb.*	Lord Carteret	
1744 *Nov.*	E. of Harrington	
1746 *Feb.*	E. Granville (Carteret) as sole Secretary	
	E. of Harrington	D. of Newcastle
Oct.	E. of Chesterfield	
1748 *Feb.*	D. of Newcastle	D. of Bedford
1751 *Jun.*		E. of Holdernesse
1754 *Mar.*	E. of Holdernesse	Sir Thomas Robinson
Nov.		Henry Fox
1756 *Dec.*		William Pitt (Chatham)
1757 *Apr.–Jun.*	Holdernesse sole Secretary until Pitt reappointed	
1761 *Mar.*	E. of Bute	
Oct.		E. of Egremont
1762 *May*	George Grenville	
Oct.	E. of Halifax	
1763 *Sep.*	E. of Sandwich	E. of Halifax
1765 *Jul.*	D. of Grafton	Henry Conway
1766 *May*	Henry Conway	D. of Richmond
1766 *Jul.*		E. of Shelburne
1768 *Mar.*	Lord Weymouth	
1768 *Oct.*	E. of Rochford	Lord Weymouth
1770 *Dec.*	E. of Sandwich	E. of Rochford
1771 *Jan.*	E. of Halifax	
1771 *Jun.*	E. of Suffolk	
1775 *Nov.*		Lord Weymouth
1779 *Oct.*	Lord Stormont	Lord Weymouth
1779 *Nov.*		Lord Hillsborough

Secretariat was reorganized in March 1782.

LORD CHANCELLORS OF ENGLAND, 1487–1707

1487 *Mar.*   John Morton, Abp of Canterbury; died, Sep. 1500

1504 *Jan.*   William Warham, Abp of Canterbury

1515 *Dec.*   Thomas Wolsey, Abp of York

1529 *Oct.*   Sir Thomas More; resigned, May 1532

1533 *Jan.*   Sir Thomas Audley; died, April 1544

1544 *May*   Thomas, Lord Wriothesley; dismissed, May 1547

1547 *Oct.*   Richard, Lord Rich; resigned, Dec. 1551

1552 *Jan.*   Thomas Goodrich, Bp of Ely; dismissed, Jul. 1553

1553 *Aug.*   Stephen Gardiner, Bp of Winchester; died, Nov. 1555

1556 *Jan.*   Nicholas Heath, Abp of York

Office vacant, Nov. 1558 to 1579

1579 *Feb.*   Sir Thomas Bromley

1587 *Apr.*   Sir Christopher Hatton

Office vacant, Nov. 1591–1603

1603 *Apr.*   Sir Thomas Egerton; died, Mar. 1617

1618 *Jan.*   Lord Verulam (Francis Bacon)

From Bacon's illness in May 1621 until 1658 the office of Chancellor was left unfilled.

1658 *Jan.*   Sir Edward Hyde (E. of Clarendon 1661)

1672 *Nov.*   Anthony Ashley Cooper, E. of Shaftesbury

1675 *Dec.*   Heneage, Lord Finch (until 1682)

1685 *Sep.*   George, Lord Jeffreys; dismissed, Dec. 1688

1697 *Apr.*   John, Lord Somers; resigned, Apr. 1700

1705 *Oct.*   William, Lord Cowper

LORD TREASURERS, 1486–1714

Since the resignation of the Duke of Shrewsbury in 1714, the office of Lord Treasurer has been held in commission; from 1721 onwards the First Lord of the Treasury has almost always been Prime Minister.

1486 *Jul.*   John, Lord Dynham

1501 *Jun.*   Thomas Howard, E. of Surrey, first D. of Norfolk 1514

1522 *Dec.*   Thomas Howard, E. of Surrey, second D. of Norfolk 1524; arrested, Dec. 1546

1547 *Feb.*   Edward Seymour, D. of Somerset; arrested, Oct. 1549

1550 *Feb.*   William Paulet, Marquess of Winchester; died, Mar. 1572

1572 *Jul.*   William Cecil, Lord Burghley; died, Aug. 1598

1599 *May*   Thomas Sackville, Lord Buckhurst, E. of Dorset from 1604; died, Apr. 1608

1608 *May*   Robert Cecil, E. of Salisbury; died, May 1612; office put in commission

1614 *Jul.*   Thomas Howard, E. of Suffolk; suspended, 1618; office again put in commission

1621 *Sep.*   Lionel, Lord Cranfield, E. of Middlesex 1622; suspended, 1624

1624 *Dec.*   James Ley, E. of Marlborough 1626

1628 *Jul.*   Richard, Lord Weston, E. of Portland 1633

1636 *Mar.*   William Juxon, Bp of London

1641–1643   In commission

1643 *Oct.*   Francis, Lord Cottington; died in Spain, 1652

1660 *Sep.*   Thomas Wriothesley, E. of Southampton; died May 1667

1667 *Jun.*   George Monck, D. of Albemarle; died, Jan. 1670

1672 *Nov.*   Thomas, Lord Clifford

1673 *Jun.*   Sir Thomas Osborne (later E. of Danby) to 1679; office again put in commission

1685 *Feb.* Laurence Hyde, E. of Rochester; resigned, Dec. 1686

Office in commission until accession of Q. Anne.

1703 *May* Sidney, Lord Godolphin (E. of Godolphin 1706)
1711 *May* Robert Harley, E. of Oxford
1714 *Jul.* 30–?13 *Oct.* Charles Talbot, D. of Shrewsbury

PRIME MINISTERS

Party labels mean little in the mid-eighteenth century and are not always given.

1730 *May 15*	Sir Robert Walpole (Whig)
1742 *Feb. 16*	Earl of Wilmington (Whig)
1743 *Aug. 27*	Henry Pelham (Whig)
1754 *Mar. 16*	Duke of Newcastle (Whig)
1756 *Nov. 16*	Duke of Devonshire (Whig)
1757 *Jul. 2*	Duke of Newcastle (II) (Whig)
1762 *May 26*	Earl of Bute (Tory)
1763 *Apr. 16*	George Grenville
1765 *Jul. 13*	Marquis of Rockingham
1766 *Jul. 30*	Earl of Chatham
1768 *Oct. 14*	Duke of Grafton
1770 *Jan. 28*	Lord North (Tory)
1782 *Mar. 27*	Marquis of Rockingham (II) (Whig)
Jul. 4	Earl of Shelburne (Whig)
1783 *Apr. 2*	Duke of Portland (Coalition)
Dec. 19	William Pitt (Tory)
1801 *Mar. 17*	Henry Addington (Tory)
1804 *May 10*	William Pitt (II) (Tory)
1806 *Feb. 10*	Lord Grenville (Whig)
1807 *Mar. 31*	Duke of Portland (II) (Tory)
1809 *Oct. 6*	Spencer Perceval (Tory)
1812 *Jun. 9*	Lord Liverpool (Tory)
1827 *Apr. 10*	George Canning (Tory)
Aug. 31	Viscount Goderich (Tory)
1828 *Jan. 22*	Duke of Wellington (Tory)
1830 *Nov. 22*	Earl Grey (Whig)
1834 *Jul. 13*	Viscount Melbourne (Whig)
Dec. 10	Sir Robert Peel (Con.)
1835 *Apr. 18*	Viscount Melbourne (II) (Whig)
1841 *Sep. 6*	Sir Robert Peel (II) (Con.)
1846 *Jun. 30*	Lord John Russell (Whig/Lib.)
1852 *Feb. 23*	Earl of Derby (Con.)
Dec. 19	Earl of Aberdeen (Peelite)
1855 *Feb. 6*	Viscount Palmerston (Lib.)
1858 *Feb. 20*	Earl of Derby (II) (Con.)
1859 *Jun. 18*	Viscount Palmerston (II) (Lib.)
1865 *Oct. 29*	Earl Russell (II) (Lib.)
1866 *Jun. 28*	Earl of Derby (III) (Con.)
1868 *Feb. 27*	Benjamin Disraeli (Con.)
Dec. 3	William Ewart Gladstone (Lib.)
1874 *Feb. 20*	Benjamin Disraeli (II); became Earl of Beaconsfield 1876 (Con.)
1880 *Apr. 23*	William E. Gladstone (II) (Lib.)
1885 *Jun. 23*	Marquis of Salisbury (Con.)
1886 *Feb. 1*	William E. Gladstone (III) (Lib.)
Jul. 25	Marquis of Salisbury (II) (Con.)
1892 *Aug. 15*	William E. Gladstone (IV) (Lib.)
1894 *Mar. 5*	Earl of Rosebery (Lib.)
1895 *Jun. 25*	Marquis of Salisbury (III) (Con./Unionist)
1902 *Jul. 12*	Arthur James Balfour (Con./Unionist)
1905 *Dec. 5*	Sir Henry Campbell Bannerman (Lib.)
1908 *Apr. 7*	Herbert Henry Asquith (Lib.)
1915 *May 26*	Herbert Henry Asquith (II) (Coalition)
1916 *Dec. 7*	David Lloyd George (Coalition)
1922 *Oct. 23*	Andrew Bonar Law (Con.)
1923 *May 22*	Stanley Baldwin (Con.)
1924 *Jan. 22*	J. Ramsay MacDonald (Lab.)
Nov. 4	Stanley Baldwin (II) (Con.)
1929 *Jun. 5*	J. Ramsay MacDonald (II) (Lab.)
1931 *Aug. 26*	J. Ramsay MacDonald (III) (National)
1935 *Jun. 7*	Stanley Baldwin (III) (National)
1937 *May 28*	A. Neville Chamberlain (National)
1940 *May 10*	Winston Churchill (Coalition)
1945 *May 23*	Winston Churchill (II) (Con.)
Jul. 26	Clement Attlee (Lab.)
1951 *Oct. 26*	Winston Churchill (III) (Con.)
1955 *Apr. 6*	Sir Anthony Eden (Con.)
1957 *Jan. 10*	M. Harold Macmillan (Con.)
1963 *Oct. 19*	Earl of Home; became Sir Alec Douglas-Home 23 Oct. (Con.)

1964 *Oct. 16*	Harold Wilson (Lab.)		1976 *Apr. 5*	L. James Callaghan (Lab.)
1970 *Jun. 19*	Edward Heath (Con.)		1979 *May 4*	Margaret Thatcher (Con.)
1974 *Mar. 4*	Harold Wilson (II) (Lab.)		1990 *Nov. 28*	John Major (Con.)

CHANCELLORS OF THE EXCHEQUER

The earliest official described as 'Chancellor of the Exchequer' appears to have been Sir Walter Mildmay, from 5 February 1559 until his death on 3 May 1589. Until 1827, however, financial responsibilities were more often entrusted to a Lord Treasurer, a Lord High Treasurer or the First Lord of the Treasury. The following list gives Chancellors who were, in effect, 'ministers of finance', responsible for presenting a budget.

1827 *Sep. 3*	John Herries		1915 *May 27*	Reginald McKenna
1828 *Jan. 22*	Henry Goulbourn		1916 *Dec. 11*	Andrew Bonar Law
1830 *Nov. 22*	Viscount Althorp (John Spencer)		1919 *Jan. 14*	Austen Chamberlain
1834 *Dec. 10*	Sir Robert Peel		1921 *Apr. 5*	Sir Robert Horne
1835 *Apr. 18*	Sir Thomas Spring Rice		1922 *Oct. 25*	Stanley Baldwin
1839 *Aug. 26*	Sir Francis Baring		1923 *Oct. 11*	Neville Chamberlain
1841 *Sep. 3*	Henry Goulburn		1924 *Jan. 23*	Philip Snowden
1846 *Jul. 6*	Sir Charles Wood		*Nov. 7*	Winston S. Churchill
1852 *Feb. 27*	Benjamin Disraeli		1929 *Jun. 8*	Philip Snowden
Dec. 28	William Gladstone		1931 *Nov. 9*	Neville Chamberlain
1855 *Feb. 28*	Sir George Cornewall Lewis		1937 *May 28*	Sir John Simon
1858 *Feb. 26*	Benjamin Disraeli		1940 *May 12*	Sir Kingsley Wood
1859 *Jun. 18*	William Gladstone		1943 *Sep. 28*	Sir John Anderson
1866 *Jul. 6*	Benjamin Disraeli		1945 *Jul. 28*	Hugh Dalton
1868 *Feb. 29*	George Ward Hunt		1947 *Nov. 17*	Sir Stafford Cripps
Dec. 9	Robert Lowe		1950 *Oct. 25*	Hugh Gaitskell
1873 *Aug. 31*	William Gladstone (also Prime Minister)		1951 *Oct. 27*	Richard Austen Butler
			1955 *Dec. 22*	M. Harold Macmillan
1874 *Feb. 21*	Sir Stafford Northcote		1957 *Jan. 14*	Peter Thorneycroft
1880 *Apr. 28*	William Gladstone (also Prime Minister)		1958 *Jan. 7*	Derick Heathcoat Amory
			1960 *Jul. 27*	John Selwyn Lloyd
1882 *Dec. 16*	Hugh Childers		1962 *Jul. 13*	Reginald Maudling
1885 *Jun. 24*	Sir Michael Hicks Beach		1964 *Oct. 16*	L. James Callaghan
1886 *Feb. 6*	Sir William Harcourt		1967 *Nov. 30*	Roy Jenkins
Feb. 3	Lord Randolph Churchill		1970 *Jun. 20*	Iain Macleod
1887 *Jan. 14*	George Goschen		*Jul. 25*	Anthony Barber
1892 *Aug. 18*	Sir William Harcourt		1974 *Mar. 5*	Denis Healey
1895 *Jun. 29*	Sir Michael Hicks Beach		1979 *May 5*	Sir Geoffrey Howe
1902 *Jul. 12*	Charles Ritchie		1983 *Jun. 11*	Nigel Lawson
1903 *Oct. 9*	Austen Chamberlain		1989 *Oct. 26*	John Major
1905 *Dec. 11*	H. Henry Asquith		1990 *Nov. 28*	Norman Lamont
1908 *Apr. 16*	David Lloyd George			

FOREIGN SECRETARIES

The Foreign Office was created during the major administrative reorganization of the spring of 1782. When the Foreign Office and Commonwealth Office were merged on 1 Oct. 1968 the post was redesignated 'Secretary of State for Foreign and Commonwealth Affairs'.

1782 *Mar. 27*	Charles J. Fox	
Jul. 17	Thomas Robinson	
1783 *Apr. 2*	Charles J. Fox	
Dec. 19	George Grenville	
23	Marquis of Carmarthen	
1791 *Jun. 8*	Lord (William) Grenville	
1801 *Feb. 20*	Lord Hawkesbury	
1804 *May 14*	Lord Harrowby	
1805 *Jan. 11*	Lord Mulgrave	
1806 *Feb. 7*	Charles J. Fox	
Sep. 24	Viscount Howick	
1807 *Mar. 25*	George Canning	
1809 *Oct. 11*	Earl Bathurst	
Dec. 6	Lord (Richard) Wellesley	
1812 *Mar. 4*	Viscount Castlereagh	
1822 *Sep. 16*	George Canning	
1827 *Apr. 30*	Lord Dudley	
1828 *Jun. 2*	Earl of Aberdeen	
1830 *Nov. 22*	Lord Palmerston	
1834 *Nov. 15*	Duke of Wellington	
1835 *Apr. 18*	Lord Palmerston	
1841 *Sep. 2*	Earl of Aberdeen	
1846 *Jul. 6*	Lord Palmerston	
1851 *Dec. 26*	Lord Granville	
1852 *Feb. 27*	Earl of Malmesbury	
Dec. 28	Lord John Russell	
1853 *Feb. 21*	Earl of Clarendon	
1858 *Feb. 26*	Earl of Malmesbury	
1859 *Jun. 18*	Lord John Russell	
1865 *Nov. 3*	Earl of Clarendon	
1866 *Jul. 6*	Lord Stanley	
1868 *Dec. 9*	Earl of Clarendon	
1870 *Jul. 6*	Lord Granville	
1874 *Feb. 21*	Earl of Derby (ex. Lord Stanley)	
1878 *Apr. 2*	Lord Salisbury	
1880 *Apr. 28*	Lord Granville	
1885 *Jun. 24*	Lord Salisbury (also Prime Minister)	
1886 *Feb. 6*	Lord Rosebery	
Aug. 3	Lord Iddesleigh (Stafford Northcote)	
1887 *Jan. 14*	Lord Salisbury (also Prime Minister)	
1892 *Aug. 18*	Lord Rosebery	
1894 *Mar. 11*	Earl of Kimberley	
1895 *Jun. 29*	Lord Salisbury (also Prime Minister)	
1900 *Nov. 12*	Lord Lansdowne	
1905 *Dec. 11*	Sir Edward Grey	
1916 *Dec. 11*	Arthur James Balfour	
1919 *Oct. 24*	Lord Curzon	
1924 *Jan. 23*	J. Ramsay MacDonald (also Prime Minister)	
Nov. 7	Austen Chamberlain	
1929 *Jun. 8*	Arthur Henderson	
1931 *Aug. 26*	Marquis of Reading	
Nov. 9	Sir John Simon	
1935 *Jun. 7*	Sir Samuel Hoare	
Dec. 22	Anthony Eden	
1938 *Mar. 1*	Lord Halifax	
1940 *Dec. 23*	Anthony Eden	
1945 *Jul. 28*	Ernest Bevin	
1951 *Mar. 12*	Herbert Morrison	
Oct. 27	Anthony Eden	
1955 *Apr. 12*	M. Harold Macmillan	
Dec. 22	John Selwyn Lloyd	
1960 *Jul. 27*	Lord Home	
1963 *Oct. 20*	Richard Austen Butler	
1964 *Oct. 16*	Patrick Gordon Walker	
1965 *Jan. 22*	Michael Stewart	
1966 *Aug. 11*	George Brown	
1968 *Mar. 16*	Michael Stewart	
1970 *Jun. 20*	Sir Alec Douglas-Home (ex Lord Home)	
1974 *Mar. 5*	L. James Callaghan	
1976 *Apr. 8*	Anthony Crosland	
1977 *Feb. 21*	David Owen	
1979 *May 5*	Lord Carrington	
1982 *Apr. 5*	Francis Pym	
1983 *Jun. 11*	Sir Geoffrey Howe	
1989 *Jul. 24*	John Major	
1989 *Oct. 26*	Douglas Hurd	

HOME SECRETARIES

The Home Office dates from 1782. Until 1794 the Home Secretary was administratively responsible for the army and until 1801 his department also attended to colonial matters.

1782 *Mar. 27*	Lord Shelburne
1782 *Jul. 10*	Thomas Townshend
1783 *Apr. 2*	Frederick North
Dec. 19	Earl Temple
23	Lord Sydney
1789 *Jun. 5*	Lord (William) Grenville
1791 *Jun. 8*	Henry Dundas
1794 *Jul. 11*	Duke of Portland
1801 *Jul. 30*	Lord Pelham
1803 *Aug. 17*	Charles Yorke
1804 *May 12*	Lord Hawkesbury
1806 *Feb. 5*	Earl Spencer
1807 *Mar. 25*	Lord Hawkesbury
1809 *Nov. 1*	Richard Ryder
1812 *Jun. 11*	Viscount Sidmouth
1822 *Jan. 17*	Robert Peel
1830 *Nov. 22*	Lord Melbourne
1834 *Dec. 15*	Henry Goulbourn
1835 *Apr. 18*	Lord John Russell
1839 *Aug. 30*	Lord Normanby
1841 *Sep. 2*	Sir James Graham
1846 *Jul. 6*	Sir George Grey
1852 *Feb. 27*	Spencer Walpole
Dec. 28	Lord Palmerston
1855 *Feb. 8*	Sir George Grey
1859 *Mar. 3*	Thomas Estcourt
Jun. 18	Sir George Cornewall Lewis
1861 *Jul. 25*	Sir George Grey
1866 *Jul. 6*	Spencer Walpole
1867 *May 17*	Gathorne Hardy
1868 *Dec. 9*	Henry Bruce
1873 *Aug. 9*	Robert Lowe
1874 *Feb. 21*	Richard Cross
1880 *Apr. 28*	Sir William Vernon Harcourt
1885 *Jun. 24*	Sir Richard Cross
1886 *Feb. 6*	Hugh Childers
Aug. 3	Henry Matthews
1892 *Aug. 18*	H. Henry Asquith
1895 *Jun. 29*	Sir Matthew Ridley
1900 *Nov. 12*	Charles Ritchie
1902 *Jul. 12*	Aretas Akers-Douglas
1905 *Dec. 11*	Herbert Gladstone
1910 *Feb. 19*	Winston S. Churchill
1911 *Oct. 24*	Reginald McKenna
1915 *May 27*	Sir John Simon
1916 *Jan. 12*	Herbert Samuel
Dec. 11	George Cave
1919 *Jan. 14*	Edward Shortt
1922 *Oct. 25*	William Bridgeman
1924 *Jan. 23*	Arthur Henderson
Nov. 7	Sir William Joynson Hicks
1929 *Jun. 8*	John Robert Clynes
1931 *Aug. 26*	Sir Herbert Samuel
1932 *Oct. 1*	Sir John Gilmour
1935 *Jun. 7*	Sir John Simon
1937 *May 28*	Sir Samuel Hoare
1939 *Sep. 4*	Sir John Anderson
1940 *Oct. 4*	Herbert Morrison
1945 *May 28*	Sir Donald Somervell
Aug. 3	James Chuter Eve
1951 *Oct. 27*	Sir David Maxwell Fyfe
1954 *Oct. 19*	Gwilym Lloyd George
1957 *Jan. 14*	Richard Austen Baker
1964 *Oct. 18*	Sir Frank Soskice
1965 *Dec. 23*	Roy Jenkins
1967 *Nov. 30*	L. James Callaghan
1970 *Jun. 20*	Reginald Maudling
1972 *Jul. 18*	Robert Carr
1974 *Mar. 5*	Roy Jenkins
1976 *Sep. 10*	Merlyn Rees
1979 *May 5*	William Whitelaw
1983 *Jun. 11*	Leon Brittan
1985 *Sep. 2*	Douglas Hurd
1989 *Oct. 26*	David Waddington
1990 *Nov. 28*	Kenneth Baker
1992 *Apr. 11*	Kenneth Clark

DEFENCE MINISTERS

Although both Churchill and Attlee were styled Ministers of Defence until 1946, a Ministry of Defence was only created at the end of 1946. With the abolition of the Admiralty, the War Office and the Air Ministry on 1 April 1964, the Minister of Defence became a Secretary of State.

DEFENCE MINISTERS 1946–64		DEFENCE SECRETARIES	
1946	Albert Victor Alexander	1964 Apr. 1	Peter Thorneycroft
1950	Emmanuel Shinwell	Oct.	Denis Healey
1951 Oct.	Winston Churchill	1970	Peter, Lord Carrington
1952 Feb.	Field Marshal Earl Alexander of Tunis	1974 Jan.	Sir Ian Gilmour
		Mar.	Roy Mason
1954	Harold Macmillan	1976	Frederick Mulley
1955 Apr.	John Selwyn Lloyd	1979 May	Francis Pym
Dec.	Sir Walter Monckton	1981	John Nott
1956 Oct.	Brigadier Antony Head	1983	Michael Heseltine
1957 Jan.	Duncan Sandys	1986	George Younger
1959	Harold Watkinson	1989	Tom King
1962	Peter Thorneycroft	1992	Malcolm Rifkind

AIR SECRETARIES

A Secretaryship of State for the Royal Air Force was created in March 1918, held briefly by Lord Rothermere and from late April until January 1919 by Lord Weir. Responsibility for the RAF then passed to Churchill as War Secretary until an independent Secretaryship for Air was created in April 1921; the post was abolished on 31 March 1964.

1921	Frederick Guest	May	Sir Archibald Sinclair
1922	Sir Samuel Hoare	1945 May	Harold Macmillan
1924 Jan.	Christopher Thomson, Baron Thomson	Aug.	William Wedgwood-Benn, Lord Stansgate
Nov.	Sir Samuel Hoare	1946	Philip Noel-Baker
1929 Apr.	Lord Thomson	1947	Arthur Henderson
1930 Oct.	William Mackenzie, Lord Amulree	1951	William Sidney, Lord De L'Isle and Dudley
1931	Charles Vane-Tempest-Stewart, Lord Londonderry	1955	Evelyn Birch
1935	Philip Cunliffe-Lister, Lord Swinton	1957	George Ward
		1960	Julian Amery
1938	Sir Kingsley Wood	1963–1964	Hugh Fraser
1940 Apr.	Sir Samuel Hoare		

WAR SECRETARIES

Until the Crimean War, there was much confusion over political control of military affairs: a Secretaryship at War had existed for 180 years, a Secretaryship of War and Colonies since 1801. Responsibility for the army was at last accorded to a single Secretary of State for War in February 1855. The post was abolished on 31 March 1964.

1855	Fox Maule-Ramsay, Lord Panmure	1918	Alfred, Viscount Milner
1858	Jonathan Peel	1919	Winston Churchill
1859	Sidney Herbert	1921	Sir William Worthington-Evans
1861	Sir George Cornwell Lewis	1922	E. of Derby
1863	George Robinson, E. of Ripon	1924 *Jan.*	Stephen Walsh
1866 *Feb.*	Spencer Cavendish, Marquess of	*Nov.*	Sir William Worthington-Evans
	Hartington	1929	Thomas Shaw
Jul.	Jonathan Peel	1931 *Aug.*	Robert, Marquess of Crewe
1867	Sir John Pakington	*Nov.*	Douglas Hogg, first Viscount
1868	Edward Cardwell		Hailsham
1874	Gathorne Hardy	1935 *Jun.*	Edward Wood, third Viscount
1878	Sir Frederick Stanley		Halifax
1880	Hugh Childers	*Nov.*	Alfred Duff Cooper
1882	Marquess of Hartington	1937	Leslie Hore-Belisha
1885	William Henry Smith	1940 *Jan.*	Oliver Stanley
1886 *Feb.*	Henry Campbell-Bannerman	*May*	Anthony Eden
Aug.	W. H. Smith	*Dec.*	Henry Margesson
1887	Edward Stanhope	1942	Sir James Grigg
1892	Henry Campbell-Bannerman	1945	John James Lawson
1895	Henry Petty-Fitzmaurice, Marquess	1946	Frederick John Bellenger
	of Lansdowne	1947	Emmanuel Shinwell
1900	William St John Brodrick	1950	John Strachey
1903	Hugh Arnold-Forster	1951	Brigadier Antony Head
1905	Richard Burdon Haldane	1956	John Hare
1912	Colonel John Seely	1958	Christopher Soames
1914 *Mar.*	H. H. Asquith (while also Prime	1960	John Profumo
	Minister)	1963 *Jun.*	Joseph Godber
Aug.	Field Marshal Earl Kitchener of	*Oct.*	James Ramsden
	Khartoum		
1916 *Jul.*	David Lloyd George		
Dec.	Edward Stanley, seventeenth E. of		
	Derby		

CHIEFS OF THE IMPERIAL GENERAL STAFF

The British Army did not have an embryonic General Staff until 1904, following the creation two years previously of the Committee of Imperial Defence. In February 1904 General Sir Neville Lyttelton, as 'Chief of the General Staff', became the sole adviser to the government on strategic questions and land operations. In September 1906 the General Staff was reorganized on the German model, its director subsequently becoming 'Chief of the Imperial General Staff (CIGS)'. This title survived until 1964.

1904–1908	Sir Neville Lyttelton	1940–1941	Sir John Dill
1908–1911	Sir William Nicholson	1941–1946	Sir Alan Brooke
1911–1914	Sir John French	1946–1948	Field Marshal Viscount
1914–1915	Sir James Murray		Montgomery of Alamein
1915–1918	Sir William Robertson	1948–1952	Sir William Slim
1918–1922	Sir Henry Wilson	1952–1955	Sir John Harding
1922–1926	Earl of Cavan	1955–1958	Sir Gerald Templer
1926–1936	Sir George Milne	1958–1961	Sir Francis Festing
1937–1939	Lord Gort VC	1961–1964	Sir Richard Hull
1939–1940	Sir Edmund Ironside		

FM Sir Richard Hull served as 'Chief of the General Staff, Ministry of Defence' until 1965 when he became 'Chief of the Defence Staff', with a Chief of the General Staff subordinate to him.

FIRST LORDS OF THE ADMIRALTY

The office of First Lord of the Admiralty – the British equivalent of a Minister of Marine – may be traced back to the formation of the Board of Admiralty in 1628. Most First Lords were civilian members of the government, but on several occasions in the eighteenth and early nineteenth centuries the post was held by distinguished admirals, notably:

1727–1733	George Byng, Viscount Torrington		**FIRST LORDS 1868–1964**	
1751–1756 &		1868	Hugh Childers	
1757–1762	George, Baron Anson	1871	George Goschen	
1766–1771	Edward, Baron Hawke	1874	George Ward Hunt	
1782–1783	Augustus, Viscount Keppel	1877	W(illiam) H(enry) Smith	
1783–1788	Richard, Viscount Howe	1880	Thomas Baring, E. of Northbrook	
1801–1804	John Jervis, E. of St Vincent	1885	Lord George Hamilton	
1805–1806	Charles Middleton, Lord Barham	1886 *Feb.*	George Robinson, Marquess of Ripon	

The constitutional position of the First Lord as a cabinet minister responsible to the Queen and to Parliament for the business of the Admiralty was defined by Letters Patent in 1869. With the creation of a unified Ministry of Defence in 1964 the post was abolished.

Aug.	Lord George Hamilton
1892	John, fifth E. Spencer
1895	George Goschen
1900	William Palmer, second E. of Selborne
1905 *Mar.*	Frederick Campbell, third E. Cawdor
Dec.	Edward Marjoribanks, second Baron Tweedmouth

1908	Reginald McKenna		1937	Alfred Duff-Cooper
1911	Winston Churchill		1938	James, seventh E. Stanhope
1915	Arthur Balfour		1939	Winston Churchill
1916	Sir Edward Carson		1940	Albert Victor Alexander
1917	Sir Eric Geddes		1945 May	Brendan Bracken
1919	Walter Long		Aug.	Albert Victor Alexander
1921	Arthur Lee		1946	George, first Viscount Hall
1922	Leo Amery		1951 May	Francis, Lord Pakenham
1924 Jan.	Frederic Thesiger, first Viscount Chelmsford		Nov.	James Thomas
			1956	Quintin Hogg, second Viscount Hailsham
Nov.	Walter Bridgeman			
1929	Albert Victor Alexander		1957	George Douglas-Hamilton, tenth E. of Selkirk
1931 Aug.	Sir Austen Chamberlain			
Nov.	Sir Bolton Eyres-Monsell		1959	Peter, sixth Baron Carrington
1936	Sir Samuel Hoare		1963	George, second E. Jellicoe

COMMANDERS-IN-CHIEF

Until the Civil War a reigning king assumed command of the army. Under Queen Elizabeth, however, Robert Dudley, Earl of Leicester, served as effective Commander-in-Chief in the Netherlands, with the title of Captain General, in 1585; and in 1588 Leicester was appointed Captain-General of the Queen's Armies and Companies in anticipation of a Spanish invasion. Thereafter the term Captain-General was frequently applied to a supreme commander of land forces. The first named Commander-in-Chief was the Parliamentarian general, Sir Thomas Fairfax, in February 1645. Oliver Cromwell was Commander-in-Chief from June 1650 until his death, seeking to make the rank inseparable from the office of Lord Protector from December 1653 onwards; but the independence of the Commander-in-Chief was re-established in May 1659. The nature and responsibilities of the post remained ill-defined; only between 1795 and 1904 was there an unbroken succession of Commanders. During that period the Commander-in-Chief occupied offices in the Horse Guards at Whitehall, which served as effective headquarters of the British Army. With the creation of the Army Council in February 1904 the post of Commander-in-Chief was abolished.

1659 May	Charles Fleetwood		1766 Aug.	John Manners, Marquess of Granby; resigned Jan. 1770
1660 Feb.	George Monck (D. of Albemarle)			
1670 Jan.	James Scott, D. of Monmouth; dismissed Sep. 1679		1778 Jun.	Gen. Jeffrey Amherst, Lord Amherst
1690 Jun.	John Churchill, E. of Marlborough; dismissed Jan. 1692		1782 Mar.	Gen. Henry Conway
			1783 Apr.	Jeffrey Amherst, Lord Amherst
1702 Mar.	John Churchill, D. of Marlborough; dismissed Dec. 1711		1795 Feb.	P. Frederick, D. of York; resigned Mar. 1809
1712 Feb.	James Butler, D. of Ormond; dismissed Sep. 1714		1809 Mar.	Gen. Sir David Dundas
			1811 May	P. Frederick, D. of York; died Jan. 1827
1714 Sep.	John Churchill, D. of Marlborough; died Jun. 1722			
			1827 Jan.	FM D. of Wellington; resigned Jan. 1828
1745 Mar.	P. William, D. of Cumberland; resigned Oct. 1757			
			1828 Feb.	Gen. Rowland Hill, Lord Hill
1757 Oct.	John Ligonier, Earl Ligonier		1842 Aug.	FM D. of Wellington; died Sep. 1852

| 1852 *Sep.* | FM Henry Hardinge, Viscount Hardinge; resigned Jul. 1856 | 1895 *Nov.* | FM Sir Garnet, Viscount Wolseley; resigned Nov. 1901 |
| 1856 *Jul.* | Gen. P. George, D. of Cambridge; resigned Jun. 1895 | 1901 *Nov.* | FM Frederick, Earl Roberts |

FIRST SEA LORDS

The use of the term 'sea lords' to describe the most senior executive officers in the Royal Navy may be traced back to the early seventeenth century. Officially they were known collectively as the Lords Commissioners of the Admiralty and were often called 'naval lords' until 1904. The First Sea Lord was the naval equivalent of the Chief of the Imperial General Staff, tendering advice on the disposition, character and strength of the fleet as well as on naval policy and strategy. The title was retained after the creation of a unified Defence Ministry, but with diminished responsibilities.

1904	Sir John Fisher (later Baron Fisher)	1938	Sir Reginald Backhouse
1910	Sir Arthur Wilson	1939	Sir Dudley Pound
1912	P. Louis of Battenberg	1943	Adm. of the Fleet Sir Andrew Cunningham
1914 *Oct.*	Adm. of the Fleet Lord Fisher		
1915 *May*	Sir Henry Jackson	1946	Adm. of the Fleet Sir John Cunningham
1916	Sir John Jellicoe		
1917	Sir Rosslyn Wemyss	1948	Adm. of the Fleet Lord Fraser of North Cape
1919	Adm. of the Fleet E. Beatty		
1927	Sir Charles Madden	1951	Adm. of the Fleet Sir Rhoderick McGrigor
1930	Sir Frederick Field		
1933	Sir Ernle Chatfield	1955–1959	Adm. of the Fleet E. Mountbatten of Burma

CHIEFS OF THE AIR STAFF

Recognition of the significance of aerial warfare led to the creation of the Air Council in the closing months of 1917. In becoming a member of the Air Council, General Sir Hugh Trenchard (later Marshal of the Royal Air Force Lord Trenchard) was appointed as the first Chief of the Air Staff, pending the amalgamation of the Royal Flying Corps and the Royal Naval Air Service to form the RAF in April 1918. The importance of the Chief of the Air Staff diminished with the institution of a Chief of the Defence Staff in 1958.

1918 *Jan.*	Sir Hugh Trenchard	1937	Sir Cyril Newall
Apr.	Sir Frederick Sykes	1940 *Sep.*	Sir Charles Portal
1919 *Feb.*	Sir Hugh Trenchard	1946 *Jan.*	Sir William Tedder
1930 *Jan.*	Sir John Salmond	1950 *Jan.*	Sir John Slessor
1933 *Mar.*	Geoffrey Salmond	1953–1956	Sir William Dickson
May	Sir Edward Ellington		

CHIEFS OF THE DEFENCE STAFF

In 1957–8 the Macmillan government strengthened co-ordination between the three services by upgrading the chairman of the Chiefs of Staff Committee, thus limiting the independence and executive responsibilities of the First Sea Lord, the CIGS and the Chief of the Air Staff.

1958	Marshal of the RAF Sir William Dickson	1976	Marshal of the RAF Sir Neil Cameron
1959	Adm. of the Fleet E. Mountbatten of Burma	1979	Adm. of the Fleet Sir Terence Lewin
1965	Field Marshal Sir Richard Hull	1982	Field Marshal Sir Edwin Bramall
1968	Marshal of the RAF Sir Charles Elworthy	1986	Adm. of the Fleet Sir John Fieldhouse
1971	Adm. of the Fleet Sir Peter Hill-Norton	1988	General Sir Anthony Walker
1973	Field Marshal Sir Michael Carver	1990	Marshal of the RAF Sir David Craig

LORD HIGH ADMIRALS

The title Lord High Admiral dates from the last years of Henry VIII's reign. With the creation of the Board of Admiralty in 1628 the office became largely honorific and was generally held in commission. Since 1828 the post has remained vacant. Only those marked with an asterisk were high-ranking naval commanders in their own right.

1540 Jul.	John, Lord Russell	1638 Apr.	Algernon Percy, E. of Northumberland
1542 Dec.	Edward Seymour, E. of Hertford		
1543 Jan.	John Dudley, E. of Warwick	1643 Dec.	Robert Rich, E. of Warwick* (office in commission, 1649)
1547 Feb.	Thomas, Lord Seymour		
1549 Oct.	John Dudley, E. of Warwick	1660 Jul.	James, D. of York* (intermittently until 1688)
1550 May	Edward, Lord Clinton		
1553 Oct.	William, Lord Howard of Effingham*	1701 Jan.	Thomas Herbert, E. of Pembroke (office in commission, 1709)
1558 Feb.	Edward, Lord Clinton	1827 Apr.	William, D. of Clarence (K. William IV)*; resigned, Sep. 1828
1585 Jul.	Charles, Lord Howard of Effingham*		
1619 Jan.	George Villiers, D. of Buckingham; murdered, Aug. 1628		

LORD CHIEF JUSTICES OF ENGLAND

This office was created in 1859 by raising the status of the Chief Justice of the Queen's Bench.

1859	Sir Alexander Cockburn	1922	Lord Hewart
1880	Lord Coleridge	1940	Viscount Caldecote
1894	Lord Russell of Killowen	1946	Lord Goddard
1900	Lord Alverstone	1958	Lord Parker of Waddington
1913	Sir Rufus Isaacs (Marquess of Reading)	1971	Lord Widgery
1921	Sir Anthony Lawrence (Lord Trevithin)	1980	Lord Lane

LORD CHANCELLORS OF GREAT BRITAIN

This office of state was created after the Act of Union in May 1707, the first incumbent being the last Lord Chancellor of England. Until 1835 there were several occasions when the office remained vacant, the Great Seal being retained by the sovereign in commission.

1707 May–Sep. 1708	Lord Cowper
1713 Apr.–Sep. 1714	Simon, Lord Harcourt
1714 Sep.–Apr. 1718	Lord Cowper
1718 May–Jan. 1725	Thomas Parker, Lord Macclesfield
1725 Jun.–Nov. 1733	Peter, Lord King
1733 Nov.–Feb. 1737	Charles, Lord Talbot of Hensol
1737 Feb.–Nov. 1756	Philip Yorke, Lord Hardwicke
1761 Jan.–Jun. 1766	Robert, Lord Henley
1766 Jul.–Jan. 1770	Charles Pratt, Lord Camden
1771 Jan.–May 1778	Henry Bathurst, Lord Apsley (E. Bathurst 1775)
1778 Jun.–Jun. 1792	Edward, Lord Thurlow (with intermission, Apr.–Dec. 1783)
1793 Jan.–Apr. 1801	Alexander Wedderburn, Lord Loughborough
1801 Apr.–Jan. 1806	John Scott, Lord Eldon
1806 Feb.–Mar. 1807	Thomas, Lord Erskine
1807 Apr.–Apr. 1827	Lord Eldon
1827 May–Nov. 1830	John Copley, Lord Lyndhurst
1830 Nov.–Nov. 1834	Henry, Lord Brougham and Vaux
1834 Nov.–Apr. 1835	Lord Lyndhurst
1836 Jan.–Sep. 1841	Charles Pepys, Lord Cottenham
1841 Sep.–Jul. 1846	Lord Lyndhurst
1846 Jul.–Jul. 1850	Lord Cottenham
1850 Jul.–Feb. 1852	Thomas Wilde, Lord Truro
1852 Feb.–Dec.	Edward Sugden, Lord St Leonards
1852 Dec.–Feb. 1858	Robert Rolfe, Lord Cranworth
1858 Feb.–Jun. 1859	Frederic Thesiger, Lord Chelmsford
1859 Jun.–Jun. 1861	John, Lord Campbell
1861 Jun.–Jul. 1865	Richard Bethell, Lord Westbury
1865 Jul.–Jul. 1866	Lord Cranworth
1866 Jul.–Feb. 1868	Lord Chelmsford
1868 Feb.–Dec.	Hugh, Lord Cairns
1868 Dec.–Oct. 1872	Wiliam Wood, Lord Hatherley
1872 Oct.–Feb. 1874	Roundell Palmer, Lord Selborne
1874 Feb.–Apr. 1880	Lord Cairns
1880 Apr.–Jun. 1885	Lord Selborne
1885 Jun.–Feb. 1886	Hardinge Giffard, Lord Halsbury
1886 Feb.–Aug.	Farrer, Lord Herschell
1886 Aug.–Aug. 1892	Lord Halsbury
1892 Aug.–Jun. 1895	Lord Herschell
1895 Jun.–Dec. 1905	Lord Halsbury
1905 Dec.–Jun. 1912	Robert Reid, Lord Loreburn
1912 Jun.–May 1915	Richard, Lord Haldane
1915 May–Dec. 1916	Stanley, Lord Buckmaster
1916 Dec.–Jan. 1919	Robert, Lord Finlay
1919 Jan.–Oct. 1922	F. E. Smith, Lord Birkenhead
1922 Oct.–Jan. 1924	George, Lord Cave
1924 Jan.–Nov.	Lord Haldane
1924 Nov.–Mar. 1928	Lord Cave
1928 Mar.–Jun. 1929	Douglas Hogg, Lord Hailsham
1929 Jun.–Jun. 1935	John, Lord Sankey
1935 Jun.–Mar. 1938	Lord Hailsham
1938 Mar.–Sep. 1939	Frederick, Lord Maugham
1939 Sep.–May 1940	Thomas Inskip, Lord Caldecote
1940 May–Jul. 1945	John, Lord Simon
1945 Jul.–Oct. 1951	William, Lord Jowitt
1951 Oct.–Oct. 1954	Gavin, Lord Simonds
1954 Oct.–Jul. 1962	David Maxwell Fyfe, Lord Kilmuir
1962 Jul.–Oct. 1964	Reginald Manningham-Buller, Lord Dilhorne
1964 Oct.–Jun. 1970	Gerald, Lord Gardiner
1970 Jun.–Mar. 1974	Quintin Hogg, Lord Hailsham of St Marylebone
1974 Mar.–May 1979	Frederick, Lord Elwyn-Jones
1979 May–May 1987	Lord Hailsham of St Marylebone
1987 Jun.–Oct.	Robert, Lord Havers
1987 Oct.–	James, Lord Mackay of Clashfern

SPEAKERS OF THE HOUSE OF COMMONS SINCE THE RESTORATION

1660	Sir Henry Grimston	1802–1816	Charles Abbot (Lord Colchester)
1661–1671	Sir Edward Turner	1817–1835	Charles Sutton (Viscount Canterbury)
1673 *Feb.*	Sir John Charlton		
1673–1677	Edward Seymour	1835–1838	James Abrrcromby (Lord Dunfermline)
1678	Sir Robert Sawyer		
1679	William Gregory	1839–1857	Charles Shaw-Lefebvre (Viscount Eversley)
1680–1681	William Williams		
1685	Sir John Trevor	1857–1872	J. Evelyn Denison (Viscount Ossington)
1689–1693	Henry Powle		
1694–1695	Paul Foley	1872–1884	Sir Henry Brand (Viscount Hampden)
1698–1699	Sir Thomas Lyttelton		
1700–1701	Robert Harley	1884–1895	Arthur Peel (Viscount Peel)
1702–1707	John Smith	1895–1905	William Gully (Viscount Selby)
		1905–1922	James Lowther (Viscount Ullswater)
	PARLIAMENT OF GREAT BRITAIN	1922–1928	John Whitley
1708–1709	Sir Richard Onslow	1928–1943	Hon. E. Algernon Fitzroy
1710	William Bromley	1943–1951	Colonel Clifton Brown (Viscount Ruffside)
1713	Sir Thomas Hanmer		
1715–1727	Spencer Compton	1951–1959	William Shepherd Morrison (Viscount Dunrossil)
1727–1761	Arthur Onslow		
1761–1769	Sir Arthur Cust	1959–1965	Sir Harry Hylton-Foster
1770–1780	Sir Frederick Norton	1965–1971	Horace King (Lord Maybray-King)
1780–1788	Charles Cornwall	1971–1976	J. Selwyn Lloyd (Lord Selwyn-Lloyd)
1788	Henry Grenville	1976–1983	George Thomas (Viscount Tonypandy)
1789–1801	Henry Addington (Visc. Sidmouth)		
		1983–1992	Bernard Weatherill
	PARLIAMENT OF THE UNITED KINGDOM	1992	Betty Boothroyd
1801	Sir John Mitford (Lord Redesdale)		

VICEROYS OF INDIA

The Governor-Generals of India bore the additional title of Viceroy from 1857 until the creation of the independent dominion of India in August 1947. The names by which they were known during their Viceregal term are printed in capital letters.

1858	Charles Canning, first E. CANNING	1880	George Robinson, first Marquess of RIPON
1862	James Bruce, eighth E. of ELGIN	1884	Frederick Blackwood, first Marquess of DUFFERIN and Ava
1864	Sir John LAWRENCE		
1869	Richard Bourke, E. of MAYO		
1872	Francis Baring, second Baron NORTHBROOK	1888	Henry Petty-Fitzmaurice, fifth Marquess of LANSDOWNE
1876	Edward Bulwer Lytton, second Baron LYTTON	1894	Victor Bruce, ninth E. of ELGIN
		1899	George Nathaniel Curzon, Baron CURZON of Kedleston

1905	Gilbert Elliott, fourth E. of MINTO	1931	Freeman Freeman-Thomas, first Marquess of WILLINGDON
1910	Charles Hardinge, first Baron HARDINGE of Penshurst	1936	Victor Hope, second Marquess of LINLITHGOW
1916	Frederic Thesiger, first Viscount CHELMSFORD	1943	Field Marshal Archibald Wavell, first Viscount WAVELL
1921	Rufus Isaacs, first Marquess of READING	1947	Rear-Admiral Lord Louis MOUNTBATTEN
1926	Edward Wood, first Baron IRWIN (later Lord Halifax)		

FOUNDATION OF EXISTING ANGLICAN DIOCESES (IN ENGLAND)

	SENIOR SEES	1542	Bristol
597	Canterbury (province, with Abp 601/2		Oxford
627	York (province, with Abp 735)		Sodor and Man (earlier a Scottish bishopric)
604	London	1836	Ripon (suffragan bishopric of York c.680)
995	Durham		
660	Winchester	1848	Manchester
		1877	St Albans
	OTHERS		Truro
604	Rochester	1880	Liverpool
669	Lichfield (archbishopric 788–803)	1882	Newcastle upon Tyne
676	Hereford	1884	Southwell
680	Worcester	1888	Wakefield
c.909	Wells (united as 'Bath & Wells' by papal authority 1345)	1905	Birmingham
			Southwark
1050	Exeter	1914	Chelmsford
1072	Lincoln (suffragan bishopric of York c.680)		St Edmundsbury and Ipswich
			Sheffield
1075	Chichester	1918	Coventry (reviving an independent
1078	Salisbury		see existing from 1121 to 1228 and
1094–1096	Norwich		thereafter linked with Lichfield until
1108	Ely		1836)
1123	Bath (see also Wells)	1920	Bradford
1133	Carlisle	1926	Blackburn
1541	Chester		Leicester
	Gloucester	1927	Derby
	Peterborough		Guildford
			Portsmouth

ARCHBISHOPS OF CANTERBURY, PRIMATES OF ALL ENGLAND

In the following lists, 'trs' denotes 'translated from'.

601/2–605	Augustine	1206–1228	Stephen Langton
605–619	Laurentius	1229–1231	Richard Wethershed
619–624	Mellitus; trs. London	1233–1240	Edmund Rich of Abingdon
624–627	Justus; trs. Rochester	1241–1270	Boniface of Savoy
627–653	Honorius	1272–1278	Robert Kilwardy
655–664	Deusdedit	1279–1292	John Pecham
669–690	Theodore 'of Tarsus'	1294–1313	Robert Winchelsey
693–731	Berhtwald	1314–1327	Walter Reynolds; trs. Worcester
731–734	Tatwine	1327–1333	Simon of Meopham
734–739	Nothelm	1333–1348	John Stratford
740–760	Cuthbert; trs. Hereford	1348–1349	Thomas Bradwardine
761–764	Bregowine	1349–1366	Simon of Islip
765–792	Jaenbehrt	1366–1368	Simon of Langham; trs. Ely
793–805	Ethelheard	1368–1374	William of Whittlesey; trs.
805–829	Wulfred		Winchester
832	Feologild	1374–1381	Simon of Sudbury; trs. London; murdered in Tower of London
833–870	Ceolnoth		
870–888	Ethelred	1381–1396	William Courtenay; trs. London
890–923	Plegmund	1396–1414	Thomas Arundel; trs. York (at St. Andrews 1397–9)
923–926	Athelm; trs. Wells		
926–941	Wulfhelm; trs. Wells	1414–1443	Henry Chichele; trs. St Davids
941–958	Odo; trs. Ramsbury	1443–1452	John Stafford; trs. Bath
958–959	Elfsige; trs. Winchester	1452–1454	John Kempe; trs. York
959	Byrthelm; trs. Wells	1454–1486	Thomas Bourchier; trs. Ely; cardinal 1467
959–988	Dunstan; trs. London		
989–990	Ethelgar; trs. Selsey	1486–1500	John Morton; trs. Ely; cardinal 1493
990–994	Sigeric; trs. Ramsbury		
995–1005	Elfric; trs. Ramsbury	1501–1503	Henry Deane; trs. Salisbury
1006–1012	Alphege; trs. Winchester; murdered Greenwich	1503–1532	William Wareham; trs. London
		1533–1553	Thomas Cranmer; martyred at Oxford 1556
1013–1020	Elfstan (Lyfing); trs. Wells		
1020–1038	Ethelnoth	1556–1558	Cardinal Reginald Pole
1038–1050	Eadsige	1559–1575	Matthew Parker
1050/1–1052	Robert of Jumieges; trs. London	1576–1583	Edmund Grindal; trs. York
1052–1070	Stigand; trs. Winchester	1583–1604	John Witgift; trs. Worcester
1070–1089	Lanfranc of Bec	1604–1610	Richard Bancroft; trs. London
1093–1109	Anselm of Bec	1611–1633	George Abbott; trs. London
1114–1122	Ralph d'Escures	1633–1645	William Laud; trs. London; executed
1123–1136	William of Corbeil		
1139–1161	Theobald of Bec	1660–1663	William Juxon; trs. London
1162–1170	Thomas Becket; murdered in Cathedral	1663–1677	Gilbert Sheldon; trs. London
		1677–1690	William Sancroft; deprived; d. 1693
1173–1184	Richard of Dover		
1184–1190	Baldwin; trs. Winchester	1691–1694	John Tillotson
1193–1205	Hubert Walter	1695–1715	Thomas Tenison; trs. Lincoln

1715–1737	William Wake; trs. Lincoln	1896–1902	Frederick Temple; trs. London
1737–1747	John Potter; trs. Oxford	1903–1928	Randall Davidson; trs. Winchester; first Archbishop to retire; d. 1930
1747–1757	Thomas Herring; trs. York		
1757–1758	Matthew Hutton; trs. York	1928–1942	Cosmo Gordon Lang; trs. York; d. 1945
1758–1768	Thomas Secker; trs. Oxford		
1768–1783	Frederick Cornwallis; trs. Lichfield	1942–1944	William Temple; trs. York
1783–1805	John Moore; trs. Bangor	1944–1961	Geoffrey Fisher; trs. London; d. 1972
1805–1828	Charles Manners Sutton; trs. Norwich		
		1961–1974	Michael Ramsey; trs. York; d. 1988
1828–1848	William Howley; trs. London		
1848–1862	John Sumner; trs. Chester	1974–1980	Donald Coggan; trs. York; retired
1862–1868	Charles Longley; trs. York	1980–1991	Robert Runcie; trs. St Albans; retired
1868–1882	Archibald Tait; trs. London		
1883–1896	Edward Benson; trs. Truro	1991	George Carey; trs. Bath and Wells

ARCHBISHOPS OF YORK, PRIMATES OF ENGLAND

625–644	Paulinus	1215	Walter de Grey; trs. Worcester
664	Cedda	1256	Sewal de Bovil
669	Wilfrid	1258	Godfrey Ludham
678	Bosa	1266	Walter Giffard; trs. Bath
706	John of Beverley; trs. Hexham	1279	William Wickwaine
718	Wilfrid II	1286	John le Romayne
732	Egbert	1298	Henry Newark
766	Ethelbert	1300	Thomas Corbridge
780	Eanbald	1306	William Greenfield
796	Eanbald II	1317	William Melton
808	Wulfsige	1342	William Zouche
837	Wigmund	1352	John Thoresby; trs. Worcester
854	Wulfheare	1374	Alexander Neville; to St Andrews
900	Ethelbald	1388	Thomas Arundel; trs. Ely; to Canterbury
928	Redweard		
931	Wulfstan I	1397	Robert Waldby; trs. Chichester
958	Osketyl	1398	Richard Scrope; trs. Lichfield; executed by Henry IV, 8 Jun. 1405
972	Oswald		
992	Ealdulf	1407	Henry Bowett; trs. Bath
1003	Wulfstan II; trs. London	1425	John Kempe; trs. London; to Canterbury
1023	Elfric Puttock		
1051	Kynesige	1452	William Booth; trs. Lichfield
1061	Ealdred; trs. Worcester	1465	George Neville; trs. Exeter
1070	Thomas of Bayeux	1476	Lawrence Booth; trs. Durham
1101	Gerard; trs. Hereford	1480	Thomas Rotherham; trs. Lincoln
1109	Thomas II	1501	Thomas Savage; trs. London
1119	Thurstan	1508	Thomas Bainbridge; trs. Durham
1143	William Fitzherbert	1514	Thomas Wolsey; trs. Lincoln; cardinal 1515
1147	Henry Murdac		
1154	Roger de Pont l'Eveque	1531	Edward Lee
1191	Geoffrey	1545	Robert Holgate; trs. Llandaff

1555	Nicholas Heath; trs. Worcester	1757	John Gilbert; trs. Salisbury
1561	Thomas Young; trs. St Davids	1761	Robert Hay Drummond
1570	Edmund Grindal; trs. London; to Canterbury	1777	William Markham; trs. Chester
		1807	Edward Vernon Harcourt; trs. Carlisle
1576	Edwin Sandys; trs. London		
1589	John Piers; trs. Salisbury	1847	Thomas Musgrave; trs. Hereford
1595	Matthew Hutton; trs. Durham	1860	Charles Longley; trs. Durham; to Canterbury
1606	Tobias Matthew; trs. Durham		
1628	George Monteigne; trs. Durham	1862	William Thomson; trs. Gloucester
	Samuel Harsnett; trs. Norwich	1891	William Magee; trs. Peterborough
1632	Richard Neile; trs. Winchester		William Maclagan; trs. Lichfield; retired
1641–1650	John Williams; trs. Lincoln		
1660	Accepted Frewen; trs. Lichfield	1908	Cosmo Gordon Lang; trs. Stepney; to Canterbury
1664	Richard Sterne; trs. Carlisle		
1683	John Dolben; trs. Rochester	1929	William Temple; trs. Manchester; to Canterbury
1688	Thomas Lamplugh; trs. Exeter		
1691	John Sharp	1942	Cyril Garbett; trs. Winchester
1714	Sir William Dawes Bart; trs. Chester	1946	Michael Ramsey; trs. Durham; to Canterbury
1724	Lancelot Blackburn; trs. Exeter		
1743	Thomas Herring; trs. Bangor, to Canterbury	1961	Donald Coggan; trs. Bradford; to Canterbury
1747	Matthew Hutton; trs. Bangor, to Canterbury	1975	Stuart Blanch; trs. Liverpool; retired
		1983	John Habgood; trs. Durham

BISHOPS OF LONDON SINCE 1086

The earliest recorded Bishop of London was Mellitus, 604–c.616. The best-known of 32 pre-Conquest bishops was Dunstan (Bp c.957–9, trs. Canterbury). London ranks in seniority immediately behind Canterbury and York, the bishop always being entitled to sit in the Lords. The following list gives the dates of consecration or enthronement.

1086–1107	Maurice	1317	Richard Newport
1108–1127	Richard de Belmeiss I	1318	Stephen Gravesend
1128–1134	Gilbert Universalis	1338–1339	Richard Bintworth
1141–1150	Robert de Siglio	1340–1354	Ralph Stratford
1152–1162	Richard de Belmeiss II	1355	Michael Northburgh
1163–1187	Gilbert Foliot; trs. Hereford	1361	Simon of Sudbury; to Canterbury
1189–1198	Richard Fitzneal	1375–1381	William Courtenay; trs. Hereford; to Canterbury
1199	William de Sainte-Mere-Eglise		
1221–1228	Eustace de Fauconberg	1382	Robert Braybrooke
1229–1241	Roger Niger	1405	Roger Walden; trs. Canterbury (Abp 1397–9, but never officiated)
1244–1259	Fulk Bassett		
1260–1262	Henry of Wingham	1406	Nicholas Bubwith; to Salisbury
1263–1273	Henry of Sandwich	1407–1421	Richard Clifford; trs. Worcester
1274	John Chishull	1422	John Kempe; trs. Chichester; to York
1280–1303	Richard Gravesend	1425	William Gray; to Lincoln
1304	Ralph Baldock	1431	Robert Fitzhugh
1313–1316	Gilbert Segrave	1436–1448	Robert Gilbert

1450	Thomas Kempe	1663–1675	Humphrey Henchman; trs. Salisbury
1489	Richard Hill	1676	Henry Compton; trs. Oxford
1496–1501	Thomas Savage; trs. Rochester; to York	1713	John Robinson; trs. Bristol
		1723	Edmund Gibson; trs. Lincoln
1502–1503	William Wareham; to Canterbury	1748	Thomas Sherlock; trs. Salisbury
1504–1505	William Barons	1761	Thomas Hayter; trs. Norwich
1506	Richard Fitzjames	1762	Richard Osbaldeston; trs. Carlisle
1522	Cuthbert Tunstall; to Durham	1764	Richard Terrick; trs. Peterborough
1530–1539	John Stokesley	1777	Robert Lowth; trs. Oxford
1540	Edmund Bonner; deprived Oct. 1549	1787	Beilby Porteus; trs. Chester
1550	Nicholas Ridley; trs. Rochester; deprived Jul. 1553	1809	John Randolph; trs. Bangor
		1813	William Howley; to Canterbury
1553	Edmund Bonner; restored; deprived May 1559	1828	Charles Blomfield; trs. Chester
		1856–1868	Archibald Tait; to Canterbury
1559	Edmund Grindal; to York	1869	John Jackson; trs. Lincoln
1570	Edwin Sandys; trs. Worcester; to York	1885	Frederick Temple; trs. Exeter; to Canterbury
1577	John Aylmer	1896	Mandell Creighton; trs. Peterborough
1594–1596	Richard Fletcher; trs. Worcester		
1597	Richard Bancroft; to Canterbury	1901	Arthur Winnington-Ingram; trs. Stepney
1604	Richard Vaughan; trs. Chester		
1607–1609	Thomas Ravis; trs. Gloucester	1939	Geoffrey Fisher; trs. Chester; to Canterbury
1610	George Abbot; trs. Lichfield; to Canterbury		
		1945	John Wand; trs. Bath and Wells
1611	John King	1956	Henry Montgomery-Campbell; trs. Guildford
1621	George Monteigne; trs. Lincoln; to Durham		
		1961	Robert Stopford; trs. Peterborough
1628	William Laud; trs. Bath; to Canterbury	1973	Gerald Ellison; trs. Chester
		1981	Graham Leonard; trs. Truro
1633	William Juxon; to Canterbury	1991	David Michael Hope; trs. Wakefield
1660	Gilbert Sheldon; to Canterbury		

BISHOPS OF DURHAM

The first recorded consecration of a Bishop of Durham was in January 1041, nearly 50 years after the establishment of the see. Earlier Northumbrian bishops were based territorially on Lindisfarne (634–875, with St Cuthbert as Bp 685–7) and Chester-le-Street (882–995); the see of Hexham (681–821) was founded as a suffragan bishopric of York. The mediaeval Bishops of Durham exercised unique powers of civil jurisdiction in England, as Counts Palatine. Durham remains the fourth see in order of seniority in England; the bishop is always entitled to sit in the House of Lords. The following list gives the dates of consecration or enthronement.

1041	Ethelric	1143–1152	William of Ste Barbe
1056	Ethelwine	1153–1195	Hugh du Puiset
1071	Walcher	1197–1208	Philip de Poitiers
1080–1096	William of Carilef	1217–1226	Richard Marsh
1099–1128	Ranulf Flambard	1228–1237	Richard Poore; trs. Salisbury
1133–1141	Geoffrey Rufus	1241	Nicholas Farnham

1249–1260	Walter Kirkham	1628	George Monteigne; trs. London; to York
1261	Robert Stichill		John Howson; trs. Oxford
1274–1283	Robert of Holy Island		
1284	Anthony Bek	1632	Thomas Morton; trs. Lichfield
1311–1316	Richard Kellaw	1660–1672	John Cosin
1318	Lewis de Beaumont	1674	Nathaniel Crew; trs. Oxford (Baron Crew 1697)
1333	Richard of Bury		
1345–1381	Thomas of Hatfield	1721	William Talbot; trs. Salisbury
1382	John Fordham; to Ely	1730	Edward Chandler; trs. Lichfield
1388	Walter Skirlaw; trs. Bath and Wells	1750	Joseph Butler; trs. Bristol
1406	Thomas Langley	1752	Richard Trevor; trs. St Davids
1438	Robert Nevill; trs. Salisbury	1771	John Egerton; trs. Lichfield
1457	Lawrence Booth; to York	1787	Thomas Thurlow; trs. Lincoln
1476–1483	William Dudley	1791	Shute Barrington; trs. Salisbury
1484	John Shirwood	1826	William van Mildert; trs. Llandaff
1494–1501	Richard Fox; trs. Bath and Wells; to Winchester	1836	Edward Maltby; trs. Chichester
		1856	Charles Longley, trs. Ripon; to York
1502	William Sever; trs. Carlisle	1860	Henry Villiers; trs. Carlisle
1507–1508	Christopher Bainbridge; to York	1861	Charles Baring; trs. Gloucester
1509	Thomas Ruthall	1879	Joseph Lightfoot
1523	Thomas Wolsey (already Card.-Abp of York)	1890	Brooke Westcott
		1901	Handley Moule
1530–1559	Cuthbert Tunstall; trs. London	1920	Herbert Hensley Henson; trs. Hereford
1561–1576	James Pilkington		
1577–1587	Richard Barnes; trs. Carlisle	1939	Alwyn Williams; to Winchester
1589	Matthew Hutton; to York	1952	A. Michael Ramsey; to York
1595	Tobias Matthew; to York	1956	Maurice Harland; trs. Lincoln
1606	William James	1966–1972	Ian Ramsey
1617	Richard Neile; trs. Lincoln; to Winchester	1973–1983	John Habgood; to York
		1984	David Jenkins

BISHOPS OF WINCHESTER

The earliest bishopric of the West Saxons was at Dorchester-on-Thames (635–60). The bishopric was divided into Winchester and Sherborne in 705, and Winchester and Ramsbury 909–1058. Best known of the pre-Conquest Bishops of Winchester were Swithin (Bp 852–62) and Ethelwold (Bp 963–84). Winchester is fifth in seniority among English sees; the bishops had considerable political influence between 1100 and 1560. The bishop is always entitled to sit in the House of Lords. The following list gives the dates of consecration or enthronement.

1070–1098	Walkelin	1262	John Gervais
1107	William Giffard	1268–1280	Nicholas of Ely; trs. Worcester
1129–1171	Henry of Blois	1282–1304	John of Pontoise
1174–1188	Richard of Ilchester	1305	Henry Woodcock
1189–1204	Godfrey de Lucy	1316	John Sandale
1205–1238	Peter des Roches	1319–1323	Rigaud of Assier
1240	William Raleigh; trs. Norwich	1324–1333	John Stratford; to Canterbury
1250–1260	Aymer de Valence	1334–1345	Adam Orleton

1346	William Edendon		1662	George Morley; trs. Worcester
1366	William of Wykeham		1684–1706	Peter Mews; trs. Bath and Wells
1404	Henry Beaufort; cardinal 1427		1707	Jonathan Trelawney; trs. Exeter
1447–1486	William Waynflete		1721	Charles Trimnell; trs. Norwich
1487–1492	Peter Courtenay; trs. Exeter		1723	Richard Willis; trs. Salisbury
1493	Thomas Langton; to Canterbury		1734	Benjamin Hoadley; trs. Salisbury
1501–1528	Richard Fox; trs. Durham		1761	John Thomas; trs. Salisbury
1529–1530	Thomas Wolsey (Card.-Abp of York, etc)		1781	Brownlow North; trs. Worcester
			1820	George Pretyman-Tomline; trs. Lincoln
1531	Stephen Gardiner; deprived Feb. 1551		1827	Charles Sumner; trs. Llandaff
1551	John Ponet; trs. Rochester		1869	Samuel Wilberforce; trs. Oxford
1553–1555	Stephen Gardiner; restored		1873	Edward Browne; trs. Ely
1556–1559	John White; trs. Lincoln		1891	Anthony Thorold; trs. Rochester
1561	Robert Horne		1895	Randall Davidson; trs. Rochester; to Canterbury
1580	John Watson			
1584	Thomas Cooper; trs. Lincoln		1903	Herbert Ryle; trs. Exeter
1594	William Wickham; trs. Lincoln		1911	Edward Talbot; trs. Southwark
1595–1596	William Day		1923	Frank Woods; trs. Peterborough
1597	Thomas Bilson; trs. Worcester		1932	Cyril Garbett; trs. Southwark; to York
1616	James Montague; trs. Bath			
1618–1626	Lancelot Andrewes; trs. Ely		1942	Mervyn Haigh; trs. Coventry
1628	Richard Neile; trs. Durham; to York		1952	Alwyn Williams; trs. Durham
			1961–1974	Sherard Allison; trs. Chelmsford
1632–1647	Walter Curle; trs. Bath and Wells		1975	John Taylor
1660	Brian Duppa; trs. Salisbury		1985	Colin James; trs. Wakefield

CARDINAL ARCHBISHOPS OF WESTMINSTER

Since 1850 Cardinal Archbishops of Westminster have been the senior Roman Catholic prelates in England and Wales.

1850	Cardinal Nicholas Wiseman		1935	Arthur Hinsley; cardinal 1937
1865	Henry Manning; cardinal 1875		1943	Bernard Griffin; cardinal 1946
1892	Herbert Vaughan; cardinal 1893		1963	John Heenan; cardinal 1965
1903	Francis Bourne; cardinal 1911		1976	Basil Hume; cardinal 1976

600	King's, Canterbury	1544	Berkhampsted	1568	St Edmund's, Ware
604	King's, Rochester	1545	Royal Grammar,	1569	Queen Elizabeth's
627	St Peter's, York		Newcastle upon Tyne		Grammar, Blackburn
914	Warwick		King Henry VIII's,	1570	St Alban's
970	King's, Ely		Coventry	1571	St Olave's, Southwark
1180	Wells Cathedral School	1546	Abp Holgate's		Harrow
1239	Dundee High		Grammar, York	1574	Ruthin, Clwyd
1240	Norwich	1549	Bromsgrove	1576	Queen Elizabeth's,
1256	Abingdon		Kirkham Grammar,		Faversham
1381	Hereford Cathedral		Preston		Burford
	School		Truro Cathedral School		Sutton Valence
1382	Winchester College	1550	Sherborne	1580	Roger Manwood's,
1400	Ipswich		Bury St Edmunds		Sandwich
1407	Oswestry	1551	King Edward VI,		Wrexham Grammar
1414	Durham		Chelmsford	1583	St Bees
1418	Sevenoaks	1552	King Edward's, Bath	1584	Oakham
1440	Eton College		King Edward's,		Uppingham
1442	City of London		Birmingham	1586	Queen Elizabeth's
1469	Royal Grammar,		King Edward's, Poole		Hospital, Bristol
	Lancaster		Bedford	1591	Queen Elizabeth's
1480	Magdalen College		Leeds Grammar		Grammar, Wakefield
	School, Oxford		Shrewsbury	1595	Wellingborough
1495	Loughborough Grammar	1553	King's New Grammar,	1596	Trinity School, Croydon
1502	King's, Macclesfield		Stratford-upon-Avon		Whitgift
1509	St Paul's		Christ's Hospital,	1597	Aldenham
1512	Giggleswick		Horsham	1599	Blundell's, Tiverton
1513	Nottingham High		King Edward's, Witley		SOME LATER
1514	Pocklington		Tonbridge		FOUNDATIONS
1515	Manchester Grammar	1554	Queen Mary's Grammar,	1619	Dulwich College
	Allhallows, Rousdon		Walsall	1659	George Heriot's
1518	Cranbrook	1555	Gresham's, Holt	1802	Ampleforth College
1519	King's, Bruton	1556	Oundle	1807	Mill Hill
1522	Bablake, Coventry	1557	Brentwood	1841	Cheltenham College
1524	Bolton		Repton		Glenalmond College
1525	Sedbergh	1560	Solihull	1843	Marlborough College
1532	Bristol Grammar		Westminster	1847	Radley College
	Stamford	1561	Kingston Grammar	1848	Lancing College
1539	Crypt, Gloucester		Merchant Taylors',	1856	Wellington College
	King's Grammar,		Northwood	1858	Ardingly
	Colchester	1562	High Wycombe	1862	Clifton College
1541	Sir George Monoux,	1563	Elizabeth College,		Haileybury
	Walthamstow		Guernsey	1865	Malvern College
	Christ's College, Brecon		Elizabeth College,		Epsom College
	King's, Chester		Buxton	1870	Fettes
	King's, Gloucester	1564	Felsted, Dunmow	1875	The Leys, Cambridge
	King's, Worcester	1565	Highgate	1893	Bedales
1542	Bristol Cathedral School	1567	Rugby	1923	Stowe
1543	Dauntsey's, Devizes		Lord William's, Thame	1934	Gordonstoun

*c.*1160	Oxford
1209	Cambridge
1411	St Andrews
1451	Glasgow
1495	Aberdeen
1583	Edinburgh
1592	Trinity College, Dublin
1832	Durham (after short-lived Cromwellian experiment in 1657)
1836	London (Univ. College 1826; King's College 1828)
1893	University of Wales (Lampeter 1822; Aberystwyth 1872; Cardiff 1883; Bangor 1884; to be joined by Swansea in 1920)
1900	Birmingham (Mason College 1880)
1903	Manchester (Institute of Science 1824; Owen's College 1851) Liverpool (Univ. College 1804)
1904	Leeds (Yorkshire College of Science 1874)
1905	Sheffield (Univ. College 1897)
1908	Queen's University, Belfast National University of Ireland, Dublin
1909	Bristol (Univ. College 1876)
1926	Reading (Univ. College 1891)
1948	Nottingham (Univ. College 1881)
1952	Southampton (Hartley Institute 1862)
1954	Hull (Univ. College 1927)
1955	Exeter (Univ. College of the South-West 1922)
1957	Leicester (Univ. College 1921)
1961	University of Sussex, Brighton
1962	Keele (Univ. College of North Staffordshire 1950)
1963	Newcastle upon Tyne (as part of Durham Univ. 1852) University of East Anglia, Norwich York

1964	Lancaster University of Strathclyde, Glasgow (Scottish College of Commerce 1845; Technical College 1886) University of Essex, Colchester
1965	University of Warwick, Coventry University of Kent, Canterbury Loughborough University of Technology
1966	Aston, Birmingham Bath Bradford (formerly Institute of Technology) City, London (Northampton Polytechnic 1891) Brunel, Uxbridge (Uxbridge Technical College 1957) Heriot-Watt, Edinburgh (School of Arts, 1821; Watt Institute 1852) University of Surrey, Guildford (Battersea Polytechnic Institute 1861)
1967	Salford (Royal Technical Institute 1896) Dundee (Univ. College 1881) Stirling
1969	Open University, Milton Keynes
1983	Buckingham (Independent Univ.; founded as Univ. College 1976)
1984	University of Ulster, Coleraine (New Univ. of Ulster 1965 and Ulster Polytechnic)

OTHER ACADEMIC INSTITUTIONS
GRANTING HIGHER DEGREES

1837	Royal College of Art, Kensington
1969	Cranfield Institute of Technology, Bedford

ENGLISH HOSPITALS

Many abbeys were responsible for founding, and occasionally maintaining, hospitals or medical hospices from the eleventh century onwards. Most were for lepers. Archbishop Lanfrance is, however, known to have endowed a general hospital, St Gregory's at Canterbury, *circa* 1080. The coming of the orders of hospitallers in the twelfth century speeded the growth of such institutions. By 1530 there were at least 25 hospitals or hospices of religious foundation in London alone. But the most rapid spread of free, charitable hospitals in England came in the mid-eighteenth century. Listed below are the best-known foundations, up to the end of George III's reign.

1123	St Bartholomew's, London	1751	Newcastle Royal
1190	St Thomas Acon, Cheapside	1752	Manchester Royal
1197	St Mary Spital ('Spitalfields')	1755	Chester
c.1220	St Thomas's, Southwark		Gloucester Infirmary
1247	St Mary's, Bethlehem, London ('Bedlam')	1766	Stafford
c.1315	The Lock, Southwark (leprosy; later, venereal diseases)		Birmingham
			Salisbury
1505	Savoy Hospital, London	1767	Addenbrooke's, Cambridge (from legacy of 1719)
1696	St Peter's, Bristol		
1720	Westminster		Leeds Infirmary
1726	Guy's	1769	Lincoln County (from initiative of 1744)
1734	St George's, Knightsbridge	1770	Radcliffe Infirmary, Oxford
1735	Bristol General	1771	Leicester Infirmary
1736	Winchester	1776	Hereford (from initiative of 1764)
1739	Foundling, Holborn	1782	Nottingham General
	Lying-In Hospital, St James's (Q. Charlotte's Maternity 1806)		Hull Royal Infirmary
		1787	Wakefield Infirmary
1740	London	1805	Moorfields ('London Dispensary for the Relief of the Poor Afflicted with Diseases of the Eye and Ear')
	York County		
1741	Exeter (Devon and Exeter 1753)		
1743	Northampton	1810	Taunton and Somerset General
1745	Middlesex	1816	Royal Waterloo Hospital for Children and Women
	Durham Infirmary		
	Liverpool Royal Infirmary		
	Shrewsbury Infirmary		LATER FOUNDATIONS
1746	Worcester Royal Infirmary	1843	Hospital for Diseases of Women, Holborn
1749	British Lying-In Hospital, Long Acre, Covent Garden	1851	Hospital for Sick Children, Great Ormond Street

---

BIRTHS AND DEATHS

A Registrar-General was first appointed in 1836 and the earliest systematic vital statistics for England and Wales were compiled for the year 1838. But no reliable figures exist for the United Kingdom as a whole before the middle of the 19th century.

See diagram opposite

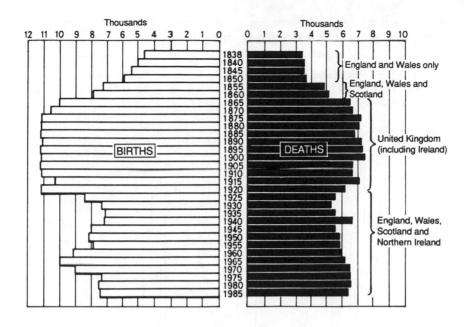

POPULATION OF THE BRITISH ISLES

Before 1801, all figures are estimates.

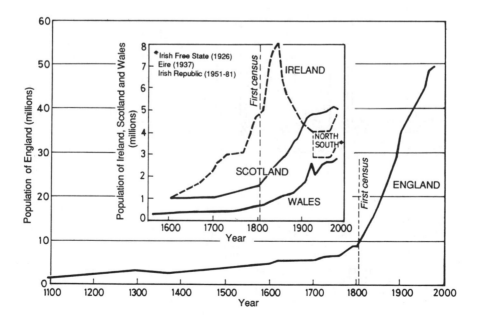

The population of sixteen towns, based from 1801 onwards on census returns but for some towns estimates before that date are also given. The census in Belfast was taken in 1926 and 1937 rather than 1921 and 1932. No figures are available for 1941.

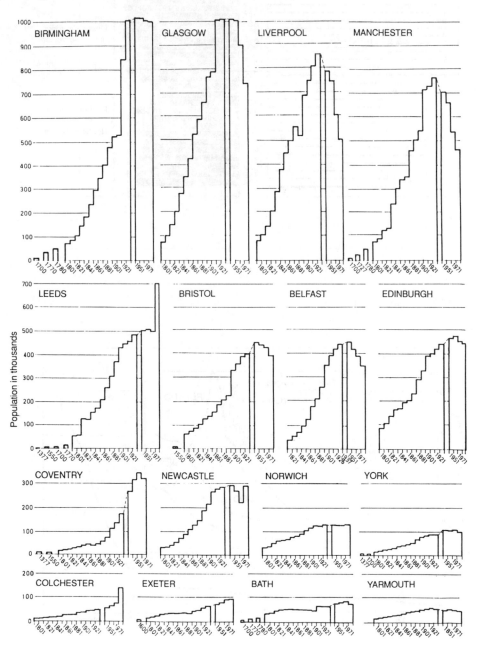

POPULATION OF LONDON

Figures before the first census (1801) are estimated.

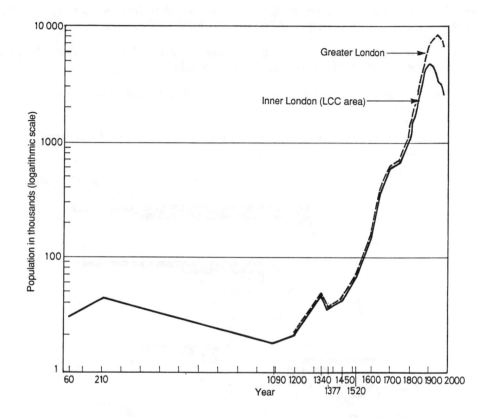

Speed of communication: stage coaches, 1710-1830. The following, for comparison, are some earlier journey times:

London to York   In about 150 AD a Roman legion on the march took 10 days, and an imperial courier 4 days. In 1605 a postboy, John Lepton, took 16 hours on the road.

York to London   In 1066 Harold must have marched his army south from York in less than 7 days, and from London to the site of the Battle of Hastings (about 50 miles) in 2 days.

Dover to London   In about 150 AD a Roman legion on the march took 4 days, and an imperial courier 36 hours. In 1605 a postboy took 9 hours.

London (Richmond) to Edinburgh   In March 1603 Sir Robert Carey, with news of King James's accession, took about 62 hours.

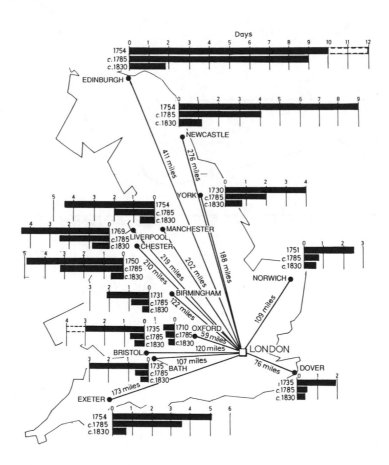

Speed of communication: express trains, 1889-1989. The shortest route to Exeter in 1889 was from Waterloo (172 miles). The GWR line from Paddington, originally by way of Bristol, was in 1903 reduced to 175 miles by new track through Westbury. The GWR ran in close competition with the Southern route until after World War 2.

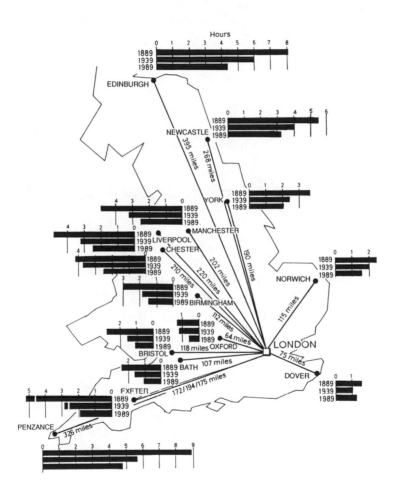

517

RAILWAY MILEAGE

Railway mileage in Great Britain (national network only). The peak of 20,312 miles was reached in 1920, falling to 18,771 by 1960 and rapidly to 12,098 by 1970.

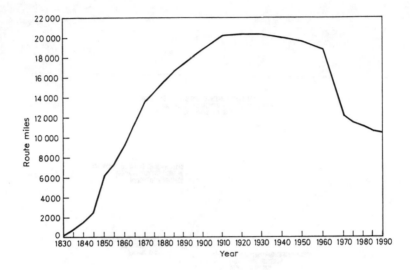

TRADE UNION MEMBERSHIP

Trade Union membership in Great Britain.

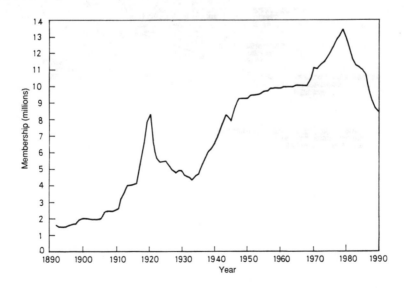

Fluctuations in the price of bread, London 1545-1925. The graphs are based on statistical tables printed in B. R. Mitchell, *Abstract of British Historical Statistics* (Cambridge University Press, 1962).

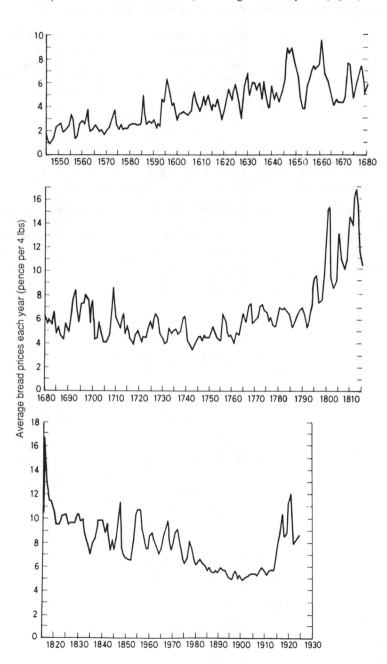

POETS LAUREATE

Ben Jonson was never officially appointed Poet Laureate, but from 1616 onwards he enjoyed a special status after receiving a pension from James I. In 1638 Jonson was succeeded as unofficial laureate by Sir William D'Avenant. The following received the title of Poet Laureate officially from their sovereign.

1668	John Dryden	1757	William Whitehead	1896	Alfred Austin
1688	Thomas Shadwell	1785	Thomas Warton	1913	Robert Bridges
1692	Nahum Tate	1790	Henry James Pye	1930	John Masefield
1715	Nicholas Rowe	1813	Robert Southey	1967	Cecil Day Lewis
1718	Laurence Eusden	1843	William Wordsworth	1972	Sir John Betjeman
1730	Colley Cibber	1850	Alfred Tennyson	1984	Ted Hughes

MASTERS OF THE KING'S / QUEEN'S MUSIC

1626	Nicholas Lanier	1786	Sir William Parsons	1924	Sir Edward Elgar
1666	Louis Grabu	1817	William Shield	1934	Sir Henry Walford Davies
1674	Nicholas Staggins	1829	Christian Kramer	1941	Sir Arnold Bax
1700	John Eccles	1834	Franz Cramer	1953	Sir Arthur Bliss
1735	Maurice Greene	1848	George Anderson	1975	Malcolm Williamson
1757	William Boyce	1870	Sir William Cusins		
1779	John Stanley	1893	Sir Walter Parratt		

PRESIDENTS OF THE ROYAL SOCIETY

1660	Sir Robert Moray	1778	Sir Joseph Banks	1913	Sir William Crookes
1662	Viscount Brouncker	1820	William Wollaston	1915	Sir Joseph Thomson OM
1677	Sir Joseph Williamson		Sir Humphrey Davy	1920	Sir Charles Sherrington
1680	Sir Christopher Wren	1827	Davies Gilbert		OM
1682	Sir John Hoskins	1830	Duke of Sussex	1925	Lord Rutherford OM
1683	Sir Cyril Wyche	1838	Marquis of Northampton	1930	Sir Frederick Hopkins OM
1684	Samuel Pepys	1848	Earl of Rosse	1935	Sir William Bragg OM
1686	Earl of Carbery	1854	Lord Wrottesley	1940	Sir Henry Dale OM
1689	Earl of Pembroke	1858	Sir Benjamin Brodie	1941	Sir William Bragg OM
1690	Sir Robert Southwell	1861	Sir Edward Sabine	1942	Sir Henry Dale OM
1695	Earl of Halifax	1871	Sir George Airy	1947	Sir Robert Robinson OM
1698	Lord Somers	1873	Sir Joseph Hooker	1951	Lord Adrian OM
1703	Sir Isaac Newton	1878	William Spottiswoode	1955	Sir Cyril Hinshelwood
1727	Sir Hans Sloane	1883	Thomas Henry Huxley		OM
1741	Martin Folkes	1885	Sir George Stokes	1960	Lord Florey OM
1752	Earl of Macclesfield	1890	Lord Kelvin	1965	Lord Blackett OM
1764	Earl of Morton	1895	Lord Lister	1970	Sir Alan Hodgkin OM
1768	Sir James Barrow	1900	Sir William Huggins	1975	Lord Todd OM
	James West	1905	Lord Rayleigh	1980	Sir Andrew Huxley OM
1772	Sir John Pringle	1908	Sir Archibald Geikie	1985	Sir George Porter

PRESIDENTS OF THE ROYAL ACADEMY

1768	Sir Joshua Reynolds	1878	Lord Leighton	1949	Sir Gerald Kelly
1792	Benjamin West	1896	Sir John Millais	1954	Sir Arthur Richardson
1805	James Wyatt		Sir Edward Poynter	1956	Sir Charles Wheeler
1806	Benjamin West	1919	Sir Aston Webb	1966	Sir Thomas Monnington
1820	Sir Thomas Lawrence	1924	Sir Frank Dicksee	1976	Sir Hugh Casson
1830	Sir Michael Shee	1928	Sir William Llewellyn	1984	Roger de Grey
1850	Sir Charles Eastlake	1938	Sir Edwin Lutyens		
1866	Sir Francis Grant	1944	Sir Alfred Munnings		

ASTRONOMERS ROYAL

1675	John Flamsteed	1811	John Pond	1955	Sir Richard Woolley
1720	Edmund Halley	1835	Sir George Airy	1972	Sir Martin Ryle
1742	James Bradley	1881	Sir William Christie	1982	Sir Francis Graham Smith
1762	Nathaniel Bliss	1910	Sir Frank Dyson		
1765	Nevil Maskeleyne	1933	Sir Harold Spencer Jones		

NOBEL PRIZE WINNERS FROM THE BRITISH COMMONWEALTH AND IRELAND

PHYSICS PRIZE

1904	Lord Rayleigh (J.W. Strutt)
1906	J.J. Thomson
1915	W.H. Bragg and
	W.L. Bragg
1917	C.G. Barkla
1927	C.T.R. Wilson
1928	O.W. Richardson
1933	P.A.M. Dirac
1935	J. Chadwick
1937	G.P. Thomson
1947	E.V. Appleton
1948	P.M.S. Blackett
1950	C.F. Powell
1951	J.D. Cockcroft (and
	E.T.S. Walton, Ireland)
1954	M. Born
1971	D. Gabor
1973	B.D. Josephson
1974	Sir Martin Ryle and
	A. Hewish
1977	Sir Nevill Mott

CHEMISTRY PRIZE

1904	W. Ramsay
1908	E. Rutherford
1921	F. Soddy
1922	F.W. Aston
1929	A. Harden
1937	W.N. Haworth
1947	R. Robinson
1952	A.J.P. Martin and
	R.L.M. Synge
1956	C.N. Hinshelwood
1957	A.R. Todd
1958	F.R. Sanger
1962	J.C. Kendrew and
	M.F. Perutz

1964	Dorothy Hodgkin
1967	R.G.W. Nirrish and
	G. Porter
1969	D.H. Barton
1971	G. Herzberg (Canada)
1973	G. Wilkinson
1975	J.W. Cornfoot (Australia)
1978	P. Mitchell
1980	F. Sanger
1982	A. Klug

PHYSIOLOGY AND MEDICINE PRIZE

1902	R. Ross
1922	A.V. Hill
1923	F.G. Banting (Canada) and
	J.J.R. Macleod (Canada)
1929	F.G. Hopkins
1932	C.S. Sherrington and
	E.D. Adrian
1936	H.H. Dale
1945	A. Fleming, E.B. Chain
	and H. Florey (Australia)
1951	M. Theiler (South Africa)
1953	H.A. Krebs
1950	F.M. Burnet (Australia)
	and P.B. Medawar
1962	M.H.F. Wilkins and
	F.H.C. Crick
1963	A.L. Hodgkin,
	A.F. Huxley and
	J.C. Eccles (Australia)
1970	Sir Bernard Katz
1972	G.R. Porter
1979	C.N. Hounsfield
1982	J.R. Vane

LITERATURE PRIZE

1907	R. Kipling
1913	Radindranath Tagore (India)
1923	W.B. Yeats (Ireland)
1925	G.B. Shaw
1932	J. Galsworthy
1948	T.S. Eliot
1950	B. Russell
1953	W.S. Churchill
1969	S. Beckett (Ireland)
1973	P.V.M. White (Australia)
1983	William Golding

ECONOMIC SCIENCES PRIZE

1972	Sir John Hicks
1974	F. Hayek
1977	J.E. Meade
1979	Sir Arthur Lewis (West Indies)

PEACE PRIZE

1903	W.R. Cremer
1925	Sir Austen Chamberlain
1933	N. Angell
1934	A. Henderson
1937	Viscount Cecil of Chelwood
1949	J. Boyd Orr
1957	Lester Pearson (Canada)
1959	P. Noel-Baker
1960	A. Luthuli (South Africa)
1974	Sean McBride (Ireland)
1976	Mrs B. Williams and Miss M. Corrigan
(1984	Archbishop D. Tutu of Rep. of South Africa.)

PRIME MINISTERS OF AUSTRALIA

From the federation of the Commonwealth of Australia in 1900.

1901 *Jan. 1*	Edmund Barton	Protectionist	1941 *Aug. 28*	Arthur Fadden	Country
1903 *Sep. 24*	Alfred Deakin	Protectionist	*Oct. 7*	John Curtin	Labor
1904 *Apr. 27*	John Watson	Labor	1945 *Jul. 5*	Frank Forde	Labor
Aug. 17	George Reid	Coalition	*12*	Ben Chifley	Labor
1905 *Jul. 8*	Alfred Deakin	Protectionist	1949 *Dec. 19*	Sir Robert	
1908 *Nov. 10*	Andrew Fisher	Labor		Menzies	Liberal
1909 *Apr. 29*	Alfred Deakin	Protectionist	1966 *Jan. 20*	Harold Holt	Liberal
1910 *Apr. 13*	Andrew Fisher	Labor	1967 *Dec. 18*	John McEwen	Country
1913 *Jun. 24*	Joseph Cook	Protectionist	1968 *Jan. 9*	John Gorton	Liberal
1914 *Sep. 5*	Andrew Fisher	Labor	1971 *Mar. 22*	William	
1915 *Oct. 27*	William Hughes	Labor		McMahon	Liberal
1923 *Feb. 9*	Stanley Bruce	Nat/Country	1972 *Dec. 2*	Gough Whitlam	Labor
1929 *Oct. 12*	James Scullin	Labor	1975 *Nov. 11*	Malcolm Fraser	Liberal
1931 *Dec. 19*	Joseph Lyons	United Australia Party	1983 *Mar. 5*	Bob Hawke	Labor
1939 *Apr. 7*	Earle Page	UAP	1990 *Dec. 19*	Paul Keating	Labor
26	Robert Menzies	UAP			

PRIME MINISTERS OF CANADA

From federation in 1867

1867 *Jul. 1*	Sir John Macdonald	Conservative	1920 *Jul. 10*	Arthur Meighen	Unionist
1873 *Nov. 7*	Alexander Mackenzie	Liberal	1921 *Dec. 29*	W.L. Mackenzie King	Liberal
1878 *Oct. 17*	Sir John Macdonald	Conservative	1926 *Jun. 25*	A. Meighen	Conservative
1891 *Jun. 16*	Sir John Abbott	Conservative	*Sep. 25*	W.L. Mackenzie King	Liberal
1892 *Dec. 5*	Sir John Thompson	Conservative	1930 *Aug. 7*	Richard Bennett	Conservative
1894 *Dec. 21*	Sir Mackenzie Bowell	Conservative	1935 *Oct. 23*	W.L. Mackenzie King	Liberal
1896 *May 1*	Sir Charles Tupper	Conservative	1948 *Nov. 15*	Louis St Laurent	Liberal
Jul. 11	Sir Wilfred Laurier	Liberal	1957 *Jun. 21*	John Diefenbaker	Conservative
1911 *Oct. 11*	Sir Robert Borden	Conservative	1963 *Apr. 22*	Lester Pearson	Liberal
1917 *Oct. 12*	Borden (continued)	Unionist	1968 *Apr. 20*	Pierre Trudeau	Liberal
			1979 *Jun. 4*	Charles Clarke	Conservative
			1980 *Mar. 3*	Pierre Trudeau	Liberal
			1984 *Jun. 30*	John Turner	Liberal
			Sep. 17	Brian Mulroney	Progressive Conservative

From the grant of responsible self-government to the colony in 1856.

1856 *May* 7	Henry Sewell	
20	William Fox	
Jun. 2	Edward Stafford	
1861 *Jul.* 12	William Fox	
1862 *Aug.* 6	Alfred Domett	
1863 *Oct.* 30	Frederick Whitaker	
1864 *Nov.* 24	Frederick Weld	
1865 *Oct.* 16	Edward Stafford	
1869 *Jun.* 28	William Fox	
1872 *Sep.* 10	Edward Stafford	
Oct. 11	George Waterhouse	
1873 *Mar.* 3	William Fox	
Apr. 8	Julius Vogel	
1875 *Jul.* 6	David Pollen	
1876 *Feb.* 15	Sir Julius Vogel	
Sep. 1	Harry Atkinson	
1877 *Oct.* 15	Sir George Grey	
1879 *Oct.* 8	John Hall	
1882 *Apr.* 21	Frederick Whitaker	
1883 *Sep.* 25	Harry Atkinson	
1884 *Aug.* 16	Sir Robert Stout	
24	Harry Atkinson	
Sep. 3	Sir Robert Stout	
1887 *Oct.* 8	Sir Harry Atkinson	

1891 *Jan.* 24	John Ballance
1893 *May* 1	Richard Seddon
1906 *Jun.* 21	William Hall-Jones
Aug. 6	Sir Joseph Ward
1912 *Mar.* 28	Thomas Mackenzie
	William Massey
1925 *May* 14	Sir Francis Bell
30	Joseph Coates
1928 *Dec.* 10	Sir Joseph Ward
1930 *May* 28	George Forbes
Dec. 6	Michael Savage
1940 *Apr.* 1	Peter Fraser
1949 *Dec.* 13	Sidney Holland
1957 *Sep.* 20	Keith Holyoake
Dec. 12	Walter Nash
1960 *Dec.* 12	Sir Keith Holyoake
1972 *Feb.* 7	John Marshall
Dec. 8	Norman Kirk
1974 *Sep.* 6	Wallace Rowling
1975 *Dec.* 12	Robert Muldoon
1984 *Jul.* 26	David Lange
1989	Geoffrey Palmer
1990 *Oct.* 15	Jim Bolger

INDEX OF TOPICS

1886, 1895–7, 1908–9, 1912–14, 1916, 1918–23
Ecclesiastical Titles Act, 1851, 1871
economic conferences, 1932–3, 1952, 1970
economic theory, 1682, 1697, 1776, 1798, 1813, 1817, 1848, 1880, 1910, 1919, 1923, 1925, 1930
ecumenical movements, 1894, 1896, 1941, 1946, 1961–2, 1966, 1980, 1982, 1989, 1992
Education Acts, 1870, 1889, 1891, 1902, 1906, 1918, 1944, 1988
education, adult, 1823, 1870, 1904, 1963; scientific, 1916; state-sponsored, 1839, 1860, 1872, 1899, 1965, 1970, 1976, 1979, 1985, 1988 (see also Education Acts)
educational theory, 1693, 1697, 1798, 1803, 1808, 1891, 1959
Egypt, British political and financial administration of, 1876, 1882–3, 1914, 1922, 1936, 1952–3, 1956
Eisteddfod, 1176, 1568
Eleanor crosses, 1291
elections, general, 1679, 1695, 1698, 1702, 1705, 1708, 1710, 1713, 1715, 1734, 1754, 1768, 1784, 1790, 1806–7, 1818, 1820, 1830–2, 1835, 1837, 1847, 1852, 1857, 1859, 1865, 1868, 1874, 1880, 1885–6, 1892, 1895, ('khaki') 1900, 1906, 1910 (Jan.), 1910 (Dec.), 1918, 1923, 1924, 1929, 1931, 1935, 1945, 1950, 1951, 1959, 1964, 1970, 1974 (Feb.), 1974 (Oct.), 1979, 1983, 1987, 1992
electricity, 1767, 1806, 1821, 1831, 1860, 1873, 1878, 1880, 1883–4, 1890
embroidery (tapestry), 910–15, 1082, 1962
emigration, 1637, 1902
Empire Games, 1930
Employment Act, 1982
enclosures, 1517, 1549, 1607, 1801, 1830
engineering, 1762, 1769, 1781, 1783, 1797
Énosis movement, 1954
Entente Cordiale, 1903–4
Entertainment National Service Administration (ENSA), 1940
environmental protection, 1951, 1958, 1989
Equal Pay Act, 1970
essays, 1597, 1625, 1823, 1881
European Community Act, 1972
European Economic Community (EEC), 1961–3, 1967, 1969–70, 1972–3, 1975, 1986, 1990
European exchange rate mechanism (ERM), 1990

European Free Trade Association (EFTA), 1959
European Parliament, 1977, 1979
evangelical movements, 1779–80, 1783, 1846, 1860, 1865, 1882, 1954, 1967 (see also Methodism)
Evening News, 1881
Everest expedition, 1953
evolution, theories of, 1858–9, 1864, 1871
exchange controls, 1932, 1947, 1979
Exchequer, 1110, 1114, 1129, 1179, 1233, 1323, 1672
Exchequer of Jews, 1194
Excise Bill, 1733
Exclusion Bills, 1679–81
exhibitions, 1802, 1851, 1857, 1862, 1888, 1901, 1908, 1924, 1940
exploration, 1768, 1770, 1778–9, 1788, 1792, 1795, 1798, 1806, 1828, 1831, 1841, 1852, 1855, 1857, 1860, 1862, 1870–1, 1874, 1877, 1879, 1901–2, 1908, 1910, 1912, 1914, 1948, 1957–8

Fabian Society, 1884, 1889
Factory Acts, 1802, 1825, 1833, 1843, 1867, 1874
fairs, 1133, 1683–4
falconry, 1274
Falklands disputes, 1771, 1955, 1982
family allowances, 1945
famine and food shortages, 1205, 1315–17, 1631, 1710, 1795–6, 1800, 1842, 1845–6
Fascists (see British Union of Fascists)
Fashoda crisis, 1898
Fenian Brotherhood, 1858, 1867, 1869–70, 1882
fenland, reclamation of, 120, 1634
festivals of arts and science, 1947, 1951, 1990
feudal obligations, 1290, 1610
Field of Cloth of Gold, 1520
Fifth Monarchy Men, 1649
films, 1896, 1913, 1933, 1936–47, 1962, 1981, 1983
Financial Times, 1888
Fine Arts Commission, Royal, 1923
fishery disputes, 1904, 1959, 1976–77
Five Boroughs (Danish-held), 877, 918
Flower Children, 1967
flying (pioneer), 1808, 1909–10, 1912, 1919, 1926, 1928, 1930, 1932, 1936–7
flying bombs (V-1), 1944–5
food and drugs protection, 1860, 1875
food rationing (see rationing)
football, 1314, 1486, 1647, 1863, 1871, 1902, 1907, 1923, 1927, 1934, 1946, 1957, 1961, 1965–6,

1981, 1985, 1989
forced loans, 1626–8
Foreign Office (Foreign Secretary), 1782, 1850, 1895, 1907
forests (and forest laws), 1079, 1180, 1189, 1216–17, 1225, 1297, 1633
forts, burhs, 887; coastal defence, 220, 270, 343, 1864; hill, 4,000–3,000 BC, 3,400–400 BC, AD 43–4, 490; Martello, 1803; Roman, 43–7, 49–51, 71, 74, 80–1, 83, 100–5, 139, 142–4, 169–75, 197, 297, 369, 383, 401; Wessex, 915–16, 919
franchise, parliamentary, 1832, 1867, 1884, 1918, 1928, 1948, 1970
free trade, 1821, 1845, 1853, 1860, 1932
friars, 1221, 1224, 1247, 1279, 1308, 1324, 1357
Friends of the People, Society of, 1792
Friends, Society of (see Quakers)
furniture, 1753, 1754, 1788

Gallipoli campaign, 1915–16
garden cities, 1898, 1905, 1920
gardening, 1621, 1685, 1715, 1718–19, 1739, 1765, 1785, 1795, 1841, 1844
'Garroters' Act, 1862
Garter, Order of the, 1348, 1519, 1953–4
gas industry, 1948
gas lighting, 1807
General Strike, 1926
general warrants, 1763
geology, 1830
German navy, at war, 1914–18, 1939–44; rivalry, 1900–13; scuttled, 1919; signed agreement limiting, 1937; surrenders, 1918
Gibraltar disputes, 1713, 1726, 1728, 1966–8
gilds (guilds), 1107, 1130, 1504
gin (and spirits), 1751, 1885
Girl Guides, 1909
'Glorious First of June' (naval battle), 1794
gold standard, 1819, 1821, 1925, 1931
goldfields, 1851, 1892
golf, 1457, 1754, 1766, 1860
Government of Ireland Act, 1920–1,
Grand Remonstrance, 1641
Great Contract, 1610–11
Great Exhibition, 1851
Great Fire (of London), 1666
Great Frost, 1683–4, 1737–40
Great Stink, 1858
Great Storm, 1703
Great Trek, 1835, 1838
Greek campaign, 1941
Greek independence, Britain and,

navy, Cromwellian, 1652–3, 1655–7
New Model Army, 1645
News of the World, 1843
newspapers, 1621, 1643, 1702, 1785,
    1788, 1791–2, 1814, 1836–7, 1855,
    1872, 1881, 1888, 1890, 1896,
    1900, 1924
Nobel prizes, 1902, 1904, 1906–8,
    1915, 1921, 1925, 1932, 1935,
    1937, 1945, 1947, 1948–50, 1952,
    1964, 1969, 1976, 1979–80, 1983
Non-Jurors, 1689–90
Nootka Sound crisis, 1789–90
North African campaign, 1940–3
North Atlantic Treaty Organization
    (NATO), 1949
The North Briton, 1762–3
Northern Ireland, government of,
    1921, 1965–6, 1968–74, 1978,
    1985
Norwegian campaign, 1940
novels, 1590, 1594, 1668, 1719,
    1721, 1726, 1740, 1748–9, 1751,
    1759, 1766–70, 1778, 1795, 1800,
    1809–11, 1813–16, 1818, 1821,
    1826, 1831, 1834 6, 1840,
    1842–5, 1848, 1851–7, 1859, 1861,
    1863–4, 1866–8, 1870, 1872,
    1874–5, 1879, 1882, 1886–9,
    1891–4, 1897–1907, 1909,
    1911–91
nuclear power, 1956, 1986
nuclear weapons, 1950, 1952, 1962
nursing, 1854, 1915, 1961

Oath of Association, 1696
obscenity, 1763–4, 1959
The Observer, 1801
Occasional Conformity Act, 1711,
    1717
occupation, British armies of, 1920,
    1923, 1925, 1929
Ochakov crisis, 1791
Official Secrets Act, 1911
oilfields, offshore, 1965–6, 1975–6,
    1988
old-age pensions, 1908–9, 1973
Olympic Games, 1908, 1924, 1948,
    1956, 1980, 1988
Ombudsman, 1966
omnibus, 1829, 1899
opera, 1656, 1689, 1691, 1711, 1726,
    1728–9, 1731, 1734, 1763, 1826,
    1858, 1884, 1909–10, 1914, 1916,
    1934, 1946–7, 1951–3, 1955, 1961,
    1970, 1973–4, 1981
operetta, 1875, 1877–8, 1881–2,
    1887–8, 1890, 1902
optical instruments, 1292, 1665,
    1684, 1758, 1957
Orange Order, 1795, 1822
oratorio, 1732, 1742–3, 1747,
    1831–2, 1887, 1900, 1973
orchestral music, 1717, 1749, 1791,
    1829, 1831–2, 1877, 1899, 1901,

1903, 1908, 1910–11, 1920,
    1922–3, 1928, 1930, 1932, 1937,
    1948–9, 1958, 1975, 1981
ordeal by water, 1166
organs (organ music), 957, 970,
    1517, 1526–30, 1572, 1641, 1668,
    1679
Orthodox Church, Greek, 1676
Osborne Judgment, 1909
Oxford Movement (*see* Tractarians)

painting, 1797, 1803, 1813, 1817,
    1822, 1827, 1844, 1858, 1870–2,
    1878, 1912, 1920, 1926, 1929–31,
    1936, 1941–4; water colour, 1804,
    1942
palaces, royal, 1097, 1128, 1163,
    1171, 1360, 1393–4, 1475, 1497,
    1501, 1514, 1531, 1616, 1618,
    1635, 1689, 1698, 1705, 1762,
    1783, 1786, 1825, 1827
Pale (Irish), 1394, 1402
Palestine, conflicts within, 1929–30,
    1933, 1936–9, 1946–8
Palestine Liberation Organization
    (PLO), 1970, 1978
papal bulls, 1155, 1570, 1581
parks, public, 1845–6; national,
    1949
Parliament, origins of, 1236, 1258,
    1265, 1270, 1304, 1309, 1311,
    1324, 1363, 1371, 1429
Parliament, All-India, 1921
Parliament Bill and Act, 1910–11
Parliament, Canada, 1957
Parliament, Irish, 1459, 1494, 1689,
    1780, 1782, 1798, 1800
Parliament, Northern Ireland, 1921
Parliament, Scottish, 1303, 1364,
    1639–40, 1672, 1703, 1707
parliamentary procedure, 1324,
    1376, 1576, 1587, 1593, 1604,
    1621, 1641–2, 1644, 1707, 1763,
    1768, 1770, 1780, 1911, 1957–8,
    1975, 1981, 1986, 1989
parliamentary reform, 1785, 1809,
    1812, 1818–19, 1821, 1829,
    1831–2, 1853–4, 1859, 1864,
    1866–8, 1884–5, 1911, 1918, 1978
Parliaments (named, chronological
    order), Model, 1295; Stamford,
    1309; York, 1322; Good, 1376;
    Merciless, 1388; Unlearned, 1404;
    (first) Long, 1406; Coventry,
    1459; Reformation, 1529–36;
    Addled, 1614; Short, 1640; Long,
    1640–53; Oxford, 1644;
    Barebones, 1653; Convention,
    1660, 1688–9; Cavalier, 1661–79
Parochial and Burgh Schoolmasters
    Act, 1861
Peace Ballot, 1935
Peasants' Revolt, 1381
peerage, life, 1957–8; renunciation
    of inherited title, 1961, 1963;

wider representation in H. of
    Lords, 1963, 1969
pencils, 1564
penicillin, 1928, 1940, 1945
People's Budget, 1909–10
'People's Democracy', Ireland (*see*
    Civil Rights Movement).
Periodicals and magazines, 1709–11,
    1726, 1731, 1745, 1762, 1823,
    1841–2, 1851, 1938
Persian oil dispute, 1951
Peterloo Massacre, 1819
Petition of Right, 1628
petrol, price of, 1926, 1939, 1974
philosophy, 1709–10, 1719, 1741–2,
    1748, 1875, 1879, 1893, 1900,
    1903, 1921–3, 1927, 1933, 1936,
    1940
photography, 1838, 1864
physics, 1906, 1912–13, 1920, 1937,
    1947–8, 1950
Picture Post, 1938
Pilgrim Fathers, 1620
Pilgrimage of Grace, 1536–7
pilgrimages, 1027, 1050, 1054, 1173,
    1179, 1980
pipe rolls, 1114, 1129–30, 1230
piracy, 1699, 1701, 1856
plague, 1361, 1528, 1563, 1592,
    1625, 1665–6 (*see also* Black
    Death)
Plaid Cymru, 1966
plantation (of Ulster), 1609
playing cards, 1463
PLUTO pipeline, 1944
Plymouth Brethren, 1830
Poet Laureate, 1668, 1688, 1813,
    1850, 1972, 1984
poetry, descriptive, 1501, 1606,
    1630, 1642, 1762, 1783, 1844,
    1897
poetry, devotional, 680, 700, 800,
    1046, 1230, 1320, 1349, 1393,
    1648, 1827
poetry, didactic, 1711
poetry, lyrical and elegiac, 1501,
    1503, 1595, 1609, 1612–13, 1633,
    1637–40, 1747, 1788, 1798,
    1807–8, 1821, 1832, 1850, 1861,
    1870, 1878, 1881, 1889, 1896,
    1911–12, 1914–18, 1935, 1940–5,
    1964
poetry, narrative and epic, 1225,
    1250, 1264, 1272, 1300, 1320,
    1360, 1362, 1370, 1381–2, 1387,
    1390, 1559, 1645–6, 1667, 1671,
    1728, 1751, 1785, 1804–5, 1808,
    1811, 1813, 1816–17, 1835, 1842,
    1849, 1853–5, 1859, 1864, 1902,
    1904, 1920, 1926, 1930
poetry, odes, 1656, 1747
police, 1749, 1829, 1836–7
political theory, 1411–12, 1436,
    1461–3, 1468, 1476, 1516
    (*Utopia*), 1531, 1599, 1627, 1642,

1896
Baltimore, Lord, George Calvert (1580–1632), 1631
Bamburgh, Northumberland, 547, 1479; Castle, 1095, 1139
Bancroft, Marie (1839–1921), 1865
Bancroft, Richard (1544–1610), Archbp, 1604
Bancroft, Squire (1841–1926), 1865
Bangkok, Ty of, 1826
Bangladesh, 1972
Bangor, Wales, 1893
Bangweulu, Lake, Zambia, 1873
Banister, John (c.1630–79), 1672
Bank, London, 1829, 1900
Bannister, Roger (1929–), 1954
Bannockburn, Scotland, battle of, 1314
Bantry Bay, Ireland, 1796
Bapaume, France, 1917
Barbados, 1966
Barber, Anthony (1920–), 1970
Barbican, London, 1982
Barcelona, 1705–6
Barham, Richard (1788–1845), 1840
Baring, Evelyn (1841–1917), 1883, 1898
Barlow, W. H. (1812–1902), 1864
Barlow, William (d.1625), 1616
Barnard Castle, Durham, 1903
Barnard, John, 1641
Barnardo, Thomas (1845–1905), 1867
Barnet, Herts., battle of, 1471
Barnett, Henrietta (1851–1936), 1906
Barnfield, Richard (1574–1627), 1594
Barnum, Phineas (1810–91), 1889
Barrett, Michael, 1868
Barrie, James (1860–1939), 1902, 1904, 1908, 1916
Barrow, R., Ireland, 1394
Barrow-in-Furness, Cumbria, 1901
Barrow-on-Solness, Cumbria, 122–39
Barry, Charles (1795–1860), 1831, 1837, 1840
Barry, Edward (1830–80), 1857
Barry, Gerald (1898–1958), 1951
Barstow, Stan (1928–), 1960
Bart, Lionel (1930–), 1960
Bartlett, Frederick (1886–1969), 1932
Barton, Elizabeth (d.1534), 1534
Basevi, George (1794–1845), 1837
Basing House, Hants., 1645
Bass, George (d.1812), 1798
Bass Strait, Australia, 1798
Basutoland (Lesotho), 1843, 1868
Bates, H. E. (1905–74), 1949
Bath, 100, 973, 1704, 1727, 1729, 1942; Abbey, 957; Theatre Royal, 1768; University of, 1966
Batten, Jean (1909–82), 1937

Battersea Power Station, London 1933
Battle Abbey, Sussex, 1067
Batum, Caucasus, 1920
Bawsey, Norfolk, 25–20 BC
Bax, Arnold (1883–1953), 1928
Baxter, Richard (1615–91), 1650
Bayeux, Normandy, 1082, 1105
Baylis, Lilian (1874–1937), 1912, 1931
Bayonne, France, 1375, 1451
Bazalgette, Joseph (1819–91), 1862, 1875
Beachy Head, Sussex, battle of, 1690
Beardsley, Aubrey (1872–98), 1894
Beaton, David (1494–1546), Archbp, 1524, 1538, 1543, 1546
Beatty, David (1871–1935), Adm., 1914, 1918
Beaufort, Henry (c.1375–1447), Cardinal Bp, 1410, 1413, 1424–31, 1435
Beaufort, Joan, Q. Consort of Scots, 1424
Beaufort, Lady Margaret (1443–1509), 1505
Beaumaris Castle, Anglesey, 1295
Beaumont, Francis (1584–1616), 1619, 1642
Beauvais, France, 1930
Bechuanaland (Botswana), 1885, 1895, 1966
Becket, St Thomas (1118–70), Archbp, 1155–6, 1162–4, 1170, 1174, 1220
Beckett, Samuel (1906–89), 1955–6, 1969
Bede, St (673–735), 703, 725, 731, 934/5
Bedford, 915, 1957
Bedford, E. of, Francis Russell (1593–1641), 1634
Bedford, Eric, 1964
Beecham, Thomas (1879–1961), 1916, 1932, 1953
Beeching, Richard (1913–85), 1962–3
Beerbohm, Max (1872–1956), 1911
Beeton, Isabella (1835–65), 1859
Beeton, Samuel (1830–72), 1852, 1859
Behn, Aphra (1640–89), 1668–9
Beirut, 1840, 1987
Belcher, John (1905–64), 1949
Belfast, 1886, 1905, 1920–1, 1941, 1965, 1969, 1976; Falls Road, 1907; Maze Prison, 1974, 1980–1, 1983; Queen's University, 1908, 1968–70
Belfast Lough, 1778
Bell, Andrew (1753–1832), 1797
Bell, George (1885–1958), Bp, 1942, 1944
Bell, Henry (1767–1830), 1812, 1820
Bell, Vanessa (1879–1961), 1930

Belling, Charles, 1912
Bellingham, John (d.1812), 1812
Belloc, Hilaire (1870–1953), 1895, 1902
Belsen, Germany, 1945
Bemis Heights, NY, battle of, 1777
Benbecula, I. of, Scotland, 1746
Bengal, India, 1767
Benghazi, Libya, 1941
Benin, Africa, 1862
Benn, Anthony (1935–), 1961, 1963
Bennett, Alan (1934–), 1968
Bennett, Arnold (1867–1931), 1902, 1908, 1910, 1923
Bentinck, George, Lord (1802–48), 1846–7
Bentley, E. Clerihew (1875–1956), 1905, 1913
Bentley, John (?1840–1903), 1903
Berber, Sudan, 1884
Berchtesgaden, Germany, 1938
Bere Castle, Wales, battle of, 1283
Berengaria (d.c.1230), Q. Consort, 1191
Bergen, Norway, 1940
Berkeley Castle, Glos., 1327
Berkeley, George (1685–1753), Bp, 1709–10, 1713
Berlin, 1912, 1940, 1944, 1948; Conference, 1884; Congress of, 1878; Ty of, 1878
Berlin, Irving (1888–1989), 1947
Bermuda(s), 1610, 1953, 1957, 1971, 1973, 1977
Bernicia (Northumbria), kingdom of, 547, 593, 642
Berwick, D. of, James Fitzjames (1670–1734), 1707
Berwick, Northumberland, 1216, 1296, 1318–19, 1333–4, 1354, 1356, 1461, 1482, 1648; Castle, 1189; pacification of, 1639; Treaties of, 1357, 1560, 1586
Besant, Walter (1836–1901), 1882
Besika Bay, Turkey, 1853, 1876
Bessemer, Henry (1813–98), 1855
Bethnal Green, London, 1649, 1943, 1945
Betjeman, John (1906–84), 1954, 1958, 1960, 1972, 1984
Betterton, Thomas (1635–1710), 1669
Bevan, Aneurin (1897–1960), 1945, 1951, 1955, 1960
Beveridge, William (1879–1963), 1909, 1942–3
Beverley, Yorks., 1377; Minster, 1220
Bevin, Ernest (1881–1951), 1928, 1943, 1945, 1947, 1951
Bewcastle, Cumbria, 700
Bidassoa, R., Spain, 1813
Bilney, Thomas (1495–1531), 1527, 1531
Birgham, Scotland, Ty of, 1290

1916
Bright, John (1811–89), 1855
Bright, Timothy (1551–1615), 1586, 1588
Brighton, Sussex, 1784, 1883, 1961, 1984; Pavilion, 1787, 1816, 1818
Brigid, St (c.450–c.523), 523
Brihuega, Spain, battle of, 1710
Brindley, James (1716–72), 1761
Bristol, 1358, 1399, 1481, 1497, 1643, 1645, 1784, 1831, 1940, 1943, 1961, 1963, 1970; Council of, 1216; Saint Paul's, 1980; Ty of, 1574; University of, 1909, 1950
British Columbia, Canada, 1871
British Guiana (Guyana), 1953
British Museum, London, 1753, 1760, 1816, 1823, 1857
Brittan, Leon (1939–), 1986
Brittany, 450, 1113, 1156, 1158, 1166, 1169, 1203, 1341–2, 1345, 1347, 1373, 1379, 1396, 1423, 1446, 1448, 1468, 1489, 1492, 1512
Britten, Benjamin (1913–76), 1936, 1945–7, 1949, 1951, 1953 4, 1957–8, 1961–2, 1976
Britton, Thomas (1644–1714), 1678
Brixton, London, 1981, 1985; prison, 1961
Brixworth, Northants., 680, 746/7, 803
Broadcasting House, London, 1932
Broadlands, Hants., 1765
Broadwater Farm Estate, London, 1985
Brock, Thomas (1847–1922), 1911
Brodie, Israel (1895–1979), 1957
Bromswold, Northants., 1071
Brontë, Anne (1820–49), 1848
Brontë, Charlotte (1816–55), 1847
Brontë, Emily (1818–48), 1847
Brook, Peter (1925–), 1946
Brooke, Rupert (1887–1915), 1911, 1915
Brooklands, Surrey, 1907
Brookner, Anita (1928–), 1984
Brougham, Henry, Lord (1778–1868), 1827
Broughton, Jack, 1743
Brown, Arthur (1886–1948), 1919
Brown, George (1914–85), 1960, 1963, 1966–8
Brown, Lancelot 'Capability' (1715–83), 1765
Brown, Louise (1978–), 1978
Brown, Pamela (1914–), 1949
Browne, Robert (c.1550–1633), 1580
Browne, Thomas (1605–82), 1646
Browning, Elizabeth Barrett (1806–61), 1850, 1857
Browning, Robert (1812–89), 1833, 1835
Brownsea I., Dorset, 1907
Bruce, Edward (d.1318), High K. of

Ireland, 1313, 1315, 1318
Bruce, Henry (1815–95), 1872
Bruce, James (1730–94), 1770
Brude (d.c.584), K. of Picts, 563
Bruges, Belgium, 1474; Truce of, 1375
Brummell, George 'Beau' (1778–1840), 1794, 1813
Brunanburh, ?Yorks., battle of, 937
Brunei, 1888, 1962
Brunel, Isambard (1806–59), 1843, 1852, 1858
Brunel University, Uxbridge, Middx, 1966
Brunswick, D. of, Charles (1713–80), 1758–9
Brussels, 1961, 1972; Heysel Stadium, 1985
Buchan, John (1875–1940), 1915–16
Buchanan, James (1791–1868), Pres. of USA, 1858, 1860
Buchman, Frank (1878–1961), 1921
Buckingham, DD of, Edward Stafford (1478–21), 1521; Humphrey Stafford (d.1483), 1483; George Villiers (1592–1628), 1614, 1617, 1623, 1625–8; George Villiers (1628–87), 1667
Buckingham Palace (House), London, 1762, 1825–6, 1837, 1910, 1914, 1962
Budapest, 1990
Buenos Aires, Argentina, 1806, 1824
Buffalo, NY, 1813
Buganda, 1886
Builth, Wales, battle of, 1282; Castle, 1295
Bulawayo, Africa, 1893
Bulganin, Nikolai (1895–1975), 1956
Buller, Redvers (1839–1908), Gen., 1900
Bulmer, Bevis (c.1540–1615), 1594
Bulwer-Lytton, Edward (1803–73), 1834–5
Bunbury, Charles (1740–1821), 1780
Bunker Hill, Mass., battle of, 1775
Bunyan, John (1628–88), 1672, 1678
Burbage, Cuthbert (1567–1636), 1598
Burbage, James (1531–97), 1576, 1593/4
Burbage, Richard (c.1571–1619), 1593/4, 1598
Burdett, Francis (1770–1844), 1810, 1818
Burford, Oxon., 1107, 1649
Burgess, Anthony (1917–), 1962–3
Burgess, Guy (1910–63), 1951
Burgh Castle, Suffolk, 270
Burgh, Elizabeth de (d.1363), 1333, 1342
Burgh, Hubert de (d.1243), 1215, 1221, 1223, 1227–9, 1231–2
Burgh-upon-Sands, Cumbria, 1307

Burghclere Chapel, Berks., 1926
Burghley, Lord, William Cecil (1520–98), 1558, 1561, 1563, 1569, 1571, 1587
Burgos, Spain, 1812
Burgoyne, John (1722–92), Gen., 1777, 1786
Burgundy, 1373, 1423–4, 1468, 1470, 1493, 1496
Burgundy, DD of, Charles (1433–77), 1468, 1474–5; John (d.1419), 1411, 1416, 1419; Philip (1396–1467), 1419–20; Philip (1478–1506), 1500, 1506
Burke, Edmund (1729–97), 1770, 1775, 1777, 1787, 1790, 1796
Burke, Robert (1820–61), 1860
Burke, Thomas (1829–82), 1882
Burlington Arcade, London, 1819
Burlington, E. of, Richard Boyle (1694–1753), 1725, 1731
Burlington House, London, Conference of, 1928
Burma, 1826, 1885–6, 1937, 1944–5, 1948
Burne-Jones, Edward (1833–98), 1875, 1880
Burney, Fanny (1752–1840), 1778, 1796
Burns, John (1858–1943), 1889
Burns, Robert (1759–96), 1786
Burrough Court, Leics., 1931
Burton, Richard (1821–90), 1857, 1862
Burton, Richard (1925–84), 1949
Burton, Robert (1577–1640), 1621
Bury, Richard de (1281–1345), Bp, 1345
Bury St Edmunds, Suffolk, 1447, 1647; Abbey, 1020, 1433
Buss, Frances (1827–94), 1870
Bute, E. of, John Stuart (1713–92), 1761–3
Butler, Edward, 1884
Butler, Joseph (1692–1752), 1736
Butler, R. A. (1902–82), 1944, 1951–2, 1956–7
Butler, Samuel (1613–80), 1662–3, 1678
Butler, Samuel (1835–1902), 1872
Butlin, William (1899–1980), 1936
Butt, Isaac (1813–70), 1870
Butterfield, William (1814–1900), 1876
Buttington I., R. Severn, battle of, 893
Byatt, A. S. (1936–), 1990
Byland, Yorks., battle of, 1322
Byng, John (1704–57), Adm., 1756–7
Byrd, William (c.1543–1623), 1563, 1572, 1575, 1588
Byrhtferth of Ramsey, 1011
Byron, George Gordon, Lord (1788–1824), 1807, 1812, 1814, 1817,

Catterick, Yorks., battle of, 600
Catuvellauni, 100 BC, 54 BC, AD 7, 43
Cavagnari, Louis (1829–79), 1879
Cave, Edward (1691–1754), 1731
Cavell, Edith (1865–1915), 1915
Cavendish, Henry (1731–1810), 1798
Cavendish, Lord Frederick (1836–1882), 1882
Cavendish Square, London, 1953
Cavour, Camille (1810–61), 1855
Cawarden, Thomas, 1545
Cawnpore, India, 1857
Caxton, William (c.1422–91), 1474, 1476/7, 1478, 1480–3, 1485
Ceawlin (d.591), K. of Wessex, 577
Cecil, Vct, Hugh (1864–1958), 1937
Cedd, St (d.664), 653
Cenwulf (d.821), K. of Mercia, 817, 821
Cerdic, K. of West Saxons, 495
Cerrito, Fanny (1817–1909), 1845
Cetewayo (d.1884), K. of Zulus, 1878–9
Ceylon (Sri Lanka), 1795–6, 1875, 1948
Chad, Lake, Africa, 1893
Chadwick, Edwin (1800–90), 1834, 1842
Chadwick, James (1891–1974), 1935
Chain, Ernest (1906–79), 1940, 1945
Chalgrove Field, Oxon., battle of, 1643
Chamberlain, Austen (1863–1937), 1903, 1921–2, 1924–5
Chamberlain, Joseph (1836–1914), 1873, 1880, 1885–7, 1891–2, 1895–9, 1901, 1903
Chamberlain, Neville (1869–1940), 1923–4, 1931–2, 1934, 1937–40
Chambers, John Graham (1843–83), 1866
Champagne, France, 1373, 1380
Chanak, Turkey, 1922
Chancellor, Richard (d.1555), 1553–5
Channel Is, 1940, 1945
Chantrey, Francis (1781–1841), 1841
Chapel Royal, London, 1516, 1553, 1572
Chapman, George (c.1559–1634), 1604–5, 1607
Charasia, Afghanistan, battle of, 1879
Charing Cross, London, 1274
Charlemagne (d.814), HRE, 789, 796
Charles V (1500–58), HRE 1507, 1519–22, 1526, 1543–4
Charles I (1600–49), K., 1616, 1619, 1623–6, 1628–9, 1631–5, 1637–49
Charles II (1630–85), K., 1630, 1641–2, 1645–6, 1649–51, 1655, 1660–3, 1665–75, 1677–9, 1681–3, 1685

Charles IV (d.1328), K. of France, 1324
Charles V (d.1380), K. of France, 1364, 1369
Charles VI (1368–1422), K. of France, 1396, 1419–20, 1422
Charles VII (d.1461), K. of France, 1418, 1421–2, 1425, 1442, 1444
Charles VIII (1470–98), K. of France, 1492
Charles Edward (1720–88), pretender, 1720, 1745–6, 1788
Charles, K. of Navarre, 1355
Charles, P. of Wales (1948–), 1948, 1958, 1969, 1981
Charleston, S. Carolina, 1706
Charlotte (1744–1818), Q. Consort, 1761–2, 1796
Charlotte (1796–1817), P. 1796, 1817
Charlottenburg, Prussia, Ty of, 1723
Chatham, E. of, William Pitt (1708–78), 1737, 1742, 1746, 1755–7, 1761, 1766–8, 1775
Chatham, Kent, 1667, 1765
Chaucer, Geoffrey (c.1343–1400), 1349, 1370, 1380, 1382, 1385, 1392, 1478
Chekhov, Anton (1860–1904), 1909
Chelsea, London, 1745, 1981
Chelsea Hospital, London, 1682
Cheltenham, Glos., 1990; GCHQ, 1984
Chepman, Walter (c.1473–1538), 1507
Chequers, Bucks., 1921, 1971, 1984
Cherbourg, France, 1418, 1443, 1450, 1944
Chesney, George (1830–95), 1871
Chester, 74, 79, 100, 216, 383, 973, 1254, 1422, 1540, 1867; battle of, 613, 616
Chester, EE of, Hugh (d.1101), 1071; Ranulf (d.1152), 1140–1, 1146–7, 1149, 1152
Chester-le-Street, Durham, 878
Chesters, Northumberland, 122–39
Chesterton, Gilbert (1874–1936), 1904, 1908
Chevy Chase (Otterburn), Northumberland, battle of, 1387
Chiang Kai-shek (1887–1975), Gen., 1943
Chichele, Henry (c.1362–1443), Archbp, 1414, 1429, 1438
Chichester, Francis (1901–72), 1966, 1967
Chichester, Sussex, 80–50 BC, AD 43; Festival Theatre, 1962
Childerley Hall, Cambs., 1647
Childers, Erskine (1870–1922), 1903
Chillianwala, India, battle of, 1849
China, 1986
Chinon, France, Truce of, 1214
Chippendale, Thomas (1718–79),

1753–4
Chippenham, Wilts., 878
Chipping Camden, Glos., 1612–13
Chislehurst, Kent, 1873
Chiswick, London, 1774, 1944; House, 1725
Christ Church College, Oxford, 1525, 1644
Christ Church, Spitalfields, London, 1715–20
Christchurch, New Zealand, 1850
Christian, Albert (1832–99), 1896
Christie, Agatha (1890–1976), 1920, 1926, 1930, 1952
Christie, John (1882–1962), 1934
Christ's College, Cambridge, 1505, 1566
Christ's Hospital, London, 1553
Churchill, Caryl (1938–), 1982
Churchill, Charles (1731–64), 1762
Churchill College, Cambridge, 1960
Churchill, Lord Randolph (1849–94), 1885–6
Churchill, Oxon., 200
Churchill, Winston (1874–1965), 1897–8, 1900, 1908–9, 1911–13, 1919, 1921, 1925, 1931–3, 1938–46, 1948, 1951–5, 1964–5
Cicely (1469–1507), P., 1474, 1482
Cirencester, Glos., 75–80; battle of, 628
Ciudad Rodrigo, Spain, 1812
Clacton, Essex, 1964
Clare, Ireland, 1828
Clare, John (1793–1864), 1827
Clarence, D. of, George (1449–78), 1469–71, 1476–8
Clarendon, EE of, Edward Hyde (1609–74), 1661, 1667; George Villiers (1800–70), 1865, 1868
Clarendon, Wilts., council of, 1164, 1166
Clark, Kenneth (1903–83), 1957
Clarke, Samuel (1675–1707), 1705–6
Classicianus, Julius, 61
Claudius (10 BC–AD 54), Rom. Emp., 43, 49
Cleland, John (1710–89), 1749
Clement VII (d.1534), Pope, 1523, 1529, 1533
Clerk-Maxwell, James (1831–79), 1873
Clerkenwell, London, 1678; gaol, 1867
Clifford, John (1876–1923), 1891
Clifford, Rosamund, 1165
Clifford, Thomas (1630–73), 1667
Clive, Robert (1725–74), 1751, 1757, 1766
Cliveden, Bucks., 1740
Clofeshoh, Councils of, 746/7, 803
Clontarf, Ireland, 1843; battle of, 1014
Clwyd, R., Wales, 1157

Clyde, R., Scotland, 81, 83, 87, 139, 1790, 1812, 1928
Clydebank, Scotland, 1934, 1938
Clydeside, Scotland, 1941
Cnut (d.1035), K. of England and Denmark, 1013–20, 1025/6–28, 1035, 1166
Coalbrookdale, Shrops., 1709, 1773
Cobbett, William (1763–1835), 1802, 1810, 1816, 1821, 1830
Cobden, Richard (1804–65), 1838, 1857, 1860
Cobham, Alan (1894–1973), 1926
Cobham, Eleanor (d.1452), D. of Gloucester, 1425, 1441
Coblenz, Germany, 1338
Cochran, Charles (1872–1951), 1911
Cockcroft, John (1897–1967), 1932, 1951
Cockerell, Christopher (1910–), 1959
Cody, Samuel (1862–1913), 1908
Coel Hen (Coel the Old), K., 425
Coggan, Donald (1909–), Archbp, 1975–6
Cokayne, William (1561–1626), 1615
Coke, Edward (1552–1634), 1600, 1616, 1628
Colchester, Essex, 80–50 BC, 34–27 BC, AD 7, 43, 49, 61; Castle, 1078; Council of, 931
Colcutt, Thomas, 1893
Coldstream, Scotland, Truce of, 1491
Coldstream, William (1908–87), 1937
Colenso, John (1814–83), Bp, 1862
Colenso, South Africa, battle of, 1899
Coleridge, Samuel Taylor (1772–1834), 1798, 1816
Colet, John (1467–1519), 1496, 1509
Coliseum Theatre, London, 1904, 1918, 1974
Collins, John (1905–80), 1945, 1958
Collins, Michael (1890–1922), 1922
Collins, Wilkie (1824–89), 1860, 1868
Colman (d.676), Bp, 664
Cologne, Germany, 1942
Colombia, 1586, 1824
Colombo, (Sri Lanka), 1796
Columba, St (c.521–97), 563, 574–5, 849/50
Columbanus, St (c.543–615), 610–15
Commius, 55 BC, 50 BC
Compiègne, France, battle of, 1430; Forest of, 1918
Compton, Edmund (1906–), 1966
Compton-Burnett, Ivy (1892–1969), 1957, 1963
Conan, D. of Brittany, 1158, 1166
Conan Doyle, Arthur (1859–1930), 1889, 1891, 1894, 1902, 1905
Congo, 1884

Congo, R., 1877, 1890
Congresbury, Somerset, 490
Congreve, William (1670–1729), 1693, 1695, 1700, 1732
Connaught, D. of, P. Arthur (1850–1942), 1921
Connaught, Ireland, 1235
Connecticut, 1635
Connolly, James (1868–1916), 1896
Connor, Ireland, battle of, 1315
Conrad, Joseph (1857–1924), 1900, 1902, 1907, 1914
Consett, Durham, 1980
Constable, John (1776–1837), 1817, 1821, 1827–8
Constance, D. of Brittany, 1166, 1181
Constans (c. 320–50), W. Emp., 343
Constantine (c.274–337), Rom. Emp., 306
Constantine III (d.411), W. Emp., 407–9
Constantine II (d.943), K. of Scots, 900, 906, 920
Constantine, Learie, Lord (1902–71), 1969
Constantinople (Istanbul), 1853, 1876–8, 1896, 1920, 1923; Ty of, 1854
Constantius I (250–306), W. Emp., 293, 296–7, 306
Constantius II (317–61), E. Emp., 353
Constitution Hill, London, 1840
Conway, R., Wales, 1211
Conway, Wales, Castle, 1399; Ty of, 1277
Cook, A. J. (1885–1931), 1926
Cook, James (1728–79), 1768–70, 1773, 1778–9
Cook, Thomas (1808–92), 1841, 1861
Cooke, William (1806–79), 1837
Coote, Eyre (1762–83), 1761
Cope, John (d.1760), Gen., 1745
Copenhagen, 1807; battle of, 1801
Corbridge, Northumberland, 80, 105, 139, 154–5, 220, 914, 1311
Corfe Castle, Dorset, 978
Corfu, I. of, 1824
Cork, Ireland, 1177, 1491, 1690, 1920
Cornbury Park, Oxon., 1588
Cornhill, London, 43–7, 1582
Cornwall, 62–8, 400, 722, 815, 1497, 1549
Cornwallis, Charles (1708–1835), Gen., 1780–1, 1790, 1792–3
Cornysh, William (c.1468–1523), 1513
Coronel, Chile, battle of, 1914
Corpus Christi College, Oxford, 1517
Corrichie, Scotland, battle of, 1562
Corrigan, Mairead (1944–), 1976

Corsica, 1793
Cort, Henry (1740–1800), 1783
Corunna, Spain, 1386, 1589, 1808–9
Coryat, Thomas (c.1577–1617), 1608
Cotentin peninsula, Normandy, 1000, 1346
Countisbury Hill, Devon, battle of, 878
Courtenay, William (d.1396), Bp, 1377
Covadonga, Philippines, battle of, 1743
Covent Garden, London, 1974, 1979; Royal Opera House (Theatre Royal), 1731–2, 1737, 1806, 1808–9, 1817, 1857–8, 1910–12, 1914, 1916, 1946, 1952, 1956–7, 1974, 1979; Russell St, 1763; Tavistock St, 1836
Coventry, 1147, 1298, 1392, 1405, 1456–7, 1459, 1790, 1939–40, 1951, 1982; Belgrade Theatre, 1958; Cathedral, 1962
Coverdale, Miles (1488–1559), 1539
Coward, Noel (1899–1973), 1924–5, 1929–31, 1941–3
Cowes, I. of Wight, 1895
Cowley, Abraham (1618–67), 1656
Cowley, Oxford, 200, 1913
Cowper, William (1731–1800), 1785
Cowton Moor, Yorks., battle of 'Standard', 1138
Crabbe, George (1754–1832), 1783
Cragside, Rothbury, Northumberland, 1880
Craig, James (1748–1812), 1795
Craig, James (Vct Craigavon, 1871–1940), 1921–2
Craik, Dinah (1826–87), 1857
Cramond, Scotland, 208–9
Cranfield, Lionel (1575–1645), 1621, 1624
Cranko, John (1927–73), 1951, 1957
Cranmer, Thomas (1489–1556), Archbp, 1533, 1536–7, 1553–4, 1556
Crécy, France, battle of, 1346
Creswell Crags, Derbys., 26,000–10,000 BC
Crete, I. of, 1897, 1940–1
Cribb, Tom (1781–1848), 1810
Criccieth Castle, Wales, 1295
Crick, Francis (1916–), 1953
Cricklade, Wilts., 887
Crimea, 1854–6
Crippen, Hawley (1862–1910), 1910
Cripps, Stafford (1889–1952), 1942, 1948, 1950
Crome, John (1768–1821), 1803
Cromer, Lord (see Baring, Evelyn)
Crompton, Richmal (1890–1969), 1922
Crompton, Samuel (1753–1827), 1779

Cromwell, Oliver (1599–1658), 1628, 1643–5, 1647–55, 1657–8, 1661
Cromwell, Richard (1626–1712), 1658–9
Cromwell, Thomas (1485–1540), 1533, 1535, 1537, 1539–40
Cronje, Piet (1835–1911), Gen., 1900
Crookes, William (1832–1919), 1865, 1873
Cropredy Bridge, Oxon., battle of, 1644
Crosland, Anthony (1918–77), 1976–7
Cross, Richard (1823–1914), 1874
Crowe, Eyre (1864–1925), 1907
Crowmer, William (d.1450), 1450
Croydon, Surrey, 1801, 1950; airport, 1926, 1930
Croyland (Crowland) Abbey, Lincs., 1470, 1486
Crozier, Eric (1914–), 1949
Cruft, Charles (1846–1938), 1885
Crystal Palace, London, 1851, 1854–5, 1857, 1872, 1902, 1936
Cubitt, Lewis 1852
Cubitt, Thomas (1788–1855), 1822
Culloden, Scotland, battle of, 1746
Cumberland, 1157, 1483
Cumberland, DD of, Ernest (1771–1851), 1837; William (1721–65), 1745–7, 1757
Cumbria, 1092, 1986, 1987
Cumming, Alexander (1733–1814), 1775
Cunedda, K. of Gwynedd, 430
Cunningham, Andrew (1883–1963), Adm., 1941, 1943
Cunobelin (Cymbeline, d.40/43), 7, 43
Curragh, Ireland, 1914
Curzon, George (1859–1925), 1892, 1897–9, 1905, 1916, 1919, 1922–3
Cuthbert, St (c.634–67), 664, 684, 875, 934/5
Cynewulf, 800
Cyprus, I. of, 1878, 1925, 1954–7, 1959–60
Cyrenaica, Libya, 1941

Dacre, Leonard, Lord (d.1573), 1570
Dal Riada, Scotland, 501, 603
Dale, Henry (1875–1968), 1936
Dalhousie, E. of, James Broun-Ramsay (1812–60), 1848–9
Dalrymple, Hew (1750–1830), Gen., 1808
Dalton, Hugh (1887–1962), 1945, 1947
Dalton, John (1766–1844), 1801, 1803
Dalyel, Thomas (1599–1685), 1666
Damascus, Syria, 1918
Dampier, William (1652–1715), 1699–1700

Danby, E. of, Thomas Osborne (1631–1712), 1673–4, 1677–8, 1695
Dandi, India, 1930
Daniel, Samuel (1562–1619), 1602
Danube, R., 1704
Dar es Salaam, Tanzania, 1877
Darby, Abraham (1677–1717), 1709
Darby, John (1800–82), 1830
Dardanelles, 1807, 1841, 1853, 1876, 1878, 1895, 1914–15
Darien isthmus, Panama, 1698–9
Darling, Grace (1815–42), 1838
Darling, R., Australia, 1828–9
Darlington, Durham, 1825
Darnel, Thomas (c.1582–1640), 1627
Darnley, Henry, Lord (1546–67), 1565–7
Dartford, Kent, 1452
Dartmoor prison, Devon, 1806
Darwin, Australia, 1861, 1928, 1930
Darwin, Charles (1809–82), 1831, 1839, 1858–9, 1871
Davenant, William (1606–68), 1656, 1661–2
David I (d.1153), K. of Scots, 1124, 1126–8, 1135–6, 1138–9, 1149, 1153
David II (1324–71), K. of Scots, 1328–9, 1334, 1341, 1346, 1354, 1357, 1363–4, 1371
David (d.1194), P. of Gwynedd, 1177
David (d.1246), P. of Gwynedd, 1240–1, 1245–6
David (d.1283), P. of Wales, 1274, 1282–3
David, St (c.462–c.547), 547
Davies, Emily (1830–1921), 1869
Davies, W. H. (1871–1940), 1908
Daviot, Gordon (Josephine Tey, 1896–1952), 1933
Davis, John (1550–1605), 1585
Davison, Emily (1872–1913), 1913
Davy, Humphry (1778–1829), 1800, 1806, 1815, 1821
Dawes, Charles (1865–1951), 1925
Day-Lewis, Cecil (1904–72), 1940
de Gaulle, Charles (1890–1970), 1962–3, 1967
de la Mare, Walter (1873–1956), 1925
de Quincey, Thomas (1785–1859), 1822
de Valera, Eamon (1882–1975), 1919
de Valois, Ninette (1898–), 1931, 1937
Dean, Christopher (1958–), 1984
Dearmer, Percy (1867–1936), 1906
Decianus Catus, 61
Dee, John (1527–1608), 1577
Dee, R., Cheshire, 757, 973
Defoe, Daniel (1660–1731), 1697, 1702–3, 1719, 1722, 1724
Deganwy, Wales, 822

Deira (Yorks.), kingdom of, 560, 593, 642
Dekker, Thomas (c.1572–1632), 1599, 1609
Delafield, E. M. (1890–1943), 1930
Delany, Mary (1700–88), 1754–5
Delcassé, Theophile (1852–1923), 1903
Delhi, India, 1857, 1877, 1911, 1921, 1983; Viceroy's House, 1931
Delius, Frederick (1862–1934), 1903–4, 1910, 1953
Dell, Ethel M. (1881–1939), 1912
Denbigh Castle, Wales, 1295
Denham, John (1615–69), 1641–2
Denham Studios, Bucks., 1932
Deptford, London, 1581, 1593, 1836
Derby, 877, 917, 1745
Derby, EE of, Edward Stanley (1799–1869), 1852, 1858–9, 1866, 1868; Edward Stanley (1826–93), 1866, 1874–5, 1877–8
Dere Street, 85
Dermot (d.1171), K. of Leinster, 1166–7, 1169, 1171
Desmond, EE of, Gerald Fitzgerald (c.1533–83), 1579; Thomas Fitzgerald (d.1468), 1462–3, 1468
Despenser, Hugh (elder, d.1326), 1321–2, 1326
Despenser, Hugh (younger, d.1326), 1318, 1321–2, 1325–6
Dettingen, Germany, battle of, 1743
Deverel, Dorset, 1,400 BC
Devlin, Bernadette (1947–), 1968–9
Devon, 400, 690, 710, 1204, 1455, 1549
Devonshire, D. of, William Cavendish (1720–64), 1756
Diaghilev, Serge (1872–1929), 1911–13, 1918–19, 1921
Diana, P. of Wales (1961–), 1981
Dickens, Charles (1812–70), 1836–8, 1841, 1843, 1846, 1849–50, 1857, 1859, 1861, 1865, 1870
Didius Gallus, 52
Dieppe, France, 1942
Digges, Dudley (1583–1639), 1626
Dilke, Charles (1810–69), 1872, 1884, 1886
Dinorben, Wales, 1400
Diocletian (245–316), Rom. Emp., 301
Dior, Christian (1905–57), 1947
Dispenser, Henry (d.1406), Bp, 1383
Disraeli, Benjamin (Lord Beaconsfield, 1804–81), 1826, 1836–7, 1844–7, 1849–50, 1852, 1858–9, 1864, 1867–8, 1870, 1872–8
Dixmude, Belgium, battle of, 1489
Dobunni, 43
Dogger Bank, 1904; battle of, 1915
Doherty, John (?1778–1854), 1829–30

Edward VII (1841–1910), K., 1841, 1860, 1863, 1869, 1873–5, 1884, 1890–1, 1900–3, 1905–10

Edward VIII (1894–1972), K. (D. of Windsor), 1911, 1921, 1927, 1931, 1936–7, 1972

Edward (d.924), K. of Wessex, 899, 902, 911, 915, 917–20, 924

Edward the Black Prince (1330–76), 1338, 1343, 1349, 1355–6, 1359, 1361–3, 1367, 1370, 1376

Edward, P. of Wales (1453–71), 1453, 1455–6, 1461, 1463, 1470–1

Edward, P. of Wales (1473–84), 1483–4

Edward (d.1057), P., 1057

Edward, D. of York (c.1373–1415), 1410, 1415

Edwin (d.632), K. of Northumbria, 616, 627, 632

Edwin (d.1069), E. of Mercia, 1062, 1066, 1068

Efailwen, Wales, 1839

Egan, Pierce (1772–1849), 1821

Egbert (d.839), K. of Wessex, 802, 815, 825, 829, 838

Egbert (d.766), Archbp, 735

Egfrith (d.685), K. of Northumbria, 672, 678, 684–5

Egypt, 1881–3, 1887; Suez Canal Zone, 1936, 1952, 1956

Eire, 1937, 1939, 1949

Eisenhower, Dwight (1890–1969), Pres. of USA, 1953, 1957, 1959

El Obeid, Sudan, battle of, 1883

Eleanor of Aquitaine (d.1204), Q. Consort, 1152, 1154, 1173–4, 1185, 1199, 1202, 1204

Eleanor of Castile (d.1290), Q. Consort, 1254, 1276, 1290–1

Eleanor of Provence (d.1291), Q. Consort, 1236, 1240, 1253

Elgar, Edward (1857–1934), 1890, 1899–1901, 1908, 1910–11, 1924

Elgin, E. of, Thomas Bruce (1766–1841), 1816

Elgin, Scotland, 1296, 1336

Eliot, George (1819–90), 1859–61, 1872, 1876

Eliot, John (1592–1632), 1626, 1629

Eliot, T. S. (1888–1965), 1917, 1922, 1930, 1935, 1939–43, 1948–9, 1953, 1958, 1981

Eliot, Thomas (c.1490–1546), 1531

Elizabeth I (1533–1603), Q., 1533, 1536, 1544, 1554, 1558, 1560, 1562–4, 1567–72, 1575, 1577–9, 1581–5, 1587–8, 1599, 1603

Elizabeth II (1926–), Q., 1926, 1942, 1947, 1952–4, 1957–61, 1964–5, 1968, 1972, 1975–7, 1982–4, 1986, 1987, 1989

Elizabeth (1900–), Q. Consort, 1923, 1951

Elizabeth of Bohemia (1596–1662),

P. 1612–13

Elizabeth of York (1466–1503), Q. Consort, 1486, 1488, 1503

Ellendun (Wroughton), Wilts., battle of, 825

Ellis, Ruth (1926–55), 1955

Ellis, William Webb (1805–72), 1823

Elmet (Leeds), kingdom of, 616

Elphinstone, William (1431–1514), Bp, 1495

Eltham Palace, London, 1424, 1474

Ely, I. of, Cambs., 1070, 1143, 1265, 1267; Abbey (Cathedral), 963, 1081, 1322

Ely, Reginald, 1446

Embankment, London, 1879

Emma (d.1052), Q. Consort, 1002, 1013, 1017, 1036–7, 1041–4, 1052

Emmet, Robert (1778–1803), 1803

Empingham, Lincs., battle of, 1470

Empson, Richard (c.1465–1510), 1509–10

Enfield, Middx, 1938

English Channel, 6,500 BC, AD 1785, 1874–5, 1909, 1959

Ennis, Ireland, 1880

Enniskillen, N. Ireland, 1912, 1987

Epirus, Greece, 1886

Epping, Essex, 1739, 1944

Epsom, Surrey, 1779

Epstein, Jacob (1880–1959), 1908, 1925, 1929, 1935, 1953, 1957, 1962

Erasmus, Desiderius (1466–1536), 1496, 1509

Eric (d.954), K. of Norway and York, 947–8, 952, 954

Eriskay I., Scotland, 1745

Ermine Street, 43–7

Erne, Lord, 1880

Esplechin, France, Truce of, 1340

Essex, 490, 527, 616, 1381, 1953; University of, 1964

Essex, EE of, Geoffrey de Mandeville (d.1144), 1141, 1143; Robert Devereux (1567–1601), 1591, 1596–7, 1599–1601; Robert Devereux (1591–1646), 1642, 1644

Etaples, France, Ty of, 1492

Ethelbald (d.757), K. of Mercia, 716, 736, 746–7, 749, 757

Ethelbert (d.616), K. of Kent, 560, 597, 604, 616

Ethelbert (d.866), K. of Wessex, 860

Ethelfleda (d.918), ruler of Mercia, 911–18

Ethelfrith (d.616), K. of Northumbria, 593, 603, 613, 616

Ethelred I (d.871), K. of Wessex, 865, 871

Ethelred II (d.1016), K., 978, 991, 994, 997, 1002, 1008, 1013–14, 1016

Ethelwold, St (c.908–84), Bp, 963,

971

Ethelwulf (d.855), K. of Wessex, 851, 853, 855

Ethiopia, 1770, 1868, 1935, 1941

Eton College, Windsor, 1440–1

Eu, Normandy, 1843

Eugène (1663–1736), P., 1704, 1709

Eugénie (1826–1920), Empress, 1855, 1869

Eustace (d.1153), P., 1151–3

Euston Arch, London, 1838

Euston station, London, 1837–8, 1848

Evans, Arthur (1851–1941), 1900

Evans, Gwynfor (1912–), 1966

Evans, Thomas (1766–1833), 1816

Everest, Mt, 1953

Evesham, Worcs., Abbey, 961; battle of, 1265

Evreux, Normandy, 1200

Exeter, 43–7, 62–8, 75–80, 690, 877, 926–30, 957, 1067, 1646, 1658, 1831, 1942; canal, 1564; Cathedral, 957, 1046; Theatre Royal, 1887

Exeter, DD of, Henry Holland (1430–75), 1455, 1468; Thomas Beaufort (d.1426), 1410, 1412

Eyre, Edward (1815–1901), 1841, 1865

Fairfax, Thomas (1612–71), Gen., 1643, 1645–6

Falaise, Normandy, 1418; battle of, 1944

Falkirk, Scotland, 1080; battle of, 1298, 1746

Falkland Is, 1770–1, 1833, 1955, 1970; battles of, 1914, 1982–3

Falkland Palace, Scotland, 1539, 1542

Falmouth, Cornwall, 1644, 1840

Faraday, Michael (1791–1867), 1827, 1831

Faringdon Castle, Oxon., 1145

Farnborough, Hants., 1860, 1908, 1954

Farne Is, Northumberland, 1838

Faroe Is, Denmark, 725

Farquhar, George (1678–1709), 1699, 1702, 1706–7

Farringdon St station, London, 1863

Fashoda (Kodok), Sudan, 1898

Fastidius, Bp, 420–30

Faughart, Ireland, 1316; battle of, 1318

Faulkner, Brian (1921–), 1974

Faversham, Kent, 1688

Fawkes, Guy (1570–1606), 1605–6

Fawley, Southampton, 1951

Fay, Frank (1870–1931), 1902

Fay, William (1872–1947), 1902

Fayrfax, Robert (1494–1521), 1504

Felix, St (d.648), Bp, 631

Felton, John (1595–1628), 1628

Gatwick airport, Sussex, 1958
Gauden, John (1605–62), Bp, 1649
Gaveston, Piers (d.1312), 1307–12
Gawilghur, India, 1803
Gay, John (1685–1732), 1728–9,
　1731, 1920
Gaza, Palestine, 1917
Geldof, Bob (1954–), 1984
Geneva, 1872, 1917, 1924;
　Conferences, 1954–5, 1958
Gentili, Aloysius (1801–48), 1835
Geoffrey, D. of Brittany (1158–86),
　1166, 1169, 1173, 1181, 1183–4,
　1186
Geoffrey D. of Nantes (d.1158),
　1152, 1156
Geoffrey of Monmouth (d.1155),
　1136
George I (1660–1727), K., 1680,
　1714, 1717, 1721–2, 1727
George II (1683–1760), K., 1714,
　1727, 1737, 1742–3, 1746, 1760
George III (1738–1820), K., 1738
　1760–2, 1764–5, 1772, 1782–3,
　1788–9, 1794–6, 1800–1, 1804,
　1807, 1811, 1817, 1820, 1823
George IV (1762–1830), K., 1762,
　1783–5, 1787, 1789, 1795–6,
　1806, 1811, 1813, 1817, 1820–1,
　1824, 1827, 1830
George V (1865–1936), K., 1910–12,
　1914, 1920–1, 1923–4, 1932–3,
　1935–6
George VI (1895–1952), K., 1923,
　1927, 1936–9, 1950–2
George of Denmark (1653–1708), P.
　Consort, 1683, 1700, 1702, 1708
George, Henry (1839–97), 1880
Georgia, USA, 1732, 1735
Geraint, K. of Dumnonia, 710
Gerald of Wales (c.1146–c.1220),
　1184/5/6, 1188–9
Gerbier, Balthazar (1591–1667),
　1649
German, Edward (1862–1936), 1902
Germanus, St (c.378–448), Bp, 429,
　446–7
Gertler, Mark (1891/2–1939), 1916
Geta (d.212), Rom. Emp., 208–9
Ghana (see also Gold Coast), 1957
Ghent, Belgium, 1340; Ty of,
　1814–15
Gibberd, Frederick (1908–), 1967
Gibbon, Edward (1737–94), 1776
Gibbons, Orlando (1583–1625),
　1612, 1622
Gibbons, Stella (1902–90), 1932
Gibbs, James (1682–1754), 1722,
　1728, 1730, 1737
Gibraltar, 1704, 1713, 1726–7, 1780,
　1966–8, 1985, 1988
Gielgud, John (1904–), 1931, 1933,
　1949, 1952
Gifford, William (1756–1826), 1809
Gilbert of Hastings, Bp, 1147

Gilbert, Henry (1817–1901), 1843
Gilbert, Humphrey (1539–83), 1572,
　1575, 1578, 1583
Gilbert, W. S. (1836–1911), 1875,
　1877–8, 1880–2, 1884–5, 1887–9,
　1893, 1896
Gildas (c.493–570), 546–50
Gill, Eric (1882–1940), 1913, 1927,
　1929, 1932
Girton College, Cambridge, 1869
Gisors, Normandy, battle of, 1198;
　Ty of, 1113
Gissing, George (1857–1903), 1886,
　1891, 1903
Gladstone, William (1809–98),
　1850, 1852–3, 1858–9, 1864,
　1866, 1868–9, 1873–6, 1879–80,
　1885–6, 1891–4, 1896
Glamorgan, 1402, 1453
Glanvill, Ranulf de (d.1190), 1180
Glasbury on Wye, Herefords., battle
　of, 1056
Glasgow, 600, 1638, 1823, 1873,
　1878, 1901, 1931, 1938, 1941,
　1951, 1982, 1990; Ibrox Park,
　1971; Royalty Theatre, 1909;
　School of Art, 1904, 1909;
　University of, 1451
Glastonbury, Somerset, 80–50 BC,
　AD 1914; Abbey, 470–500, 688,
　1184, 1276
Glencoe, Scotland, 1692
Glendower, Owen (c.1350–c.1415),
　1400–5, 1410
Glenfinnan, Scotland, 1745
Glenshiel, Scotland, 1719
Globe Theatre, London, 1598, 1613
Gloucester, 43–7, 62–8, 90–8, 877,
　1216, 1378, 1541–2, 1643, 1780,
　1977, 1983; Cathedral, 1089,
　1337, 1724; Ty of, 1240
Gloucester, EE of, Gilbert (d.1295),
　1265, 1267; Robert (d.1147), 1136,
　1138–9, 1141, 1143, 1147
Glubb, John (1897–1986), Gen.,
　1956
Glyndebourne, Sussex, 1934
Goderich, Vct, Frederick Robinson
　(1782–1859), 1827–8
Godesberg, Germany, 1938
Godfrey, Edmund Berry (1622–78),
　1678
Godiva, Lady (d.1080), 1043
Gododdin (Votadini), 400, 430
Godolphin, Sidney (1645–1712),
　1702, 1704, 1710
Godwin, E. of Wessex (d.1053),
　1020, 1035–6, 1040, 1051–3
Gold Coast (Ghana), 1618, 1872,
　1898, 1946
Golding, William (1911–), 1954,
　1956, 1959, 1964, 1980, 1983
Goldsmith, Oliver (1730–74), 1762,
　1766, 1770, 1773
Gollancz, Victor (1893–1967), 1936

Gooch, Graham (1953–), 1990
Good Hope, Cape of, 1806, 1813
Goodman's Fields Theatre, London,
　1731–2, 1741
Goodwin, Francis, 1604
Goodwood, Sussex, 1802
Goose Green, E. Falkland, battle of,
　1982
Gorbachev, Mikhail (1931–), 1989
Gordon, Charles (1833–85), Gen.,
　1874, 1884–5
Gordon Walker, Patrick (1907–80),
　1964–5
Gore, Charles (1853–1932), Bp,
　1889, 1892
Gore, Spencer (1850–1906), 1877
Gorham, G. C. (1787–1857), 1850
Goschen, George (1831–1907),
　1887–8
Gosden Common, Surrey, 1745
Gosforth, Cumbria, 901–15
Gosson, Stephen (1554–1624), 1579
Gow, Ian (1937–90), 1990
Gower, John (c.1330–1408), 1381,
　1390
Gower peninsula, Wales, 400, 1231
Gowrie, E. of, John Ruthven (1577–
　1600), 1600
Gowrie House, Perth, 1600
Grace, W. G. (1848–1916), 1864,
　1871, 1876, 1908
Grafton, D. of, Augustus Fitzroy
　(1735–1811), 1768–9
Grafton Galleries, London, 1911–12
Graham, Billy (1918–), 1954
Graham, Thomas (1805–69), 1830
Grahame, Kenneth (1859–1932),
　1908
Grahn, Lucille (1819–1907), 1845
Grangemouth, Scotland, 1975
Grant, Duncan (1885–1978), 1930
Grantham, Lincs., 1938; battle of,
　1643
Granville, E., George Leveson-
　Gower (1815–91), 1859, 1870,
　1880, 1883
Grately, Hants., 926–30
Gratian, Count, 343
Grattan, Henry (1746–1820), 1782
Graupius, Mons, Scotland, battle of,
　84
Gravelines, France, 1439, 1588
Graves, Robert (1895–1985),
　1916–17, 1929, 1934, 1947–8
Gravesend, Kent, 1377, 1661
Gray, John de (1214), Bp, 1205–6
Gray, Simon (1936–), 1981
Gray, Stephen (c.1690–1736), 1732
Gray, Thomas (1716–71), 1747, 1751
Great Lakes, Canada, 1756
Green, John (1837–83), 1874
Green Park, London, 1749
Greene, Graham (1904–91),
　1938–40, 1948, 1955, 1958, 1973
Greene, Robert (1558–92), 1592

Greenham Common, Berks., 1980, 1983
Greenland, 1585
Greensted, Essex, 1013
Greenwich, London, 1661, 1714, 1967; Palace, 1491, 1522, 1527, 1553, 1579, 1616, 1695; Peace of, 1543
Greenwood, Walter (1903–74), 1933
Gregory, Augusta, Lady (1852–1932), 1902, 1904
Gregory I (d.604), Pope, 597
Grein, Jacob (1862–1935), 1891–2
Grenada, I. of, 1762, 1763, 1974, 1983
Grenville, George (1712–70), 1763–4
Grenville, Richard (1542–91), 1591
Grenville, William, Lord (1759–1834), 1806–7
Gresham College, London, 1596, 1660
Gresham, Thomas (1519–79), 1571
Grey, E., Charles (1764–1845), 1806, 1830, 1832, 1834
Grey, Jane (1537–54), 1553–4
Grey, Vct, Edward Grey (1862–1933), 1905–6, 1914–16
Greyfriars, Canterbury, 1224
Griffiths, James (1890–1975), 1964
Grimaldi, Joseph (1779–1837), 1806, 1828
Grimes Graves, Norfolk, 3,000–2,400 BC
Grimes, William (1905–88), 1954
Grimthorpe, Yorks., 1,400 BC
Grindal, Edmund (1519–83), Archbp, 1575, 1577, 1583
Grisi, Carlotta (1819–99), 1845
Grocyn, William (1442–1519), 1493
Grosmont, Wales, battle of, 1405
Grosseteste, Robert (c.1175–1253), Bp, 1229, 1234, 1253
Grosvenor Gallery, London, 1877
Gruffyd ap Llewelyn (d.1063), P. of Gwynedd, 1039, 1046, 1052, 1055, 1058, 1063
Grunwick Works, London, 1977
Guadeloupe, I. of, 1759, 1979
Guernsey, I. of, 1372
Guiana, 1616
Guildford, Surrey, 1966, 1974; Cathedral, 1961
Guildhall, London, 1411
Guildhall School of Music, London, 1880
Guinea, Africa, 1567–8
Guinegate, France, battle of 'Spurs', 1513
Guinevere, Q., 1191
Guinness, Alec (1914–), 1957
Guise, D. of, Henri (1550–88), 1583
Guizot, François (1787–1874), 1848
Gujerat, India, 1849
Gundulf (1024–1108), Bp, 1078
Gurney, Henry (1898–1951), 1951

Guthrie, James (1859–1930), 1878
Guthrum (d.889/90), K. of Danes, 877–8, 886
Guyana (see also British Guiana), 1966
Guy's Hospital, London, 1725
Gwithian, Cornwall, 1,400 BC
Gwynedd, Wales, 430, 918, 1063, 1071
Gwynne, Nell (1650–87), 1667
Gyrth Godwinsson (d.1066), 1051, 1057, 1066

Hadfield, James, 1800
Hadley, John (1682–1744), 1731
Hadley Wood, Herts., 1971
Hadrian (76–138), Rom. Emp., 122
Hadrian VI (d.1523), Pope, 1522–3
Hadrian's Wall, 122–39, 158, 162–3, 200, 206, 216, 297, 367, 369, 410, 537
Haggard, H. Rider (1856–1925), 1886–7
Hague, The, Ty of, 1625
Haig, Douglas (1861–1928), Gen., 1915
Hailes Abbey, Glos., 1246
Hainault, Belgium, 1337, 1339, 1424–5
Haldane, Vct, Richard Burdon (1856–1928), 1905, 1907, 1912
Hales, Stephen (1677–1761), 1727
Halfdan (d.877), K. of Danes, 865, 875–7
Halidon Hill, Northumberland, battle of, 1333
Halifax, Nova Scotia, 1917
Halifax, Vcts, Charles Wood (1839–1934), 1894; Edward Wood (1881–1959), 1929, 1937–9
Hall, Henry (1898–1989), 1932
Hall, Peter (1930–), 1955, 1960, 1973
Hall, Willis (1929–), 1960
Halley, Edmond (1656–1742), 1676–7, 1705
Hambledon, Hants., 1763
Hambledon Hill, Dorset, 4,000–3,000 BC
Hamburg, Germany, 1943
Hamilton, James, Lord (1606–49), 1638
Hamilton, Ontario, 1930
Hamilton, Scotland, 1967
Hammersmith, London, 1890
Hammerstein, Oscar (1895–1960), 1947
Hampden, John (1594–1643), 1636–8, 1642–3
Hampshire, 490
Hampstead Garden Suburb, London, 1906
Hampton Court Palace, 1514, 1524, 1531, 1647, 1765; Conference of, 1604; Ty of, 1562

Handel, Georg Friedrich (1685–1759), 1711, 1713, 1717, 1726, 1731–1734, 1739, 1742–3, 1747, 1749
Handley, Tommy (1902–49), 1939
Hanover, 1727, 1742, 1756–7, 1837; Ty of, 1725
Hanseatic League, 1388, 1468, 1474
Hansom, Joseph (1803–82), 1834
Hanway, Jonas (1712–86), 1778
Harby, Northants., 1290, 1291
Harcourt, William (1827–1904), 1880, 1894, 1896
Hardie, James Keir (1856–1915), 1893, 1906
Hardwick, Philip (1792–1870), 1838
Hardy, Thomas (1752–1832), 1792, 1794
Hardy, Thomas (1840–1928), 1872, 1874, 1878, 1880, 1887, 1891, 1895, 1904
Hare, David (1947–), 1985
Harewood, E. of, George (1923–), 1949
Harfleur, Normandy, 1415–16, 1440
Hargreaves, James (c.1720–78), 1764
Harington, James (1611–77), 1656
Hariot, Thomas (1560–1621), 1586, 1588, 1631
Harlech Castle, Wales, 1295, 1409, 1647
Harold (d.1066), K. of Norway, 1066
Harold I (d.1040), K., 1035–7, 1040
Harold II (d.1066), K., 1043, 1051, 1053, 1055, 1060, 1062–6
Harringay Stadium, London, 1954
Harrison, George (1943–), 1963, 1967, 1970
Harrison, John (1693–1776), 1735
Harrods store, London, 1983
Harrow, Middx, 1952
Harrow School, Middx, 1571
Hart, Watson, 1932
Harthacnut (d.1042), K. of Denmark and England, 1028, 1035, 1037, 1040–2
Hartington, Spencer Cavendish, Lord (1833–1908), 1875
Hartlepool, Cleveland, 1914
Hartley, L. P. (1895–1972), 1946–7, 1953
Harvard, John (1607–38), 1636
Harvard University, Mass., 1638
Harvey, William (1578–1657), 1619, 1628, 1651
Harwell, Oxon., 1947
Hastein, Danish leader, 892
Hastenbeck, Germany, battle of, 1757
Hastings, Lady Flora (d.1839), 1839
Hastings, Sussex, 771, 1377; battle of, 1066
Hastings, Warren (1732–1818),

1773, 1787–8, 1795
Hatchett, Charles (1765–1847), 1800
Hatfield Chase, Yorks., battle of, 632
Hatton, Christopher (1540–91), 1587
Haughey, Charles (1925–), 1980
Havelock Ellis, Henry (1859–1939), 1897
Hawaii, 1794
Hawarden, Cheshire, 1868
Hawke, Edward (1705–81), Adm., 1759
Hawkins, John (1532–95), 1562, 1564–5, 1567–8, 1595
Hawkshaw, John (1811–91), 1886
Hawksmoor, Nicholas (1661–1736), 1702, 1705, 1715–20, 1735, 1745
Hay, Ian (1876–1952), 1915
Hay, Will (1888–1949), 1937
Haydn, Franz Joseph (1732–1809), 1791
Haymarket, London, Queen's (King's), later Her (His) Majesty's, Theatre, 1705, 1737, 1815, 1845, 1847; Theatre Royal, 1943
Haynau, Julius (1786–1853), Gen., 1850
Hayward Gallery, London, 1968
Hazlitt, William (1778–1830), 1825, 1828
Headington, Oxford, 200, 1478
Healey, Denis (1917–), 1974
Healy, Timothy (1855–1931), 1922
Heath, Edward (1916–), 1965, 1970–4
Heath, F. G. (1843–1913), 1904
Heath, Nicholas (1501–78), Archbp, 1556
Heather, William (1563–1627), 1627
Heathrow airport, London, 1946, 1952
Heaviside, Oliver (1850–1925), 1902
Hebrides Is, Scotland, 860, 1263, 1266, 1939
Hedgeley Moor, Northumberland, battle of, 1464
Hedley, William (1770–1843), 1813
Heligoland Bight, Germany, battle of, 1914
Heligoland, Germany, 1814, 1884; Ty of, 1890
Helpmann, Robert (1909–88), 1946
Hemming, Edward, 1685
Henderson, Arthur (1863–1935), 1903, 1915–16, 1929, 1931
Hendon, Middx, 1876
Hengist (d.?488), 430
Hengistbury Head, Dorset, 450 BC
Henley, Oxon., 1829, 1839
Henri IV (1553–1610), K. of France, 1589, 1591
Henrietta Maria (1609–69), Q. Consort, 1624–6, 1634, 1642–4
Henry V (1081–1125), HRE, 1114,

1124
Henry I (1068–1135), K., 1091, 1096, 1100–1, 1104–5, 1121, 1124, 1133, 1135
Henry II (1133–89), K., 1133, 1142–4, 1149–60, 1163–74, 1177–80, 1182–9
Henry III (1207–72), K., 1216, 1220, 1227, 1229–30, 1233–45, 1247, 1252–5, 1257–67, 1272
Henry IV (1366–1413), K., 1387, 1398–1400, 1402–4, 1409
Henry V (1387–1422), K., 1399, 1401, 1403, 1405, 1407–22, 1415
Henry VI (1421–71), K., 1422, 1429–33, 1437, 1439–41, 1444–6, 1450–3, 1455–6, 1458–61, 1463, 1465, 1470–1
Henry VII (1457–1509), K., 1471, 1483, 1485–6, 1489, 1492–3, 1496–7, 1500–1, 1503, 1506, 1509, 1519
Henry VIII (1491–1547), K., 1491, 1503–4, 1509, 1511, 1513, 1516–17, 1519–22, 1524–9, 1531–4, 1536–7, 1540–4, 1546–7
Henry (1155–83), Young K., 1158, 1160, 1169–70, 1173, 1182–3
Henry (1594–1612), P. of Wales, 1610, 1612
Henry of Almain (d.1271), 1264, 1266
Henry of Blois (d.1171), Bp, 1126, 1129, 1139, 1141, 1153
Henry of Huntingdon (d.1155), 1154
Henry, Patrick (1736–99), 1765
Henryson, Robert (c.1424–c.1506), 1490
Henty, G. A. (1832–1902), 1884, 1898
Henze, Hans (1926–), 1958
Hepplewhite, George (c.1730–86), 1788
Herat, Afghanistan, 1856
Hereford, 760; Cathedral, 1260, 1290, 1724
Hereward 'the Wake', 1070–1
Herrick, Robert (1591–1674), 1648
Herschel, William (1738–1822), 1800
Hertford, Synod of, 672
Hertfordshire, 490
Hesdin, France, Truce of, 1463
Heseltine, Michael (1933–), 1986, 1990
Hess, Myra (1890–1965), 1939
Hess, Rudolf (1894–1987), 1941
Hetherington, James, 1797
Hexham, Northumberland, 1570; battle of, 1464
Hick, Graeme (1966–), 1988
Hick, John (1922–), 1978
Higden, Ranulf (d.1364), 1364, 1387
High Beech, Essex, 1928
Highcliffe Castle, Bournemouth,

1907
Highgate, London, 1626
Hilda, St (614–80), 657
Hill, Rowland (1795–1879), 1840
Hillary, Edmund (1919–), 1953
Hillary, William (1771–1847), 1824
Hilliard, Nicholas (1547–1619), 1572
Hillsborough, Belfast, Accord of, 1985
Hilton Hotel, London, 1963
Hilton, John (1599–1657), 1652
Hilton, Walter (d.1396), 1396
Hingston Down, Cornwall, battle of, 838
Hinkler, Bert (1892–1933), 1928
Hinsley, Arthur (1865–1943), Cardinal Archbp, 1941
Hinton St Mary, Dorset, 360
Hispaniola, I. of, 1562
Hitchcock, Alfred (1899–1980), 1930, 1938
Hitchin, Herts., 1869
Hitler, Adolf (1889–1945), 1937–40, 1942
Hoadly, Benjamin (1676–1761), Bp, 1717
Hoare, Samuel (1880–1959), 1931, 1935
Hobart, Tasmania, Constitutional Convention of, 1897
Hobbes, Thomas (1588–1679), 1641, 1651
Hobbs, Jack (1882–1963), 1926, 1934
Hobson, John (1858–1940), 1902
Hoccleve, Thomas (c.1369–1426), 1411–12
Hoddinott, Alan (1929–), 1981
Hodgkin, Dorothy (1910–), 1955, 1964
Hogarth, William (1697–1764), 1733–5, 1743–5, 1751
Hogg, Quintin (1843–1902), 1882
Hoggart, Richard (1918–), 1957
Holbeach Hall, Staffs., 1605
Holbein, Hans (1497–1543), 1526, 1532
Holden, Charles (1875–1960), 1929, 1934
Holdenby House, Northants., 1647
Holford Square, London, 1902
Holinshed, Raphael (d.?1582), 1577
Holkham Hall, Norfolk, 1734
Holland, Henry (1746–1806), 1783–4, 1787
Holland, John (1840–1914), 1898
Holloway, London, 1921; prison, 1955
Holman Hunt, Henry (1823–1910), 1848
Holst, Gustav (1874–1934), 1920, 1923
Holy River, Sweden, battle of, 1025/6

Holyhead, Wales, 369, 1850
Holyrood Abbey, Edinburgh, 1128, 1385, 1437
Holyrood House, Edinburgh, 1501, 1565–6
Homildon Hill, Northumberland, battle of, 1402
Hong Kong, 1841–2, 1856, 1941, 1967, 1989
Honorius (384–423), W. Emp., 410
Hood, Robin, 1230, 1362
Hooke, Robert (1635–1703), 1656–9, 1661–2
Hope, Anthony (1863–1933), 1894
Hopkins, Frederick (1861–1947), 1906
Hopkins, Gerard Manley (1844–89), 1918
Hopkins, Matthew (d.1647), 1647
Hoppner, John (1758–1810), 1786
Horne Tooke, John (1736–1812), 1801
Horniman, Annie (1860–1937), 1908
Horsa (d?455), 430, 455
Hounsfield, Godfrey (1919–), 1979
Hounslow Heath, London, 1686
Housesteads, Northumberland, 122–39
Housman, A. E. (1859–1936), 1896
Hove, Sussex, 1,800 –1,400 BC
Howard, Catherine (1523–42), Q. Consort, 1540, 1542
Howard, Ebenezer (1850–1928), 1898, 1905, 1920
Howard of Effingham, Charles, Lord (1536–1624), 1587, 1596
Howard, Frances (1592–1632), 1613, 1616
Howard, Leslie (1893–1943), 1941, 1943
Howard, Michael (1941–), 1990
Howard, Trevor (1916–88), 1945
Howe, E., Richard (1726–99), Adm., 1794, 1797
Howe, Geoffrey (1926–), 1979, 1983, 1989–90
Hoxne, Suffolk, battle of, 869
Huddersfield, 1817
Huddleston, Trevor (1913–), Bp, 1957
Hudson Bay, Canada, 1610
Hudson, Henry (c.1561–1611), 1610–11
Hudson, William (1841–1922), 1904, 1925
Hugh, St (c.1135–1200), Bp, 1178, 1186, 1200, 1220
Hughes, Richard (1900–76), 1961
Hughes, Ted (1930–), 1984
Hughes, Thomas (1822–96), 1857
Humber, R., Yorks., 270–90, 430, 490, 1069
Hume, Basil (1923–), Cardinal Archbp, 1976, 1980
Hume, David (1711–76), 1739,

1741–2, 1748
Humphrey (c.1390–1447), D. of Gloucester, 1422–6, 1430–1, 1435, 1447
Hungerford, Thomas (d.1398), 1377
Hunne, Richard (d.1514), 1514
Hunsdon, Lord, George Carey (1547–1603), 1597; Henry Carey (1524–96), 1569–70, 1583
Hunt, G. W. (1829–1904), 1877
Hunt, Henry (1773–1835), 1819
Hunt, John (1910–), 1953
Hunt, Leigh (1754–1859), 1808
Huntcliff, Yorks., 369
Huntingdon, Cambs., 1628; Castle, 1068
Huntingdon, Countess of, Selina (1707–91), 1748, 1779
Huntly, E. of, George Gordon (1510–62), 1562
Hurd, Douglas (1930–), 1989–90
Huskisson, William (1770–1830), 1823, 1828, 1830
Hussein (1935–), K. of Jordan, 1958
Hutton, Leonard (1916–90), 1938, 1953
Huxley, Aldous (1894–1963), 1921, 1925, 1928, 1932, 1936, 1948
Huxley, Thomas (1825–95), 1858, 1870, 1889
Hyde Park, London, 1850–1, 1855, 1857, 1866, 1885, 1925, 1933, 1971, 1982
Hywel Dda (d.949/50), P. of Gwynedd, 949/50

Ibsen, Henrik (1828–1906), 1880, 1891
Iceland, 795
Iceni, 25–20 BC, AD 43–7, 61
Ida, K. of Bernicia, 547
Idle, R., Yorks., battle of, 616
Île d'Yeu, Brittany, 1795
Île-de-France, 1441
Illtud, St, 470–500
Imjin R., Korea, battle of, 1951
Imperial Institute, London, 1893
Imphal, India, battle of, 1944
Inchtuthil, Scotland, 83, 87
India, 1756–7, 1761, 1790, 1792–3, 1799, 1818–19, 1845–6, 1856–8, 1875, 1877, 1921, 1929–32, 1935, 1942, 1947, 1983
Indore, India, 1818
Indulf (d.c.962), K. of Scots, 954
Ine (d.726), K. of Wessex, 688, 694, 710, 722
Inkerman, Crimea, battle of, 1854
Innocent III (d.1216), Pope, 1206, 1208, 1212–13, 1215
Inonu, Ismet (1884–1973), Pres. of Turkey, 1943
Invergordon, Scotland, 1931
Inverlochy, Scotland, battle of, 1645
Iona, I. of, Scotland, 563, 664, 780,

795, 802, 806–7, 980
Ionesco, Eugene (1912–), 1960
Ionian Is, 1864
Ipswich, Suffolk, 25–20 BC, AD 991, 1525
Iran, 1941
Iraq, 1927, 1932, 1990, 1991, (see also Mesopotamia)
Ireland, English Pale in, 1394, 1401
Ireland, 432, 610–15, 841, 1155, 1169–72, 1185, 1315–17, 1366, 1380, 1394–5, 1459, 1468, 1494, 1541, 1579, 1599, 1601–3, 1609, 1649, 1689–91, 1728, 1778, 1780, 1782, 1791, 1796–8, 1800–1, 1803, 1823, 1833, 1836, 1838, 1840, 1845–6, 1850, 1858, 1866–70, 1869, 1877, 1879–82, 1885–6, 1920 (see also Eire, Irish Free State, N. Ireland, Ulster)
Ireton, Henry (1611–51), Gen., 1647–8, 1661
Irish Free State, 1921–2, 1925, 1933–5, 1937 (see also Eire)
Irrawaddy, R., Burma, 1945
Irving, Henry (1838–1905), 1878
Irwin, Lord (see Halifax, Vcts, Edward Wood)
Isabel of Angoulême (d.1246), Q. Consort, 1200
Isabella of France (1296–1358), Q. Consort of Edward II, 1304, 1308, 1319, 1325–7, 1330
Isabella of France (1389–1409), Q. Consort of Richard II, 1396
Isandhlwana, Africa, battle of, 1879
Isherwood, Christopher (1904–86), 1935, 1939, 1964
Isle of Dogs, London, 1802, 1893, 1983, 1988
Islington, London, 1907
Ismailia, Egypt, 1952
Israel, 1956
Issigonis, Alec (1906–88), 1959
Istanbul, 1936
Itelezi, Africa, battle of, 1879
Ivar 'the Boneless', K. of Danes, 865, 869
Iveagh, E. of, Edward Guinness (1847–1927), 1928
Ivinghoe Beacon, Bucks., 1,400 BC, 800–450 BC
Ivry, France, Pact of, 1177

Jack 'the Ripper', 1888
Jackson, Barry (1869–1971), 1913, 1929, 1946
Jacobsen, Arne (1902–71), 1966
Jacomb-Hood, J. W. (1852–1914), 1922
Jacqueline of Hainault (1401–36), 1423–5
Jamaica, West Indies, 1655, 1955–6, 1962
James Bay, Canada, 1611

James, C. (1893–1953), 1938
James I (1394–1437), K. of Scots, 1406, 1423–5, 1437
James II (1430–60), K. of Scots, 1437, 1440, 1452, 1460
James III (1452–88), K. of Scots, 1460, 1466, 1468, 1479, 1482, 1484, 1488
James IV (1473–1513), K. of Scots, 1474, 1488, 1493, 1495, 1503, 1506, 1513
James V (1512–42), K. of Scots, 1513, 1524, 1532, 1538–9, 1542
James VI and I (1566–1625), K., 1566–7, 1573, 1582, 1589, 1599–1600, 1603–4, 1606–7, 1610–11, 1614, 1616–25, 1635
James II (1633–1701), K., 1647, 1661, 1673, 1678–80, 1683, 1685–91, 1701
James Edward (1688–1766), Pretender, 1688, 1701–2, 1708, 1714–16, 1722
James, M. R. (1832–1936), 1904
James, Naomi (1949–), 1978
James, William (1842–1910), 1902
Jameson, Leander (1853–1917), 1891, 1893, 1895–6
Jamestown, Virginia, 1607, 1610, 1619
Jamieson, Penelope (1942–), Bp, 1990
Jardine, Douglas (1900–58), 1933
Jarrow, Northumberland, 794, 1936; Abbey, 674, 685, 716
Jeans, James (1877–1946), 1926
Jedburgh, Scotland, 1523; Abbey, 1138
Jeffrey, Francis (1773–1850), 1802
Jeffreys, George (1648–89), Judge, 1685
Jeffries, John (1744–1819), 1785
Jellahabad, India, 1842
Jenkins, David (1925–), Bp, 1984
Jenkins, Robert, Cap., 1738–9
Jenkins, Roy (1920–), 1959, 1965, 1974, 1981
Jenkinson, Anthony (c.1530–1611), 1588
Jenner, Edward (1749–1823), 1796
Jerome, Jerome K. (1859–1927), 1889
Jersey, I. of, 1646, 1649
Jerusalem, 1185, 1841, 1917, 1929; King David Hotel, 1946
Jesus College, Cambridge, 1496
Jewel, John (1522–71), Bp, 1559, 1562
Joan (1210–38), Q. Consort of Alexander II, K. of Scots, 1221
Joan (1321–62), Q. Consort of David II, K. of Scots, 1328
Joan of Navarre (d.1437), Q. Consort, 1403
Joan (d.1237), P. Consort of

Gwynedd, 1206
Joan of Kent (1328–85), P. of Wales, 1361
Joan of Arc, St (d.1431), 1429–31
Joanna (1479–1555), Q. of Castile, 1506
Jocelyn of Brakelond (c.1155–1215), 1205
Jockey Club, London, 1750
Jodrell Bank, Cheshire, 1957
Johannesburg, South Africa, 1892, 1900
John (1165–1216), K., 1177, 1184–5, 1191–5, 1199–1200, 1211–16
John II (d.1364), K. of France, 1346, 1356, 1358, 1360, 1364
John (1388–1435), D. of Bedford, 1416, 1422–3, 1426–7, 1433–5
John of Gaunt (1340–99), D. of Lancaster, 1362, 1369, 1372–4, 1376–7, 1384, 1386–7, 1389, 1393, 1399
John of Ashendon (d?1379), 1345, 1348
John of Gaddesden, 1316
John Paul II (1920–), Pope, 1979, 1982, 1989
John of Salisbury (1115/20–1180), 1159, 1162–3, 1170, 1172/3
John XXIII, (1881–1963), Pope, 1961
John, Augustus (1878–1961), 1908, 1913–14, 1926, 1940
John, Gwen (1876–1939), 1926
Johnson, Amy (1903–41), 1930, 1936
Johnson, Celia (1908–82), 1945
Johnson, Samuel (1709–84), 1737–8, 1755, 1759, 1763–4, 1779
Jones, Henry Arthur (1851–1929), 1882, 1895–6
Jones, Inigo (1573–1652), 1616, 1618
Jones, Paul (1742–92), 1778
Jonson, Ben (1572–1637), 1597, 1605–6, 1609–10, 1614, 1616
Jordan, 1923, 1946, 1956–8, 1970, 1984
Joyce, George, (c.1620–70), 1647
Joyce, James (1882–1941), 1914, 1922
Juan Carlos (1938–), K. of Spain, 1986
Julian (c.331–63), Rom. Emp., 355, 359–60
Julian of Norwich (c.1342–c.1416), 1393
Julius Verus, 154–5
Jutes, 447–50, 490
Jutland, battle of, 1916
Juxon, William (1582–1663), Bp, 1633, 1636

Kabul, Afghanistan, 1841–2, 1878–80, 1919
Kagoshima, Japan, 1864
Kamehameha, K. of Polynesia, 1794

Kandahar, Afghanistan, 1879–80
Karachi, Pakistan, 1929
Karsavina, Tamara (1885–1978), 1911
Kay, John (c.1703–64), 1733
Kealakelua Bay, Hawaii, 1779
Kean, Edmund (?1787–1833), 1814, 1833
Keats, John (1795–1821), 1818, 1820–1
Keble College, Oxford, 1870, 1876
Keble, John (1792–1866), 1827, 1833
Keele, Staffs., 1967; University College, 1949
Keeler, Christine (1942–), 1963
Kells, Ireland, 780, 807; Synod of, 1152
Kelly, Ned (1855–80), 1880
Kelso, Scotland, 1523, 1542; Abbey, 1126
Kelvin, William, Lord (see Thomson, William)
Kemal Attaturk, Mustafa (1881–1938), 1922, 1936
Kemble, John (1757–1823), 1782, 1817
Kempe, Margery (c.1373–c.1439), 1438
Kempe, William (c.1568–c.1608), 1600
Kendall, James (1889–1978), 1915
Kenilworth Castle, Warwicks., 1265–6, 1327, 1450, 1456, 1575
Kennedy, John (1917–63), Pres. of USA, 1962
Kennedy, Margaret (1896–1967), 1924
Kenneth II (d.995), K. of Scots, 971
Kenneth MacAlpin (d.858), K. of Dal Riada, 843
Kennington, Eric (1888–1960), 1917
Kennington, London, 1848
Kennington Oval, London, 1845, 1872, 1880, 1938, 1953
Kensington, London, 1946, 1980
Kensington Palace, London, 1689, 1694, 1702, 1704, 1760, 1837
Kent, 55–54 BC, AD 430, 490, 695, 776, 796–8, 1381, 1450–1; University of, 1965
Kent, D. of, Victoria (1786–1861), 1819
Kent, DD of, P. Edward (1767–1820), 1819; P. George (1902–42), 1942
Kent, William (1685–1745), 1734, 1739
Kentigern (Mungo, c.525–c.612), St, 600
Kent's Cavern, Devon, 26,000–10,000 BC
Kenwood House, London, 1764, 1928
Kenya, 1902, 1920, 1952, 1959,

1963
Kenyon, Kathleen (1906–78), 1952
Kett, Robert (1514–49), 1549
Kettering, Northants., 1792
Kew Gardens, London, 1841, 1844, 1987
Keyes, Sidney (1922–43), 1942–3
Keynes, J. Maynard (1883–1946), 1919, 1925, 1930
Khartoum, Sudan, 1884–5, 1898
Khrushchev, Nikita (1894–1971), 1956
Khyber Pass, 1879
Kidd, William (c.1645–1701), Cap., 1699, 1701
Kidder, Francis, 1868
Kiel, Germany, Ty of, 1814
Kildare, EE of, Garrett Fitzgerald (c.1456–1513), 1478, 1495–6, 1504; Thomas Fitzgerald (1513–37), 1534, 1537; Thomas Fitzgerald (d.1478), 1470
Killala, Ireland, 1798
Killiecrankie, Scotland, battle of, 1689
Killigrew, Thomas (1612–83), 1662–3
Killingworth colliery, Northumberland, 1814
Kimberley, E. of, John Wodehouse (1826–1902), 1894–6
Kimberley, South Africa, 1869, 1899–1900
Kimbolton House, Cambs., 1536, 1707
King, William (1663–1712), 1710
Kinglake, Alexander (1805–91), 1844
King's College, Cambridge, 1441, 1446, 1918
King's College, London, 1828
King's Cross station, London, 1852, 1879, 1987
King's Enham, Hants., 1008
King's Lynn, Norfolk, 1915
King's Mountain, battle of, 1780
King's Rd, London, 1966
Kingsley, Charles (1819–75), 1850, 1854–5, 1863, 1866
Kingston, Surrey, 925; Ty of, 1217
Kingsway, London, 1905, 1941
Kinnock, Neil (1942–), 1983
Kinross, Scotland, 1963
Kinsale, Ireland, 1601–2, 1689–90
Kipling, Rudyard (1865–1936), 1886, 1888–9, 1892, 1895, 1897–8, 1901–2, 1907
Kiralfy, Imre (d.1919), 1908
Kirk o'Field, Edinburgh, 1567
Kismayu, Kenya, 1924
Kitchener, Horatio (1850–1916), Gen., 1896, 1898, 1900–1, 1914, 1916
Klosterzeven, Germany, Convention of, 1757

Kneller, Godfrey (1646–1723), 1694–5, 1702
Knight, Laura (1877–1970), 1936
Knockdoe, Ireland, battle of, 1504
Knollys, Lettice (1540–1634), Countess of Essex, 1578
Knossos, Crete, 1900
Knott, Ralph (1878–1929), 1922
Knox, John (?1512–72), 1547, 1555, 1558–60
Koestler, Arthur (1905–83), 1945
Kohima, India, battle of, 1944
Korda, Alexander (1893–1956), 1932–3, 1937
Korea, 1950
Kossuth, Lajos (1802–94), 1851
Kowloon, China, 1858, 1898
Kreisler, Fritz (1875–1962), 1910
Kruger, Paulus (1825–1904), 1881, 1896, 1899
Kuala Lumpur, Malaysia, 1989
Kumasi, Ghana, 1874, 1896
Kut, Iraq, 1915–17
Kuwait, 1899, 1928, 1961, 1991
Kyle, Scotland, 750

La Hogue, Normandy, battle of, 1692
La Rochelle, France, 1214, 1293, 1372, 1627–8
Lady Margaret Hall, Oxford, 1879
Ladysmith, South Africa, 1899–1900
Lafayette, Marie Joseph (1757–1834), 1781
Laffeldt, Netherlands, battle of, 1747
Lagos Bay, Nigeria, 1759
Laing's Neck, South Africa, battle of, 1881
Lake, Vct, Gerard (1744–1808), Gen., 1797
Lamb, Charles (1775–1834), 1807, 1823
Lamb, Henry (1883–1960), 1914
Lamb, Mary (1764–1847), 1807
Lambarde, William (1536–1601), 1576
Lambeth, London, 1610
Lambeth Palace, London, 1988; Conferences, 1867, 1888
Lamont, Norman (1942–), 1990
Lancashire, 1947
Lancaster Bay, Canada, 1818
Lancaster House, London, 1979
Lancaster, James (1555–1618), 1591
Lancaster, Joseph (1778–1838), 1803, 1808
Lancaster, University of, 1964
Land's End, Cornwall, 330–320 BC
Landseer, Edwin (1802–73), 1837
Lane, Allen (1902–70), 1935
Lane, Elizabeth (1905–), 1965
Lane, Lupino (1892–1959), 1937
Lanercost, Cumbria, 1306
Lanfranc (d.1089), Archbp, 1070–7,

1087, 1089
Lang, Cosmo (1864–1945), Archbp, 1941
Langland, William (c.1330–86), 1362
Langport, Somerset, battle of, 1645
Langside, Scotland, battle of, 1568
Langton, Stephen (d.1228), Archbp, 1206, 1213, 1215, 1217
Lansbury, George (1859–1940), 1912, 1921, 1932
Lansdowne, Henry, Lord (1845–1927), 1900, 1903, 1917
Largs, Scotland, battle of, 1263
Larkin, Philip (1922–1985), 1964
Lasdun, Denys (1914–), 1969
Laszlo, Philip (1869–1937), 1925
Latimer, Hugh (1485–1555), Bp, 1539, 1554–5
Latinius Postumus, Gen., 259
Laud, William (1573–1645), Archbp, 1628, 1633, 1637–8, 1640–1, 1645
Lauderdale, D. of, John Maitland (1616–82), 1667
Laughton, Charles (1899–1962), 1933
Lausanne, Switzerland, Conference, 1922, 1923; Ty of, 1923
Laval, Pierre (1883–1945), 1935
Lavardin, France, Ty of, 1448
Lawes, Henry (1596–1662), 1656
Lawes, John (1814–1900), 1843
Lawrence, D. H. (1885–1930), 1911, 1913, 1916, 1921, 1926, 1928–9, 1960
Lawrence, T. E. (1888–1935), 1917, 1926, 1929
Lawrence, Thomas (1769–1830), 1814
Lawson, Nigel (1932–), 1983, 1989
Layard, Henry (1817–94), 1845
Lazamon, 1200
Le Carré, John (1931–), 1963, 1982–3, 1986
Le Goulet, France, Ty of, 1200
Le Havre, France, 1562
Le Mans, France, 1425, 1448
Lea, R., 894–5
Leake, Notts., Ty of, 1318
Leakey, Louis (1903–72), 1959, 1964
Leakey, Mary (1913–), 1959, 1964
Leakey, Richard (1944–), 1972
Leamington, Warks., 1872
Lean, David (1908–91), 1945, 1957, 1962
Lear, Edward (1812–88), 1846
Leather, Diane (1934–), 1954
Leeds, Yorks., 1643, 1816, 1837, 1858, 1879, 1931; Headingley, 1930, 1981; University of, 1874, 1904, 1915
Leicester, 130, 877, 1530, 1645
Leicester, EE of, Robert (d.1168), 1153; Robert Dudley (1532–88),

1560, 1569, 1575, 1578, 1585–8
Leicestershire, 1607
Leigh, Vivien (1913–67), 1951
Leinster, Ireland, 1207, 1394
Leith, Lothian, 1544, 1559, 1561
Lely, Peter (1618–80), 1647, 1661, 1666–7
Lenglen, Suzanne (1899–1938), 1919
Lenin, Vladimir (1870–1924), 1902
Lennon, John (1940–80), 1963, 1967, 1970
Lennox, E. of, Matthew Stewart (1516–71), 1570–1
Leo X (d.1521), Pope, 1521
Leo XIII (1810–1903), Pope, 1887, 1896
Leofric, E. of Mercia (d.1057), 1017, 1035, 1043, 1057
Leofwine Godwinsson (d.1066), 1051, 1057, 1066
Leopold I (1790–1865), K. of Belgium, 1862
Leopold II (1835–1909), K. of Belgium, 1890
Leslie, David (1601–82), Gen., 1645, 1650
Letchworth, Herts., 1905
Leven, E. of, Alexander Leslie (1580–1661), 1639, 1644
Lewes, Sussex, Abbey, 1077; battle of, 1264
Lewis, Alun (1915–44), 1942
Lewis, C. S. (1898–1963), 1941–2
Lewis (Ludwig) IV (c.1283–1347), HRE, 1337–8
Lewis, Wyndham (1884–1957), 1913
Lewisham, London, 1977
Lexington, Mass., 1775
Leyton, Essex, 1965; cricket ground, 1932
Leytonstone, Essex, 1882
Lhasa, Tibet, Ty of, 1903
Libya, 1971, 1984, 1986
Lichfield House, London, 1835
Lichfield, Staffs., 788, 803, 1075
Liddell, Eric (1920–45), 1924
Liddington, Wilts., 500
Liège, Belgium, 1702
Lieven, Dorothea (1786–1857), 1812
Lilburne, John (1614–57), 1645, 1649–50
Lille, France, 1708, 1918
Lillywhite, Frederick (1829–66), 1859
Limassol, Cyprus, 1954
Limehouse, London, 1832
Limerick, Ireland, 967, 1177, 1920; Ty of, 1691
Limoges, France, 1370
Linacre, Thomas (c.1467–1524), 1518
Lincoln, 43–7, 71, 75–80, 90–8, 877, 1140, 1149, 1255; battles of, 1141, 1217; Castle, 1068; Cathedral, 1072–3, 1208, 1255

Lincoln, E. of, John de la Pole (c.1464–87), 1484, 1487
Lincoln's Inn Theatre, London, 1661, 1695
Lind, Jenny (1820–87), 1847
Lindemann, Frederick (Lord Cherwell, 1886–1957), 1926
Lindisfarne (Holy Island), Northumberland, 634, 698, 793
Lindsay, David (1486–1555), 1540
Lindsey (Lincolns.), kingdom of, 627
Linlithgow Palace, Scotland, 1540, 1542
Lintot, Barnaby (1675–1736), 1712
Lionel, D. of Clarence (1338–68), 1342, 1361–2, 1366
Lisbon, 1147, 1809
Lisle Castle, France, 1513
Lister, Joseph (1827–1912), 1867
Little Gidding, Cambs., 1646
Little Woodbury, Wilts., 800–450 BC
Liverpool, 1816, 1830, 1840, 1886, 1893, 1896, 1937, 1940, 1954, 1980; Cathedral, 1903, 1978; Playhouse, 1911; RC Cathedral, 1967; Toxteth, 1981; University of, 1881, 1884
Liverpool, E. of, Robert Jenkinson (1770–1828), 1812, 1822, 1827
Livingstone, David (1813–73), 1841, 1852, 1855, 1870–1, 1873
Livingstone, Ken (1945–), 1981
Llandaff Cathedral, Wales, 1957
Llandrinio, Wales, 1806
Llantwit Major, Wales, 470–500
Llewelyn the Great (1173–1240), P. of Gwynedd, 1194, 1200–1, 1206, 1208, 1211–16, 1218–19, 1231, 1233–4, 1240
Llewelyn (d.1282), P. of Wales, 1246, 1255, 1257–8, 1260, 1262, 1265, 1274–8, 1282
Lleyn peninsula, Wales, 400
Lloyd George, David (1863–1945), 1901, 1907–9, 1911, 1915–19, 1922, 1925
Lloyd Webber, Andrew (1948–), 1970, 1972–3, 1978, 1981
Lloyd's, London, 1692
Locarno, Switzerland, Ty of, 1925
Lochleven Castle, Scotland, 1567–8
Locke, John, 1555
Locke, John (1632–1704), 1689–90, 1693
Locke, Matthew (1622–77), 1661
Lockerbie, Scotland, 1988
Lockhart, John (1794–1854), 1837–8
Lodge, David (1935–), 1975, 1984, 1988
Lodge, Oliver (1851–1940), 1884
Lodge, Thomas (1552–1625), 1590
Loire, R., France, 1356, 1380
Lollius Urbicus, 139

London, Jack (1876–1916), 1903
London, 871, 886, 1066, 1141, 1215–16, 1326, 1377, 1381, 1392, 1459, 1471, 1517, 1563, 1580, 1592, 1665–6, 1688, 1736, 1810, 1823, 1829, 1848–9, 1854–5, 1882, 1886–8, 1915, 1918, 1932, 1939–41, 1944–5, 1952, 1962, 1968, 1975, 1981–4; City of, 43–7, 1580, 1594, 1857, 1866, 1940; City Temple, 1917; City University, 1966; Conferences, 1867, 1871, 1884, 1921, 1930, 1934, 1939, 1953–5; Conventions, 1884, 1924; Councils of, 1050, 1075, 1102, 1129; County Hall, 1922; Docklands, 1981, 1986–7; Docks, 1802, 1805, 1889, 1911–12, 1950; Exhibitions, 1851, 1886; Law Courts, 1874; Roman, 43–7, 61, 75–80, 100, 122, 130, 200, 296, 1954; Tower of, 1078, 1088, 1255, 1381, 1465, 1471, 1478, 1483, 1499, 1535–6, 1553–4, 1603, 1645, 1685, 1747, 1763, 1810, 1885; Treaties of, 1423, 1474, 1518, 1758, 1827, 1831, 1839, 1870, 1913, 1915, 1930; UN Assembly, 1946; University of, 1836, 1900
London Bridge, 43–7, 1582, 1831, 1836
London Library, 1841
London Medical School for Women, 1875
London Mint, 1300
London School of Economics, 1895, 1969
London Stock Exchange, 1773, 1929, 1986, 1990
London Transport building, 1929
London Zoological Society (Zoo), 1826
Londonderry, N. Ireland, 1689, 1968–9, 1972, 1976
Longchamp, William (d.1197), Bp, 1189–91, 1194
Longleat House, Wilts., 1568, 1574
Loos, France, battle of, 1915
Lopez, Roderigo (d.1594), 1594
Lord, Thomas (1755–1832), 1787
Lord's Cricket Ground, London, 1787, 1806, 1814, 1864, 1938, 1945, 1950, 1962, 1975, 1990
Lothian, 600, 954, 973, 1019–20, 1054
Loubet, Emile (1838–1929), 1903
Loudounhill, Scotland, battle of, 1307
Lough Swilly, Ireland, 1798
Loughborough, Leics., 1817; University of, 1966
Loughgal, N. Ireland, 1987
Louis, K. of Franks, 936, 939, 946
Louis VI, K. of France, 1111, 1116,

Louis VII (d.1180), K. of France, 1144, 1151–2, 1158–9, 1169, 1173, 1177, 1179–80

Louis VIII (d.1226), K. of France, 1216–17, 1224

Louis IX, St (1214–70), K. of France, 1243, 1263–4

Louis XI (1423–83), K. of France, 1462, 1467, 1475

Louis XII (1462–1515), K. of France, 1514

Louis XIV (1638–1715), K. of France, 1668, 1670, 1697, 1701, 1703, 1709

Louis Philippe (1773–1850), K. of France, 1843, 1848

Louisburg, Canada, 1758

Louth, Lincs., 1536

Louvain, Belgium, 1516

Louviers, Normandy, Ty of, 1195

Lovat, Simon Fraser, Lord (1667–1747), 1747

Lovelace, Richard (1618–58), 1649

Lovell, Francis, Lord (1454–?), 1486–7

Lovett, William (1800–77), 1836

Lowe, Robert (1811–92), 1868, 1873

Lowestoft, Suffolk, 1665

Lubbock, John (1834–1913), 1870–1

Lübeck, Germany, 1945

Lucas, Charles, 1854

Lucknow, India, 1857

Ludford Bridge, Shrops., battle of, 1459

Ludlow, Shrops., 1459; Castle, 1502–3

Lullingstone, Kent, 360

Lumphanan, Scotland, battle of, 1057

Lunardi, Vincenzo (1759–1806), 1784

Luneberg Heath, Germany, 1945

Lusaka, Zambia, 1979

Lutyens, Edwin (1869–1944), 1906, 1920, 1925, 1927, 1931

Luwum, Janani (1922–77), Archbp, 1977

Luxor, Egypt, 1922

Lyceum Hall, London, 1802

Lyceum Theatre, London, 1878, 1951

Lydford, Berks., 1581

Lydgate, John (c.1370–1449), 1412, 1420, 1424

Lydney, Glos., 361

Lyell, Charles (1797–1875), 1830

Lyme Regis, Dorset, 1685

Lynmouth, Devon, 1952

Lyric Theatre, Hammersmith, London, 1918, 1925

Maamtrasna, Ireland, 1882

Macaulay, Rose (1881–1958), 1926

Macaulay, Thomas, Lord (1800–59), 1842, 1848

Macbeth (d.1057), K. of Scots, 1040, 1050, 1054, 1057

McCabe, John (1939–), 1975

McCallum, R. B. (1898–1973), 1947

McCarthy, John (1957–), 1991

McCartney, Paul (1942–), 1963, 1967, 1970

Macdermott, 'Great' (Gilbert Farrell, 1845–1901), 1877

Macdonald, Claud (1852–1915), 1900

Macdonald, Flora (1722–90), 1746

Macdonald, Ramsay (1866–1937), 1900, 1911, 1924, 1929, 1931, 1934–5

McDouall, John, 1861

Macintosh, Charles (1766–1843), 1823

Mackenzie, Compton (1883–1972), 1913

Mackenzie, George (1636–91), 1682

Mackenzie King, W. L. (1874–1950), 1943

Mackenzie, William (1795–1861), 1837

Mackerras, Charles (1925–), 1951

Mackintosh, Charles (1868–1928), 1904, 1909

Maclean, Donald (1913–83), 1951

Macleod, Iain (1913–70), 1952, 1959, 1961, 1970

Macmillan, Harold (1894–1986), 1954–60, 1962–3, 1984

Macmillan, Kirkpatrick (1813–78), 1834, 1839

McNaughton, Daniel, 1843

MacNeice, Louis (1907–63), 1939, 1963

Macready, William (1793–1873), 1816, 1851

McTaggart, John (1866–1925), 1921

McWhirter, Ross (1925–75), 1975

Madagascar, 1890

Madox Brown, Ford (1821–93), 1855, 1877

Madras, India, 1761

Madresfield, Worcs., 1836

Madrid, 1623, 1812

Maeatae, 185, 197, 210–11

Maelsechnail II, High K. of Ireland, 980, 999

Maes Howe, Orkney, 3000–2400 BC

Maes Moydog, Wales, battle of, 1295

Mafeking, South Africa, 1899–1900

Magdala, Ethiopia, 1868

Magdalen College, Oxford, 1448, 1478, 1490, 1687

Magellan Strait, 1578

Magersfontein, South Africa, battle of, 1899

Magnentius, W. Emp., 350, 353

Magnus VI (1238–80), K. of Norway, 1266

Magus Muir, Scotland, 1679

Maharatta, India, 1819

Mahdi, Mohammed El (1840–85), 1883–5

Maiden Castle, Dorset, 4,000–3,000 BC, 800–450 BC, AD 43–7, 1934

Maidstone, Kent, 1837, 1868

Maine, Cuthbert (d.1577), 1577

Maine, France, 1113, 1199, 1203, 1445–6, 1448

Maiwand, Afghanistan, battle of, 1880

Major, John (1943–), 1989–91

Makarios III (1913–77), Archbp, 1956, 1959

Malawi (see also Nyasaland), 1964

Malaya, 1867, 1941, 1949, 1951–4, 1957

Malcolm I (943–54), K. of Scots, 945, 948

Malcolm II (c.954–1034), K. of Scots, 1019–20, 1027

Malcolm III (c.1031–93), K. of Scots, 1054, 1057–8, 1061, 1070, 1072, 1080, 1091, 1093

Malcolm IV (1141–65), K. of Scots, 1153, 1157, 1160, 1164–5

Maldon, Essex, 916; battle of, 991

Malestroit, France, Truce of, 1343

Mallock, William (1849–1923), 1877

Malmesbury, Wilts., 1153; Abbey, 939, 957

Malory, Thomas (d.1471), 1471

Malplaquet, France, battle of, 1709

Malta, 1800, 1803, 1814, 1878, 1942–3, 1956, 1971–2

Malthus, Thomas (1766–1834), 1798

Malvern, Worcs., 1929, 1941; Priory, 1450

Man, I. of, 500, 632, 1000, 1266, 1313, 1333, 1397, 1829

Manchester, 1761, 1801, 1817, 1830, 1836, 1838, 1842, 1846, 1851, 1866–7, 1888, 1890, 1903, 1908, 1939–40, 1945, 1988; Belle Vue, 1926; Chat Moss airport, 1929; Gaiety Theatre, 1908; John Rylands Library, 1899; Moss Side, 1981; Old Trafford, 1981; St Peter's Fields, 1819; Town Hall, 1877; University of, 1948

Manchester Ship Canal, 1894

Mandalay, Burma, 1885, 1945

Mandeville, Sir John, 1375

Manning, Henry (1808–92), Cardinal, 1850, 1884

Manningham, John (1576–1622), 1602

Mannyng, Robert (d.c.1338), 1303

Manor Park, London, 1948

Mansfeld, Count, Ernst (1580–1626), 1624–5

Mansfield, Katherine (1888–1923), 1920

Mansfield, William Murray (1705–93), 1772

Mansion House, London, 1890

Map, Walter (c.1140–c.1209), 1192

Mar, EE of, John Erskine (1510–72), 1571–2; John Erskine (1675–1732), 1715

Marbeck, John (c.1510–85), 1550

Marchand, Jean (1863–1934), Col., 1898

Marconi, Guglielmo (1874–1937), 1901, 1920

Marconi House, London, 1922

Mare, Peter de la, 1376

Margaret (1240–75), Q. Consort of Scots, 1251, 1255

Margaret of Anjou (1429–82), Q. Consort, 1444–6, 1448, 1456–7 1460–3, 1470–1, 1475

Margaret of France (d.1308), Q. Consort, 1299

Margaret of Norway (c.1283–90), Q. of Scots, 1286, 1289–90

Margaret, St (c.1046–93), Q. Consort of Scots, 1070, 1093

Margaret Tudor (1489–1541), Q. Consort of Scots, 1503, 1515, 1524

Margaret, P. of France, 1158, 1160

Margaret (d.1503), D. of Burgundy, 1465, 1493

Marie, D. of Edinburgh (1853–1920), 1874

Markham, Beryl (1902–86), 1936

Markievicz, Countess, Constance (1868–1927), 1918

Marlborough, D. of, Sarah (1660–1744), 1692, 1702, 1707–10

Marlborough, D. of, John Churchill (1650–1722), 1685, 1688–90, 1692, 1698, 1701–6, 1709, 1711–12, 1714, 1722

Marlborough House, London, 1709

Marlowe, Christopher (1564–93), 1587/8, 1592–3

Marne, R., France, battle of, 1914

Marryat, Frederick (1792–1848), 1834, 1836

Marsh, Adam (d.1259), 1247

Marsh, Edward (1872–1953), 1912

Marshal, William (c.1146–1219), E. of Pembroke, 1205, 1207, 1212, 1216–17, 1219

Marshall, George (1880–1959), 1947

Marston Moor, Yorks., battle of, 1644

Martin, Archer (1910–), 1952

Marvell, Andrew (1621–78), 1677

Mary I (1516–58), Q., 1516, 1536, 1544, 1550, 1553–4, 1558

Mary II (1662–94), Q., 1677, 1689, 1692, 1694–5

Mary (1542–87), Q. of Scots, 1542–3, 1548, 1561, 1565–9, 1571–3, 1584, 1586–7

Mary of Modena (1658–1718), Q.

Consort, 1673, 1685, 1688

Mary of Guise (1515–60), Q. Consort of Scots, 1538, 1554, 1559–60

Mary Stuart (1631–60), P. of Orange, 1641–2

Mary (1457–82), D. of Burgundy, 1476, 1480

Mary Tudor, D. of Suffolk (1496–1533), 1507, 1514

Maryland, USA, 1631, 1649

Marylebone Cricket Club, London, 1787–8

Masefield, John (1878–1967), 1902, 1910–11

Maserfelth (?Oswestry, Shrops.), battle of, 642

Masham, Abigail (1671–1734), 1707

Masham, Samuel (1679–1758), Col., 1707

Mashonaland, Zimbabwe, 1889

Maskelyne, Nevil (1732–1811), 1767

Massachusetts, 1620, 1630, 1635, 1774

Massinger, Philip (1583–1640), 1623, 1634

Masters, John (1914–), 1954

Matabeleland, South Africa, 1888, 1893

Matapan, Cape, Greece, battle of, 1941

Mathghamhain (d.976), K. of W. Munster, Ireland, 967

Matilda (1102–67), Empress, 1114, 1127–8, 1137, 1139, 1141–3, 1148, 1167

Matilda (d.1118), Q. Consort of Henry I, 1100, 1118

Matilda, Q. Consort of Stephen, 1141

Matthew, Robert (1911–66), 1951

Matthews, Stanley (1915–90), 1934, 1965

Maudit, John, 1311

Maudling, Reginald (1917–79), 1962, 1972

Maudslay, Henry (1771–1831), 1797

Maugham, Benjamin, 1865

Maugham, W. Somerset (1875–1965), 1915, 1919, 1932, 1944

Mauritius, I. of, 1814

Mauron, Brittany, battle of, 1351

Maximian (d.310), Rom. Emp., 289

Maximilian I (1459–1519), HRE, 1480, 1489, 1494, 1506, 1513, 1518–19

Maximus (d.388), W. Emp., 382–3, 388

Maxwell, Robert (1923–91), 1991

Maxwell Davies, Peter (1934–), 1973

Mayer, Robert (1879–1986), 1923

Mayfair, London, 1736, 1978

Maynooth, Ireland, 1795, 1845

Mayo, E. of, Richard Bourke (1822–72), 1872

Mayo, Ireland, 1880

Meare, Somerset, 80–50 BC

Mearns, Andrew (1857–1925), 1883

Meaux, France, 1421–2, 1439

Medina del Campo, Spain, Ty of, 1489

Medway, R., Kent, 43, 999, 1667

Meerut, India, 1857

Mehemet Ali (c.1769–1849), 1840

Melba, Nellie (1861–1931), 1920

Melbourne, Australia, 1837, 1860, 1877, 1880, 1956

Melbourne, William Lamb, Lord (1779–1848), 1834–5, 1837, 1839, 1841

Mellaart, James (1925–), 1961

Mellifont Abbey, Ireland, 1142

Melrose Abbey, Scotland, 1136, 1385

Melun, France, 1420

Menai Straits, Wales, 1850

Mendelssohn, Felix (1809–47), 1829, 1832, 1846

Mendip, Somerset, caves, 26,000–10,000 BC; mines, 49

Mendoza, Bernardino de, 1583–4

Menzies, Robert (1894–1978), 1956

Mercia, earldom of, 1017; kingdom of, 585, 628, 653–4, 657, 665–70, 691, 716, 757, 825, 867, 874, 918, 957

Meredith, George (1828–1909), 1859, 1862, 1864, 1867, 1875, 1879, 1883, 1885, 1895

Meres, Francis (1565–1647), 1598

Mermaid Theatre, London, 1959

Mersey, R., Lancs., 919

Merseyside, Lancs., 1941

Merton College, Oxford, 1264, 1274, 1311

Merton, Surrey, Council of, 1236

Merton, Walter de (d.1277), 1264

Mesolongion, Greece, 1824

Mesopotamia, 1920 (see also Iraq)

Messines, France, battle of, 1917

Metternich, Clemens (1773–1859), P., 1814, 1848

Meulan, France, 1419

Mexico, 1824

Meyerbeer, Giacomo (1791–1864), 1858

Mid-Ulster, N. Ireland, 1969

Middleham, Yorks., 1484

Middleton, Hugh (1560–1631), 1613

Middleton, Thomas (1580–1627), 1608, 1616, 1630

Midlothian, Scotland, 1879

Mildenhall, Suffolk, 360

Mile End, London, 1381

Miles, Bernard (1907–91), 1959

Milford Haven, Dyfed, 1171, 1405, 1485

Mill, James (1773–1836), 1829

Mill, John Stuart (1806–73), 1843,

Nashe, Thomas (1567–1601), 1594, 1597

Nasr-ed-din (1829–1926), Shah, 1873

Nassau, Bahamas, 1962, 1985

Nasser, Gamal (1918–70), 1956

Natal, South Africa, 1843, 1856, 1884, 1893

National Gallery, London, 1824, 1837, 1939

National Portrait Gallery, London, 1859, 1896

National Theatre, London, 1951, 1969, 1976

National Westminster Tower, London, 1980

Natural History Museum, London, 1873

Naunton, Robert (1563–1635), 1618

Navarino, Greece, battle of, 1827

Neagle, Anna (1904–86), 1937

Neath Abbey, Glamorgan, 1326

Neave, Airey (1916–1979), 1979

Nechtan (d.c.732), K. of Picts, 717

Nectaridus, Count, 367

Nefyn, Wales, 1284

Neilson, James (1792–1865), 1827

Nejd, Arabia, 1879

Nelson, Horatio, Lord (1758–1805), Adm., 1797–8, 1801, 1805

Nennius, 800, 829/30

Nerina, Nadia (1927–), 1960

Nesbit, Edith (1858–1924), 1899

Ness, R., Scotland, 563

Netherlands, 1493, 1496, 1506, 1575, 1585–7, 1692, 1695

Netter, Thomas (c.1377–1430), 1430

Nettleham, Lincs., 1301

Neuilly, France, Ty of, 1919

Neuve Chapelle, France, battle of, 1915

Neville, Anne (1456–85), Q. Consort, 1470, 1472

Neville, George (d.1476), Archbp, 1467

Neville, Isabel (1453–76), D. of Clarence, 1469

Neville's Cross, Durham, battle of, 1346

Nevison, John (1639–84), 1684

New (Albery) Theatre, London, 1944

New Brunswick, Canada, 1867

New College, Oxford, 1379, 1382

New Cross, London, 1954

New Forest, Hants., 1079

New Lanark, Scotland, 1800

New Orleans, battle of, 1815

New River canal, London, 1613

New Romney, Kent, 1921

New South Wales, Australia, 1880, 1885

New York, 1664, 1667, 1776; Metropolitan Opera House, 1949

New Zealand, 1769, 1840–1, 1845, 1852, 1856, 1860–1, 1868, 1880

Newark, New Jersey, 1813

Newark, Notts., 1216

Newbery, John (c.1550–85), 1584

Newburn, Northumberland, battle of, 1640

Newbury, Berks., battles of, 1643–4

Newby, P. H. (1918–), 1969

Newcastle, D. of, Thomas Pelham (1693–1768), 1724, 1754, 1756–7, 1762

Newcastle-upon-Tyne, Northumberland, 1080, 1095, 1215, 1244, 1334, 1640, 1646, 1849, 1878, 1891, 1935

Newfoundland, 1481, 1858, 1901, 1919, 1933, 1941

Newgate, London, 1868; prison, 1820

Newham, London, City airport, 1987; Ronan Point, 1968

Newman, John Henry (1801–90), Cardinal, 1833, 1841, 1845, 1864, 1866

Newmarket, Suffolk, 1634, 1647, 1671, 1809

Newnham College, Cambridge, 1871

Newport, Christopher (1565–1617), 1606–7

Newport, Wales, 1839

Newstead, Scotland, 81, 105, 139, 160, 185

Newton, Isaac (1642–1727), 1669, 1683–4, 1686, 1705–6

Niall (c.379–c.405), K. of Ireland, 405

Nicholas I (1796–1855), Tsar, 1844, 1853

Nicholas II (1868–1918), Tsar, 1896, 1908

Nicolson, Arthur (1849–1928), 1906

Niger, R., Africa, 1795, 1805, 1885

Nigeria, 1898, 1960

Nightingale, Florence (1820–1910), 1854, 1907

Nijinsky, Vaslav (1890–1950), 1911

Nile, R., 1864, 1874; battle of, 1798

Nine Elms, London, 1974

Ninian, St (d.c.432), 397

Nixon, Richard (1913–), Pres. of USA, 1971

Noel-Baker, Philip (1889–1982), 1959

Nombre de Dios, Panama, 1572

Nonsuch Palace, London, Ty of, 1585

Nootka Sound, Vancouver, 1789–90

Norden, John (1548–1623), 1593

Nore, Kent, 1797

Norfolk, 1549, 1649

Norfolk, DD of, Thomas Howard (1473–1554), 1523, 1536, 1540, 1542; Thomas Howard (1536–72), 1569–72; Thomas Mowbray (d.1399), 1387, 1398

Norfolk House, London, 1738

Norham Castle, Northumberland, 1209, 1291, 1497, 1513

Normandy, 1944

Normandy, Duchy of, 1000, 1091, 1096, 1102, 1104–6, 1137, 1144, 1150–1, 1169, 1199, 1204, 1346, 1369, 1419–20, 1434, 1449–50, 1522, 1589, 1591

Norris, John (1547–97), 1586, 1589, 1595

North Antrim, N. Ireland, 1970

North Creake, Norfolk, 25–20 BC

North Foreland, Kent, battle of, 1653

North, Frederick, Lord (1732–92), 1770, 1773–4, 1780, 1782–3

North London Collegiate School, 1870

North Sea, 1965–6, 1988

North, Thomas (c.1535–c.1603), 1579

Northampton, 1215, 1264; Assize of, 1176; battle of, 1460; Council of, 1164; Ty of, 1328

Northamptonshire, 1607

Northcote, Stafford (1818–87), 1874, 1881

Northern Ireland, 1920–1, 1925, 1966, 1968–70, 1971–6, 1979–80, 1985, 1987

Northey island, Essex, 991

Northumberland, DD of, Alan Percy (1880–1930), 1922; John Dudley (1502–53), 1546, 1549, 1551–3

Northumberland, EE of, Henry Percy (1341–1408), 1402–3, 1405, 1408; Henry Percy (c.1449–89), 1489; Thomas Percy (1528–72), 1569; Robert de Mowbray, 1095

Northumberland, 1139, 1157 (see also Northumbria)

Northumbria, kingdom of, 593, 603, 613/16, 627, 632, 634, 641–2, 867, 875–6, (see also Bernicia, Deira); earldom of, 1017

Northumbria, 914, 918, 947–8, 957, (see also Northumberland)

Norton, Thomas (1532–84), 1561

Norwich, Norfolk, 1531, 1580, 1600, 1785, 1810, 1942, 1963; Castle, 1075; Cathedral, 1096, 1321; City Hall, 1938

Notre Dame, Paris, 1625

Notting Hill, London, 1958, 1976

Nottingham, 867, 877, 1336, 1387, 1642, 1811, 1817, 1958; Castle, 1068

Nova Scotia, Canada, 1763, 1867

Novello, Ivor (1893–1951), 1935, 1939

Noyes, Geoffrey de, 1208

Nullarbor Plain, Australia, 1841

Nuremberg, Germany, Ty of, 1294

Nyasaland (Malawi), 1953, 1964

557

1840
Parnell, Charles (1846–91), 1877, 1880–2, 1884–5, 1887, 1889–90
Parr, Catherine (1512–48), Q. Consort, 1542
Parry, William (d.1585), 1585
Parsons, Charles (1854–1931), 1884
Parsons, Robert (1546–1610), 1580
Partick, Scotland, 1872
Pas-de-Calais, France, 1944
Passchendaele, Belgium, battle of, 1917
Passfield, Lord (see Webb, Sidney)
Paston family, 1420
Patay, France, battle of, 1429
Pater, Walter (1839–94), 1873, 1885
Paterson, James (1854–1932), 1878
Patras, Greece, 1944
Patrick, St (d.?461), 431, 455
Patterson, Paul (1947–), 1983
Paul, Lewis (c.1700–59), 1760
Paul, Roman official, 353
Paul VI (1897–1978), Pope, 1966, 1970
Paulinus (d.644), Bp, 627, 632
Paviland Cave, Wales, 26,000-10,000 BC
Pavilion Theatre, London, 1896
Paxton, Joseph (1801–65), 1851
Peacock, Thomas (1785–1866), 1816, 1818, 1831
Pearl Harbor, USA, 1941
Pearson, J. L. (1817–97), 1880
Pecham, John (d.1292), Archbp, 1279
Pecock, Reginald (1395–c.1460), 1455
Pedro (d.1369), K. of Castile, 1367
Peel, Robert (1788–1850), 1819, 1822–3, 1834–5, 1839, 1841–6, 1850
Peiho, R., China, 1859
Peking (Beijing), 1859–60, 1900, 1986; Convention of, 1898; Treaties of, 1860, 1984
Pelagians, 429, 446–7
Pelagius, 425
Pelham, Henry (1696–1754), 1724, 1743, 1746–7, 1754
Peloponnese, Greece, 1941, 1944
Pembroke, EE of, Aymer de Valence (d.1324), 1317; Jasper Tudor (1431–95), 1453; Richard de Clare, 'Strongbow' (c.1130–76), 1170–1; Richard Marshal (d.1234), 1232–4; William Herbert (1501–70), 1557; William Marshal II (d.1231), 1223
Pembroke, Wales, 400, 1215, 1219, 1684; Castle, 1093–4, 1648
Penang I., Malaysia, 1786
Penda (d.654), K. of Mercia, 628, 632, 642, 654
Penn, William (1644–1718), 1668, 1681, 1693

Penn-in-the-Rocks, Sussex, 1930
Pennine Mts, 154–5, 197, 1816
Penruddock, John (1619–56), Col., 1655
Penry, John (d.1593), 1593
Pentridge, Derbys., 1817
Penzance, Cornwall, 1595
People's Palace, London, 1887
Pepys, Samuel (1633–1709), 1660, 1669, 1686, 1825
Perceval, Spencer (1762–1812), 1809, 1812
Percy, Henry 'Hotspur' (1363–1403), 1388, 1401–3
Perivale Hoover factory, London, 1932
Péronne, France, 1917–18
Perreal, Jean, 1516
Perrers, Alice (d.1400), 1369–70, 1375–6
Perrot, John (1527–92), 1573
Perrot, Jules (1810–94), 1845
Perry, Fred (1909–), 1934
Pershore Abbey, Worcs, 961
Persia (see also Iran), 1873, 1899, 1907
Perth, Scotland, 1313, 1335, 1559, 1715; pacification of, 1573; Ty of, 1266
Pertinax, 185, 187
Peter I (1672–1725), Tsar, 1698
Peter Martyr (1500–62), 1548
Peterborough, Cambs., 1541–2, 1938; Abbey, 963, 1070; Cathedral, 1117
Peterborough, E. of, Charles Mordaunt (1658–1735), 1705–6
Peterhead, Scotland, 1715
Petilius Cerealis, 61, 71
Petty, William (1623–87), 1682
Pevensey, Sussex, 343, 1066
Philadelphia, Pennsylvania, 1774, 1777–8
Philby, Kim (1911–88), 1963
Philip II (1527–98), K. of Spain, 1554
Philip II (1165–1223), K. of France, 1180, 1186–9, 1192, 1195, 1198–1200, 1202, 1204, 1206, 1214
Philip III (1245–85), K. of France, 1273
Philip IV (1268–1314), K. of France, 1286, 1294
Philip VI (1293–1350), K. of France, 1329, 1331, 1337, 1346
Philip, P., D. of Edinburgh (1921–), 1947, 1955–6
Philiphaugh, Scotland, battle of, 1645
Philippa of Hainault (c.1314–69), Q. Consort, 1326, 1328, 1369
Phoenix Park, Dublin, 1882
Picardy, France, 1369, 1522–3, 1914
Picasso, Pablo (1881–1973), 1919
Picquigny, France, Ty of, 1475

Pierce, R. (1884–1968), 1938
Pigott, Richard (c.1828–89), 1889
Pilleth, Wales, battle of, 1402
Pilltown, Ireland, battle of, 1462
Pinero, Arthur (1855–1934), 1885, 1893, 1898
Pinewood studios, Bucks., 1936
Pinkie, Scotland, battle of, 1546
Pinter, Harold (1930–), 1958, 1960, 1965, 1976
Piper, John (1903–), 1934, 1942, 1962, 1967
Piraeus, Greece, 1850, 1941
Pitman, Isaac (1813–97), 1837
Pitt, William (1759–1806), 1782–6, 1789–91, 1793–5, 1798–9, 1801, 1804, 1806
Pitt-Rivers, Augustus (1827–1900), Gen., 1882
Plassey, India, battle of, 1757
Plate, R., battle of, 1939
Platorius Nepos, 122
Playfair, Nigel (1874–1934), 1918
Playford, John (1623–86), 1650
Plimsoll, Samuel (1824–98), 1876
Plummer, John (d.c.1462), 1444
Plymouth, Devon, 800–450 BC, 330–320 BC, AD 1568, 1577–8, 1580, 1586, 1591, 1595, 1617, 1620, 1830, 1919, 1941, 1955, 1966–7; Theatre Royal, 1982
Pocahontas (1593/7–1617), P. 1617
Poitiers, France, 1372; battle of, 1356
Poitou, 1206, 1224, 1242, 1259, 1372
Poldhu, Cornwall, 1901
Pole, Reginald (1500–58), Cardinal Archbp, 1536, 1540, 1555–6, 1558
Pompeius Falco, 118
Pompidou, Georges (1911–74), 1971
Pondicherry, India, 1761
Pontefract, Yorks., 1319, 1321–2; Castle, 1400
Pontnewydd cave, Wales, 200,000 BC
Pontoise, France, 1419, 1437, 1441
Poona, India, 1819, 1933–4
Pope, Alexander (1688–1744), 1711–12, 1714, 1728
Poplar, London, 1921
Popper, Karl (1902–), 1945
Porson, Richard (1759–1808), 1794
Port Arthur (Lu-ta), China, 1897–8
Port Hamilton, Korea, 1885
Port Moresby, New Guinea, 1883
Port Said, Egypt, 1956
Port Stanley, E. Falkland, 1982
Portchester, Hants, 270
Portland, Dorset, 786
Portland, D. of, William Bentinck (1738–1809), 1783, 1807, 1809
Porto Bello, Panama, 1739
Portree, I. of Skye, 1746
Portsmouth, Hants., 1101, 1338,

1926, 1930–1, 1937
Sadler's Wells Theatre, London, 1828, 1931, 1935, 1975
Sahagun, Spain, battle of, 1808
St Albans, Herts., 80–50 BC, AD 1326, 1381; battles of, 1455, 1461; Cathedral, 1077; Roman, 43–7, 51, 61, 75–80, 220, 270–90
St Andrews, Scotland, 1304, 1546–7, 1754; Abbey, 761, 834; University of, 1413
St Anne, Limehouse, London, 1715–20
St Bartholomew, Smithfield, London, Hospital, 1123, 1544; Priory, 1123, 1133
St Catherine's College, Cambridge, 1966
St David's, Wales, 547, 1081
St George-in-the-East, London, 1715–20, 1859
St George's Chapel, Windsor, 1348, 1474, 1519
St George's Hill, Weybridge, Surrey, 1649
St Germain, France, Ty of, 1919
St Giles's Cathedral, Edinburgh, 1637
St Helena, I. of, 1676–7, 1815
St James's Palace, London, 1532, 1558, 1630, 1677, 1683, 1736–7, 1743, 1912, 1920, 1924; Chapel Royal, 1840
St James's Sq., London, 1984
St James's Theatre, London, 1951
St John, Smith Sq., London, 1715–20
St John's College, Cambridge, 1509
St John's, Newfoundland, 1583
St Just in Penwith, Cornwall, 1375
St Katharine's Dock, London, 1828, 1973
St Lawrence Seaway, Canada, 1959
St Leger, Barry (1737–89), Col., 1778
St Lucia Bay, South Africa, 1884
St Lucia, West Indies, 1797, 1803, 1814
St Malo, Brittany, 1230, 1379
St Martin-in-the-Fields, London, 1722
St Martin's Lane, London, 1754
St Mary, Deerhurst, Glos., 970
St Mary, Putney, London, 1647
St Mary's Hospital, London, 1928, 1982
St Mawgan, Cornwall, 300 BC
St Michael's Mount, Cornwall, 330–20 BC, AD 1473–4
St Nazaire, France, 1942
St Omer, France, 1313
St Pancras, London, Hotel, 1868; station hall, 1874; town hall, 1960
St Paul's Cathedral, London, 604, 1087, 1395, 1458, 1561, 1580, 1666, 1675, 1697, 1789, 1951;

1981
St Paul's School, London, 1509
St Peter and St Wilfrid, Ripon, Yorks., 1456
St Petersburg, 1874; Convention, 1907
St Stephen, Walbrook, London, 1672, 1953
St Stephen's Chapel, Westminster, 1298
St Vincent, E., John Jervis (1735–1823), Adm., 1797
Salamanca, Spain, 1808; battle of, 1812
Salerno, Italy, 1943
Salford, Lancs., 1890; University of, 1967
Salisbury, Countess of, Margaret (1471–1541), 1541
Salisbury, E. of, Robert Cecil (1563–1612), 1612
Salisbury, Mqs of, James Cecil (1830–1904), 1876–8, 1881, 1884–7, 1889, 1891–3, 1895–1902
Salisbury (Harare), Zimbabwe, 1890–1
Salisbury, Wilts., 1075, 1075–8, 1220, 1258, 1289, 1483; Council of, 1086
Salonika (Thessaloniki), Greece, 1915, 1918
Samoa, 1887
Sampson, Richard (1470–1554), 1516
Samuel, Herbert (1870–1963), 1920–1, 1925–6, 1943
San Carlos Bay, E. Falkland, 1982
San Francisco, USA, 1579; Conference, 1945
San Juan de Ulloa, Mexico, battle of, 1568
San Sebastian, Spain, 1813
Sancroft, William (1617–93), Archbp, 1688–9
Sandringham House, Norfolk, 1936, 1952
Sands, Bobby (1954–81), 1981
Sandwich Is, 1778
Sandwich, Kent, 851, 1009, 1048, 1217, 1457, 1460
Sanger, Frederick (1918–), 1980
Sankey, Ira (1840–1908), 1873
Santa Cruz, Panama, 1797
Santa Cruz, Tenerife, 1657
Saragossa, Spain, battle of, 1710
Saratoga, NY, 1777
Sarawak, 1888, 1962
Sargent, John (1856–1925), 1898, 1900, 1913, 1926
Sassoon, Siegfried (1886–1967), 1917–18
Savannah, Georgia, 1733, 1778
Savoy Palace, London, 1377, 1381
Savoy Theatre, London, 1881, 1896
Sawtrey, William (d.1401), 1401

Saxe, Maurice (1696–1750), Marshal, 1745, 1747
Saxon Shore, 270, 343
Saxons, 220, 430, 447–50, 455, 490
Saxton, Christopher (c.1533–96), 1575
Say, James Fiennes, Lord (d.1450), 1450
Sayers, Dorothy L. (1893–1957), 1923, 1934, 1943
Sayers, Tom (1826–65), 1860
Scapa Flow, Scotland, 1918–19, 1939
Scarborough, Yorks., 1312, 1914; Library Theatre, 1973
Schleswig-Holstein, 1863–4
Schomberg, D. of, Frederick (1615–90), 1689
Scilly Is, 1646
Scofield, Paul (1922–), 1946
Scone, Scotland, 906, 1296, 1306, 1357
Scot, Michael (c.1175–c.1235), 1220
Scotland, 81–4, 1296–1307, 1332–7, 1354, 1356–7, 1385, 1457, 1557, 1559–60, 1607, 1610, 1616, 1618, 1638–40, 1650, 1689, 1692, 1695, 1703–7, 1715, 1726, 1745–6, 1843, 1861, 1872, 1878, 1888–9, 1929, 1986
Scott, C. P. (1846–1932), 1872
Scott, Elizabeth (1898–1972), 1928
Scott, George Gilbert (1811–78), 1868, 1872
Scott, Giles Gilbert (1880–1960), 1903, 1933–4, 1978
Scott, Paul (1920–78), 1966
Scott, Robert (1868–1912), Cap., 1901–2, 1910, 1912
Scott, Walter (1771–1832), 1802–3, 1805, 1808, 1810, 1814–16, 1818, 1821, 1824, 1826–7
Scrope, Henry, Lord (d.1415), 1415
Scrope, Richard (d.1405), Archbp, 1405
Scutari (Uskudar), Turkey, 1854
Sebastopol, Crimea, 1854–6
Sedgemoor, Somerset, battle of, 1685
Seeley, John Robert (1834–95), 1866, 1883
Segu, Nigeria, 1795
Seine, R., France, 1416
Selby, Yorks., 1976
Selden, John (1584–1654), 1617, 1632
Selfridge's store, London, 1909
Sellar, W. C. (1898–1951), 1930
Selsdon Park Hotel, Croydon, 1970
Selsey, Sussex, 477, 1075
Selwyn Lloyd, John (1904–78), 1955–6, 1959–60, 1962
Seoul, S. Korea, 1988
Seringapatam, India, battles of, 1792, 1799
Severn, R., 49–51, 577, 628, 757,

784, 1772, 1789, 1886
Severn Road Bridge, Glos., 1966
Severus (146–211), Rom. Emp., 192, 196–7, 208–9, 211
Sèvres, France, Ty of, 1920
Seychelles Is, 1956
Seymour, Jane (1509–37), Q. Consort, 1536–7
Seymour, Thomas (1508–49), 1549
Seymour, William (1588–1660), 1610
Shackleton, Ernest (1874–1922), 1902, 1908–9, 1914
Shadwell, Thomas (1642–96), 1688
Shaffer, Peter (1926–), 1958, 1964, 1979, 1987
Shaftesbury, EE of, Anthony Ashley Cooper (1621–83), 1667, 1673, 1675, 1678–82; Anthony Ashley Cooper (1801–85), 1842, 1843, 1876, 1884
Shakespeare, William (1564–1616), 1590, 1592–1611, 1613, 1616, 1623
Sharp, Cecil (1859–1924), 1911
Sharp, James (1618–79), Archbp, 1679
Shaw, G. B. (1856–1950), 1889, 1892, 1894–5, 1897, 1899–1900, 1905–6, 1909, 1913–14, 1921, 1923–5, 1928–9, 1951
Shaxton, Nicholas (1485–1556), Bp, 1539
Sheen Palace, Surrey, 1497
Sheerness, Kent, 1667
Sheffield, Yorks., 1903, 1945; Hillsborough Stadium, 1989; University of, 1905
Shelburne, E. of, William Petty (1737–1805), 1782–3
Sheldonian Theatre, Oxford, 1664, 1791, 1864
Shelley, Mary (1797–1851), 1818
Shelley, Percy (1792–1822), 1813, 1820–1
Shepherd, Edward (16?–1747), 1731–2, 1736
Shepherd's Bush studios, London, 1927
Sheppard, Jack (1703–24), 1724
Sheppey, Kent, 835
Shepstone, Theophilus 1877
Sherborne, Dorset, 1075
Sherburn-in-Elmet, Yorks., 1321
Sheridan, Richard (1751–1816), 1775, 1777, 1779
Sheriff, R. C. (1896–1975), 1928
Sheriffmuir, Scotland, battle of, 1715
Sherrington, Charles (1857–1952), 1932
Shetland Is, Scotland, 860, 1468, 1472
Shillibeer, George (1797–1866), 1829
Shirley, Anthony (1565–1635), 1613
Shoreditch, London, 1576

Shrapnel, Henry (1761–1842), Maj., 1803
Shrewsbury, EE of, Charles Talbot (1660–1718), 1694, 1714; Robert de Belleme (d.c.1113), 1102, 1111–12; Roger de Montgomery (d.1094), 1075
Shrewsbury, Shrops., 1214, 1387, 1398; battle of, 1403
Shute, John, 1563
Siam (Thailand), 1893
Sicily, 1860, 1943
Sickert, Walter (1860–1942), 1886, 1911–12
Siddons, Sarah (1755–1831), 1775, 1782, 1784, 1812
Sidgwick, Henry (1838–1900), 1874, 1882
Sidi Barrani, Egypt, 1940
Sidney, Algernon (?1622–83), 1683
Sidney, Henry (1529–86), 1566
Sidney, Philip (1554–86), 1586
Sidney St, London, 1911
Sierra Leone, 1562, 1808, 1882
Sigismund (1368–1437), HRE, 1416
Sigtuna, Sweden, 1015
Sihtric (d.927), K. of York, 914, 920, 927
Silbury Hill, Wilts., 3,000–2,400 BC
Silchester, Hants., 51, 80–50 BC, AD 130, 296, 360
Sillitoe, Alan (1928–), 1958
Silures, 49, 51, 74
Silvertown, London, 1917
Simeon, Charles (1759–1836), 1783
Simnel, Lambert (c.1477–c.1534), 1487
Simon, John (1873–1954), 1926, 1930–1, 1937
Simonstown, South Africa, 1975
Simpson, Thomas (1710–61), 1737
Simpson, Wallis (1896–1986), D. of Windsor, 1931, 1936–7
Sims, George, 1883
Sinclair, Clive (1940–), 1985
Singapore, 1819, 1942, 1945, 1959, 1962, 1968
Sinope, Turkey, 1853
Siraj-ud-Daula (d.1757), 1756–7
Sitwell, Edith (1887–1964), 1915, 1923
Siward, E. of Northumbria (d.1055), 1023, 1035, 1054–5
Skara Brae, Orkney, 3000–2400 BC
Skegness, Lincs., 1936, 1988
Skelton, John (c.1460–1529), 1523
Skipton, Yorks., 1944
Skye, I. of, Scotland, 795
Slade School of Fine Art, London, 1871
Slater, James, 1864
Sligo, Ireland, 1979
Slim, William (1891–1970), Gen., 1944–5
Sluys, Netherlands, battle of, 1340

Smethwick, W. Midlands, 1964
Smirke, Robert (1781–1867), 1823
Smith, Adam (1723–90), 1776
Smith, Ian (1919–), 1964–6, 1968, 1977
Smith, John (1580–1631), 1607, 1616
Smith, Keith (1890–1955), 1919
Smith, Maggie (1934–), 1964
Smith, Ross (1892–1922), 1919
Smith, Sidney (1764–1840), Adm., 1799
Smithfield, London, 1123, 1133, 1362, 1381, 1401, 1555
Smollett, Tobias (1721–71), 1748, 1751, 1771
Smuts, Jan (1870–1950), Gen. 1899, 1917
Smyrna (Izmir), Turkey, 1922
Smyth, Ethel (1858–1944), 1909, 1916
Smythson, Robert (c.1535–1614), 1568, 1574, 1580
Snettisham, Norfolk, 25–20 BC
Snow, C. P. (1905–80), 1940, 1947, 1951, 1954, 1959, 1964, 1970
Snowden, Philip (1864–1937), 1929, 1931
Soames, Christopher, Lord (1920–87), 1979
Soane, John (1753–1837), 1795, 1814
Sobrahan, India, battle of, 1846
Soddy, Frederick (1877–1956), 1904, 1913, 1921
Soho, London, 1676
Solent, The, 1929, 1944
Solway Moss, Cumbria, battle of, 1542
Solway, R., 105, 122, 613/16, 1778
Somaliland, 1884
Somers, George (1554–1610), 1610
Somers, John, Lord (1651–1716), 1694, 1697, 1700, 1710
Somerset, 658
Somerset, DD of, Edmund Beaufort (c.1406–55), 1446, 1448–50, 1452–3, 1455; Henry Beaufort (c.1436–64), 1460, 1464; John Beaufort (1404–44), 1443; Edward Seymour (c.1506–52), 1544–50, 1552
Somerset House, London, 1547–50
Somerville College, Oxford, 1879
Somerville, John (1560–83), 1583
Somme, R., France, battles of, 1916, 1918
Sophia (1630–1714), Electress, 1701, 1714
South Africa, 1835, 1838, 1877, 1899–1903
South Australia, 1850
South Cadbury, Somerset, 490
South Georgia, I. of, 1982
South Kensington, London, 1862
South Pole, 1909, 1912

Southampton, Hants., 296, 495, 842, 1338, 1415, 1936, 1940; Old Green, 1299
Southend, Essex, 1889, 1948
Southey, Robert (1774–1843), 1805, 1813
Southwark, London, 1450, 1676, 1849–50, 1861
Southwell, Notts., 1646; Minster, 1108
Southwell, Robert (1561–95), 1595
Southwick, Sussex, 1651
Southwold Bay, Suffolk, battle of, 1672
Soviet Union, 1987
Spa Fields, Clerkenwell, London, 1779, 1816
Spark, Muriel (1918–), 1957, 1960–1, 1963, 1965, 1974
Speaight, Robert (1904–76), 1935
Spee, Maximilian von (1861–1914), Adm., 1914
Speenhamland, Berks., 1795
Speke, John (1827–64), 1857
Spence, Basil (1907–76), 1962–4
Spencer, Herbert (1820–1903), 1850, 1862, 1873
Spencer, Stanley (1891–1959), 1923, 1926, 1932, 1941
Spenser, Edmund (?1552–99), 1579, 1595
Speymouth, Scotland, 1650
Spion Kop, South Africa, battle of, 1900
Spitalfields, London, 1719
Spithead, Hants., 1797, 1887, 1896
Spode, Josiah (1754–1827), 1800
Spurgeon, Charles (1834–92), 1857
Stainmore, Yorks., 971; battle of, 954
Stalin, Joseph (1879–1953), 1942–5
Stalybridge, Lancs., 1862
Stamford Bridge, Yorks., battle of, 1066
Stamford, Lincs., 877, 1309; University of, 1334
Stane Street, 43–7
Stanegate, 85
Stanford, Charles (1852–1924), 1884
Stanhope, Vct, James (1675–1721), 1710, 1714, 1716–17
Stanley, Henry (1841–1904), 1870–1, 1874, 1877, 1890
Stanley, William (145?–95), 1495
Staple How, Yorks., 800–450 BC
Stapledon, Walter (d.1326), Bp, 1323, 1326
Star Carr, Yorks., 8,300 BC
Starr, Ringo (1940–), 1963, 1967, 1970
Steel, David (1938–), 1976–8
Steele, Richard (1672–1729), 1709, 1711
Steelyard, London, 1157, 1474
Steenkerk, Netherlands, battle of, 1692
Steer, Wilson (1860–1942), 1886
Stein, Marion (1926–), 1949
Stenness, Orkney, 3,000–2,400 BC
Stephen (c.1100–1154), K., 1135–7, 1139, 1141–2, 1145, 1147, 1149, 1152–4
Stephen Harding, St (d.1133), 1119
Stephen, Leslie (1832–1904), 1882, 1900
Stephens, James (1825–1901), 1858
Stephenson, George (1781–1848), 1814, 1829, 1830
Stephenson, Robert (1803–59), 1849–50
Stepney, London, 1867
Sterne, Laurence (1713–68), 1759, 1767–8
Stevenson, Robert Louis (1850–94), 1879, 1881–3, 1886, 1893
Stewart, Michael (1906–89), 1965–6, 1968
Stigand (d.1070), Archbp, 1043–4, 1070
Stilicho (d.408), Gen., 396–8, 401
Stirling Bridge, Scotland, battle of, 1297
Stirling, Scotland, 1452, 1487, 1571, 1639; Castle, 1299, 1304, 1313, 1337
Stockport, Lancs., 1817
Stockton, Cleveland, 1825
Stockwell, London, 1890
Stoke, Notts., battle of, 1487
Stoke-on-Trent, Staffs., 1800
Stonecutter's I., China, 1858
Stonehenge, Wilts., 3,000–2,400 BC, 2,400 BC, 2,300 BC, 1,800–1,400 BC, AD 1136
Stonyhurst School, Lancs., 1794
Stopes, Marie (1880–1958), 1916, 1921
Stoppard, Tom (1937–), 1967, 1981–2
Storey, David (1933–), 1962
Stormberg, South Africa, battle of, 1899
Stow, John (1525–1605), 1580, 1598
Stow-on-the-Wold, Glos., 1646
Strachey, John (1901–63), 1932
Strachey, Lytton (1880–1932), 1918, 1921
Strafford, E. of, Thomas Wentworth (1593–1641), 1628, 1633, 1639–41
Strand Inn, London, 1292
Strangford Lough, Ireland, battle of, 877
Stratford, John (d.1348), Archbp, 1330, 1333, 1339–41
Stratford, Robert (d.1362), Bp, 1340
Stratford-upon-Avon, Warks., 1616; Memorial Theatre 1926, 1928, 1932, 1946, 1952, 1960
Strathclyde, kingdom of, 400, 600, 900, 945
Stravinsky, Igor (1882–1971), 1912, 1935
Street, George (1824–81), 1874
Stresa, Italy, Conference, 1935
Strode, Richard, 1512
Struma, R. (Strymon), Greece, battle of, 1917
Strutt, Jebediah (1726–97), 1759
Stuart, Arbella (1575–1615), 1610–11, 1615
Stuart, James (1713–88), 1794
Stubbs, George (1724–1806), 1766
Stubbs, John (1541–91), 1579
Studley Royal, Yorks., 1718–19
Sturt, Charles (1795–1869), 1828–9
Stuttgart, Germany, 1944
Suckling, John (1609–41), 1638, 1646
Sudan, 1883–5, 1896, 1898–9, 1953
Sudbury, Simon (d.1381), Archbp, 1381
Suetonius Paulinus, 58, 60–1
Suez Canal, 1869, 1875, 1915, 1956
Suffolk, 1874
Suffolk, DD of, Charles Brandon (1484–1545), 1514, 1522–3, 1530; William de la Pole (1396–1450), 1444, 1446, 1450
Suffolk, EE of, Edmund de la Pole (c.1472–1513), 1506, 1513; Michael de la Pole (c.1330–89), 1383, 1385–7; Thomas Howard (1561–1626), 1618
Sullivan, Arthur (1842–1900), 1875, 1877–8, 1880–2, 1884–5, 1887–9, 1893, 1896, 1951
Sumatra, 1601
Summerhill Creek, New South Wales, 1851
Sunderland, E. of, Charles Spencer (1675–1722), 1706, 1710
Sunderland, Tyne and Wear, 1986
Sunningdale Conference, Berks., 1973
Surrey, University of, 1966
Surrey, E. of, Thomas Howard (1443–1524), 1513
Surtees, Robert (1805–64), 1838
Sussex, 490, 680, 771, 1987; University of, 1961, 1964
Sutherland, Graham (1903–80), 1942, 1949, 1951, 1954, 1962
Sutton Hoo, Suffolk, 621–30, 1939
Swan, Joseph (1828–1914), 1860, 1864, 1878, 1880
Swan Theatre, London, 1597
Swanscombe, Kent, 250,000 BC
Swansea, Wales, 1136
Swein, K. of Denmark, 1070
Swein (d.1036), K. of Norway, 1028
Swein (d.1014), K. of Denmark, 994
Swein Godwinsson, (d.1052), E., 1043, 1046, 1049–51
Swift, Jonathan (1667–1745), 1701, 1704, 1714, 1725–6

1738), 1709, 1714, 1716, 1721, 1730
Towton, Yorks., battle of, 1461
Toynbee, Arnold (1889–1975), 1934, 1961
Toynbee Hall, London, 1884
Tradescant, John (c.1585–1638), 1617
Trafalgar, battle of, 1805
Trafalgar Sq., London, 1840, 1887, 1956, 1958–61, 1976
Tranby Croft, Yorks., 1891
Transkei, South Africa, 1877
Transport House, London, 1928
Transvaal, South Africa, 1852, 1877, 1880–1, 1884, 1895, 1899–1900, 1906
Travellers' Club, London, 1831
Travers, Ben (1886–1980), 1926–8, 1976
Tree, Herbert (1853–1917), 1914
Trent, R., battle of, 678
Trenton, New Jersey, battle of, 1776
Trevelyan, G. M. (1876–1962), 1926, 1944
Trevisa, John (c.1340–1402), 1387
Trevisker, Cornwall, 1,400 BC
Trevithick, Richard (1771–1833), 1801, 1804
Trianon, France, Ty of, 1920
Trincomalee, Sri Lanka, 1795
Trinidad, West Indies, 1797, 1962
Trinity College, Cambridge, 1546, 1676
Trinity House, London, 1514
Trinovantes, 100 BC, 54 BC, 34–27 BC, AD 7, 61
Tripoli, Libya, 1943
Trollope, Anthony (1815–82), 1855, 1857, 1861, 1864, 1867, 1869
Trollope, Frances (1780–1863), 1832
Tromp, Cornelis (1629–91), Adm., 1652–3
Tromso Fjord, Norway, 1944
Trotsky, Leon (1879–1940), 1902
Troyes, France, Treaties of, 1420–1, 1564
Truman, Christine (1941–), 1961
Truro, Cornwall, 1646; Cathedral, 1880
Tuam, Ireland, See of, 1152
Tubbs, Ralph (1912–), 1951
Tudor, Gwilym, 1400
Tudor, Owen (c.1399–1461), 1429, 1461
Tudor, Rhys, 1400
Tull, Jethro (1674–1741), 1701, 1733
Tunbridge Wells, Kent, 1895
Tunis, 1943
Tunstall, Cuthbert (1474–1559), Bp, 1527, 1552
Turin, Italy, Ty of, 1855
Turkana, Lake, Kenya, 1972
Turkey, 1853–4, 1876–8, 1922
Turnbull, William (c.1410–54), Bp,

1451
Turner, Ben (1863–1942), 1928
Turner, J. M. W. (1775–1851), 1797, 1803–4, 1813, 1839, 1844
Turnham Green, London, 1696
Turpin, Dick (1705–39), 1739
Tussaud, Marie (1761–1850), 1802
Tut'ankhamun (d.c.1,340 BC), 1922, 1972
Tutbury Castle, Staffs., 1569
Tweed, R., Scotland, 81, 1640
Twickenham, Middlesex, 1415
Tyburn, London, 1537, 1577, 1581, 1586, 1594–5, 1661, 1724–5, 1760
Tyler, Wat (d.1381), 1381
Tynan, Kenneth (1927–80), 1970
Tyndale, William (1494–1536), 1526, 1530, 1539
Tyne, R., Northumberland, 105, 122, 122–39, 270–90, 1849
Tyrconnell, EE of, Richard Talbot (1630–91), 1687; Rory O'Donnell (1575–1608), 1607
Tyrell, William (14?–1502), 1502
Tyrone, EE of, Hugh O'Neill (1540–1616), 1594–6, 1598, 1601, 1603, 1607; Shane O'Neill (c.1515–67), 1562, 1567

Uganda, 1890, 1893–4, 1962, 1972, 1976, 1977
Ujiji, Tanzania, 1871
Ulpius Marcellus, 180, 185
Ulster, 1177, 1594, 1609, 1797, 1912–14, 1956, 1969
Ulster, EE of, Richard de Burgh (d.1326), 1315; William de Burgh (d.1333), 1333
Ulundi, Africa, battle of, 1879
University College, Cambridge, 1965
University College, London, 1826, 1871
University College, Oxford, 1280
Ur, Iraq, 1922
Urban II (d.1099), Pope, 1095
USA, 1939
Usk, Gwent, battle of, 1405; Castle, 1233
Ussher, James (1581–1656), Archbp, 1650
Utrecht, Netherlands, treaties of, 1474, 1712–13
Uxbridge, Middlesex, 1645

Valencia, Spain, 1706
Van Diemen's Gulf, Australia, 1861
Van Dyck, Anthony (1599–1641), 1632, 1634, 1637
Vanbrugh, John (1664–1726), 1696–7, 1702, 1705, 1707
Vancouver, George (1758–98), Cap., 1791, 1794
Varah, Chad (1911–), 1953
Varius Marcellus, 197
Varna, Bulgaria, 1854

Vaughan, Henry (1621–95), 1646
Vaughan Williams, Ralph (1872–1958), 1906, 1910, 1924, 1931, 1948, 1951
Venezuela, 1902, 1903
Venlo, Netherlands, 1702
Venn, John (1759–1813), 1799
Ventris, Michael (1922–56), 1952
Vera Cruz, Mexico, 1862
Vereeniging, South Africa, 1902
Vergil, Polydore (c.1470–c.1555), 1506
Vermuyden, Cornelius (c.1594–1683), 1634
Vernon, Edward (1684–1757), 1739, 1741
Verona, Italy, Congress of, 1821
Versailles, France, treaties of, 1783, 1919
Vertue, Robert, 1519
Verwoerd, Hendrik (1901–66), 1961
Vesey, Elizabeth (1715–91), 1754–5
Vespasian (d.79), Rom. Emp., 43
Vettius Bolanus, 68
Vexin, Normandy, 1151, 1160, 1195, 1198, 1200
Victoria and Albert Museum, London, 1909
Victoria (1819–1901), Q., 1819, 1837–40, 1842–4, 1848, 1850–1, 1854–5, 1857–60, 1862, 1864, 1866, 1868, 1870–2, 1876–7, 1887, 1893–7, 1899–1901
Victoria (1840–1901), P., German Empress, 1858
Victoria, Australia, 1850
Victoria Falls, Africa, 1855
Victoria Land, Antarctica, 1841
Victoria Palace Theatre, London, 1937
Victoria Park, London, 1845
Victorinus, Gen., 277–8
Vienna, 1955; Congress of, 1814–15; Treaties of, 1731
Vigo Bay, Spain, 1702–4
Vimeiro, Portugal, battle of, 1808
Vimy Ridge, France, battle of, 1917
Virginia, USA, 1585, 1607, 1781
Virius Lupus, 197
Vitoria, Spain, battle of, 1813
Voltaire, François (1694–1778), 1726
Volusenus, Gaius, 55 BC
Vortigern, K., 425, 430
Votadini, 81, 400

Waddell, Helen (1889–1965), 1927
Wade, George (1673–1748), Gen., 1726
Wade, John (1788–1875), 1831
Wadi Halfa, Sudan, 1884
Wagner, Richard (1813–83), 1877, 1914
Wain, John (1925–), 1953, 1958
Waitangi, New Zealand, Ty of, 1840

Waite, Terry (1939–), 1987, 1991
Wakefield, Gibbon (1796–1862), 1829
Wakefield, Yorks., 1450; battle of, 1460
Walbrook, Anton (1900–68), 1937
Walcher (d.1080), Bp, 1076, 1080
Walcher (d.1135), Prior, 1092, 1108–12
Walcheren, Netherlands, 1809
Wales, 18,000–14,000 BC, AD 169 75, 400, 430, 632, 757, 784, 822, 893, 900, 1055–6, 1063, 1094, 1098, 1108, 1136, 1165, 1167, 1177, 1200–1, 1211–13, 1215–16, 1223, 1231, 1233–4, 1240–1, 1245–7, 1255, 1257–8, 1260, 1262, 1274–7, 1282–4, 1287–8, 1301, 1400–5, 1407–9, 1536, 1543, 1811, 1839, 1842, 1889, 1983; University of, 1893
Walker, John (1781–1859), 1827
Wallace, Alfred (1820–1913), 1858
Wallace Collection, London, 1900
Wallace, Edgar (1875–1932), 1928
Wallace, William (d.1305), 1297–8, 1304–5
Waller, Edmund (1606–87), 1645
Wallingford, Oxon, 887, 1152; Castle, 1192; Ty of, 1153
Wallis, Barnes (1887–1979), 1943
Wallis, John (1616–1703), 1655
Wallsend, Northumberland, 122–39
Walpole, Horace (1717–97), 1785
Walpole, Hugh (1884–1941), 1911, 1930
Walpole, Robert (1676–1745), 1708, 1715, 1717, 1721, 1724–5, 1731, 1733–4, 1737–40, 1742
Walsingham, Francis (1532–90), 1573
Walsingham, Thomas (d.?1422), 1376
Walsingham, Norfolk, 1980
Walter of Coutances (d.1207), Archbp, 1191
Walter of Guisborough, 1312, 1347
Walter of Henley, 1272
Walter, Hubert (d.1205), Archbp, 1193, 1205
Walter, John (1739–1812), 1785
Walter, Lucy (1631–59), 1662
Waltham Abbey, Essex, 1060, 1540
Waltheof, E. of Northumbria (d.1076), 1075–6
Walton, Ernest (1903–), 1932, 1951
Walton, Izaak (1593–1683), 1653
Walton, William (1902–83), 1923, 1931, 1937
Walton-on-Naze, Essex, 1338
Walvis Bay, Africa, 1878
Wandsworth, Surrey, 1801
Wansdyke, 490
Wantage, Berks., 997
Wapping, London, 1682, 1843,

1986–7
Warbeck, Perkin (c.1474–99), 1491–7, 1499
Wardlaw, Henry (c.1370–1440), Bp, 1413
Ware, Herts., 894, 1784
Ware, Samuel 1819
Wareham, Dorset, 887
Wareham, William (1450–1532), Archbp, 1503, 1527, 1532
Warrenpoint, N. Ireland, 1979
Warwick, Castle, 1068; University of, 1965
Warwick, EE of, Edward (1475–99), 1485, 1487, 1499; Richard Neville (1428–71), 1453, 1455–6, 1458–61, 1467, 1469–71; Thomas Beauchamp (d.1401), 1387–8, 1397
Wash, The, 430, 1216
Washington, DC, 1814, 1860, 1941, 1950; Conferences, 1887, 1927; Treaties of, 1846, 1871, 1921
Washington, George (1732–99), 1755, 1776, 1792
Wastell, John (d.1515), 1490
Water Newton, Cambs., 360
Waterford, Ireland, 1170, 1210, 1394, 1495
Waterhouse, Alfred (1830–1905), 1873, 1877
Waterhouse, Keith (1929–), 1960
Waterloo, battle of, 1815
Waterloo Bridge, London, 1817, 1879
Waterloo station, London, 1922
Watling Street, 43–7
Wat's Dyke, 757, 784
Watson, James (1928–), 1953
Watson, Richard (1737–1816), 1796
Watson-Watt, Robert (1892–1973), 1935
Watt, James (1736–1819), 1769, 1781
Watts, Isaac (1674–1748), 1707
Waugh, Evelyn (1903–66), 1928, 1930, 1942, 1945, 1952, 1955, 1957, 1961
Wavell, Archibald (1883–1950), Gen., 1940–1
Waverley Abbey, Hants., 1129
Waynflete, William (d.1486), 1448
Weatherby, James, 1773
Weaver, John (1673–1760), 1717, 1721
Webb, Aston (1849–1930), 1909, 1910
Webb, Beatrice (1858–1943), 1894
Webb, Mary (1881–1927), 1917
Webb, Matthew (1848–83), 1875
Webb, Sidney (1859–1947), 1894, 1930
Weber, Carl von (1786–1826), 1826
Wedgwood, Josiah (1730–95), 1769, 1775

Wedgwood, Ralph, 1806
Wei-hai-wei, China, 1898, 1930
Welles, Orson (1915–85), 1950
Wellesley, Mqs of, Richard (1760–1842), 1798, 1812, 1822
Wellington, D. of, Arthur Wellesley (1769–1852), 1803, 1808–10, 1812–15, 1821, 1827–30, 1832, 1834, 1848, 1852
Wells, H. G. (1866–1946), 1895, 1897–9, 1901, 1905, 1909–10, 1916, 1920, 1933
Wells Cathedral, Somerset, 1180, 1306
Welshpool, Wales, 1400
Welwyn Garden City, Herts., 1920
Wembley Stadium, London, 1923–4, 1948, 1955, 1966, 1985
Wentworth, Peter (c.1524–96), 1576, 1587, 1593
Weobley, Herefords., 1835
Wesel, Germany, 1945
Wesley, Charles (1707–88), 1729, 1735
Wesley, John (1703–91), 1729, 1735, 1738, 1784
Wessex, 3,000–2,400 BC; kingdom of, 495, 577, 628, 635, 658, 690, 694, 710, 736, 752, 796, 870–1, 877–8, 911, 925, 1016; earldom of, 1017
West Africa, 1884
West Ham (Newham), 1893
West Kennet, Wilts., 3,000–2,400 BC
Westerley, Robert (fl.1430–61), 1441
Western Australia, 1890
Westminster, 1306, 1867; Assembly of, 1643; Council of, 1163; H. of Commons, 1941, 1950, 1975, 1989; Palace of, 1360, 1605; Treaties of, 1527, 1654, 1674, 1742, 1756
Westminster Abbey, 616, 957, 1060, 1065–6, 1220, 1245, 1269, 1291, 1378, 1395, 1503, 1519, 1557, 1745, 1920, 1947, 1950–1
Westminster Cathedral, 1903, 1913
Westminster Hall, 1097, 1393–4, 1509, 1649, 1657, 1710, 1788, 1885, 1982
Westminster School, 1560
Westmorland, 1157
Westmorland, E. of, Charles Nevill (1542/3–1601), 1569
Wexford, Ireland, 1169, 1649, 1798
Weymouth, Dorset, 1471, 1506
Wheathampstead, Herts., 54 BC
Wheatstone, Charles (1802–75), 1837
Wheeler, Mortimer (1890–1976), 1934
Whipsnade Zoo, Beds., 1931
Whistler, James (1834–1903), 1863, 1871–2, 1878, 1886